PYTHON

IN A NUTSHELL

PYTHON

IN A NUTSHELL

Alex Martelli

O'REILLY®

Beijing • Cambridge • Farnham • Köln • Paris • Sebastopol • Taipei • Tokyo

Python in a Nutshell
by Alex Martelli

Published by O'Reilly & Associates, Inc., 1005 Gravenstein Highway North, Sebastopol, CA 95472.

O'Reilly & Associates books may be purchased for educational, business, or sales promotional use. Online editions are also available for most titles (*safari.oreilly.com*). For more information, contact our corporate/institutional sales department: 800-998-9938 or *corporate@oreilly.com*.

Editors: Paula Ferguson and Laura Lewin

Production Editor: Emily Quill

Cover Designer: Emma Colby

Interior Designer: Bret Kerr

Printing History:

   March 2003:   First Edition.

ISBN: 0-596-00188-6
[M]

Table of Contents

Part I. Getting Started with Python

Part II. Core Python Language and Built-ins

Part III. Python Library and Extension Modules

Part IV. Network and Web Programming

Part V. Extending and Embedding

Preface

The Python programming language manages to reconcile many apparent contradictions: it's both elegant and pragmatic, simple and powerful, a high-level language that doesn't get in your way when you want to fiddle with bits and bytes, suitable for programming novices and great for experts too.

This book is aimed at programmers with some previous exposure to Python, as well as experienced programmers coming to Python for the first time from other programming languages. The book is a quick reference to Python itself, the most important parts of its vast standard library, and some of the most popular and useful third-party modules, covering a range of applications including web and network programming, GUIs, XML handling, database interactions, and high-speed numeric computing. It focuses on Python's cross-platform capabilities and covers the basics of extending Python and embedding it in other applications, using either C or Java.

How This Book Is Organized

This book has five parts, as follows:

Part I, *Getting Started with Python*

- Chapter 1, *Introduction to Python*, covers the general characteristics of the Python language and its implementations, and discusses where to get help and information.

- Chapter 2, *Installation*, explains how to obtain and install Python.

- Chapter 3, *The Python Interpreter*, covers the Python interpreter program, its command-line options, and its use for running Python programs and in interactive sessions. The chapter also mentions text editors that are particularly suitable for editing Python programs, and examines some full-fledged integrated development environments, including IDLE, which comes free with standard Python.

Part II, *Core Python Language and Built-ins*

- Chapter 4, *The Python Language*, covers Python syntax, built-in data types, expressions, statements, and how to write and call functions.

- Chapter 5, *Object-Oriented Python*, explains object-oriented programming in Python.

- Chapter 6, *Exceptions*, covers how to deal with errors and abnormal conditions in Python programs.

- Chapter 7, *Modules*, covers the ways in which Python lets you group code into modules and packages, and how to define and import modules.

- Chapter 8, *Core Built-ins*, is a reference to built-in data types and functions, and some of the most fundamental modules in the standard Python library.

- Chapter 9, *Strings and Regular Expressions*, covers Python's powerful string-processing facilities, including regular expressions.

Part III, *Python Library and Extension Modules*

- Chapter 10, *File and Text Operations*, explains how to deal with files and text processing using built-in Python file objects, modules from Python's standard library, and platform-specific extensions for rich text I/O.

- Chapter 11, *Persistence and Databases*, introduces Python's serialization and persistence mechanisms, as well as Python's interfaces to DBM databases and relational (SQL-based) databases.

- Chapter 12, *Time Operations*, covers how to deal with times and dates in Python, using the standard library and popular extensions.

- Chapter 13, *Controlling Execution*, explains how to achieve advanced execution control in Python, including execution of dynamically generated code, restricted execution environments, and control of garbage collection.

- Chapter 14, *Threads and Processes*, covers Python's functionality for concurrent execution, both via multiple threads running within one process and via multiple processes running on a single machine.

- Chapter 15, *Numeric Processing*, shows Python's features for numeric computations, both in standard library modules and in the popular extension package called Numeric.

- Chapter 16, *Tkinter GUIs*, explains how to develop graphical user interfaces in Python with the Tkinter package included with the standard Python distribution, and mentions other alternative Python GUI frameworks.

- Chapter 17, *Testing, Debugging, and Optimizing*, deals with Python tools and approaches that help ensure your programs do what they're meant to do, find and correct errors in your programs, and check and enhance performance.

Part IV, *Network and Web Programming*

- Chapter 18, *Client-Side Network Protocol Modules*, covers many modules in Python's standard library that help you write network client programs.

- Chapter 19, *Sockets and Server-Side Network Protocol Modules*, explains Python's interfaces to low-level network mechanisms (sockets), standard Python library modules that help you write network server programs, and asynchronous (event-driven) network programming with standard modules and popular extensions.

- Chapter 20, *CGI Scripting and Alternatives*, covers the basics of CGI programming and how to perform CGI programming in Python with standard Python library modules. The chapter also mentions alternatives to CGI programming for server-side web programming through Python extensions.

- Chapter 21, *MIME and Network Encodings*, shows how to process email and other network-structured and encoded documents in Python.

- Chapter 22, *Structured Text: HTML*, covers Python library modules that let you process and generate HTML documents.

- Chapter 23, *Structured Text: XML*, covers Python library modules and popular extensions that let you process, modify, and generate XML documents.

Part V, *Extending and Embedding*

- Chapter 24, *Extending and Embedding Classic Python*, shows how to code Python extension modules using C and other classic compiled languages, and how to embed Python in applications coded in such languages.

- Chapter 25, *Extending and Embedding Jython*, shows how to use Java classes from the Jython implementation of Python, and how to embed Jython in applications coded in Java.

- Chapter 26, *Distributing Extensions and Programs*, covers the tools that let you package Python extensions, modules, and applications for distribution.

Conventions Used in This Book

The following conventions are used throughout this book.

Reference Conventions

In the function/method reference entries, when feasible, each optional parameter is shown with a default value using the Python syntax *name=value*. Built-in functions need not accept named parameters, so parameter names are not significant. Some optional parameters are best explained in terms of their presence or absence, rather than through default values. In such cases, a parameter is indicated as being optional by enclosing it in brackets ([ ]). When more than one argument is optional, the brackets are nested.

Typographic Conventions

Italic
    Used for filenames, program names, URLs, and to introduce new terms.

Constant Width
    Used for all code examples, as well as for commands and all items that appear in code, including keywords, methods, functions, classes, and modules.

Constant Width Italic
> Used to show text that can be replaced with user-supplied values in code examples.

Constant Width Bold
> Used for commands that must be typed on the command line, and occasionally for emphasis in code examples or to indicate code output.

How to Contact Us

We have tested and verified the information in this book to the best of our ability, but you may find that features have changed (or even that we have made mistakes!). Please let us know about any errors you find, as well as your suggestions for future editions, by writing to:

> O'Reilly & Associates
> 1005 Gravenstein Highway North
> Sebastopol, CA 95472
> (800) 928-9938 (in the United States or Canada)
> (707) 829-0515 (international or local)
> (707) 829-0104 (fax)

There is a web page for this book, which lists errata, examples, and any additional information. You can access this page at:

> *http://www.oreilly.com/catalog/pythonian/*

To ask technical questions or comment on the book, send email to:

> *bookquestions@oreilly.com*

For more information about books, conferences, resource centers, and the O'Reilly Network, see the O'Reilly web site at:

> *http://www.oreilly.com*

Acknowledgments

My heartfelt thanks to everybody who helped me out on this book. Many Python beginners, practitioners, and experts have read drafts of parts of the book and have given me feedback to help make it clearer and more precise, accurate, and readable. Out of those, for the quality and quantity of their feedback, I must single out for special thanks Andrea Babini, Andrei Raevsky, Anna Ravenscroft, and my fellow Python Business Forum board members Jacob Hallén and Laura Creighton.

Some Python experts gave me indispensable help in specific areas: Aahz on threading, Itamar Shtull-Trauring on Twisted, Mike Orr on Cheetah, Eric Jones and Paul Dubois on Numeric, and Tim Peters on threading, testing, performance issues, and optimization.

I was also blessed with a wonderful group of technical reviewers: Fred Drake of Python Labs, co-author of *Python & XML* (O'Reilly) and Grand Poobah of Python's excellent free documentation; Magnus Lie Hetland, author of *Practical·*

Python (Apress); Steve Holden, author of *Python Web Programming* (New Riders); and last but not least Sue Giller, whose observations as a sharp-eyed, experienced, non-Pythonista programmer were particularly useful in the pursuit of clarity and precision. The book's editor, Paula Ferguson, went above and beyond the call of duty in her work to make this book clearer and more readable.

My family and friends have been patient and supportive throughout the time it took me to write this book: particular thanks for that to my children Flavia and Lucio, my partner Marina, my sister Elisabetta, and my father Lanfranco.

Getting Started with Python

Introduction to Python

Python is a general-purpose programming language. It has been around for quite a while: Guido van Rossum, Python's creator, started developing Python back in 1990. This stable and mature language is very high level, dynamic, object-oriented, and cross-platform—all characteristics that are very attractive to developers. Python runs on all major hardware platforms and operating systems, so it doesn't constrain your platform choices.

Python offers high productivity for all phases of the software life cycle: analysis, design, prototyping, coding, testing, debugging, tuning, documentation, deployment, and, of course, maintenance. Python's popularity has seen steady, unflagging growth over the years. Today, familiarity with Python is an advantage for every programmer, as Python is likely to have some useful role to play as a part of any software solution.

Python provides a unique mix of elegance, simplicity, and power. You'll quickly become productive with Python, thanks to its consistency and regularity, its rich standard library, and the many other modules that are readily available for it. Python is easy to learn, so it is quite suitable if you are new to programming, yet at the same time it is powerful enough for the most sophisticated expert.

The Python Language

The Python language, while not minimalist, is rather spare, for good pragmatic reasons. When a language offers one good way to express a design idea, supplying other ways has only modest benefits, while the cost in terms of language complexity grows with the number of features. A complicated language is harder to learn and to master (and to implement efficiently and without bugs) than a simpler one. Any complications and quirks in a language hamper productivity in software maintenance, particularly in large projects, where many developers cooperate and often maintain code originally written by others.

3

Python is simple, but not simplistic. It adheres to the idea that if a language behaves a certain way in some contexts, it should ideally work similarly in all contexts. Python also follows the principle that a language should not have convenient shortcuts, special cases, ad hoc exceptions, overly subtle distinctions, or mysterious and tricky under-the-covers optimizations. A good language, like any other designed artifact, must balance such general principles with taste, common sense, and a high degree of practicality.

Python is a general-purpose programming language, so Python's traits are useful in any area of software development. There is no area where Python cannot be part of an optimal solution. "Part" is an important word here—while many developers find that Python fills all of their needs, Python does not have to stand alone. Python programs can cooperate with a variety of other software components, making it an ideal language for gluing together components written in other languages.

Python is a very-high-level language. This means that Python uses a higher level of abstraction, conceptually farther from the underlying machine, than do classic compiled languages, such as C, C++, and Fortran, which are traditionally called high-level languages. Python is also simpler, faster to process, and more regular than classic high-level languages. This affords high programmer productivity and makes Python an attractive development tool. Good compilers for classic compiled languages can often generate binary machine code that runs much faster than Python code. However, in most cases, the performance of Python-coded applications proves sufficient. When it doesn't, you can apply the optimization techniques covered in Chapter 17 to enhance your program's performance while keeping the benefits of high programming productivity.

Python is an object-oriented programming language, but it lets you develop code using both object-oriented and traditional procedural styles, mixing and matching as your application requires. Python's object-oriented features are like those of C++, although they are much simpler to use.

The Python Standard Library and Extension Modules

There is more to Python programming than just the Python language: the standard Python library and other extension modules are almost as important for effective Python use as the language itself. The Python standard library supplies many well-designed, solid, 100% pure Python modules for convenient reuse. It includes modules for such tasks as data representation, string and text processing, interacting with the operating system and filesystem, and web programming. Because these modules are written in Python, they work on all platforms supported by Python.

Extension modules, from the standard library or from elsewhere, let Python applications access functionality supplied by the underlying operating system or other software components, such as graphical user interfaces (GUIs), databases, and networks. Extensions afford maximal speed in computationally intensive tasks, such as XML parsing and numeric array computations. Extension modules that are not coded in Python, however, do not necessarily enjoy the same cross-platform portability as pure Python code.

You can write special-purpose extension modules in lower-level languages to achieve maximum performance for small, computationally intensive parts that you originally prototyped in Python. You can also use tools such as SWIG to make existing C/C++ libraries into Python extension modules, as we'll see in Chapter 24. Finally, you can embed Python in applications coded in other languages, exposing existing application functionality to Python scripts via dedicated Python extension modules.

This book documents many modules, both from the standard library and from other sources, in areas such as client- and server-side network programming, GUIs, numerical array processing, databases, manipulation of text and binary files, and interaction with the operating system.

Python Implementations

Python currently has two production-quality implementations, CPython and Jython, and one experimental implementation, Python .NET. This book primarily addresses CPython, which I refer to as just Python for simplicity. However, the distinction between a language and its implementations is an important one.

CPython

Classic Python (a.k.a., CPython, often just called Python) is the fastest, most up-to-date, most solid and complete implementation of Python. CPython is a compiler, interpreter, and set of built-in and optional extension modules, coded in standard C. CPython can be used on any platform where the C compiler complies with the ISO/IEC 9899:1990 standard (i.e., all modern, popular platforms). In Chapter 2, I'll explain how to download and install CPython. All of this book, except Chapter 24 and a few sections explicitly marked otherwise, applies to CPython.

Jython

Jython is a Python implementation for any Java Virtual Machine (JVM) compliant with Java 1.2 or better. Such JVMs are available for all popular, modern platforms. To use Jython well, you need some familiarity with fundamental Java classes. You do not have to code in Java, but documentation and examples for existing Java classes are couched in Java terms, so you need a nodding acquaintance with Java to read and understand them. You also need to use Java supporting tools for tasks such as manipulating .jar files and signing applets. This book deals with Python, not with Java. For Jython usage, you should complement this book with *Jython Essentials*, by Noel Rappin and Samuele Pedroni (O'Reilly), possibly *Java in a Nutshell*, by David Flanagan (O'Reilly), and, if needed, some of the many other Java resources available.

Choosing Between CPython and Jython

If your platform is able to run both CPython and Jython, how do you choose between them? First of all, don't choose—download and install them both. They coexist without problems, and they're free. Having them both on your machine costs only some download time and a little extra disk space.

To experiment, learn, and try things out, you will most often use CPython, as it's faster. To develop and deploy, your best choice depends on what extension modules you want to use and how you want to distribute your programs. CPython applications are generally faster, particularly if they can make good use of suitable extension modules, such as Numeric (covered in Chapter 15). The development of CPython versions is faster than that of Jython versions: at the time of writing, for example, the next scheduled release is 2.2 for Jython, but 2.3 for CPython.

However, as you'll see in Chapter 25, Jython can use any Java class as an extension module, whether the class comes from a standard Java library, a third-party library, or a library you develop yourself. A Jython-coded application is a 100% pure Java application, with all of Java's deployment advantages and issues, and runs on any target machine having a suitable JVM. Packaging opportunities are also identical to Java's.

Jython and CPython are both good, faithful implementations of Python, reasonably close in terms of usability and performance. Given these pragmatic issues, either one may enjoy decisive practical advantages in a specific scenario. Thus, it is wise to become familiar with the strengths and weaknesses of each, to be able to choose optimally for each development task.

Python .NET

The experimental Python .NET is a Python implementation for the Microsoft .NET platform, with an architecture similar to Jython's, but targeting Microsoft Intermediate Language (MSIL) rather than JVM bytecode. Python .NET is not as mature as CPython or Jython, but when it is ready for production use, Python .NET may become a great way to develop for .NET, like Jython is for the JVM. For information on Python .NET and links to download it, see *http://www.activestate.com/Initiatives/NET/Research.html*.

Licensing and Price Issues

Current releases of CPython are covered by the CNRI Open Source GPL-Compatible License, allowing free use of Python for both commercial and free-software development (*http://www.python.org/2.2.1/license.html*). Jython's license is similarly liberal. Anything you download from the main Python and Jython sites will not cost you a penny. These licenses do not constrain what licensing and pricing conditions you can use for software you develop using the tools, libraries, and documentation they cover.

However, not everything Python-related is totally free from licensing costs or hassles. Many third-party Python sources, tools, and extension modules that you can freely download have liberal licenses, similar to that of Python itself. Others, however, are covered by the GNU Public License (GPL) or Lesser GPL (LGPL), constraining the licensing conditions you are allowed to place on derived works. Commercially developed modules and tools may require you to pay a fee, either unconditionally or if you use them for profit.

There is no substitute for careful examination of licensing conditions and prices. Before you invest time and energy into any software component, check that you can live with its license. Often, especially in a corporate environment, such legal matters may involve consulting a lawyer. Modules and tools covered in this book, unless I explicitly say otherwise, can be taken to be, at the time of this writing, freely downloadable, open source, and covered by a liberal license akin to Python's. However, I claim no legal expertise, and licenses can change over time, so double-checking is always prudent.

Python Development and Versions

Python is developed by the Python Labs of Zope Corporation, which consists of half a dozen core developers headed by Guido van Rossum, Python's inventor, architect, and Benevolent Dictator For Life (BDFL). This title means that Guido has the final say on what becomes part of the Python language and standard libraries.

Python intellectual property is vested in the Python Software Foundation (PSF), a non-profit corporation devoted to promoting Python, with dozens of individual members (nominated for their contributions to Python, and including all of the Python core team) and corporate sponsors. Most PSF members have commit privileges to Python's CVS tree on SourceForge (*http://sf.net/cvs/?group_id=5470*), and most Python CVS committers are members of the PSF.

Proposed changes to Python are detailed in public documents called Python Enhancement Proposals (PEPs), debated (and sometimes advisorily voted upon) by Python developers and the wider Python community, and finally approved or rejected by Guido, who takes debate and votes into account but is not bound by them. Hundreds of people contribute to Python development, through PEPs, discussion, bug reports, and proposed patches to Python sources, libraries, and documentation.

Python Labs releases minor versions of Python (2.*x*, for growing values of *x*) about once or twice a year. 2.0 was released in October 2000, 2.1 in April 2001, and 2.2 in December 2001. Python 2.3 is scheduled to be released in early 2003. Each minor release adds features that make Python more powerful and simpler to use, but also takes care to maintain backward compatibility. One day there will be a Python 3.0 release, which will be allowed to break backward compatibility to some extent. However, that release is still several years in the future, and no specific plans for it currently exist.

Each minor release 2.*x* starts with alpha releases, tagged as 2.*x*a0, 2.*x*a1, and so on. After the alphas comes at least one beta release, 2.*x*b1, and after the betas at least one release candidate, 2.*x*rc1. By the time the final release of 2.*x* comes out, it is always solid, reliable, and well tested on all major platforms. Any Python programmer can help ensure this by downloading alphas, betas, and release candidates, trying them out on existing Python programs, and filing bug reports for any problem that might emerge.

Once a minor release is out, most of the attention of the core team switches to the next minor release. However, a minor release normally gets successive point releases (i.e., 2.x.1, 2.x.2 and so on) that add no functionality but can fix errors, port Python to new platforms, enhance documentation, and add optimizations and tools.

The Python Business Forum (*http://python-in-business.org*) is an international society of companies that base their business on Python. The Forum, among other activities, tests and maintains special Python releases (known as "Python-in-a-tie") that Python Labs certifies for industrial-strength robustness.

This book focuses on Python 2.2 (and all its point releases), the most stable and widespread release at the time of this writing, and the basis of the current "Python-in-a-tie" efforts. It also mentions a few changes scheduled to appear in Python 2.3, and documents the parts of the language and libraries that are new in 2.2 and thus cannot be used with the previous 2.1 release. Python 2.1 is still important because it's used in widely deployed Zope 2.x releases (the current Zope releases, 3.x, rely on Python 2.2 and later). Also, at the time of this writing, the released version of Jython supports only Python 2.1, not yet Python 2.2.

Among older releases of Python, the only one with a large installed base is 1.5.2, which is part of most installations of Red Hat Linux Releases 6.x and 7.x. However, this book does not address Python 1.5.2, which is over three years old and should not be used for any new development. Python's backward compatibility is good: current versions of Python are able to properly process just about any valid Python 1.5.2 program.

Python Resources

The richest of all Python resources is the Internet. The starting point is Python's site, *http://www.python.org*, which is full of interesting links that you will want to explore. And *http://www.jython.org* is a must if you have any interest in Jython.

Documentation

Python and Jython come with good documentation. The manuals are available in many formats, suitable for viewing, searching, and printing. You can browse the manuals on the Web at *http://www.python.org/doc/current/*. You can find links to the various formats you can download at *http://www.python.org/doc/current/download.html*, and *http://www.python.org/doc/* has links to a large variety of documents. For Jython, *http://www.jython.org/docs/* has links to Jython-specific documents as well as general Python ones. The Python FAQ (Frequently Asked Questions) is at *http://www.python.org/doc/FAQ.html*, and the Jython-specific FAQ is at *http://www.jython.org/cgi-bin/faqw.py?req=index*.

Most Python documentation (including this book) assumes some software development knowledge. However, Python is quite suitable for first-time programmers, so there are exceptions to this rule. A few good introductory online texts are:

- Josh Cogliati's "Non-Programmers Tutorial For Python," available at *http://www.honors.montana.edu/~jjc/easytut/easytut/*
- Alan Gauld's "Learning to Program," available at *http://www.crosswinds.net/~agauld/*
- Allen Downey and Jeffrey Elkner's "How to Think Like a Computer Scientist (Python Version)," available at *http://www.ibiblio.org/obp/thinkCSpy/*

Newsgroups and Mailing Lists

The URL *http://www.python.org/psa/MailingLists.html* has links to Python-related mailing lists and newsgroups. Always use plain-text format, not HTML, in all messages to mailing lists and newsgroups.

The Usenet newsgroup for Python discussions is *comp.lang.python*. The newsgroup is also available as a mailing list. To subscribe, send a message whose body is the word subscribe to *python-list-request@python.org*. Python-related announcements are posted to *comp.lang.python.announce*. To subscribe to its mailing-list equivalent, send a message whose body is the word subscribe to *python-announce-list-request@python.org*. To subscribe to Jython's mailing list, visit *http://lists.sf.net/lists/listinfo/jython-users*. To ask for individual help with Python, email your question to *python-help@python.org*. For questions and discussions about using Python to teach or learn programming, write to *tutor@python.org*.

Special Interest Groups

Discussions on specialized subjects related to Python take place on the mailing lists of Python Special Interest Groups (SIGs). *http://www.python.org/sigs/* has a list of active SIGs and pointers to general and specific information about them. Over a dozen SIGs are active at the time of this writing. Here are a few examples:

http://www.python.org/sigs/c++-sig/
 Bindings between C++ and Python

http://www.python.org/sigs/i18n-sig/
 Internationalization and localization of Python programs

http://www.python.org/sigs/image-sig/
 Image processing in Python

Python Business Forum

The Python Business Forum (PBF), at *http://www.python-in-business.org/*, is an international society of companies that base their business on Python. The PBF was formed quite recently, but the site already offers interesting information about business uses of Python.

Python Journal

The Python Journal, *http://pythonjournal.cognizor.com/*, is a free online publication focusing on Python, how to use it, and its applications.

Extension Modules and Python Sources

A good starting point to explore the world of available Python extensions and sources is "The Vaults of Parnassus," available at *http://www.vex.net/parnassus/*. It contains over 1,000 classified and commented links. By following these links, you can find and download most freely available Python modules and tools.

The standard Python source distribution contains excellent Python source code in the standard library and in the Demos and Tools directories, as well as C source for the many built-in extension modules. Even if you have no interest in building Python from source, I suggest you download and unpack the Python source distribution for study purposes.

Many Python modules and tools covered in this book also have dedicated sites. References to these sites are included in the appropriate chapters in this book.

The Python Cookbook

ActiveState has built a collaborative web site at *http://www.activestate.com/ASPN/Python/Cookbook* that contains a living collection of Python recipes. Each recipe contains some Python code, with comments and discussion, contributed by volunteers and enriched with the contributions of readers, under the editorial supervision of David Ascher. All code is covered by a license similar to Python's. Everyone is invited to participate as author and reader in this interesting and useful community endeavor. Hundreds of recipes from the site, edited, commented, and grouped into chapters with introductions by well-known Python experts, are published by O'Reilly as the *Python Cookbook*, edited by Alex Martelli and David Ascher.

Books and Magazines

Although the Net is a rich source of information, books and magazines still have their place (if you and I didn't agree on this, I wouldn't be writing this book, and you wouldn't be reading it). At the time of this writing, the only magazine entirely devoted to Python is *Py* (for updated information, visit *http://www.pyzine.com/*).

Books about Python and Jython are more numerous. Here are a few that I recommend:

- If you are just starting to learn Python (but have some previous programming experience), *Learning Python*, by Mark Lutz and David Ascher (O'Reilly), will serve you well. It sticks to the basics of Python's language and core libraries, covering clearly and in depth each of the subjects it touches.
- *Python Web Programming*, by Steve Holden (New Riders), teaches the basics of both Python and many other technologies that help you build dynamic web

sites, including TCP/IP, HTTP, HTML, XML, and relational databases. The book offers substantial examples, including a complete database-backed site.

- *Python Programming on Win32*, by Mark Hammond and Andy Robinson (O'Reilly), is indispensable for optimal Python use on Windows. The book details platform-specific extensions to Python for COM, ActiveScripting, Win32 API calls, and integration with Windows applications. The current edition uses Python's old 1.5.2 version, but everything also applies to Python's current version.

- *Jython Essentials*, by Samuele Pedroni and Noel Rappin (O'Reilly), is a rich and concise book on Jython, suitable if you already have some Java knowledge. For effective Jython use, I also suggest *Java in a Nutshell*, by David Flanagan (O'Reilly).

- *Python Essential Reference*, by David Beazley (New Riders), is a concise but complete reference to the Python language and its standard libraries.

- *Python Standard Library*, by Fredrik Lundh (O'Reilly), offers terse and usable coverage of all modules in the standard Python library, with over 300 well-commented scripts to show how you can use each module. The amount and quality of examples stands out as the book's outstanding feature.

- For a massive, wide-ranging treatise on Python applications and techniques, including many large examples, you can't beat *Programming Python*, by Mark Lutz (O'Reilly).

- For a very concise summary reference and reminder of Python's essentials, check out *Python Pocket Reference*, also by Mark Lutz (O'Reilly).

2

Installation

You can install Python, in both classic (CPython) and JVM (Jython) versions, on most platforms. With a suitable development system (C for CPython, Java for Jython), you can install Python from its source code distribution. On popular platforms, you also have the alternative of installing from a prebuilt binary distribution.

Installing CPython from a binary distribution is faster, saves you substantial work on some platforms, and is the only possibility if you have no suitable C development system. Installing from a source code distribution gives you more control and flexibility, and is the only possibility if you can't find a suitable prebuilt binary distribution for your platform. Even if you install from binaries, I recommend you also download the source distribution, which includes examples and demos that may be missing from prebuilt binary packages.

Installing Python from Source Code

To install Python from source code, you need a platform with an ISO-compliant C compiler and ancillary tools such as *make*. On Windows, the normal way to build Python is with the Microsoft product Visual C++.

To download Python source code, visit *http://www.python.org* and follow the link labeled Download. The latest version at the time of this writing is:

```
http://www.python.org/ftp/python/2.2.2/Python-2.2.2.tgz
```

The *.tgz* file extension is equivalent to *.tar.gz* (i.e., a *tar* archive of files, compressed by the powerful and popular *gzip* compressor).

Windows

On Windows, installing Python from source code can be a chore unless you are already familiar with Microsoft Visual C++ and used to working at the Windows command line (i.e., in the text-oriented windows known as MS-DOS Prompt or Command Prompt, depending on your version of Windows).

If the following instructions give you trouble, I suggest you skip ahead to the material on installing Python from binaries later in this chapter. It may be a good idea, on Windows, to do an installation from binaries anyway, even if you also install from source code. This way, if you notice anything strange while using the version you installed from source code, you can double-check with the installation from binaries. If the strangeness goes away, it must have been due to some quirk in your installation from source code, and then you know you must double-check the latter.

In the following sections, for clarity, I assume you have made a new directory named *C:\Py* and downloaded *Python-2.2.2.tgz* there. Of course, you can choose to name and place the directory as it best suits you.

Uncompressing and unpacking the Python source code

You can uncompress and unpack a *.tgz* file with programs *tar* and *gunzip*. If you do not have *tar* and *gunzip*, you can download the collection of utilities *ftp://ftp.objectcentral.com/winutils.zip* into *C:\Py*. If you do not have other ways to unpack a ZIP file, download *ftp://ftp.th-soft.com/UNZIP.EXE* into *C:\Py*. Open an MS-DOS Prompt window and give the following commands:

```
C:\> My Documents>cd \Py
C:\Py> unzip winutils
    [unzip lists the files it is unpacking - omitted here]
C:\Py> gunzip Python-2.2.2.tgz
C:\Py> tar xvf Python-2.2.2.tar
    [tar lists the files it is unpacking - omitted here]
C:\Py>
```

Commercial programs WinZip (*http://www.winzip.com*) and PowerArchiver (*http://www.powerarchiver.com*) can also uncompress and unpack *.tgz* archives. Whether via *gunzip* and *tar*, a commercial program, or some other program, you now have a directory *C:\Py\Python-2.2.2*, the root of a tree that contains the entire standard Python distribution in source form.

Building the Python source code with Microsoft Visual C++

Open the workspace file *C:\Py\Python-2.2.2\PCbuild\pcbuild.dsw* with Microsoft Visual C++, for example by starting Windows Explorer, going to directory *C:\Py\Python-2.2.2\PCbuild*, and double-clicking on file *pcbuild.dsw*.

Choose Build → Set Active Configuration → python Win32 Release, then Build → Build python.exe. Visual C++ builds projects *pythoncore* and *python*, making files *python22.dll* and *python.exe* in *C:\Py\Python-2.2.2\PCbuild*. You can also build other subprojects (for example with Build → Batch Build...). However, to build subprojects *_tkinter*, *bsddb*, *pyexpat*, and *zlib*, you first need to download other open source packages and install them in the *C:\Py* directory. Follow the instructions in *C:\Py\Python-2.2.2\PCbuild\readme.txt* if you want to build every Python package that is in the distribution.

Building Python for debugging

You can also, optionally, build the debug versions, as well as the release versions, of the Python packages.

With Visual C++, an executable (*.exe*) built for release can interoperate fully only with dynamic load libraries (DLLs) also built for release, while an executable built for debugging interoperates fully only with DLLs also built for debugging. Trying to mix and match can cause program crashes and assorted strangeness. To help you avoid accidentally mixing parts built for release with others built for debugging, the Python workspace appends a *_d* to the name of debugging executables and DLLs. For example, when you build for debugging, *pythoncore* produces *python22_d.dll* and *python* produces *python22_d.exe*.

What makes the debugging and release Visual C++ builds incompatible is the choice of runtime library. Executables and DLLs can fully interoperate only by using the same runtime library, and the runtime library must in turn be a DLL. You can tweak Project → Settings → C/C++ → Code Generation → Use run-time library, setting all projects to use Multithreaded DLL (*MSVCRT.DLL*) (also remove the _DEBUG definition in C/C++ → Code Generation → Preprocessor). I recommend you do this only if you are experienced with Microsoft Visual C++ and have special, advanced requirements. Otherwise, resigning yourself to keeping two separate and distinct release and debugging "worlds" is the simplest approach.

Installing after the build

python22.dll (or *python22_d.dll*, if you want to run a debug-mode *python_d.exe*) must be in a directory from which Windows loads DLLs when needed. Suitable directories depend on your version of Windows: for example, *c:\windows\system* is one possibility. If you don't copy *python22.dll* to a suitable directory, you can run Python only when the current directory is the directory in which *python22.dll* resides.

Similarly, *python.exe* must be in a directory in which Windows looks for executables, normally a directory listed in the Windows environment variable named PATH. How to set PATH and other environment variables depends on your version of Windows, as mentioned in Chapter 3. Python can locate other files, such as the standard library modules, according to various strategies. *C:\Py\Python-2.2.2\PC\ readme.txt* documents the various possibilities.

Building Python for Cygwin

Python 2.2 is also available as a part of the free Cygwin Unix-like environment for Windows—see *http://cygwin.com/* for more information. Cygwin runs on top of Windows. However, Cygwin is quite similar to Linux and other free Unix-like environments in many respects. In particular, Cygwin uses the popular, free *gcc* C/C++ compiler and associated tools, such as *make*. Building Python from source code on Cygwin is therefore similar to building from source code on Unix-like environments, even though Cygwin runs on Windows.

Unix-like Platforms

On Unix-like platforms, installing Python from source code is not a particularly complicated procedure. In the following sections, for clarity, I assume you have created a new directory named *~/Py* and downloaded *Python-2.2.2.tgz* there. Of course, you can choose to name and place the directory as it best suits you.

Uncompressing and unpacking the Python source code

You can uncompress and unpack a *.tgz* file with programs *tar* and *gunzip*. If you have the popular GNU version of *tar*, you can just type the following at a shell prompt:

```
$ cd ~/Py
$ tar xzf Python-2.2.2.tgz
```

You now have a directory *~/Py/Python-2.2.2*, the root of a tree that contains the entire standard Python distribution in source form.

Configuring, building, and testing

You will find detailed notes in file *~/Py/Python-2.2.2/README* under the heading "Build instructions," and I strongly suggest reading those notes. In the simplest case, however, all you need to get started may be to give the following commands at a shell prompt:

```
$ cd ~/Py/Python-2.2.2
$ ./configure
    [configure writes much information - snipped here]
$ make
    [make takes quite a while, and emits much information]
```

If you run *make* without running *./configure* first, *make* will implicitly run *./configure* for you. When *make* finishes, you should test that the Python you have just built works as expected, as follows:

```
$ make test
    [takes quite a while, emits much information]
```

Most likely, *make test* will confirm that your build is working, but also inform you that some tests have been skipped because optional modules were missing.

Some of the modules are platform-specific (e.g., some only work on machines running SGI's Irix operating system), so you should not worry about them if your machine just doesn't support them. However, other modules get skipped during the build procedure because they depend on other open source packages that may not be installed on your machine. For example, module _tkinter, needed to run the Tkinter GUI package covered in Chapter 16, can be built only if *./configure* is able to find an installation of Tcl/Tk 8.0 or later on your machine. See *~/Py/ Python-2.2.2/README* for more details, and also for specific caveats regarding many different Unix and Unix-like platforms.

Building from source code lets you tweak your configuration in several useful ways. For example, you can build Python in a special way that will help you track down memory leaks if you develop C-coded Python extensions, covered in Chapter 24. Again, *~/Py/Python-2.2.2/README* is a good source of information about the configuration options you can use.

Installing after the build

By default, *./configure* prepares Python for installation in */usr/local/bin* and */usr/ local/lib*. You can change these settings by running *./configure* with option --prefix before running *make*. For example, if you want a private installation of Python in subdirectory *py22* of your home directory, run:

```
$ cd ~/Py/Python-2.2.2
$ ./configure --prefix=~/py22
```

and continue with *make* as in the previous section. Once you're done building and testing Python, to perform the actual installation of all files, run:

```
$ make install
```

The user running *make install* must have write permissions on the target directories. Depending on your choice of target directories and the permissions set on those directories, you may therefore need to *su* to *root*, *bin*, or some other special user when you run *make install*.

Apple Macintosh

Jack Jansen's page on MacPython, *http://www.cwi.nl/~jack/macpython.html*, is an indispensable resource for any Macintosh Python user. The page includes pointers to specially packaged Python 2.2.2 source code for Macintosh (requiring the CodeWarrior Pro 7 C compiler), prebuilt binaries for both Mac OS X and older Mac OS 9, and a wealth of other Macintosh-specific resources.

Installing Python from Binaries

If your platform is popular and current, you may find a prebuilt and packaged binary version of Python ready for installation. Binary packages are typically self-installing, either directly as executable programs, or via appropriate system tools, such as the RedHat Package Manager (RPM) on Linux and the Microsoft Installer (MSI) on Windows. Once you have downloaded a package, install it by running the program and interactively choosing installation parameters, such as the directory where Python is to be installed.

To download Python binaries, visit *http://www.python.org* and follow the link labeled Download. At the time of this writing, the only binary installer directly available from the main Python site is a Windows installer executable:

```
http://www.python.org/ftp/python/2.2.2/Python-2.2.2.exe
```

Many third parties supply free binary Python installers for other platforms. For Linux distributions, see *http://rpmfind.net* if your distribution is RPM-based (RedHat, Mandrake, SUSE, and so on) or *http://www.debian.org* for Debian. The site *http://www.python.org/download/* provides links to binary distributions for Macintosh, OS/2, Amiga, RISC OS, QNX, VxWorks, IBM AS/400, Sony PlayStation 2, and Sharp Zaurus. Older Python versions, mainly 1.5.2, are also usable and functional, though not as powerful and polished as the current Python 2.2.2. The download page provides links to 1.5.2 installers for older or less popular platforms (MS-DOS, Windows 3.1, Psion, BeOS, etc.).

ActivePython (*http://www.activestate.com/Products/ActivePython*) is a binary package of Python 2.2 for 32-bit versions of Windows and x86 Linux.

Installing Jython

To install Jython, you need a Java Virtual Machine (JVM) that complies with Java 1.1 or higher. See *http://www.jython.org/platform.html* for advice on JVMs for your platform.

To download Jython, visit *http://www.jython.org* and follow the link labeled Download. The latest version at the time of this writing is:

```
http://prdownloads.sf.net/jython/jython-21.class
```

In the following section, for clarity, I assume you have created a new directory named *C:\Jy* and downloaded *jython-21.class* there. Of course, you can choose to name and place the directory as it best suits you. On Unix-like platforms, in particular, the directory name will more likely be something like *~/Jy*.

The Jython installer *.class* file is a self-installing program. Open an MS-DOS Prompt window (or a shell prompt on a Unix-like platform), change directory to *C:\Jy*, and run your Java interpreter on the Jython installer. Make sure to include directory *C:\Jy* in the Java CLASSPATH. With most releases of Sun's Java Development Kit (JDK), for example, you can run:

```
C:\Jy> java -cp . jython-21
```

This runs a GUI installer that lets you choose destination directory and options. If you want to avoid the GUI, you can use the -o switch on the command line. The switch lets you specify the installation directory and options directly on the command line. For example:

```
C:\Jy> java -cp . jython-21 -o C:\Jython-2.1 demo lib source
```

installs Jython, with all optional components (demos, libraries, and source code), in directory *C:\Jython-2.1*. The Jython installation builds two small, useful command files. One, run as *jython* (named *jython.bat* on Windows), runs the interpreter. The other, run as *jythonc*, compiles Python source into JVM byte-code. You can add the Jython installation directory to your PATH, or copy these command files into any directory on your PATH.

You may want to use Jython with different JDKs on the same machine. For example, while JDK 1.4 is best for most development, you may also need to use JDK 1.1 occasionally in order to compile applets that can run on browsers that support only Java 1.1. In such cases, you could share a single Jython installation among multiple JVMs. However, to avoid confusion and accidents, I suggest you perform separate installations from the same Jython download on each JVM you want to support. Suppose, for example, that you have JDK 1.4 installed in *C:\Jdk14* and JDK 1.1 installed in *C:\Jdk11*. In this case, you could use the commands:

```
C:\Jy> \Jdk14\java -cp . jython-21 -o C:\Jy21-14 demo lib source
C:\Jy> \Jdk11\java -cp . jython-21 -o C:\Jy21-11 demo lib source
```

With these installations, you could then choose to work off *C:\Jy21-14* most of the time (e.g., by placing it in your PATH), and *cd* to *C:\Jy21-11* when you specifically need to compile applets with JDK 1.1.

3

The Python Interpreter

To develop software systems in Python, you produce text files that contain Python source code and documentation. You can use any text editor, including those in Integrated Development Environments (IDEs). You then process the source files with the Python compiler and interpreter. You can do this directly, or implicitly inside an IDE, or via another program that embeds Python. The Python interpreter also lets you execute Python code interactively, as do IDEs.

The python Program

The Python interpreter program is run as *python* (it's named *python.exe* on Windows). *python* includes both the interpreter itself and the Python compiler, which is implicitly invoked, as needed, on imported modules. Depending on your system, the program may have to be in a directory listed in your PATH environment variable. Alternatively, as with any other program, you can give a complete pathname to it at the command (shell) prompt, or in the shell script (or *.BAT* file, shortcut target, etc.) that runs it.* On Windows, you can also use Start → Programs → Python 2.2 → Python (command line).

Environment Variables

Besides PATH, other environment variables affect the *python* program. Some environment variables have the same effects as options passed to *python* on the command line; these are documented in the next section. A few provide settings not available via command-line options:

---

* This may involve using quotes, if the pathname contains spaces—again, this depends on your operating system.

PYTHONHOME

The Python installation directory. A *lib* subdirectory, containing the standard Python library modules, should exist under this directory. On Unix-like systems, the standard library modules should be in subdirectory *lib/python-2.2* for Python 2.2, *lib/python-2.3* for Python 2.3, and so on.

PYTHONPATH

A list of directories, separated by colons on Unix-like systems and by semicolons on Windows. Modules are imported from these directories. This extends the initial value for Python's sys.path variable. Modules, importing, and the sys.path variable are covered in Chapter 7.

PYTHONSTARTUP

The name of a Python source file that is automatically executed each time an interactive interpreter session starts. No such file is run if this variable is not set, or if it is set to the path of a file that is not found. The PYTHONSTARTUP file is not used when you run a Python script: it is used only when you start an interactive session.

How you set and examine environment variables depends on your operating system: shell commands, persistent startup shell files (e.g., *AUTOEXEC.BAT* on Windows), or other approaches (e.g., Start → Settings → Control Panel → System → Environment on Windows/NT, 2000, and XP). Some Python versions for Windows also look for this information in the registry, in addition to the environment. On Macintosh systems, the Python interpreter is started through the PythonInterpreter icon and configured through the EditPythonPrefs icon. See *http://www.python.org/doc/current/mac/mac.html* for information about Python on the Mac.

Command-Line Syntax and Options

The Python interpreter command-line syntax can be summarized as follows:

> [*path*]python {*options*} [-c *command* | *file* | -] {*arguments*}

Here, brackets ([ ]) denote something that is optional, braces ({ }) enclose items of which 0 or more may be present, and vertical bars (|) show a choice between alternatives (with none of them also being a possibility).

options are case-sensitive short strings, starting with a hyphen, that ask *python* for a non-default behavior. Unlike most Windows programs, *python* only accepts options starting with a hyphen, not with a slash. Python consistently uses slashes for file paths, as in Unix. The most useful options are listed in Table 3-1. Each option's description gives the environment variable (if any) that, when set to any value, requests the same behavior.

Table 3-1. Python frequently used command-line options

Option	Meaning (and equivalent environment variable)
-h	Prints a full list of options and summary help, then terminates
-i	Ensures an interactive session, no matter what (PYTHONINSPECT)
-O	Optimizes generated bytecode (PYTHONOPTIMIZE)
-OO	Like -O, but also removes documentation strings from the bytecode

Table 3-1. Python frequently used command-line options (continued)

Option	Meaning (and equivalent environment variable)
-Q *arg*	Controls the behavior of division operator / on integers
-S	Omits the normally implicit import site on startup
-t	Warns about inconsistent usage of tabs and blank spaces
-tt	Like -tt, but raises an error rather than a warning
-u	Uses unbuffered binary files for standard output and standard error (PYTHONUNBUFFERED)
-U	Treats all literal strings as Unicode literals
-v	Verbosely traces import and cleanup actions (PYTHONVERBOSE)
-V	Prints the Python version number, then terminates
-W *arg*	Adds an entry to the warnings filter (covered in Chapter 17)
-x	Excludes (skips) the first line of the main script's source

-i is used to get an interactive session immediately after running some script, with variables still intact and available for inspection. You do not need it for normal interactive sessions. -t and -tt ensure that your tabs and spaces in Python sources are used consistently (see Chapter 4 for more information about whitespace usage in Python).

-0 and -00 yield small savings of time and space in bytecode generated for modules you import: expect about 10% to 20% improvement in runtime, depending on your platform and coding style. However, with -00, documentation strings will not be available. -Q determines the behavior of division operator / used between two integer operands (division is covered in Chapter 4). -W adds an entry to the warnings filter (warnings are covered in Chapter 17).

-u uses binary mode for standard output (and standard error). Some platforms, such as Windows, distinguish binary and text modes. Binary mode is needed when binary data is emitted to standard output, as in some Common Gateway Interface (CGI) scripts. -u also ensures that output is performed immediately, rather than buffered to enhance performance. This is necessary when delays due to buffering could cause problems, as in certain Unix pipelines.

After the options, if any, comes an indication of what Python program is to be run. A file path is that of a Python source or bytecode file to run, complete with file extension, if any. On any platform, you may use a slash (/) as the separator between components in this path. On Windows only, you may alternatively use a backslash (\). Instead of a file path, you can use -c *command* to execute a Python code string *command*. *command* normally contains spaces, so you need quotes around it to satisfy your operating system's shell or command-line processor. Some shells (e.g., *bash*) let you enter multiple lines as a single argument, so that *command* can be a series of Python statements. Other shells (e.g., Windows shells) limit you to a single line; *command* can then be one or more simple statements separated by semicolons (;), as discussed in Chapter 4. A hyphen, or the lack of any token in this position, tells the interpreter to read program source from standard input— normally, an interactive session. You need an explicit hyphen only if arguments follow. *arguments* are arbitrary strings: the Python application being run can access the strings as sys.argv.

For example, on a standard Windows installation of Python 2.2, you can enter the following at an MS-DOS Prompt (or Command Prompt):

```
C:\> python22\python -c "import time; print time.asctime( )"
```

to have Python emit the current date and time. On an installation of Python from sources, on Cygwin, Linux, OpenBSD, or other Unix-like systems, you can enter the following at a shell prompt:

```
$ /usr/local/bin/python -v
```

to start an interactive session with verbose tracing of import and cleanup. In each case, you can start the command with just *python* (you do not have to specify the full path to the Python executable) if the directory of the Python executable is in your PATH environment variable.

Interactive Sessions

When you run *python* without a script argument, *python* enters an interactive session and prompts you to enter Python statements or expressions. Interactive sessions are useful to explore, to check things out, and to use Python as a very powerful, extensible interactive calculator.

When you enter a complete statement, Python executes it. When you enter a complete expression, Python evaluates it. If the expression has a result, Python outputs a string representing the result, and also assigns the result to the variable named _ (a single underscore) so that you can easily use that result in another expression. The prompt string is >>> when Python expects a statement or expression, and ... when a statement or expression has been started but not yet completed. For example, Python prompts you with ... when you have opened a parenthesis on a previous line and have not closed it yet.

An interactive session is terminated by end-of-file on standard input (Ctrl-Z on Windows, Ctrl-D on Unix-like systems). The statement raise SystemExit also ends the session, as does a call to sys.exit( ), either interactively or in code being run (SystemExit and Python exception handling are covered in Chapter 6).

Line-editing and history facilities depend in part on how Python was built: if the optional readline module was included, the features of the GNU readline library are available. Windows NT, 2000, and XP have a simple but usable history facility for interactive text-mode programs like *python*. Windows 95, 98, and ME don't. You can use other line-editing and history facilities by installing the Alternative ReadLine package for Windows (*http://newcenturycomputers.net/projects/readline.html*) or pyrepl for Unix (*http://starship.python.net/crew/mwh/hacks/pyrepl.html*).

Python Development Environments

The Python interpreter's built-in interactive mode is the simplest development environment for Python. It is a bit primitive, but it is lightweight, has a small footprint, and starts fast. Together with an appropriate text editor (as discussed later in this chapter) and line-editing and history facilities, it is a usable and popular development environment. However, there are a number of other development environments that you can also use.

IDLE

Python's Integrated DeveLopment Environment (IDLE) comes with the standard Python distribution. IDLE is a cross-platform, 100% pure Python application based on Tkinter (see Chapter 16). IDLE offers a Python shell, similar to interactive Python interpreter sessions but richer in functionality. It also includes a text editor optimized to edit Python source code, an integrated interactive debugger, and several specialized browsers/viewers.

Other Free Cross-Platform Python IDEs

IDLE is mature, stable, easy to use, and rich in functionality. Promising new Python IDEs that share IDLE's free and cross-platform nature are emerging. Red Hat's Source Navigator (*http://sources.redhat.com/sourcenav/*) supports many languages. It runs on Linux, Solaris, HPUX, and Windows. Boa Constructor (*http://boa-constructor.sf.net/*) is Python-only and still beta-level, but well worth trying out. Boa Constructor includes a GUI builder for the wxWindows cross-platform GUI toolkit.

Platform-Specific Free Python IDEs

Python is cross-platform, and this book focuses on cross-platform tools and components. However, Python also provides good platform-specific facilities, including IDEs, on many platforms it supports. For the Macintosh, MacPython includes an IDE (see *http://www.python.org/doc/current/mac/mac.html*). On Windows, ActivePython includes the PythonWin IDE. PythonWin is also available as a free add-on to the standard Python distribution for Windows, part of Mark Hammond's powerful win32all extensions (see *http://starship.python.net/ crew/mhammond*).

Commercial Python IDEs

Several companies sell commercial Python IDEs, both cross-platform and platform-specific. You must pay for them if you use them for commercial development and, in most cases, even if you develop free software. However, they offer support contracts and rich arrays of tools. If you have funding for software tool purchases, it is worth looking at these in detail and trying out their free demos or evaluations. Most work on Linux and Windows.

Secret Labs (*http://www.pythonware.com*) offers a Python IDE called PythonWorks. It includes a GUI designer for Tkinter (covered in Chapter 16). Archaeopterix sells a Python IDE, Wing, notable for its powerful source-browsing and remote-debugging facilities (*http://archaeopterix.com/wingide*). theKompany sells a Python IDE, BlackAdder, that includes a GUI builder for the PyQt GUI toolkit (*http://www.thekompany.com/products/blackadder*).

ActiveState (*http://www.activestate.com*) has two Python IDE products. Komodo is built on top of Mozilla (*http://www.mozilla.org*) and includes remote debugging capabilities. Visual Python is for Windows only, and lets you use Microsoft's multi-language Visual Studio .NET IDE for Python development.

Free Text Editors with Python Support

You can edit Python source code with any text editor, even simplistic ones such as *notepad* on Windows or *ed* on Linux. Powerful free editors also support Python, with extra features such as syntax-based colorization and automatic indentation. Cross-platform editors let you work in uniform ways on different platforms. Good programmers' text editors also let you run, from within the editor, tools of your choice on the source code you're editing.

Top of the league for sheer editing power is a classic, *emacs* (*http://www.emacs. org*, and *http://www.python.org/emacs* for Python-specific add-ons). However, *emacs* is not the easiest editor to use, nor is it lightweight. My personal favorite is another classic, *vim* (*http://www.vim.org*), the modern, improved version of the traditional Unix editor *vi*. *vim* is fast, lightweight, Python-programmable, and runs everywhere in both text-mode and GUI versions. *vim*, like *vi*, has a modal design, which lets you use normal keys for cursor movement and text changes when in command mode. Some love this as an ergonomic trait, minimizing finger travel. Others find it confusing and detest it. Newer editors challenge the classic ones. SciTE (*http://www.scintilla.org*) builds on the Scintilla programming language editor component. FTE (*http://fte.sf.net*) is also worth trying.

Other advanced free editors with Python syntax support are platform-specific. On Windows, try SynEdit (*http://www.mkidesign.com/syneditinfo.html*). On Unix-like systems, try Glimmer (*http://glimmer.sf.net*), and Cooledit (*http://cooledit.sf.net*), which also offers Python programmability, like *vim*, but without *vim*'s modal architecture.

Running Python Programs

Whatever tools you use to produce your Python application, you can see your application as a set of Python source files. A *script* is a file that you can run directly. A *module* is a file that you can import (as covered in Chapter 7) to provide functionality to other files or to interactive sessions. A Python file can be both a module and a script, exposing functionality when imported, but also suitable for being run directly. A useful and widespread convention is that Python files that are primarily meant to be imported as modules, when run directly, should execute self-test operations. Testing is covered in Chapter 17.

The Python interpreter automatically compiles Python source files as needed. Python source files normally have extension *.py*. Python saves the compiled byte-code file for each module in the same directory as the module's source, with the same basename and extension *.pyc* (or *.pyo* if Python is run with option -0). Python does not save the compiled bytecode form of a script when you run the script directly; rather, Python recompiles the script each time you run it. Python saves bytecode files only for modules you import. It automatically rebuilds each module's bytecode file whenever necessary, for example when you edit the module's source. Eventually, for deployment, you may package Python modules using tools covered in Chapter 26.

You can run Python code interactively, with the Python interpreter or an IDE. Normally, however, you initiate execution by running a top-level script. To run a script, you give its path as an argument to *python*, as covered earlier in this chapter. Depending on your operating system, you can invoke *python* directly, from a shell script, or in a command file. On Unix-like systems, you can make a Python script directly executable by setting the file's permission bits x and r and beginning the script with a so-called *shebang* line, which is a first line of the form:

```
#!/usr/bin/env python {options}
```

providing a path to the *python* program.

On Windows, you can associate file extensions *.py*, *.pyc*, and *.pyo* with the Python interpreter in the Windows registry. Most Python versions for Windows perform this association when installed. You can then run Python scripts with the usual Windows mechanisms, such as double-clicking on their icons. On Windows, when you run a Python script by double-clicking on the script's icon, Windows automatically closes the text-mode console associated with the script as soon as the script terminates. If you want the console to linger in order to allow the user to read the script's output on the screen, you need to ensure the script doesn't terminate too soon, for example by using the following as the script's last statement:

```
raw_input('Press Enter to terminate')
```

This is not necessary when you run the script from a pre-existing console (also known as a MS-DOS Prompt or Command Prompt window).

On Windows, you can also use extension *.pyw* and interpreter program *pythonw. exe* instead of *.py* and *python.exe*. The *w* variants run Python without a text-mode console, and thus without standard input and output. These variants are appropriate for scripts that rely on GUIs. You normally use them only when the script is fully debugged, to keep standard output and error available for information, warnings, and error messages during development.

Applications coded in other languages may embed Python, controlling the execution of Python code for their own purposes. We examine this subject further in Chapter 24.

The Jython Interpreter

The *jython* interpreter built during installation (see Chapter 2) is run similarly to the *python* program:

```
[path]jython {options} [ -j jar | -c command | file | - ] {arguments}
```

-j *jar* tells *jython* that the main script to run is *__run__.py* in the *.jar* file. Options -i, -S, and -v are the same as for *python*. --help is like *python*'s -h, and --version is like *python*'s --V. Instead of environment variables, *jython* uses a text file named *registry* in the installation directory to record properties with structured names. Property python.path, for example, is the Jython equivalent of Python's environment variable PYTHONPATH. You can also set properties with *jython* command-line options, in the form -D *name=value*.

Core Python Language and Built-ins

The Python Language

4

This chapter is a quick guide to the Python language. To learn Python from scratch, I suggest you start with *Learning Python*, by Mark Lutz and David Ascher (O'Reilly). If you already know other programming languages and just want to learn the specifics of Python, this chapter is for you. I'm not trying to teach Python here, so we're going to cover a lot of ground at a pretty fast pace.

Lexical Structure

The lexical structure of a programming language is the set of basic rules that govern how you write programs in that language. It is the lowest-level syntax of the language and specifies such things as what variable names look like and what characters are used for comments. Each Python source file, like any other text file, is a sequence of characters. You can also usefully see it as a sequence of lines, tokens, or statements. These different syntactic views complement and reinforce each other. Python is very particular about program layout, especially with regard to lines and indentation, so you'll want to pay attention to this information if you are coming to Python from another language.

Lines and Indentation

A Python program is composed of a sequence of *logical lines*, each made up of one or more *physical lines*. Each physical line may end with a comment. A pound sign (#) that is not inside a string literal begins a comment. All characters after the # and up to the physical line end are part of the comment, and the Python interpreter ignores them. A line containing only whitespace, possibly with a comment, is called a *blank line*, and is ignored by the interpreter. In an interactive interpreter session, you must enter an empty physical line (without any whitespace or comment) to terminate a multiline statement.

In Python, the end of a physical line marks the end of most statements. Unlike in other languages, Python statements are not normally terminated with a delimiter, such as a semicolon (;). When a statement is too long to fit on a single physical line, you can join two adjacent physical lines into a logical line by ensuring that the first physical line has no comment and ends with a backslash (\). Python also joins adjacent physical lines into one logical line if an open parenthesis ((), bracket ([), or brace ({) has not yet been closed. Triple-quoted string literals can also span physical lines. Physical lines after the first one in a logical line are known as *continuation lines*. The indentation issues covered next do not apply to continuation lines, but only to the first physical line of each logical line.

Python uses indentation to express the block structure of a program. Unlike other languages, Python does not use braces or begin/end delimiters around blocks of statements: indentation is the only way to indicate such blocks. Each logical line in a Python program is indented by the whitespace on its left. A block is a contiguous sequence of logical lines, all indented by the same amount; the block is ended by a logical line with less indentation. All statements in a block must have the same indentation, as must all clauses in a compound statement. Standard Python style is to use four spaces per indentation level. The first statement in a source file must have no indentation (i.e., it must not begin with any whitespace). Additionally, statements typed at the interactive interpreter prompt >>> (covered in Chapter 3) must have no indentation.

A tab is logically replaced by up to 8 spaces, so that the next character after the tab falls into logical column 9, 17, 25, etc. Don't mix spaces and tabs for indentation, since different tools (e.g., editors, email systems, printers) treat tabs differently. The -t and -tt options to the Python interpreter (covered in Chapter 3) ensure against inconsistent tab and space usage in Python source code. You can configure any good editor to expand tabs to spaces so that all Python source code you write contains only spaces, not tabs. You then know that all tools, including Python itself, are going to be consistent in handling the crucial matter of indentation in your source files.

Tokens

Python breaks each logical line into a sequence of elementary lexical components, called *tokens*. Each token corresponds to a substring of the logical line. The normal token types are *identifiers*, *keywords*, *operators*, *delimiters*, and *literals*, as covered in the following sections. Whitespace may be freely used between tokens to separate them. Some whitespace separation is needed between logically adjacent identifiers or keywords; otherwise, they would be parsed as a single, longer identifier. For example, printx is a single identifier—to write the keyword print followed by identifier x, you need to insert some whitespace (e.g., print x).

Identifiers

An *identifier* is a name used to identify a variable, function, class, module, or other object. An identifier starts with a letter (A to Z or a to z) or underscore (_) followed by zero or more letters, underscores, and digits (0 to 9). Case is significant in Python: lowercase and uppercase letters are distinct. Punctuation characters such as @, $, and % are not allowed in identifiers.

Normal Python style is to start class names with an uppercase letter and other identifiers with a lowercase letter. Starting an identifier with a single leading underscore indicates by convention that the identifier is meant to be private. Starting an identifier with two leading underscores indicates a strongly private identifier; if the identifier also ends with two trailing underscores, the identifier is a language-defined special name. The identifier _ (a single underscore) is special in interactive interpreter sessions: the interpreter binds _ to the result of the last expression statement evaluated interactively, if any.

Keywords

Python has 28 keywords (29 in Python 2.3 and later), which are identifiers that Python reserves for special syntactic uses. Keywords are composed of lowercase letters only. You cannot use keywords as regular identifiers. Some keywords begin simple statements or clauses of compound statements, while other keywords are used as operators. All the keywords are covered in detail in this book, either later in this chapter or in Chapters 5, 6, or 7. The keywords in Python are:

and	del	for	is	raise
assert	elif	from	lambda	return
break	else	global	not	try
class	except	if	or	while
continue	exec	import	pass	yield[a]
def	finally	in	print	

[a] Only in Python 2.3 and later (or Python 2.2 with from __future__ import generators).

Operators

Python uses non-alphanumeric characters and character combinations as operators. Python recognizes the following operators, which are covered in detail later in this chapter:

```
+    -    *    /    %    **    //    <<    >>    &
|    ^    ~    <    <=    >    >=    <>    !=    ==
```

Delimiters

Python uses the following symbols and symbol combinations as delimiters in expressions, lists, dictionaries, various aspects of statements, and strings, among other purposes:

```
(      )      [      ]      {      }
,      :      .             =      ;
+=     -=     *=     /=      //=    %=
&=     |=     ^=     >>=     <<=    **=
```

The period (.) can also appear in floating-point and imaginary literals. A sequence of three periods (...) has a special meaning in slices. The last two rows of the table list the augmented assignment operators, which serve lexically as delimiters but also perform an operation. I'll discuss the syntax for the various delimiters when I introduce the objects or statements with which they are used.

The following characters have special meanings as part of other tokens:

```
'     "    #    \
```

The characters @, $, and ?, all control characters except whitespace, and all characters with ISO codes above 126 (i.e., non-ASCII characters, such as accented letters), can never be part of the text of a Python program except in comments or string literals.

Literals

A *literal* is a data value that appears directly in a program. The following are all literals in Python:

```
42             # Integer literal
3.14           # Floating-point literal
1.0J           # Imaginary literal
'hello'        # String literal
"world"        # Another string literal
"""Good
night"""       # Triple-quoted string literal
```

Using literals and delimiters, you can create data values of other types:

```
[ 42, 3.14, 'hello' ]   # List
( 100, 200, 300 )       # Tuple
{ 'x':42, 'y':3.14 }    # Dictionary
```

The syntax for literals and other data values is covered in detail later in this chapter, when we discuss the various data types supported by Python.

Statements

You can consider a Python source file as a sequence of simple and compound statements. Unlike other languages, Python has no declarations or other top-level syntax elements.

Simple statements

A *simple statement* is one that contains no other statements. A simple statement lies entirely within a logical line. As in other languages, you may place more than one simple statement on a single logical line, with a semicolon (;) as the separator. However, one statement per line is the usual Python style, as it makes programs more readable.

Any expression can stand on its own as a simple statement; we'll discuss expressions in detail later in this chapter. The interactive interpreter shows the result of an expression statement entered at the prompt (>>>), and also binds the result to a variable named _. Apart from interactive sessions, expression statements are useful only to call functions (and other callables) that have side effects (e.g., that perform output or change global variables).

An *assignment* is a simple statement that assigns a value to a variable, as we'll discuss later in this chapter. Unlike in some other languages, an assignment in Python is a statement, and therefore can never be part of an expression.

Compound statements

A *compound statement* contains other statements and controls their execution. A compound statement has one or more *clauses*, aligned at the same indentation. Each clause has a *header* that starts with a keyword and ends with a colon (:), followed by a *body*, which is a sequence of one or more statements. When the body contains multiple statements, also known as a *block*, these statements should be placed on separate logical lines after the header line and indented rightward from the header line. The block terminates when the indentation returns to that of the clause header (or further left from there). Alternatively, the body can be a single simple statement, following the : on the same logical line as the header. The body may also be several simple statements on the same line with semicolons between them, but as I've already indicated, this is not good Python style.

Data Types

The operation of a Python program hinges on the data it handles. All data values in Python are represented by objects, and each object, or value, has a *type*. An object's type determines what operations the object supports, or, in other words, what operations you can perform on the data value. The type also determines the object's attributes and items (if any) and whether the object can be altered. An object that can be altered is known as a *mutable object*, while one that cannot be altered is an *immutable object*. I cover object attributes and items in detail later in this chapter.

The built-in type(*obj*) accepts any object as its argument and returns the type object that represents the type of *obj*. Another built-in function, isinstance(*obj*,*type*), returns True if object *obj* is represented by type object *type*; otherwise, it returns False (built-in names True and False were introduced in Python 2.2.1; in older versions, 1 and 0 are used instead).

Python has built-in objects for fundamental data types such as numbers, strings, tuples, lists, and dictionaries, as covered in the following sections. You can also create user-defined objects, known as *classes*, as discussed in detail in Chapter 5.

Numbers

The built-in number objects in Python support integers (plain and long), floating-point numbers, and complex numbers. All numbers in Python are immutable objects, meaning that when you perform an operation on a number object, you always produce a new number object. Operations on numbers, called arithmetic operations, are covered later in this chapter.

Integer literals can be decimal, octal, or hexadecimal. A decimal literal is represented by a sequence of digits where the first digit is non-zero. An octal literal is specified with a 0 followed by a sequence of octal digits (0 to 7). To indicate a hexadecimal literal, use 0x followed by a sequence of hexadecimal digits (0 to 9 and A to F, in either upper- or lowercase). For example:

```
1, 23, 3493              # Decimal integers
01, 027, 06645           # Octal integers
0x1, 0x17, 0xDA5         # Hexadecimal integers
```

Any kind of integer literal may be followed by the letter L or l to denote a long integer. For instance:

```
1L, 23L, 99999333493L          # Long decimal integers
01L, 027L, 01351033136165L     # Long octal integers
0x1L, 0x17L, 0x17486CBC75L     # Long hexadecimal integers
```

Use uppercase L here, not lowercase l, which may look like the digit 1. The difference between a long integer and a plain integer is that a long integer has no predefined size limit: it may be as large as memory allows. A plain integer takes up a few bytes of memory and has minimum and maximum values that are dictated by machine architecture. sys.maxint is the largest available plain integer, while -sys.maxint-1 is the largest negative one. On typical 32-bit machines, sys.maxint is 2147483647.

A floating-point literal is represented by a sequence of decimal digits that includes a decimal point (.), an exponent part (an e or E, optionally followed by + or -, followed by one or more digits), or both. The leading character of a floating-point literal cannot be e or E: it may be any digit or a period (.) (prior to Python 2.2, a leading 0 had to be immediately followed by a period). For example:

```
0., 0.0, .0, 1., 1.0, 1e0, 1.e0, 1.0e0
```

A Python floating-point value corresponds to a C double and shares its limits of range and precision, typically 53 bits of precision on modern platforms. (Python currently offers no way to find out this range and precision.)

A complex number is made up of two floating-point values, one each for the real and imaginary parts. You can access the parts of a complex object z as read-only attributes z.real and z.imag. You can specify an imaginary literal as a floating-point or decimal literal followed by a j or J:

```
0j, 0.j, 0.0j, .0j, 1j, 1.j, 1.0j, 1e0j, 1.e0j, 1.0e0j
```

The j at the end of the literal indicates the square root of -1, as commonly used in electrical engineering (some other disciplines use i for this purpose, but Python has chosen j). There are no other complex literals; constant complex numbers are denoted by adding or subtracting a floating-point literal and an imaginary one.

Note that numeric literals do not include a sign: a leading + or -, if present, is a separate operator, as discussed later in this chapter.

Sequences

A *sequence* is an ordered container of items, indexed by non-negative integers. Python provides built-in sequence types for strings (plain and Unicode), tuples, and lists. Library and extension modules provide other sequence types, and you can write yet others yourself (as discussed in Chapter 5). Sequences can be manipulated in a variety of ways, as discussed later in this chapter.

Strings

A built-in string object is an ordered collection of characters used to store and represent text-based information. Strings in Python are *immutable*, meaning that when you perform an operation on a string, you always produce a new string object rather than mutating the existing string. String objects provide numerous methods, as discussed in detail in Chapter 9.

A string literal can be quoted or triple-quoted. A quoted string is a sequence of zero or more characters enclosed in matching quote characters, single (') or double ("). For example:

```
'This is a literal string'
"This is another string"
```

The two different kinds of quotes function identically; having both allows you to include one kind of quote inside of a string specified with the other kind without needing to escape them with the backslash character (\):

```
'I\'m a Python fanatic'         # a quote can be escaped
"I'm a Python fanatic"          # this way is more readable
```

To have a string span multiple lines, you can use a backslash as the last character of the line to indicate that the next line is a continuation:

```
"A not very long string\
that spans two lines"           # comment not allowed on previous line
```

To make the string output on two lines, you must embed a newline in the string:

```
"A not very long string\n\
that prints on two lines"       # comment not allowed on previous line
```

Another approach is to use a triple-quoted string, which is enclosed by matching triplets of quote characters (''' or """):

```
"""An even bigger
string that spans
three lines"""                  # comments not allowed on previous lines
```

In a triple-quoted string literal, line breaks in the literal are preserved as newline characters in the resulting string object.

The only character that cannot be part of a triple-quoted string is an unescaped backslash, while a quoted string cannot contain an unescaped backslash, a line-end, and the quote character that encloses it. The backslash character starts an escape sequence, which lets you introduce any character in either kind of string. Python's string escape sequences are listed in Table 4-1.

Table 4-1. String escape sequences

Sequence	Meaning	ASCII/ISO code
\<newline>	End of line is ignored	None
\\	Backslash	0x5c
\'	Single quote	0x27
\"	Double quote	0x22
\a	Bell	0x07

Table 4-1. String escape sequences (continued)

Sequence	Meaning	ASCII/ISO code
\b	Backspace	0x08
\f	Form feed	0x0c
\n	Newline	0x0a
\r	Carriage return	0x0d
\t	Tab	0x09
\v	Vertical tab	0x0b
\DDD	Octal value DDD	As given
\xXX	Hexadecimal value XX	As given
\other	Any other character	0x5c + as given

A variant of a string literal is a raw string. The syntax is the same as for quoted or triple-quoted string literals, except that an r or R immediately precedes the leading quote. In raw strings, escape sequences are not interpreted as in Table 4-1, but are literally copied into the string, including backslashes and newline characters. Raw string syntax is handy for strings that include many backslashes, as in regular expressions (see Chapter 9). A raw string cannot end with an odd number of backslashes: the last one would be taken as escaping the terminating quote.

Unicode string literals have the same syntax as other string literals, plus a u or U immediately before the leading quote character. Unicode string literals can use \u followed by four hexadecimal digits to denote Unicode characters, and can also include the kinds of escape sequences listed in Table 4-1. Unicode literals can also include the escape sequence \N{name}, where name is a standard Unicode name as per the list at *http://www.unicode.org/charts/*. For example, \N{Copyright Sign} indicates a Unicode copyright sign character (©). Raw Unicode string literals start with ur, not ru.

Multiple string literals of any kind (quoted, triple-quoted, raw, Unicode) can be adjacent, with optional whitespace in between. The compiler concatenates such adjacent string literals into a single string object. If any literal in the concatenation is Unicode, the whole result is Unicode. Writing a long string literal in this way lets you present it readably across multiple physical lines, and gives you an opportunity to insert comments about parts of the string. For example:

```
marypop = ('supercalifragilistic'    # Open paren -> logical line continues
           'expialidocious')          # Indentation ignored in continuation
```

The result here is a single word of 34 characters.

Tuples

A *tuple* is an immutable ordered sequence of items. The items of a tuple are arbitrary objects and may be of different types. To specify a tuple, use a series of expressions (the *items* of the tuple) separated by commas (,). You may optionally place a redundant comma after the last item. You may group tuple items with parentheses, but the parentheses are needed only where the commas would otherwise have another meaning (e.g., in function calls) or to denote empty or nested tuples. A tuple with exactly two items is also often called a pair. To create a tuple of one item (a singleton), add a comma to the end of the expression. An empty tuple is denoted by an empty pair of parentheses. Here are some tuples, all enclosed in optional parentheses:

```
(100,200,300)          # Tuple with three items
(3.14,)                # Tuple with one item
()                     # Empty tuple
```

You can also call the built-in tuple to create a tuple. For example:

```
tuple('wow')
```

This builds a tuple equal to:

```
('w', 'o', 'w')
```

tuple( ) without arguments creates and returns an empty tuple. When *x* is a sequence, tuple(*x*) returns a tuple whose items are the same as the items in sequence *x*.

Lists

A *list* is a mutable ordered sequence of items. The items of a list are arbitrary objects and may be of different types. To specify a list, use a series of expressions (the *items* of the list) separated by commas (,) and within brackets ([ ]). You may optionally place a redundant comma after the last item. An empty list is denoted by an empty pair of brackets. Here are some example lists:

```
[42,3.14,'hello']      # List with three items
[100]                  # List with one item
[]                     # Empty list
```

You can also call the built-in list to create a list. For example:

```
list('wow')
```

This builds a list equal to:

```
['w', 'o', 'w']
```

list( ) without arguments creates and returns an empty list. When *x* is a sequence, list(*x*) creates and returns a new list whose items are the same as the items in sequence *x*. You can also build lists with list comprehensions, as discussed later in this chapter.

Dictionaries

A *mapping* is an arbitrary collection of objects indexed by nearly arbitrary values called *keys*. Mappings are mutable and, unlike sequences, are unordered.

Python provides a single built-in mapping type, the dictionary type. Library and extension modules provide other mapping types, and you can write others yourself (as discussed in Chapter 5). Keys in a dictionary may be of different types, but they must be *hashable* (see function hash in "Built-in Functions" in Chapter 8). Values in a dictionary are arbitrary objects and may be of different types. An *item* in a dictionary is a key/value pair. You can think of a dictionary as an associative array (also known in some other languages as a hash).

To specify a dictionary, use a series of pairs of expressions (the pairs are the items of the dictionary) separated by commas (,) within braces ({ }). You may optionally place a redundant comma after the last item. Each item in a dictionary is written *key*:*value*, where *key* is an expression giving the item's key and *value* is an expression giving the item's value. If a key appears more than once in a dictionary, only one of the items with that key is kept in the dictionary. In other words, dictionaries do not allow duplicate keys. An empty dictionary is denoted by an empty pair of braces. Here are some dictionaries:

```
{ 'x':42, 'y':3.14, 'z':7 }    # Dictionary with three items and string keys
{ 1:2, 3:4 }                   # Dictionary with two items and integer keys
{ }                            # Empty dictionary
```

In Python 2.2 and up, you can call the built-in dict to create a dictionary. For example:

```
dict([[1,2],[3,4]])
```

This builds a dictionary equal to:

```
{1:2,3:4}
```

dict( ) without arguments creates and returns an empty dictionary. When the argument *x* to dict is a mapping, dict returns a new dictionary object with the same keys and values as *x*. When *x* is a sequence, the items in *x* must be pairs, and dict(*x*) returns a dictionary whose items (key/value pairs) are the same as the items in sequence *x*. If a key appears more than once in *x*, only the last item with that key is kept in the resulting dictionary.

None

The built-in type None denotes a null object. None has no methods or other attributes. You can use None as a placeholder when you need a reference but you don't care about what object you refer to, or when you need to indicate that no object is there. Functions return None as their result unless they have specific return statements coded to return other values.

Callables

In Python, callable types are those whose instances support the function call operation (see "Expressions and Operators" later in this chapter). Functions are obviously callable, and Python provides built-in functions (see Chapter 8) and also supports user-defined functions (see "Functions" later in this chapter). Generators, which are new as of Python 2.2, are also callable (see "Generators" later in this chapter).

Types are also callable. Thus, the dict, list, and tuple built-ins discussed earlier are in fact types. Prior to Python 2.2, these names referred to factory functions for creating objects of these types. As of Python 2.2, however, they refer to the type objects themselves. Since types are callable, this change does not break existing programs. See Chapter 8 for a complete list of built-in types.

As we'll discuss in Chapter 5, class objects are callable. So are methods, which are functions bound to class attributes. Finally, class instances whose classes supply __call__ methods are also callable.

Boolean Values

Prior to Python 2.3, there is no explicit Boolean type in Python. However, every data value in Python can be evaluated as a truth value: true or false. Any non-zero number or non-empty string, tuple, list, or dictionary evaluates as true. Zero (of any numeric type), None, and empty strings, tuples, lists, and dictionaries evaluate as false. Python also has a number of built-in functions that return Boolean results.

Built-in names True and False were introduced in Python 2.2.1 to represent true and false; in older versions of Python, 1 and 0 are used instead. Throughout the rest of this book, I will use True and False to represent true and false. If you are using a version of Python older than 2.2.1, you'll need to substitute 1 and 0 when using examples from this book.

Python 2.2.1 also introduced a new built-in function named bool. When this function is called with any argument, it considers the argument's value in a Boolean context and returns False or True accordingly.

In Python 2.3, bool becomes a type (a subclass of int) and True and False are the values of that type. The only substantial effect of this innovation is that the string representations of Boolean values become 'True' and 'False', while in earlier versions they are '1' and '0'.

The 2.2.1 and 2.3 changes are handy because they let you speak of functions and expressions as "returning True or False" or "returning a Boolean." The changes also let you write clearer code when you want to return a truth value (e.g., return True instead of return 1).

Variables and Other References

A Python program accesses data values through references. A *reference* is a name that refers to the specific location in memory of a value (object). References take the form of variables, attributes, and items. In Python, a variable or other reference has no intrinsic type. The object to which a reference is bound at a given time does have a type, however. Any given reference may be bound to objects of different types during the execution of a program.

Variables

In Python, there are no declarations. The existence of a variable depends on a statement that *binds* the variable, or, in other words, that sets a name to hold a reference to some object. You can also *unbind* a variable by resetting the name so it no longer holds a reference. Assignment statements are the most common way to bind variables and other references. The del statement unbinds references.

Binding a reference that was already bound is also known as *rebinding* it. Whenever binding is mentioned in this book, rebinding is implicitly included except where it is explicitly excluded. Rebinding or unbinding a reference has no effect on the object to which the reference was bound, except that an object disappears when nothing refers to it. The automatic cleanup of objects to which there are no references is known as *garbage collection*.

You can name a variable with any identifier except the 29 that are reserved as Python's keywords (see "Keywords" earlier in this chapter). A variable can be global or local. A *global variable* is an attribute of a module object (Chapter 7 covers modules). A *local variable* lives in a function's local namespace (see "Functions" later in this chapter).

Object attributes and items

The distinction between attributes and items of an object is in the syntax you use to access them. An *attribute* of an object is denoted by a reference to the object, followed by a period (.), followed by an identifier called the *attribute name* (i.e., x.y refers to the attribute of object x that is named y).

An *item* of an object is denoted by a reference to the object, followed by an expression within brackets ([ ]). The expression in brackets is called the *index* or *key* to the item, and the object is called the *container* of the item (i.e., x[y] refers to the item at key or index y in container object x).

Attributes that are callable are also known as *methods*. Python draws no strong distinction between callable and non-callable attributes, as other languages do. General rules about attributes also apply to callable attributes (methods).

Accessing nonexistent references

A common programming error is trying to access a reference that does not exist. For example, a variable may be unbound, or an attribute name or item index may not be valid for the object to which you apply it. The Python compiler, when it analyzes and compiles source code, diagnoses only syntax errors. Compilation does not diagnose semantic errors such as trying to access an unbound attribute, item, or variable. Python diagnoses semantic errors only when the errant code executes, i.e., at runtime. When an operation is a Python semantic error, attempting it raises an exception (see Chapter 6). Accessing a nonexistent variable, attribute, or item, just like any other semantic error, raises an exception.

Assignment Statements

Assignment statements can be plain or augmented. Plain assignment to a variable (e.g., name=value) is how you create a new variable or rebind an existing variable to a new value. Plain assignment to an object attribute (e.g., obj.attr=value) is a request to object obj to create or rebind attribute attr. Plain assignment to an item in a container (e.g., obj[key]=value) is a request to container obj to create or rebind the item with index key.

Augmented assignment (e.g., name+=value) cannot, per se, create new references. Augmented assignment can rebind a variable, ask an object to rebind one of its existing attributes or items, or request the target object to modify itself (an object may, of course, create arbitrary new references while responding to requests). When you make a request to an object, it is up to the object to decide whether to honor the request or raise an exception.

Plain assignment

A plain assignment statement in the simplest form has the syntax:

```
target = expression
```

The target is also known as the left-hand side, and the expression as the right-hand side. When the assignment statement executes, Python evaluates the right-hand side expression, then binds the expression's value to the left-hand side target. The binding does not depend on the type of the value. In particular, Python draws no strong distinction between callable and non-callable objects, as some other languages do, so you can bind functions, methods, types, and other callables to variables.

Details of the binding do depend on the kind of target, however. The target in an assignment may be an identifier, an attribute reference, an indexing, or a slicing:

- An identifier is a variable's name: assignment to an identifier binds the variable with this name.

- An attribute reference has the syntax *obj.name*. *obj* is an expression denoting an object, and *name* is an identifier, called an *attribute name* of the object. Assignment to an attribute reference asks object *obj* to bind its attribute named *name*.

- An indexing has the syntax *obj[expr]*. *obj* and *expr* are expressions denoting any objects. Assignment to an indexing asks container *obj* to bind its item selected by the value of *expr*, also known as the index or key of the item.

- A slicing has the syntax *obj[start:stop]* or *obj[start:stop:stride]*. *obj*, *start*, *stop*, and *stride* are expressions denoting any objects. *start*, *stop*, and *stride* are all optional (i.e., *obj[:stop]* is also a syntactically correct slicing, equivalent to *obj[None:stop:None]*). Assignment to a slicing asks container *obj* to bind or unbind some of its items.

We'll come back to indexing and slicing targets later in this chapter when we discuss operations on lists and dictionaries.

When the target of the assignment is an identifier, the assignment statement specifies the binding of a variable. This is never disallowed: when you request it, it takes place. In all other cases, the assignment statement specifies a request to an object to bind one or more of its attributes or items. An object may refuse to create or rebind some (or all) attributes or items, raising an exception if you attempt a disallowed creation or rebinding.

There can be multiple targets and equals signs (=) in a plain assignment. For example:

```
a = b = c = 0
```

binds variables a, b, and c to the value 0. Each time the statement executes, the right-hand side expression is evaluated once. Each target gets bound to the single object returned by the expression, just as if several simple assignments executed one after the other.

The target in a plain assignment can list two or more references separated by commas, optionally enclosed in parentheses or brackets. For example:

```
a, b, c = x
```

This requires x to be a sequence with three items, and binds a to the first item, b to the second, and c to the third. This kind of assignment is called an unpacking assignment, and, in general, the right-hand side expression must be a sequence with exactly as many items as there are references in the target; otherwise, an exception is raised. Each reference in the target is bound to the corresponding item in the sequence. An unpacking assignment can also swap references:

```
a, b = b, a
```

This rebinds a to refer to what b was bound to, and vice versa.

Augmented assignment

An augmented assignment differs from a plain assignment in that, instead of an equals sign (=) between the target and the expression, it uses an *augmented operator*: a binary operator followed by =. The augmented operators are +=, -=, *=, /=, //=, %=, **=, |=, >>=, <<=, &=, and ^=. An augmented assignment can have only one target on the left-hand side; that is, augmented assignment doesn't support multiple targets.

In an augmented assignment, just as in a plain one, Python first evaluates the right-hand side expression. Then, if the left-hand side refers to an object that has a special method for the appropriate in-place version of the operator, Python calls the method with the right-hand side value as its argument. It is up to the method to modify the left-hand side object appropriately and return the modified object (Chapter 5 covers special methods). If the left-hand side object has no appropriate in-place special method, Python applies the corresponding binary operator to the left-hand side and right-hand side objects, then rebinds the target reference to the operator's result. For example, x+=y is like x=x.__iadd__(y) when x has special method __iadd__. Otherwise x+=y is like x=x+y.

Augmented assignment never creates its target reference: the target must already be bound when augmented assignment executes. Augmented assignment can rebind the target reference to a new object or modify the same object to which the target reference was already bound. Plain assignment, in contrast, can create or rebind the left-hand side target reference, but it never modifies the object, if any, to which the target reference was previously bound. The distinction between objects and references to objects is crucial here. For example, x=x+y does not modify the object to which name x was originally bound. Rather, it rebinds the name x to refer to a new object. x+=y, in contrast, modifies the object to which name x is bound when that object has special method __iadd__; otherwise, x+=y rebinds the name x, just like x=x+y.

del Statements

Despite its name, a del statement does not delete objects: rather, it unbinds references. Object deletion may follow as a consequence, by garbage collection, when no more references to an object exist.

A del statement consists of the keyword del, followed by one or more target references separated by commas (,). Each target can be a variable, attribute reference, indexing, or slicing, just like for assignment statements, and must be bound at the time del executes. When a del target is an identifier, the del statement specifies the unbinding of the variable. As long as the identifier is bound, unbinding it is never disallowed: when requested, it takes place.

In all other cases, the del statement specifies a request to an object to unbind one or more of its attributes or items. An object may refuse to unbind some (or all) attributes or items, raising an exception if a disallowed unbinding is attempted (see also __delattr__ in Chapter 5). Unbinding a slicing normally has the same effect as assigning an empty sequence to that slice, but it is up to the container object to implement this equivalence.

Expressions and Operators

An *expression* is a phrase of code that the Python interpreter can evaluate to produce a value. The simplest expressions are literals and identifiers. You build other expressions by joining subexpressions with the operators and/or delimiters in Table 4-2. This table lists the operators in decreasing order of precedence, so operators with higher precedence are listed before those with lower precedence. Operators listed together have the same precedence. The A column lists the associativity of the operator, which can be L (left-to-right), R (right-to-left), or NA (non-associative).

In Table 4-2, *expr*, *key*, *f*, *index*, *x*, and *y* indicate any expression, while *attr* and *arg* indicate identifiers. The notation ,... indicates that commas join zero or more repetitions, except for string conversion, where one or more repetitions are allowed. A trailing comma is also allowed and innocuous in all such cases, except with string conversion, where it's forbidden.

Table 4-2. Operator precedence in expressions

Operator	Description	A
`expr,...`	String conversion	NA
{key:expr,...}	Dictionary creation	NA
[expr,...]	List creation	NA
(expr,...)	Tuple creation or simple parentheses	NA
f(expr,...)	Function call	L
x[index:index]	Slicing	L
x[index]	Indexing	L
x.attr	Attribute reference	L
x**y	Exponentiation (x to yth power)	R
~x	Bitwise NOT	NA
+x, -x	Unary plus and minus	NA
x*y, x/y, x//y, x%y	Multiplication, division, truncating division, remainder	L
x+y, x-y	Addition, subtraction	L
x<<y, x>>y	Left-shift, right-shift	L

Table 4-2. Operator precedence in expressions (continued)

Operator	Description	A
x&y	Bitwise AND	L
x^y	Bitwise XOR	L
x|y	Bitwise OR	L
x<y, x<=y, x>y, x>=y, x<>y, x!=y, x==y	Comparisons (less than, less than or equal, greater than, greater than or equal, inequality, equality)[a]	NA
x is y, x is not y	Identity tests	NA
x in y, x not in y	Membership tests	NA
not x	Boolean NOT	NA
x and y	Boolean AND	L
x or y	Boolean OR	L
lambda arg,...: expr	Anonymous simple function	NA

[a] Note that <> and != are alternate forms of the same operator, where != is the preferred version and <> is obsolete.

You can *chain* comparisons, implying a logical and. For example:

```
a < b <= c < d
```

has the same meaning as:

```
a < b and b <= c and c < d
```

The chained form is more readable and evaluates each subexpression only once.

Operators and and or short-circuit their operands' evaluation: the right-hand operand evaluates only if its value is needed to get the truth value of the entire and or or operation. In other words, x and y first evaluates x and if x is false, the result is x; otherwise, the result is y. By the same token, x or y first evaluates x and if x is true, the result is x; otherwise, the result is y. Note that and and or don't force their results to be True or False, but rather return one or the other of their operands. This lets you use these operators more generally, not just in Boolean contexts. and and or, because of their short-circuiting semantics, differ from all other operators, which fully evaluate all operands before performing the operation. As such, and and or let the left operand act as a guard for the right operand.

Numeric Operations

Python supplies the usual numeric operations, as you've just seen in Table 4-2. All numbers are immutable objects, so when you perform a numeric operation on a number object, you always produce a new number object. You can access the parts of a complex object z as read-only attributes z.real and z.imag. Trying to rebind these attributes on a complex object raises an exception.

Note that a number's optional + or - sign, and the + that joins a floating-point literal to an imaginary one to make a complex number, are not part of the literals' syntax. They are ordinary operators, subject to normal operator precedence rules (see Table 4-2). This is why, for example, -2**2 evaluates to -4: exponentiation has higher precedence than unary minus, so the whole expression parses as -(2**2), not as (-2)**2.

Coercion and Conversions

You can perform arithmetic operations and comparisons between any two numbers. If the operands' types differ, *coercion* applies: Python converts the operand with the smaller type to the larger type. The types, in order from smallest to largest, are integers, long integers, floating-point numbers, and complex numbers.

You can also perform an explicit conversion by passing a numeric argument to any of the built-ins: int, long, float, and complex. int and long drop their argument's fractional part, if any (e.g., int(9.8) is 9). Converting from a complex number to any other numeric type drops the imaginary part. You can also call complex with two arguments, giving real and imaginary parts.

Each built-in type can also take a string argument with the syntax of an appropriate numeric literal with two small extensions: the argument string may start with a sign and, for complex numbers, may sum or subtract real and imaginary parts. int and long can also be called with two arguments: the first one a string to convert, and the second one the *radix*, an integer between 2 and 36 to use as the base for the conversion (e.g., int('101',2) returns 5, the value of '101' in base 2).

Arithmetic Operations

If the right operand of /, //, or % is 0, Python raises a runtime exception. The // operator, introduced in Python 2.2, performs truncating division, which means it returns an integer result (converted to the same type as the wider operand) and ignores the remainder, if any. When both operands are integers, the / operator behaves like // if you are using Python 2.1 and earlier or if the switch -Qold was used on the Python command line (-Qold is the default in Python 2.2). Otherwise, / performs true division, returning a floating-point result (or a complex result, if either operand is a complex number). To have / perform true division on integer operands in Python 2.2, use the switch -Qnew on the Python command line or begin your source file with the statement:

```
from future import division
```

This ensures that operator / works without truncation on any type of operands.

To ensure that your program's behavior does not depend on the -Q switch, use // (in Python 2.2 and later) to get truncating division. When you do not want truncation, ensure that at least one operand is not an integer. For example, instead of a/b, use 1.*a/b to avoid making any assumption on the types of a and b. To check whether your program has version dependencies in its use of division, use the switch -Qwarn on the Python command line (in Python 2.2 and later) to get warnings about uses of / on integer operands.

The built-in divmod function takes two numeric arguments and returns a pair whose items are the quotient and remainder, thus saving you from having to use both // for the quotient and % for the remainder.

An exponentiation operation, $a**b$, raises an exception if a is less than zero and b is a floating-point value with a non-zero fractional part. The built-in pow(a,b) function returns the same result as $a**b$. With three arguments, pow(a,b,c) returns the same result as $(a**b)\%c$, but faster.

Comparisons

All objects, including numbers, can also be compared for equality (==) and inequality (!=). Comparisons requiring order (<, <=, >, >=) may be used between any two numbers except complex ones, for which they raise runtime exceptions. All these operators return Boolean values (True or False).

Bitwise Operations on Integers

Integers and long integers can be considered strings of bits and used with the bitwise operations shown in Table 4-2. Bitwise operators have lower priority than arithmetic operators. Positive integers are extended by an infinite string of 0 bits on the left. Negative integers are represented in two's complement notation, and therefore are extended by an infinite string of 1 bits on the left.

Sequence Operations

Python supports a variety of operations that can be applied to sequence types, including strings, lists, and tuples.

Sequences in General

Sequences are containers with items accessible by indexing or slicing, as we'll discuss shortly. The built-in len function takes a container as an argument and returns the number of items in the container. The built-in min and max functions take one argument, a non-empty sequence (or other iterable) whose items are comparable, and they return the smallest and largest items in the sequence, respectively. You can also call min and max with multiple arguments, in which case they return the smallest and largest arguments, respectively.

Coercion and conversions

There is no implicit coercion between different sequence types except that normal strings are coerced to Unicode strings if needed. Conversion to strings is covered in detail in Chapter 9. You can call the built-in tuple and list functions with a single argument (a sequence or other iterable) to get an instance of the type you're calling, with the same items in the same order as in the argument.

Concatenation

You can concatenate sequences of the same type with the + operator. You can also multiply any sequence S by an integer n with the * operator. The result of S*n or n*S is the concatenation of n copies of S. If n is zero or less than zero, the result is an empty sequence of the same type as S.

Sequence membership

The x in S operator tests to see whether object x equals any item in the sequence S. It returns True if it does and False if it doesn't. Similarly, the x not in S operator is just like not (x in S).

Indexing a sequence

The *n*th item of a sequence *S* is denoted by an *indexing*: $S[n]$. Indexing in Python is zero-based (i.e., the first item in *S* is $S[0]$). If *S* has *L* items, the index *n* may be 0, 1, ... up to and including *L*-1, but no larger. *n* may also be -1, -2, ... down to and including -*L*, but no smaller. A negative *n* indicates the same item in *S* as *L+n* does. In other words, $S[-1]$ is the last element of *S*, $S[-2]$ is the next-to-last one, and so on. For example:

```
x = [1,2,3,4]
x[1]            # 2
x[-1]           # 4
```

Using an index greater than or equal to *L* or less than -*L* raises an exception. Assigning to an item with an invalid index also raises an exception. You can add elements to a list, but to do so you assign to a slice, not an item, as we'll discuss shortly.

Slicing a sequence

You can denote a subsequence of *S* with a *slicing*, using the syntax $S[i:j]$, where *i* and *j* are integers. $S[i:j]$ is the subsequence of *S* from the *i*th item, included, to the *j*th item, excluded. Note that in Python, all ranges include the lower bound and exclude the upper bound. A slice can be an empty subsequence if *j* is less than *i* or if *i* is greater than or equal to *L*, the length of *S*. You can omit *i* if it is equal to 0, so that the slice begins from the start of *S*, and you can omit *j* if it is greater than or equal to *L*, so that the slice extends all the way to the end of *S*. You can even omit both indices to mean the entire sequence: $S[:]$. Either or both indices may be less than 0. A negative index indicates the same spot in *S* as *L+n*, just as in indexing. An index greater than or equal to *L* means the end of *S*, while a negative index less than or equal to -*L* means the start of *S*. Here are some examples:

```
x = [1,2,3,4]
x[1:3]          # [2,3]
x[1:]           # [2,3,4]
x[:2]           # [1,2]
```

Slicing can also use the extended syntax $S[i:j:k]$. In Python 2.2, built-in sequences do not support extended-form slicing, but in Python 2.3 they do. Even in Python 2.2 and earlier, however, user-defined sequences can optionally support extended-form slicing. *k* is the *stride* of the slice, or the distance between successive indices. For example, $S[i:j]$ is equivalent to $S[i:j:1]$, $S[::2]$ is the subsequence of *S* that includes all items that have an even index in *S*, and $S[::-1]$ has the same items as *S*, but in reverse order.

Strings

String objects are immutable, so attempting to rebind or delete an item or slice of a string raises an exception. The items of a string object are strings of length 1. The slices of a string object are its substrings. String objects have several methods, which are covered in Chapter 9.

Tuples

Tuple objects are immutable, so attempting to rebind or delete an item or slice of a tuple raises an exception. The items of a tuple are arbitrary objects, and may be of different types. The slices of a tuple are also tuples. Tuples have no normal methods.

Lists

List objects are mutable, so you may rebind or delete items and slices of a list. The items of a list are arbitrary objects, and may be of different types. The slices of a list are also lists.

Modifying a list

You can modify a list by assigning to an indexing. For instance:

```
x = [1,2,3,4]
x[1] = 42                    # x is now [1,42,2,3]
```

Another way to modify a list object L is to use a slice of L as the target (left-hand side) of an assignment statement. The right-hand side of the assignment must also be a list. The left-hand side slice and the right-hand side list may each be of any length, which means that assigning to a slice can add items to the list or remove items from the list. For example:

```
x = [1,2,3,4]
x[1:3] = [22,33,44]        # x is now [1,22,33,44,4]
x[1:4] = [2,3]             # x back to [1,2,3,4]
```

Here are some important special cases:

- Using the empty list [ ] as the right-hand side expression removes the target slice from L. In other words, L[i:j]=[ ] has the same effect as del L[i:j].
- Using an empty slice of L as the left-hand side target inserts the items of the right-hand side list at the appropriate spot in L. In other words, L[i:i]=['a','b'] inserts the items 'a' and 'b' after item i in L.
- Using a slice that covers the entire list object, L[:], as the left-hand side target totally replaces the content of L.

You can delete an item or a slice from a list with del. For instance:

```
x = [1,2,3,4,5]
del x[1]                    # x is now [1,3,4,5]
del x[1:3]                  # x is now [1,5]
```

In-place operations on a list

List objects define in-place versions of the + and * operators, which are used via augmented assignment statements. The augmented assignment statement L+=L1 has the effect of adding the items of list L1 to the end of L, while L*=n has the effect of adding n copies of L to the end of L.

List methods

List objects provide several methods, as shown in Table 4-3. *Non-mutating methods* return a result without altering the object to which they apply, while *mutating methods* may alter the object to which they apply. Many of the mutating methods behave like assignments to appropriate slices of the list. In Table 4-3, *L* and *l* indicate any list object, *i* any valid index in *L*, and *x* any object.

Table 4-3. List object methods

Method	Description
Non-mutating methods	
L.count(x)	Returns the number of occurrences of x in L
L.index(x)	Returns the index of the first occurrence of item x in L or raises an exception if L has no such item
Mutating methods	
L.append(x)	Appends item x to the end of L
L.extend(l)	Appends all the items of list l to the end of L
L.insert(i,x)	Inserts item x at index i in L
L.remove(x)	Removes the first occurrence of item x from L
L.pop([i])	Returns the value of the item at index i and removes it from L; if i is omitted, removes and returns the last item
L.reverse( )	Reverses, in-place, the items of L
L.sort([f])	Sorts, in-place, the items of L, comparing items by f; if f is omitted, cmp is used as comparison function

All mutating methods of list objects except pop return None. The sort method takes one optional argument. If present, the argument must be a function that, when called with any two list items as arguments, returns -1, 0, or 1, depending on whether the first item is to be considered less than, equal to, or greater than the second item for sorting purposes. Passing the argument slows down the sort, although it makes it easy to sort small lists in flexible ways. The decorate-sort-undecorate idiom, presented in Chapter 17, is faster (and often less error-prone) than passing an argument to sort, and it's at least as flexible.

Dictionary Operations

Python provides a variety of operations that can be applied to dictionaries. Since dictionaries are containers, the built-in len function can take a dictionary as its single argument and return the number of items (key/value pairs) in the dictionary object.

Dictionary Membership

In Python 2.2 and later, the k in D operator tests to see whether object k is one of the keys of the dictionary D. It returns True if it is and False if it isn't. Similarly, the k not in D operator is just like not (k in D).

Indexing a Dictionary

The value in a dictionary D that is currently associated with key k is denoted by an *indexing*: D[k]. Indexing with a key that is not present in the dictionary raises an exception. For example:

```
d = { 'x':42, 'y':3.14, 'z':7 }
d['x']                    # 42
d['z']                    # 7
d['a']                    # raises exception
```

Plain assignment to a dictionary indexed with a key that is not yet in the dictionary (e.g., D[newkey]=value) is a valid operation that adds the key and value as a new item in the dictionary. For instance:

```
d = { 'x':42, 'y':3.14, 'z':7 }
d['a'] = 16               # d is now {'x':42,'y':3.14,'z':7,'a':16}
```

The del statement, in the form del D[k], removes from the dictionary the item whose key is k. If k is not a key in dictionary D, del D[k] raises an exception.

Dictionary Methods

Dictionary objects provide several methods, as shown in Table 4-4. Non-mutating methods return a result without altering the object to which they apply, while mutating methods may alter the object to which they apply. In Table 4-4, D and D1 indicate any dictionary object, k any valid key in D, and x any object.

Table 4-4. Dictionary object methods

Method	Description
Non-mutating methods	
D.copy()	Returns a (shallow) copy of the dictionary
D.has_key(k)	Returns True if k is a key in D, otherwise returns False
D.items()	Returns a copy of the list of all items (key/value pairs) in D
D.keys()	Returns a copy of the list of all keys in D
D.values()	Returns a copy of the list of all values in D
D.iteritems()	Returns an iterator on all items (key/value pairs) in D
D.iterkeys()	Returns an iterator on all keys in D
D.itervalues()	Returns an iterator on all values in D
D.get(k[,x])	Returns D[k] if k is a key in D, otherwise returns x (or None, if x is not given)
Mutating methods	
D.clear()	Removes all items from D
D.update(D1)	For each k in D1, sets D[k] equal to D1[k]
D.setdefault(k[,x])	Returns D[k] if k is a key in D; otherwise sets D[k] equal to x and returns x
D.popitem()	Removes and returns an arbitrary item (key/value pair)

The items, keys, and values methods return their resulting lists in arbitrary order. If you call more than one of these methods without any intervening change to the dictionary, however, the order of the results is the same for all. The iteritems, iterkeys, and itervalues methods, which are new as of Python 2.2, return iterators equivalent to these lists (iterators are discussed later in this chapter). An iterator consumes less memory than a list, but you are not allowed to modify a dictionary while iterating on one of its iterators. Iterating on the list returned by items, keys, or values carries no such constraint. Iterating directly on a dictionary D is exactly like iterating on D.iterkeys( ).

The popitem method can be used for destructive iteration on a dictionary. Both items and popitem return dictionary items as key/value pairs, but using popitem consumes less memory, as it does not rely on a separate list of items. The memory savings make the idiom usable for a loop on a huge dictionary, if it's okay to destroy the dictionary in the course of the loop. In Python 2.2 and later, iterating directly on the dictionary (or on iterkeys or iteritems) also consumes modest amounts of memory, and does not destroy the dictionary you're iterating on.

The setdefault method returns the same result as get, but if k is not a key in D, setdefault also has the side effect of binding D[k] to the value x.

The print Statement

A print statement is denoted by the keyword print followed by zero or more expressions separated by commas. print is a handy, simple way to output values in text form. print outputs each expression x as a string that's just like the result of calling str(x) (covered in Chapter 8). print implicitly outputs a space between expressions, and it also implicitly outputs \n after the last expression, unless the last expression is followed by a trailing comma (,). Here are some examples of print statements:

```
letter = 'c'
print "give me a", letter, "..."        # prints: give me a c ...
answer = 42
print "the answer is:", answer          # prints: the answer is: 42
```

The destination of print's output is the file or file-like object that is the value of the stdout attribute of the sys module (covered in Chapter 8). You can control output format more precisely by performing string formatting yourself, with the % operator or other string manipulation techniques, as covered in Chapter 9. You can also use the write or writelines methods of file objects, as covered in Chapter 10. However, print is very simple to use, and simplicity is an important advantage in the common case where all you need are the simple output strategies that print supplies.

Control Flow Statements

A program's *control flow* is the order in which the program's code executes. The control flow of a Python program is regulated by conditional statements, loops, and function calls. This section covers the if statement and for and while loops; functions are covered later in this chapter. Raising and handling exceptions also affects control flow; exceptions are covered in Chapter 6.

The if Statement

Often, you need to execute some statements only if some condition holds, or choose statements to execute depending on several mutually exclusive conditions. The Python compound statement if, which uses if, elif, and else clauses, lets you conditionally execute blocks of statements. Here's the syntax for the if statement:

```
if expression:
    statement(s)
elif expression:
    statement(s)
elif expression:
    statement(s)
...
else expression:
    statement(s)
```

The elif and else clauses are optional. Note that unlike some languages, Python does not have a switch statement, so you must use if, elif, and else for all conditional processing.

Here's a typical if statement:

```
if x < 0: print "x is negative"
elif x % 2: print "x is positive and odd"
else: print "x is even and non-negative"
```

When there are multiple statements in a clause (i.e., the clause controls a block of statements), the statements are placed on separate logical lines after the line containing the clause's keyword (known as the *header line* of the clause) and indented rightward from the header line. The block terminates when the indentation returns to that of the clause header (or further left from there). When there is just a single simple statement, as here, it can follow the : on the same logical line as the header, but it can also be placed on a separate logical line, immediately after the header line and indented rightward from it. Many Python practitioners consider the separate-line style more readable:

```
if x < 0:
    print "x is negative"
elif x % 2:
    print "x is positive and odd"
else:
    print "x is even and non-negative"
```

You can use any Python expression as the condition in an if or elif clause. When you use an expression this way, you are using it in a *Boolean context*. In a Boolean context, any value is taken as either true or false. As we discussed earlier, any non-zero number or non-empty string, tuple, list, or dictionary evaluates as true. Zero (of any numeric type), None, and empty strings, tuples, lists, and dictionaries evaluate as false. When you want to test a value x in a Boolean context, use the following coding style:

```
if x:
```

This is the clearest and most Pythonic form. Don't use:

```
if x is True:
if x == True:
if bool(x):
```

There is a crucial difference between saying that an expression "returns True" (meaning the expression returns the value 1 intended as a Boolean result) and saying that an expression "evaluates as true" (meaning the expression returns any result that is true in a Boolean context). When testing an expression, you care about the latter condition, not the former.

If the expression for the if clause evaluates as true, the statements following the if clause execute, and the entire if statement ends. Otherwise, the expressions for any elif clauses are evaluated in order. The statements following the first elif clause whose condition is true, if any, are executed, and the entire if statement ends. Otherwise, if an else clause exists, the statements following it are executed.

The while Statement

The while statement in Python supports repeated execution of a statement or block of statements that is controlled by a conditional expression. Here's the syntax for the while statement:

```
while expression:
    statement(s)
```

A while statement can also include an else clause and break and continue statements, as we'll discuss shortly.

Here's a typical while statement:

```
count = 0
while x > 0:
    x = x // 2          # truncating division
    count += 1
print "The approximate log2 is", count
```

First, *expression*, which is known as the *loop condition*, is evaluated. If the condition is false, the while statement ends. If the loop condition is satisfied, the statement or statements that comprise the *loop body* are executed. When the loop body finishes executing, the loop condition is evaluated again, to see if another iteration should be performed. This process continues until the loop condition is false, at which point the while statement ends.

The loop body should contain code that eventually makes the loop condition false, or the loop will never end unless an exception is raised or the loop body executes a break statement. A loop that is in a function's body also ends if a return statement executes in the loop body, as the whole function ends in this case.

The for Statement

The for statement in Python supports repeated execution of a statement or block of statements that is controlled by an iterable expression. Here's the syntax for the for statement:

```
for target in iterable:
    statement(s)
```

Note that the in keyword is part of the syntax of the for statement and is functionally unrelated to the in operator used for membership testing. A for statement can also include an else clause and break and continue statements, as we'll discuss shortly.

Here's a typical for statement:

```
for letter in "ciao":
    print "give me a", letter, "..."
```

iterable may be any Python expression suitable as an argument to built-in function iter, which returns an iterator object (explained in detail in the next section). *target* is normally an identifier that names the *control variable* of the loop; the for statement successively rebinds this variable to each item of the iterator, in order. The statement or statements that comprise the *loop body* execute once for each item in *iterable* (unless the loop ends because an exception is raised or a break or return statement is executed).

A target with multiple identifiers is also allowed, as with an unpacking assignment. In this case, the iterator's items must then be sequences, each with the same length, equal to the number of identifiers in the target. For example, when *d* is a dictionary, this is a typical way to loop on the items in *d*:

```
for key, value in d.items():
    if not key or not value: del d[key]      # keep only true keys and values
```

The items method returns a list of key/value pairs, so we can use a for loop with two identifiers in the target to unpack each item into key and value.

If the iterator has a mutable underlying object, that object must not be altered while a for loop is in progress on it. For example, the previous example cannot use iteritems instead of items. iteritems returns an iterator whose underlying object is d, so therefore the loop body cannot mutate d (by del d[key]). items returns a list, though, so d is not the underlying object of the iterator and the loop body can mutate d.

The control variable may be rebound in the loop body, but is rebound again to the next item in the iterator at the next iteration of the loop. The loop body does not execute at all if the iterator yields no items. In this case, the control variable is not bound or rebound in any way by the for statement. If the iterator yields at least one item, however, when the loop statement terminates, the control variable remains bound to the last value to which the loop statement has bound it. The following code is thus correct, as long as someseq is not empty:

```
for x in someseq:
    process(x)
print "Last item processed was", x
```

Iterators

An *iterator* is any object *i* such that you can call *i*.next( ) without any arguments. *i*.next( ) returns the next item of iterator *i*, or, when iterator *i* has no more items, raises a StopIteration exception. When you write a class (see Chapter 5), you can allow instances of the class to be iterators by defining such a method next. Most iterators are built by implicit or explicit calls to built-in function iter, covered in Chapter 8. Calling a generator also returns an iterator, as we'll discuss later in this chapter.

The for statement implicitly calls iter to get an iterator. The following statement:

```
for x in c:
    statement(s)
```

is equivalent to:

```
_temporary_iterator = iter(c)
while True:
    try: x = _temporary_iterator.next( )
    except StopIteration: break
    statement(s)
```

Thus, if iter(c) returns an iterator *i* such that *i*.next( ) never raises StopIteration (an *infinite iterator*), the loop for x in c: never terminates (unless the statements in the loop body contain suitable break or return statements or propagate exceptions). iter(c), in turn, calls special method c.__iter__( ) to obtain and return an iterator on c. We'll talk more about the special method __iter__ in Chapter 5.

Iterators were first introduced in Python 2.2. In earlier versions, for x in S: required S to be a sequence that was indexable with progressively larger indices 0, 1, ..., and raised an IndexError when indexed with a too-large index. Thanks to iterators, the for statement can now be used on a container that is not a sequence, such as a dictionary, as long as the container is iterable (i.e., it defines an __iter__ special method so that function iter can accept the container as the argument and return an iterator on the container). Built-in functions that used to require a sequence argument now also accept any iterable.

range and xrange

Looping over a sequence of integers is a common task, so Python provides built-in functions range and xrange to generate and return integer sequences. The simplest, most idiomatic way to loop *n* times in Python is:

```
for i in xrange(n):
    statement(s)
```

range(x) returns a list whose items are consecutive integers from 0 (included) up to x (excluded). range(x,y) returns a list whose items are consecutive integers from x (included) up to y (excluded). The result is the empty list if x is greater than or equal to y. range(x,y,step) returns a list of integers from x (included) up to y (excluded), such that the difference between each two adjacent items in the list is step. If step is less than 0, range counts down from x to y. range returns the empty list when x is greater than or equal to y and step is greater than 0, or when x is less than or equal to *y* and *step* is less than 0. If *step* equals 0, range raises an exception.

While range returns a normal list object, usable for all purposes, xrange returns a special-purpose object, specifically intended to be used in iterations like the for statement shown previously. xrange consumes less memory than range for this specific use. Leaving aside memory consumption, you can use range wherever you could use xrange.

List comprehensions

A common use of a for loop is to inspect each item in a sequence and build a new list by appending the results of an expression computed on some or all of the items inspected. The expression form, called a *list comprehension*, lets you code this common idiom concisely and directly. Since a list comprehension is an expression (rather than a block of statements), you can use it directly wherever you need an expression (e.g., as an actual argument in a function call, in a return statement, or as a subexpression for some other expression).

A list comprehension has the following syntax:

```
[ expression for target in iterable lc-clauses ]
```

target and *iterable* are the same as in a regular for statement. You must enclose the *expression* in parentheses if it indicates a tuple.

lc-clauses is a series of zero or more clauses, each with one of the following forms:

```
for target in iterable
if expression
```

target and *iterable* in each for clause of a list comprehension have the same syntax as those in a regular for statement, and the *expression* in each if clause of a list comprehension has the same syntax as the *expression* in a regular if statement.

A list comprehension is equivalent to a for loop that builds the same list by repeated calls to the resulting list's append method. For example (assigning the list comprehension result to a variable for clarity):

```
result1 = [x+1 for x in some_sequence]
```

is the same as the for loop:

```
result2 = [ ]
for x in some_sequence:
    result2.append(x+1)
```

Here's a list comprehension that uses an if clause:

```
result3 = [x+1 for x in some_sequence if x>23]
```

which is the same as a for loop that contains an if statement:

```
result4 = [ ]
for x in some_sequence:
    if x>23:
        result4.append(x+1)
```

And here's a list comprehension that uses a for clause:

```
result5 = [x+y for x in alist for y in another]
```

which is the same as a for loop with another for loop nested inside:

```
result6 = [ ]
for x in alist:
    for y in another:
        result6.append(x+y)
```

As these examples show, the order of for and if in a list comprehension is the same as in the equivalent loop, but in the list comprehension the nesting stays implicit.

The break Statement

The break statement is allowed only inside a loop body. When break executes, the loop terminates. If a loop is nested inside other loops, break terminates only the innermost nested loop. In practical use, a break statement is usually inside some clause of an if statement in the loop body so that it executes conditionally.

One common use of break is in the implementation of a loop that decides if it should keep looping only in the middle of each loop iteration:

```
while True:                    # this loop can never terminate naturally
    x = get_next( )
    y = preprocess(x)
    if not keep_looping(x, y): break
    process(x, y)
```

The continue Statement

The continue statement is allowed only inside a loop body. When continue executes, the current iteration of the loop body terminates, and execution continues with the next iteration of the loop. In practical use, a continue statement is usually inside some clause of an if statement in the loop body so that it executes conditionally.

The continue statement can be used in place of deeply nested if statements within a loop. For example:

```
for x in some_container:
    if not seems_ok(x): continue
    lowbound, highbound = bounds_to_test( )
    if x<lowbound or x>=highbound: continue
    if final_check(x):
        do_processing(x)
```

This equivalent code does conditional processing without continue:

```
for x in some_container:
    if seems_ok(x):
        lowbound, highbound = bounds_to_test( )
        if lowbound<=x<highbound:
            if final_check(x):
                do_processing(x)
```

Both versions function identically, so which one you use is a matter of personal preference.

The else Clause on Loop Statements

Both the while and for statements may optionally have a trailing else clause. The statement or statements after the else execute when the loop terminates naturally (at the end of the for iterator or when the while loop condition becomes false), but not when the loop terminates prematurely (via break, return, or an exception). When a loop contains one or more break statements, you often need to check whether the loop terminates naturally or prematurely. You can use an else clause on the loop for this purpose:

```
for x in some_container:
    if is_ok(x): break          # item x is satisfactory, terminate loop
else:
    print "Warning: no satisfactory item was found in container"
    x = None
```

The pass Statement

The body of a Python compound statement cannot be empty—it must contain at least one statement. The pass statement, which performs no action, can be used as a placeholder when a statement is syntactically required but you have nothing specific to do. Here's an example of using pass in a conditional statement as a part of somewhat convoluted logic, with mutually exclusive conditions being tested:

```
if condition1(x):
    process1(x)
elif x>23 or condition2(x) and x<5:
    pass                        # nothing to be done in this case
elif condition3(x):
    process3(x)
else:
    process_default(x)
```

The try Statement

Python supports exception handling with the try statement, which includes try, except, finally, and else clauses. A program can explicitly raise an exception with the raise statement. As we'll discuss in detail in Chapter 6, when an exception is raised, normal control flow of the program stops and Python looks for a suitable exception handler.

Functions

Most statements in a typical Python program are organized into functions. A *function* is a group of statements that executes upon request. Python provides many built-in functions and allows programmers to define their own functions. A request to execute a function is known as a *function call*. When a function is called, it may be passed arguments that specify data upon which the function performs its computation. In Python, a function always returns a result value, either None or a value that represents the results of its computation. Functions defined within class statements are also called *methods*. Issues specific to methods are covered in Chapter 5; the general coverage of functions in this section, however, also applies to methods.

In Python, functions are objects (values) and are handled like other objects. Thus, you can pass a function as an argument in a call to another function. Similarly, a function can return another function as the result of a call. A function, just like any other object, can be bound to a variable, an item in a container, or an attribute of an object. Functions can also be keys into a dictionary. For example, if you need to quickly find a function's inverse given the function, you could define a dictionary whose keys and values are functions and then make the dictionary bidirectional (using some functions from module math, covered in Chapter 15):

```
inverse = {sin:asin, cos:acos, tan:atan, log:exp}
for f in inverse.keys( ): inverse[inverse[f]] = f
```

The fact that functions are objects in Python is often expressed by saying that functions are first-class objects.

The def Statement

The def statement is the most common way to define a function. def is a single-clause compound statement with the following syntax:

```
def function-name(parameters):
    statement(s)
```

function-name is an identifier. It is a variable that gets bound (or rebound) to the function object when def executes.

parameters is an optional list of identifiers, called *formal parameters* or just param-eters, that are used to represent values that are supplied as arguments when the function is called. In the simplest case, a function doesn't have any formal param-eters, which means the function doesn't take any arguments when it is called. In this case, the function definition has empty parentheses following *function-name*.

When a function does take arguments, *parameters* contains one or more identi-fiers, separated by commas (,). In this case, each call to the function supplies values, known as *arguments*, that correspond to the parameters specified in the function definition. The parameters are local variables of the function, as we'll discuss later in this section, and each call to the function binds these local vari-ables to the corresponding values that the caller supplies as arguments.

The non-empty sequence of statements, known as the *function body*, does not execute when the def statement executes. Rather, the function body executes later, each time the function is called. The function body can contain zero or more occurrences of the return statement, as we'll discuss shortly.

Here's an example of a simple function that returns a value that is double the value passed to it:

```
def double(x):
    return x*2
```

Parameters

Formal parameters that are simple identifiers indicate *mandatory parameters*. Each call to the function must supply a corresponding value (argument) for each mandatory parameter.

In the comma-separated list of parameters, zero or more mandatory parameters may be followed by zero or more *optional parameters*, where each optional parameter has the syntax:

```
identifier=expression
```

The def statement evaluates the *expression* and saves a reference to the value returned by the expression, called the *default value* for the parameter, among the attributes of the function object. When a function call does not supply an argument corresponding to an optional parameter, the call binds the parameter's identifier to its default value for that execution of the function.

Note that the same object, the default value, gets bound to the optional parameter whenever the caller does not supply a corresponding argument. This can be tricky when the default value is a mutable object and the function body alters the parameter. For example:

```
def f(x, y=[ ]):
    y.append(x)
    return y
print f(23)              # prints: [23]
prinf f(42)             # prints: [23,42]
```

The second print statement prints [23,42] because the first call to f altered the default value of y, originally an empty list [ ], by appending 23 to it. If you want y to be bound to a new empty list object each time f is called with a single argument, use the following:

```
def f(x, y=None):
    if y is None: y = [ ]
    y.append(x)
    return y
print f(23)              # prints: [23]
prinf f(42)             # prints: [42]
```

At the end of the formal parameters, you may optionally use either or both of the special forms *identifier1* and **identifier2*. If both are present, the one with two asterisks must be last. *identifier1* indicates that any call to the function may supply extra positional arguments, while **identifier2* specifies that any call to the function may supply extra named arguments (positional and named arguments are covered later in this chapter). Every call to the function binds *identifier1* to a tuple whose items are the extra positional arguments (or the empty tuple, if there are none). *identifier2* is bound to a dictionary whose items are the names and values of the extra named arguments (or the empty dictionary, if there are none). Here's how to write a function that accepts any number of arguments and returns their sum:

```
def sum(*numbers):
    result = 0
```

```
    for number in numbers: result += number
    return result
print sum(23,42)            # prints: 65
```

The ** form also lets you construct a dictionary with string keys in a more read-able fashion than with the standard dictionary creation syntax:

```
def adict(**kwds): return kwds
print adict(a=23, b=42)     # prints: {'a':23, 'b':42}
```

Note that the body of function adict is just one simple statement, and therefore we can exercise the option to put it on the same line as the def statement. Of course, it would be just as correct (and arguably more readable) to code function adict using two lines instead of one:

```
def adict(**kwds):
    return kwds
```

Attributes of Function Objects

The def statement defines some attributes of a function object. The attribute func_name, also accessible as __name__, is a read-only attribute (trying to rebind or unbind it raises a runtime exception) that refers to the identifier used as the function name in the def statement. The attribute func_defaults, which you may rebind or unbind, refers to the tuple of default values for the optional parameters (or the empty tuple, if the function has no optional parameters).

Another function attribute is the *documentation string*, also known as a *docstring*. You may use or rebind a function's docstring attribute as either func_doc or __doc__. If the first statement in the function body is a string literal, the compiler binds that string as the function's docstring attribute. A similar rule applies to classes (see Chapter 5) and modules (see Chapter 7). Docstrings most often span multiple physical lines, and are therefore normally specified in triple-quoted string literal form. For example:

```
def sum(*numbers):
    '''Accept arbitrary numerical arguments and return their sum.

    The arguments are zero or more numbers.  The result is their sum.'''

    result = 0
    for number in numbers: result += number
    return result
```

Documentation strings should be part of any Python code you write. They play a role similar to that of comments in any programming language, but their applica-bility is wider since they are available at runtime. Development environments and other tools may use docstrings from function, class, and module objects to remind the programmer how to use those objects. The doctest module (covered in Chapter 17) makes it easy to check that the sample code in docstrings is accurate and correct.

To make your docstrings as useful as possible, you should respect a few simple conventions. The first line of a docstring should be a concise summary of the function's purpose, starting with an uppercase letter and ending with a period. It should not mention the function's name, unless the name happens to be a natural-language word that comes naturally as part of a good, concise summary of the function's operation. If the docstring is multiline, the second line should be empty, and the following lines should form one or more paragraphs, separated by empty lines, describing the function's expected arguments, preconditions, return value, and side effects (if any). Further explanations, bibliographical references, and usage examples (to be checked with doctest) can optionally follow toward the end of the docstring.

In addition to its predefined attributes, a function object may be given arbitrary attributes. To create an attribute of a function object, bind a value to the appropriate attribute references in an assignment statement after the def statement has executed. For example, a function could count how many times it is called:

```
def counter():
    counter.count += 1
    return counter.count
counter.count = 0
```

Note that this is not common usage. More often, when you want to group together some state (data) and some behavior (code), you should use the object-oriented mechanisms covered in Chapter 5. However, the ability to associate arbitrary attributes with a function can sometimes come in handy.

The return Statement

The return statement in Python is allowed only inside a function body, and it can optionally be followed by an expression. When return executes, the function terminates and the value of the expression is returned. A function returns None if it terminates by reaching the end of its body or by executing a return statement that has no expression.

As a matter of style, you should not write a return statement without an expression at the end of a function body. If some return statements in a function have an expression, all return statements should have an expression. return None should only be written explicitly to meet this style requirement. Python does not enforce these stylistic conventions, but your code will be clearer and more readable if you follow them.

Calling Functions

A function call is an expression with the following syntax:

```
function-object(arguments)
```

function-object may be any reference to a function object; it is most often the function's name. The parentheses denote the function-call operation itself. arguments, in the simplest case, is a series of zero or more expressions separated by commas (,), giving values for the function's corresponding formal parameters. When a function is called, the parameters are bound to these values, the function body executes, and the value of the function-call expression is whatever the function returns.

The semantics of argument passing

In traditional terms, all argument passing in Python is *by value*. For example, if a variable is passed as an argument, Python passes to the function the object (value) to which the variable currently refers, not the variable itself. Thus, a function cannot rebind the caller's variables. However, if a mutable object is passed as an argument, the function may request changes to that object since Python passes the object itself, not a copy. Rebinding a variable and mutating an object are totally different concepts in Python. For example:

```
def f(x, y):
    x = 23
    y.append(42)
a = 77
b = [99]
f(a, b)
print a, b                # prints: 77 [99, 42]
```

The print statement shows that a is still bound to 77. Function f's rebinding of its parameter x to 23 has no effect on f's caller, and in particular on the binding of the caller's variable, which happened to be used to pass 77 as the parameter's value. However, the print statement also shows that b is now bound to [99,42]. b is still bound to the same list object as before the call, but that object has mutated, as f has appended 42 to that list object. In either case, f has not altered the caller's bindings, nor can f alter the number 77, as numbers are immutable. However, f can alter a list object, as list objects are mutable. In this example, f does mutate the list object that the caller passes to f as the second argument by calling the object's append method.

Kinds of arguments

Arguments that are just expressions are called *positional arguments*. Each positional argument supplies the value for the formal parameter that corresponds to it by position (order) in the function definition.

In a function call, zero or more positional arguments may be followed by zero or more *named arguments* with the following syntax:

```
identifier=expression
```

The *identifier* must be one of the formal parameter names used in the def statement for the function. The *expression* supplies the value for the formal parameter of that name.

A function call must supply, via either a positional or a named argument, exactly one value for each mandatory parameter, and zero or one value for each optional parameter. For example:

```
def divide(divisor, dividend): return dividend // divisor
print divide(12,94)                  # prints: 7
print divide(dividend=94, divisor=12)        # prints: 7
```

As you can see, the two calls to divide are equivalent. You can pass named arguments for readability purposes when you think that identifying the role of each argument and controlling the order of arguments enhances your code's clarity.

A more common use of named arguments is to bind some optional parameters to specific values, while letting other optional parameters take their default values:

```
def f(middle, begin='init', end='finis'): return begin+middle+end
print f('tini', end='')                  # prints: inittini
```

Thanks to named argument end='', the caller can specify a value, the empty string '', for f's third parameter, end, and still let f's second parameter, begin, use its default value, the string 'init'.

At the end of the arguments in a function call, you may optionally use either or both of the special forms *seq and **dict. If both are present, the one with two asterisks must be last. *seq passes the items of seq to the function as positional arguments (after the normal positional arguments, if any, that the call gives with the usual simple syntax). seq may be any sequence or iterable. **dict passes the items of dict to the function as named arguments, where dict must be a dictionary whose keys are all strings. Each item's key is a parameter name, and the item's value is the argument's value.

Sometimes you want to pass an argument of the form *seq or **dict when the formal parameters use similar forms, as described earlier under "Parameters." For example, using the function sum defined in that section (and shown again here), you may want to print the sum of all the values in dictionary d. This is easy with *seq:

```
def sum(*numbers):
    result = 0
    for number in numbers: result += number
    return result
print sum(*d.values())
```

However, you may also pass arguments of the form *seq or **dict when calling a function that does not use similar forms in its formal parameters.

Namespaces

A function's formal parameters, plus any variables that are bound (by assignment or by other binding statements) in the function body, comprise the function's *local namespace*, also known as *local scope*. Each of these variables is called a *local variable* of the function.

Variables that are not local are known as *global variables* (in the absence of nested definitions, which we'll discuss shortly). Global variables are attributes of the module object, as covered in Chapter 7. If a local variable in a function has the same name as a global variable, whenever that name is mentioned in the function body, the local variable, not the global variable, is used. This idea is expressed by saying that the local variable hides the global variable of the same name throughout the function body.

The global statement

By default, any variable that is bound within a function body is a local variable of the function. If a function needs to rebind some global variables, the first statement of the function must be:

```
global identifiers
```

where *identifiers* is one or more identifiers separated by commas (,). The identifiers listed in a global statement refer to the global variables (i.e., attributes of the module object) that the function needs to rebind. For example, the function counter that we saw in "Attributes of Function Objects" could be implemented using global and a global variable rather than an attribute of the function object as follows:

```
_count = 0
def counter( ):
    global _count
    _count += 1
    return _count
```

Without the global statement, the counter function would raise an UnboundLocalError exception because _count would be an uninitialized (unbound) local variable. Note also that while the global statement does enable this kind of programming, it is neither elegant nor advisable. As I mentioned earlier, when you want to group together some state and some behavior, the object-oriented mechanisms covered in Chapter 5 are typically the best approach.

You don't need global if the function body simply uses a global variable, including changing the object bound to that variable if the object is mutable. You need to use a global statement only if the function body rebinds a global variable. As a matter of style, you should not use global unless it's strictly necessary, as its presence will cause readers of your program to assume the statement is there for some useful purpose.

Nested functions and nested scopes

A def statement within a function body defines a *nested function*, and the function whose body includes the def is known as an *outer function* to the nested one. Code in a nested function's body may access (but not rebind) local variables of an outer function, also known as *free variables* of the nested function. This nested-scope access is automatic in Python 2.2 and later. To request nested-scope access in Python 2.1, the first statement of the module must be:

```
from __future__ import nested_scopes
```

The simplest way to let a nested function access a value is often not to rely on nested scopes, but rather to explicitly pass that value as one of the function's arguments. The argument's value can be bound when the nested function is defined by using the value as the default for an optional argument. For example:

```
def percent1(a, b, c):                 # works with any version
    def pc(x, total=a+b+c): return (x*100.0) / total
    print "Percentages are ", pc(a), pc(b), pc(c)
```

Here's the same functionality using nested scopes:

```
def percent2(a, b, c):                 # needs 2.2 or "from future import"
    def pc(x): return (x*100.0) / (a+b+c)
    print "Percentages are", pc(a), pc(b), pc(c)
```

In this specific case, percent1 has a slight advantage: the computation of *a+b+c* happens only once, while percent2's inner function pc repeats the computation three times. However, if the outer function were rebinding its local variables between calls to the nested function, repeating this computation might be an advantage. It's therefore advisable to be aware of both approaches, and choose the most appropriate one case by case.

A nested function that accesses values from outer local variables is known as a *closure*. The following example shows how to build a closure without nested scopes (using a default value):

```
def make_adder_1(augend):          # works with any version
    def add(addend, _augend=augend): return addend+_augend
    return add
```

Here's the same closure functionality using nested scopes:

```
def make_adder_2(augend):          # needs 2.2 or "from future import"
    def add(addend): return addend+augend
    return add
```

Closures are an exception to the general rule that the object-oriented mechanisms covered in Chapter 5 are the best way to bundle together data and code. When you need to construct callable objects, with some parameters fixed at object construction time, closures can be simpler and more effective than classes. For example, the result of make_adder_1(7) is a function that accepts a single argument and adds 7 to that argument (the result of make_adder_2(7) behaves in just the same way). You can also express the same idea as lambda x: x+7, using the lambda form covered in the next section. A closure is a "factory" for any member of a family of functions distinguished by some parameters, such as the value of argument *augend* in the previous examples, and this may often help you avoid code duplication.

lambda Expressions

If a function body contains a single return *expression* statement, you may choose to replace the function with the special lambda expression form:

```
lambda parameters: expression
```

A lambda expression is the anonymous equivalent of a normal function whose body is a single return statement. Note that the lambda syntax does not use the return keyword. You can use a lambda expression wherever you would use a reference to a function. lambda can sometimes be handy when you want to use a simple function as an argument or return value. Here's an example that uses a lambda expression as an argument to the built-in filter function:

```
aList = [1,2,3,4,5,6,7,8,9]
low = 3
high = 7
filter(lambda x,l=low,h=high: h>x>l, aList)     # returns: [4, 5, 6]
```

As an alternative, you can always use a local def statement that gives the function object a name. You can then use this name as the argument or return value. Here's the same filter example using a local def statement:

```
aList = [1,2,3,4,5,6,7,8,9]
low = 3
```

```
high = 7
def test(value, l=low, h=high):
    return h>value>l
filter(test, aList)                              # returns: [4, 5, 6]
```

Generators

When the body of a function contains one or more occurrences of the keyword yield, the function is called a *generator*. When a generator is called, the function body does not execute. Instead, calling the generator returns a special iterator object that wraps the function body, the set of its local variables (including its parameters), and the current point of execution, which is initially the start of the function.

When the next method of this iterator object is called, the function body executes up to the next yield statement, which takes the form:

yield *expression*

When a yield statement executes, the function is frozen with its execution state and local variables intact, and the expression following yield is returned as the result of the next method. On the next call to next, execution of the function body resumes where it left off, again up to the next yield statement. If the function body ends or executes a return statement, the iterator raises a StopException to indicate that the iterator is finished. Note that return statements in a generator cannot contain expressions, as that is a syntax error.

yield is always a keyword in Python 2.3 and later. In Python 2.2, to make yield a keyword in a source file, use the following line as the first statement in the file:

from __future__ import generators

In Python 2.1 and earlier, you cannot define generators.

Generators are often handy ways to build iterators. Since the most common way to use an iterator is to loop on it with a for statement, you typically call a generator like this:

for *avariable* in *somegenerator*(*arguments*):

For example, say that you want a sequence of numbers counting up from 1 to *N* and then down to 1 again. A generator helps:

```
def updown(N):
    for x in xrange(1,N): yield x
    for x in xrange(N,0,-1): yield x
for i in updown(3): print i                     # prints: 1 2 3 2 1
```

Here is a generator that works somewhat like the built-in xrange function, but returns a sequence of floating-point values instead of a sequence of integers:

```
def frange(start, stop, step=1.0):
    while start < stop:
        yield start
        start += step
```

frange is only somewhat like xrange, because, for simplicity, it makes arguments start and stop mandatory, and silently assumes step is positive (by default, like xrange, frange makes step equal to 1).

Generators are more flexible than functions that return lists. A generator may build an iterator that returns an infinite stream of results that is usable only in loops that terminate by other means (e.g., via a break statement). Further, the generator-built iterator performs *lazy evaluation*: the iterator computes each successive item only when and if needed, just in time, while the equivalent function does all computations in advance and may require large amounts of memory to hold the results list. Therefore, in Python 2.2 and later, if all you need is the ability to iterate on a computed sequence, it is often best to compute the sequence in a generator, rather than in a function that returns a list. If the caller needs a list that contains all the items produced by a generator $G(arguments)$, the caller can use the following code:

```
resulting_list = list(G(arguments))
```

Recursion

Python supports recursion (i.e., a Python function can call itself), but there is a limit to how deep the recursion can be. By default, Python interrupts recursion and raises a RecursionLimitExceeded exception (covered in Chapter 6) when it detects that the stack of recursive calls has gone over a depth of 1,000. You can change the recursion limit with function setrecursionlimit of module sys, covered in Chapter 8.

However, changing this limit will still not give you unlimited recursion; the absolute maximum limit depends on the platform, particularly on the underlying operating system and C runtime library, but it's typically a few thousand. When recursive calls get too deep, your program will crash. Runaway recursion after a call to setrecursionlimit that exceeds the platform's capabilities is one of the very few ways a Python program can crash—really crash, hard, without the usual safety net of Python's exception mechanisms. Therefore, be wary of trying to fix a program that is getting RecursionLimitExceeded exceptions by raising the recursion limit too high with setrecursionlimit. Most often, you'd be better advised to look for ways to remove the recursion or, at least, to limit the depth of recursion that your program needs.

5

Object-Oriented Python

Python is an object-oriented programming language. Unlike some other object-oriented languages, Python doesn't force you to use the object-oriented paradigm exclusively. Python also supports procedural programming with modules and functions, so you can select the most suitable programming paradigm for each part of your program. Generally, the object-oriented paradigm is suitable when you want to group state (data) and behavior (code) together in handy packets of functionality. It's also useful when you want to use some of Python's object-oriented mechanisms covered in this chapter, such as inheritance or special methods. The procedural paradigm, based on modules and functions, tends to be simpler and is more suitable when you don't need any of the benefits of object-oriented programming. With Python, you often mix and match the two paradigms.

Python 2.2 and 2.3 are in transition between two slightly different object models. This chapter starts by describing the classic object model, which was the only one available in Python 2.1 and earlier and is still the default model in Python 2.2 and 2.3. The chapter then covers the small differences that define the powerful new-style object model and discusses how to use the new-style object model with Python 2.2 and 2.3. Because the new-style object model builds on the classic one, you'll need to understand the classic model before you can learn about the new model. Finally, the chapter covers special methods for both the classic and new-style object models, as well as metaclasses for Python 2.2 and later.

The new-style object model will become the default in a future version of Python. Even though the classic object model is still the default, I suggest you use the new-style object model when programming with Python 2.2 and later. Its advantages over the classic object model, while small, are measurable, and there are practically no compensating disadvantages. Therefore, it's simpler just to stick to the new-style object model, rather than try to decide which model to use each time you code a new class.

Classic Classes and Instances

A *classic class* is a Python object with several characteristics:

- You can call a class object as if it were a function. The call creates another object, known as an *instance* of the class, that knows what class it belongs to.
- A class has arbitrarily named attributes that you can bind and reference.
- The values of class attributes can be data objects or function objects.
- Class attributes bound to functions are known as *methods* of the class.
- A method can have a special Python-defined name with two leading and two trailing underscores. Python invokes such *special methods*, if they are present, when various kinds of operations take place on class instances.
- A class can *inherit* from other classes, meaning it can delegate to other class objects the lookup of attributes that are not found in the class itself.

An instance of a class is a Python object with arbitrarily named attributes that you can bind and reference. An instance object implicitly delegates to its class the lookup of attributes not found in the instance itself. The class, in turn, may delegate the lookup to the classes from which it inherits, if any.

In Python, classes are objects (values), and are handled like other objects. Thus, you can pass a class as an argument in a call to a function. Similarly, a function can return a class as the result of a call. A class, just like any other object, can be bound to a variable (local or global), an item in a container, or an attribute of an object. Classes can also be keys into a dictionary. The fact that classes are objects in Python is often expressed by saying that classes are first-class objects.

The class Statement

The class statement is the most common way to create a class object. class is a single-clause compound statement with the following syntax:

```
class classname[(base-classes)]:
    statement(s)
```

classname is an identifier. It is a variable that gets bound (or rebound) to the class object after the class statement finishes executing.

base-classes is an optional comma-delimited series of expressions whose values must be class objects. These classes are known by different names in different languages; you can think of them as the *base classes*, *superclasses*, or *parents* of the class being created. The class being created is said to *inherit* from, *derive* from, *extend*, or *subclass* its base classes, depending on what language you are familiar with. This class is also known as a *direct subclass* or *descendant* of its base classes.

The subclass relationship between classes is transitive. If *C1* subclasses *C2*, and *C2* subclasses *C3*, *C1* subclasses *C3*. Built-in function issubclass(*C1*, *C2*) accepts two arguments that are class objects: it returns True if *C1* subclasses *C2*, otherwise it returns False. Any class is considered a subclass of itself; therefore issubclass(*C*, *C*) returns True for any class *C*. The way in which the base classes of a class affect the functionality of the class is covered later in this chapter.

The syntax of the class statement has a small, tricky difference from that of the def statement covered in Chapter 4. In a def statement, parentheses are mandatory between the function's name and the colon. To define a function without formal parameters, use a statement such as:

```
def name( ):
    statement(s)
```

In a class statement, the parentheses are mandatory if the class has one or more base classes, but they are forbidden if the class has no base classes. Thus, to define a class without base classes, use a statement such as:

```
class name:
    statement(s)
```

The non-empty sequence of statements that follows the class statement is known as the *class body*. A class body executes immediately, as part of the class statement's execution. Until the body finishes executing, the new class object does not yet exist and the *classname* identifier is not yet bound (or rebound). The "Metaclasses" section later in this chapter provides more details about what happens when a class statement executes.

Finally, note that the class statement does not create any instances of a class, but rather defines the set of attributes that are shared by all instances when they are created.

The Class Body

The body of a class is where you normally specify the attributes of the class; these attributes can be data objects or function objects.

Attributes of class objects

You typically specify an attribute of a class object by binding a value to an identifier within the class body. For example:

```
class C1:
    x = 23
print C1.x                          # prints: 23
```

Class object C1 now has an attribute named x, bound to the value 23, and C1.x refers to that attribute.

You can also bind or unbind class attributes outside the class body. For example:

```
class C2: pass
C2.x = 23
print C2.x                          # prints: 23
```

However, your program is more readable if you bind, and thus create, class attributes with statements inside the class body. Any class attributes are implicitly shared by all instances of the class when those instances are created, as we'll discuss shortly.

The class statement implicitly defines some class attributes. Attribute __name__ is the *classname* identifier string used in the class statement. Attribute __bases__ is the tuple of class objects given as the base classes in the class statement (or the empty tuple, if no base classes are given). For example, using the class C1 we just created:

```
print C1.__name__, C1.__bases__          # prints: C1, ()
```

A class also has an attribute __dict__, which is the dictionary object that the class uses to hold all of its other attributes. For any class object C, any object x, and any identifier S (except __name__, __bases__, and __dict__), C.S=x is equivalent to C.__dict__['S']=x. For example, again referring to the class C1 we just created:

```
C1.y = 45
C1.__dict__['z'] = 67
print C1.x, C1.y, C1.z                    # prints: 23, 45, 67
```

There is no difference between class attributes created in the class body, outside of the body by assigning an attribute, or outside of the body by explicitly binding an entry in C.__dict__.

In statements that are directly in a class's body, references to attributes of the class must use a simple name, not a fully qualified name. For example:

```
class C3:
    x = 23
    y = x + 22                            # must use just x, not C3.x
```

However, in statements that are in methods defined in a class body, references to attributes of the class must use a fully qualified name, not a simple name. For example:

```
class C4:
    x = 23
    def amethod(self):
        print C4.x                        # must use C4.x, not just x
```

Note that attribute references (i.e., an expression like C.S) have richer semantics than attribute binding. These references are covered in detail later in this chapter.

Function definitions in a class body

Most class bodies include def statements, as functions (called methods in this context) are important attributes for class objects. A def statement in a class body obeys the rules presented in "Functions" in Chapter 4. In addition, a method defined in a class body always has a mandatory first parameter, conventionally named self, that refers to the instance on which you call the method. The self parameter plays a special role in method calls, as covered later in this chapter.

Here's an example of a class that includes a method definition:

```
class C5:
    def hello(self):
        print "Hello"
```

A class can define a variety of special methods (methods with names that have two leading and two trailing underscores) relating to specific operations. We'll discuss special methods in great detail later in this chapter.

Class-private variables

When a statement in a class body (or in a method in the body) uses an identifier starting with two underscores (but not ending with underscores), such as __ident, the Python compiler implicitly changes the identifier into _classname__ident, where classname is the name of the class. This lets a class use private names for attributes, methods, global variables, and other purposes, without the risk of accidentally duplicating names used elsewhere.

By convention, all identifiers starting with a single underscore are also intended as private to the scope that binds them, whether that scope is or isn't a class. The Python compiler does not enforce privacy conventions, however: it's up to Python programmers to respect them.

Class documentation strings

If the first statement in the class body is a string literal, the compiler binds that string as the documentation string attribute for the class. This attribute is named __doc__ and is known as the *docstring* of the class. See "Attributes of Function Objects" in Chapter 4 for more information on docstrings.

Instances

When you want to create an instance of a class, call the class object as if it were a function. Each call returns a new instance object of that class:

```
anInstance = C5()
```

You can call built-in function isinstance(I,C) with a class object as argument C. In this case, isinstance returns True if object I is an instance of class C or any subclass of C. Otherwise, isinstance returns False.

__init__

When a class has or inherits a method named __init__, calling the class object implicitly executes __init__ on the new instance to perform any instance-specific initialization that is needed. Arguments passed in the call must correspond to the formal parameters of __init__. For example, consider the following class:

```
class C6:
    def __init__(self,n):
        self.x = n
```

Here's how to create an instance of the C6 class:

```
anotherInstance = C6(42)
```

As shown in the C6 class, the __init__ method typically contains statements that bind instance attributes. An __init__ method must either not return a value or return the value None; any other return value raises a TypeError exception.

The main purpose of __init__ is to bind, and thus create, the attributes of a newly created instance. You may also bind or unbind instance attributes outside __init__, as you'll see shortly. However, your code will be more readable if you initially bind all attributes of a class instance with statements in the __init__ method.

When __init__ is absent, you must call the class without arguments, and the newly generated instance has no instance-specific attributes. See "Special Methods" later in this chapter for more details about __init__.

Attributes of instance objects

Once you have created an instance, you can access its attributes (data and methods) using the dot (.) operator. For example:

```
anInstance.hello()                      # prints: Hello
print anotherInstance.x                 # prints: 42
```

Attribute references such as these have fairly rich semantics in Python and are covered in detail later in this section.

You can give an instance object an arbitrary attribute by binding a value to an attribute reference. For example:

```
class C7: pass
z = C7()
z.x = 23
print z.x                               # prints: 23
```

Instance object z now has an attribute named x, bound to the value 23, and z.x refers to that attribute. Note that the __setattr__ special method, if present, intercepts every attempt to bind an attribute. __setattr__ is covered in "Special Methods" later in this chapter.

Creating an instance implicitly defines two instance attributes. For any instance z, z.__class__ is the class object to which z belongs, and z.__dict__ is the dictionary that z uses to hold all of its other attributes. For example, for the instance z we just created:

```
print z.__class__.__name__, z.__dict__    # prints: C7, {'x':23}
```

You may rebind (but not unbind) either or both of these attributes, but this is rarely necessary.

For any instance object z, any object x, and any identifier S (except __class__ and __dict__), z.S=x is equivalent to z.__dict__['S']=x (unless a __setattr__ special method intercepts the binding attempt). For example, again referring to the instance z we just created:

```
z.y = 45
z.__dict__['z'] = 67
print z.x, z.y, z.z                     # prints: 23, 45, 67
```

There is no difference between instance attributes created in __init__, by assigning to attributes, or by explicitly binding an entry in z.__dict__.

The factory-function idiom

It is common to want to create instances of different classes depending upon some condition or to want to avoid creating a new instance if an existing one is available for reuse. You might consider implementing these needs by having __init__ return a particular object, but that isn't possible because Python raises an exception when __init__ returns any value other than None. The best way to implement flexible object creation is by using an ordinary function, rather than by calling the class object directly. A function used in this role is known as a *factory function*.

Calling a factory function is a more flexible solution, as such a function may return an existing reusable instance or create a new instance by calling whatever class is appropriate. Say you have two almost-interchangeable classes (SpecialCase and NormalCase) and you want to flexibly generate either one of them, depending on an argument. The following appropriateCase factory function allows you to do just that (the role of the self parameters is covered in "Bound and Unbound Methods" later in this chapter):

```
class SpecialCase:
    def amethod(self): print "special"
class NormalCase:
    def amethod(self): print "normal"
def appropriateCase(isnormal=1):
    if isnormal: return NormalCase( )
    else: return SpecialCase( )
aninstance = appropriateCase(isnormal=0)
aninstance.amethod( )                        # prints "special", as desired
```

Attribute Reference Basics

An *attribute reference* is an expression of the form *x.name*, where *x* is any expression and *name* is an identifier called the *attribute name*. Many kinds of Python objects have attributes, but an attribute reference has special rich semantics when *x* refers to a class or instance. Remember that methods are attributes too, so everything I say about attributes in general also applies to attributes that are callable (i.e., methods).

Say that x is an instance of class C, which inherits from base class B. Both classes and the instance have several attributes (data and methods) as follows:

```
class B:
    a = 23
    b = 45
    def f(self): print "method f in class B"
    def g(self): print "method g in class B"
class C(B):
    b = 67
    c = 89
    d = 123
    def g(self): print "method g in class C"
    def h(self): print "method h in class C"
x = C( )
x.d = 77
x.e = 88
```

Some attribute names are special. For example, C.__name__ is the string 'C', the class name. C.__bases__ is the tuple (B,), the tuple of C's base classes. x.__class__ is the class C, the class to which x belongs. When you refer to an attribute with one of these special names, the attribute reference looks directly into a special dedicated slot in the class or instance object and fetches the value it finds there. Thus, you can never unbind these attributes. Rebinding them is allowed, so you can change the name or base classes of a class or the class of an instance on the fly, but this is an advanced technique and rarely necessary.

Both class C and instance x each have one other special attribute, a dictionary named __dict__. All other attributes of a class or instance, except for the few special ones, are held as items in the __dict__ attribute of the class or instance.

Apart from special names, when you use the syntax x.name to refer to an attribute of instance x, the lookup proceeds in two steps:

1. When 'name' is a key in x.__dict__, x.name fetches and returns the value at x.__dict__['name']

2. Otherwise, x.name delegates the lookup to x's class (i.e., it works just the same as x.__class__.name)

Similarly, lookup for an attribute reference C.name on a class object C also proceeds in two steps:

1. When 'name' is a key in C.__dict__, C.name fetches and returns the value at C.__dict__['name']

2. Otherwise, C.name delegates the lookup to C's base classes, meaning it loops on C.__bases__ and tries the name lookup on each

When these two lookup procedures do not find an attribute, Python raises an AttributeError exception. However, if x's class defines or inherits special method __getattr__, Python calls x.__getattr__('name') rather than raising the exception.

Consider the following attribute references:

```
print x.e, x.d, x.c, x.b. x.a          # prints: 88, 77, 89, 67, 23
```

x.e and x.d succeed in step 1 of the first lookup process, since 'e' and 'd' are both keys in x.__dict__. Therefore, the lookups go no further, but rather return 88 and 77. The other three references must proceed to step 2 of the first process and look in x.__class__ (i.e., C). x.c and x.b succeed in step 1 of the second lookup process, since 'c' and 'b' are both keys in C.__dict__. Therefore, the lookups go no further, but rather return 89 and 67. x.a gets all the way to step 2 of the second process, looking in C.__bases__[0] (i.e., B). 'a' is a key in B.__dict__, therefore x.a finally succeeds and returns 23.

Note that the attribute lookup steps happen only when you refer to an attribute, not when you bind an attribute. When you bind or unbind an attribute whose name is not special, only the __dict__ entry for the attribute is affected. In other words, in the case of attribute binding, there is no lookup procedure involved.

Bound and Unbound Methods

Step 1 of the class attribute reference lookup process described in the previous section actually performs an additional task when the value found is a function. In this case, the attribute reference does not return the function object directly, but rather wraps the function into an *unbound method object* or a *bound method object*. The key difference between unbound and bound methods is that an unbound method is not associated with a particular instance, while a bound method is.

In the code in the previous section, attributes f, g, and h are functions; therefore an attribute reference to any one of them returns a method object wrapping the respective function. Consider the following:

```
print x.h, x.g, x.f, C.h, C.g, C.f
```

This statement outputs three bound methods, represented as strings like:

```
<bound method C.h of <__main__.C instance at 0x8156d5c>>
```

and then three unbound ones, represented as strings like:

```
<unbound method C.h>
```

We get bound methods when the attribute reference is on instance x, and unbound methods when the attribute reference is on class C.

Because a bound method is already associated with a specific instance, you call the method as follows:

```
x.h( )                    # prints: method h in class C
```

The key thing to notice here is that you don't pass the method's first argument, self, by the usual argument-passing syntax. Rather, a bound method of instance x implicitly binds the self parameter to object x. Thus, the body of the method can access the instance's attributes as attributes of self, even though we don't pass an explicit argument to the method.

An unbound method, however, is not associated with a specific instance, so you must specify an appropriate instance as the first argument when you invoke an unbound method. For example:

```
C.h(x)                    # prints: method h in class C
```

You call unbound methods far less frequently than you call bound methods. The main use for unbound methods is for accessing overridden methods, as discussed in "Inheritance" later in this chapter.

Unbound method details

As we've just discussed, when an attribute reference on a class refers to a function, a reference to that attribute returns an unbound method that wraps the function. An unbound method has three attributes in addition to those of the function object it wraps: im_class is the class object supplying the method, im_func is the wrapped function, and im_self is always None. These attributes are all read-only, meaning that trying to rebind or unbind any of them raises an exception.

You can call an unbound method just as you would call its im_func function, but the first argument in any call must be an instance of im_class or a descendant. In other words, a call to an unbound method must have at least one argument, which corresponds to the first formal parameter (conventionally named self).

Bound method details

As covered earlier in "Attribute Reference Basics," an attribute reference on an instance *x*, such as *x.f*, delegates the lookup to *x*'s class when '*f*' is not a key in *x*.__dict__. In this case, when the lookup finds a function object, the attribute reference operation creates and returns a bound method that wraps the function. Note that when the attribute reference finds a function object in *x*.__dict__ or any other kind of callable object by whatever route, the attribute reference operation does not create a bound method. The bound method is created only when a function object is found as an attribute in the instance's class.

A bound method is similar an unbound method, in that it has three read-only attributes in addition to those of the function object it wraps. Like with an unbound method, im_class is the class object supplying the method, and im_func is the wrapped function. However, in a bound method object, attribute im_self refers to *x*, the instance from which the method was obtained.

A bound method is used like its im_func function, but calls to a bound method do not explicitly supply an argument corresponding to the first formal parameter (conventionally named self). When you call a bound method, the bound method passes im_self as the first argument to im_func, before other arguments (if any) are passed at the point of call.

Let's follow the conceptual steps in a typical method call with the normal syntax *x.name(arg)*. *x* is an instance object, *name* is an identifier naming one of *x*'s methods (a function-valued attribute of *x*'s class), and *arg* is any expression. Python checks if '*name*' is a key in *x*.__dict__, but it isn't. So Python finds *name* in *x*.__class__ (possibly, by inheritance, in one of its __bases__). Python notices that the value is a function object, and that the lookup is being done on instance *x*. Therefore, Python creates a bound method object whose im_self attribute refers to *x*. Then, Python calls the bound method object with *arg* as the only actual argument. The bound method inserts im_self (i.e., *x*) as the first actual argument and *arg* becomes the second one. The overall effect is just like calling:

```
x.__class__.__dict__['name'](x, arg)
```

When a bound method's function body executes, it has no special namespace relationship to either its self object or any class. Variables referenced are local or global, just as for any other function, as covered in "Namespaces" in Chapter 4. Variables do not implicitly indicate attributes in self, nor do they indicate attributes in any class object. When the method needs to refer to, bind, or unbind an attribute of its self object, it does so by standard attribute-reference syntax (e.g., self.name). The lack of implicit scoping may take some getting used to (since Python differs in this respect from many other object-oriented languages), but it results in clarity, simplicity, and the removal of potential ambiguities.

Bound method objects are first-class objects, and you can use them wherever you can use a callable object. Since a bound method holds references to the function it wraps and to the self object on which it executes, it's a powerful and flexible alternative to a closure (covered in "Nested functions and nested scopes" in Chapter 4). An instance object with special method __call__ (covered in "Special Methods" later in this chapter) offers another viable alternative. Each of these constructs lets you bundle some behavior (code) and some state (data) into a single callable object. Closures are simplest, but limited in their applicability. Here's the closure from Chapter 4:

```
def make_adder_as_closure(augend):
    def add(addend, _augend=augend): return addend+_augend
    return add
```

Bound methods and callable instances are richer and more flexible. Here's how to implement the same functionality with a bound method:

```
def make_adder_as_bound_method(augend):
    class Adder:
        def __init__(self, augend): self.augend = augend
        def add(self, addend): return addend+self.augend
    return Adder(augend).add
```

Here's how to implement it with a callable instance (an instance with __call__):

```
def make_adder_as_callable_instance(augend):
    class Adder:
        def __init__(self, augend): self.augend = augend
        def __call__(self, addend): return addend+self.augend
    return Adder(augend)
```

From the viewpoint of the code that calls the functions, all of these functions are interchangeable, since all return callable objects that are polymorphic (i.e., usable in the same ways). In terms of implementation, the closure is simplest; the bound method and callable instance use more flexible and powerful mechanisms, but there is really no need for that extra power in this case.

Inheritance

When you use an attribute reference C.name on a class object C, and 'name' is not a key in C.__dict__, the lookup implicitly proceeds on each class object that is in C.__bases__, in order. C's base classes may in turn have their own base classes. In this case, the lookup recursively proceeds up the inheritance tree, stopping when 'name' is found. The search is depth-first, meaning that it examines the ancestors of each base class of C before considering the next base class of C. Consider the following example:

```
class Base1:
    def amethod(self): print "Base1"
class Base2(Base1): pass
class Base3:
    def amethod(self): print "Base3"
class Derived(Base2, Base3): pass
aninstance = Derived( )
aninstance.amethod( )                   # prints: "Base1"
```

In this case, the lookup for amethod starts in Derived. When it isn't found there, lookup proceeds to Base2. Since the attribute isn't found in Base2, lookup then proceeds to Base2's ancestor, Base1, where the attribute is found. Therefore, the lookup stops at this point and never considers Base3, where it would also find an attribute with the same name.

Overriding attributes

As we've just seen, the search for an attribute proceeds up the inheritance tree and stops as soon as the attribute is found. Descendent classes are examined before their ancestors, meaning that when a subclass defines an attribute with the same name as one in a superclass, the search finds the definition when it looks at the subclass and stops there. This is known as the subclass *overriding* the definition in the superclass. Consider the following:

```
class B:
    a = 23
    b = 45
    def f(self): print "method f in class B"
    def g(self): print "method g in class B"
class C(B):
    b = 67
    c = 89
    d = 123
    def g(self): print "method g in class C"
    def h(self): print "method h in class C"
```

In this code, class C overrides attributes b and g of its superclass B.

Delegating to superclass methods

When a subclass C overrides a method f of its superclass B, the body of C.f often wants to delegate some part of its operation to the superclass's implementation of the method. This can be done using an unbound method, as follows:

```
class Base:
    def greet(self, name): print "Welcome ", name
class Sub(Base):
    def greet(self, name):
        print "Well Met and",
        Base.greet(self, name)
x = Sub( )
x.greet('Alex')
```

The delegation to the superclass, in the body of Sub.greet, uses an unbound method obtained by attribute reference Base.greet on the superclass, and therefore passes all attributes normally, including self. Delegating to a superclass implementation is the main use of unbound methods.

One very common use of such delegation occurs with special method __init__. When an instance is created in Python, the __init__ methods of base classes are not automatically invoked, as they are in some other object-oriented languages. Thus, it is up to a subclass to perform the proper initialization by using delegation if necessary. For example:

```
class Base:
    def __init__(self):
        self.anattribute = 23
class Derived(Base):
    def __init__(self):
        Base.__init__(self)
        self.anotherattribute = 45
```

If the __init__ method of class Derived didn't explicitly call that of class Base, instances of Derived would miss that portion of their initialization, and thus such instances would lack attribute anattribute.

"Deleting" class attributes

Inheritance and overriding provide a simple and effective way to add or modify class attributes (methods) non-invasively (i.e., without modifying the class in which the attributes are defined), by adding or overriding the attributes in subclasses. However, inheritance does not directly support similar ways to delete (hide) base classes' attributes non-invasively. If the subclass simply fails to define (override) an attribute, Python finds the base class's definition. If you need to perform such deletion, possibilities include:

- Overriding the method and raising an exception in the method's body
- Eschewing inheritance, holding the attributes elsewhere than in the subclass's __dict__, and defining __getattr__ for selective delegation
- Using the new-style object model and overriding __getattribute__ to similar effect

The last two techniques here are demonstrated in "__getattribute__" later in this chapter.

New-Style Classes and Instances

Most of what I have covered so far in this chapter also holds for the new-style object model introduced in Python 2.2. New-style classes and instances are first-class objects just like classic ones, both can have arbitrary attributes, you call a class to create an instance of the class, and so on. In this section, I'm going to cover the few differences between the new-style and classic object models.

In Python 2.2 and 2.3, a class is new-style if it inherits from built-in type object directly or indirectly (i.e., if it subclasses any built-in type, such as list, dict, file, object, and so on). In Python 2.1 and earlier, a class cannot inherit from a built-in type, and built-in type object does not exist. In "Metaclasses" later in this chapter, I cover other ways to make a class new-style, ways that you can use in Python 2.2 or later whether a class has superclasses or not.

As I said at the beginning of this chapter, I suggest you get into the habit of using new-style classes when you program in Python 2.2 or later. The new-style object model has small but measurable advantages, and there are practically no compensating disadvantages. It's simpler just to stick to the new-style object model, rather than try to decide which model to use each time you code a new class.

The Built-in object Type

As of Python 2.2, the built-in object type is the ancestor of all built-in types and new-style classes. The object type defines some special methods (as documented in "Special Methods" later in this chapter) that implement the default semantics of objects:

__new__, __init__
> You can create a direct instance of object, and such creation implicitly uses the static method __new__ of type object to create the new instance, and then uses the new instance's __init__ method to initialize the new instance. object.__init__ ignores its arguments and performs no operation whatsoever, so you can pass arbitrary arguments to type object when you call it to create an instance of it: all such arguments will be ignored.

__delattr__, __getattribute__, __setattr__
> By default, an object handles attribute references as covered earlier in this chapter, using these methods of object.

__hash__, __repr__, __str__
> An object can be passed to functions hash and repr and to type str.

A subclass of object may override any of these methods and/or add others.

Class-Level Methods

The new-style object model allows two kinds of class-level methods that do not exist in the classic object model: static methods and class methods. Class-level methods exist only in Python 2.2 and later, but in these versions you can also have such methods in classic classes. This is the only feature of the new-style object model that is also fully functional with classic classes in Python 2.2 and later.

Static methods

A *static method* is a method that you can call on a class, or on any instance of the class, without the special behavior and constraints of ordinary methods, bound and unbound, on the first argument. A static method may have any signature: it may have no arguments, and the first argument, if any, plays no special role. You can think of a static method as an ordinary function that you're able to call normally, despite the fact that it happens to be bound to a class attribute. While it is never necessary to define static methods (you could always define a function instead), some programmers consider them to be an elegant alternative to such functions whose purpose is tightly bound to some specific class.

You build a static method by calling built-in type staticmethod and binding its result to a class attribute. Like all binding of class attributes, this is normally done in the body of the class, but you may also choose to perform it elsewhere. The only argument to staticmethod is the function to invoke when Python calls the static method. The following example shows how to define and call a static method:

```
class AClass(object):
    def astatic( ): print 'a static method'
    astatic = staticmethod(astatic)
anInstance = AClass( )
AClass.astatic( )              # prints: a static method
anInstance.astatic( )          # prints: a static method
```

This example uses the same name for the function passed to staticmethod and for the attribute bound to staticmethod's result. This style is not mandatory, but it's a good idea, and I recommend that you use it.

Class methods

A *class method* is a method that you can call on a class or on any instance of the class. Python binds the method's first argument to the class on which you call the method, or the class of the instance on which you call the method; it does not bind it to the instance, as for normal bound methods. There is no equivalent of unbound methods for class methods. The first formal argument of a class method is conventionally named cls. While it is never necessary to define class methods (you could always alternatively define a function that takes the class object as its first argument), some programmers consider them to be an elegant alternative to such functions.

You build a class method by calling built-in type classmethod and binding its result to a class attribute. Like all binding of class attributes, this is normally done in the body of the class, but you may also choose to perform it elsewhere. The only argument to classmethod is the function to invoke when Python calls the class method. Here's how to define and call a class method:

```
class ABase(object):
    def aclassmet(cls): print 'a class method for', cls.__name__
    aclassmet = classmethod(aclassmet)
class ADeriv(ABase): pass
bInstance = ABase()
dInstance = ADeriv()
ABase.aclassmet()          # prints: a class method for ABase
bInstance.aclassmet()      # prints: a class method for ABase
ADeriv.aclassmet()         # prints: a class method for ADeriv
dInstance.aclassmet()      # prints: a class method for ADeriv
```

This example uses the same name for the function passed to classmethod and for the attribute bound to classmethod's result. This style is not mandatory, but it's a good idea, and I recommend that you use it.

New-Style Classes

All features of classic classes, covered earlier in this chapter, also apply to new-style classes. New-style classes also have some additional features with regard to the __init__ special method, and they all have a __new__ static method.

__init__

A new-style class C that inherits __init__ from object without overriding it lets you pass arbitrary arguments when you call C, but ignores all of those arguments. This behavior can be somewhat surprising. I suggest you override __init__ in all new-style classes that directly subclass object, even in those rare cases in which your own class's __init__ has no task to perform. For example:

```
class C(object):
    def __init__(self): pass
    # rest of class body omitted
```

Now instantiating C() without arguments works, but mistakenly trying to pass an argument (e.g., C('xyz')) raises an exception. If class C did not override __init__, a call C('xyz') would silently ignore the erroneous argument. It's generally best not to silently ignore errors.

__new__

Each new-style class has a static method named __new__. When you call C(*args,**kwds) to create a new instance of a new-style class C, Python invokes C.__new__(C,*args,**kwds). Python uses __new__'s return value x as the newly created instance. Then, Python calls C.__init__(x,*args,**kwds), but only when x is indeed an instance of C (otherwise, x's state is as __new__ had left it). Thus, for a new-style class C, the statement x=C(23) is equivalent to the following code:

```
x = C.__new__(C, 23)
if isinstance(x, C): C.__init__(x, 23)
```

object.__new__ creates a new, uninitialized instance of the class it receives as its first argument, and ignores any other arguments. When you override __new__ within the class body, you do not need to add __new__=staticmethod(__new__), as you normally would: Python recognizes the name __new__ and treats it specially in this context. In those rare cases in which you rebind C.__new__ later, outside the body of class C, you do need to use C.__new__=staticmethod(whatever).

__new__ has most of the flexibility of a factory function, as covered earlier in this chapter. __new__ may choose to return an existing instance or to make a new one, as appropriate. When __new__ does need to create a new instance, it most often delegates creation by calling object.__new__ or the __new__ method of another built-in type that is a superclass of C. The following example shows how to override static method __new__ in order to implement a version of the Singleton design pattern:

```
class Singleton(object):
    _singletons = { }
    def __new__(cls, *args, **kwds):
        if not cls._singletons.has_key(cls):
            cls._singletons[cls] = object.__new__(cls)
        return cls._singletons[cls]
```

Any subclass of Singleton (that does not further override __new__) has exactly one instance. If the subclass defines an __init__ method, the subclass must ensure its __init__ is safe when called repeatedly (at each creation request) on the one and only class instance.

New-Style Instances

All features of instances of classic classes, covered earlier in this chapter, also apply to instances of new-style classes. In addition, new-style classes may define attributes called properties and a special attribute named __slots__ that affects access to instance attributes. The new-style object model also adds a special method __getattribute__ that is more general than the __getattr__ special method present in both the classic and new-style object models. It also has different semantics for per-instance definition of special methods.

Properties

A property is an instance attribute with special functionality. You reference, bind, or unbind the attribute with the normal syntax (e.g., print *x*.prop, *x*.prop=23, del *x*.prop). However, rather than following the usual semantics for attribute reference, binding, and unbinding, these accesses call methods on instance *x* that you specify when defining the property using the built-in type property. Here's how to define a read-only property:

```
class Rectangle(object):
    def __init__(self, width, heigth):
        self.width = width
        self.heigth = heigth
    def getArea(self):
        return self.width * self.heigth
    area = property(getArea, doc='area of the rectangle')
```

Each instance *r* of class Rectangle has a synthetic read-only attribute *r*.area, computed on the fly in method *r*.getArea( ) by multiplying the sides of the rectangle. The docstring Rectangle.area.__doc__ is 'area of the rectangle'. The property is read-only (attempts to rebind or unbind it fail) because we only specify a get method in the call to property.

Properties perform tasks that are similar to those of special methods __getattr__, __setattr__, and __delattr__ (covered in "Special Methods" later in this chapter), but in a faster and simpler way. You build a property by calling built-in type property and binding its result to a class attribute. Like all binding of class attributes, this is normally done in the body of the class, but you may also choose to perform it elsewhere. Within the body of a class *C*, use the following syntax:

```
attrib = property(fget=None, fset=None, fdel=None, doc=None)
```

When *x* is an instance of *C* and you reference *x.attrib*, Python calls on *x* the method you passed as argument *fget* to the property constructor, without arguments. When you assign *x.attrib = value*, Python calls the method you passed as argument *fset*, with *value* as the only argument. When you perform del *x.attrib*, Python calls the method you passed as argument *fdel*, without arguments. Python uses the argument you passed as *doc* as the docstring of the attribute. All arguments to property are optional. When an argument is missing, the corresponding operation is forbidden. For example, in the Rectangle example, we made property area read-only, because we passed only argument *fget*, not arguments *fset* and *fdel*.

To obtain similar results for a classic class in Python 2.1, we need to define special methods __getattr__ and __setattr__ and in each of them test for attribute name 'area' and handle it specifically. The following example shows how to simulate a read-only property in Python 2.1:

```
class Rectangle:
    def __init__(self, width, heigth):
        self.width = width
        self.heigth = heigth
    def getArea(self):
        return self.width * self.heigth
```

```
def __getattr__(self, name):
    if name=='area': return self.getArea( )
    raise AttributeError, name
def __setattr__(self, name, value):
    if name=='area':
        raise AttributeError, "can't bind attribute"
    self.__dict__[name] = value
```

__slots__

Normally, each instance object *x* of any class *C* has a dictionary *x*.__dict__ that Python uses to let you bind arbitrary attributes on *x*. To save some memory (at the cost of letting *x* have only a predefined set of attribute names), you can define in class *C* a class attribute named __slots__, which is a sequence (normally a tuple) of strings (normally identifiers).When class *C* has an attribute __slots__, a direct instance *x* of class *C* has no *x*.__dict__, and any attempt to bind on *x* any attribute whose name is not in *C*.__slots__ raises an exception. Using __slots__ lets you reduce memory consumption for small instance objects that can do without the ability to have arbitrarily named attributes. Note that __slots__ is worth adding only to classes that can have so many instances that saving a few tens of bytes per instance is important—typically classes that can have millions, not mere thousands, of instances alive at the same time. Unlike most other class attributes, __slots__ works as I've just described only if some statement in the class body binds it as a class attribute. Any later alteration, rebinding, or unbinding of __slots__ has no effect, nor does inheriting __slots__ from a base class. Here's how to add __slots__ to the Rectangle class defined earlier, to get smaller (though less flexible) instances:

```
class OptimizedRectangle(Rectangle):
    __slots__ = 'width', 'heigth'
```

We do not need to define a slot for the area property. __slots__ does not constrain properties, only ordinary instance attributes—the attributes that would reside in the instance's __dict__ if __slots__ wasn't defined.

__getattribute__

All references to instance attributes for new-style instances proceed through special method __getattribute__. This method is supplied by base class object, where it implements all the details of object attribute reference semantics as documented earlier in this chapter. However, you may override __getattribute__ for special purposes, such as hiding inherited class attributes (e.g., methods) for your subclass's instances. The following example shows one way to implement a list without append in the new-style object model:

```
class listNoAppend(list):
    def __getattribute__(self, name):
        if name == 'append': raise AttributeError, name
        return list.__getattribute__(self, name)
```

An instance *x* of class listNoAppend is almost indistinguishable from a built-in list object, except that performance is substantially worse, and any reference to *x*. append raises an exception.

The following example shows how to implement `__getattr__`, `__setattr__`, and `__delattr__` so that `__getattr__` is called on every attribute reference, just like `__getattribute__` is for new-style instances:

```
class AttributeWatcher:
    def __init__(self):
        # note the caution to avoid triggering __setattr__, and the
        # emulation of Python's name-mangling for a private attribute
        self.__dict__['_AttributeWatcher__mydict']={ }
    def __getattr__(self, name):
        # as well as tracing every call, for demonstration purposes we
        # also fake "having" any requested attribute, EXCEPT special
        # methods (__getattr__ is also invoked to ask for them: check by
        # trying a few operations on an AttributeWatcher instance).
        print "getattr", name
        try: return self.__mydict[name]
        except KeyError:
            if name.startswith('__') and name.endswith('__'):
                raise AttributeError, name
            else: return 'fake_'+name
    def __setattr__(self, name, value):
        print "setattr", name, value
        self.__mydict[name] = value
    def __delattr__(self, name):
        print "delattr", name
        try: del self.__mydict[name]
        except KeyError: pass
```

Per-instance methods

Both the classic and new-style object models allow an instance to have instance-specific bindings for all attributes, including callable attributes (methods). For a method, just like for any other attribute, an instance-specific binding hides a class-level binding: attribute lookup does not even look at the class if it finds a binding directly in the instance. In both object models, an instance-specific binding for a callable attribute does not perform any of the transformations detailed in "Bound and Unbound Methods" earlier in this chapter. In other words, the attribute reference returns exactly the same callable object that was earlier bound directly to the instance attribute.

Classic and new-style object models do differ on per-instance binding of the special methods that Python invokes implicitly as a result of various operations, as covered in "Special Methods" later in this chapter. In the classic object model, an instance may usefully override a special method, and Python uses the per-instance binding even when invoking the method implicitly. In the new-style object model, implicit use of special methods always relies on the class-level binding of the special method, if any. The following code shows this difference between classic and new-style object models:

```
def fakeGetItem(idx): return idx
class Classic: pass
c = Classic( )
c.__getitem__ = fakeGetItem
```

```
print c[23]                        # prints: 23
class NewStyle(object): pass
n = NewStyle()
n.__getitem__ = fakeGetItem
print n[23]                        # results in:
# Traceback (most recent call last):
#    File "<stdin>", line 1, in ?
# TypeError: unindexable object
```

The semantics of the classic object model in this regard are sometimes handy for tricky and somewhat obscure purposes. However, the new-style object model's approach regularizes and simplifies the relationship between classes and meta-classes, covered in "Metaclasses" later in this chapter.

Inheritance in the New-Style Object Model

In the new-style object model, inheritance works similarly to the way it works in the classic object model. One key difference is that a new-style class can inherit from a built-in type. The new-style object model, like the classic one, supports multiple inheritance. However, a class may directly or indirectly subclass multiple built-in types only if those types are specifically designed to allow this level of mutual compatibility. Python does not support unconstrained inheritance from multiple arbitrary built-in types. Normally, a new-style class only subclasses at most one substantial built-in type; this means at most one built-in type in addition to object, which is the superclass of all built-in types and new-style classes and imposes no constraints on multiple inheritance.

Method resolution order

In the classic object model, method and attribute lookup (also called *resolution order*) among direct and indirect base classes proceeds left-first, depth-first. While very simple, this rule may produce undesired results when multiple base classes inherit from the same common base class and override different subsets of the common base class's methods; in this case, the overrides of the rightmost base class are hidden in the lookup. For example, if A subclasses B and C in that order, and B and C each subclass D, the classic lookup proceeds in the conceptual order A, B, D, C, D. Since Python looks up D before C, any method defined in class D, even if class C overrides it, is therefore found only in the base class D version. This issue causes few practical problems only because such an inheritance pattern, also known as a diamond-shaped inheritance graph, is rarely used in the classic Python object model.

In the new-style object model, however, all types directly or indirectly subclass object. Therefore, any multiple inheritance gives diamond-shaped inheritance graphs, and the classic resolution order would often produce problems. Python's new-style object model changes the resolution order by leaving in the lookup sequence only the rightmost occurrence of any given class. Using the example from the previous paragraph, when class D is new-style (e.g., D directly subclasses object), the resolution order for class A becomes A, B, C, D, object, and no anomalies arise. Figure 5-1 shows the classic and new-style method resolution orders for the case of a diamond-shaped inheritance graph.

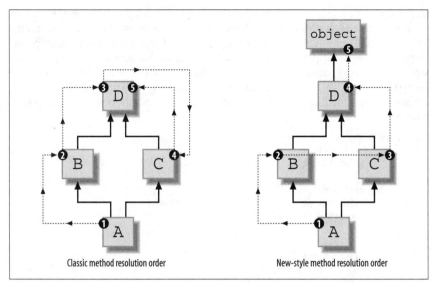

Figure 5-1. Classic and new-style method resolution order

Each new-style class and built-in type has a special read-only class attribute called __mro__, which is the tuple of types used for method resolution, in order. You can reference __mro__ only on classes, not on instances, and, since __mro__ is a read-only attribute, you cannot rebind or unbind it.

Cooperative superclass method calling

As we saw earlier in this chapter, when a subclass overrides a method, the overriding method often wants to delegate part of its operation to the superclass's implementation of the same method. The simple solution that is idiomatic in Python's classic object model (calling the superclass's version directly with unbound method syntax) is imperfect in cases of multiple inheritance with diamond-shaped graphs. Consider the following definitions:

```
class A(object):
    def met(self):
        print 'A.met'
class B(A):
    def met(self):
        print 'B.met'
        A.met(self)
class C(A):
    def met(self):
        print 'C.met'
        A.met(self)
class D(B,C):
    def met(self):
        print 'D.met'
        B.met(self)
        C.met(self)
```

In this code, when we call D( ).met( ), A.met ends up being called twice. How can we ensure that each ancestor's implementation of the method is called once, and only once? This problem turns out to be rather hard to solve without some special help. The special help that Python 2.2 provides is the new built-in type super. super(aclass, obj) returns a special superobject of object obj. When we look up an attribute (e.g., a method) in this superobject, the lookup begins after class aclass in obj's method resolution order. We can therefore rewrite the previous code as:

```
class A(object):
    def met(self):
        print 'A.met'
class B(A):
    def met(self):
        print 'B.met'
        super(B,self).met( )
class C(A):
    def met(self):
        print 'C.met'
        super(C,self).met( )
class D(B,C):
    def met(self):
        print 'D.met'
        super(D,self).met( )
```

Now, D( ).met( ) results in exactly one call to each class's version of met. If you get into the habit of always coding superclass calls with super, your classes will fit smoothly even in complicated inheritance structures. There are no ill effects whatsoever if the inheritance structure turns out to be simple instead (as long as your code only runs on Python 2.2 and later, of course).

Special Methods

A class may define or inherit special methods (i.e., methods whose names begin and end with double underscores). Each special method relates to a specific operation. Python implicitly invokes a special method whenever you perform the related operation on an instance object. In most cases, the method's return value is the operation's result, and attempting an operation when its related method is not present raises an exception. Throughout this section, I will point out the cases in which these general rules do not apply. In the following, x is the instance of class C on which you perform the operation, and y is the other operand, if any. The formal argument self of each method also refers to instance object x.

General-Purpose Special Methods

Some special methods relate to general-purpose operations. A class that defines or inherits these methods allows its instances to control such operations. These operations can be divided into the following categories:

Initialization and finalization
    An instance can control its initialization (a frequent need) via special method __init__, and/or its finalization (a rare need) via __del__.

Representation as string
An instance can control how Python represents it as a string via special methods __repr__, __str__, and __unicode__.

Comparison, hashing, and use in a Boolean context
An instance can control how it compares with other objects (methods __lt__ and __cmp__), how dictionaries use it as a key (__hash__), and whether it evaluates to true or false in Boolean contexts (__nonzero__).

Attribute reference, binding, and unbinding
An instance can control access to its attributes (reference, binding, unbinding) by defining special methods __getattribute__, __getattr__, __setattr__, and __delattr__.

Callable instances
An instance is callable, just like a function object, if it has the special method __call__.

The rest of this section documents the general-purpose special methods.

__call__   __call__(self[,*args*...])

When you call *x*([*args*...]), Python translates the operation into a call to *x*.__call__(([*args*...]). The formal arguments for the call operation are the same as for the __call__ method, minus the first argument. The first argument, conventionally called self, refers to *x*, and Python supplies it implicitly and automatically, just as in any other call to a bound method.

__cmp__   __cmp__(self,*other*)

Any comparison, when its specific special method (__lt__, __gt__, etc.) is absent or returns NotImplemented, calls *x*.__cmp__(*y*) instead, as do built-in function cmp(*x*,*y*) and the sort method of list objects. __cmp__ should return -1 if *x* is less than *y*, 0 if *x* is equal to *y*, 1 if *x* is greater than *y*. When __cmp__ is also absent, order comparisons (<, <=, >, >=) raise exceptions. Equality comparisons (==, !=), in this case, become identity checks: *x*==*y* evaluates id(*x*)==id(*y*) (i.e., *x* is *y*).

__del__   __del__(self)

Just before *x* disappears because of garbage collection, Python calls *x*.__del__() to let *x* finalize itself. If __del__ is absent, Python performs no special finalization upon garbage-collecting *x* (this is the usual case, as very few classes need to define __del__). Python ignores the return value of __del__. Python performs no implicit call to __del__ methods of class *C*'s superclasses. *C*.__del__ must explicitly perform any needed finalization.

For example, when class *C* has a base class *B* to finalize, the code in *C*.__del__ must call *B*.__del__(self) (or better, for new-style classes, super(*C*, self).__del__()). __del__ is generally not the best approach when you need timely and guaranteed finalization. For such needs, use the try/finally statement covered in Chapter 6.

__delattr__

__delattr__(self,*name*)

At every request to unbind attribute *x.y* (typically, a del statement del *x.y*), Python calls *x*.__delattr__('*y*'). All the considerations discussed for __setattr__ also apply to __delattr__. Python ignores the return value of __delattr__. If __delattr__ is absent, Python usually translates del *x.y* into del *x*.__dict__['*y*'].

__eq__,
__ge__,
__gt__,
__le__,
__lt__,
__ne__

__eq__(self,*other*)
__ge__(self,*other*)
__gt__(self,*other*)
__le__(self,*other*)
__lt__(self,*other*)
__ne__(self,*other*)

Comparisons *x*==*y*, *x*>=*y*, *x*>*y*, *x*<=*y*, *x*<*y*, and *x*!=*y*, respectively, call the special methods listed here, which should return False or True (in Python 2.2.1 and later; 0 or 1 in Python 2.2, 2.1, and earlier). Each method may return NotImplemented to tell Python to handle the comparison in alternative ways (e.g., Python may then try *y*>*x* in lieu of *x*<*y*).

__getattr__

__getattr__(self,*name*)

When attribute *x.y* is accessed but not found by the usual procedure (i.e., where AttributeError would normally be raised), Python calls *x*.__getattr__('*y*') instead. Python does not call __getattr__ for attributes found by normal means (i.e., as keys in *x*.__dict__ or via *x*.__class__). If you want Python to call __getattr__ on every attribute reference, keep the attributes elsewhere (e.g., in another dictionary referenced by an attribute with a private name, as shown earlier in this chapter), or else write a new-style class and override __getattribute__ instead. __getattr__ should raise AttributeError if it cannot find *y*.

__get attribute__

__getattribute__(self,*name*)   Python 2.2 and later

At every request to access attribute *x.y*, if *x* is an instance of new-style class *C*, Python calls *x*.__getattribute__('*y*'), which must obtain and return the attribute value or else raise AttributeError. The normal semantics of attribute access (using *x*.__dict__, *C*.__slots__, *C*'s class attributes, *x*.__getattr__) are all due to object.__getattribute__.

If class *C* overrides __getattribute__, it must implement all of the attribute access semantics it wants to offer. Most often, the most convenient way to implement attribute access semantics is by delegating (e.g., calling object.__getattribute__(self, ...) as part of the operation of your override of __getattribute__). Note that a class that overrides __getattribute__ makes attribute access on instances of the class quite slow, since your overriding code is called on every such attribute access.

__hash__   __hash__(self)

The hash(x) built-in function call, and using x as a dictionary key (typically, D[x] where D is a dictionary), call x.__hash__(). __hash__ must return a 32-bit int such that x==y implies hash(x)==hash(y), and must always return the same value for a given object.

When __hash__ is absent, hash(x) and using x as a dictionary key call id(x) instead, as long as __cmp__ and __eq__ are also absent.

Any x such that hash(x) returns a result, rather than raising an exception, is known as a *hashable object*. When __hash__ is absent, but __cmp__ or __eq__ is present, hash(x) and using x as a dictionary key raise an exception. In this case, x is not hashable and cannot be a dictionary key.

You normally define __hash__ only for immutable objects that also define __cmp__ and/or __eq__. Note that, if there exists any y such that x==y, even if y is of a different type, and both x and y are hashable, you must ensure that hash(x)==hash(y).

__init__   __init__(self[,*args*...])

When a call C([*args*...]) creates instance x of class C Python calls x.__init__([*args*...]) to let x initialize itself. If __init__ is absent, you must call class C without arguments, C(), and x has no instance-specific attributes upon creation (note that __init__ is never absent for a new-style class, since such a class inherits __init__ from object unless it redefines it). __init__ must return None. Python performs no implicit call to __init__ methods of class C's superclasses. C.__init__ must explicitly perform any needed initialization. For example, when class C has a base class B to initialize without arguments, the code in C.__init__ must explicitly call B.__init__(self) (or better, for new-style classes, call super(C, self).__init__()).

__new__   __new__(cls[,*args*...])   Python 2.2 and later

When you call C([*args*...]) and C is a new-style class, Python will obtain the new instance x that you are creating by invoking C.__new__(C,[*args*...]). __new__ is a static method that every new-style class has (often simply inheriting it from object) and it can return any value x. In other words, __new__ is not constrained to returning a new instance of C, although normally it is expected to do so. If, and only if, the value x that __new__ returns is indeed an instance of C (whether a new or previously existing one), Python continues after calling __new__ by implicitly calling __init__ on x.

__nonzero__   __nonzero__(self)

When evaluating x as true or false (see "Boolean Values" in Chapter 4), for example on a call to bool(x) in Python 2.2.1 and later, Python calls x.__nonzero__(), which should return True or False. When __nonzero__ is not present, Python calls __len__ instead, and takes *x* as false when *x*.__len__() returns 0. When neither __nonzero__ nor __len__ is present, Python always takes *x* as true.

__repr__   __repr__(self)

The repr(*x*) built-in function call, the `x` expression form, and the interactive interpreter (when *x* is the result of an expression statement) call *x*.__repr__() to obtain an official, complete string representation of *x*. If __repr__ is absent, Python uses a default string representation. __repr__ should return a string with unambiguous information on *x*. Ideally, when feasible, the string should be an expression such that eval(repr(*x*))==*x*.

__setattr__   __setattr__(self, *name*, *value*)

At every request to bind attribute *x.y* (typically, an assignment statement *x.y=value*), Python calls *x*.__setattr__('*y*',*value*). Python always calls __setattr__ for any attribute binding on *x*; a major difference from __getattr__ (__setattr__ is closer to new-style classes' __getattribute__ in this sense). To avoid recursion, when *x*.__setattr__ binds *x*'s attributes, it must modify *x*.__dict__ directly (e.g., by *x*.__dict__[*name*]=*value*), or better, for a new-style class, delegate (e.g., call super(C, *x*).__setattr__('*y*',*value*)). Python ignores the return value of __setattr__. If __setattr__ is absent, Python usually translates *x.y=z* into *x*.__dict__['*y*']=*z*.

__str__   __str__(self)

The str(*x*) built-in type and the print *x* statement call *x*.__str__() to obtain an informal, concise string representation of *x*. If __str__ is absent, Python calls *x*.__repr__ instead. __str__ should return a conveniently human-readable string, even if it entails some approximation.

__unicode__   __unicode__(self)   Python 2.2 and later

The unicode(*x*) built-in type call, in Python 2.2 and later, invokes *x*.__unicode__(), if present, in preference to *x*.__str__(). If a class supplies both special methods __unicode__ and __str__, the two should return equivalent strings (of Unicode and plain string type respectively).

Special Methods for Containers

An instance can be a *container* (either a sequence or a mapping, but not both, as they are mutually exclusive concepts). For maximum usefulness, containers should provide not just special methods __getitem__, __setitem__, __delitem__,

__len__, __contains__, and __iter__, but also a few non-special methods, as discussed in the following sections.

Sequences

In each item access special method, a sequence that has L items should accept any integer *key*, such that 0<=*key*<L. For compatibility with built-in sequences, a negative index *key*, 0>*key*>=-L, should be equivalent to *key*+L. When *key* has an invalid type, the method should raise TypeError. When *key* is a value of a valid type, but out of range, the method should raise IndexError. In Python 2.1, and also in later Python versions for classes that do not define __iter__, the for statement relies on these requirements, as do built-in functions that take sequences as arguments.

A sequence should also allow concatenation by + and repetition by *. A sequence should therefore have special methods __add__, __mul__, __radd__, and __rmul__, covered in "Special Methods for Numeric Objects" later in this chapter. Mutable sequences should also have __iadd__ and __imul__, and the non-special methods covered in "List methods" in Chapter 4: append, count, index, insert, extend, pop, remove, reverse, and sort.

Mappings

A mapping's item access special methods should raise KeyError, rather than IndexError, when they receive an invalid *key* argument value of a valid type. A mapping should define the non-special methods covered in "Dictionary Methods" in Chapter 4: copy, get, has_key, items, keys, values, iteritems, iterkeys, and itervalues. Special method __iter__ should be equivalent to iterkeys. A mutable mapping should also define methods clear, popitem, setdefault, and update.

Sets

Sets, scheduled to be introduced in Python 2.3, can be seen as rather peculiar kinds of containers—containers that are neither sequences nor mappings, and cannot be indexed, but do have a length (number of elements) and are iterable. Unfortunately, the interface of sets (and even the final decision about introducing them in Python 2.3) is still not stable as of this writing. Therefore, I do not consider sets in this book.

Container slicing

When you reference, bind, or unbind a slicing such as x[i:j] or x[i:j:k] on a container x, Python calls x's applicable item access special method, passing as *key* an object of a built-in type called a *slice object*. A slice object has attributes start, stop, and step. Each attribute is None if the corresponding value is omitted in the slice syntax. For example, del x[:3] calls x.__delitem__(y), and y is a slice object such that y.stop is 3, y.start is None, and y.step is None. It is up to container object x to appropriately interpret the slice object argument passed to x's special methods.

Some built-in types, such as list and tuple, define now-deprecated special methods __getslice__, __setslice__, and __delslice__. For an instance x of such a type, slicing *x* with only one colon, as in *x*[*i*:*j*], calls a slice-specific special method. Slicing *x* with two colons, as in *x*[*i*:*j*:*k*], calls an item access special method with a slice object argument. For example:

```
class C:
    def __getslice__(self, i, j): print 'getslice', i, j
    def __getitem__(self, index): print 'getitem', index
x = C()
x[12:34]
x[56:78:9]
```

The first slicing calls *x*.__getslice__(12,34), and the second calls *x*.__getitem__ (slice(56,78,9)). It's best to avoid defining the slice-specific special methods in your classes, but you may need to override them if your class subclasses list or tuple and you want to provide special functionality when an instance of your class is sliced. Note that built-in sequences do not yet support slicing with two colons up to Python 2.2: this functionality is scheduled to be introduced in Python 2.3.

Container methods

Special methods __getitem__, __setitem__, __delitem__, __iter__, __len__, and __contains__ expose container functionality.

__contains__   __contains__(self,*item*)

The Boolean test *y* in *x* calls *x*.__contains__(*y*). When *x* is a sequence, __contains__ should return True when *y* equals the value of an item in the sequence. When *x* is a mapping, __contains__ should return True when *y* equals the value of a key in the mapping. Otherwise, __contains__ should return False. If __contains__ is absent, Python performs *y* in *x* as follows, taking time proportional to len(*x*):

```
for z in x:
    if y==z: return True
return False
```

__delitem__   __delitem__(self,*key*)

For a request to unbind an item or slice of *x* (typically del *x*[*key*]), Python will call *x*.__delitem__(*key*). A container *x* should have __delitem__ only if *x* is mutable, so that items (and possibly slices) can be removed.

__getitem__   __getitem__(self,*key*)

When *x*[*key*] is accessed (i.e., when container *x* is indexed or sliced), Python calls *x*.__getitem__(*key*). All containers should have __getitem__.

__iter__   __iter__(self)

For a request to loop on all items of *x* (typically for *item* in *x*), Python calls *x*.__iter__() to obtain an iterator on *x*. The built-in

---

function iter(x) also calls x.__iter__( ). If __iter__ is absent and x is a sequence, iter(x) synthesizes and returns an iterator object that wraps x and returns x[0], x[1], and so on, until one of these item accesses raises IndexError to indicate the end of the sequence.

__len__   __len__(self)

The len(x) built-in function call, and other built-in functions that need to know how many items are in container x, call x.__len__( ). __len__ should return an int, the number of items in x. Python also calls x.__len__( ) to evaluate x in a Boolean context, if __nonzero__ is absent. Absent __nonzero__, a container is taken as false if and only if the container is empty (i.e., the container's length is 0).

__setitem__   __setitem__(self,key,value)

For a request to bind an item or slice of x (typically an assignment x[key]=value), Python calls x.__setitem__(key,value). A container x should have __setitem__ only if x is mutable, so that items, and possibly slices, can be added and/or rebound.

Special Methods for Numeric Objects

An instance may support numeric operations by means of many special methods. Some classes that are not numbers also support some of the following special methods, in order to overload operators such as + and *. For example, sequences should have special methods __add__, __mul__, __radd__, and __rmul__, as mentioned earlier in this chapter.

__abs__,   __abs__(self)
__invert__,   __invert__(self)
__neg__,   __neg__(self)
__pos__   __pos__(self)

Unary operators abs(x), ~x, -x, and +x, respectively, call these methods.

__add__,   __add__(self,other)
__div__,   __div__(self,other)
__floordiv__,   __floordiv__(self,other)
__mod__,   __mod__(self,other)
__mul__,   __mul__(self,other)
__sub__,   __sub__(self,other)
__truediv__   __truediv__(self,other)

Operators x+y, x/y, x//y, x%y, x*y, x-y, and x/y, respectively, call these methods. The operator / calls __truediv__, if present, instead of __div__, in the situations where division is non-truncating, as covered in "Arithmetic Operations" in Chapter 4.

__and__, __lshift__, __or__, __rshift__, __xor__	`__and__(self,other)` `__lshift__(self,other)` `__or__(self,other)` `__rshift__(self,other)` `__xor__(self,other)`
	Operators x&y, x<<y, x|y, x>>y, and x^y, respectively, call these methods.

__coerce__	`__coerce__(self,other)`
	For any numeric operation with two operands x and y, Python invokes x.__coerce__(y). __coerce__ should return a pair with x and y converted to acceptable types. __coerce__ returns None when it cannot perform the conversion. In such cases, Python will call y.__coerce__(x). This special method is now deprecated: new Python classes should not implement it, but instead deal with whatever types they can accept directly in the special methods of the relevant numeric operations. However, if a class does supply __coerce__, Python still calls it for backward compatibility.

__complex__, __float__, __int__, __long__	`__complex__(self)` `__float__(self)` `__int__(self)` `__long__(self)`
	Built-in types complex(x), float(x), int(x), and long(x), respectively, call these methods.

__divmod__	`__divmod__(self,other)`
	Built-in function divmod(x,y) calls x.__divmod__(y). __divmod__ should return a pair (quotient,remainder) equal to (x//y,x%y).

__hex__, __oct__	`__hex__(self)` `__oct__(self)`
	Built-in function hex(x) calls x.__hex__( ). Built-in function oct(x) calls x.__oct__( ). Each of these special methods should return a string representing the value of x, in base 16 and 8 respectively.

__iadd__, __idiv__, __ifloordiv__, __imod__, __imul__, __isub__, __itruediv__	`__iadd__(self,other)` `__idiv__(self,other)` `__ifloordiv__(self,other)` `__imod__(self,other)` `__imul__(self,other)` `__isub__(self,other)` `__itruediv__(self,other)`
	The augmented assignments x+=y, x/=y, x//=y, x%=y, x*=y, x-=y, and x/=y, respectively, call these methods. Each method should modify x in-place and return self. Define these methods when x is mutable (i.e., when x can change in-place).

`__iand__,` `__ilshift__,` `__ior__,` `__irshift__,` `__ixor__`	`__iand__(self,other)` `__ilshift__(self,other)` `__ior__(self,other)` `__irshift__(self,other)` `__ixor__(self,other)` Augmented assignments $x\&=y$, $x<<=y$, $x|=y$, $x>>=y$, and $x^\wedge=y$, respectively, call these methods. Each method should modify x in-place and return self.
`__ipow__`	`__ipow__(self,other)` Augmented assignment $x**=y$ calls $x.\_\_ipow\_\_(y)$. `__ipow__` should modify x in-place and return self.
`__pow__`	`__pow__(self,other[,modulo])` $x**y$ and $pow(x,y)$ both call $x.\_\_pow\_\_(y)$, while $pow(x,y,z)$ calls $x.\_\_pow\_\_(y,z)$. $x.\_\_pow\_\_(y,z)$ should return a value equal to the expression $x.\_\_pow\_\_(y)\%z$.
`__radd__,` `__rdiv__,` `__rmod__,` `__rmul__,` `__rsub__`	`__radd__(self,other)` `__rdiv__(self,other)` `__rmod__(self,other)` `__rmul__(self,other)` `__rsub__(self,other)` Operators $y+x$, y/x, $y\%x$, $y*x$, and $y-x$, respectively, call these methods when y doesn't have a needed method `__add__`, `__div__`, and so on.
`__rand__,` `__rlshift__,` `__ror__,` `__rrshift__,` `__rxor__`	`__rand__(self,other)` `__rlshift__(self,other)` `__ror__(self,other)` `__rrshift__(self,other)` `__rxor__(self,other)` Operators $y\&x$, $y<<x$, $y|x$, $y>>x$, and $y^\wedge x$, respectively, call these methods when y doesn't have needed method `__and__`, `__lshift__`, and so on.
`__rdivmod__`	`__rdivmod__(self,other)` Built-in function $divmod(y,x)$ calls $x.\_\_rdivmod\_\_(y)$ when y doesn't have `__divmod__`. `__rdivmod__` should return a pair (`remainder,quotient`).
`__rpow__`	`__rpow__(self,other)` $y**x$ and $pow(y,x)$ call $x.\_\_rpow\_\_(y)$, when y doesn't have `__pow__`. There is no three-argument form in this case.

Object-Oriented

Metaclasses

Any object, even a class object, has a type. In Python, types and classes are also first-class objects. The type of a class object is also known as the class's *metaclass.*[*] An object's behavior is determined largely by the type of the object. This also holds for classes: a class's behavior is determined largely by the class's metaclass. Metaclasses are an advanced subject, and you may want to skip the rest of this chapter on first reading. However, fully grasping metaclasses can help you obtain a deeper understanding of Python, and sometimes it can even be useful to define your own custom metaclasses.

The distinction between classic and new-style classes relies on the fact that each class's behavior is determined by its metaclass. In other words, the reason classic classes behave differently from new-style classes is that classic and new-style classes are object of different types (metaclasses):

```
class Classic: pass
class Newstyle(object): pass
print type(Classic)              # prints: <type 'class'>
print type(Newstyle)             # prints: <type 'type'>
```

The type of `Classic` is object `types.ClassType` from standard module types, while the type of `Newstyle` is built-in object type. type is also the metaclass of all Python built-in types, including itself (i.e., `print type(type)` also prints `<type 'type'>`).

How Python Determines a Class's Metaclass

To execute a class statement, Python first collects the base classes into a tuple *t* (an empty one, if there are no base classes) and executes the class body in a temporary dictionary *d*. Then, Python determines the metaclass *M* to use for the new class object *C* created by the class statement.

When '`__metaclass__`' is a key in *d*, *M* is *d*['`__metaclass__`']. Thus, you can explicitly control class *C*'s metaclass by binding the attribute `__metaclass__` in *C*'s class body. Otherwise, when *t* is non-empty (i.e., when *C* has one or more base classes), *M* is type(*t*[0]), the metaclass of *C*'s first base class. This is why inheriting from object indicates that *C* is a new-style class. Since type(object) is type, a class *C* that inherits from object (or some other built-in type) gets the same metaclass as object (i.e., type(*C*), *C*'s metaclass, is also type) Thus, being a new-style class is synonymous with having type as the metaclass.

When *C* has no base classes, but the current module has a global variable named `__metaclass__`, *M* is the value of that global variable. This lets you make classes without base classes default to new-style classes, rather than classic classes, throughout a module. Just place the following statement toward the start of the module body:

```
__metaclass_ = type
```

---

[*] Strictly speaking, the type of a class *C* could be said to be the metaclass only of instances of *C*, rather than of *C* itself, but this exceedingly subtle terminological distinction is rarely, if ever, observed in practice.

Failing all of these, in Python 2.2 and 2.3, M defaults to types.ClassType. This last default of defaults clause is why classes without base classes are classic classes by default, when __metaclass__ is not bound in the class body or as a global variable of the module.

How a Metaclass Creates a Class

Having determined M, Python calls M with three arguments: the class name (a string), the tuple of base classes t, and the dictionary d. The call returns the class object C, which Python then binds to the class name, completing the execution of the class statement. Note that this is in fact an instantiation of type M, so the call to M executes M.__init__(C,namestring,t,d), where C is the return value of M.__new__(M,namestring,t,d), just as in any other similar instantiation of a new-style class (or built-in type).

After class object C is created, the relationship between class C and its type (type(C), normally M) is the same as that between any object and its type. For example, when you call class C (to create an instance of C), M.__call__ executes, with class object C as the first actual argument.

Note the benefit of the new-style approach described in the section "Per-instance methods" earlier in this chapter. Calling C to instantiate it must execute the metaclass's M.__call__, whether or not C has a per-instance attribute (method) __call__ (i.e., independently of whether instances of C are or aren't callable). This requirement is simply incompatible with the classic object model, where per-instance methods override per-class ones—even for implicitly called special methods. The new-style approach avoids having to make the relationship between a class and its metaclass an ad hoc special case. Avoiding ad hoc special cases is a key to Python's power: Python has few, simple, general rules, and applies them consistently.

Defining and using your own metaclasses

It's easy to define metaclasses in Python 2.2 and later, by inheriting from type and overriding some methods. You can also perform most of these tasks with __new__, __init__, __getattribute__, and so on, without involving metaclasses. However, a custom metaclass can be faster, since special processing is done only at class creation time, which is a rare operation. A custom metaclass also lets you define a whole category of classes in a framework that magically acquires whatever interesting behavior you've coded, quite independently of what special methods the classes may choose to define. Moreover, some behavior of class objects can be customized only in metaclasses. The following example shows how to use a metaclass to change the string format of class objects:

```
class MyMeta(type):
    def __str__(cls): return "Beautiful class '%s'"%cls.__name__
class MyClass:
    __metaclass__ = MyMeta
x = MyClass()
print type(x)
```

Strictly speaking, classes that instantiate your own custom metaclass are neither classic nor new-style: the semantics of classes and of their instances is entirely defined by their metaclass. In practice, your custom metaclasses will almost invariably subclass built-in type. Therefore, the semantics of the classes that instantiate them are best thought of as secondary variations with respect to the semantics of new-style classes.

A substantial custom metaclass example

Suppose that, programming in Python, we miss C's struct type: an object that is just a bunch of data attributes with fixed names. Python lets us easily define an appropriate Bunch class, apart from the fixed names:

```
class Bunch(object):
    def __init__(self, **fields): self.__dict__ = fields
p = Bunch(x=2.3, y=4.5)
print p                       # prints: <__main__.Bunch object at 0x00AE8B10>
```

However, a custom metaclass lets us exploit the fact that the attribute names are fixed at class creation time. The code shown in Example 5-1 defines a metaclass, metaMetaBunch, and a class, MetaBunch, that let us write code like the following:

```
class Point(MetaBunch):
    """ A point has x and y coordinates, defaulting to 0.0, and a color,
        defaulting to 'gray' -- and nothing more, except what Python and
        the metaclass conspire to add, such as __init__ and __repr__
    """
    x = 0.0
    y = 0.0
    color = 'gray'
# example uses of class Point
q = Point()
print q                       # prints: Point()
p = Point(x=1.2, y=3.4)
print p                       # prints: Point(y=3.399999999, x=1.2)
```

In this code, the print statements print readable string representations of our Point instances. Point instances are also quite memory-lean, and their performance is basically the same as for instances of the simple class Bunch in the previous example (no extra overhead due to special methods getting called implicitly). Note that Example 5-1 is quite substantial, and following all its details requires understanding aspects of Python covered later in this book, such as strings (Chapter 9) and module warnings (Chapter 17).

Example 5-1. The metaMetaBunch metaclass

```
import warnings
class metaMetaBunch(type):
    """
    metaclass for new and improved "Bunch": implicitly defines __slots__,
    __init__ and __repr__ from variables bound in class scope.
    A class statement for an instance of metaMetaBunch (i.e., for a class
    whose metaclass is metaMetaBunch) must define only class-scope data
    attributes (and possibly special methods, but NOT __init__ and
    __repr__!). metaMetaBunch removes the data attributes from class
    scope, snuggles them instead as items in a class-scope dict named
```

Example 5-1. The metaMetaBunch metaclass (continued)

```
    __dflts__, and puts in the class a __slots__ with those attributes'
    names, an __init__ that takes as optional keyword arguments each of
    them (using the values in __dflts__ as defaults for missing ones), and
    a __repr__ that shows the repr of each attribute that differs from its
    default value (the output of __repr__ can be passed to __eval__ to
    make an equal instance, as per the usual convention in the matter, if
    each of the non-default-valued attributes respects the convention too)
    """
    def __new__(cls, classname, bases, classdict):
        """ Everything needs to be done in __new__, since type.__new__ is
            where __slots__ are taken into account.
        """
        # define as local functions the __init__ and __repr__ that we'll
        # use in the new class
        def __init__(self, **kw):
            """ Simplistic __init__: first set all attributes to default
                values, then override those explicitly passed in kw.
            """
            for k in self.__dflts__: setattr(self, k, self.__dflts__[k])
            for k in kw: setattr(self, k, kw[k])
        def __repr__(self):
            """ Clever __repr__: show only attributes that differ from the
                respective default values, for compactness.
            """
            rep = ['%s=%r' % (k, getattr(self, k)) for k in self.__dflts__
                        if getattr(self, k) != self.__dflts__[k]
                  ]
            return '%s(%s)' % (classname, ', '.join(rep))
        # build the newdict that we'll use as class-dict for the new class
        newdict = { '__slots__':[ ], '__dflts__':{ },
            '__init__':__init__, '__repr__':__repr__, }
        for k in classdict:
            if k.startswith('__') and k.endswith('__'):
                # special methods: copy to newdict, warn about conflicts
                if k in newdict:
                    warnings.warn("Can't set attr %r in bunch-class %r"
                        % (k, classname))
                else:
                    newdict[k] = classdict[k]
            else:
                # class variables, store name in __slots__, and name and
                # value as an item in __dflts__
                newdict['__slots__'].append(k)
                newdict['__dflts__'][k] = classdict[k]
        # finally delegate the rest of the work to type.__new__
        return type.__new__(cls, classname, bases, newdict)
class MetaBunch(object):
    """ For convenience: inheriting from MetaBunch can be used to get
        the new metaclass (same as defining __metaclass__ yourself).
    """
    __metaclass__ = metaMetaBunch
```

6

Exceptions

Python uses exceptions to communicate errors and anomalies. An *exception* is an object that indicates an error or anomalous condition. When Python detects an error, it raises an exception; that is, it signals the occurrence of an anomalous condition by passing an exception object to the exception-propagation mechanism. Your code can also explicitly raise an exception by executing a raise statement.

Handling an exception means receiving the exception object from the propagation mechanism and performing whatever actions are needed to deal with the anomalous situation. If a program does not handle an exception, it terminates with an error traceback message. However, a program can handle exceptions and keep running despite errors or other abnormal conditions.

Python also uses exceptions to indicate some special situations that are not errors, and are not even abnormal occurrences. For example, as covered in Chapter 4, an iterator's next method raises the exception StopIteration when the iterator has no more items. This is not an error, and it is not even an anomalous condition, since most iterators run out of items eventually.

The try Statement

The try statement provides Python's exception-handling mechanism. It is a compound statement that can take one of two different forms:

- A try clause followed by one or more except clauses
- A try clause followed by exactly one finally clause

try/except

Here's the syntax for the try/except form of the try statement:

```
try:
    statement(s)
except [expression [, target]]:
    statement(s)
[else:
    statement(s)]
```

This form of the try statement has one or more except clauses, as well as an optional else clause.

The body of each except clause is known as an *exception handler*. The code executes if the *expression* in the except clause matches an exception object that propagates from the try clause. *expression* is an optional class or tuple of classes that matches any exception object of one of the listed classes or any of their subclasses. The optional *target* is an identifier that names a variable that Python binds to the exception object just before the exception handler executes. A handler can also obtain the current exception object by calling the exc_info function of module sys (covered in Chapter 8).

Here is an example of the try/except form of the try statement:

```
try: 1/0
except ZeroDivisionError: print "caught divide-by-0 attempt"
```

If a try statement has several except clauses, the exception propagation mechanism tests the except clauses in order: the first except clause whose expression matches the exception object is used as the handler. Thus, you must always list handlers for specific cases before you list handlers for more general cases. If you list a general case first, the more specific except clauses that follow will never enter the picture.

The last except clause may lack an expression. This clause handles any exception that reaches it during propagation. Such unconditional handling is a rare need, but it does occur, generally in wrapper functions that must perform some extra task before reraising an exception, as we'll discuss later in the chapter.

Note that exception propagation terminates when it finds a handler whose expression matches the exception object. Thus, if a try statement is nested in the try clause of another try statement, a handler established by the inner try is reached first during propagation, and therefore is the one that handles the exception, if it matches the expression. For example:

```
try:
    try: 1/0
    except: print "caught an exception"
except ZeroDivisionError:
    print "caught divide-by-0 attempt"
# prints: caught an exception
```

In this case, it does not matter that the handler established by clause except ZeroDivisionError: in the outer try clause is more specific and appropriate than the catch-all except: in the inner try clause. The outer try does not even enter into the picture because the exception doesn't propagate out of the inner try.

The optional else clause of try/except executes only if the try clause terminates normally. In other words, it does not execute if an exception propagates from the try clause or if the try clause exits with a break, continue, or return statement. The handlers established by try/except cover only the try clause, not the else clause. The else clause is useful to avoid accidentally handling unexpected exceptions. For example:

```
print repr(value), "is ",
try:
    value + 0
except TypeError:
    # not a number, maybe a string, Unicode, UserString...?
    try:
        value + ''
    except TypeError:
        print "neither a number nor a string"
    else:
        print "a string or string-like value"
else:
    print "a number of some kind"
```

try/finally

Here's the syntax for the try/finally form of the try statement:

```
try:
    statement(s)
finally:
    statement(s)
```

This form has exactly one finally clause, and it cannot have an else clause.

The finally clause establishes what is known as a *clean-up handler*. The code always executes after the try clause terminates in any way. When an exception propagates from the try clause, the try clause terminates, the clean-up handler executes, and the exception keeps propagating. When no exception occurs, the clean-up handler executes anyway, whether the try clause reaches its end or exits by executing a break, continue, or return statement.

Clean-up handlers established with try/finally offer a robust and explicit way to specify finalization code that must always execute, no matter what, to ensure consistency of program state and/or external entities (e.g., files, databases, network connections). Here is an example of the try/finally form of the try statement:

```
f = open(someFile, "w")
try:
    do_something_with_file(f)
finally:
    f.close()
```

Note that the try/finally form is distinct from the try/except form: a try statement cannot have both except and finally clauses, as execution order might be ambiguous. If you need both exception handlers and a clean-up handler, nest a try statement in the try clause of another try statement to define execution order explicitly and unambiguously.

A finally clause cannot directly contain a continue statement, but it may contain a break or return statement. Such usage, however, makes your program less clear, as exception propagation stops when such a break or return executes. Most programmers would not normally expect propagation to be stopped in a finally clause, so this usage may confuse people who are reading your code.

Exception Propagation

When an exception is raised, the exception-propagation mechanism takes control. The normal control flow of the program stops, and Python looks for a suitable exception handler. Python's try statement establishes exception handlers via its except clauses. The handlers deal with exceptions raised in the body of the try clause, as well as exceptions that propagate from any of the functions called by that code, directly or indirectly. If an exception is raised within a try clause that has an applicable except handler, the try clause terminates and the handler executes. When the handler finishes, execution continues with the statement after the try statement.

If the statement raising the exception is not within a try clause that has an applicable handler, the function containing the statement terminates, and the exception propagates upward to the statement that called the function. If the call to the terminated function is within a try clause that has an applicable handler, that try clause terminates, and the handler executes. Otherwise, the function containing the call terminates, and the propagation process repeats, unwinding the stack of function calls until an applicable handler is found.

If Python cannot find such a handler, by default the program prints an error message to the standard error stream (the file sys.stderr). The error message includes a traceback that gives details about functions terminated during propagation. You can change Python's default error-reporting behavior by setting sys.excepthook (covered in Chapter 8). After error reporting, Python goes back to the interactive session, if any, or terminates if no interactive session is active. When the exception class is SystemExit, termination is silent and includes the interactive session, if any.

Here are some functions that we can use to see exception propagation at work.

```
def f():
    print "in f, before 1/0"
    1/0                        # raises a ZeroDivisionError exception
    print "in f, after 1/0"

def g():
    print "in g, before f()"
    f()
    print "in g, after f()"
```

```
def h():
    print "in h, before g()"
    try:
        g()
        print "in h, after g()"
    except ZeroDivisionError:
        print "ZD exception caught"
    print "function h ends"
```

Calling the h function has the following results:

```
>>> h()
in h, before g()
in g, before f()
in f, before 1/0
ZD exception caught
function h ends
```

Function h establishes a try statement and calls function g within the try clause. g, in turn, calls f, which performs a division by 0, raising an exception of class ZeroDivisionError. The exception propagates all the way back to the except clause in h. Functions f and g terminate during the exception propagation phase, which is why neither of their "after" messages is printed. The execution of h's try clause also terminates during the exception propagation phase, so its "after" message isn't printed either. Execution continues after the handler, at the end of h's try/except block.

The raise Statement

You can use the raise statement to raise an exception explicitly. raise is a simple statement with the following syntax:

```
raise [expression1[, expression2]]
```

Only an exception handler (or a function that a handler calls, directly or indirectly) can use raise without any expressions. A plain raise statement reraises the same exception object that the handler received. The handler terminates, and the exception propagation mechanism keeps searching for other applicable handlers. Using a raise without expressions is useful when a handler discovers that it is unable to handle an exception it receives, so the exception should keep propagating.

When only *expression1* is present, it can be an instance object or a class object. In this case, if *expression1* is an instance object, Python raises that instance. When *expression1* is a class object, raise instantiates the class without arguments and raises the resulting instance. When both expressions are present, *expression1* must be a class object. raise instantiates the class, with *expression2* as the argument (or multiple arguments if *expression2* is a tuple), and raises the resulting instance.

Here's an example of a typical use of the raise statement:

```
def crossProduct(seq1, seq2):
    if not seq1 or not seq2:
```

```
raise ValueError, "Sequence arguments must be non-empty"
return [ (x1, x2) for x1 in seq1 for x2 in seq2 ]
```
The crossProduct function returns a list of all pairs with one item from each of its sequence arguments, but first it tests both arguments. If either argument is empty, the function raises ValueError, rather than just returning an empty list as the list comprehension would normally do. Note that there is no need for crossProduct to test if seq1 and seq2 are iterable: if either isn't, the list comprehension itself will raise the appropriate exception, presumably a TypeError. Once an exception is raised, be it by Python itself or with an explicit raise statement in your code, it's up to the caller to either handle it (with a suitable try/except statement) or let it propagate further up the call stack.

Use the raise statement only to raise additional exceptions for cases that would normally be okay but your specifications define to be errors. Do not use raise to duplicate the error checking and diagnostics Python already and implicitly does on your behalf.

Exception Objects

Exceptions are instances of subclasses of the built-in Exception class. For backward compatibility, Python also lets you use strings, or instances of any class, as exception objects, but such usage risks future incompatibility and gives no benefits. An instance of any subclass of Exception has an attribute args, the tuple of arguments used to create the instance. args holds error-specific information, usable for diagnostic or recovery purposes.

The Hierarchy of Standard Exceptions

All exceptions that Python itself raises are instances of subclasses of Exception. The inheritance structure of exception classes is important, as it determines which except clauses handle which exceptions.

The SystemExit class inherits directly from Exception. Instances of SystemExit are normally raised by the exit function in module sys (covered in Chapter 8).

Other standard exceptions derive from StandardError, a direct subclass of Exception. Three subclasses of StandardError, like StandardError itself and Exception, are never instantiated directly. Their purpose is to make it easier for you to specify except clauses that handle a broad range of related errors. These subclasses are:

ArithmeticError
> The base class for exceptions due to arithmetic errors (i.e., OverflowError, ZeroDivisionError, FloatingPointError)

LookupError
> The base class for exceptions that a container raises when it receives an invalid key or index (i.e., IndexError, KeyError)

EnvironmentError
> The base class for exceptions due to external causes (i.e., IOError, OSError, WindowsError)

Standard Exception Classes

Common runtime errors raise exceptions of the following classes:

AssertionError
> An assert statement failed.

AttributeError
> An attribute reference or assignment failed.

FloatingPointError
> A floating-point operation failed. Derived from ArithmeticError.

IOError
> An I/O operation failed (e.g., the disk is full, a file was not found, or needed permissions were missing). Derived from EnvironmentError.

ImportError
> An import statement (covered in Chapter 7) cannot find the module to import or cannot find a name specifically requested from the module.

IndentationError
> The parser encountered a syntax error due to incorrect indentation. Derived from SyntaxError.

IndexError
> An integer used to index a sequence is out of range (using a non-integer as a sequence index raises TypeError). Derived from LookupError.

KeyError
> A key used to index a mapping is not in the mapping. Derived from LookupError.

KeyboardInterrupt
> The user pressed the interrupt key (Ctrl-C, Ctrl-Break, or Delete, depending on the platform).

MemoryError
> An operation ran out of memory.

NameError
> A variable was referenced, but its name is not bound.

NotImplementedError
> Raised by abstract base classes to indicate that a concrete subclass must override a method.

OSError
> Raised by functions in module os (covered in Chapters 10 and 14) to indicate platform-dependent errors. Derived from EnvironmentError.

OverflowError
> The result of an operation on an integer is too large to fit into an integer (operator << does not raise this exception: rather, it drops excess bits). Derived from ArithmeticError. Python 2.1 only; in 2.2 and 2.3, too-large integer results implicitly become long integers, without raising exceptions.

SyntaxError
> The parser encountered a syntax error.

SystemError

An internal error within Python itself or some extension module. You should report this to the authors and maintainers of Python, or of the extension in question, with all possible details to allow reproducing it.

TypeError

An operation or function was applied to an object of an inappropriate type.

UnboundLocalError

A reference was made to a local variable, but no value is currently bound to that local variable. Derived from NameError.

UnicodeError

An error occurred while converting Unicode to a string or vice versa.

ValueError

An operation or function was applied to an object that has a correct type but an inappropriate value, and nothing more specific (e.g., KeyError) applies.

WindowsError

Raised by functions in module os (covered in Chapters 10 and 14) to indicate Windows-specific errors. Derived from OsError.

ZeroDivisionError

A divisor (the right-hand operand of a /, //, or % operator or the second argument to built-in function divmod) is 0. Derived from ArithmeticError.

Custom Exception Classes

You can subclass any of the standard exception classes in order to define your own exception class. Typically, such a subclass adds nothing more than a docstring:

```
class InvalidAttribute(AttributeError):
    "Used to indicate attributes that could never be valid"
```

Given the semantics of try/except, raising a custom exception class such as InvalidAttribute is almost the same as raising its standard exception superclass, AttributeError. Any except clause able to handle AttributeError can handle InvalidAttribute just as well. In addition, client code that knows specifically about your InvalidAttribute custom exception class can handle it specifically, without having to handle all other cases of AttributeError if it is not prepared for those. For example:

```
class SomeFunkyClass(object):
    "much hypothetical functionality snipped"
    def __getattr__(self, name):
        "this __getattr__ only clarifies the kind of attribute error"
        if name.startswith('_'):
            raise InvalidAttribute, "Unknown private attribute "+name
        else:
            raise AttributeError, "Unknown attribute "+name
```

Now client code can be more selective in its handlers. For example:

```
s = SomeFunkyClass( )
try:
```

```
        value = getattr(s, thename)
    except InvalidAttribute, err
        warnings.warn(str(err))
        value = None
    # other cases of AttributeError just propagate, as they're unexpected
```

A special case of custom exception class that you may sometimes find useful is one that wraps another exception and adds further information. To gather information about a pending exception, you can use the exc_info function from module sys (covered in Chapter 8). Given this, your custom exception class could be defined as follows:

```
import sys
class CustomException(Exception):
    "Wrap arbitrary pending exception, if any, in addition to other info"
    def __init__(self, *args):
        Exception.__init__(self, *args)
        self.wrapped_exc = sys.exc_info()
```

You would then typically use this class in a wrapper function such as:

```
def call_wrapped(callable, *args, **kwds):
    try: return callable(*args, **kwds)
    except: raise CustomException, "Wrapped function propagated exception"
```

Error-Checking Strategies

Most programming languages that support exceptions are geared to raise exceptions only in very rare cases. Python's emphasis is different. In Python, exceptions are considered appropriate whenever they make a program simpler and more robust. A common idiom in other languages, sometimes known as "look before you leap" (LBYL), is to check in advance, before attempting an operation, for all circumstances that might make the operation invalid. This is not ideal, for several reasons:

- The checks may diminish the readability and clarity of the common, mainstream cases where everything is okay.
- The work needed for checking may duplicate a substantial part of the work done in the operation itself.
- The programmer might easily err by omitting some needed check.
- The situation might change between the moment the checks are performed and the moment the operation is attempted.

The preferred idiom in Python is generally to attempt the operation in a try clause and handle the exceptions that may result in except clauses. This idiom is known as "it's easier to ask forgiveness than permission" (EAFP), a motto widely credited to Admiral Grace Murray Hopper, co-inventor of COBOL, and shares none of the defects of "look before you leap." Here is a function written using the LBYL idiom:

```
def safe_divide_1(x, y):
    if y==0:
        print "Divide-by-0 attempt detected"
```

```
        return None
    else:
        return x/y
```

With LBYL, the checks come first, and the mainstream case is somewhat hidden at the end of the function.

Here is the equivalent function written using the EAFP idiom:

```
def safe_divide_2(x, y):
    try:
        return x/y
    except ZeroDivisionError:
        print "Divide-by-0 attempt detected"
        return None
```

With EAFP, the mainstream case is up front in a try clause, and the anomalies are handled in an except clause.

EAFP is most often the preferable error-handling strategy, but it is not a panacea. In particular, you must be careful not to cast too wide a net, catching errors that you did not expect and therefore did not mean to catch. The following is a typical case of such a risk (built-in function getattr is covered in Chapter 8):

```
def trycalling(obj, attrib, default, *args, **kwds):
    try: return getattr(obj, attrib)(*args, **kwds)
    except AttributeError: return default
```

The intention of function trycalling is to try calling a method named attrib on object obj, but to return default if obj has no method thus named. However, the function as coded does not do just that. It also hides any error case where AttributeError is raised inside the implementation of the sought-after method, silently returning default in those cases. This may hide bugs in other code. To do exactly what is intended, the function must take a little bit more care:

```
def trycalling(obj, attrib, default, *args, **kwds):
    try: method = getattr(obj, attrib)
    except AttributeError: return default
    else: return method(*args, **kwds)
```

This implementation of trycalling separates the getattr call, placed in the try clause and therefore watched over by the handler in the except clause, from the call of the method, placed in the else clause and therefore free to propagate any exceptions it may need to. Using EAFP in the most effective way involves frequent use of the else clause on try/except statements.

Handling Errors in Large Programs

In large programs, it is especially easy to err by making your try/except statements too wide, particularly once you have convinced yourself of the power of EAFP as a general error-checking strategy. A try/except is too wide when it catches too many different errors or an error that can occur in too many different places. The latter is a problem if you need to distinguish exactly what happened and where, and the information in the traceback is not sufficient to pinpoint such details (or you discard some or all of the information in the traceback object). For effective error handling, you have to keep a clear distinction between errors and anomalies that you expect (and thus know exactly how to handle), and unexpected errors and anomalies, which indicate a bug somewhere in your program.

Some errors and anomalies are not really erroneous, and perhaps not even all that anomalous: they are just special cases, perhaps rare but nevertheless quite expected, which you choose to handle via EAFP rather than via LBYL to avoid LBYL's many intrinsic defects. In such cases, you should just handle the anomaly, in most cases without even logging or reporting it. Be very careful, under these circumstances, to keep the relevant try/except constructs as narrow as feasible. Use a small try clause that doesn't call too many other functions, and very specific exception-class lists in the except clauses.

Errors and anomalies that depend on user input or other external conditions not under your control are always expected to some extent, precisely because you have no control on their underlying causes. In such cases, you should concentrate your effort on handling the anomaly gracefully, normally reporting and logging its exact nature and details, and generally keep your program running with undamaged internal and persistent states. The width of try/except clauses under such circumstances should also be reasonably narrow, although this is not quite as crucial as when you use EAFP to structure your handling of not-really-erroneous special cases.

Lastly, entirely unexpected errors and anomalies indicate bugs in your program's design or coding. In most cases, the best strategy regarding such errors is to avoid try/except and just let the program terminate with error and traceback messages. (You might even want to log such information and/or display it more suitably with an application-specific hook in sys.excepthook, as we'll discuss shortly.) If your program must keep running at all costs, even under such circumstances, try/except statements that are quite wide may be appropriate, with the try clause guarding function calls that exercise vast swaths of program functionality and broad except clauses.

In the case of a long-running program, make sure all details of the anomaly or error are logged to some persistent place for later study (and that some indication gets displayed, too, so that you know such later study is necessary). The key is making sure that the program's persistent state can be reverted to some undamaged, internally consistent point. The techniques that enable long-running programs to survive some of their own bugs are known as checkpointing and transactional behavior, but they are not covered further in this book.

Logging Errors

When Python propagates an exception all the way to the top of the stack without finding an applicable handler, the interpreter normally prints an error traceback to the standard error stream of the process (sys.stderr) before terminating the program. You can rebind sys.stderr to any file-like object usable for output in order to divert this information to a destination more suitable for your purposes.

When you want to change the amount and kind of information output on such occasions, rebinding sys.stderr is not sufficient. In such cases, you can assign your own function to sys.excepthook, and Python will call it before terminating the program due to an unhandled exception. In your exception-reporting function, you can output whatever information you think will later help you diagnose and debug the problem to whatever destinations you please. For example, you might use module traceback (covered in Chapter 17) to help you format stack traces. When your exception-reporting function terminates, so does your program.

The assert Statement

The assert statement allows you to introduce debugging code into a program. assert is a simple statement with the following syntax:

```
assert condition[,expression]
```

When you run Python with the optimize flag (-O, as covered in Chapter 3), assert is a null operation: the compiler generates no code. Otherwise, assert evaluates *condition*. If *condition* is satisfied, assert does nothing. If *condition* is not satisfied, assert instantiates AssertionError with *expression* as the argument (or without arguments, if there is no *expression*) and raises the resulting instance.

assert statements are an effective way to document your program. When you want to state that a significant condition *C* is known to hold at a certain point in a program's execution, assert *C* is better than a comment that just states *C*. The advantage of assert is that when the condition does not in fact hold, assert alerts you to the problem by raising AssertionError.

The __debug__ Built-in Variable

When you run Python without option -O, the __debug__ built-in variable is True. When you run Python with option -O, __debug__ is False. Also, with option -O, the compiler generates no code for an if statement whose condition is __debug__.

To exploit this optimization, surround the definitions of functions that you call only in assert statements with if __debug__. This technique makes compiled code smaller and faster when Python is run with -O, and enhances program clarity by showing that the functions exist only to perform sanity checks.

7

Modules

A typical Python program is made up of several source files. Each source file corresponds to a *module*, which packages program code and data for reuse. Modules are normally independent of each other so that other programs can reuse the specific modules they need. A module explicitly establishes dependencies upon another module by using import or from statements. In some other programming languages, global variables can provide a hidden conduit for coupling between modules. In Python, however, global variables are not global to all modules, but instead such variables are attributes of a single module object. Thus, Python modules communicate in explicit and maintainable ways.

Python also supports *extensions*, which are components written in other languages, such as C, C++, or Java, for use with Python. Extensions are seen as modules by the Python code that uses them (called client code). From the client code viewpoint, it does not matter whether a module is 100% pure Python or an extension. You can always start by coding a module in Python. Later, if you need better performance, you can recode some modules in a lower-level language without changing the client code that uses the modules. Chapters 24 and 25 discuss writing extensions in C and Java.

This chapter discusses module creation and loading. It also covers grouping modules into *packages*, which are modules that contain other modules, forming a hierarchical, tree-like structure. Finally, the chapter discusses using Python's distribution utilities (distutils) to prepare packages and modules for distribution and to install distributed packages and modules.

Module Objects

A module is a Python object with arbitrarily named attributes that you can bind and reference. The Python code for a module named *aname* normally resides in a file named *aname.py*, as covered in "Module Loading" later in this chapter.

In Python, modules are objects (values) and are handled like other objects. Thus, you can pass a module as an argument in a call to a function. Similarly, a function can return a module as the result of a call. A module, just like any other object, can be bound to a variable, an item in a container, or an attribute of an object. For example, the sys.modules dictionary, covered later in this chapter, holds module objects as its values.

The import Statement

You can use any Python source file as a module by executing an import statement in some other code. import has the following syntax:

```
import modname [as varname][,...]
```

The import keyword is followed by one or more module specifiers, separated by commas. In the simplest and most common case, *modname* is an identifier, the name of a variable that Python binds to the module object when the import statement finishes. In this case, Python looks for the module of the same name to satisfy the import request. For example:

```
import MyModule
```

looks for the module named MyModule and binds the variable named MyModule in the current scope to the module object. *modname* can also be a sequence of identifiers separated by dots (.) that names a module in a package, as covered in later in this chapter.

When as *varname* is part of an import statement, Python binds the variable named *varname* to the module object, but the module name that Python looks for is *modname*. For example:

```
import MyModule as Alias
```

looks for the module named MyModule and binds the variable named Alias in the current scope to the module object. *varname* is always a simple identifier.

Module body

The body of a module is the sequence of statements in the module's source file. There is no special syntax required to indicate that a source file is a module; any valid source file can be used as a module. A module's body executes immediately the first time the module is imported in a given run of a program. During execution of the body, the module object already exists and an entry in sys.modules is already bound to the module object.

Attributes of module objects

An import statement creates a new namespace that contains all the attributes of the module. To access an attribute in this namespace, use the name of the module object as a prefix:

```
import MyModule
a = MyModule.f( )
```

or:

```
import MyModule as Alias
a = Alias.f( )
```

Most attributes of a module object are bound by statements in the module body. When a statement in the body binds a variable (a global variable), what gets bound is an attribute of the module object. The normal purpose of a module body is exactly that of creating the module's attributes: def statements create and bind functions, class statements create and bind classes, assignment statements bind attributes of any type.

You can also bind and unbind module attributes outside the body (i.e., in other modules), generally using attribute reference syntax M.*name* (where M is any expression whose value is the module, and identifier *name* is the attribute name). For clarity, however, it's usually best to bind module attributes in the module body.

The import statement implicitly defines some module attributes as soon as it creates the module object, before the module's body executes. The __dict__ attribute is the dictionary object that the module uses as the namespace for its attributes. Unlike all other attributes of the module, __dict__ is not available to code in the module as a global variable. All other attributes in the module are entries in the module's __dict__, and they are available to code in the modules as global variables. Attribute __name__ is the module's name, and attribute __file__ is the filename from which the module was loaded, if any.

For any module object M, any object x, and any identifier string S (except __dict__), binding M.S=x is equivalent to binding M.__dict__['S']=x. An attribute reference such as M.S is also substantially equivalent to M.__dict__['S']. The only difference is that when 'S' is not a key in M.__dict__, accessing M.__dict__['S'] directly raises KeyError, while accessing M.S raises AttributeError instead. Module attributes are also available to all code in the module's body as global variables. In other words, within the module body, S used as a global variable is equivalent to M.S (i.e., M.__dict__['S']) for both binding and reference.

Python built-ins

Python offers several built-in objects (covered in Chapter 8). All built-in objects are attributes of a preloaded module named __builtin__. When Python loads a module, the module automatically gets an extra attribute named __builtins__, which refers to either module __builtin__ or to __builtin__'s dictionary. Python may choose either, so don't rely on __builtins__. If you need to access module __builtin__ directly, use an import __builtin__ statement. Note the difference between the name of the attribute and the name of the module: the former has an extra s. When a global variable is not found in the current module, Python looks for the identifier in the current module's __builtins__ before raising NameError.

The lookup is the only mechanism that Python uses to let your code implicitly access built-ins. The built-ins' names are not reserved, nor are they hardwired in Python itself. Since the access mechanism is simple and documented, your own code can use the mechanism directly (in moderation, or your program's clarity and simplicity will suffer). Thus, you can add your own built-ins or substitute your functions for the normal built-in ones. You can restrict an untrusted module by controlling what built-ins the untrusted module sees (as covered in Chapter 13). The following example shows how you can wrap a built-in function with your own function (_import_ and reload are both covered later in this chapter):

```
# reload takes a module object; let's make it accept a string as well
import __builtin__
_reload = __builtin__.reload          # save the original built-in
def reload(mod_or_name):
    if isinstance(mod_or_name, str):      # if argument is a string
        mod_or_name = __import__(mod_or_name)  # get the module instead
    return _reload(mod_or_name)         # invoke the real built-in
__builtin__.reload = reload            # override built-in with wrapper
```

Module documentation strings

If the first statement in the module body is a string literal, the compiler binds that string as the module's documentation string attribute, named _doc_. Documentation strings are also called *docstrings*. See "Attributes of Function Objects" in Chapter 4 for more information on docstrings.

Module-private variables

No variable of a module is really private. However, by convention, starting an identifier with a single underscore (_), such as _secret, indicates that the identifier is meant to be private. In other words, the leading underscore communicates to client-code programmers that they should not access the identifier directly.

Development environments and other tools rely on the leading-underscore naming convention to discern which attributes of a module are public (i.e., part of the module's interface) and which ones are private (i.e., to be used only within the module). It is good programming practice to distinguish between private and public attributes by starting the private ones with _, for clarity and to get maximum benefit from tools.

It is particularly important to respect the convention when you write client code that uses modules written by others. In other words, avoid using any attributes in such modules whose names start with _. Future releases of the modules will no doubt maintain their public interface, but are quite likely to change private implementation details.

The from Statement

Python's from statement lets you import specific attributes from a module into the current namespace. from has two syntax variants:

```
from modname import attrname [as varname][,...]
from modname import *
```

A from statement specifies a module name, followed by one or more attribute specifiers separated by commas. In the simplest and most common case, *attrname* is an identifier that names a variable that Python binds to the attribute of the same name in the module named *modname*. For example:

```
from MyModule import f
```

modname can also be a sequence of identifiers separated by dots (.) that names a module within a package, as covered later in this chapter.

When as *varname* is part of a from statement, Python binds the variable named *varname* to the attribute, but the module attribute from which the variable gets its value is *attrname*. For example:

```
from MyModule import f as foo
```

attrname and *varname* are always simple identifiers.

Code that is directly inside a module body (not in the body of a function or class) may use an asterisk (*) in a from statement:

```
from MyModule import *
```

The * requests that all attributes of module *modname* be bound as global variables in the importing module. When the module has an attribute named __all__, the attribute's value is the list of the attributes that are bound by this type of from statement. Otherwise, this type of from statement binds all attributes of *modname* except those beginning with underscores. Since from M import * may bind an arbitrary set of global variables, it can have unforeseen and undesired side effects, such as hiding built-ins and rebinding variables you still need. Thus, you should use the * form of from very sparingly and only from modules that are explicitly documented as supporting such usage.

In general, the import statement is a better choice than the from statement. I suggest you think of the from statement, and particularly from M import *, as conveniences meant only for occasional use in interactive Python sessions. If you always access module M with the statement import M, and always access M's attributes with explicit syntax M.A, your code will be slightly less concise, but far clearer and more readable. from is a good idea only for modules whose documentation explicitly specifies from support (such as module Tkinter, covered in Chapter 16). Another good use of from is to import specific modules from a package, as we'll discuss in "Packages" later in this chapter.

Module Loading

Module-loading operations rely on attributes of the built-in sys module (covered in Chapter 8). The module-loading process described here is carried out by built-in function __import__. Your code can call __import__ directly, with the module name string as an argument. __import__ returns the module object or raises ImportError if the import fails.

To import a module named *M*, __import__ first checks dictionary sys.modules, using string *M* as the key. When key *M* is in the dictionary, __import__ returns the corresponding value as the requested module object. Otherwise, __import__ binds sys.modules[M] to a new empty module object with a __name__ of *M*, then looks for the right way to initialize (load) the module, as covered in "Searching the Filesystem for a Module" later in this section.

Thanks to this mechanism, the loading operation takes place only the first time a module is imported in a given run of the program. When a module is imported again, the module is not reloaded, since __import__ finds and returns the module's entry in sys.modules. Thus, all imports of a module after the first one are extremely fast because they're just dictionary lookups.

Built-in Modules

When a module is loaded, __import__ first checks whether the module is built-in. Built-in modules are listed in tuple sys.builtin_module_names, but rebinding that tuple does not affect module loading. A built-in module, like any other Python extension, is initialized by calling the module's initialization function. The search for built-in modules also finds frozen modules and modules in platform-specific locations (e.g., resources on the Mac, the Registry in Windows).

Searching the Filesystem for a Module

If module M is not built-in or frozen, __import__ looks for M's code as a file on the filesystem. __import__ looks in the directories whose names are the items of list sys.path, in order. sys.path is initialized at program startup, using environment variable PYTHONPATH (covered in Chapter 3) if present. The first item in sys.path is always the directory from which the main program (script) is loaded. An empty string in sys.path indicates the current directory.

Your code can mutate or rebind sys.path, and such changes affect what directories __import__ searches to load modules. Changing sys.path does not affect modules that are already loaded (and thus already listed in sys.modules) when sys.path is changed.

If a text file with extension .pth is found in the PYTHONHOME directory at startup, its contents are added to sys.path, one item per line. .pth files can also contain blank lines and comment lines starting with the character #, as Python ignores any such lines. .pth files can also contain import statements, which Python executes, but no other kinds of statements.

When looking for the file for module M in each directory along sys.path, Python considers the following extensions in the order listed:

1. .pyd and .dll (Windows) or .so (most Unix-like platforms), which indicate Python extension modules. (Some Unix dialects use different extensions; e.g., .sl is the extension used on HP-UX.)

2. .py, which indicates pure Python source modules.

3. .pyc (or .pyo, if Python is run with option -O), which indicates bytecode-compiled Python modules.

Upon finding source file M.py, Python compiles it to M.pyc (or M.pyo) unless the bytecode file is already present, is newer than M.py, and was compiled by the same version of Python. Python saves the bytecode file to the filesystem in the same directory as M.py (if permissions on the directory allow writing) so that future runs will not needlessly recompile. When the bytecode file is newer than the source file, Python does not recompile the module.

Once Python has the bytecode file, either from having constructed it by compilation or by reading it from the filesystem, Python executes the module body to initialize the module object. If the module is an extension, Python calls the module's initialization function.

The Main Program

Execution of a Python application normally starts with a top-level script (also known as the *main program*), as explained in Chapter 3. The main program executes like any other module being loaded except that Python keeps the bytecode in memory without saving it to disk. The module name for the main program is always __main__, both as the __name__ global variable (module attribute) and as the key in sys.modules. You should not normally import the same *.py* file that is in use as the main program. If you do, the module is loaded again, and the module body is executed once more from the top in a separate module object with a different __name__.

Code in a Python module can test whether the module is being used as the main program by checking if global variable __name__ equals '__main__'. The idiom:

```
if __name__=='__main__':
```

is often used to guard some code so that it executes only when the module is run as the main program. If a module is designed only to be imported, it should normally execute unit tests when it is run as the main program, as covered in Chapter 17.

The reload Function

As I explained earlier, Python loads a module only the first time you import the module during a program run. When you develop interactively, you need to make sure that your modules are reloaded each time you edit them (some development environments provide automatic reloading).

To reload a module, pass the module object (*not* the module name) as the only argument to built-in function reload. reload(M) ensures the reloaded version of M is used by client code that relies on import M and accesses attributes with the syntax M.A. However, reload(M) has no effect on other references bound to previous values of M's attributes (e.g., with the from statement). In other words, already-bound variables remain bound as they were, unaffected by reload. reload's inability to rebind such variables is a further incentive to avoid from.

Circular Imports

Python lets you specify circular imports. For example, you can write a module *a.py* that contains import b, while module *b.py* contains import a. In practice, you are typically better off avoiding circular imports, since circular dependencies are fragile and hard to manage. If you decide to use a circular import for some reason, you need to understand how circular imports work in order to avoid errors in your code.

Say that the main script executes import a. As discussed earlier, this import statement creates a new empty module object as sys.modules['a'], and then the body of module a starts executing. When a executes `import b`, this creates a new empty module object as `sys.modules['b']`, and then the body of module b starts executing. The execution of a's module body is now suspended until b's module body finishes.

Now, when b executes `import a`, the `import` statement finds `sys.modules['a']` already defined and therefore binds global variable a in module b to the module object for module a. Since the execution of a's module body is currently suspended, module a may be only partly populated at this time. If the code in b's module body tries to access some attribute of module a that is not yet bound, an error results.

If you do insist on keeping a circular import in some case, you must carefully manage the order in which each module defines its own globals, imports the other module, and accesses the globals of the other module. Generally, you can have greater control on the sequence in which things happen by grouping your statements into functions and calling those functions in a controlled order, rather than just relying on sequential execution of top-level statements in module bodies. However, removing circular dependencies is almost always easier than ensuring bomb-proof ordering while keeping such circular dependencies.

sys.modules Entries

The built-in `__import__` function never binds anything other than a module object as a value in `sys.modules`. However, if `__import__` finds an entry that is already in `sys.modules`, it will try to use that value, whatever type of object it may be. The `import` and `from` statements rely on the `__import__` function, so therefore they too can end up using objects that are not modules. This lets you set class instances as entries in `sys.modules`, and take advantage of features such as their `__getattr__` and `__setattr__` special methods, covered in Chapter 5. This advanced technique lets you import module-like objects whose attributes can in fact be computed on the fly. Here's a trivial toy-like example:

```
class TT:
    def __getattr__(self, name): return 23
import sys
sys.modules[__name__] = TT()
```

When you import this code as a module, you get a module-like object that appears to have any attribute name you try to get from it, and all attribute names correspond to the integer value 23.

Custom Importers

You can rebind the `__import__` attribute of module `__builtin__` to your own custom importer function by wrapping the `__import__` function using the technique shown earlier in this chapter. Such rebinding influences all `import` and `from` statements that execute after the rebinding. A custom importer must implement the same interface as the built-in `__import__`, and is often implemented with some help from the functions exposed by built-in module `imp`. Custom importer functions are an advanced and rarely used technique.

Packages

A *package* is a module that contains other modules. Modules in a package may be subpackages, resulting in a hierarchical tree-like structure. A package named *P* resides in a subdirectory, also called *P*, of some directory in sys.path. The module body of *P* is in the file *P/__init__.py*. You must have a file named *P/__init__.py*, even if it's empty (representing an empty module body), in order to indicate to Python that directory *P* is indeed a package. Other *.py* files in directory *P* are the modules of package *P*. Subdirectories of *P* containing *__init__.py* files are subpackages of *P*. Nesting can continue to any depth.

You can import a module named *M* in package *P* as *P.M*. More dots let you navigate a hierarchical package structure. A package is always loaded before a module in the package is loaded. If you use the syntax import *P.M*, variable *P* is bound to the module object of package *P*, and attribute *M* of object *P* is bound to module *P.M*. If you use the syntax import *P.M* as *V*, variable *V* is bound directly to module *P.M*.

Using from *P* import *M* to import a specific module *M* from package *P* is fully acceptable programming practice. In other words, the from statement is specifically okay in this case.

A module *M* in a package *P* can import any other module *X* of *P* with the statement import *X*. Python searches the module's own package directory before searching the directories in sys.path. However, this applies only to sibling modules, not to ancestors or other more-complicated relationships. The simplest, cleanest way to share objects (such as functions or constants) among modules in a package *P* is to group the shared objects in a file named *P/Common.py*. Then you can import Common from every module in the package that needs to access the objects, and then refer to the objects as Common.*f*, Common.*K*, and so on.

The Distribution Utilities (distutils)

Python modules, extensions, and applications can be packaged and distributed in several forms:

Compressed archive files
Generally *.zip* for Windows and *.tar.gz* or *.tgz* for Unix-based systems, but both forms are portable

Self-unpacking or self-installing executables
Normally *.exe* for Windows

Platform-specific installers
For example, *.msi* on Windows, *.rpm* and *.srpm* on Linux, and *.deb* on Debian GNU/Linux

When you distribute a package as a self-installing executable or platform-specific installer, a user can then install the package simply by running the installer. How to run such an installer program depends on the platform, but it no longer matters what language the program was written in.

When you distribute a package as an archive file or as an executable that unpacks but does not install itself, it does matter that the package was coded in Python. In this case, the user must first unpack the archive file into some appropriate directory, say *C:\Temp\MyPack* on a Windows machine or *~/MyPack* on a Unix-like machine. Among the extracted files there should be a script, conventionally named *setup.py*, that uses the Python facility known as the *distribution utilities* (package distutils). The distributed package is then almost as easy to install as a self-installing executable would be. The user opens a command-prompt window and changes to the directory into which the archive is unpacked. Then the user runs, for example:

```
C:\Temp\MyPack> python setup.py install
```

The *setup.py* script, run with this install command, installs the package as a part of the user's Python installation, according to the options specified in the setup script by the package's author. distutils, by default, provides tracing information when the user runs *setup.py*. Option --quiet, placed right before the install command, hides most details (the user still sees error messages, if any). The following command:

```
C:\> python setup.py --help
```

gives help on distutils.

When you are installing a package prepared with distutils, you can, if you wish, exert detailed control over how distutils performs installations. You can record installation options in a text file with extension *.cfg*, called a config file, so that distutils applies your favorite installation options by default. Such customization can be done on a systemwide basis, for a single user, or even for a single package installation. For example, if you want an installation with minimal amounts of output to be your systemwide default, create the following text file named *pydistutils.cfg*:

```
[global]
quiet=1
```

Place this file in the same directory in which the distutils package resides. On a typical Python 2.2 installation on Windows, for example, the file is *C:\Python22\Lib\distutils\pydistutils.cfg*. Chapter 26 provides more information on using distutils to prepare Python modules, packages, extensions, and applications for distribution.

8

Core Built-ins

The term *built-in* has more than one meaning in Python. In most contexts, a built-in is any object directly accessible to a Python program without an import statement. Chapter 7 showed the mechanism that Python uses to allow this direct access. Built-in types in Python include numbers, sequences, dictionaries, functions (covered in Chapter 4), classes (covered in Chapter 5), the standard exception classes (covered in Chapter 6), and modules (covered in Chapter 7). The built-in file object is covered in Chapter 10, and other built-in types covered in Chapter 13 are intrinsic to Python's internal operation. This chapter provides additional coverage of the core built-in types, and it also covers the built-in functions available in module __builtin__.

As I mentioned in Chapter 7, some modules are called built-in because they are an integral part of the Python standard library, even though it takes an import statement to access them. Built-in modules are distinct from separate, optional add-on modules, also called Python *extensions*. This chapter documents the following core built-in modules: sys, getopt, copy, bisect, UserList, UserDict, and UserString. Chapter 9 covers some string-related core built-in modules, while Parts III and IV of the book cover many other useful built-in modules.

Built-in Types

This section documents Python's core built-in types, like int, float, and dict. Note that prior to Python 2.2, these names referred to factory functions for creating objects of these types. As of Python 2.2, however, they refer to actual type objects. Since you can call type objects just as if they were functions, this change does not break existing programs.

classmethod   classmethod(*function*)   Python 2.2 and later

Creates and returns a class method object. In practice, you call this built-in type only within a class body. See "Class methods" in Chapter 5.

complex   complex(*real*,*imag*=0)

Converts any number, or a suitable string, to a complex number. *imag* may be present only when *real* is a number, and is the imaginary part of the resulting complex number.

dict   dict(*x*={ })   Python 2.2 and later

Returns a new dictionary object with the same items as argument *x*. When *x* is a dictionary, dict(*x*) returns a copy of *x*, like *x*.copy( ) does. Alternatively, *x* can be a sequence of pairs, that is, a sequence whose items are sequences with two items each. In this case, dict(*x*) returns a dictionary whose keys are the first items of each pair in *x*, while the corresponding values are the corresponding second items. In other words, when *x* is a sequence, c=dict(*x*) has the same effect as the following:

```
c = { }
for key, value in x: c[key] = value
```

file, open   file(*path*,*mode*='r',*bufsize*=-1)
                      open(*filename*,*mode*='r',*bufsize*=-1)

Opens or creates a file and returns a new file object. In Python 2.2 and later, open is a synonym for the built-in type file. In Python 2.1 and earlier, open was a built-in function and file was not a built-in name at all. See "File Objects" in Chapter 10.

float   float(*x*)

Converts any number, or a suitable string, to a floating-point number.

int   int(*x*[,*radix*])

Converts any number, or a suitable string, to an int. When *x* is a number, int truncates toward 0, dropping any fractional part. *radix* may be present only when *x* is a string. *radix* is the conversion base, between 2 and 36, with 10 as the default. *radix* can be explicitly passed as 0: the base is then 8, 10, or 16, depending on the form of string *x*, just like for integer literals, as covered in "Numbers" in Chapter 4.

Core Built-ins

list

    `list(seq=[])`

    Returns a new list object with the same items as the iterable object *seq*, in the same order. When *seq* is a list, `list(seq)` returns a copy of *seq*, like *seq*`[:]` does.

long

    `long(x[,radix])`

    Converts any number, or a suitable string, to a `long`. The rules regarding the *radix* argument are exactly the same as for `int`.

object

    `object(*args,**kwds)`

    Creates and returns a new instance of the most fundamental type. Such direct instances of type `object` have no useful functionality so there is never a practical reason to create one, although Python does let you call `object` for regularity. `object` accepts and ignores any positional and named arguments.

property

    `property(fget=None,fset=None,fdel=None,`
    `doc=None)`   *Python 2.2 and later*

    Creates and returns a property accessor. In practice, you call this built-in type only within a class body. See "Properties" in Chapter 5.

staticmethod

    `staticmethod(function)`   *Python 2.2 and later*

    Creates and returns a static method object. In practice, you call this built-in type only within a class body. See "Static methods" in Chapter 5.

str

    `str(obj)`

    Returns a concise and readable string representation of *obj*. If *obj* is a string, `str` returns *obj*. See also `repr` later in this chapter and `__str__` in Chapter 5.

super

    `super(cls,obj)`   *Python 2.2 and later*

    Returns a super object of object *obj* (which must be an instance of class *cls* or of a subclass of *cls*), suitable for calling superclass methods. In practice, you call this built-in type only within a method's code. See "Cooperative superclass method calling" in Chapter 5.

tuple

    `tuple(seq)`

    Returns a tuple with the same items as the iterable object *seq*, in the same order. When *seq* is a tuple, `tuple` returns *seq* itself, like *seq*`[:]` does.

| **type** | type(*obj*) |

Returns the type object that represents the type of *obj* (i.e., the most-derived type object of which *obj* is an instance). All classic instance objects have the same type (InstanceType), even when they are instances of different classes; use isinstance (covered later in this chapter) to check whether an instance belongs to a particular class. In the new-style object model, however, type(*x*) is *x*.__class__ for any *x*.

Checking type(*x*) for equality or identity to some other type object is known as type-checking. Type-checking is rarely appropriate in production Python code because it interferes with polymorphism. The normal idiom in Python is to try to use *x* as if it were of the type you expect, handling any problems with a try/except statement, as discussed in Chapter 6. When you must type-check, typically for debugging purposes, use isinstance instead. isinstance(*x*,*atype*) is a somewhat lesser evil than type(*x*) is *atype*, since at least it accepts an *x* that is an instance of any subclass of *atype*, not just a direct instance of *atype* itself.

| **unicode** | unicode(*string*[,*codec*[,*errors*]]) |

Returns the Unicode string object obtained by decoding *string*. *codec* names the codec to use. If *codec* is missing, unicode uses the default codec (generally 'ascii'). *errors*, if present, is a string that specifies how to handle decoding errors. See also "Unicode" in Chapter 9, particularly for information about codecs and *errors*, and __unicode__ in Chapter 5.

Built-in Functions

This section documents the Python functions available in module __builtin__ in alphabetical order. Note that the names of these built-ins are not reserved words. Thus, your program can bind for its own purposes, in local or global scope, an identifier that has the same name as a built-in function. Names bound in local or global scope have priority over names bound in built-in scope, so local and global names hide built-in ones. You can also rebind names in built-in scope, as covered in Chapter 7. You should avoid hiding built-ins that your code might need.

| **__import__** | __import__(*module_name*[,*globals*[,*locals*[,*fromlist*]]]) |

Loads the module named by string *module_name* and returns the resulting module object. *globals*, which defaults to the result of globals( ), and *locals*, which defaults to the result of locals( ) (both covered in this section), are dictionaries that __import__ treats as read-only and uses only to get context for package-relative imports, covered in "Packages" in Chapter 7. *fromlist* defaults to an empty list, but can be a list of strings that name the module attributes to be imported in a `from` statement. See "Module Loading" in Chapter 7 for more details on module loading.

In practice, when you call `__import__`, you generally pass only the first argument, except in the rare and dubious case in which you use `__import__` for a package-relative import. When you replace the built-in `__import__` function with your own in order to provide special import functionality, you may have to take *globals*, *locals*, and *fromlist* into account.

abs	`abs(x)`

Returns the absolute value of number *x*. When *x* is complex, abs returns the square root of *x*.imag**2+*x*.real**2. Otherwise, abs returns -*x* if *x* is less than 0, or *x* if *x* is greater than or equal to 0. See also `__abs__` in Chapter 5.

apply	`apply(func,args=( ),keywords={ })`

Calls a function (or other callable object) and returns its result. apply's behavior is exactly the same as *func(*args,**keywords)*. The * and ** forms are covered in "Functions" in Chapter 4. In almost all cases of practical interest, you can just use the syntax *func(*args,**keywords)* and avoid apply.

bool	`bool(x)`	Python 2.2 and later

Returns 0, also known as False, if argument *x* evaluates as false; returns 1, also known as True, if argument *x* evaluates as true. See also "Boolean Values" in Chapter 4. In Python 2.3, bool becomes a type (a subclass of int), and built-in names False and True refer to the only two instances of type bool. They are still numbers with values of 0 and 1 respectively, but str(True) becomes 'True', and str(False) becomes 'False', while in Python 2.2 the corresponding strings are '0' and '1' respectively.

buffer	`buffer(obj,offset=0,size=-1)`

Creates and returns a buffer object referring to *obj*'s data. *obj* must be of a type that supports the buffer call interface, such as a string or array. For more on buffer, see Chapter 13.

callable	`callable(obj)`

Returns True if *obj* can be called, otherwise False. An object can be called if it is a function, method, class, type, or an instance with a `__call__` method. See also `__call__` in Chapter 5.

chr	`chr(code)`

Returns a string of length 1, a single character corresponding to integer *code* in the ASCII/ISO encoding. See also ord and unichr in this section.

cmp	cmp(*x*,*y*)
	Returns 0 when *x* equals *y*, -1 when *x* is less than *y*, or 1 when *x* is greater than *y*. See also __cmp__ in Chapter 5.

coerce	coerce(*x*,*y*)
	Returns a pair whose two items are numbers *x* and *y* converted to a common type. See "Coercion and Conversions" in Chapter 4.

compile	compile(*string*,*filename*,*kind*)
	Compiles a string and returns a code object usable by exec or eval. compile raises SyntaxError when *string* is not syntactically valid Python. When *string* is a multiline compound statement, the last character must be '\n'. *kind* must be 'eval' when *string* is an expression and the result is meant for eval, otherwise *kind* must be 'exec'. *filename* must be a string, and is used only in error messages (if and when errors occur). See also eval in this section and "Dynamic Execution and the exec Statement" in Chapter 13.

delattr	delattr(*obj*,*name*)
	Removes attribute *name* from *obj*. delattr(*obj*,'ident') is like del *obj*.ident. If *obj* has an attribute named *name* just because its type or class has it (as is normally the case, for example, with methods of *obj*), you cannot delete that attribute from *obj* itself. You may or may not be able to delete that attribute from the type or class itself, depending on what the type or class allows. If you can, *obj* would cease to have the attribute, and so would every other object of that type or class.

dir	dir([*obj*])
	Called without arguments, dir( ) returns the sorted list of all variable names that are bound in the current scope. dir(*obj*) returns the sorted list of all names of attributes of *obj*. In Python 2.1 and earlier, dir does not return attributes that *obj* gets from its type or by inheritance. In Python 2.2 and later, dir returns all attributes, including ones that are inherited and from its type. See also vars in this section.

divmod	divmod(*dividend*,*divisor*)
	Divides two numbers and returns a pair whose items are the quotient and remainder. See also __divmod__ in Chapter 5.

eval	eval(*expr*,[*globals*[,*locals*]])
	Returns the result of an expression. *expr* may be a code object ready for evaluation or a string. In the case of a string, eval gets a code object by calling compile(*expr*, 'string', 'eval'). eval evaluates

the code object as an expression, using the *globals* and *locals* dictionaries as namespaces. When both arguments are missing, eval uses the current namespace. eval cannot execute statements; it can only evaluate expressions. For more information on eval, see Chapter 13.

execfile

execfile(*filename*,[*globals*[,*locals*]])

execfile is a shortcut for the following statement:

    exec open(*filename*).read( ) in *globals*, *locals*

See "Dynamic Execution and the exec Statement" in Chapter 13.

filter

filter(*func*,*seq*)

Constructs a list from those elements of *seq* for which *func* is true. *func* can be any callable object that accepts a single argument or None. *seq* must be a sequence, iterator, or other iterable object. When *func* is a callable object, filter calls *func* on each item of *seq* and returns the list of items for which *func*'s result is true, like this:

    [*item* for *item* in *seq* if *func*(*item*)]

When *seq* is a string or tuple, filter's result is also a string or tuple, rather than a list. When *func* is None, filter tests for true items like this:

    [*item* for *item* in *seq* if *item*]

getattr

getattr(*obj*,*name*[,*default*])

Returns *obj*'s attribute named by string *name*. getattr(*obj*,'ident') is like *obj*.ident. When *default* is present and *name* is not found in *obj*, getattr returns *default* instead of raising AttributeError. See also "Attribute Reference Basics" in Chapter 5.

globals

globals( )

Returns the __dict__ of the calling module (i.e., the dictionary used as the global namespace at the point of call). See also locals in this section.

hasattr

hasattr(*obj*,*name*)

Returns False if *obj* has no attribute *name* (i.e., if getattr(*obj*,*name*) raises AttributeError). Otherwise, hasattr returns True. See also "Attribute Reference Basics" in Chapter 5.

hash

hash(*obj*)

Returns the hash value for *obj*. *obj* can be a dictionary key only if *obj* can be hashed. All numbers that compare equal have the same hash value, even if they are of different types. If the type of *obj* does not define equality comparison, hash(*obj*) returns id(*obj*). See also __hash__ in Chapter 5.

hex hex(*x*)

Converts integer *x* to a hexadecimal string representation. See also __hex__ in Chapter 5.

id id(*obj*)

Returns the integer value that denotes the identity of *obj*. The id of *obj* is unique and constant during *obj*'s lifetime, but may be reused at any later time after *obj* is garbage-collected. When a type or class does not define equality comparison, Python uses id to compare and hash instances. For any objects *x* and *y*, the identity check *x* is *y* has the same result as id(*x*)==id(*y*).

input input(*prompt*='')

input(*prompt*) is a shortcut for eval(raw_input(*prompt*)). In other words, input prompts the user for a line of input, evaluates the resulting string as an expression, and returns the expression's result. The implicit eval may raise SyntaxError or other exceptions. input is therefore rather user-unfriendly and not appropriate for most programs, but it can be handy for experiments and your own test scripts. See also eval and raw_input in this section.

intern intern(*string*)

Ensures that *string* is held in the table of interned strings and returns *string* itself or a copy. Interned strings compare for equality faster than other strings, but garbage collection cannot recover the memory used for interned strings, so interning too many strings might slow down your program.

isinstance isinstance(*obj*,*cls*)

Returns True when *obj* is an instance of class *cls* (or any subclass of *cls*) or when *cls* is a type object and *obj* is an object of that type. Otherwise it returns False.

Since Python 2.2.1, *cls* can also be a tuple whose items are classes or types. In this case, isinstance returns True if *obj* is an instance of any of the items of tuple *cls*, otherwise isinstance returns False.

issubclass issubclass(*cls1*,*cls2*)

Returns True if *cls1* is a direct or indirect subclass of *cls2*, otherwise returns False. *cls1* and *cls2* must be types or classes.

iter iter(*obj*)
iter(*func*,*sentinel*)

Creates and returns an iterator: an object with a next method that you can call repeatedly to get one item at a time (see "Iterators" in Chapter 4). When called with one argument, iter(*obj*) normally

Core Built-ins

returns *obj*.__iter__( ). When *obj* is a sequence without a special method __iter__, iter(*obj*) is equivalent to the following simple generator:

```
def iterSequence(obj):
    i = 0
    while 1:
        try: yield obj[i]
        except IndexError: raise StopIteration
        i += 1
```

See also "Generators" in Chapter 4 and __iter__ in Chapter 5.

When called with two arguments, the first argument must be callable without arguments, and iter(*func,sentinel*) is equivalent to the following simple generator:

```
def iterSentinel(func, sentinel):
    while 1:
        item = func( )
        if item == sentinel: raise StopIteration
        yield item
```

As discussed in Chapter 4, the statement for *x* in *obj* is equivalent to for *x* in iter(*obj*). iter is *idempotent*. In other words, when *x* is an iterator, iter(*x*) is *x*, as long as *x* supplies an __iter__ method whose body is just return self, as an iterator should.

---

len   len(*container*)

Returns the number of items in *container*, which is a sequence or a mapping. See also __len__ in Chapter 5.

---

locals   locals( )

Returns a dictionary that represents the current local namespace. Treat the returned dictionary as read-only; trying to modify it may or may not affect the values of local variables and might raise an exception. See also globals and vars in this section.

---

map   map(*func,seq,*seqs*)

Applies *func* to every item of *seq* and returns a list of the results. When map is called with *n*+1 arguments, the first one, *func*, can be any callable object that accepts *n* arguments, or None. The remaining arguments to map must be iterable. When *func* is callable, map repeatedly calls *func* with *n* arguments (one corresponding item from each iterable) and returns the list of results. Thus, map(*func, seq*) is the same as:

[*func(item)* for *item* in *seq*]

When *func* is None, map returns a list of tuples, each with *n* items (one item from each iterable); this is similar to zip, covered in this section. When the iterable objects have different lengths, however, map conceptually pads the shorter ones with None, while zip conceptually truncates the longer ones.

---

max

max(*s*,**args*)

Returns the largest item in the only argument *s* (*s* must be iterable) or the largest of multiple arguments.

min

min(*s*,**args*)

Returns the smallest item in the only argument *s* (*s* must be iterable) or the smallest of multiple arguments.

oct

oct(*x*)

Converts integer *x* to an octal string representation. See also __oct__ in Chapter 5.

ord

ord(*ch*)

Returns the ASCII/ISO integer code between 0 and 255 (inclusive) for the single-character string *ch*. When *ch* is Unicode, ord returns an integer code between 0 and 65534 (inclusive). See also chr and unichr in this section.

pow

pow(*x*,*y*[,*z*])

When *z* is present, pow(*x*,*y*,*z*) returns *x***y%*z*. When *z* is missing, pow(*x*,*y*) returns *x***y. See also __pow__ in Chapter 5.

range

range([*start*,]*stop*[,*step*=1])

Returns a list of integers in arithmetic progression:

    [*start*, *start*+*step*, *start*+2**step*, ...]

When *start* is missing, it defaults to 0. When *step* is missing, it defaults to 1. When *step* is 0, range raises ValueError. When *step* is greater than 0, the last item is the largest *start*+*i**step strictly less than *stop*. When *step* is less than 0, the last item is the smallest *start*+*i**step strictly greater than *stop*. The result is an empty list when *start* is greater than or equal to *stop* and *step* is greater than 0, or when *start* is less than or equal to *stop* and *step* is less than 0. Otherwise, the first item of the result list is always *start*.

raw_input

raw_input(*prompt*='')

Writes *prompt* to standard output, reads a line from standard input, and returns the line (without \n) as a string. When at end-of-file, raw_input raises EOFError. See also input in this section.

reduce

reduce(*func*,*seq*[,*init*])

Applies *funct* to the items of *seq*, from left to right, to reduce the sequence to a single value. *func* must be callable with two arguments. reduce calls *func* on the first two items of *seq*, then on the result of the first call and the third item, and so on. reduce returns

Core Built-ins

the result of the last such call. When *init* is present, it is used before *seq*'s first item, if any. When *init* is missing, *seq* must be non-empty. When *init* is missing and *seq* has only one item, reduce returns *seq*[0]. Similarly, when *init* is present and *seq* is empty, reduce returns *init*. The built-in reduce is equivalent to:

```
def reduce_equivalent(func,seq,init=None):
    if init is None: init, seq = seq[0], seq[1:]
    for item in seq: init = func(init,item)
    return init
```

A typical use of reduce is to compute the sum of a sequence of numbers:

```
thesum = reduce(operator.add, seq, 0)
```

reload

reload(*module*)

Reloads and reinitializes module object *module*, and returns *module*. See "The reload Function" in Chapter 7.

repr

repr(*obj*)

Returns a complete and unambiguous string representation of *obj*. When feasible, repr returns a string that eval can use to create a new object with the same value as *obj*. See also str in this section and __repr__ in Chapter 5.

round

round(*x*,*n*=0)

Returns a float whose value is number *x* rounded to *n* digits after the decimal point (i.e., the multiple of $10**-n$ that is closest to *x*). When two such multiples are equally close to *x*, round returns the one that is farther from 0. Since today's computers represent floating-point numbers in binary, not in decimal, most of round's results are not exact.

setattr

setattr(*obj*,*name*,*value*)

Binds *obj*'s attribute *name* to *value*. setattr(*obj*,'*ident*',*val*) is like *obj*.*ident*=*val*. See also "Assignment Statements" in Chapter 4 and "Attribute Reference Basics" in Chapter 5.

slice

slice([*start*,]*stop*[,*step*])

Creates and returns a slice object with read-only attributes start, stop, and step bound to the respective argument values, each defaulting to None when missing. Such a slice is meant to signify the same set of indices as range(*start*,*stop*,*step*). Slicing syntax *obj*[*start*:*stop*:*step*] passes such a slice object as the argument to the __getitem__, __setitem__, or __delitem__ method of object obj, as appropriate. It is up to *obj* to interpret the slice objects that its methods receive. See also "Container slicing" in Chapter 5.

unichr	unichr(*code*)
	Returns a Unicode string whose single character corresponds to *code*, where *code* is an integer between 0 and 65536 (inclusive). See also chr and ord in this section.
vars	vars([*obj*])
	When called with no argument, vars( ) returns a dictionary that represents all variables that are bound in the current scope (exactly like locals, covered in this section). This dictionary should be treated as read-only. vars(*obj*) returns a dictionary that represents all attributes currently bound in *obj*, as covered in dir in this section. This dictionary may or may not be modifiable, depending on the type of *obj*.
xrange	xrange([*start*,]*stop*[,*step*=1])
	Returns a sequence object whose items are integers in arithmetic progression. The arguments are the same as for range, covered in this section. While range creates and returns a normal list object, xrange returns a sequence object of a special type, meant only for use in a for statement. xrange consumes less memory than range for this specific, frequent use, although the performance difference is usually small.
zip	zip(*seq*,**seqs*)
	Returns a list of tuples, where the *n*th tuple contains the *n*th element from each of the argument sequences. zip is called with *n* iterable objects as arguments (where *n* is greater than 0). If the iterable objects have different lengths, zip returns a list as long as the shortest iterable, ignoring trailing items in the other iterable objects. See also map in this section.

The sys Module

The attributes of the sys module are bound to data and functions that provide information on the state of the Python interpreter or that affect the interpreter directly. This section documents the most frequently used attributes of sys, in alphabetical order.

argv	The list of command-line arguments passed to the main script. argv[0] is the name or full path of the main script, or '-c' if the -c option was used. See "The getopt Module" later in this chapter for a good way to use sys.argv.

displayhook   displayhook(*value*)

In interactive sessions, the Python interpreter calls displayhook, passing it the result of each expression-statement entered. The default displayhook does nothing if *value* is None, otherwise it preserves and displays *value*:

```
if value is not None:
    __builtin__._ = value
    print repr(value)
```

You can rebind sys.displayhook in order to change interactive behavior. The original value is available as sys.__displayhook__.

excepthook   excepthook(*type,value,traceback*)

When an exception is not caught by any handler, Python calls excepthook, passing it the exception class, exception object, and traceback object, as covered in Chapter 6. The default excepthook displays the error and traceback. You can rebind sys.excepthook to change what is displayed for uncaught exceptions (just before Python returns to the interactive loop or terminates). The original value is also available as sys.__excepthook__.

exc_info   exc_info( )

If the current thread is handling an exception, exc_info returns a tuple whose three items are the class, object, and traceback for the exception. If the current thread is not handling any exception, exc_info returns (None,None,None). A traceback object indirectly holds references to all variables of all functions that propagated the exception. Thus, if you hold a reference to the traceback object (for example, indirectly, by binding a variable to the whole tuple that exc_info returns), Python has to retain in memory data that might otherwise be garbage-collected. So you should make sure that any binding to the traceback object is of short duration. To ensure that the binding gets removed, you can use a try/finally statement (discussed in Chapter 6).

exit   exit(*arg=0*)

Raises a SystemExit exception, which normally terminates execution after executing cleanup handlers installed by try/finally statements. If *arg* is an integer, Python uses *arg* as the program's exit code: 0 indicates successful termination, while any other value indicates unsuccessful termination of the program. Most platforms require exit codes to be between 0 and 127. If *arg* is not an integer, Python prints *arg* to sys.stderr, and the exit code of the program is 1 (i.e., a generic unsuccessful termination code).

getdefault encoding	getdefaultencoding( )
	Returns the name of the default codec used to encode and decode Unicode and string objects (normally 'ascii'). Unicode, codecs, encoding, and decoding are covered in Chapter 9.
getrefcount	getrefcount(*object*)
	Returns the reference count of *object*. Reference counts are covered in "Garbage Collection" in Chapter 13.
getrecursion limit	getrecursionlimit( )
	Returns the current limit on the depth of Python's call stack. See also "Recursion" in Chapter 4 and setrecursionlimit in this section.
_getframe	_getframe(*depth*=0)
	Returns a frame object from the call stack. When *depth* is 0, the result is the frame of _getframe's caller. When *depth* is 1, the result is the frame of the caller's caller, and so forth. The leading _ in _getframe's name is a reminder that it's a private system function, to be used for internal specialized purposes. Chapter 17 covers ways in which you can use frame objects for debugging.
maxint	The largest integer in this version of Python (at least 2147483647). Negative integers can go down to -maxint-1, due to 2's complement notation.
modules	A dictionary whose items are the names and module objects for all loaded modules. See Chapter 7 for more information on sys. modules.
path	A list of strings that specifies the directories that Python searches when looking for a module to load. See Chapter 7 for more information on sys.path.
platform	A string that names the platform on which this program is running. Typical values are brief operating system names, such as 'sunos5', 'linux2', and 'win32'.
ps1, ps2	ps1 and ps2 specify the primary and secondary interpreter prompt strings, initially '>>> ' and '... ', respectively. These attributes exist only in interactive interpreter sessions. If you bind either attribute to a non-string object, Python prompts by calling str( ) on the object each time a prompt is output. This feature lets you create dynamic prompting by coding a class that defines __str__ and assigning an instance of that class to sys.ps1 and/or sys.ps2.

setdefault encoding	setdefaultencoding(*name*)
	Sets the default codec used to encode and decode Unicode and string objects (normally 'ascii'). setdefaultencoding is meant to be called only from *sitecustomize.py* during startup; the site module removes this attribute from sys. You can call reload(sys) to make this attribute available again, but this is not considered good programming practice. Unicode, codecs, encoding, and decoding are covered in Chapter 9. The site and sitecustomize modules are covered in Chapter 13.
setprofile	setprofile(*profilefunc*)
	Sets a global profile function, a callable object that Python then calls at each function entry and return. Profiling is covered in Chapter 17.
setrecursion limit	setrecursionlimit(*limit*)
	Sets the limit on the depth of Python's call stack (the default is 1000). The limit prevents runaway recursion from crashing Python. Raising the limit may be necessary for programs that rely on deep recursion, but most platforms cannot support very large limits on call-stack depth. Lowering the limit may help you check, during debugging, that your program is gracefully degrading under situations of almost-runaway recursion. See also "Recursion" in Chapter 4.
settrace	settrace(*tracefunc*)
	Sets a global trace function, a callable object that Python then calls as each logical source line executes. Chapter 17 covers tracing.
stdin, stdout, stderr	stdin, stdout, and stderr are predefined file objects that correspond to Python's standard input, output, and error streams. You can rebind stdout and stderr to file-like objects (objects that supply a write method accepting a string argument) to redirect the destination of output and error messages. You can rebind stdin to a file-like object open for reading (one that supplies a readline method returning a string) to redirect the source from which built-in functions raw_input and input read. The original values are available as __stdin__, __stdout__, and __stderr__. Chapter 10 covers file objects and streams.
tracebacklimit	The maximum number of levels of traceback displayed for unhandled exceptions. By default, this attribute is not set (i.e., there is no limit). When sys.tracebacklimit is less than or equal to 0, traceback information is suppressed and only the exception type and value are printed.

version	A string that describes the Python version, build number and date, and C compiler used. version[:3] is '2.1' for Python 2.1, '2.2' for 2.2, and so on.

The getopt Module

The getopt module helps parse the command-line options and arguments passed to a Python program, available in sys.argv. The getopt module distinguishes arguments proper from options: options start with '-' (or '--' for long-form options). The first non-option argument terminates option parsing (similar to most Unix commands, and differently from GNU and Windows commands). Module getopt supplies a single function, also called getopt.

getopt	getopt(*args,options,long_options*=[ ])
	Parses command-line options. *args* is usually sys.argv[1:]. *options* is a string: each character is an option letter, followed by ':' if the option takes a parameter. *long_options* is a list of strings, each a long-option name, without the leading '--', followed by '=' if the option takes a parameter.
	When getopt encounters an error, it raises GetoptError, an exception class supplied by the getopt module. Otherwise, getopt returns a pair (*opts,args_proper*), where *opts* is a list of pairs of the form (*option,parameter*) in the same order in which options are found in *args*. Each *option* is a string that starts with a single hyphen for a short-form option or two hyphens for a long-form one; each *parameter* is also a string (an empty string for options that don't take parameters). *args_proper* is the list of program argument strings that are left after removing the options.

The copy Module

As discussed in Chapter 4, assignment in Python does not copy the right-hand side object being assigned. Rather, assignment adds a reference to the right-hand side object. When you want a copy of object *x*, you can ask *x* for a copy of itself. If *x* is a list, *x*[:] is a copy of *x*. If *x* is a dictionary, *x*.copy( ) returns a copy of *x*.

The copy module supplies a copy function that creates and returns a copy of most types of objects. Normal copies, such as *x*[:] for a list *x* and copy.copy(*x*), are also known as shallow copies. When *x* has references to other objects (e.g., items or attributes), a normal copy of *x* has distinct references to the same objects. Sometimes, however, you need a deep copy, where referenced objects are copied recursively. Module copy supplies a deepcopy(*x*) function that performs a deep copy and returns it as the function's result.

copy	copy(*x*) Creates and returns a copy of *x* for *x* of most types (copies of modules, classes, frames, arrays, and internal types are not supported). If *x* is immutable, copy.copy(*x*) may return *x* itself as an optimization. A class can customize the way copy.copy copies its instances by having a special method __copy__(self) that returns a new object, a copy of self.
| **deepcopy** | deepcopy(*x*,[*memo*])<br><br>Makes a deep copy of *x* and returns it. Deep copying implies a recursive walk over a directed graph of references. A precaution is needed to preserve the graph's shape: when references to the same object are met more than once during the walk, distinct copies must not be made. Rather, references to the same copied object must be used. Consider the following simple example:<br><br>```
sublist = [1,2]
original = [sublist, sublist]
thecopy = copy.deepcopy(original)
```<br><br>original[0] is original[1] is True (i.e., the two items of list original refer to the same object). This is an important property of original and therefore must be preserved in anything that claims to be a copy of it. The semantics of copy.deepcopy are defined to ensure that thecopy[0] is thecopy[1] is also True in this case. In other words, the shapes of the graphs of references of original and thecopy are the same. Avoiding repeated copying has an important beneficial side effect: preventing infinite loops that would otherwise occur if the graph has cycles.<br><br>copy.deepcopy accepts a second, optional argument *memo*, which is a dictionary that maps the id( ) of objects already copied to the new objects that are their copies. *memo* is passed by recursive calls of deepcopy to itself, but you may also explicitly pass it (normally as an originally empty dictionary) if you need to keep such a correspondence map between the identities of originals and copies of objects.<br><br>A class can customize the way copy.deepcopy copies its instances by having a special method __deepcopy__(self,*memo*) that returns a new object, a deep copy of self. When __deepcopy__ needs to deep copy some referenced object *subobject*, it must do so by calling copy.deepcopy(*subobject*,*memo*). When a class has no special method __deepcopy__, copy.deepcopy on an instance of that class tries to call special methods __getinitargs__, __getstate__, and __setstate__, which are covered in "Pickling instance objects" in Chapter 11. |
```

The bisect Module

The bisect module uses a bisection algorithm to keep a list in sorted order as items are inserted. bisect's operation is faster than calling a list's sort method after each insertion. This section documents the main functions supplied by bisect.

bisect   bisect(*seq*,*item*,*lo*=0,*hi*=sys.maxint)

Returns the index *i* into *seq* where *item* should be inserted to keep *seq* sorted. In other words, *i* is such that each item in *seq*[:*i*] is less than or equal to *item*, and each item in *seq*[*i*:] is greater than or equal to *item*. *seq* must be a sorted sequence. For any sorted sequence *seq*, *seq*[bisect(*seq*,*y*)-1]==*y* is equivalent to *y* in *seq*, but faster if len(*seq*) is large. You may pass optional arguments *lo* and *hi* to operate on the slice *seq*[*lo*:*hi*].

insort   insort(*seq*,*item*,*lo*=0,*hi*=sys.maxint)

Like *seq*.insert(bisect(*seq*,*item*),*item*). In other words, *seq* must be a sorted mutable sequence, and insort modifies *seq* by inserting *item* at the right spot, so that *seq* remains sorted. You may pass optional arguments *lo* and *hi* to operate on the slice *seq*[*lo*:*hi*].

Module bisect also supplies functions bisect_left, bisect_right, insort_left, and insort_right for explicit control of search and insertion strategies into sequences that contain duplicates. bisect is a synonym for bisect_right, and insort is a synonym for insort_right.

The UserList, UserDict, and UserString Modules

The UserList, UserDict, and UserString modules each supply one class, with the same name as the respective module, that implements all the methods needed for the class's instances to be mutable sequences, mappings, and strings, respectively. When you need such polymorphism, you can subclass one of these classes and override some methods rather than have to implement everything yourself. In Python 2.2 and later, you can subclass built-in types list, dict, and str directly, to similar effect (see "New-Style Classes and Instances" in Chapter 5). However, these modules can still be handy if you need to create a classic class in order to keep your code compatible with Python 2.1 or earlier.

Each instance of one of these classes has an attribute called data that is a Python object of the corresponding built-in type (list, dict, and str, respectively). You can instantiate each class with an argument of the appropriate type (the argument is copied, so you can later modify it without side effects). UserList and UserDict can also be instantiated without arguments to create initially empty containers.

Module UserString also supplies class MutableString, which is very similar to class UserString except that instances of MutableString are mutable. Instances of MutableString and its subclasses cannot be keys into a dictionary. Instances of both UserString and MutableString can be Unicode strings rather than plain strings: just use a Unicode string as the initializer argument at instantiation time.

If you subclass UserList, UserDict, UserString, or MutableString and then override __init__, make sure the __init__ method you write can also be called with one argument of the appropriate type (as well as without arguments for UserList and UserDict). Also be sure that your __init__ method explicitly and appropriately calls the __init__ method of the superclass, as usual.

For maximum efficiency, you can arrange for your subclass to inherit from the appropriate built-in type when feasible (i.e., when your program runs with Python 2.2), but keep the ability to fall back to these modules when necessary (i.e., when your program runs with Python 2.1). Here is a typical idiom you can use for this purpose:

```
try:                        # can we subclass list?
    class _Temp(list):
        pass
except:                     # no: use UserList.UserList as base class
    from UserList import UserList as BaseList
else:                       # yes: remove _Temp and use list as base class
    del _Temp
    BaseList = list
class AutomaticallyExpandingList(BaseList):
    """a list such that you can always set L[i]=x even for a large i:
       L automatically grows, if needed, to make i a valid index."""
    def __setitem__(self, idx, val):
        self.extend((1+idx-len(self))*[None])
        BaseList.__setitem__(self, idx, val)
```

9

Strings and Regular Expressions

Python supports plain and Unicode strings extensively, with statements, operators, built-in functions, methods, and dedicated modules. This chapter covers the methods of string objects, talks about string formatting, documents the `string`, `pprint`, and `repr` modules, and discusses issues related to Unicode strings.

Regular expressions let you specify pattern strings and allow searches and substitutions. Regular expressions are not easy to master, but they are a powerful tool for processing text. Python offers rich regular expression functionality through the built-in `re` module, as documented in this chapter.

Methods of String Objects

Plain and Unicode strings are immutable sequences, as covered in Chapter 4. All immutable-sequence operations (repetition, concatenation, indexing, slicing) apply to strings. A string object *s* also supplies several non-mutating methods, as documented in this section. Unless otherwise noted, each method returns a plain string when *s* is a plain string, or a Unicode string when *s* is a Unicode string. Terms such as letters, whitespace, and so on refer to the corresponding attributes of the `string` module, covered later in this chapter. See also the later section "Locale Sensitivity."

---

capitalize   `s.capitalize( )`

Returns a copy of *s* where the first character, if a letter, is uppercase, and all other letters, if any, are lowercase.

---

center   `s.center(n)`

Returns a string of length `max(len(s),n)`, with a copy of *s* in the central part, surrounded by equal numbers of spaces on both sides (e.g., `'ciao'.center(2)` is `'ciao'`, `'ciao'.center(7)` is `' ciao '`).

count	`s.count(`*sub,start*`=0,`*end*`=sys.maxint)`
	Returns the number of occurrences of substring *sub* in `s[`*start:end*`]`.
encode	`s.encode(`*codec*`=None,`*errors*`='strict')`
	Returns a plain string obtained from s with the given codec and error handling. See "Unicode" later in this chapter for more details.
endswith	`s.endswith(`*suffix,start*`=0,`*end*`=sys.maxint)`
	Returns True when `s[`*start:end*`]` ends with *suffix*, otherwise False.
expandtabs	`s.expandtabs(`*tabsize*`=8)`
	Returns a copy of s where each tab character is changed into one or more spaces, with tab stops every *tabsize* characters.
find	`s.find(`*sub,start*`=0,`*end*`=sys.maxint)`
	Returns the lowest index in s where substring *sub* is found, such that *sub* is entirely contained in `s[`*start:end*`]`. For example, `'banana'.find('na')` is 2, as is `'banana'.find('na',1)`, while `'banana'.find('na',3)` is 4, as is `'banana'.find('na',-2)`. find returns -1 if *sub* is not found.
index	`s.index(`*sub,start*`=0,`*end*`=sys.maxint)`
	Like find, but raises ValueError when *sub* is not found.
isalnum	`s.isalnum( )`
	Returns True when len(s) is greater than 0 and all characters in s are letters or decimal digits. When s is empty, or when at least one character of s is neither a letter nor a decimal digit, isalnum returns False.
isalpha	`s.isalpha( )`
	Returns True when len(s) is greater than 0 and all characters in s are letters. When s is empty, or when at least one character of s is not a letter, isalpha returns False.
isdigit	`s.isdigit( )`
	Returns True when len(s) is greater than 0 and all characters in s are decimal digits. When s is empty, or when at least one character of s is not a digit, isdigit returns False.

islower

`s.islower( )`

Returns True when all letters in s are lowercase. When s has no letters, or when at least one letter of s is uppercase, islower returns False.

isspace

`s.isspace( )`

Returns True when len(s) is greater than 0 and all characters in s are whitespace. When s is empty, or when at least one character of s is not whitespace, isspace returns False.

istitle

`s.istitle( )`

Returns True when letters in s are titlecase: a capital letter at the start of each contiguous sequence of letters, all other letters lowercase (e.g., 'King Lear'.istitle( ) is True). When s has no letters, or when at least one letter of s violates the titlecase constraint, istitle returns False (e.g., '1900'.istitle( ) and 'Troilus and Cressida'. istitle( ) are False).

isupper

`s.isupper( )`

Returns True when all letters in s are uppercase. When s has no letters, or when at least one letter of s is lowercase, isupper returns False.

join

`s.join(seq)`

Returns the string obtained by concatenating the items of seq, which must be a sequence of strings, and interposing a copy of s between each pair of items (e.g., ''.join([str(x) for x in range(7)]) is '0123456').

ljust

`s.ljust(n)`

Returns a string of length max(len(s),n), with a copy of s at the start, followed by zero or more trailing spaces.

lower

`s.lower( )`

Returns a copy of s with all letters, if any, converted to lowercase.

lstrip

`s.lstrip(x=None)`

Returns a copy of s with leading whitespace, if any, removed. Since Python 2.2.2, you can optionally pass a string x as an argument, in which case lstrip removes characters found in x rather than removing whitespace.

replace	`s.replace(old,new,maxsplit=sys.maxint)` Returns a copy of s with the first *maxsplit* (or fewer, if there are fewer) non-overlapping occurrences of substring *old* replaced by string *new* (e.g., `'banana'.replace('a','e',2)` is `'benena'`).
rfind	`s.rfind(sub,start=0,end=sys.maxint)` Returns the highest index in s where substring *sub* is found, such that *sub* is entirely contained in `s[start:end]`. `rfind` returns -1 if *sub* is not found.
rindex	`s.rindex(sub,start=0,end=sys.maxint)` Like `rfind`, but raises `ValueError` if *sub* is not found.
rjust	`s.rjust(n)` Returns a string of length `max(len(s),n)`, with a copy of s at the end, preceded by zero or more leading spaces.
rstrip	`s.rstrip(x=None)` Returns a copy of s with trailing whitespace, if any, removed. Since Python 2.2.2, you can optionally pass a string *x* as an argument, in which case `rstrip` removes characters found in *x* rather than removing whitespace.
split	`s.split(sep=None,maxsplit=sys.maxint)` Returns a list *L* of up to *maxsplit*+1 strings. Each item of *L* is a "word" from s, where string *sep* separates words. When s has more than *maxsplit* words, the last item of *L* is the substring of s that follows the first *maxsplit* words. When *sep* is None, any string of whitespace separates words (e.g., `'four score and seven years ago'.split(None,3)` is `['four', 'score', 'and', 'seven years ago']`).
splitlines	`s.splitlines(keepends=False)` Like `s.split('\n')`. When *keepends* is true, however, the trailing `'\n'` is included in each item of the resulting list.
startswith	`s.startswith(prefix,start=0,end=sys.maxint)` Returns `True` when `s[start:end]` starts with *prefix*, otherwise `False`.
strip	`s.strip(x=None)` Returns a copy of s with both leading and trailing whitespace removed. Since Python 2.2.2, you can optionally pass a string *x* as an argument, in which case `strip` removes characters found in *x* rather than removing whitespace.

swapcase	`s.swapcase()`
	Returns a copy of s with all uppercase letters converted to lowercase and vice versa.

title	`s.title()`
	Returns a copy of s transformed to titlecase: a capital letter at the start of each contiguous sequence of letters, with all other letters, if any, lowercase.

translate	`s.translate(table,deletechars='')`
	Returns a copy of s where all characters occurring in string *deletechars* are removed, and the remaining characters are mapped through translation-table *table*. When s is a plain string, *table* must be a plain string of length 256. When s is a Unicode string, *table* must be a Unicode string of length 65536. Each character c is mapped to character `table[ord(c)]`. A plain-string *table* is most often built using function `string.maketrans`, covered later.

upper	`s.upper()`
	Returns a copy of s with all letters, if any, converted to uppercase.

The string Module

The `string` module supplies functions that duplicate each method of string objects, as covered in the previous section. Each function takes the string object as its first argument. Module `string` also has several useful string-valued attributes:

ascii_letters
> The string `ascii_lowercase+ascii_uppercase`

ascii_lowercase
> The string `'abcdefghijklmnopqrstuvwxyz'`

ascii_uppercase
> The string `'ABCDEFGHIJKLMNOPQRSTUVWXYZ'`

digits
> The string `'0123456789'`

hexdigits
> The string `'0123456789abcdefABCDEF'`

letters
> The string `lowercase+uppercase`

lowercase
> A string containing all characters that are deemed lowercase letters: at least `'abcdefghijklmnopqrstuvwxyz'`, but more letters (e.g., accented ones) may be present, depending on the active locale

Strings

octdigits
> The string `'01234567'`

punctuation
> The string `'!"#$%&\'()*+,-./:;<=>?@[\\]^_'{|}~'` (i.e., all ASCII characters that are deemed punctuation characters in the "C" locale; does not depend on what locale is active)

printable
> The string of those characters that are deemed printable (i.e., digits, letters, punctuation, and whitespace)

uppercase
> A string containing all characters that are deemed uppercase letters: at least `'ABCDEFGHIJKLMNOPQRSTUVWXYZ'`, but more letters (e.g., accented ones) may be present, depending on the active locale

whitespace
> A string containing all characters that are deemed whitespace: at least space, tab, linefeed, and carriage return, but more characters (e.g., control characters) may be present, depending on the active locale

You should not rebind these attributes, since other parts of the Python library may rely on them and the effects of rebinding them would be undefined.

Locale Sensitivity

The locale module is covered in Chapter 10. Locale setting affects some attributes of module string (letters, lowercase, uppercase, whitespace). Through these attributes, locale setting also affects functions of module string and methods of plain-string objects that deal with classification of characters as letters, and conversion between upper- and lowercase, such as capitalize, isalnum, and isalpha. The corresponding methods of Unicode strings are not affected by locale setting.

The maketrans Function

The method translate of plain strings, covered earlier in this chapter, takes as its first argument a plain string of length 256 that it uses as a translation table. The easiest way to build translation tables is to use the maketrans function supplied by module string.

maketrans	maketrans(*from,onto*)
	Returns a translation table, which is a plain string of length 256 that provides a mapping from characters in ascending ASCII order to another set of characters. *from* and *onto* must be plain strings, with len(*from*) equal to len(*onto*). Each character in string *from* is mapped to the character at the corresponding position in string *onto*. For each character not listed in *from*, the translation table maps the character to itself. To get an identity table that maps each character to itself, call maketrans('','').

With the `translate` string method, you can delete characters as well as translate them. When you use `translate` just to delete characters, the first argument you pass to `translate` should be the identity table. Here's an example of using the `maketrans` function and the string method `translate` to delete vowels:

```
import string
identity = string.maketrans('','')
print 'some string'.translate(identity,'aeiou')    # prints: sm strng
```

Here are examples of turning all other vowels into a's and also deleting s's:

```
intoas = string.maketrans('eiou','aaaa')
print 'some string'.translate(intoas)              # prints: sama strang
print 'some string'.translate(intoas,'s')          # prints: ama trang
```

String Formatting

In Python, a string-formatting expression has the syntax:

format % values

where *format* is a plain or Unicode string containing format specifiers and *values* is any single object or a collection of objects in a tuple or dictionary. Python's string-formatting operator has roughly the same set of features as the C language's `printf` and operates in a similar way. Each format specifier is a substring of *format* that starts with a percent sign (%) and ends with one of the conversion characters shown in Table 9-1.

Table 9-1. String-formatting conversion characters

Character	Output format	Notes
d, i	Signed decimal integer	Value must be number
u	Unsigned decimal integer	Value must be number
o	Unsigned octal integer	Value must be number
x	Unsigned hexadecimal integer (lowercase letters)	Value must be number
X	Unsigned hexadecimal integer (uppercase letters)	Value must be number
e	Floating-point value in exponential form (lowercase e for exponent)	Value must be number
E	Floating-point value in exponential form (uppercase E for exponent)	Value must be number
f, F	Floating-point value in decimal form	Value must be number
g, G	Like e or E when *exp* is greater than 4 or less than the precision; otherwise like f or F	*exp* is the exponent of the number being converted
c	Single character	Value can be integer or single-character string
r	String	Converts any value with `repr`
s	String	Converts any value with `str`
%	Literal % character	Consumes no value

Between the % and the conversion character, you can specify a number of optional modifiers, as we'll discuss shortly.

The result of a formatting expression is a string that is a copy of *format* where each format specifier is replaced by the corresponding item of *values* converted to a string according to the specifier. Here are some simple examples:

```
x = 42
y = 3.14
z = "george"
print 'result = %d' % x            # prints: result = 42
print 'answers are: %d %f' % (x,y)  # prints: answers are: 42 3.14
print 'hello %s' % z               # prints: hello george
```

Format Specifier Syntax

A format specifier can include numerous modifiers that control how the corresponding item in *values* is converted to a string. The components of a format specifier, in order, are:

- The mandatory leading % character that marks the start of the specifier
- An optional item name in parentheses (e.g. (*name*))
- Zero or more optional conversion flags:
    - #, which indicates that the conversion uses an alternate form (if any exists for its type)
    - 0, which indicates that the conversion is zero-padded
    - -, which indicates that the conversion is left-justified
    - a space, which indicates that a space is placed before a positive number
    - +, which indicates that the numeric sign (+ or -) is included before any numeric conversion
- An optional minimum width of the conversion, specified using one or more digits or an asterisk (*), which means that the width is taken from the next item in *values*
- An optional precision for the conversion, specified with a dot (.) followed by zero or more digits or a *, which means that the width is taken from the next item in *values*
- A mandatory conversion type from Table 9-1

Item names must be given either in all format specifiers in *format* or in none of them. When item names are present, *values* must be a mapping (often the dictionary of a namespace, e.g., *vars( )*), and each item name is a key in *values*. In other words, each format specifier corresponds to the item in *values* keyed by the specifier's item name. When item names are present, you cannot use * in any format specifier.

When item names are absent, *values* must be a tuple; when there is just one item, *values* may be the item itself instead of a tuple. Each format specifier corresponds to an item in *values* by position, and *values* must have exactly as many items as *format* has specifiers (plus one extra for each width or precision given by *). When the width or precision component of a specifier is given by *, the * consumes one item in *values*, which must be an integer and is taken as the number of characters to use as minimum width or precision of the conversion.

Common String-Formatting Idioms

It is quite common for *format* to contain several occurrences of %s and for *values* to be a tuple with exactly as many items as *format* has occurrences of %s. The result is a copy of *format* where each %s is replaced with str applied to the corresponding item of *values*. For example:

```
'%s+%s is %s'%(23,45,68)            # results in: '23+45 is 68'
```

You can think of %s as a fast and concise way to put together a few values, converted to string form, into a larger string. For example:

```
oneway = 'x' + str(j) + 'y' + str(j) + 'z'
another = 'x%sy%sz' % (j, j)
```

After this code is executed, variables oneway and another will always be equal, but the computation of another, done via string formatting, is measurably faster. Which way is clearer and simpler is a matter of habit: get used to the string-formatting idiom, and it will come to look simpler and clearer.

Apart from %s, other reasonably common format specifiers are those used to format floating-point values: %f for decimal formatting, %e for exponential formatting, and %g for either decimal or exponential formatting, depending on the number's magnitude. When formatting floating-point values, you normally specify width and/or precision modifiers. A width modifier is a number right after the % that gives the minimum width for the resulting conversion; you generally use a width modifier if you're formatting a table for display in a fixed-width font. A precision modifier is a number following a dot (.) right before the conversion type letter; you generally use a precision modifier in order to fix the number of decimal digits displayed for a number, to avoid giving a misleading impression of excessive precision and wasting display space. For example:

```
'%.2f'%(1/3.0)                      # results in: '0.33'
'%s'%(1/3.0)                        # results in: '0.333333333333'
```

With %s, you cannot specify how many digits to display after the decimal point. It is important to avoid giving a mistaken impression of very high precision when you know that your numeric results are only accurate to a few digits. Displaying high precision values might mislead people examining those results into believing the results are much more accurate than is in fact the case.

The pprint Module

The pprint module pretty-prints complicated data structures, with formatting that may be more readable than that supplied by built-in function repr (see Chapter 8). To fine-tune the formatting, you can instantiate the PrettyPrinter class supplied by module pprint and apply detailed control, helped by auxiliary functions also supplied by module pprint. Most of the time, however, one of the two main functions exposed by module pprint suffices.

pformat	pformat(*obj*)
	Returns a string representing the pretty-printing of *obj*.

pprint	pprint(*obj*,*stream*=sys.stdout)
	Outputs the pretty-printing of *obj* to file object *stream*, with a terminating newline.

The following statements are the same:

```
print pprint.pformat(x)
pprint.pprint(x)
```

Either of these constructs will be roughly the same as print x in many cases, such as when the string representation of x fits within one line. However, with something like x=range(30), print x displays x in two lines, breaking at an arbitrary point, while using module pprint displays x over 30 lines, one line per item. You can use module pprint when you prefer the module's specific display effects to the ones of normal string representation.

The repr Module

The repr module supplies an alternative to the built-in function repr (see Chapter 8), with limits on length for the representation string. To fine-tune the length limits, you can instantiate or subclass the Repr class supplied by module repr and apply detailed control. Most of the time, however, the main function exposed by module repr suffices.

repr	repr(*obj*)
	Returns a string representing *obj*, with sensible limits on length.

Unicode

Plain strings are converted into Unicode strings either explicitly, with the unicode built-in, or implicitly, when you pass a plain string to a function that expects Unicode. In either case, the conversion is done by an auxiliary object known as a *codec* (for coder-decoder). A codec can also convert Unicode strings to plain strings either explicitly, with the encode method of Unicode strings, or implicitly.

You identify a codec by passing the codec name to unicode or encode. When you pass no codec name and for implicit conversion, Python uses a default encoding, normally 'ascii'. (You can change the default encoding in the startup phase of a Python program, as covered in Chapter 13; see also setdefaultencoding in Chapter 8.) Every conversion has an explicit or implicit argument *errors*, a string specifying how conversion errors are to be handled. The default is 'strict', meaning any error raises an exception. When *errors* is 'replace', the conversion replaces each character causing an error with '?' in a plain-string result or with u'\ufffd' in a Unicode result. When *errors* is 'ignore', the conversion silently skips characters that cause errors.

The codecs Module

The mapping of codec names to codec objects is handled by the codecs module. This module lets you develop your own codec objects and register them so that they can be looked up by name, just like built-in codecs. Module codecs also lets you look up any codec explicitly, obtaining the functions the codec uses for encoding and decoding, as well as factory functions to wrap file-like objects. Such advanced facilities of module codecs are rarely used, and are not covered further in this book.

The codecs module, together with the encodings package, supplies built-in codecs useful to Python developers dealing with internationalization issues. Any supplied codec can be installed as the default by module sitecustomize, or can be specified by name when converting explicitly between plain and Unicode strings. The codec normally installed by default is 'ascii', which accepts only characters with codes between 0 and 127, the 7-bit range of the American Standard Code for Information Interchange (ASCII) that is common to most encodings. A popular codec is 'latin-1', a fast, built-in implementation of the ISO 8859-1 encoding that offers a one-byte-per-character encoding of all special characters needed for Western European languages.

The codecs module also supplies codecs implemented in Python for most ISO 8859 encodings, with codec names from 'iso8859-1' to 'iso8859-15'. On Windows systems only, the codec named 'mbcs' wraps the platform's multibyte character set conversion procedures. In Python 2.2, many codecs are added to support Asian languages. Module codecs also supplies several standard code pages (codec names from 'cp037' to 'cp1258'), Mac-specific encodings (codec names from 'mac-cyrillic' to 'mac-turkish'), and Unicode standard encodings 'utf-8' and 'utf-16' (the latter also have specific big-endian and little-endian variants 'utf-16-be' and 'utf-16-le'). For use with UTF-16, module codecs also supplies attributes BOM_BE and BOM_LE, byte-order marks for big-endian and little-endian machines respectively, and BOM, byte-order mark for the current platform.

Module codecs also supplies two functions to make it easier to deal with encoded text during input/output operations.

EncodedFile   EncodedFile(*file,datacodec,filecodec*=None,*errors*='strict')

Wraps the file-like object *file*, returning another file-like object *ef* that implicitly and transparently applies the given encodings to all data read from or written to the file. When you write a string *s* to *ef*, *ef* first decodes *s* with the codec named by *datacodec*, then encodes the result with the codec named by *filecodec*, and lastly writes it to *file*. When you read a string, *ef* applies *filecodec* first, then *datacodec*. When *filecodec* is None, *ef* uses *datacodec* for both steps in either direction.

For example, if you want to write strings that are encoded in latin-1 to sys.stdout and have the strings come out in utf-8, use the following:

```
import sys, codecs
sys.stdout = codecs.EncodedFile(sys.stdout,'latin-1',
                                             'utf-8')
```

---

open   open(*filename*,*mode*='rb',*encoding*=None,*errors*='strict', *buffering*=1)

Uses the built-in function open (covered in Chapter 10) to supply a file-like object that accepts and/or provides Unicode strings to/ from Python client code, while the underlying file can either be in Unicode (when *encoding* is None) or use the codec named by *encoding*. For example, if you want to write Unicode strings to file *uni.txt* and have the strings implicitly encoded as latin-1 in the file, replacing with '?' any character that cannot be encoded in Latin-1, use the following:

```
import codecs
flout = codecs.open('uni.txt','w','latin-1','replace')

# now you can write Unicode strings directly to flout
flout.write(u'élève')
flout.close( )
```

The unicodedata Module

The unicodedata module supplies easy access to the Unicode Character Database. Given any Unicode character, you can use functions supplied by module unicodedata to obtain the character's Unicode category, official name (if any), and other, more exotic information. You can also look up the Unicode character (if any) corresponding to a given official name. Such advanced facilities are rarely needed, and are not covered further in this book.

Regular Expressions and the re Module

A *regular expression* is a string that represents a pattern. With regular expression functionality, you can compare that pattern to another string and see if any part of the string matches the pattern.

The re module supplies all of Python's regular expression functionality. The compile function builds a regular expression object from a pattern string and optional flags. The methods of a regular expression object look for matches of the regular expression in a string and/or perform substitutions. Module re also exposes functions equivalent to a regular expression's methods, but with the regular expression's pattern string as their first argument.

Regular expressions can be difficult to master, and this book does not purport to teach them—I cover only the ways in which you can use them in Python. For general coverage of regular expressions, I recommend the book *Mastering Regular Expressions*, by Jeffrey Friedl (O'Reilly). Friedl's book offers thorough coverage of regular expressions at both the tutorial and advanced levels.

Pattern-String Syntax

The pattern string representing a regular expression follows a specific syntax:

- Alphabetic and numeric characters stand for themselves. A regular expression whose pattern is a string of letters and digits matches the same string.

- Many alphanumeric characters acquire special meaning in a pattern when they are preceded by a backslash (\).

- Punctuation works the other way around. A punctuation character is self-matching when escaped, and has a special meaning when unescaped.

- The backslash character itself is matched by a repeated backslash (i.e., the pattern \\).

Since regular expression patterns often contain backslashes, you generally want to specify them using raw-string syntax (covered in Chapter 4). Pattern elements (e.g., r'\t', which is equivalent to the non-raw string literal '\\t') do match the corresponding special characters (e.g., the tab character '\t'). Therefore, you can use raw-string syntax even when you do need a literal match for some such special character.

Table 9-2 lists the special elements in regular expression pattern syntax. The exact meanings of some pattern elements change when you use optional flags, together with the pattern string, to build the regular expression object. The optional flags are covered later in this chapter.

Table 9-2. Regular expression pattern syntax

Element	Meaning
.	Matches any character except \n (if DOTALL, also matches \n)
^	Matches start of string (if MULTILINE, also matches after \n)
$	Matches end of string (if MULTILINE, also matches before \n)
*	Matches zero or more cases of the previous regular expression; greedy (match as many as possible)
+	Matches one or more cases of the previous regular expression; greedy (match as many as possible)
?	Matches zero or one case of the previous regular expression; greedy (match one if possible)
*?, +?, ??	Non-greedy versions of *, +, and ? (match as few as possible)
{m,n}	Matches m to n cases of the previous regular expression (greedy)
{m,n}?	Matches m to n cases of the previous regular expression (non-greedy)
[...]	Matches any one of a set of characters contained within the brackets
		Matches expression either preceding it or following it
(...)	Matches the regular expression within the parentheses and also indicates a group
(?iLmsux)	Alternate way to set optional flags; no effect on match

Table 9-2. Regular expression pattern syntax (continued)

Element	Meaning
(?:...)	Like (...), but does not indicate a group
(?P<id>...)	Like (...), but the group also gets the name *id*
(?P=*id*)	Matches whatever was previously matched by group named *id*
(?#...)	Content of parentheses is just a comment; no effect on match
(?=...)	Lookahead assertion; matches if regular expression ... matches what comes next, but does not consume any part of the string
(?!...)	Negative lookahead assertion; matches if regular expression ... does not match what comes next, and does not consume any part of the string
(?<=...)	Lookbehind assertion; matches if there is a match for regular expression ... ending at the current position (... must match a fixed length)
(?<!...)	Negative lookbehind assertion; matches if there is no match for regular expression ... ending at the current position (... must match a fixed length)
number	Matches whatever was previously matched by group numbered *number* (groups are automatically numbered from 1 up to 99)
\A	Matches an empty string, but only at the start of the whole string
\b	Matches an empty string, but only at the start or end of a word (a maximal sequence of alphanumeric characters; see also \w)
\B	Matches an empty string, but not at the start or end of a word
\d	Matches one digit, like the set [0-9]
\D	Matches one non-digit, like the set [^0-9]
\s	Matches a whitespace character, like the set [\t\n\r\f\v]
\S	Matches a non-white character, like the set [^ \t\n\r\f\v]
\w	Matches one alphanumeric character; unless LOCALE or UNICODE is set, \w is like [a-zA-Z0-9_]
\W	Matches one non-alphanumeric character, the reverse of \w
\Z	Matches an empty string, but only at the end of the whole string
\\\	Matches one backslash character

Common Regular Expression Idioms

'.*' as a substring of a regular expression's pattern string means "any number of repetitions (zero or more) of any character." In other words, '.*' matches any substring of a target string, including the empty substring. '.+' is similar, but it matches only a non-empty substring. For example:

    'pre.*post'

matches a string containing a substring 'pre' followed by a later substring 'post', even if the latter is adjacent to the former (e.g., it matches both 'prepost' and 'pre23post'). On the other hand:

    'pre.+post'

matches only if 'pre' and 'post' are not adjacent (e.g., it matches 'pre23post' but does not match 'prepost'). Both patterns also match strings that continue after the 'post'.

To constrain a pattern to match only strings that end with 'post', end the pattern with \Z. For example:

```
r'pre.*post\Z'
```

matches 'prepost', but not 'preposterous'. Note that we need to express the pattern with raw-string syntax (or escape the backslash \ by doubling it into \\), as it contains a backslash. Using raw-string syntax for all regular expression pattern literals is good practice in Python, as it's the simplest way to ensure you'll never fail to escape a backslash.

Another frequently used element in regular expression patterns is \b, which matches a word boundary. If you want to match the word 'his' only as a whole word and not its occurrences as a substring in such words as 'this' and 'history', the regular expression pattern is:

```
r'\bhis\b'
```

with word boundaries both before and after. To match the beginning of any word starting with 'her', such as 'her' itself but also 'hermetic', but not words that just contain 'her' elsewhere, such as 'ether', use:

```
r'\bher'
```

with a word boundary before, but not after, the relevant string. To match the end of any word ending with 'its', such as 'its' itself but also 'fits', but not words that contain 'its' elsewhere, such as 'itsy', use:

```
r'its\b'
```

with a word boundary after, but not before, the relevant string. To match whole words thus constrained, rather than just their beginning or end, add a pattern element \w* to match zero or more word characters. For example, to match any full word starting with 'her', use:

```
r'\bher\w*'
```

And to match any full word ending with 'its', use:

```
r'\w*its\b'
```

Sets of Characters

You denote sets of characters in a pattern by listing the characters within brackets ([ ]). In addition to listing single characters, you can denote a range by giving the first and last characters of the range separated by a hyphen (-). The last character of the range is included in the set, which is different from other Python ranges. Within a set, special characters stand for themselves, except \,], and -, which you must escape (by preceding them with a backslash) when their position is such that, unescaped, they would form part of the set's syntax. In a set, you can also denote a class of characters by escaped-letter notation, such as \d or \S. However, \b in a set denotes a backspace character, not a word boundary. If the first character in the set's pattern, right after the [, is a caret (^), the set is *complemented*. In other words, the set matches any character except those that follow ^ in the set pattern notation.

A frequent use of character sets is to match a word, using a definition of what characters can make up a word that differs from \w's default (letters and digits). To match a word of one or more characters, each of which can be a letter, an apostrophe, or a hyphen, but not a digit (e.g., 'Finnegan-O'Hara'), use:

```
r"[a-zA-z'\-]+"
```

It's not strictly necessary to escape the hyphen with a backslash in this case, since its position makes it syntactically unambiguous. However, the backslash makes the pattern somewhat more readable, by visually distinguishing the hyphen that you want to have as a character in the set from those used to denote ranges.

Alternatives

A vertical bar (|) in a regular expression pattern, used to specify alternatives, has low precedence. Unless parentheses change the grouping, | applies to the whole pattern on either side, up to the start or end of the string, or to another |. A pattern can be made up of any number of subpatterns joined by |. To match such a regular expression, the first subpattern is tried first, and if it matches, the others are skipped. If the first subpattern does not match, the second subpattern is tried, and so on. | is neither greedy nor non-greedy, as it doesn't take into consideration the length of the match.

If you have a list L of words, a regular expression pattern that matches any of the words is:

```
'|'.join([r'\b%s\b' % word for word in L])
```

If the items of L can be more-general strings, not just words, you need to escape each of them with function re.escape, covered later in this chapter, and you probably don't want the \b word boundary markers on either side. In this case, use the regular expression pattern:

```
'|'.join(map(re.escape,L))
```

Groups

A regular expression can contain any number of groups, from none up to 99 (any number is allowed, but only the first 99 groups are fully supported). Parentheses in a pattern string indicate a group. Element (?P<id>...) also indicates a group, and in addition gives the group a name, id, that can be any Python identifier. All groups, named and unnamed, are numbered from left to right, 1 to 99, with group number 0 indicating the whole regular expression.

For any match of the regular expression with a string, each group matches a substring (possibly an empty one). When the regular expression uses |, some of the groups may not match any substring, although the regular expression as a whole does match the string. When a group doesn't match any substring, we say that the group does not *participate* in the match. An empty string '' is used to represent the matching substring for a group that does not participate in a match, except where otherwise indicated later in this chapter.

For example:

```
r'(.+)\1+\Z'
```

matches a string made up of two or more repetitions of any non-empty substring. The (.+) part of the pattern matches any non-empty substring (any character, one or more times), and defines a group thanks to the parentheses. The \1+ part of the pattern matches one or more repetitions of the group, and the \Z anchors the match to end-of-string.

Optional Flags

A regular expression pattern element with one or more of the letters "iLmsux" between (? and) lets you set regular expression options within the regular expression's pattern, rather than by the *flags* argument to function compile of module re. Options apply to the whole regular expression, no matter where the options element occurs in the pattern. For clarity, options should always be at the start of the pattern. Placement at the start is mandatory if x is among the options, since x changes the way Python parses the pattern.

Using the explicit *flags* argument is more readable than placing an options element within the pattern. The *flags* argument to function compile is a coded integer, built by bitwise ORing (with Python's bitwise OR operator, |) one or more of the following attributes of module re. Each attribute has both a short name (one uppercase letter), for convenience, and a long name (an uppercase multiletter identifier), which is more readable and thus normally preferable:

I *or* IGNORECASE
> Makes matching case-insensitive

L *or* LOCALE
> Causes \w, \W, \b, and \B matches to depend on what the current locale deems alphanumeric

M *or* MULTILINE
> Makes the special characters ^ and $ match at the start and end of each line (i.e., right after/before a newline), as well as at the start and end of the whole string

S *or* DOTALL
> Causes the special character . to match any character, including a newline

U *or* UNICODE
> Makes \w, \W, \b, and \B matches depend on what Unicode deems alphanumeric

X *or* VERBOSE
> Causes whitespace in the pattern to be ignored, except when escaped or in a character set, and makes a # character in the pattern begin a comment that lasts until the end of the line

For example, here are three ways to define equivalent regular expressions with function compile, covered later in this chapter. Each of these regular expressions matches the word "hello" in any mix of upper- and lowercase letters:

```
import re
r1 = re.compile(r'(?i)hello')
r2 = re.compile(r'hello', re.I)
r3 = re.compile(r'hello', re.IGNORECASE)
```

The third approach is clearly the most readable, and thus the most maintainable, even though it is slightly more verbose. Note that the raw-string form is not necessary here, since the patterns do not include backslashes. However, using raw strings is still innocuous, and is the recommended style for clarity.

Option re.VERBOSE (or re.X) lets you make patterns more readable and understandable by appropriate use of whitespace and comments. Complicated and verbose regular expression patterns are generally best represented by strings that take up more than one line, and therefore you normally want to use the triple-quoted raw-string format for such pattern strings. For example:

```
repat_num1 = r'(0[0-7]*|0x[\da-fA-F]+|[1-9]\d*)L?\Z'
repat_num2 = r'''(?x)                # pattern matching integer numbers
              (0 [0-7]*      | # octal: leading 0, then 0+ octal digits
              0x [\da-f-A-F]+ | # hex: 0x, then 1+ hex digits
              [1-9] \d*      ) # decimal: leading non-0, then 0+ digits
              L?\Z             # optional trailing L, then end of string
              '''
```

The two patterns defined in this example are equivalent, but the second one is made somewhat more readable by the comments and the free use of whitespace to group portions of the pattern in logical ways.

Match Versus Search

So far, we've been using regular expressions to match strings. For example, the regular expression with pattern r'box' matches strings such as 'box' and 'boxes', but not 'inbox'. In other words, a regular expression match can be considered as implicitly anchored at the start of the target string, as if the regular expression's pattern started with \A.

Often, you're interested in locating possible matches for a regular expression anywhere in the string, without any anchoring (e.g., find the r'box' match inside such strings as 'inbox', as well as in 'box' and 'boxes'). In this case, the Python term for the operation is a *search*, as opposed to a match. For such searches, you use the search method of a regular expression object, while the match method only deals with matching from the start. For example:

```
import re
r1 = re.compile(r'box')
if r1.match('inbox'): print 'match succeeds'
else print 'match fails'                          # prints: match fails
if r1. search('inbox'): print 'search succeeds'    # prints: search succeeds
else print 'search fails'
```

Anchoring at String Start and End

The pattern elements ensuring that a regular expression search (or match) is anchored at string start and string end are \A and \Z respectively. More traditionally, elements ^ for start and $ for end are also used in similar roles. ^ is the same as \A, and $ is the same as \Z, for regular expression objects that are not multiline (i.e., that do not contain pattern element (?m) and are not compiled with the flag re.M or re.MULTILINE). For a multiline regular expression object, however, ^

anchors at the start of any line (i.e., either at the start of the whole string or at the position right after a newline character \n). Similarly, with a multiline regular expression, $ anchors at the end of any line (i.e., either at the end of the whole string or at the position right before \n). On the other hand, \A and \Z anchor at the start and end of the whole string whether the regular expression object is multiline or not. For example, here's how to check if a file has any lines that end with digits:

```
import re
digatend = re.compile(r'\d$', re.MULTILINE)
if re.search(open('afile.txt').read()): print "some lines end with digits"
else: print "no lines end with digits"
```

A pattern of r'\d\n' would be almost equivalent, but in that case the search would fail if the very last character of the file were a digit not followed by a terminating end-of-line character. With the example above, the search succeeds if a digit is at the very end of the file's contents, as well as in the more usual case where a digit is followed by an end-of-line character.

Regular Expression Objects

A regular expression object *r* has the following read-only attributes detailing how *r* was built (by function compile of module re, covered later in this chapter):

flags
> The *flags* argument passed to compile, or 0 when *flags* is omitted

groupindex
> A dictionary whose keys are group names as defined by elements (?P<*id*>); the corresponding values are the named groups' numbers

pattern
> The pattern string from which *r* is compiled

These attributes make it easy to get back from a compiled regular expression object to its pattern string and flags, so you never have to store those separately.

A regular expression object *r* also supplies methods to locate matches for *r*'s regular expression within a string, as well as to perform substitutions on such matches. Matches are generally represented by special objects, covered in the later "Match Objects" section.

findall	*r*.findall(*s*)
	When *r* has no groups, findall returns a list of strings, each a substring of *s* that is a non-overlapping match with *r*. For example, here's how to print out all words in a file, one per line:

```
import re
reword = re.compile(r'\w+')
for aword in reword.findall(open('afile.txt').read()):
    print aword
```

When *r* has one group, findall also returns a list of strings, but each is the substring of *s* matching *r*'s group. For example, if you want to print only words that are followed by whitespace (not

Strings

punctuation), you need to change only one statement in the previous example:

```
reword = re.compile('(\w+)\s')
```

When r has n groups (where n is greater than 1), findall returns a list of tuples, one per non-overlapping match with r. Each tuple has n items, one per group of r, the substring of s matching the group. For example, here's how to print the first and last word of each line that has at least two words:

```
import re
first_last = re.compile(r'^\W*(\w+)\b.*\b(\w+)\W*$',
                        re.MULTILINE)
for first, last in \
first_last.findall(open('afile.txt').read()):
    print first, last
```

match   r.match(s,start=0,end=sys.maxint)

Returns an appropriate match object when a substring of s, starting at index start and not reaching as far as index end, matches r. Otherwise, match returns None. Note that match is implicitly anchored at the starting position start in s. To search for a match with r through s, from start onwards, call r.search, not r.match. For example, here's how to print all lines in a file that start with digits:

```
import re
digs = re.compile(r'\d+')
for line in open('afile.txt'):
    if digs.match(line): print line,
```

search   r.search(s,start=0,end=sys.maxint)

Returns an appropriate match object for the leftmost substring of s, starting not before index start and not reaching as far as index end, that matches r. When no such substring exists, search returns None. For example, to print all lines containing digits, one simple approach is as follows:

```
import re
digs = re.compile(r'\d+')
for line in open('afile.txt'):
    if digs.search(line): print line,
```

split   r.split(s,maxsplit=0)

Returns a list L of the splits of s by r (i.e., the substrings of s that are separated by non-overlapping, non-empty matches with r). For example, to eliminate all occurrences of substring 'hello' from a string, in any mix of lowercase and uppercase letters, one way is:

```
import re
rehello = re.compile(r'hello', re.IGNORECASE)
astring = ''.join(rehello.split(astring))
```

When *r* has *n* groups, *n* more items are interleaved in *L* between each pair of splits. Each of the *n* extra items is the substring of *s* matching *r*'s corresponding group in that match, or None if that group did not participate in the match. For example, here's one way to remove whitespace only when it occurs between a colon and a digit:

```
import re
re_col_ws_dig = re.compile(r'(:)\s+(\d)')
astring = ''.join(re_col_ws_dig.split(astring))
```

If *maxsplit* is greater than 0, at most *maxsplit* splits are in *L*, each followed by *n* items as above, while the trailing substring of *s* after *maxsplit* matches of *r*, if any, is *L*'s last item. For example, to remove only the first occurrence of substring 'hello' rather than all of them, change the last statement in the first example above to:

```
astring = ''.join(rehello.split(astring, 1))
```

---

sub   `r.sub(repl,s,count=0)`

Returns a copy of *s* where non-overlapping matches with *r* are replaced by *repl*, which can be either a string or a callable object, such as a function. An empty match is replaced only when not adjacent to the previous match. When *count* is greater than 0, only the first *count* matches of *r* within *s* are replaced. When *count* equals 0, all matches of *r* within *s* are replaced. For example, here's another way to remove only the first occurrence of substring 'hello' in any mix of cases:

```
import re
rehello = re.compile(r'hello', re.IGNORECASE)
astring = rehello.sub('', astring, 1)
```

Without the final 1 argument to method sub, this example would remove all occurrences of 'hello'.

When *repl* is a callable object, *repl* must accept a single argument (a match object) and return a string to use as the replacement for the match. In this case, sub calls *repl*, with a suitable match-object argument, for each match with *r* that sub is replacing. For example, to uppercase all occurrences of words starting with 'h' and ending with 'o' in any mix of cases, you can use the following:

```
import re
h_word = re.compile(r'\bh\w+o\b', re.IGNORECASE)
def up(mo): return mo.group(0).upper( )
astring = h_word.sub(up, astring)
```

Method sub is a good way to get a callback to a callable you supply for every non-overlapping match of *r* in *s*, without an explicit loop, even when you don't need to perform any substitution. The following example shows this by using the sub method to build a function that works just like method findall for a regular expression without groups:

```
import re
def findall(r, s):
```

```
result = [ ]
def foundOne(mo): result.append(mo.group( ))
r.sub(foundOne, s)
return result
```

The example needs Python 2.2, not just because it uses lexically nested scopes, but because in Python 2.2 re tolerates *repl* returning None and treats it as if it returned '', while in Python 2.1 re was more pedantic and insisted on *repl* returning a string.

When *repl* is a string, sub uses *repl* itself as the replacement, except that it expands back references. A *back reference* is a substring of *repl* of the form \g<*id*>, where *id* is the name of a group in *r* (as established by syntax (?P<*id*>) in *r*'s pattern string), or *dd*, where *dd* is one or two digits, taken as a group number. Each back reference, whether named or numbered, is replaced with the substring of *s* matching the group of *r* that the back reference indicates. For example, here's how to enclose every word in braces:

```
import re
grouped_word = re.compile('(\w+)')
astring = grouped_word.sub(r'{\1}', astring)
```

subn   `r.subn(repl,s,count=0)`

subn is the same as sub, except that subn returns a pair (*new_string*, *n*) where *n* is the number of substitutions that subn has performed. For example, to count the number of occurrences of substring 'hello' in any mix of cases, one way is:

```
import re
rehello = re.compile(r'hello', re.IGNORECASE)
junk, count = rehello.subn('', astring)
print 'Found', count, 'occurrences of "hello"'
```

Match Objects

Match objects are created and returned by methods match and search of a regular expression object. There are also implicitly created by methods sub and subn when argument *repl* is callable, since in that case a suitable match object is passed as the actual argument on each call to *repl*. A match object *m* supplies the following attributes detailing how *m* was created:

pos
> The *start* argument that was passed to search or match (i.e., the index into *s* where the search for a match began)

endpos
> The *end* argument that was passed to search or match (i.e., the index into *s* before which the matching substring of *s* had to end)

lastgroup
> The name of the last-matched group (None if the last-matched group has no name, or if no group participated in the match)

lastindex
> The integer index (1 and up) of the last-matched group (None if no group participated in the match)

re
> The regular expression object r whose method created m

string
> The string s passed to match, search, sub, or subn

A match object m also supplies several methods.

---

end, span, start   *m*.end(*groupid*=0)
    m.span(*groupid*=0)
    m.start(*groupid*=0)

> These methods return the delimiting indices, within *m*.string, of the substring matching the group identified by *groupid*, where *groupid* can be a group number or name. When the matching substring is *m*.string[*i*:*j*], *m*.start returns *i*, *m*.end returns *j*, and *m*.span returns (*i*, *j*). When the group did not participate in the match, *i* and *j* are -1.

---

expand   *m*.expand(*s*)

> Returns a copy of *s* where escape sequences and back references are replaced in the same way as for method *r*.sub, covered in the previous section.

---

group   *m*.group(*groupid*=0,**groupids*)

> When called with a single argument *groupid* (a group number or name), group returns the substring matching the group identified by *groupid*, or None if that group did not participate in the match. The common idiom *m*.group( ), also spelled *m*.group(0), returns the whole matched substring, since group number 0 implicitly means the whole regular expression.

> When group is called with multiple arguments, each argument must be a group number or name. group then returns a tuple with one item per argument, the substring matching the corresponding group, or None if that group did not participate in the match.

---

groups   *m*.groups(*default*=None)

> Returns a tuple with one item per group in *r*. Each item is the substring matching the corresponding group, or *default* if that group did not participate in the match.

Strings

groupdict   *m*.groupdict(*default*=None)

Returns a dictionary whose keys are the names of all named groups in *r*. The value for each name is the substring matching the corresponding group, or *default* if that group did not participate in the match.

Functions of Module re

The re module supplies the attributes listed in the earlier section "Optional Flags." It also provides a function that corresponds to each method of a regular expression object (findall, match, search, split, sub, and subn), each with an additional first argument, a pattern string that the function implicitly compiles into a regular expression object. It's generally preferable to compile pattern strings into regular expression objects explicitly and call the regular expression object's methods, but sometimes, for a one-off use of a regular expression pattern, calling functions of module re can be slightly handier. For example, to count the number of occurrences of substring 'hello' in any mix of cases, one function-based way is:

```
import re
junk, count = re.subn(r'(?i)hello', '', astring)
print 'Found', count, 'occurrences of "hello"'
```

In cases such as this one, regular expression options (here, for example, case insensitivity) must be encoded as regular expression pattern elements (here, (?i)), since the functions of module re do not accept a *flags* argument.

Module re also supplies error, the class of exceptions raised upon errors (generally, errors in the syntax of a pattern string), and two additional functions.

compile   compile(*pattern*,*flags*=0)

Creates and returns a regular expression object, parsing string *pattern* as per the syntax covered in the section "Pattern-String Syntax," and using integer *flags* as in the section "Optional Flags," both earlier in this chapter.

escape   escape(*s*)

Returns a copy of string *s* where each non-alphanumeric character is escaped (i.e., preceded by a backslash \). This is handy when you need to match string *s* literally as part (or all) of a regular expression pattern string.

III

Python Library and Extension Modules

File and Text Operations

This chapter covers dealing with files and the filesystem in Python. A *file* is a stream of bytes that a program can read and/or write, while a *filesystem* is a hierarchical repository of files on a particular computer system. Because files are such a core programming concept, several other chapters also contain material about handling files of specific kinds.

In Python, the os module supplies many of the functions that operate on the filesystem, so this chapter starts by introducing the os module. The chapter then proceeds to cover operations on the filesystem, including comparing, copying, and deleting directories and files, working with file paths, and accessing low-level file descriptors.

Next, this chapter discusses the typical ways Python programs read and write data, via built-in file objects and the polymorphic concept of file-like objects (i.e., objects that are not files, but still behave to some extent like files). Python file objects directly support the concept of *text files*, which are streams of characters encoded as bytes. The chapter also covers Python's support for data in compressed form, such as archives in the popular ZIP format.

While many modern programs rely on a graphical user interface (GUI), text-based, non-graphical user interfaces are often still useful, as they are simple, fast to program, and lightweight. This chapter concludes with material about text input and output in Python, including information about presenting text that is understandable to different users, no matter where they are or what language they speak. This is known as *internationalization* (often abbreviated *i18n*).

The os Module

The os module is an umbrella module that presents a reasonably uniform cross-platform view of the different capabilities of various operating systems. The module provides functionality for creating files, manipulating files and directories, and creating, managing, and destroying processes. This chapter covers the file-system-related capabilities of the os module, while Chapter 14 covers the process-related capabilities.

The os module supplies a name attribute, which is a string that identifies the kind of platform on which Python is being run. Possible values for name are 'posix' (all kinds of Unix-like platforms), 'nt' (all kinds of 32-bit Windows platforms), 'mac', 'os2', and 'java'. You can often exploit unique capabilities of a platform, at least in part, through functions supplied by os. This book deals with cross-platform programming, however, not with platform-specific functionality, so I do not cover parts of os that exist only on one kind of platform, nor do I cover platform-specific modules. All functionality covered in this book is available at least on both 'posix' and 'nt' platforms. However, I do cover any differences among the ways in which each given piece of functionality is provided on different platforms.

OSError Exceptions

When a request to the operating system fails, os raises an exception, an instance of OSError. os also exposes class OSError with the name os.error. Instances of OSError expose three useful attributes:

errno
> The numeric error code of the operating system error

strerror
> A string that summarily describes the error

filename
> The name of the file on which the operation failed (for file-related functions only)

os functions can also raise other standard exceptions, typically TypeError or ValueError, when the error is that they have been called with invalid argument types or values and the underlying operating system functionality has not even been attempted.

The errno Module

The errno module supplies symbolic names for error code numbers. To handle possible system errors selectively, based on error codes, use errno to enhance your program's portability and readability. For example, here's how you might handle only "file not found" errors, while propagating others:

```
try: os.some_os_function_or_other( )
except OSError, err:
    import errno
    # check for "file not found" errors
    if err.errno != errno.ENOENT: raise          # reraise other cases
    # proceed with the specific case you can handle
    print "Warning: file", err.filename, "not found -- continuing"
```

errno also supplies a dictionary named errorcode: the keys are error code numbers, and the corresponding names are the error names, such as 'ENOENT'. Displaying errno.errorcode[err.errno], as part of your diagnosis of some os.error instance err, can often make diagnosis clearer and more understandable to readers who are specialists of the specific platform.

Filesystem Operations

Using the os module, you can manipulate the filesystem in a variety of ways: creating, copying, and deleting files and directories, comparing files, and examining filesystem information about files and directories. This section documents the attributes and methods of the os module that you use for these purposes, and also covers some related modules that operate on the filesystem.

Path-String Attributes of the os Module

A file or directory is identified by a string, known as its *path*, whose syntax depends on the platform. On both Unix-like and Windows platforms, Python accepts Unix syntax for paths, with slash (/) as the directory separator. On non-Unix-like platforms, Python also accepts platform-specific path syntax. On Windows, for example, you can use backslash (\) as the separator. However, you do need to double up each backslash to \\ in normal string literals or use raw-string syntax as covered in Chapter 4. In the rest of this chapter, for brevity, Unix syntax is assumed in both explanations and examples.

Module os supplies attributes that provide details about path strings on the current platform. You should typically use the higher-level path manipulation operations covered in "The os.path Module" later in this chapter, rather than lower-level string operations based on these attributes. However, the attributes may still be useful at times:

curdir
    The string that denotes the current directory ('.' on Unix and Windows)

defpath
    The default search path used if the environment lacks a PATH environment variable

linesep
    The string that terminates text lines ('\n' on Unix, '\r\n' on Windows)

extsep
    The string that separates the extension part of a file's name from the rest of the name ('.' on Unix and Windows)

pardir
    The string that denotes the parent directory ('..' on Unix and Windows)

pathsep
    The separator between paths in lists of paths, such as those used for the environment variable PATH (':' on Unix, ';' on Windows)

sep
    The separator of path components ('/' on Unix, '\\' on Windows)

Permissions

Unix-like platforms associate nine bits with each file or directory, three each for the file's owner (user), its group, and anybody else, indicating whether the file or directory can be read, written, and executed by the specified subject. These nine bits are known as the file's *permission bits*, part of the file's *mode* (a bit string that also includes other bits describing the file). These bits are often displayed in octal notation, which groups three bits in each digit. For example, a mode of 0664 indicates a file that can be read and written by its owner and group, but only read, not written, by anybody else. When any process on a Unix-like system creates a file or directory, the operating system applies to the specified mode a bit mask known as the process's *umask*, which can remove some of the permission bits.

Non-Unix-like platforms handle file and directory permissions in very different ways. However, the functions in Python's standard library that deal with permissions accept a *mode* argument according to the Unix-like approach described in the previous paragraph. The implementation on each platform maps the nine permission bits in a way appropriate for the given platform. For example, on versions of Windows that distinguish only between read-only and read-write files and do not distinguish file ownership, a file's permission bits show up as either 0666 (read-write) or 0444 (read-only). On such a platform, when a file is created, the implementation looks only at bit 0200, making the file read-write if that bit is 0 or read-only if that bit is 1.

File and Directory Functions of the os Module

The os module supplies several functions to query and set file and directory status.

access	access(*path*,*mode*)
	Returns True if file *path* has all of the permissions encoded in integer *mode*, otherwise False. *mode* can be os.F_OK to test for file existence, or one or more of os.R_OK, os.W_OK, and os.X_OK (with the bitwise-OR operator | joining them if more than one) to test permissions to read, write, and execute the file.
	access does not use the standard interpretation for its *mode* argument, covered in "Permissions" earlier in this chapter. access tests only if this specific process's real user and group identifiers have the requested permissions on the file. If you need to study a file's permission bits in more detail, see function stat in this section.
chdir	chdir(*path*)
	Sets the current working directory to *path*.
chmod	chmod(*path*,*mode*)
	Changes the permissions of file *path*, as encoded in integer *mode*. *mode* can be zero or more of os.R_OK, os.W_OK, and os.X_OK (with the bitwise-OR operator | joining them if more than one) to set

permission to read, write, and execute. On Unix-like platforms, *mode* can also be a richer bit pattern, as covered in "Permissions" earlier in this chapter.

getcwd

getcwd( )

Returns the path of the current working directory.

listdir

listdir(*path*)

Returns a list whose items are the names of all files and subdirectories found in directory *path*. The returned list is in arbitrary order, and does not include the special directory names '.' and '..'.

The dircache module also supplies a function named listdir, which works like os.listdir, with two enhancements. First, dircache.listdir returns a sorted list. Further, dircache caches the list it returns, so repeated requests for lists of the same directory are faster if the directory's contents have not changed in the meantime. dircache automatically detects changes, so the list that dircache.listdir returns is always up to date.

makedirs, mkdir

makedirs(*path*,*mode*=0777)
mkdir(*path*,*mode*=0777)

makedirs creates all directories that are part of *path* and do not yet exist. mkdir creates only the rightmost directory of *path*. Both functions use *mode* as permission bits of directories they create. Both functions raise OSError if creation fails or if a file or directory named *path* already exists.

remove, unlink

remove(*path*)
unlink(*path*)

Removes the file named *path* (see rmdir later in this section to remove a directory). unlink is a synonym of remove.

removedirs

removedirs(*path*)

Loops from right to left over the directories that are part of *path*, removing each one. The loop ends when a removal attempt raises an exception, generally because a directory is not empty. removedirs does not propagate the exception as long as it has removed at least one directory.

rename

rename(*source*,*dest*)

Renames the file or directory named *source* to *dest*.

renames

renames(*source*,*dest*)

Like rename, except that renames attempts to create all intermediate directories needed for *dest*. After the renaming, renames tries to remove empty directories from path *source* using removedirs. It does not propagate any resulting exception, since it's not an error if the starting directory of *source* does not become empty after the renaming.

rmdir   rmdir(*path*)

Removes the directory named *path* (raises OSError if it is not empty).

stat   stat(*path*)

Returns a value *x* that is a tuple of 10 integers that provide information about a file or subdirectory *path*. See "The stat Module" later in this chapter for details about using the returned tuple. In Python 2.2 and later, *x* is of type stat_result. You can still use *x* as a tuple, but you can also access *x*'s items as read-only attributes *x*.st_mode, *x*.st_ino, and so on, using as attribute names the lowercase versions of the names of constants listed later in Table 10-1.

A module named statcache also supplies a function named stat, like os.stat but with an enhancement: the returned tuple (or stat_result instance) is cached, so repeated requests about the same file run faster. statcache cannot detect changes automatically, so you should use it only for stable files that do not change in the time between stat requests.

tempnam,   tempnam(*dir*=None,*prefix*=None)
tmpnam   tmpnam( )

Returns an absolute path usable as the name of a new temporary file. If *dir* is None, the path uses the directory normally used for temporary files on the current platform; otherwise the path uses *dir*. If *prefix* is not None, it should be a short string to be prefixed to the temporary file's name. tempnam never returns the name of any already existing file. Your program must create the temporary file, use the file, and remove the file when done, as in the following snippet:

```
import os
def work_on_temporary_file(workfun):
    nam = os.tempnam( )
    fil = open(nam, 'rw+')
    try:
        workfun(fil)
    finally:
        fil.close( )
        os.remove(nam)
```

tmpnam is a synonym for tempnam. However, tmpnam does not accept arguments, and always behaves like tempnam(None,None). tempnam and tmpnam are potential weaknesses in your program's security, and recent versions of Python emit a warning the first time your program calls these functions to alert you to this fact. See Chapter 17 for information about ways in which your program can interact with warnings.

utime	utime(*path,times*=None)
	Sets the accessed and modified times of file or directory *path*. If *times* is None, utime uses the current time. Otherwise, *times* must be a pair of numbers (in seconds since the epoch, as covered in Chapter 12) in the order (*accessed, modified*).

The os.path Module

The os.path module supplies functions to analyze and transform path strings.

abspath	abspath(*path*)
	Returns a normalized absolute path equivalent to *path*, just like:
	os.path.normpath(os.path.join(os.getcwd( ),*path*))
	For example, os.path.abspath(os.curdir) always returns the same string as os.getcwd( ).

basename	basename(*path*)
	Returns the base name part of *path*, just like os.path.split(*path*)[1]. For example, os.path.basename('b/c/d.e') returns 'd.e'.

commonprefix	commonprefix(*list*)
	Accepts a list of strings and returns the longest string that is a prefix of all items in the list. Unlike other functions in os.path, commonprefix works on arbitrary strings, not just on paths.

dirname	dirname(*path*)
	Returns the directory part of *path*, just like os.path.split(*path*)[0]. For example, os.path.basename('b/c/d.e') returns 'b/c'.

exists	exists(*path*)
	Returns True when *path* names an existing file or directory, otherwise False. In other words, os.path.exists(*x*) always returns the same result as os.access(*x*,os.F_OK).

expandvars	expandvars(*path*)
	Returns a copy of string *path*, replacing each substring of the form "$*name*" or "${*name*}" with the value of environment variable *name*. The replacement is an empty string if *name* does not exist in the environment.

getatime,	getatime(*path*)
getmtime,	getmtime(*path*)
getsize	getsize(*path*)
	Each of these functions returns an attribute from the result of os.stat(*path*), respectively the attributes st_atime, st_mtime, and st_size. See "The stat Module" later in this chapter for more information about these attributes.

isabs	isabs(*path*)
	Returns True when *path* is absolute. A path is absolute when it starts with a slash /, or, on some non-Unix-like platforms, with a drive designator followed by os.sep. When *path* is not absolute, isabs returns False.

isfile	isfile(*path*)
	Returns True when *path* names an existing regular file (in Unix, however, isfile also follows symbolic links), otherwise False.

isdir	isdir(*path*)
	Returns True when *path* names an existing directory (in Unix, however, isdir also follows symbolic links), otherwise False.

islink	islink(*path*)
	Returns True when *path* names a symbolic link. Otherwise (always, on platforms that don't support symbolic links) islink returns False.

ismount	ismount(*path*)
	Returns True when *path* names a mount point. Otherwise (always, on platforms that don't support mount points) ismount returns False.

join	join(*path*,*paths)
	Returns a string that joins the argument strings with the appropriate path separator for the current platform. For example, on Unix, exactly one slash character / separates adjacent path components. If any argument is an absolute path, join ignores all previous components. For example:

```
    print os.path.join('a/b', 'c/d','e/f')
    # on Unix prints: a/b/c/d/e/f
    print os.path.join('a/b', '/c/d', 'e/f')
    # on Unix prints: /c/d/e/f
```

The second call to os.path.join ignores its first argument 'a/b', since its second argument '/c/d' is an absolute path.

normcase

normcase(*path*)

Returns a copy of *path* with case normalized for the current platform. On case-sensitive filesystems (as typical in Unix), *path* is returned unchanged. On case-insensitive filesystems, all letters in the returned string are lowercase. On Windows, normcase also converts each / to a \.

normpath

normpath(*path*)

Returns a normalized pathname equivalent to *path*, removing redundant separators and path-navigation aspects. For example, on Unix, normpath returns 'a/b' when *path* is any of 'a//b', 'a/./b', or 'a/c/../b'. normpath converts path separators as appropriate for the current platform. For example, on Windows, the returned string uses \ as the separator.

split

split(*path*)

Returns a pair of strings (*dir*,*base*) such that join(*dir*,*base*) equals *path*. *base* is the last pathname component and never contains a path separator. If *path* ends in a separator, *base* is ''. *dir* is the leading part of *path*, up to the last path separator, shorn of trailing separators. For example, os.path.split('a/b/c/d') returns the pair ('a/b/c','d').

splitdrive

splitdrive(*path*)

Returns a pair of strings (*drv*,*pth*) such that *drv+pth* equals *path*. *drv* is either a drive specification or ''. *drv* is always '' on platforms that do not support drive specifications, such as Unix. For example, on Windows, os.path.splitdrive('c:d/e') returns the pair ('c:','d/e').

splitext

splitext(path)

Returns a pair of strings (*root*,*ext*) such that *root+ext* equals *path*. *ext* either is '', or starts with a '.' and has no other '.' or path separator. For example, os.path.splitext('a/b.c') returns the pair ('a/b','.c').

walk

walk(*path*,*func*,*arg*)

Calls *func*(*arg*,*dirpath*,*namelist*) for each directory in the tree whose root is directory *path*, starting with *path* itself. In each such call to *func*, *dirpath* is the path of the directory being visited, and *namelist* is the list of *dirpath*'s contents as returned by os.listdir. *func* may modify *namelist* in-place (e.g., with del) to avoid visiting certain parts of the tree: walk further calls *func* only for subdirectories remaining in *namelist* after *func* returns, if any. *arg* is provided only for *func*'s convenience: walk just receives *arg*, and passes *arg* back to *func* each time walk calls *func*. A typical use of os.path. walk is to print all files and subdirectories in a tree:

```
import os
def print_tree(tree_root_dir):
    def printall(junk, dirpath, namelist):
        for name in namelist:
            print os.path.join(dirpath, name)
    os.path.walk(tree_root_dir, printall, None)
```

The stat Module

Accessing items in the tuple returned by os.stat by their numeric indices is not advisable. The order of the tuple's 10 items is guaranteed, but using numeric literals to index into the tuple is not readable. The stat module supplies attributes whose values are indices into the tuple returned by os.stat. Table 10-1 lists the attributes of module stat and the meaning of corresponding items.

Table 10-1. Items of a stat tuple

Item	stat attribute	Meaning
0	ST_MODE	Protection and other mode bits
1	ST_INO	Inode number
2	ST_DEV	Device ID
3	ST_NLINK	Number of hard links
4	ST_UID	User ID of owner
5	ST_GID	Group ID of owner
6	ST_SIZE	Size in bytes
7	ST_ATIME	Time of last access
8	ST_MTIME	Time of last modification
9	ST_CTIME	Time of last status change

In Python 2.2, os.stat returns an instance of type stat_result, whose 10 items are also accessible as attributes named st_mode, st_ino, and so on—the lowercase versions of the stat attributes listed in Table 10-1.

For example, to print the size in bytes of file *path*, you can use any of:

```
import os, stat

print os.path.getsize(path)
print os.stat(path)[6]
print os.stat(path)[stat.ST_SIZE]
print os.stat(path).st_size          # only in Python 2.2 and later
```

Time values are in seconds since the epoch, as covered in Chapter 12 (int on most platforms, float on the Macintosh). Platforms unable to give a meaningful value for an item use a dummy value for that item.

Module stat also supplies functions that examine the ST_MODE item to determine the kind of file. os.path also supplies functions for such tasks, which operate directly on the file's *path*. The functions supplied by stat are faster when performing several tests on the same file: they require only one os.stat call at the start of a series of tests, while the functions in os.path ask the operating system for the information at each test. Each function returns True if *mode* denotes a file of the given kind, otherwise False.

S_ISDIR(*mode*)
> Is the file a directory

S_ISCHR(*mode*)
> Is the file a special device-file of the character kind

S_ISBLK(*mode*)
> Is the file a special device-file of the block kind

S_ISREG(*mode*)
> Is the file a normal file (not a directory, special device-file, and so on)

S_ISFIFO(*mode*)
> Is the file a FIFO (i.e., a named pipe)

S_ISLNK(*mode*)
> Is the file a symbolic link

S_ISSOCK(*mode*)
> Is the file a Unix-domain socket

Except for stat.S_ISDIR and stat.S_ISREG, the other functions are meaningful only on Unix-like systems, since most other platforms do not keep special files such as devices in the same namespace as regular files.

Module stat supplies two more functions that extract relevant parts of a file's *mode* (*x*[ST_MODE], or *x*.st_mode, in the result *x* of function os.stat).

S_IFMT	S_IFMT(*mode*)
	Returns those bits of *mode* that describe the kind of file (i.e., those bits that are examined by functions S_ISDIR, S_ISREG, etc.).

S_IMODE	S_IMODE(*mode*)
	Returns those bits of *mode* that can be set by function os.chmod (i.e., the permission bits and, on Unix-like platforms, other special bits such as the set-user-id flag).

The filecmp Module

The filecmp module supplies functionality to compare files and directories.

cmp	cmp(*f1*,*f2*,*shallow*=True,*use_statcache*=False)
	Compares the files named by path strings *f1* and *f2*. If the files seem equal, cmp returns True, otherwise False. If *shallow* is true, files are deemed equal if their stat tuples are equal. If *shallow* is false, cmp reads and compares files with equal stat tuples. If *use_statcache* is false, cmp obtains file information via os.stat; if *use_statcache* is true, cmp calls statcache.stat instead. cmp remembers what files have already been compared and does not repeat comparisons unless some file has changed, but *use_statcache* makes cmp believe that no file ever changes.
cmpfiles	cmpfiles(*dir1*,*dir2*,*common*,*shallow*=True,*use_statcache*=False)
	Loops on sequence *common*. Each item of *common* is a string naming a file present in both directories *dir1* and *dir2*. cmpfiles returns a tuple with three lists of strings: (*equal*,*diff*,*errs*). *equal* is the list of names of files equal in both directories, *diff* the list of names of files that differ between directories, and *errs* the list of names of files that could not be compared (not existing in both directories or no permission to read them). Arguments *shallow* and *use_statcache* are just as for function cmp.
dircmp	class dircmp(*dir1*,*dir2*,*ignore*=('RCS','CVS','tags'), *hide*=('.','..'))
	Creates a new directory-comparison instance object, comparing directories named *dir1* and *dir2*, ignoring names listed in *ignore*, and hiding names listed in *hide*. A dircmp instance *d* exposes three methods:

d.report( )
> Outputs to sys.stdout a comparison between *dir1* and *dir2*

d.report_partial_closure( )
> Outputs to sys.stdout a comparison between *dir1* and *dir2* and their common immediate subdirectories

d.report_full_closure( )
> Outputs to sys.stdout a comparison between *dir1* and *dir2* and their common subdirectories, recursively

A dircmp instance *d* supplies several attributes, computed just in time (i.e., only if and when needed, thanks to a __getattr__ special method) so that using a dircmp instance suffers no unnecessary overhead. *d*'s attributes are:

d.common
> Files and subdirectories that are in both *dir1* and *dir2*

d.common_dirs
> Subdirectories that are in both *dir1* and *dir2*

d.common_files

    Files that are in both *dir1* and *dir2*

d.common_funny

    Names that are in both *dir1* and *dir2* for which os.stat reports an error or returns different kinds for the versions in the two directories

d.diff_files

    Files that are in both *dir1* and *dir2* but with different contents

d.funny_files

    Files that are in both *dir1* and *dir2* but could not be compared

d.left_list

    Files and subdirectories that are in *dir1*

d.left_only

    Files and subdirectories that are in *dir1* and not in *dir2*

d.right_list

    Files and subdirectories that are in *dir2*

d.right_only

    Files and subdirectories that are in *dir2* and not in *dir1*

d.same_files

    Files that are in both *dir1* and *dir2* with the same contents

d.subdirs

    A dictionary whose keys are the strings in common_dirs: the corresponding values are instances of dircmp for each subdirectory

The shutil Module

The shutil module (an abbreviation for *shell utilities*) supplies functions to copy files and to remove an entire directory tree.

copy

copy(*src*,*dst*)

Copies the contents of file *src*, creating or overwriting file *dst*. If *dst* is a directory, the target is a file with the same base name as *src* in directory *dst*. copy also copies permission bits, but not last-access and modification times.

copy2

copy2(*src*,*dst*)

Like copy, but also copies times of last access and modification.

copyfile

copyfile(*src*,*dst*)

Copies the contents only of file *src*, creating or overwriting file *dst*.

copyfileobj	copyfileobj(*fsrc,fdst,bufsize*=16384)
	Copies file object *fsrc*, which must be open for reading, to file object *fdst*, which must be open for writing. Copies no more than *bufsize* bytes at a time if *bufsize* is greater than 0. File objects are covered later in this chapter.
copymode	copymode(*src,dst*)
	Copies permission bits of file or directory *src* to file or directory *dst*. Both *src* and *dst* must exist. Does not modify *dst*'s contents, nor any other aspect of file or directory status.
copystat	copystat(*src,dst*)
	Copies permission bits and times of last access and modification of file or directory *src* to file or directory *dst*. Both *src* and *dst* must exist. Does not modify *dst*'s contents, nor any other aspect of file or directory status.
copytree	copytree(*src,dst,symlinks*=False)
	Copies the whole directory tree rooted at *src* into the destination directory named by *dst*. *dst* must not already exist, as copytree creates it. copytree copies each file by using function copy2. When *symlinks* is true, copytree creates symbolic links in the new tree when it finds symbolic links in the source tree. When *symlinks* is false, copytree follows each symbolic link it finds, and copies the linked-to file with the link's name. On platforms that do not have the concept of a symbolic link, such as Windows, copytree ignores argument *symlinks*.
rmtree	rmtree(*path,ignore_errors*=False,*onerror*=None)
	Removes the directory tree rooted at *path*. When *ignore_errors* is true, rmtree ignores errors. When *ignore_errors* is false and *onerror* is None, any error raises an exception. When *onerror* is not None, it must be callable with parameters *func*, *path*, and *excp*. *func* is the function raising an exception (os.remove or os.rmdir), *path* the path passed to *func*, and *excp* the tuple of information that sys.exc_info( ) returns. If *onerror* raises any exception *x*, rmtree terminates, and exception *x* propagates.

File Descriptor Operations

The os module supplies functions to handle *file descriptors*, integers that the operating system uses as opaque handles to refer to open files. Python file objects, covered in the next section, are almost invariably better for input/output tasks, but sometimes working at file-descriptor level lets you perform some operation more rapidly or elegantly. Note that file objects and file descriptors are not inter-changeable in any way.

You can get the file descriptor *n* of a Python file object *f* by calling *n*=*f*.fileno( ). You can wrap a new Python file object *f* around an open file descriptor *fd* by calling *f*=os.fdopen(*fd*). On Unix-like and Windows platforms, some file descrip-tors are preallocated when a process starts: 0 is the file descriptor for the process's standard input, 1 for the process's standard output, and 2 for the process's stan-dard error.

os provides the following functions for working with file descriptors.

close   close(*fd*)

Closes file descriptor *fd*.

---

dup   dup(*fd*)

Returns a file descriptor that duplicates file descriptor *fd*.

---

dup2   dup2(*fd*,*fd2*)

Duplicates file descriptor *fd* to file descriptor *fd2*. If file descriptor *fd2* is already open, dup2 first closes *fd2*.

---

fdopen   fdopen(*fd*,*mode*='r',*bufsize*=-1)

Returns a Python file object wrapping file descriptor *fd*. *mode* and *bufsize* have the same meaning as for Python's built-in open, covered in the next section.

---

fstat   fstat(*fd*)

Returns a tuple *x* (*x* is a stat_result instance in Python 2.2 and later), with information about the file open on file descriptor *fd*. "The stat Module" earlier in this chapter covers the format of *x*'s contents.

---

lseek   lseek(*fd*,*pos*,*how*)

Sets the current position of file descriptor *fd* to the signed integer byte offset *pos*, and returns the resulting byte offset from the start of the file. *how* indicates the reference (point 0): when *how* is 0, the reference is the start of the file; when 1, the current position; and when 2, the end of the file. In particular, lseek(*fd*,0,1) returns the current position's byte offset from the start of the file, without affecting the current position. Normal disk files support such seeking operations, but calling lstat on a file that does not support seeking (e.g., a file open for output to a terminal) raises an exception.

open   open(*file*,*flags*,*mode*=0777)

Returns a file descriptor, opening or creating a file named *file*. If open creates the file, it uses *mode* as the file's permission bits. *flags* is an int, normally obtained by bitwise ORing one or more of the following attributes of os:

O_RDONLY, O_WRONLY, O_RDWR
> Opens *file* for read-only, write-only, or read-write respectively (mutually exclusive: exactly one of these attributes must be in *flags*)

O_NDELAY, O_NONBLOCK
> Opens *file* in non-blocking (no-delay) mode, if the platform supports this

O_APPEND
> Appends any new data to *file*'s previous contents

O_DSYNC, O_RSYNC, O_SYNC, O_NOCTTY
> Sets synchronization mode accordingly, if the platform supports this

O_CREAT
> Creates *file*, if *file* does not already exist

O_EXCL
> Raises an exception if *file* already exists

O_TRUNC
> Throws away previous contents of *file* (incompatible with O_RDONLY)

O_BINARY
> Open *file* in binary rather than text mode on non-Unix platforms (innocuous and without effect on Unix and Unix-like platforms)

pipe   pipe( )

Creates a pipe and returns a pair of file descriptors (*r*,*w*) open for reading and writing respectively.

read   read(*fd*,*n*)

Reads up to *n* bytes from file descriptor *fd* and returns them as a string. Reads and returns *m*<*n* bytes when only *m* more bytes are currently available for reading from the file. In particular, returns the empty string when no more bytes are currently available from the file, typically because the file is ended.

write   write(*fd*,*str*)

Writes all bytes from string *str* to file descriptor *fd*, and returns the number of bytes written (i.e., len(*str*)).

File Objects

As discussed earlier in this chapter, file is a built-in type in Python. With a file object, you can read and/or write data to a file as seen by the underlying operating system. Python reacts to any I/O error related to a file object by raising an instance of built-in exception class IOError. Errors that cause this exception include open failing to open or create a file, calling a method on a file object to which that method doesn't apply (e.g., calling write on a read-only file object or calling seek on a non-seekable file), and I/O errors diagnosed by a file object's methods. This section documents file objects, as well as some auxiliary modules that help you access and deal with their contents.

Creating a File Object with open

You normally create a Python file object with the built-in open, which has the following syntax:

```
open(filename,mode='r',bufsize=-1)
```

open opens the file named by *filename*, which must be a string that denotes any path to a file. open returns a Python file object, which is an instance of the built-in type file. Calling file is just like calling open, but file was first introduced in Python 2.2. If you explicitly pass a *mode* string, open can also create *filename* if the file does not already exist (depending on the value of *mode*, as we'll discuss in a moment). In other words, despite its name, open is not limited to opening existing files, but is also able to create new ones if needed.

File mode

mode is a string that denotes how the file is to be opened (or created). mode can have the following values:

'r'
    The file must already exist, and it is opened in read-only mode.

'w'
    The file is opened in write-only mode. The file is truncated and overwritten if it already exists, or created if it does not exist.

'a'
    The file is opened in write-only mode. The file is kept intact if it already exists, and the data you write is appended to what's already in the file. The file is created if it does not exist. Calling *f*.seek is innocuous, but has no effect.

'r+'
    The file must already exist and is opened for both reading and writing, so all methods of *f* can be called.

'w+'
    The file is opened for both reading and writing, so all methods of *f* can be called. The file is truncated and overwritten if it already exists, or created if it does not exist.

'a+'

The file is opened for both reading and writing, so all methods of f can be called. The file is kept intact if it already exists, and the data you write is appended to what's already in the file. The file is created if it does not exist. Calling f.seek has no effect if the next I/O operation on f writes data, but works normally if the next I/O operation on f reads data.

Binary and text modes

The *mode* string may also have any of the values just explained followed by a b or t. b denotes binary mode, while t denotes text mode. When the *mode* string has neither b nor t, the default is text mode (i.e., 'r' is like 'rt', 'w' is like 'wt', and so on).

On Unix, there is no difference between binary and text modes. On other platforms, when a file is open in text mode, '\n' is returned each time the string that is the value of os.linesep (the line termination string) is encountered while reading the file. Conversely, a copy of os.linesep is written each time you write '\n' to the file.

This widespread convention, originally developed in the C language, lets you read and write text files on any platform, without worrying about the platform's line-separation conventions. However, except on Unix platforms, you do have to know (and tell Python, by passing the proper *mode* argument to open) whether a file is binary or text. In this chapter, for simplicity, I use \n to refer to the line termination string, but remember that the string is in fact os.linesep in files on the filesystem, translated to and from \n in memory only for files opened in text mode.

Python 2.3 will introduce a new concept, known as *universal newlines*, letting you open a text file for reading in mode 'u' when you don't know how line separators are encoded in the file. This is useful, for example, when you share files across a network between machines with different operating systems. Mode 'u' guesses what line separator string to use based on each file's contents. However, mode 'u' is not available in Python 2.2 and earlier.

Buffering

bufsize is an integer that denotes what buffering you request for the file. When *bufsize* is less than 0, the operating system's default is used. Normally, this default is line buffering for files that correspond to interactive consoles, and some reasonably sized buffer, such as 8192 bytes, for other files. When *bufsize* equals 0, the file is unbuffered; the effect is as if the file's buffer were flushed every time you write anything to the file. When *bufsize* equals 1, the file is line-buffered, which means the file's buffer is flushed every time you write \n to the file. When *bufsize* is greater than 1, the file uses a buffer of about *bufsize* bytes, rounded up to some reasonable amount. On some platforms, you can change the buffering for files that are already open, but there is no cross-platform way to do this.

Sequential and non-sequential access

A file object f is inherently sequential (i.e., a stream of bytes). When you read from a file, you get bytes in the sequential order in which the bytes are present in the file. When you write to a file, the bytes you write are put in the file in the sequential order in which you write them.

To allow non-sequential access, the built-in file object keeps track of its current position (i.e., the position on the underlying file where the next read or write operation will start transferring data). When you open a file, the file's initial current position is at the start of the file. Any call to f.write on a file object f opened with a *mode* of 'a' or 'a+' always sets f's current position to the end of the file before writing data to f. Whenever you read or write some number n of bytes on file object f, f's current position advances by n. You can query the current position by calling f.tell, and change the current position by calling f.seek, both covered in the next section.

Attributes and Methods of File Objects

A file object f supplies the attributes and methods documented in this section.

close	f.close( ) Closes the file. You can call no other method on f after f.close. Multiple calls to f.close are allowed and innocuous.
closed	f.closed is a read-only attribute that is True if f.close( ) has been called, otherwise False.
flush	f.flush( ) Requests that f's buffer be written out to the operating system, ensuring that the file as seen by the system has exactly the contents that Python's code has written to f. Depending on the platform and on the nature of f's underlying file, f.flush may or may not be able to ensure the desired effect.
isatty	f.isatty( ) Returns True if f's file is an interactive terminal, otherwise False.
fileno	f.fileno( ) Returns an integer, the file descriptor of f's file at operating system level. File descriptors were covered in "File Descriptor Operations" earlier in this chapter.
mode	f.mode is a read-only attribute that is the value of the *mode* string used in the open call that created f.

name	f.name is a read-only attribute that is the value of the *filename* string used in the open call that created f.
read	f.read(*size*=-1)
	Reads up to *size* bytes from f's file and returns them as a string. read reads and returns less than *size* bytes if the file ends before *size* bytes are read. When *size* is less than 0, read reads and returns all bytes up to the end of the file. read returns an empty string only if the file's current position is at the end of the file or if *size* equals 0.
readline	f.readline(*size*=-1)
	Reads and returns one line from f's file, up to the end of line (\n) included. If *size* is greater than or equal to 0, readline reads no more than about *size* bytes. In this case, the returned string may not end with \n. \n may also be absent if readline reads up to the end of the file without finding \n. readline returns an empty string only if the file's current position is at the end of the file or if *size* equals 0.
readlines	f.readlines(*size*=-1)
	Reads and returns a list of all lines in f's file, each a string ending in \n. If *size*>0, readlines stops and returns the list after collecting data for a total of about *size* bytes, rather than reading all the way to the end of the file.
seek	f.seek(*pos*,*how*=0)
	Sets f's current position to the signed integer byte offset *pos* from a reference point. *how* indicates the reference point: when *how* is 0, the reference is the start of the file; when it is 1, the reference is the current position; and when it is 2, the reference is the end of the file. When f is opened in text mode, the effects of f.seek may not be as expected, due to the implied translations between os.linesep and \n. This troublesome effect does not occur on Unix platforms, nor when f is opened in binary mode, nor when f.seek is called with a *pos* that is the result of a previous call to f.tell and *how* is 0. When f is opened in mode 'a' or 'a+', all data written to f is appended to the data that is already in f, regardless of calls to f.seek.
softspace	f.softspace is a read-write attribute that is used internally by the print statement to keep track of its own state. A file object does not alter nor interpret softspace in any way: it just lets the attribute be freely read and written, and print takes care of the rest.

tell	f.tell( )
	Returns f's current position, an integer offset in bytes from the start of the file.
truncate	f.truncate([*size*])
	Truncates f's file. When *size* is present, truncates the file to be at most *size* bytes. When *size* is absent, uses f.tell( ) as the file's new size.
write	f.write(*str*)
	Writes the bytes of string *str* to the file.
writelines	f.writelines(*lst*)
	Like:
	`    for line in lst: f.write(line)`
	It does not matter whether the strings in sequence *lst* are lines: despite its name, method writelines just writes the strings to the file, one after another, without alterations or additions.
xreadlines	f.xreadlines( )
	Like xreadlines.xreadlines(f), as covered in "The xreadlines Module" later in this chapter. Method xreadlines will be deprecated in Python 2.3.

Iteration on File Objects

A file object f open for text-mode reading supports iteration. In other words, iter(f) returns an iterator whose items are the file's lines, so that the loop:

```
for line in f:
```

iterates on each line of the file. Interrupting such a loop prematurely (e.g., with break) leaves the file's current position with an arbitrary value. Calling methods that modify f's state, such as f.seek, during such a loop has an undefined effect. On the plus side, such a loop has very good performance, since these specifications allow the loop to use internal buffering to minimize I/O. Iteration on file objects is available only in Python 2.2 and later.

File-Like Objects and Polymorphism

An object x is file-like when it behaves *polymorphically* to a file, meaning that a function (or some other subset of a program) can use x as if x were a file. Code that uses such an object (known as client code of that object) typically receives the object as an argument or obtains it by calling a factory function that returns the object as the result. If the only method that a client-code function calls on *x* is *x*.read( ), without arguments, all that *x* needs to supply in order to be file-like for that function is a method read that is callable without arguments and returns a string. Other client-code functions, however, may need *x* to implement a broader subset of file object methods. Thus, file-like objects and polymorphism are not absolute concepts, but are instead relative to demands placed upon an object by client code.

Polymorphism is a powerful aspect of object-oriented programming, and file-like objects are an excellent example of polymorphism. A client-code module that writes to or reads from files can automatically be reused for data residing elsewhere, as long as the module does not break polymorphism by the dubious practice of type testing. When we discussed the built-ins type and isinstance in Chapter 8, I mentioned that type testing is often best avoided, since it blocks the normal polymorphism that Python otherwise supplies. Sometimes you may have no choice. For example, the marshal module, covered in Chapter 11, demands real file objects. Therefore, if your client code needs to use marshal, your code must also deal with real file objects, not just file-like ones. However, such situations are rare. Most often, supporting polymorphism in your client code takes nothing more than some care in avoiding type testing.

You can implement a file-like object by coding your own class, as covered in Chapter 5, and defining the specific methods needed by client code, such as read. A file-like object *f1* need not implement all the attributes and methods of a true file object *f*. If you can determine which methods client code calls on *f1*, you can choose to implement only that subset. For example, when *f1* is only meant to be written, *f1* doesn't need methods read, readline, and readlines.

When you implement a file-like object *f1*, make sure that *f1*.softspace can be read and written if you want *f1* to be usable by print. You need not alter nor interpret softspace in any way. Note that this behavior is the default when you write *f1*'s class in Python. You need to take specific care only when *f1*'s class overrides special methods __getattr__ and __setattr__ or otherwise controls access to its instances' attributes (e.g., by defining __slots__) as covered in Chapter 5. For example, if your class is a new-style class and defines __slots__, your class must have a slot named softspace, assuming you want instances of your class to be usable with the print statement.

If the main reason you want to use a file-like object instead of a real file object is to keep the data in memory, you can often make use of modules StringIO and cStringIO, covered later in this chapter. These modules supply file-like objects that hold data in memory while behaving polymorphically to file objects to a wide extent.

Auxiliary Modules for File I/O

File objects supply all functionality that is strictly needed for file I/O. There are some auxiliary Python library modules, however, that offer convenient supplementary functionality, making I/O even easier and handier in several important special cases.

The fileinput Module

The fileinput module lets you loop over all the lines in a list of text files. Performance is quite good, comparable to the performance of direct iteration on each file, since fileinput uses internal buffering to minimize I/O. Therefore, you can use module fileinput for line-oriented file input whenever you find the module's rich functionality convenient, without worrying about performance. The input function is the main function of module fileinput, and the module also provides a FileInput class that supports the same functionality as the module's functions.

close	close( )
	Closes the whole sequence, so that iteration stops and no file remains open.

FileInput	class FileInput(*files*=None,*inplace*=0,*backup*='',*bufsize*=0)
	Creates and returns an instance *f* of class FileInput. Arguments are the same as for fileinput.input, and methods of *f* have the same names, arguments, and semantics as functions of module fileinput. *f* also supplies a method readline, which reads and returns the next line. You can use class FileInput explicitly, rather than the single implicit instance used by the functions of module fileinput, when you want to nest or otherwise mix loops that read lines from more than one sequence of files.

filelineno	filelineno( )
	Returns the number of lines read so far from the file now being read. For example, returns 1 if the first line has just been read from the current file.

filename	filename( )
	Returns the name of the file being read, or None if no line has been read yet.

input	input(*files*=None,*inplace*=0,*backup*='',*bufsize*=0)
	Returns the sequence of lines in the files, suitable for use in a for loop. *files* is a sequence of filenames to open and read one after the other, in order. Filename '-' means standard input (sys.stdin). If *files* is a string, it's a single filename to open and read. If *files* is None, input uses sys.argv[1:] as the list of filenames If the sequence of filenames is empty, input reads sys.stdin.
	The sequence object that input returns is an instance of class FileInput; that instance is also the global state of module input, so all other functions of module fileinput operate on the same shared state. Each function of module fileinput corresponds directly to a method of class FileInput.

When *inplace* is false (the default), input just reads the files. When *inplace* is true, however, input moves each file being read (except standard input) to a backup file, and redirects standard output (sys.stdout) to write to the file being read. This operation lets you simulate overwriting files in-place. If *backup* is a string starting with a dot, input uses *backup* as the extension of the backup files and does not remove the backup files. If *backup* is an empty string (the default), input uses extension *.bak*, and deletes each backup file when the file is closed.

bufsize is the size of the internal buffer that input uses to read lines from the input files. If *bufsize* is 0, input uses a buffer of 8192 bytes.

isfirstline   isfirstline( )

Returns True or False, just like filelineno( )==1.

isstdin   isstdin( )

Returns True if the file now being read is sys.stdin, otherwise False.

lineno   lineno( )

Returns the total number of lines read so far since the call to input.

nextfile   nextfile( )

Closes the file now being read, so that the next line to be read will be the first one of the following file.

The linecache Module

The linecache module lets you read a given line (specified by number) from a file with a given name. The module keeps an internal cache, so if you need to read several lines from a file, the operation is cheaper than opening and examining the file each time. Module linecache exposes the following functions.

checkcache   checkcache( )

Ensures that the module's cache holds no stale data, but rather reflects what's on the filesystem. Call checkcache when the files you're reading may have changed on the filesystem, if you need to ensure that future calls to getline return updated information.

clearcache   clearcache( )

Drops the module's cache so that the memory can be reused for other purposes. Call clearcache when you don't need to perform any more reading for now.

getline   getline(*filename*,*lineno*)

Reads and returns the *lineno* line from the text file named *filename*, including the trailing \n. For any error, getline does not raise exceptions, but rather returns the empty string ''. If *filename* is not found, getline also looks for the file in the directories listed in sys.path.

The struct Module

The struct module lets you pack binary data into a string, and then unpack the bytes of such a string back into the data they represent. Such operations can be useful for various kinds of low-level programming. Most often, you use module struct to interpret data records from binary files having some specified format or to prepare records to be written to such binary files. The module's name comes from C's keyword struct, which is usable for related purposes. On any error, functions of module struct raise exceptions that are instances of exception class struct.error, the only class that the module supplies.

Operations of module struct rely on struct format strings, which are ordinary strings that follow a specified syntax. The first character of a format string can specify the byte order, size, and alignment of packed data:

@   Native byte order, native data sizes, and native alignment for the current plat-
    form; this is the default, if the first character is none of the characters listed
    here (note that format P in Table 10-2 is available only for this kind of format
    string)

=   Native byte order for the current platform, but standard size and alignment

<   Little-endian byte order (like Intel platforms), standard size and alignment

>, ! Big-endian byte order (network-standard), standard size and alignment

Standard sizes are indicated in Table 10-2. Standard alignment means that there is no forced alignment and that explicit pad bytes are used if needed. Native sizes and alignment are whatever the platform's C compiler uses. Native byte order is either little-endian or big-endian, depending on the current platform.

After the optional leading character, a format string is made up of one or more format characters that can be preceded by an optional count (an integer represented by its decimal digits). The possible format characters are shown in Table 10-2. For most format characters, the count indicates repetition (e.g., '3h' is exactly the same as 'hhh'). When the format character is s or p, indicating a string, the count is not a repetition, but rather the total number of bytes occupied by the string. Whitespace can be freely and innocuously used between formats, but not between a count and its format character.

Table 10-2. Format characters for struct

Character	C type	Python type	Standard size
B	unsigned char	int	1 byte
b	signed char	int	1 byte
c	char	str (length 1)	1 byte
d	double	float	8 bytes
f	float	float	4 bytes
H	unsigned short	int	2 bytes
h	signed short	int	2 bytes
I	unsigned int	long	4 bytes
i	signed int	int	4 bytes
L	unsigned long	long	4 bytes
l	signed long	int	4 bytes
P	void*	int	N/A
p	char[ ]	string	N/A
s	char[ ]	string	N/A
x	padding byte	no value	1 byte

Format s denotes a fixed-length string, exactly as long as its count (the Python string is truncated or padded with copies of the null character '\0', if needed). Format p denotes a Pascal-like string: the first byte is the number of significant characters, and the characters start from the second byte. The count indicates the total number of bytes, including the length byte.

Module struct supplies the following functions.

calcsize calcsize(*fmt*)

Returns the size in bytes of the structure corresponding to format string *fmt*.

pack pack(*fmt*,**values*)

Packs the given values according to format string *fmt* and returns the resulting string. *values* must match in number and types the values required by *fmt*.

unpack unpack(*fmt*,*str*)

Unpacks binary string *str* according to format string *fmt* and returns a tuple of values. len(*str*) must be equal to struct. calcsize(*fmt*).

The xreadlines Module

The xreadlines module will be deprecated in Python 2.3. You should avoid it in Python 2.2, since directly iterating on a file object is at least as fast. If you need to support Python 2.1, module xreadlines and the xreadlines method of file objects are a good choice in terms of input performance. Module fileinput, covered earlier in this chapter, is a good compromise if your code needs to support many different versions of Python, and still get good performance. The xreadlines module supplies one function.

---

xreadlines   xreadlines(*f*)

Accepts argument *f*, which must be a file object or a file-like object with a readlines method like that of file objects. Returns a sequence object *x* that is usable in a for statement or as the argument to built-in functions such as filter. *x* represents the same sequence of strings as *f*.readlines( ), but *x* does so in a lazy way, limiting memory consumption. xreadlines is to readlines much like xrange is to range.

The StringIO and cStringIO Modules

You can implement file-like objects by writing Python classes that supply the methods you need. If all you want is for data to reside in memory rather than on a file as seen by the operating system, you can use the StringIO or cStringIO module. The two modules are almost identical: each supplies a factory function to create in-memory file-like objects. The difference between them is that objects created by module StringIO are instances of class StringIO.StringIO. You may inherit from this class to create your own customized file-like objects, overriding the methods that you need to specialize. Objects created by module cStringIO, on the other hand, are instances of a special-purpose type, not of a class. Performance is much better when you can use cStringIO, but inheritance is not feasible. Furthermore, cStringIO does not support Unicode.

Each module supplies a factory function named StringIO that creates a file-like object *fl*.

StringIO   StringIO(*str*='')

Creates and returns an in-memory file-like object *fl*, with all methods and attributes of a built-in file object. The data contents of *fl* are initialized to be a copy of argument *str*, which must be a plain string for the StringIO factory function in cStringIO, while it can be a plain or Unicode string for the function in StringIO.

Besides all methods and attributes of built-in file objects, as covered in "Attributes and Methods of File Objects" earlier in this chapter, *fl* supplies one supplementary method, getvalue.

getvalue   *fl*.getvalue( )

Returns the current data contents of *fl* as a string. You cannot call *fl*.getvalue after you call *fl*.close: close frees the buffer that *fl* internally keeps, and getvalue needs to access the buffer to yield its result.

Compressed Files

Although storage space and transmission bandwidth are increasingly cheap and abundant, in many cases you can save such resources, at the expense of some computational effort, by using compression. Since computational power grows cheaper and more abundant even faster than other resources, such as bandwidth, compression's popularity keeps growing. Python makes it easy for your programs to support compression by supplying dedicated modules for compression as part of every Python distribution.

The gzip Module

The gzip module lets you read and write files compatible with those handled by the powerful GNU compression programs *gzip* and *gunzip*. The GNU programs support several compression formats, but module gzip supports only the highly effective native *gzip* format, normally denoted by appending the extension *.gz* to a filename. Module gzip supplies the GzipFile class and an open factory function.

GzipFile   class GzipFile(*filename*=None,*mode*=None,*compresslevel*=9,
                              fileobj=None)

Creates and returns a file-like object *f* that wraps the file or file-like object *fileobj*. *f* supplies all methods of built-in file objects except seek and tell. Thus, *f* is not seekable: you can only access *f* sequentially, whether for reading or writing. When *fileobj* is None, *filename* must be a string that names a file: GzipFile opens that file with the given *mode* (by default, 'rb'), and *f* wraps the resulting file object. *mode* should be one of 'ab', 'rb', 'wb', or None. If *mode* is None, *f* uses the mode of *fileobj* if it is able to find out the mode; otherwise it uses 'rb'. If *filename* is None, *f* uses the filename of *fileobj* if able to find out the name; otherwise it uses ''. *compresslevel* is an integer between 1 and 9: 1 requests modest compression but fast operation, and 9 requests the best compression feasible, even if that requires more computation.

File-like object *f* generally delegates all methods to the underlying file-like object *fileobj*, transparently accounting for compression as needed. However, *f* does not allow non-sequential access, so *f* does not supply methods seek and tell. Moreover, calling *f*.close does *not* close *fileobj* when *f* was created with an argument *fileobj* that is not None. This behavior of *f*.close is very important when *fileobj* is an instance of StringIO.StringIO, since it means you can call *fileobj*.getvalue after *f*.close to get the compressed data as a string. This behavior also means that you have to call *fileobj*.close explicitly after calling *f*.close.

---

open   open(*filename*,*mode*='rb',*compresslevel*=9)

Like GzipFile(*filename*,*mode*,*compresslevel*), but *filename* is mandatory and there is no provision for passing an already opened *fileobj*.

Say that you have some function *f(x)* that writes data to a text file object *x*, typically by calling *x*.write and/or *x*.writelines. Getting *f* to write data to a *gzip*-compressed text file instead is easy:

```
import gzip
underlying_file = open('x.txt.gz', 'wb')
compressing_wrapper = gzip.GzipFile(fileobj=underlying_file, mode='wt')
f(compressing_wrapper)
compressing_wrapper.close( )
underlying_file.close( )
```

This example opens the underlying binary file *x.txt.gz* and explicitly wraps it with gzip.GzipFile, and thus, at the end, we need to close each object separately. This is necessary because we want to use two different modes: the underlying file must be opened in binary mode (any translation of line endings would produce an invalid compressed file), but the compressing wrapper must be opened in text mode because we want the implicit translation of os.linesep to \n. Reading back a compressed text file, for example to display it on standard output, is similar:

```
import gzip, xreadlines
underlying_file = open('x.txt.gz', 'rb')
uncompressing_wrapper = gzip.GzipFile(fileobj= underlying_file, mode='rt')
for line in xreadlines.xreadlines(uncompressing_wrapper):
    print line,
uncompressing_wrapper.close( )
underlying_file.close( )
```

This example uses module xreadlines, covered earlier in this chapter, because GzipFile objects (at least up to Python 2.2) are not iterable like true file objects, nor do they supply an xreadlines method. GzipFile objects do supply a readlines method that closely emulates that of true file objects, and therefore module xreadlines is able to produce a lazy sequence that wraps a GzipFile object and lets us iterate on the GzipFile object's lines.

The zipfile Module

The zipfile module lets you read and write ZIP files (i.e., archive files compatible with those handled by popular compression programs *zip* and *unzip*, *pkzip* and *pkunzip*, *WinZip*, and so on). Detailed information on the formats and capabilities of ZIP files can be found at *http://www.pkware.com/appnote.html* and *http://www.info-zip.org/pub/infozip/*. You need to study this detailed information in order to perform advanced ZIP file handing with module zipfile.

Module zipfile can't handle ZIP files with appended comments, multidisk ZIP files, or *.zip* archive members using compression types besides the usual ones, known as stored (when a file is copied to the archive without compression) and deflated (when a file is compressed using the ZIP format's default algorithm). For invalid *.zip* file errors, functions of module zipfile raise exceptions that are instances of exception class zipfile.error. Module zipfile supplies the following classes and functions.

is_zipfile	is_zipfile(*filename*) Returns True if the file named by string *filename* appears to be a valid ZIP file, judging by the first few bytes of the file; otherwise returns False.

ZipInfo	class ZipInfo(*filename*='NoName',*date_time*=(1980,1,1,0,0,0))
	
	Methods getinfo and infolist of ZipFile instances return instances of ZipInfo to supply information about members of the archive. The most useful attributes supplied by a ZipInfo instance *z* are:
	
	comment
	    A string that is a comment on the archive member
	
	compress_size
	    Size in bytes of the compressed data for the archive member
	
	compress_type
	    An integer code recording the type of compression of the archive member
	
	date_time
	    A tuple with 6 integers recording the time of last modification to the file: the items are year, month, day (1 and up), hour, minute, second (0 and up)
	
	file_size
	    Size in bytes of the uncompressed data for the archive member
	
	filename
	    Name of the file in the archive

ZipFile	class ZipFile(*filename*,*mode*='r',*compression*=zipfile.ZIP_STORED) Opens a ZIP file named by string *filename*. *mode* can be 'r', to read an existing ZIP file; 'w', to write a new ZIP file or truncate and rewrite an existing one; or 'a', to append to an existing file.

When *mode* is 'a', *filename* can name either an existing ZIP file (in which case new members are added to the existing archive) or an existing non-ZIP file. In the latter case, a new ZIP file–like archive is created and appended to the existing file. The main purpose of this latter case is to let you build a self-unpacking *.exe* file (i.e., a Windows executable file that unpacks itself when run). The existing file must then be a fresh copy of an unpacking *.exe* prefix, as supplied by *www.info-zip.org* or by other purveyors of ZIP file compression tools.

compression is an integer code that can be either of two attributes of module zipfile. zipfile.ZIP_STORED requests that the archive use no compression, and zipfile.ZIP_DEFLATED requests that the archive use the *deflation* mode of compression (i.e., the most usual and effective compression approach used in *.zip* files).

A ZipFile instance *z* supplies the following methods.

close   z.close( )

Closes archive file *z*. Make sure the close method is called, or else an incomplete and unusable ZIP file might be left on disk. Such mandatory finalization is generally best performed with a try/ finally statement, as covered in Chapter 6.

getinfo   z.getinfo(*name*)

Returns a ZipInfo instance that supplies information about the archive member named by string *name*.

infolist   z.infolist( )

Returns a list of ZipInfo instances, one for each member in archive *z*, in the same order as the entries in the archive itself.

namelist   z.namelist( )

Returns a list of strings, the names of each member in archive *z*, in the same order as the entries in the archive itself.

printdir   z.printdir( )

Outputs a textual directory of the archive *z* to file sys.stdout.

read   z.read(*name*)

Returns a string containing the uncompressed bytes of the file named by string *name* in archive *z*. *z* must be opened for 'r' or 'a'. When the archive does not contain a file named *name*, read raises an exception.

testzip   `z.testzip( )`

Reads and checks the files in archive z. Returns a string with the name of the first archive member that is damaged, or None when the archive is intact.

write   `z.write(filename,arcname=None,compress_type=None)`

Writes the file named by string *filename* to archive z, with archive member name *arcname*. When *arcname* is None, write uses *filename* as the archive member name. When *compress_type* is None, write uses z's compression type; otherwise, *compress_type* is zipfile. ZIP_STORED or zipfile.ZIP_DEFLATED, and specifies how to compress the file. z must be opened for 'w' or 'a'.

writestr   `z.writestr(zinfo,bytes)`

zinfo must be a ZipInfo instance specifying at least *filename* and *date_time*. *bytes* is a string of bytes. writestr adds a member to archive z, using the metadata specified by *zinfo* and the data in *bytes*. z must be opened for 'w' or 'a'. When you have data in memory and need to write the data to the ZIP file archive z, it's simpler and faster to use z.writestr rather than z.write. The latter approach would require you to write the data to disk first, and later remove the useless disk file. The following example shows both approaches, each encapsulated into a function, polymorphic to each other:

```
import zipfile
def data_to_zip_direct(z, data, name):
    import time
    zinfo = zipfile.ZipInfo(name, time.localtime( )[:6])
    z.writestr(zinfo, data)
def data_to_zip_indirect(z, data, name):
    import os
    flob = open(name, 'wb')
    flob.write(data)
    flob.close( )
    z.write(name)
    os.unlink(name)
zz = zipfile.ZipFile('z.zip', 'w', zipfile.ZIP_DEFLATED)
data = 'four score\nand seven\nyears ago\n'
data_to_zip_direct(zz, data, 'direct.txt')
data_to_zip_indirect(zz, data, 'indirect.txt')
zz.close( )
```

Besides being faster and more concise, data_to_zip_direct is handier because, by working in memory, it doesn't need to have the current working directory be writable, as data_to_zip_indirect does. Of course, method write also has its uses, but that's mostly when you already have the data in a file on disk, and just want to add the file to the archive. Here's how you can print a list of all files contained in the ZIP file archive created by the previous example, followed by each file's name and contents:

```
import zipfile
zz = zipfile.ZipFile('z.zip')
zz.printdir()
for name in zz.namelist():
    print '%s: %r' % (name, zz.read(name))
zz.close()
```

The zlib Module

The zlib module lets Python programs use the free InfoZip *zlib* compression library (see *http://www.info-zip.org/pub/infozip/zlib/*), Version 1.1.3 or later. Module zlib is used by modules gzip and zipfile, but the module is also available directly for any special compression needs. This section documents the most commonly used functions supplied by module zlib.

Module zlib also supplies functions to compute Cyclic-Redundancy Check (CRC) checksums, in order to detect possible damage in compressed data. It also provides objects that can compress and decompress data incrementally, and thus enable you to work with data streams that are too large to fit in memory at once. For such advanced functionality, consult the Python library's online reference.

Note that files containing data compressed with zlib are not automatically interchangeable with other programs, with the exception of files that use the zipfile module and therefore respect the standard format of ZIP file archives. You could write a custom program, with any language able to use InfoZip's free *zlib* compression library, in order to read files produced by Python programs using the zlib module. However, if you do need to interchange compressed data with programs coded in other languages, I suggest you use modules gzip or zipfile instead. Module zlib may be useful when you want to compress some parts of data files that are in some proprietary format of your own, and need not be interchanged with any other program except those that make up your own application.

compress   compress(*str*,*level*=6)

Compresses string *str* and returns the string of compressed data. *level* is an integer between 1 and 9: 1 requests modest compression but fast operation, and 9 requests compression as good as feasible, thus requiring more computation.

decompress   decompress(*str*)

Decompresses the compressed data string *str* and returns the string of uncompressed data.

Text Input and Output

Python presents non-GUI text input and output channels to your programs as file objects, so you can use the methods of file objects (covered in "File Objects" earlier in this chapter) to manipulate these channels.

Standard Output and Standard Error

The sys module, covered in Chapter 8, has attributes stdout and stderr, file objects to which you can write. Unless you are using some sort of shell redirection, these streams connect to the terminal in which your script is running. Nowadays, actual terminals are rare: the terminal is generally a screen window that supports text input/output (e.g., an MS-DOS Prompt console on Windows or an *xterm* window on Unix).

The distinction between sys.stdout and sys.stderr is a matter of convention. sys.stdout, known as your script's standard output, is where your program emits results. sys.stderr, known as your script's standard error, is where error messages go. Separating program results from error messages helps you use shell redirection effectively. Python respects this convention, using sys.stderr for error and warning messages.

The print Statement

Programs that output results to standard output often need to write to sys.stdout. Python's print statement can be a convenient alternative to sys.stdout.write. The print statement has the following syntax:

```
print [>>fileobject,] expressions [,]
```

The normal destination of print's output is the file or file-like object that is the value of the stdout attribute of the sys module. However, when >>*fileobject,* is present right after keyword print, the statement uses the given *fileobject* instead of sys.stdout. *expressions* is a list of zero or more expressions separated by commas (,). print outputs each expression, in order, as a string (using the built-in str, covered in Chapter 8), with a space to separate strings. After all expressions, print by default outputs '\n' to terminate the line. When a trailing comma is present at the end of the statement, however, print does not output the closing '\n'.

print works well for the kind of informal output used during development to help you debug your code. For production output, you often need more control of formatting than print affords. You may need to control spacing, field widths, the number of decimals for floating-point values, and so on. In this case, prepare the output as a string with the string-formatting operator % covered in Chapter 9. Then, you can output the resulting string, normally with the write method of the appropriate file object.

When you want to direct print's output to another file, you can temporarily change sys.stdout. The following example shows a general-purpose redirection function that you can use for such a temporary change:

```
def redirect(func, *args, **kwds):
    """redirect(func, …) -> (output string result, func's return value)

    func must be a callable that outputs results to standard output.
    redirect captures those results in memory and returns a pair, with
    the results as the first item and func's return value as the second
    one.
    """
    import sys, cStringIO
    save_out = sys.stdout
    sys.stdout = cStringIO.StringIO( )
    try:
        retval = func(*args, **kwds)
        return sys.stdout.getvalue( ), retval
    finally:
        sys.stdout.close( )
        sys.stdout = save_out
```

When all you want is to output some text values to a file object *f* that isn't the current value of sys.stdout, you won't normally perform complicated manipulations as shown in the previous example. Rather, for such simple purposes, just calling *f*.write is usually best.

Standard Input

The sys module provides the stdin attribute, which is a file object from which you can read text. When you need a line of text from the user, call the built-in function raw_input (covered in Chapter 8), optionally with a string argument to use as a prompt.

When the input you need is not a string (for example, when you need a number), you can use built-in function input. However, input is unsuitable for most programs. More often, you use raw_input to obtain a string from the user, then other built-ins, such as int or float, to get a number from the string. You can also use eval (normally preceded by compile, for better control of error diagnostics), as long as you trust the user totally. A malicious user can easily exploit eval to breach security and cause damage. When you do have to use eval on untrusted input, be sure to use the restricted-execution tools covered in Chapter 13.

The getpass Module

Occasionally, you want the user to input a line of text in such a way that somebody looking at the screen cannot see what the user is typing. This often occurs when you're asking the user for a password. The getpass module provides the following functions.

getpass   getpass(*prompt*='Password: ')

                      Like raw_input, except that the line of text the user inputs in response is not echoed to the screen while the user is typing it. Also, getpass's default *prompt* is different from raw_input's.

getuser	getuser( )
	Returns the current user's username. First, getuser tries to get the username as the value of one of environment variables LOGNAME, USER, LNAME, and USERNAME, in this order. If none of these variables are keys in os.environ, getuser tries asking the operating system for the username.

Richer-Text I/O

The tools we have covered so far support the minimal subset of text I/O functionality that all platforms supply. Most platforms also offer richer-text I/O capabilities, such as responding to single keypresses (not just to entire lines of text) and showing text in any spot of the terminal (not just sequentially).

Python extensions and core Python modules let you access platform-specific functionality. Unfortunately, various platforms expose this functionality in different ways. To develop cross-platform Python programs with rich-text I/O functionality, you may need to wrap different modules uniformly, importing platform-specific modules conditionally (usually with the try/except idiom covered in Chapter 6).

The readline Module

The readline module wraps the GNU Readline Library. Readline lets the user edit text lines during interactive input, and also recall previous lines for further editing and re-entry. GNU Readline is widely installed on Unix-like platforms, and is available at *http://cnswww.cns.cwru.edu/~chet/readline/rltop.html*. A Windows port (*http://starship.python.net/crew/kernr/*) is available, but not widely deployed. Chris Gonnerman's module, Alternative Readline for Windows, implements a subset of Python's standard readline module (using a small dedicated *.pyd* file instead of GNU Readline) and can be freely downloaded from *http://newcenturycomputers. net/projects/readline.html*.

When either readline module is loaded, Python uses Readline for all line-oriented input, such as raw_input. The interactive Python interpreter always tries loading readline to enable line editing and recall for interactive sessions. You can call functions supplied by module readline to control advanced functionality, particularly the history functionality for recalling lines entered in previous sessions, and the completion functionality for context-sensitive completion of the word being entered. See *http://cnswww.cns.cwru.edu/~chet/readline/rltop.html#Documentation* for GNU Readline documentation, with details on configuration commands. Alternative Readline also supports history, but the completion-related functions it supplies are dummy ones: these functions don't perform any operation, and exist only for compatibility with GNU Readline.

get_history_ length	get_history_length( ) Returns the number of lines of history that are saved to the history file. When the returned value is less than 0, all lines in the history are saved.
parse_and_ bind	parse_and_bind(*readline_cmd*) Gives Readline a configuration command. To let the user hit Tab to request completion, call parse_and_bind('tab: complete'). See the GNU Readline documentation for other useful values of *readline_ cmd*.
read_history_ file	read_history_file(*filename*='~/.history') Loads history lines from the text file whose name or path is *filename*.
read_init_file	read_init_file(*filename*=None) Makes Readline load a text file, where each line is a configuration command. When *filename* is None, Readline loads the same file as last time.
set_completer	set_completer(*f*=None) Sets the completion function. When *f* is None, Readline disables completion. Otherwise, when the user enters a partial word *start* and then hits Tab, Readline calls *f*(*start,i*), where *i* is an int, initially 0. *f* returns the *i*th possible word that begins with *start*, or None when there are no more. Readline calls *f* repeatedly, with *i* set to 0, 1, 2, ..., until *f* returns None.
set_history_ length	set_history_length(*x*) Sets the number of lines of history that are saved to the history file. When *x* is less than 0, all lines in the history are saved.
write_history_ file	write_history_file(*filename*='~/.history') Saves history lines to the text file whose name or path is *filename*.

An example of a completion function is in module rlcompleter. In an interactive interpreter session (or, more practically, in the startup file that the interpreter runs at the start of each interactive session, as covered in Chapter 3), you can enter:

```
import readline, rlcompleter
readline.parse_and_bind('tab: complete')
```

Now, for the rest of this interactive session, you can hit Tab during line editing and get completion for global names and object attributes.

Console I/O

Terminals today are most often text windows on a graphical screen. You may also use a true terminal or the console (main screen) of a personal computer in text mode. All kinds of terminals in use today support advanced text I/O functionality, but you access this functionality in platform-dependent ways. The curses package works only on Unix-like platforms (there are persistent rumors of Windows ports of it, but I've never found a working one). Modules msvcrt, WConio, and Console work only on Windows.

The curses package

The traditional Unix approach to advanced terminal I/O is named *curses*, for obscure historical reasons.[*] The Python package curses affords reasonably simple use, but still lets you exert detailed control if required. I cover a small subset of curses, enough to let you write programs with rich text I/O functionality. See also Eric Raymond's tutorial *Curses Programming with Python*, available at *http://py-howto.sourceforge.net/curses/curses.html*, for more information. Whenever I mention the screen in this section, I mean the screen of the terminal (for example, the text window of a terminal-emulator program).

The simplest and most effective way to use curses is through the curses.wrapper module, which supplies a single function.

---

wrapper   wrapper(*func*,**args*)

Performs curses initialization, calls *func*(stdscr,**args*), performs curses finalization (setting the terminal back to normal behavior), and finally returns *func*'s result. The first argument that wrapper passes to *func* is stdscr, an object of type curses.Window that represents the whole terminal screen. wrapper ensures that the terminal is set back to normal behavior, whether *func* terminates normally or by propagating an exception.

func should be a function that performs all the tasks in your program that may need curses functionality. In other words, *func* normally contains (or more commonly calls, directly or indirectly, functions containing) all of your program's functionality, save perhaps for some non-interactive initialization and/or finalization tasks.

---

curses models text and background colors of characters as character attributes. Colors available on the terminal are numbered from 0 to curses.COLORS. Function color_content takes a color number n as its argument, and returns a tuple (r,g,b) of integers between 0 and 1000 giving the amount of each primary color in n.

---

[*] "curses" does describe well the typical utterances of programmers faced with this rich, complicated approach.

Function color_pair takes a color number *n* as its argument, and returns an attribute code that you can pass to various methods of a curses.Window object in order to display text in that color.

curses lets you create multiple instances of type curses.Window, each corresponding to a rectangle on the screen. You can also create exotic variants, such as instances of Panel, which are polymorphic with Window but not tied to a fixed screen rectangle. You do not need such advanced functionality in simple curses programs: just use the Window object stdscr that curses.wrapper gives you. Call w.refresh() to ensure that changes made to any Window instance *w*, including stdscr, show up on screen. curses can buffer the changes until you call refresh. An instance *w* of Window supplies, among many others, the following frequently used methods.

addstr	w.addstr([*y,x,*]*str*[,*attr*])
	Puts the characters in string *str*, with attribute *attr*, on *w* at the given coordinates (*x,y*), overwriting any previous contents. All curses functions and methods accept coordinate arguments in reverse order, with *y* (the row number) before *x* (the column number). If you omit *y,x*, addstr uses *w*'s current cursor coordinates. If you omit *attr*, addstr uses *w*'s current default attribute. In any case, addstr, when done adding the string, sets *w*'s current cursor coordinates to the end of the string it has added.
clrtobot, clrtoeol	w.clrtobot( ) w.clrtoeol( )
	clrtoeol writes blanks from *w*'s current cursor coordinates to the end of the line. clrtobot, in addition, also blanks all lines lower down on the screen.
delch	w.delch([*y,x*])
	Deletes one character from *w* at the given coordinates (*x,y*). If you omit the *y,x* arguments, delch uses *w*'s current cursor coordinates. In any case, delch does not change *w*'s current cursor coordinates. All the following characters in line *y*, if any, shift left by one.
deleteln	w.deleteln( )
	Deletes from *w* the entire line at *w*'s current cursor coordinates, and scrolls up by one line all lines lower down on the screen.
erase	w.erase( )
	Writes spaces to the entire terminal screen.
getch	w.getch( )
	Returns an integer *c* corresponding to a user keystroke. *c* between 0 and 255 represents an ordinary character, while *c* greater than 255

represents a special key. curses supplies names for special keys, so you can test *c* for equality with such readable constants as curses. KEY_HOME (the Home special key), curses.KEY_LEFT (the left-arrow special key), and so on. The list of all curses special-key names (about 100 of them) is in Python's free documentation, specifically, in the *Python Library Reference*, Section *6.13.3 Constants*, for current versions of Python. If you have set window *w* to no-delay mode by calling *w*.nodelay(True), *w*.getch raises an exception if no keystroke is ready. By default, however, *w*.getch waits until the user hits a key.

getyx   `w.getyx( )`

Returns *w*'s current cursor coordinates as a tuple (*y*,*x*).

insstr   `w.insstr([y,x,]str[,attr])`

Inserts the characters in string *str*, with attribute *attr*, on *w* at the given coordinates (*x*,*y*), shifting the rest of line rightwards. Any characters that shift beyond the end of line are dropped. If you omit *y*,*x*, insstr uses *w*'s current cursor coordinates. If you omit *attr*, insstr uses *w*'s current default attribute. In any case, when done inserting the string, insstr sets *w*'s current cursor coordinates to the first character of the string it has inserted.

move   `w.move(y,x)`

Moves *w*'s cursor to the given coordinates (*x*,*y*).

nodelay   `w.nodelay(flag)`

Sets *w* to no-delay mode when *flag* is true, resets *w* back to normal mode when *flag* is false. No-delay mode affects method *w*.getch.

refresh   `w.refresh( )`

Updates window *w* on-screen with all changes the program has effected on *w*.

The curses.textpad module supplies the Textpad class, which lets you support advanced input.

Textpad   `class Textpad(window)`

Creates and returns an instance *t* of class Textpad that wraps the curses window instance *window*. Instance *t* has one frequently used method:

t.edit( )

Lets the user perform interactive editing on the contents of the window instance that *t* wraps. The editing session supports simple Emacs-like key bindings: normal characters overwrite the window's previous contents, arrow keys move the cursor, Ctrl-H deletes the character to the cursor's left. When the user hits Ctrl-G, the editing session ends, and edit returns the window's contents as a single string, with newlines as line separators.

The msvcrt module

The msvcrt module, available only on Windows, supplies functions that let Python programs access a few proprietary extras supplied by the Microsoft Visual C++'s runtime library *msvcrt.dll*. Some msvcrt functions let you read user input character by character, rather than reading a full line at a time.

getch, getche

getch( )
getche( )

Reads and returns one character from keyboard input, waiting if no character is yet available for reading. getche also echoes the character to screen (if printable), while getch doesn't. When the user presses a special key (arrows, function keys, etc.), it's seen as two characters: first a chr(0) or chr(224), then a second character that, together with the first one, defines what special key the user pressed. Here's how to find out what getch returns for any key:

```
import msvcrt
print "press z to exit, or any other key to see code"
while 1:
    c = msvcrt.getch( )
    if c == 'z': break
    print "%d (%r)" % (c, c)
```

kbhit

kbhit( )

Returns True when a character is available for reading (getch, if called, would return immediately), otherwise False (getch, if called, would wait).

ungetch

ungetch(*c*)

Ungets character *c*: the next call to getch or getche returns *c*. It's an error to call ungetch twice without intervening calls to getch or getche.

The WConio and Console modules

Two Windows-specific extension modules supply single-character keyboard input (like msvcrt) and the ability to paint characters in specified positions of the text screen. Chris Gonnerman's Windows Console I/O module is small, simple, and easy to use. Module WConio can be freely downloaded from *http://newcenturycomputers.net/projects/wconio.html*. Fredrik Lundh's Console module is very complete and functionally rich. Module Console can be freely downloaded from *http://www.effbot.org/efflib/console/*.

Interactive Command Sessions

The cmd module offers a simple way to handle interactive sessions of commands. Each command is a line of text. The first word of each command is a verb defining the requested action. The rest of the line is passed as an argument to the method that implements the action that the verb requests.

Module cmd supplies class Cmd to use as a base class, and you define your own subclass of cmd.Cmd. The subclass supplies methods with names starting with do_ and help_, and may also optionally override some of Cmd's methods. When the user enters a command line such as *verb and the rest*, as long as the subclass defines a method named do_*verb*, Cmd.onecmd calls:

```
self.do_verb('and the rest')
```

Similarly, as long as the subclass defines a method named help_*verb*, Cmd.do_help calls it when the command line starts with either 'help *verb*' or '?*verb*'. Cmd, by default, also shows suitable error messages if the user tries to use, or asks for help about, a verb for which the subclass does not define a needed method.

Methods of Cmd Instances

An instance *c* of a subclass of class Cmd supplies the following methods (many of these methods are meant to be overridden by the subclass).

---

cmdloop   c.cmdloop(*intro*=None)

Performs an entire interactive session of line-oriented commands. cmdloop starts by calling *c*.preloop( ), then outputs string *intro* (*c*.intro, if *intro* is None). Then *c*.cmdloop enters a loop. In each iteration of the loop, cmdloop reads line *s* with *s*=raw_input(*c*.prompt). When standard input reaches end-of-file, cmdloop sets *s*='EOF'. If *s* is not 'EOF', cmdloop preprocesses string *s* with *s*=*c*.precmd(*s*), then calls *flag*=*c*.onecmd(*s*). When onecmd returns a true value, this is a tentative request to terminate the command loop. Now cmdloop calls *flag*=*c*.postcmd(*flag*,*s*) to check if the loop should terminate. If *flag* is now true, the loop terminates; otherwise another iteration of the loop executes. If the loop is to terminate, cmdloop calls *c*.postloop( ), then terminates. This structure of cmdloop is probably easiest to understand by showing Python code equivalent to the method just described:

```
def cmdloop(self, intro=None):
    self.preloop()
    if intro is None: intro = self.intro
    print intro
    while True:
        try: s = raw_input(self.prompt)
        except EOFError: s = `EOF'
        else: s = self.precmd(s)
        flag = self.onecmd(s)
        flag = self.postcmd(flag, s)
        if flag: break
    self.postloop()
```

cmdloop is a good example of the design pattern known as
Template Method. Such a method performs little substantial work
itself; rather, it structures and organizes calls to other methods.
Subclasses may override the other methods, to define the details of
class behavior within the overall framework thus established.
When you inherit from Cmd, you almost never override method
cmdloop, since cmdloop's structure is the main thing you get by
subclassing Cmd.

default   c.default(s)

c.onecmd calls c.default(s) when there is no method c.do_verb for
the first word verb of line s. Subclasses often override default. The
base class Cmd.default method prints an error message.

do_help   c.do_help(verb)

c.onecmd calls c.do_help(verb) when command line s starts with
'help verb' or '?verb'. Subclasses rarely override do_help. The
Cmd.do_help method calls method help_verb if the subclass
supplies it, otherwise it displays the docstring of method do_verb if
the subclass supplies that method with a non-empty docstring. If
the subclass does not supply either source of help, Cmd.do_help
outputs a message to inform the user that no help is available on
verb.

emptyline   c.emptyline()

c.onecmd calls c.emptyline() when command line s is empty or
blank. Unless a subclass overrides this method, the base-class
method Cmd.emptyline is called and re-executes the last non-blank
command line seen, stored in the attribute c.lastcmd of c.

onecmd   c.onecmd(s)

c.cmdloop calls c.onecmd(s) for each command line s that the user
inputs. You can also call onecmd directly, if you have independently
obtained a line s that you need to process as a command.
Normally, subclasses do not override method onecmd. Cmd.onecmd
unconditionally sets c.lastcmd=s. Then, onecmd calls do_verb if s

starts with the word *verb* and if the subclass supplies such a method, or else methods emptyline or default, as explained earlier. In any case, Cmd.onecmd returns the result of whatever other method it ends up calling, to be interpreted by postcmd as a termination-request flag.

postcmd
c.postcmd(*flag*,s)

c.cmdloop calls c.postcmd(*flag*,s) for each command line s, after c.onecmd(s) has returned value *flag*. If *flag* is true, the command just executed is posing a conditional request to terminate the command loop. If postcmd returns a true value, cmdloop's loop terminates. Unless your subclass overrides this method, the base-class method Cmd.postcmd is called, and returns *flag* itself as the method's result.

postloop
c.postloop( )

c.cmdloop calls c.postloop( ) when cmdloop's loop terminates. Unless your subclass overrides this method, the base-class method Cmd.postloop is called, and does nothing at all.

precmd
c.precmd(s)

c.cmdloop calls s=c.precmd(s) to preprocess each command line s. The current leg of the loop bases all further processing on the string that precmd returns. Unless your subclass overrides this method, the base-class method Cmd.precmd is called, and returns s itself as the method's result.

preloop
c.preloop( )

c.cmdloop calls c.preloop( ) before cmdloop's loop begins. Unless your subclass overrides this method, the base class Cmd.preloop method is called, and does nothing at all.

Attributes of Cmd Instances

An instance c of a subclass of class Cmd supplies the following attributes:

identchars
> A string that contains all characters that can be part of a verb; by default, c.identchars contains letters, digits, and underscore (_)

intro
> The message that cmdloop outputs first, when called with no argument

lastcmd
> The last non-blank command line seen by onecmd

prompt
> The string that cmdloop uses to prompt the user for interactive input. You almost always bind c.prompt explicitly, or override prompt as a class attribute of your subclass, because the default Cmd.prompt is just '(Cmd) '.

use_rawinput
> When false (default is true), cmdloop prompts and inputs via calls to methods of sys.stdout and sys.stdin, rather than via raw_input

Other attributes of Cmd instances, which are not covered here, let you exert fine-grained control on many formatting details of help messages.

A Cmd Example

The following example shows how to use cmd.Cmd to supply the verbs print (to output the rest of the line) and stop (to end the loop):

```
import cmd

class X(cmd.Cmd):
    def do_print(self, rest): print rest
    def help_print(self): print "print (any string): outputs (any string)"
    def do_stop(self, rest): return 1
    def help_stop(self): print "stop: terminates the command loop"

if __name__=='__main__': X().cmdloop()
```

A session using this example might proceed as follows:

```
C:\>\python22\python \examples\chapter19\CmdEx.py
(Cmd) help
Documented commands (type help <topic>):
============================================
print           stop
Undocumented commands:
==========================
help
(Cmd) help print
print (whatever): outputs string (whatever)
(Cmd) print hi there
hi there
(Cmd) stop
```

Internationalization

Most programs present some information to users as text. Such text should be understandable and acceptable to the user. For example, in some countries and cultures, the date "March 7" can be concisely expressed as "3/7". Elsewhere, "3/7" indicates "July 3", and the string that means "March 7" is "7/3". In Python, such cultural conventions are handled with the help of standard module locale.

Similarly, a greeting can be expressed in one natural language by the string "Benvenuti", while in another language the string to use is "Welcome". In Python, such translations are handled with the help of standard module gettext.

Both kinds of issues are commonly called *internationalization* (often abbreviated *i18n*, as there are 18 letters between *i* and *n* in the full spelling). This is actually a misnomer, as the issues also apply to programs used within one nation by users of different languages or cultures.

The locale Module

Python's support for cultural conventions is patterned on that of C, slightly simplified. In this architecture, a program operates in an environment of cultural conventions known as a *locale*. The locale setting permeates the program and is typically set early on in the program's operation. The locale is not thread-specific, and module locale is not thread-safe. In a multithreaded program, set the program's locale before starting secondary threads.

If a program does not call locale.setlocale, the program operates in a neutral locale known as the C locale. The C locale is named from this architecture's origins in the C language, and is similar, but not identical, to the U.S. English locale. Alternatively, a program can find out and accept the user's default locale. In this case, module locale interacts with the operating system (via the environment, or in other system-dependent ways) to establish the user's preferred locale. Finally, a program can set a specific locale, presumably determining which locale to set on the basis of user interaction, or via persistent configuration settings such as a program initialization file.

A locale setting is normally performed across the board, for all relevant categories of cultural conventions. This wide-spectrum setting is denoted by the constant attribute LC_ALL of module locale. However, the cultural conventions handled by module locale are grouped into categories, and in some cases a program can choose to mix and match categories to build up a synthetic composite locale. The categories are identified by the following constant attributes of module locale:

LC_COLLATE
> String sorting: affects functions strcoll and strxfrm in locale

LC_CTYPE
> Character types: affects aspects of module string (and string methods) that have to do with letters, lowercase, and uppercase

LC_MESSAGES
> Messages: may affect messages displayed by the operating system, for example function os.strerror and module gettext

LC_MONETARY
> Formatting of currency values: affects function locale.localeconv

LC_NUMERIC
> Formatting of numbers: affects functions atoi, atof, format, localeconv, and str in locale

LC_TIME
> Formatting of times and dates: affects function time.strftime

The settings of some categories (denoted by the constants LC_CTYPE, LC_TIME, and LC_MESSAGES) affect some of the behavior of other modules (string, time, os, and gettext, as indicated). The settings of other categories (denoted by the constants LC_COLLATE, LC_MONETARY, and LC_NUMERIC) affect only some functions of locale.

Module locale supplies functions to query, change, and manipulate locales, as well as functions that implement the cultural conventions of locale categories LC_COLLATE, LC_MONETARY, and LC_NUMERIC.

atof
atof(*str*)

Converts string *str* to a floating-point value according to the current LC_NUMERIC setting.

atoi
atoi(*str*)

Converts string *str* to an integer according to the LC_NUMERIC setting.

format
format(*fmt,num,grouping*=0)

Returns the string obtained by formatting number *num* according to the format string *fmt* and the LC_NUMERIC setting. Except for cultural convention issues, the result is like *fmt%num*. If *grouping* is true, format also groups digits in the result string according to the LC_NUMERIC setting. For example:

```
>>> locale.setlocale(locale.LC_NUMERIC,'en')
'English_United States.1252'
>>> locale.format('%s',1000*1000)
'1000000'
>>> locale.format('%s',1000*1000,1)
'1,000,000'
```

When the numeric locale is U.S. English, and argument *grouping* is true, format supports the convention of grouping digits by threes with commas.

getdefaultlocale
getdefaultlocale(*envvars*=['LANGUAGE','LC_ALL',
                    'LC_TYPE','LANG'])

Examines the environment variables whose names are specified by argument *envvars*, in order. The first variable found in the environment determines the default locale. getdefaultlocale returns a pair of strings (*lang,encoding*) compliant with RFC 1766 (except for the 'C' locale), such as ('en_US','ISO8859-1'). Each item of the pair may be None if gedefaultlocale is unable to discover what value the item should have.

getlocale
getlocale(*category*=LC_TYPE)

Returns a pair of strings (*lang,encoding*) with the current setting for the given *category*. The category cannot be LC_ALL.

localeconv   localeconv( )

Returns a dictionary *d* containing the cultural conventions specified by categories LC_NUMERIC and LC_MONETARY of the current locale.
While LC_NUMERIC is best used indirectly via other functions of
module locale, the details of LC_MONETARY are accessible only
through *d*. Currency formatting is different for local and international use. The U.S. currency symbol, for example, is '$' for local
use only. '$' would be ambiguous in international use, since the
same symbol is also used for other currencies called "dollars"
(Canadian, Australian, Hong Kong, etc.). In international use,
therefore, the U.S. currency symbol is the unambiguous string
'USD'. The keys into *d* to use for currency formatting are the
following strings:

'currency_symbol'
: Currency symbol to use locally

'frac_digits'
: Number of fractional digits to use locally

'int_curr_symbol'
: Currency symbol to use internationally

'int_frac_digits'
: Number of fractional digits to use internationally

'mon_decimal_point'
: String to use as the "decimal point" for monetary values

'mon_grouping'
: List of digit grouping numbers for monetary values

'mon_thousands_sep'
: String to use as digit-groups separator for monetary values

'negative_sign', 'positive_sign'
: String to use as the sign symbol for negative (positive) monetary values

'n_cs_precedes', 'p_cs_precedes'
: True if the currency symbol comes before negative (positive)
monetary values

'n_sep_by_space', 'p_sep_by_space'
: True if a space goes between sign and negative (positive)
monetary values

'n_sign_posn', 'p_sign_posn'
: Numeric code to use to format negative (positive) monetary
values:

0   The value and the currency symbol are placed inside
    parentheses

1   The sign is placed before the value and the currency
    symbol

2   The sign is placed after the value and the currency symbol

3   The sign is placed immediately before the value

4   The sign is placed immediately after the value

CHAR_MAX

> The current locale does not specify any convention for this formatting

d[`'mon_grouping'`] is a list of numbers of digits to group when formatting a monetary value. When *d*[`'mon_grouping'`][`-1`] is 0, there is no further grouping beyond the indicated numbers of digits. When *d*[`'mon_grouping'`][`-1`] is locale.CHAR_MAX, grouping continues indefinitely, as if *d*[`'mon_grouping'`][`-2`] were endlessly repeated. locale.CHAR_MAX is a constant used as the value for all entries in *d* for which the current locale does not specify any convention.

normalize

normalize(*localename*)

Returns a string, suitable as an argument to setlocale, that is the normalized equivalent to *localename*. If normalize cannot normalize string *localename*, then normalize returns *localename* unchanged.

resetlocale

resetlocale(*category*=LC_ALL)

Sets the locale for *category* to the default given by getdefaultlocale.

setlocale

setlocale(*category*,*locale*=None)

Sets the locale for *category* to the given *locale*, if not None, and returns the setting (the existing one when *locale* is None; otherwise, the new one). *locale* can be a string, or a pair of strings (*lang*,*encoding*). When *locale* is the empty string `''`, setlocale sets the user's default locale.

str

str(*num*)

Like locale.format(`'%f'`,*num*).

strcoll

strcoll(*str1*,*str2*)

Like cmp(*str1*,*str2*), but according to the LC_COLLATE setting.

strxfrm

strxfrm(*str*)

Returns a string *sx* such that the built-in comparison (e.g., by cmp) of strings so transformed is equivalent to calling locale.strcoll on the original strings. strxfrm lets you use the decorate-sort-undecorate (DSU) idiom for sorts that involve locale-conformant string comparisons. However, if all you need is to sort a list of strings in a locale-conformant way, strcoll's simplicity can make it faster. The following example shows two ways of performing such a sort; in this case, the simple variant is often faster than the DSU one:

```
import locale
# simpler and often faster
def locale_sort_simple(list_of_strings):
```

```
list_of_strings.sort(locale.strcoll)
# less simple and often slower
def locale_sort_DSU(list_of_strings):
    auxiliary_list = [(locale.strxfrm(s),s) for s in
                      list_of_strings]
    auxiliary_list.sort()
    list_of_strings[:] = [s for junk, s in auxiliary_list]
```

The gettext Module

A key issue in internationalization is the ability to use text in different natural languages, a task also called *localization*. Python supports localization via module gettext, inspired by GNU *gettext*. Module gettext is optionally able to use the latter's infrastructure and APIs, but is simpler and more general. You do not need to install or study GNU *gettext* to use Python's gettext effectively.

Using gettext for localization

gettext does not deal with automatic translation between natural languages. Rather, gettext helps you extract, organize, and access the text messages that your program uses. Use each string literal subject to translation, also known as a *message*, as the argument of a function named _ (underscore) rather than using it directly. gettext normally installs a function named _ in the __builtin__ module. To ensure that your program can run with or without gettext, conditionally define a do-nothing function, also named _, that just returns its argument unchanged. Then, you can safely use _('*message*') wherever you would normally use the literal '*message*'. The following example shows how to start a module for conditional use of gettext:

```
try: _
except NameError:
    def _(s): return s
def greet(): print _('Hello world')
```

If some other module has installed gettext before you run the previous code, function greet outputs a properly localized greeting. Otherwise, greet outputs the string 'Hello world' unchanged.

Edit your sources, decorating all message literals with function _. Then, use any of various tools to extract messages into a text file (normally named *messages.pot*), and distribute the file to the people who translate messages into the natural languages you support. Python supplies a script *pygettext.py* (in directory *Tools/ i18n* in the Python source distribution) to perform message extraction on your Python sources.

Each translator edits *messages.pot* and produces a text file of translated messages with extension *.po*. Compile the *.po* files into binary files with extension *.mo*, suitable for fast searching, using any of various tools. Python supplies a script *Tools/ i18n/msgfmt.py* usable for this purpose. Finally, install each *.mo* file with a suitable name in an appropriate directory.

Conventions about which directories and names are suitable and appropriate differ among platforms and applications. gettext's default is subdirectory *share/locale/<lang>/LC_MESSAGES/* of directory *sys.prefix*, where *<lang>* is the language's code (normally two letters). Each file is typically named *<name>.mo*, where *<name>* is the name of your application or package.

Once you have prepared and installed your *.mo* files, you normally execute from somewhere in your application code such as the following:

```
import os, gettext
os.environ.setdefault('LANG', 'en')          # application-default language
gettext.install('your_application_name')
```

This ensures that calls such as _('message') henceforward return the appropriate translated strings. You can choose different ways to access gettext functionality in your program, for example if you also need to localize C-coded extensions, or to switch back and forth between different languages during a run. Another important consideration is whether you're localizing a whole application, or just a package that is separately distributed.

Essential gettext functions

Module gettext supplies many functions; this section documents the ones that are most often used.

install	install(*domain*,*localedir*=None,*unicode*=False)
	Installs in Python's built-in namespace a function named _ that performs translations specified by file *<lang>/LC_MESSAGES/<domain>.mo* in directory *localedir*, with language code *<lang>* as per getdefaultlocale. When *localedir* is None, install uses directory os.path.join(sys.prefix,'share','locale'). When *unicode* is true, function _ accepts and returns Unicode strings rather than plain strings.
translation	translation(*domain*,*localedir*=None,*languages*=None)
	Searches for a *.mo* file similarly to function install. When *languages* is None, translation looks in the environment for the *lang* to use, like install. However, *languages* can also be a list of one or more *lang* names separated by colons (:), in which case translation uses the first of these names for which it finds a *.mo* file. Returns an instance object that supplies methods gettext (to translate a plain string), ugettext (to translate a Unicode string), and install (to install gettext or ugettext under name _ into Python's built-in namespace).
	Function translation offers more detailed control than install, which is like translation(*domain*,*localedir*).install(*unicode*). With translation, you can localize a single package without affecting the built-in namespace by binding name _ on a per-module basis, for example with:
	`_ = translation(domain).ugettext`

translation also lets you switch globally between several languages, since you can pass an explicit *languages* argument, keep the resulting instance, and call the install method of the appropriate language as needed:

```
import gettext
translators = { }
def switch_to_language(lang, domain='my_app',
                       use_unicode=False):
    if not translators.has_key(lang):
        translators[lang] = \
        gettext.translation(domain, languages=lang)
    translators[lang].install(use_unicode)
```

Persistence and Databases

Python supports a variety of ways of making data persistent. One such way, known as *serialization*, involves viewing the data as a collection of Python objects. These objects can be saved, or *serialized*, to a byte stream, and later loaded and recreated, or *deserialized*, back from the byte stream. Object persistence layers on top of serialization and adds such features as object naming. This chapter covers the built-in Python modules that support serialization and object persistence.

Another way to make data persistent is to store it in a database. One simple type of database is actually just a file format that uses keyed access to enable selective reading and updating of relevant parts of the data. Python supplies modules that support several variations of this file format, known as DBM, and these modules are covered in this chapter.

A relational database management system (RDBMS), such as MySQL or Oracle, provides a more powerful approach to storing, searching, and retrieving persistent data. Relational databases rely on dialects of Structured Query Language (SQL) to create and alter a database's schema, insert and update data in the database, and query the database according to search criteria. This chapter does not provide any reference material on SQL. For that purpose, I recommend *SQL in a Nutshell*, by Kevin Kline (O'Reilly). Unfortunately, despite the existence of SQL standards, no two RDBMSes implement exactly the same SQL dialect.

The Python standard library does not come with an RDBMS interface. However, many free third-party modules let your Python programs access a specific RDBMS. Such modules mostly follow the Python Database API 2.0 standard, also known as the DBAPI. This chapter covers the DBAPI standard and mentions some of the third-party modules that implement it.

Serialization

Python supplies a number of modules that deal with I/O operations that serialize (save) entire Python objects to various kinds of byte streams, and deserialize (load and recreate) Python objects back from such streams. Serialization is also called *marshaling*.

The marshal Module

The marshal module supports the specific serialization tasks needed to save and reload compiled Python files (*.pyc* and *.pyo*). marshal only handles instances of fundamental built-in data types: None, numbers (plain and long integers, float, complex), strings (plain and Unicode), code objects, and built-in containers (tuples, lists, dictionaries) whose items are instances of elementary types. marshal does not handle instances of user-defined types, nor classes and instances of classes. marshal is faster than other serialization modules. Code objects are supported only by marshal, not by other serialization modules. Module marshal supplies the following functions.

dump, dumps	dump(*value,fileobj*) dumps(*value*) dumps returns a string representing object *value*. dump writes the same string to file object *fileobj*, which must be opened for writing in binary mode. dump(*v,f*) is just like *f*.write(dumps(*v*)). *fileobj* cannot be a file-like object: it must be an instance of type file.
load, loads	load(*fileobj*) loads(*str*) loads creates and returns the object *v* previously dumped to string *str*, so that, for any object *v* of a supported type, *v* equals loads(dumps(*v*)). If *str* is longer than dumps(*v*), loads ignores the extra bytes. load reads the right number of bytes from file object *fileobj*, which must be opened for reading in binary mode, and creates and returns the object *v* represented by those bytes. *fileobj* cannot be a file-like object: it must be an instance of type file.

Functions load and dump are complementary. In other words, a sequence of calls to load(*f*) deserializes the same values previously serialized when *f*'s contents were created by a sequence of calls to dump(*v,f*). Objects that are dumped and loaded in this way can be instances of any mix of supported types.

Suppose you need to analyze several text files, whose names are given as your program's arguments, and record where each word appears in those files. The data you need to record for each word is a list of (*filename, line-number*) pairs. The following example uses marshal to encode lists of (*filename, line-number*) pairs as strings and store them in a DBM-like file (as covered later in this chapter). Since those lists contain tuples, each made up of a string and a number, they are within marshal's abilities to serialize.

```
import fileinput, marshal, anydbm
wordPos = { }
for line in fileinput.input( ):
    pos = fileinput.filename( ), fileinput.filelineno( )
    for word in line.split( ):
        wordPos.setdefault(word,[ ]).append(pos)
dbmOut = anydbm.open('indexfilem','n')
for word in wordPos:
    dbmOut[word] = marshal.dumps(wordPos[word])
dbmOut.close( )
```

We also need marshal to read back the data stored to the DBM-like file *indexfilem*, as shown in the following example:

```
import sys, marshal, anydbm, linecache
dbmIn = anydbm.open('indexfilem')
for word in sys.argv[1:]:
    if not dbmIn.has_key(word):
        sys.stderr.write('Word %r not found in index file\n' % word)
        continue
    places = marshal.loads(dbmIn[word])
    for fname, lineno in places:
        print "Word %r occurs in line %s of file %s:" % (word,lineno,fname)
        print linecache.getline(fname, lineno),
```

The pickle and cPickle Modules

The pickle and cPickle modules supply factory functions, named Pickler and Unpickler, to generate objects that wrap file-like objects and supply serialization mechanisms. Serializing and deserializing via these modules is also known as *pickling* and *unpickling*. The difference between the modules is that in pickle, Pickler and Unpickler are classes, so you can inherit from these classes to create customized serializer objects, overriding methods as needed. In cPickle, Pickler and Unpickler are factory functions, generating instances of special-purpose types, not classes. Performance is therefore much better with cPickle, but inheritance is not feasible. In the rest of this section, I'll be talking about module pickle, but everything applies to cPickle too.

Note that in releases of Python older than the ones covered in this book, unpickling from an untrusted data source was a security risk—an attacker could exploit this to execute arbitrary code. No such weaknesses are known in Python 2.1 and later.

Serialization shares some of the issues of deep copying, covered in "The copy Module" in Chapter 8. Module pickle deals with these issues in much the same way as module copy does. Serialization, like deep copying, implies a recursive walk over a directed graph of references. pickle preserves the graph's shape when the same object is encountered more than once, meaning that the object is serialized only the first time, and other occurrences of the same object serialize references to a single copy. pickle also correctly serializes graphs with reference cycles. However, this implies that if a mutable object *o* is serialized more than once to the same Pickler instance *p*, any changes to *o* after the first serialization of *o* to *p* are not saved. For clarity and simplicity, I recommend you avoid altering objects that are being serialized while serialization to a single Pickler instance is in progress.

pickle can serialize in either an ASCII format or a compact binary one. Although the ASCII format is the default for backward compatibility, you should normally request binary format, as it saves both time and storage space. When you reload objects, pickle transparently recognizes and uses either format. I recommend you always specify binary format: the size and speed savings can be substantial, and binary format has basically no downside except loss of compatibility with very old versions of Python.

pickle serializes classes and functions by name, not by value. pickle can therefore deserialize a class or function only by importing it from the same module where the class or function was found when pickle serialized it. In particular, pickle can serialize and deserialize classes and functions only if they are top-level names for their module (i.e., attributes of their module). For example, consider the following:

```
def adder(augend):
    def inner(addend, augend=augend): return addend+augend
    return inner
plus5 = adder(5)
```

This code binds a closure to name plus5 (as covered in "Nested functions and nested scopes" in Chapter 4), which is a nested function inner plus an appropriate nested scope. Therefore, trying to pickle plus5 raises a pickle. PicklingError exception: a function can be pickled only when it is top-level, and function inner, whose closure is bound to name plus5 in this code, is not top-level, but rather nested inside function adder. Similar issues apply to other uses of nested functions, and also to nested classes (i.e., classes that are not top-level).

Functions of pickle and cPickle

Modules pickle and cPickle expose the following functions.

dump, dumps	dump(*value,fileobj,bin*=0) dumps(*value,bin*=0) dumps returns a string representing object *value*. dump writes the same string to file-like object *fileobj*, which must be opened for writing. dump(*v,f,bin*) is like *f*.write(dumps(*v,bin*)). If *bin* is true, dump uses binary format, so *f* must be open in binary mode. dump(*v,f,bin*) is also like Pickler(*f,bin*).dump(*v*).
load, loads	load(*fileobj*) loads(*str*) loads creates and returns the object *v* represented by string *str*, so that for any object *v* of a supported type, *v*==loads(dumps(*v*)). If

str is longer than dumps(*v*), loads ignores the extra bytes. load reads the right number of bytes from file-like object *fileobj* and creates and returns the object *v* represented by those bytes. If two calls to dump are made in sequence on the same file, two later calls to load from that file deserialize the two objects that dump serialized. load and loads transparently support pickles performed in either binary or ASCII mode. If data is pickled in binary format, the file must be open in binary format for both dump and load. load(*f*) is like Unpickler(*f*).load( ).

Pickler   Pickler(*fileobj*,*bin*=0)

Creates and returns an object *p* such that calling *p*.dump is equivalent to calling function dump with the *fileobj* and *bin* argument values passed to Pickler. To serialize many objects to a file, Pickler is more convenient and faster than repeated calls to dump. You can subclass pickle.Pickler to override Pickler methods (particularly method persistent_id) and create your own persistence framework. However, this is an advanced issue, and is not covered further in this book.

Unpickler   Unpickler(*fileobj*)

Creates and returns an object *u* such that calling *u*.load is equivalent to calling function load with the *fileobj* argument value passed to Unpickler. To deserialize many objects from a file, Unpickler is more convenient and faster than repeated calls to function load. You can subclass pickle.Unpickler to override Unpickler methods (particularly the method persistent_load) and create your own persistence framework. However, this is an advanced issue, and is not covered further in this book.

A pickling example

The following example handles the same task as the marshal example shown earlier, but uses cPickle instead of marshal to encode lists of (*filename*, *line-number*) pairs as strings:

```python
import fileinput, cPickle, anydbm
wordPos = { }
for line in fileinput.input( ):
    pos = fileinput.filename( ), fileinput.filelineno( )
    for word in line.split( ):
        wordPos.setdefault(word,[ ]).append(pos)
dbmOut = anydbm.open('indexfilep','n')
for word in wordPos:
    dbmOut[word] = cPickle.dumps(wordPos[word], 1)
dbmOut.close( )
```

We can use either cPickle or pickle to read back the data stored to the DBM-like file *indexfilep*, as shown in the following example:

```
import sys, cPickle, anydbm, linecache
dbmIn = anydbm.open('indexfilep')
for word in sys.argv[1:]:
    if not dbmIn.has_key(word):
        sys.stderr.write('Word %r not found in index file\n' % word)
        continue
    places = cPickle.loads(dbmIn[word])
    for fname, lineno in places:
        print "Word %r occurs in line %s of file %s:" % (word,lineno,fname)
        print linecache.getline(fname, lineno),
```

Pickling instance objects

In order for pickle to reload an instance object *x*, pickle must be able to import *x*'s class from the same module in which the class was defined when pickle saved the instance. By default, to save the instance-specific state of *x*, pickle saves *x*.__dict__, and then, to restore state, reloads *x*.__dict__. Therefore, all instance attributes (values in *x*.__dict__) must be instances of types suitable for pickling and unpickling (i.e., a pickleable object). A class can supply special methods to control this process.

By default, pickle does not call *x*.__init__ to restore instance object *x*. If you do want pickle to call *x*.__init__, *x*'s class must supply the special method __getinitargs__. In this case, when pickle saves *x*, pickle then calls *x*.__getinitargs__( ), which must return a tuple *t*. When pickle later reloads *x*, pickle calls *x*.__init__(*t) (i.e., the items of tuple *t* are passed as positional arguments to *x*.__init__). When *x*.__init__ returns, pickle restores *x*.__dict__, overriding attribute values bound by *x*.__init__. Method __getinitargs__ is therefore useful only when *x*.__init__ has other tasks to perform in addition to the task of giving initial values to *x*'s attributes.

When *x*'s class has a special method __getstate__, pickle calls *x*.__getstate__( ), which normally returns a dictionary *d*. pickle saves *d* instead of *x*.__dict__. When pickle later reloads *x*, it sets *x*.__dict__ from *d*. When *x*'s class supplies special method __setstate__, pickle calls *x*.__setstate__(*d*) for whatever *d* was saved, rather than *x*.__dict__.update(*d*). When *x*'s class supplies both methods __getstate__ and __setstate__, __getstate__ may return any pickleable object *y*, not just a dictionary, since *pickle* reloads *x* by calling *x*.__setstate__(*y*). A dictionary is often the handiest type of object for this purpose. As mentioned in "The copy Module" in Chapter 8, special methods __getinitargs__, __getstate__, and __setstate__ are also used to control the way instance objects are copied and deep-copied. If a new-style class defines __slots__, the class should also define __getstate__ and __setstate__, otherwise the class's instances are not pickleable.

Pickling customization with the copy_reg module

You can control how pickle serializes and deserializes objects of an arbitrary type (not class) by registering factory and reduction functions with module copy_reg.

This is useful when you define a type in a C-coded Python extension. Module copy_reg supplies the following functions.

constructor	constructor(*fcon*) Adds *fcon* to the table of safe constructors, which lists all factory functions that pickle may call. *fcon* must be callable, and is normally a function.
pickle	pickle(*type*,*fred*,*fcon*=None) Registers function *fred* as the reduction function for type *type*, where *type* must be a type object (not a class). To save any object *o* of type *type*, module pickle calls *fred*(*o*) and saves fred's result. *fred*(*o*) must return a pair (*fcon*,*t*) or a tuple (*fcon*,*t*,*d*), where *fcon* is a safe constructor and *t* is a tuple. To reload *o*, pickle calls *o*=*fcon*(*t). Then, if *fred* returned a *d*, pickle uses *d* to restore *o*'s state, as in "Pickling of instance objects" (*o*.__setstate__(*d*) if *o* supplies __setstate__, otherwise *o*.__dict__.update(*d*)). If *fcon* is not None, pickle also calls constructor(*fcon*) to register *fcon* as a safe constructor.

The shelve Module

The shelve module orchestrates modules cPickle (or pickle, when cPickle is not available in the current Python installation), cStringIO (or StringIO, when cStringIO is not available in the current Python installation), and anydbm (and its underlying modules for access to DBM-like archive files, as discussed later in this chapter) in order to provide a lightweight persistence mechanism.

shelve supplies a function open that is polymorphic to anydbm.open. The mapping object *s* returned by shelve.open is less limited than the mapping object *a* returned by anydbm.open. *a*'s keys and values must be strings. *s*'s keys must also be strings, but *s*'s values may be of any type or class that pickle can save and restore. pickle customizations (e.g., copy_reg, __getinitargs__, __getstate__, and __setstate__) also apply to shelve, since shelve delegates serialization to pickle.

Beware a subtle trap when you use shelve and mutable objects. When you operate on a mutable object held in a shelf, the changes don't take unless you assign the changed object back to the same index. For example:

```
import shelve
s = shelve.open('data')
s['akey'] = range(4)
print s['akey']                  # prints: [0, 1, 2, 3]
s['akey'].append('moreover')     # trying direct mutation
print s['akey']                  # doesn't take; prints: [0, 1, 2, 3]
```

```
x = s['akey']                  # fetch the object
x.append('moreover')           # perform mutation
s['akey'] = x                  # store the object back
print s['akey']                # now it takes, prints: [0, 1, 2, 3, 'moreover']
```

The following example handles the same task as the pickling example earlier, but uses shelve to persist lists of (*filename*, *line-number*) pairs:

```
import fileinput, shelve
wordPos = { }
for line in fileinput.input( ):
    pos = fileinput.filename( ), fileinput.filelineno( )
    for word in line.split( ):
        wordPos.setdefault(word,[ ]).append(pos)
shOut = shelve.open('indexfiles','n')
for word in wordPos:
    shOut[word] = wordPos[word]
shOut.close( )
```

We must use shelve to read back the data stored to the DBM-like file *indexfiles*, as shown in the following example:

```
import sys, shelve, linecache
shIn = shelve.open('indexfiles')

for word in sys.argv[1:]:
    if not shIn.has_key(word):
        sys.stderr.write('Word %r not found in index file\n' % word)
        continue
    places = shIn[word]
    for fname, lineno in places:
        print "Word %r occurs in line %s of file %s:" % (word,lineno,fname)
        print linecache.getline(fname, lineno),
```

These two examples are the simplest and most direct of the various equivalent pairs of examples shown throughout this section. This reflects the fact that module shelve is higher level than the modules used in previous examples.

DBM Modules

A DBM-like file is a file that contains a set of pairs of strings (*key*,*data*), with support for fetching or storing the data given a key, known as *keyed access*. DBM-like files were originally supported on early Unix systems, with functionality roughly equivalent to that of access methods popular on other mainframe and minicomputers of the time, such as ISAM, the Indexed-Sequential Access Method. Today, several different libraries, available for many platforms, let programs written in many different languages create, update, and read DBM-like files.

Keyed access, while not as powerful as the data access functionality of relational databases, may often suffice for a program's needs. And if DBM-like files are sufficient, you may end up with a program that is smaller, faster, and more portable than one that uses an RDBMS.

The classic *dbm* library, whose first version introduced DBM-like files many years ago, has limited functionality, but tends to be available on most Unix platforms. The GNU version, *gdbm*, is richer and also widespread. The BSD version, *dbhash*, offers superior functionality. Python supplies modules that interface with each of these libraries if the relevant underlying library is installed on your system. Python also offers a minimal DBM module, dumbdbm (usable anywhere, as it does not rely on other installed libraries), and generic DBM modules, which are able to automatically identify, select, and wrap the appropriate DBM library to deal with an existing or new DBM file. Depending on your platform, your Python distribution, and what *dbm*-like libraries you have installed on your computer, the default Python build may install some subset of these modules. In general, at a minimum, you can rely on having module dbm on Unix-like platforms, module dbhash on Windows, and dumbdbm on any platform.

The anydbm Module

The anydbm module is a generic interface to any other DBM module. anydbm supplies a single factory function.

open	open(*filename*,*flag*='r',*mode*=0666)

Opens or creates the DBM file named by *filename* (a string that can denote any path to a file, not just a name), and returns a suitable mapping object corresponding to the DBM file. When the DBM file already exists, open uses module whichdb to determine which DBM library can handle the file. When open creates a new DBM file, open chooses the first available DBM module in order of preference: dbhash, gdbm, dbm, and dumbdbm.

flag is a one-character string that tells open how to open the file and whether to create it, as shown in Table 11-1. *mode* is an integer that open uses as the file's permission bits if open creates the file, as covered in "Permissions" in Chapter 10. Not all DBM modules use *flags* and *mode*, but for portability's sake you should always supply appropriate values for these arguments when you call anydbm.open.

Table 11-1. flag values for anydbm.open

Flag	Read-only?	If file exists	If file does not exist
'r'	yes	open opens the file	open raises error
'w'	no	open opens the file	open raises error
'c'	no	open opens the file	open creates the file
'n'	no	open truncates the file	open creates the file

anydbm.open returns a mapping object *m* that supplies a subset of the functionality of dictionaries (covered in Chapter 4). *m* only accepts strings as keys and values, and the only mapping methods *m* supplies are *m*.has_key and *m*.keys. However, you can bind, rebind, access, and unbind items in *m* with the same indexing syntax *m*[*key*] that you would use if *m* were a dictionary. If *flag* is `'r'`, open returns a mapping *m* that is read-only so that you can only access *m*'s items, not bind, rebind, or unbind them. One extra method that *m* supplies is *m*.close, with the same semantics as the close method of a built-in file object. You should ensure *m*.close( ) is called when you're done using *m*. The try/finally statement (covered in Chapter 6) is the best way to ensure finalization.

The dumbdbm Module

The dumbdbm module supplies minimal DBM functionality and mediocre performance. dumbdbm's only advantage is that you can use it anywhere, since dumbdbm does not rely on any library. You don't normally import dumbdbm; rather, import anydbm, and let anydbm supply your program with the best DBM module available, defaulting to dumbdbm if nothing better is available on the current Python installation. The only case in which you import dumbdbm directly is the rare one in which you need to create a DBM-like file that you can later read from any Python installation. Module dumbdbm supplies an open function and an exception class error that are polymorphic to those anydbm supplies.

The dbm, gdbm, and dbhash Modules

The dbm module exists only on Unix platforms, where it can wrap any of the *dbm*, *ndbm*, and *gdbm* libraries, since each supplies a *dbm*-compatibility interface. You never import dbm directly; rather, you import anydbm, and let anydbm supply your program with the best DBM module available, defaulting to dbm if appropriate. Module dbm supplies an open function and an exception class error that are polymorphic to those anydbm supplies.

The gdbm module wraps the GNU DBM library, *gdbm*. The gdbm.open function accepts other values for the *flag* argument, and returns a mapping object *m* supplying a few extra methods. You may need to import gdbm directly, if you need to access non-portable functionality. I do not cover gdbm specifics in this book, since the book is focused on cross-platform Python.

The dbhash module wraps the BSD DBM library in a DBM-compatible way. The dbhash.open function accepts other values for the *flag* argument, and returns a mapping object *m* supplying a few extra methods. You may choose to import dbhash directly, if you need to access non-portable functionality. For full access to the BSD DB functionality, however, you can also import bsddb, covered in "The Berkeley DB Module" later in this chapter.

The whichdb Module

The whichdb module attempts to guess which of the several DBM modules are available. whichdb supplies a single function.

whichdb   whichdb(*filename*)

Opens the file specified by *filename* and determines which DBM-like package created the file. whichdb returns None if the file does not exist or cannot be opened and read. whichdb returns '' if the file exists and can be opened and read, but it cannot be determined which DBM-like package created the file (i.e., the file is not a DBM file). whichdb returns a string naming a module, such as 'dbm', 'dumbdbm', or 'dbhash', if it can determine which module can read the DBM-like file named by *filename*.

Examples of DBM-Like File Use

Keyed access is quite suitable when your program needs to record, in a persistent way, the equivalent of a Python dictionary, with strings as both keys and values. For example, suppose you need to analyze several text files, whose names are given as your program's arguments, and record where each word appears in those files. In this case, the keys are words, and, therefore, intrinsically strings. The data you need to record for each word is a list of (*filename, line-number*) pairs. However, you can encode the data as a string in several ways, for example by exploiting the fact that the path separator string os.pathsep (covered in Chapter 10) does not normally appear in filenames. (Note that more solid, general, and reliable approaches to the general issue of encoding data as strings are covered in "Serialization" earlier in this chapter.) With this simplification, the program that records word positions in files might be as follows:

```python
import fileinput, os, anydbm
wordPos = { }
sep = os.pathsep
for line in fileinput.input( ):
    pos = '%s%s%s'%(fileinput.filename( ), sep, fileinput.filelineno( ))
    for word in line.split( ):
        wordPos.setdefault(word,[ ]).append(pos)
dbmOut = anydbm.open('indexfile','n')
sep2 = sep * 2
for word in wordPos:
    dbmOut[word] = sep2.join(wordPos[word])
dbmOut.close( )
```

We can read back the data stored to the DBM-like file *indexfile* in several ways. The following example accepts words as command-line arguments and prints the lines where the requested words appear:

```python
import sys, os, anydbm, linecache
dbmIn = anydbm.open('indexfile')
sep = os.pathsep
sep2 = sep * 2
for word in sys.argv[1:]:
    if not dbmIn.has_key(word):
        sys.stderr.write('Word %r not found in index file\n' % word)
```

```
    continue
places = dbmIn[word].split(sep2)
for place in places:
    fname, lineno = place.split(sep)
    print "Word %r occurs in line %s of file %s:" % (word,lineno,fname)
    print linecache.getline(fname, int(lineno)),
```

The Berkeley DB Module

Python comes with the *bsddb* module, which wraps the Berkeley Database library
(also known as BSD DB) if that library is installed on your system and your
Python installation is built to support it. With the BSD DB library, you can create
hash, binary tree, or record-based files that generally behave like dictionaries. On
Windows, Python includes a port of the BSD DB library, thus ensuring that
module *bsddb* is always usable. To download BSD DB sources, binaries for other
platforms, and detailed documentation on BSD DB, see *http://www.sleepycat.com*.
Module *bsddb* supplies three factory functions, btopen, hashopen, and rnopen.

btopen,	btopen(*filename,flag*='r',**many_other_optional_arguments*)
hashopen,	hashopen(*filename,flag*='r',**many_other_optional_arguments*)
rnopen	rnopen(*filename,flag*='r',**many_other_optional_arguments*)

btopen opens or creates the binary tree format file named by
filename (a string that denotes any path to a file, not just a name),
and returns a suitable BTree object to access and manipulate the
file. Argument *flag* has exactly the same values and meaning as for
anydbm.open. Other arguments indicate low-level options that allow
fine-grained control, but are rarely used.

hashopen and rnopen work the same way, but open or create hash
format and record format files, returning objects of type Hash and
Record. hashopen is generally the fastest format and makes sense
when you are using keys to look up records. However, if you also
need to access records in sorted order, use btopen, or if you need to
access records in the same order in which you originally wrote
them, use rnopen. Using hashopen does not keep records in order in
the file.

An object *b* of any of the types BTree, Hash, and Record can be indexed as a
mapping, with both keys and values constrained to being strings. Further, *b* also
supports sequential access through the concept of a *current record*. *b* supplies the
following methods.

close	*b*.close( )
	Closes *b*. Call no other method on *b* after *b*.close( ).

first	`b.first()`
	Sets *b*'s current record to the first record, and returns a pair (*key,value*) for the first record. The order of records is arbitrary, except for BTree objects, which ensure records are sorted in alphabetical order of their keys. `b.first()` raises KeyError if *b* is empty.

has_key	`b.has_key(key)`
	Returns True if string *key* is a key in *b*, otherwise returns False.

keys	`b.keys()`
	Returns the list of *b*'s key strings. The order is arbitrary, except for BTree objects, which return keys in alphabetical order.

last	`b.last()`
	Sets *b*'s current record to the last record and returns a pair (*key,value*) for the last record. Type Hash does not supply method last.

next	`b.next()`
	Sets *b*'s current record to the next record and returns a pair (*key,value*) for the next record. `b.next()` raises KeyError if *b* has no next record.

previous	`b.previous()`
	Sets *b*'s current record to the previous record and returns a pair (*key,value*) for the previous record. Type Hash does not supply method previous.

set_location	`b.set_location(key)`
	Sets *b*'s current record to the item with string key *key*, and returns a pair (*key,value*). If *key* is not a key in *b*, and *b* is of type BTree, `b.set_location(key)` sets *b*'s current record to the item whose key is the smallest key larger than *key* and returns that key/value pair. For other object types, set_location raises KeyError if *key* is not a key in *b*.

Examples of Berkeley DB Use

The Berkeley DB is suited to tasks similar to those for which DBM-like files are appropriate. Indeed, anydbm uses dbhash, the DBM-like interface to the Berkeley DB, to create new DBM-like files. In addition, the Berkeley DB can also use other file formats when you use module bsddb explicitly. The binary tree format, while not quite as fast as the hashed format when all you need is keyed access, is excellent when you also need to access keys in alphabetical order.

The following example handles the same task as the DBM example shown earlier, but uses bsddb rather than anydbm:

```
import fileinput, os, bsddb
wordPos = { }
sep = os.pathsep
for line in fileinput.input( ):
    pos = '%s%s%s'%(fileinput.filename( ), sep, fileinput.filelineno( ))
    for word in line.split( ):
        wordPos.setdefault(word,[ ]).append(pos)
btOut = bsddb.btopen('btindex','n')
sep2 = sep * 2
for word in wordPos:
    btOut[word] = sep2.join(wordPos[word])
btOut.close( )
```

The differences between this example and the DBM one are minimal: writing a new binary tree format file with bsddb is basically the same task as writing a new DBM-like file with anydbm. Reading back the data using bsddb.btopen('btindex') rather than anydbm.open('indexfile') is similarly trivial. To illustrate the extra features of binary trees regarding access to keys in alphabetical order, we'll perform a slightly more general task. The following example treats its command-line arguments as specifying the beginning of words, and prints the lines in which any word with such a beginning appears:

```
import sys, os, bsddb, linecache
btIn = bsddb.btopen('btindex')
sep = os.pathsep
sep2 = sep * 2

for word in sys.argv[1:]:
    key, pos = btIn.set_location(word)
    if not key.startswith(word):
        sys.stderr.write('Word-start %r not found in index file\n' % word)
    while key.startswith(word):
        places = pos.split(sep2)
        for place in places:
            fname, lineno = place.split(sep)
            print "%r occurs in line %s of file %s:" % (word,lineno,fname)
            print linecache.getline(fname, int(lineno)),
        try: key, pos = btIn.next( )
        except IndexError: break
```

This example exploits the fact that btIn.set_location sets btIn's current position to the smallest key larger than *word*, when *word* itself is not a key in btIn. When *word* is a word-beginning, and keys are words, this means that set_location sets the current position to the first word, in alphabetical order, that starts with *word*. The tests with *key*.startswith(*word*) let us check that we're still scanning words with that beginning, and terminate the while loop when that is no longer the case. We perform the first such test in an if statement, right before the while, because we want to single out the case where no word at all starts with the desired beginning, and output an error message in that specific case.

The Python Database API (DBAPI) 2.0

As I mentioned earlier, the Python standard library does not come with an RDBMS interface, but there are many free third-party modules that let your Python programs access specific databases. Such modules mostly follow the Python Database API 2.0 standard, also known as the DBAPI.

At the time of this writing, Python's DBAPI Special Interest Group (SIG) was busy preparing a new version of the DBAPI (possibly to be known as 3.0 when it is ready). Programs written against DBAPI 2.0 should work with minimal or no changes with the future DBAPI 3.0, although 3.0 will no doubt offer further enhancements that future programs will be able to take advantage of.

If your Python program runs only on Windows, you may prefer to access databases by using Microsoft's ADO package through COM. For more information on using Python on Windows, see the book *Python Programming on Win32*, by Mark Hammond and Andy Robinson (O'Reilly). Since ADO and COM are platform-specific, and this book focuses on cross-platform use of Python, I do not cover ADO nor COM further in this book.

After importing a DBAPI-compliant module, you call the module's connect function with suitable parameters. connect returns an instance of class Connection, which represents a connection to the database. This instance supplies commit and rollback methods to let you deal with transactions, a close method to call as soon as you're done with the database, and a cursor method that returns an instance of class Cursor. This instance supplies the methods and attributes that you'll use for all database operations. A DBAPI-compliant module also supplies exception classes, descriptive attributes, factory functions, and type-description attributes.

Exception Classes

A DBAPI-compliant module supplies exception classes Warning, Error, and several subclasses of Error. Warning indicates such anomalies as data truncation during insertion. Error's subclasses indicate various kinds of errors that your program can encounter when dealing with the database and the DBAPI-compliant module that interfaces to it. Generally, your code uses a statement of the form:

```
try:
    ...
except module.Error, err:
    ...
```

in order to trap all database-related errors that you need to handle without terminating.

Thread Safety

When a DBAPI-compliant module has an attribute threadsafety that is greater than 0, the module is asserting some specific level of thread safety for database interfacing. Rather than relying on this, it's safer and more portable to ensure that a single thread has exclusive access to any given external resource, such as a database, as outlined in Chapter 14.

Parameter Style

A DBAPI-compliant module has an attribute paramstyle that identifies the style of markers to use as placeholders for parameters. You insert such markers in SQL statement strings that you pass to methods of Cursor instances, such as method execute, in order to use runtime-determined parameter values. Say, for example, that you need to fetch the rows of database table *ATABLE* where field *AFIELD* equals the current value of Python variable *x*. Assuming the cursor instance is named *c*, you could perform this task by using Python's string formatting operator % as follows:

```
c.execute('SELECT * FROM ATABLE WHERE AFIELD=%r' % x)
```

However, this is not the recommended approach. This approach generates a different statement string for each value of *x*, requiring such statements to be parsed and prepared anew each time. With parameter substitution, you pass to execute a single statement string, with a placeholder instead of the parameter value. This lets execute perform parsing and preparation just once, giving potentially better performance. For example, if a module's paramstyle attribute is 'qmark', you can express the above query as:

```
c.execute('SELECT * FROM ATABLE WHERE AFIELD=?', [x])
```

The read-only attribute paramstyle is meant to inform your program about the way to use parameter substitution with that module. The possible values of paramstyle are:

format
> The marker is %s, as in string formatting. A query looks like:
>
>  ```
>  c.execute('SELECT * FROM ATABLE WHERE AFIELD=%s', [x])
>  ```

named
> The marker is :*name* and parameters are named. A query look like:
>
>  ```
>  c.execute('SELECT * FROM ATABLE WHERE AFIELD=:x', {'x':x})
>  ```

numeric
> The marker is :*n*, giving the parameter's number. A query looks like:
>
>  ```
>  c.execute('SELECT * FROM ATABLE WHERE AFIELD=:1', [x])
>  ```

pyformat
> The marker is %(*name*)s and parameters are named. A query looks like:
>
>  ```
>  c.execute('SELECT * FROM ATABLE WHERE AFIELD=%(x)s', {'x':x})
>  ```

qmark
> The marker is ?. A query looks like:
>
>  ```
>  c.execute('SELECT * FROM ATABLE WHERE AFIELD=?', [x])
>  ```

When paramstyle does not imply named parameters, the second argument of method execute is a sequence. When parameters are named, the second argument of method execute is a dictionary.

Factory Functions

Parameters passed to the database via placeholders must typically be of the right type. This means Python numbers (integers or floating-point values), strings (plain or Unicode), and None to represent SQL NULL. Python has no specific types to represent dates, times, and binary large objects (BLOBs). A DBAPI-compliant module supplies factory functions to build such objects. The types used for this purpose by most DBAPI-compliant modules are those supplied by module mxDateTime, covered in Chapter 12, and strings or buffer types for BLOBs. The factory functions are as follows.

Binary	Binary(*string*)
	Returns an object representing the given *string* of bytes as a BLOB.
Date	Date(*year,month,day*)
	Returns an object representing the specified date.
DateFromTicks	DateFromTicks(*s*)
	Returns an object representing the date that is *s* seconds after the epoch of module time, covered in Chapter 12. For example, DateFromTicks(time.time()) is today's date.
Time	Time(*hour,minute,second*)
	Returns an object representing the specified time.
TimeFromTicks	TimeFromTicks(*s*)
	Returns an object representing the time that is *s* seconds after the epoch of module time, covered in Chapter 12. For example, TimeFromTicks(time.time()) is the current time.
Timestamp	Timestamp(*year,month,day,hour,minute,second*)
	Returns an object representing the specified date and time.
TimestampFrom Ticks	TimestampFromTicks(*s*)
	Returns an object representing the date and time that is *s* seconds after the epoch of module time, covered in Chapter 12. For example, TimestampFromTicks(time.time()) is the current date and time.

Type Description Attributes

A Cursor instance's attribute description describes the types and other characteristics of each column of a query. Each column's type (the second item of the tuple describing the column) equals one of the following attributes of the DBAPI-compliant module:

BINARY
> Describes columns containing BLOBs

DATETIME
> Describes columns containing dates, times, or both

NUMBER
> Describes columns containing numbers of any kind

ROWID
> Describes columns containing a row-identification number

STRING
> Describes columns containing text of any kind

A cursor's description, and in particular each column's type, is mostly useful for introspection about the database your program is working with. Such introspection can help you write general modules that are able to work with databases that have different schemas, schemas that may not be fully known at the time you are writing your code.

The connect Function

A DBAPI-compliant module's connect function accepts arguments that vary depending on the kind of database and the specific module involved. The DBAPI standard recommends, but does not mandate, that connect accept named arguments. In particular, connect should at least accept optional arguments with the following names:

database
> Name of the specific database to connect

dsn
> Data-source name to use for the connection

host
> Hostname on which the database is running

password
> Password to use for the connection

user
> Username for the connection

Connection Objects

A DBAPI-compliant module's connect function returns an object x that is an instance of class Connection. x supplies the following methods.

---

close   x.close( )

> Terminates the database connection and releases all related resources. Call close as soon as you're done with the database, since keeping database connections uselessly open can be a serious resource drain on the system.

---

commit	x.commit( )
	Commits the current transaction in the database. If the database does not support transactions, x.commit( ) is an innocuous no-op.

cursor	x.close( )
	Returns a new instance of class Cursor, covered later in this section.

rollback	x.rollback( )
	Rolls back the current transaction in the database. If the database does not support transactions, x.rollback( ) raises an exception. The DBAPI recommends, but does not mandate, that for databases that do not support transactions class Connection supplies no rollback method, so that x.rollback( ) raises AttributeError. You can test whether transaction support is present with hasattr(x,'rollback').

Cursor Objects

A Connection instance provides a cursor method that returns an object c that is an instance of class Cursor. A SQL cursor represents the set of results of a query and lets you work with the records in that set, in sequence, one at a time. A cursor as modeled by the DBAPI is a richer concept, since it also represents the only way in which your program executes SQL queries in the first place. On the other hand, a DBAPI cursor allows you only to advance in the sequence of results (some relational databases, but not all, also provide richer cursors that are able to go backward as well as forward), and does not support the SQL clause WHERE CURRENT OF CURSOR. These limitations of DBAPI cursors enable DBAPI-compliant modules to provide cursors even on RDBMSes that provide no real SQL cursors at all. An instance of class Cursor c supplies many attributes and methods; the most frequently used ones are documented here.

close	c.close( )
	Closes the cursor and releases all related resources.

description	A read-only attribute that is a sequence of seven-item tuples, one per column in the last query executed:
	name, typecode, displaysize, internalsize, precision, scale, nullable
	c.description is None if the last operation on c was not a query or returned no usable description of the columns involved. A cursor's description is mostly useful for introspection about the database your program is working with. Such introspection can help you

write general modules that are able to work with databases that
have different schemas, including schemas that may not be fully
known at the time you are writing your code.

execute   `c.execute(statement,parameters=None)`

Executes a SQL *statement* on the database with the given
parameters. *parameters* is a sequence when the module's
paramstyle is `'format'`, `'numeric'`, or `'qmark'`, and a dictionary
when `'named'` or `'pyformat'`.

executemany   `c.executemany(statement,*parameters)`

Executes a SQL *statement* on the database, once for each item of
the given *parameters*. *parameters* is a sequence of sequences when
the module's paramstyle is `'format'`, `'numeric'`, or `'qmark'`, and a
sequence of dictionaries when `'named'` or `'pyformat'`. For example,
the statement:

```
c.executemany('UPDATE atable SET x=? WHERE y=?',
              (12,23),(23,34))
```

that uses a module whose paramstyle is `'qmark'` is equivalent to,
but probably faster than, the two statements:

```
c.execute('UPDATE atable SET x=12 WHERE y=23')
c.execute('UPDATE atable SET x=23 WHERE y=34')
```

fetchall   `c.fetchall()`

Returns all remaining result rows from the last query as a sequence
of tuples. Raises an exception if the last operation was not a SELECT
query.

fetchmany   `c.fetchmany(n)`

Returns up to *n* remaining result rows from the last query as a
sequence of tuples. Raises an exception if the last operation was
not a SELECT query.

fetchone   `c.fetchone()`

Returns the next result row from the last query as a tuple. Raises an
exception if the last operation was not a SELECT query.

rowcount   A read-only attribute that specifies the number of rows fetched or
affected by the last operation, or -1 if the module is unable to
determine this value.

DBAPI-Compliant Modules

Whatever relational database you want to use, there's at least one (and often more than one) DBAPI-compliant module that you can download from the Internet. All modules listed in the following sections, except mxODBC, have liberal licenses that are mostly similar to Python's license (the SAP DB, however, is licensed under GPL) and that let you use them freely in either open source or closed source programs. mxODBC can be used freely for noncommercial purposes, but you must purchase a license for any commercial use. There are so many relational databases that it's impossible to list them all, but here are some of the most popular ones:

ODBC

Open DataBase Connectivity (ODBC) is a popular standard that lets you connect to many different relational databases, including ones not otherwise supported by DBAPI-compliant modules, such as Microsoft Jet (also known as the Access database). The Windows distribution of Python contains an odbc module, but the module is unsupported and complies to an older version of the DBAPI, not to the current version 2.0. On either Unix or Windows, use mxODBC, available at *http://www.lemburg.com/files/Python/ mxODBC.html*. mxODBC's paramstyle is 'qmark'. Its connect function accepts three optional arguments, named *dsn*, *user*, and *password*.

Oracle

Oracle is a widespread, commercial RDBMS. To interface to Oracle, I recommend module DCOracle2, available at *http://www.zope.org/Members/matt/ dco2*. DCOracle2's paramstyle is 'numeric'. Its connect function accepts a single optional, unnamed argument string with the syntax:

```
'user/password@service'
```

Microsoft SQL Server

To interface to Microsoft SQL Server, I recommend module mssqldb, available at *http://www.object-craft.com.au/projects/mssql/*. mssqldb's paramstyle is 'qmark'. Its connect function accepts three arguments, named *dsn*, *user*, and *passwd*, as well as an optional *database* argument.

DB2

For IBM DB/2, try module DB2, available at *ftp://people.linuxkorea.co.kr/pub/ DB2/*. DB2's paramstyle is 'format'. Its connect function accepts three optional arguments, named *dsn*, *uid*, and *pwd*.

MySQL

MySQL is a widespread, open source RDBMS. To interface to MySQL, try MySQLdb, available at *http://sourceforge.net/projects/mysql-python*. MySQLdb's paramstyle is 'format'. Its connect function accepts four optional arguments, named *db*, *host*, *user*, and *passwd*.

PostgreSQL

PostgreSQL is an excellent open source RDBMS. To interface to PostgreSQL, I recommend psycopg, available at *http://initd.org/Software/psycopg*. psycopg's paramstyle is 'pyformat'. Its connect function accepts a single mandatory argument, named *dsn*, with the syntax:

```
'host=host dbname=dbname user=username password=password'
```

SAP DB

SAP DB, once known as Adabas, is a powerful RDBMS that used to be closed source, but is now open source. SAP DB comes with sapdbapi, available at *http://www.sapdb.org/sapdbapi.html*, as well as other useful Python modules. sapdbapi's paramstyle is 'pyformat'. Its connect function accepts three mandatory arguments, named *user*, *password*, and *database*, and an optional argument named *host*.

Gadfly

Gadfly, available at *http://gadfly.sf.net*, is not an interface to some other RDBMS, but rather a complete RDBMS engine written in Python. Gadfly supports a large subset of standard SQL. For example, Gadfly lacks NULL, but it does support VIEW, which is a crucial SQL feature that engines such as MySQL still lack at the time of this writing. Gadfly can run as a daemon server, to which clients connect with TCP/IP. Alternatively, you can run the Gadfly engine directly in your application's process, if you don't need other processes to be able to access the same database concurrently.

The gadfly module has several discrepancies from the DBAPI 2.0 covered in this chapter because Gadfly implements a variant of the older DBAPI 1.0. The concepts are quite close, but several details differ. The main differences are:

- gadfly does not supply custom exception classes, so Gadfly operations that fail raise normal Python exceptions, such as IOError, NameError, etc.
- gadfly does not supply a paramstyle attribute. However, the module behaves as if it supplied a paramstyle of 'qmark'.
- gadfly does not supply a function named connect; use the gadfly.gadfly or gadfly.client.gfclient functions instead.
- gadfly does not supply factory functions for data types.
- Gadfly cursors do not supply the executemany method. Instead, in the specific case in which the SQL statement is an INSERT, the execute method optionally accepts as its second argument a list of tuples and inserts all the data.
- Gadfly cursors do not supply the rowcount method.

The gadfly module supplies the following functions.

gadfly	gadfly.gadfly(*dbname,dirpath*)
	Returns a connection object for the database named *dbname*, which must have been previously created in the directory indicated by string *dirpath*. The database engine runs in the same process as your application.

gfclient	gadfly.client.gfclient(*policyname, port, password, host*)
	Returns a connection object for the database served by a gfserve process on the given *host* and *port*. *policyname* identifies the level of access required, and is often 'admin' to specify unlimited access.

12

Time Operations

A Python program can handle time in several ways. Time intervals are represented by floating-point numbers, in units of seconds (a fraction of a second is the fractional part of the interval). Particular instants in time are expressed in seconds since a reference instant, known as the *epoch*. (Midnight, UTC, of January 1, 1970, is a popular epoch used on both Unix and Windows platforms.) Time instants often also need to be expressed as a mixture of units of measurement (e.g., years, months, days, hours, minutes, and seconds), particularly for I/O purposes.

This chapter covers the time module, which supplies Python's core time-handling functionality. The time module strongly depends on the system C library. The chapter also presents the sched and calendar modules and the essentials of the popular extension module mx.DateTime. mx.DateTime has more uniform behavior across platforms than time, which helps account for its popularity.

Python 2.3 will introduce a new datetime module to manipulate dates and times in other ways. At *http://starship.python.net/crew/jbauer/normaldate/*, you can download Jeff Bauer's *normalDate.py*, which gains simplicity by dealing only with dates, not with times. Neither of these modules is further covered in this book.

The time Module

The underlying C library determines the range of dates that the time module can handle. On Unix systems, years 1970 and 2038 are the typical cut-off points, a limitation that mx.DateTime lets you avoid. Time instants are normally specified in UTC (Coordinated Universal Time, once known as GMT, or Greenwich Mean Time). Module time also supports local time zones and Daylight Saving Time (DST), but only to the extent that support is supplied by the underlying C system library.

As an alternative to seconds since the epoch, a time instant can be represented by a tuple of nine integers known as a time-tuple. Items in time-tuples are covered in Table 12-1. All items are integers, and therefore time-tuples cannot keep track of fractions of a second. In Python 2.2 and later, the result of any function in module time that used to return a time-tuple is now of type struct_time. You can still use the result as a tuple, but you can also access the items as read-only attributes *x*.tm_year, *x*.tm_mon, and so on, using the attribute names listed in Table 12-1. Wherever a function used to require a time-tuple argument, you can now pass an instance of struct_time or any other sequence whose items are nine integers in the applicable ranges.

Table 12-1. Tuple form of time representation

Item	Meaning	Field name	Range	Notes
0	Year	tm_year	1970–2038	Wider on some platforms
1	Month	tm_mon	1–12	1 is January; 12 is December
2	Day	tm_mday	1–31	
3	Hour	tm_hour	0–23	0 is midnight; 12 is noon
4	Minute	tm_min	0–59	
5	Second	tm_sec	0–61	60 and 61 for leap seconds
6	Weekday	tm_wday	0–6	0 is Monday; 6 is Sunday
7	Year day	tm_yday	1–366	Day number within the year
8	DST flag	tm_isdst	−1 to 1	-1 means library determines DST

To translate a time instant from "a seconds since the epoch" floating-point value into a time-tuple, pass the floating-point value to a function (e.g., localtime) that returns a time-tuple with all nine items valid. When you convert in the other direction, mktime ignores items six (tm_wday) and seven (tm_yday) of the tuple. In this case, you normally set item eight (tm_isdst) to -1, so that mktime itself determines whether to apply Daylight Saving Time (DST).

Module time supplies the following functions and attributes.

asctime asctime([*tupletime*])

Accepts a time-tuple and returns a 24-character string such as 'Tue Dec 10 18:07:14 2002'. asctime( ) without arguments is like asctime(localtime(time( ))) (i.e., it formats the current time instant).

clock clock( )

Returns the current CPU time as a floating-point number of seconds. To measure computational costs of different approaches, it is generally better to use the results of time.clock rather than those of time.time. On Unix-like platforms, the reason is that the results of time.clock, using CPU time rather than elapsed time, are less dependent than those of time.time on unpredictable factors due to machine load. On Windows, this reason does not apply, as Windows has no concept of CPU time, but there is another reason: time.clock uses the higher-precision performance counter machine clock. The epoch (the time corresponding to a 0.0 result from time.clock) is arbitrary, but differences between the results of successive calls to time.clock in the same process are accurate.

ctime

ctime([*secs*])

Like asctime(localtime(*secs*)) (i.e., accepts an instant expressed in seconds since the epoch and returns a 24-character string form of that time instant). ctime() without arguments is like asctime(localtime(time())) (i.e., it formats the current time instant).

gmtime

gmtime([*secs*])

Accepts an instant expressed in seconds since the epoch and returns a nine-item time-tuple *t* with the UTC time (DST, the last item of *t*, is always 0). gmtime() without arguments is like gmtime(time()) (i.e., it returns the nine-item time-tuple for the current time instant).

localtime

localtime([*secs*])

Accepts an instant expressed in seconds since the epoch and returns a nine-item tuple *t* with the local time (DST, the last item of *t*, is set to 0 or 1, depending on whether DST applies to instant *secs* according to local rules). localtime() without arguments is like localtime(time()) (i.e., it returns the nine-item time-tuple for the current time instant).

mktime

mktime(*tupletime*)

Accepts an instant expressed as a nine-item tuple in local time and returns a floating-point value with the instant expressed in seconds since the epoch. DST, the last item in *tupletime*, is meaningful: set it to 0 to get solar time, to 1 to get Daylight Saving Time, or to -1 to let mktime compute whether DST is in effect or not at the given instant.

sleep

sleep(*secs*)

Suspends the calling thread for *secs* seconds (*secs* is a floating-point number and can indicate a fraction of a second). The calling thread may start executing again before *secs* seconds (if some signal wakes it up) or after a longer suspension (depending on system scheduling of processes and threads).

strftime

strftime(*fmt*[,*tupletime*])

Accepts an instant expressed as a nine-item tuple in local time and returns a string that represents *tupletime* as specified by string *fmt*. If you omit *tupletime*, strftime uses localtime(time()) instead (i.e., it formats the current time instant in the local time zone). The syntax of string *format* is similar to the syntax speci- fied in "String Formatting" in Chapter 9. However, conversion characters are different, as shown in Table 12-2, and refer to the time instant specified by *tupletime*. Specifying width and precision explicitly works on some platforms, but not on all.

Table 12-2. Conversion characters for strftime

Type char	Meaning	Special notes
a	Weekday name, abbreviated	Depends on locale
A	Weekday name, full	Depends on locale
b	Month name, abbreviated	Depends on locale
B	Month name, full	Depends on locale
c	Complete date and time representation	Depends on locale
d	Day of the month	Between 1 and 31
H	Hour (24-hour clock)	Between 0 and 23
I	Hour (12-hour clock)	Between 1 and 12
j	Day of the year	Between 1 and 366
m	Month number	Between 1 and 12
M	Minute number	Between 0 and 59
p	'AM' or 'PM' equivalent	Depends on locale
S	Second number	Between 0 and 61
U	Week number (Sunday first weekday)	Between 0 and 53
w	Weekday number	0 is Sunday, up to 6
W	Week number (Monday first weekday)	Between 0 and 53
x	Complete date representation	Depends on locale
X	Complete time representation	Depends on locale
y	Year number within century	Between 0 and 99
Y	Year number	1970 to 2038, or wider
Z	Name of time zone	Empty if no time zone exists
%	A literal % character	Encoded as %%

You can obtain dates as formatted by asctime (e.g., 'Tue Dec 10 18:07:14 2002') with the format string:

```
'%a %b %d %H:%M:%S %Y'
```

You can obtain dates compliant with RFC 822 (e.g., 'Tue, 10 Dec 2002 18:07:14 EST') with the format string:

```
'%a, %d %b %Y %H:%M:%S %Z'
```

strptime   strptime(*str*,*fmt*='%a %b %d %H:%M:%S %Y')

Parses *str* according to format string *fmt*, and returns the instant in time-tuple format. With Python 2.2 and earlier, strptime is not available on all platforms. However, a pure Python implementation is available at *http://aspn.activestate.com/ASPN/Python/Cookbook/Recipe/56036*. In Python 2.3, the pure Python implementation will be used as a fallback on platforms that provide no other, so that time.strptime will always be available.

time	time( )
	Returns the current time instant, a floating-point number of seconds since the epoch. On some platforms, the precision of time measurements is as low as one second.

timezone	Attribute time.timezone is the offset in seconds of the local time zone (without DST) from UTC (greater than 0 in the Americas and less than 0 in most of Europe, Asia, and Africa).

tzname	Attribute time.tzname is a pair of locale-dependent strings, the names of the local time zone without and with DST, respectively.

The sched Module

The sched module supplies a class that implements an event scheduler. sched supplies a scheduler class.

scheduler	class scheduler(*timefunc,delayfunc*)
	An instance *s* of scheduler is initialized with two functions, which *s* then uses for all time-related operations. *timefunc* must be callable without arguments to get the current time instant (in any unit of measure), meaning that you can pass time.time. *delayfunc* must be callable with one argument (a time duration, in the same units *timefunc* returns), and it should delay for about that amount of time, meaning you can pass time.sleep. scheduler also calls *delayfunc* with argument 0 after each event, to give other threads a chance; again, this is compatible with the behavior of time.sleep.

A scheduler instance *s* supplies the following methods.

cancel	*s*.cancel(*event_token*)
	Removes an event from *s*'s queue of scheduled events. *event_token* must be the result of a previous call to *s*.enter or *s*.enterabs, and the event must not yet have happened; otherwise cancel raises RuntimeError.

empty	*s*.empty( )
	Returns True if *s*'s queue of scheduled events is empty, otherwise False.

enterabs   *s*.enterabs(*when,priority,func,args*)

Schedules a future event (i.e., a callback to *func(*args)*) at time *when*. *when* is expressed in the same units of measure used by the time functions of *s*. If several events are scheduled for the same instant, *s* executes them in increasing order of *priority*. enterabs returns an event token *t*, which you may later pass to *s*.cancel to cancel this event.

enter   *s*.enter(*delay,priority,func,args*)

Like enterabs, except that argument *delay* is a relative time (the difference from the current instant, in the same units of measure), while enterabs's argument *when* is an absolute time (a future instant).

run   *s*.run( )

Runs all scheduled events. *s*.run loops until *s*.empty( ), using *delayfunc* as passed on *s*'s initialization to wait for the next scheduled event, and then executes the event. If a callback *func* raises an exception, *s* propagates it, but *s* keeps its own state, removing from the schedule the event whose callback raised. If a callback *func* takes longer to run than the time available before the next scheduled event, *s* falls behind, but keeps executing scheduled events in order and never drops events. You can call *s*.cancel to drop an event explicitly if that event is no longer of interest.

The calendar Module

The calendar module supplies calendar-related functions, including functions to print a text calendar for any given month or year. By default, calendar considers Monday the first day of the week and Sunday the last one. You can change this setting by calling function calendar.setfirstweekday. calendar handles years in the range supported by module time, typically 1970 to 2038. Module calendar supplies the following functions.

calendar   calendar(*year,w=2,l=1,c=6*)

Returns a multiline string with a calendar for year *year* formatted into three columns separated by *c* spaces. *w* is the width in characters of each date; each line has length 21*w*+18+2*c*. *l* is the number of lines used for each week.

firstweekday   firstweekday( )

Returns the current setting for the weekday that starts each week. By default, when calendar is first imported, this is 0, meaning Monday.

isleap	`isleap(year)` Returns True if *year* is a leap year, otherwise False.
leapdays	`leapdays(y1,y2)` Returns the total number of leap days in the years in range(*y1*,*y2*).
month	`month(year,month,w=2,l=1)` Returns a multiline string with a calendar for month *month* of year *year*, one line per week plus two header lines. *w* is the width in characters of each date; each line has length 7*w+6. *l* is the number of lines for each week.
monthcalendar	`monthcalendar(year,month)` Returns a list of lists of integers. Each sublist represents a week. Days outside month *month* of year *year* are represented by a placeholder value of 0; days within the given month are represented by their dates, from 1 on up.
monthrange	`monthrange(year,month)` Returns a pair of integers. The first item is the code of the weekday for the first day of the month *month* in year *year*; the second item is the number of days in the month. Weekday codes are 0 (Monday) to 6 (Sunday); month numbers are 1 (January) to 12 (December).
prcal	`prcal(year,w=2,l=1,c=6)` Like print calendar.calendar(*year*,*w*,*l*,*c*).
prmonth	`prmonth(year,month,w=2,l=1)` Like print calendar.month(*year*,*month*,*w*,*l*).
setfirstweekday	`setfirstweekday(weekday)` Sets the first day of each week to the weekday code *weekday*. Weekday codes are 0 (Monday) to 6 (Sunday). Module calendar also supplies attributes MONDAY, TUESDAY, WEDNESDAY, THURSDAY, FRIDAY, SATURDAY, and SUNDAY, whose values are the integers 0 to 6. Use these attributes when you mean weekday codes (e.g., calendar.FRIDAY instead of 4), to make your code clearer and more readable.
timegm	`timegm(tupletime)` The inverse of time.gmtime: accepts a time instant in time-tuple form and returns the same instant as a floating-point number of seconds since the epoch.

weekday	weekday(*year*,*month*,*day*)
	Returns the weekday code for the given date. Weekday codes are 0 (Monday) to 6 (Sunday); month numbers are 1 (January) to 12 (December).

The mx.DateTime Module

DateTime is one of the modules in the mx package made available by eGenix GmbH. mx is open source, and at the time of this writing, mx.DateTime has liberal license conditions similar to those of Python itself. mx.DateTime's popularity stems from its functional richness and cross-platform portability. I present only an essential subset of mx.DateTime's rich functionality here; the module comes with detailed documentation about its advanced time and date handling features.

Date and Time Types

Module DateTime supplies several date and time types whose instances are immutable (and therefore suitable as dictionary keys). Type DateTime represents a time instant and includes an absolute date, which is the number of days since an epoch of January 1, year 1 CE, according to the Gregorian calendar (0001-01-01 is day 1), and an absolute time, which is a floating-point number of seconds since midnight. Type DateTimeDelta represents an interval of elapsed time, which is a floating-point number of seconds. Class RelativeDateTime lets you specify dates in relative terms, such as "next Monday" or "first day of next month." DateTime and DateTimeDelta are covered in detail later in this section, but RelativeDateTime is not.

Date and time types supply customized string conversion, invoked via the built-in str or automatically during implicit conversion (e.g., in a print statement). The resulting strings are in standard ISO 8601 formats, such as:

```
YYYY-MM-DD HH:MM:SS.ss
```

For finer-grained control of string formatting, use method strftime. Function DateTimeFrom constructs DateTime instances from strings. Submodules of module mx.DateTime supply other formatting and parsing functions, using different standards and conventions.

The DateTime Type

Module DateTime supplies factory functions to build instances of type DateTime, which in turn supply methods, attributes, and arithmetic operators.

Factory functions for DateTime

Module `DateTime` supplies many factory functions that produce `DateTime` instances. Several of these factory functions can also be invoked through synonyms. The most commonly used factory functions are the following.

DateTime, Date, Timestamp	`DateTime(`*year,month=1,day=1,hour=0,minute=0,second=0.0*`)`
	
	Creates and returns a `DateTime` instance representing the given absolute time. `Date` and `Timestamp` are synonyms of `DateTime`. *day* can be less than 0 to denote days counted from the end of the month: -1 is the last day of the month, -2 the next to last day, and so on. For example:
	
	    `print mx.DateTime.DateTime(2002,12,-1)`
	    `# prints: 2002-12-31 00:00:00.00`
	
	second is a floating-point value and can include an arbitrary fraction of a second.

DateTimeFrom, TimestampFrom	`DateTimeFrom(`**args,**kwds*`)` Creates and returns a `DateTime` instance built from the given arguments. `TimestampFrom` is a synonym of `DateTimeFrom`. `DateTimeFrom` can parse strings that represent a date and/or time. `DateTimeFrom` can also accept named arguments, taking the same names as those of the arguments of function `DateTime`.
DateTimeFrom AbsDays	`DateTimeFromAbsDays(`*days*`)` Creates and returns a `DateTime` instance representing an instant *days* days after the epoch. *days* is a floating-point number and can include an arbitrary fraction of a day.
DateTimeFrom COMDate	`DateTimeFromCOMDate(`*comdate*`)` Creates and returns a `DateTime` instance representing the COM-format date *comdate*. *comdate* is a floating-point number and can include an arbitrary fraction of a day. The COM date epoch is midnight of January 1, 1900.
DateFromTicks	`DateFromTicks(`*secs*`)` Creates and returns a `DateTime` instance representing midnight, local time, of the day of instant *secs*. *secs* is an instant as represented by the `time` module (i.e., seconds since `time`'s epoch).
gmt, utc	`gmt( )` Creates and returns a `DateTime` instance representing the current GMT time. `utc` is a synonym of `gmt`.

gmtime, utctime	gmtime(*secs*=None)
	Creates and returns a DateTime instance representing the GMT time of instant *secs*. *secs* is an instant as represented by the time module (i.e., seconds since time's epoch). When *secs* is None, gmtime uses the current instant as returned by function time.time. utctime is a synonym of gmtime.

localtime	localtime(*secs*=None)
	Creates and returns a DateTime instance representing the local time of instant *secs*. *secs* is an instant as represented by the time module (i.e., seconds since time's epoch). When *secs* is None, localtime uses the current instant as returned by function time.time.

mktime	mktime(*timetuple*)
	Creates and returns a DateTime instance representing the instant indicated by nine-item tuple *timetuple*, which is in the format used by module time.

now	now( )
	Creates and returns a DateTime instance representing the current local time.

TimestampFrom Ticks	TimestampFromTicks(*secs*)
	Creates and returns a DateTime instance representing the local time of instant *secs*. *secs* is an instant as represented by the time module (i.e., seconds since time's epoch).

today	today(*hour*=0,*minute*=0,*second*=0.0)
	Creates and returns a DateTime instance representing the local time for the given time (the default is midnight) of today's date.

Methods of DateTime instances

The most commonly used methods of a DateTime instance *d* are the following.

absvalues	*d*.absvalues( )
	Returns a pair (*ad*,*at*) where *ad* is an integer representing *d*'s absolute date and *at* is a floating-point number representing *d*'s absolute time.

COMDate	*d*.COMDate( )
	Returns *d*'s instant in COM format (i.e., a floating-point number that is the number of days and fraction of a day since midnight of January 1, 1900).
gmticks	*d*.gmticks( )
	Returns a floating-point value representing *d*'s instant as seconds (and fraction) since module time's epoch, assuming *d* is represented in GMT.
gmtime	*d*.gmtime( )
	Returns a DateTime instance *d1* representing *d*'s instant in GMT, assuming *d* is represented in local time.
gmtoffset	*d*.gmtoffset( )
	Returns a DateTimeDelta instance representing the time zone of *d*, assuming *d* is represented in local time. gmtoffset returns negative values in the Americas, positive ones in most of Europe, Asia, and Africa.
localtime	*d*.localtime( )
	Returns a DateTime instance *d1* representing *d*'s instant in local time, assuming *d* is represented in GMT.
strftime, Format	*d*.strftime(*fmt*="%c")
	Returns a string representing *d* as specified by string *fmt*. The syntax of *fmt* is the same as in time.strftime, covered in "The time Module" earlier in this chapter. Format is a synonym of strftime.
ticks	*d*.ticks( )
	Returns a floating-point number representing *d*'s instant as seconds (and fraction) since module time's epoch, assuming *d* is represented in local time.
tuple	*d*.tuple( )
	Returns *d*'s instant as a nine-item tuple, in the format used by module time.

Attributes of DateTime instances

The most commonly used attributes of a DateTime instance *d* are the following (all read-only):

absdate
   d's absolute date, like *d*.absvalues( )[0]

absdays
   A floating-point number representing days (and fraction of a day) since the epoch

abstime
   d's absolute time, like *d*.absvalues( )[1]

date
   A string in format 'YYYY-MM-DD', the standard ISO format for the date of *d*

day
   An integer between 1 and 31, the day of the month of *d*

day_of_week
   An integer between 0 and 6, the day of the week of *d* (Monday is 0)

day_of_year
   An integer between 1 and 366, the day of the year of *d* (January 1 is 1)

dst
   An integer between -1 and 1, indicating whether DST is in effect on date *d*, assuming *d* is represented in local time (-1 is unknown, 0 is no, 1 is yes)

hour
   An integer between 0 and 23, the hour of the day of *d*

iso_week
   A three-item tuple (*year, week, day*) with the ISO week notation for *d* (*week* is week-of-year; *day* is between 1, Monday, and 7, Sunday)

minute
   An integer between 0 and 59, the minute of the hour of *d*

month
   An integer between 1 and 12, the month of the year of *d*

second
   A floating-point number between 0.0 and 60.0, the second of the minute of *d* (DateTime instances do not support leap seconds)

year
   An integer, the year of *d* (1 is 1 CE, 0 is 1 BCE)

Arithmetic on DateTime instances

You can use binary operator - (minus) between two DateTime instances *d1* and *d2*. In this case, *d1-d2* is a DateTimeDelta instance representing the elapsed time between *d1* and *d2*, which is greater than 0 if *d1* is later than *d2*. You can use binary operators + and - between a DateTime instance *d* and a number *n*. *d+n*, *d-n*, and *n+d* are all DateTime instances differing from *d* by *n* (or *-n*) days (and fraction of a day, if *n* is a floating-point number), and *n-d* is arbitrarily defined to be equal to *d-n*.

The DateTimeDelta Type

Instances of type `DateTimeDelta` represent differences between time instants. Internally, a `DateTimeDelta` instance stores a floating-point number that represents a number of seconds (and fraction of a second).

Factory functions for DateTimeDelta

Module `DateTime` supplies many factory functions that produce `DateTimeDelta` instances. Some of these factory functions can be invoked through one or more synonyms. The most commonly used are the following.

DateTimeDelta	`DateTimeDelta(days,hours=0.0,minutes=0.0,seconds=0.0)`
	Creates and returns a `DateTimeDelta` instance by the formula:
	$seconds+60.0*(minutes+60.0*(hours+24.0*days))$
DateTimeDelta From	`DateTimeDeltaFrom(*args,**kwds)`
	Creates and returns a `DateTimeDelta` instance from the given arguments. See the `DateTimeFrom` factory function for type `DateTime` earlier in this chapter.
DateTimeDelta FromSeconds	`DateTimeDeltaFromSeconds(seconds)`
	Like `DateTimeDelta(0,0,0,seconds)`.
TimeDelta, Time	`TimeDelta(hours=0.0,minutes=0.0,seconds=0.0)`
	Like `DateTimeDelta(0,hours,minutes,seconds)`. Function `TimeDelta` is guaranteed to accept named arguments. `Time` is a synonym for `TimeDelta`.
TimeDeltaFrom, TimeFrom	`TimeDeltaFrom(*args,**kwds)`
	Like `DateTimeDeltaFrom`, except that the first positional numeric arguments, if any, indicate hours, not days as for `DateTimeDeltaFrom`. `TimeFrom` is a synonym for `TimeDeltaFrom`.
TimeFromTicks	`TimeFromTicks(secs)`
	Creates and returns a `DateTimeDelta` instance for the amount of time between the instant *secs* (in the format used by the `time` module) and midnight of the same day as that of the instant *secs*.

Methods of DateTimeDelta instances

The most commonly used methods of a `DateTimeDelta` instance *d* are the following.

absvalues   `d.absvalues()`

Returns a pair (*ad*,*at*) where *ad* is an integer (*d*'s number of days), *at* is a floating-point number (*d*'s number of seconds modulo 86400), and both have the same sign.

strftime, Format   `d.strftime(`*fmt*`="%c")`

Returns a string representing *d* as specified by string *fmt*. The syntax of *fmt* is the same as in `time.strftime`, covered in "The time Module" earlier in this chapter, but not all specifiers are meaningful. The result of `d.strftime` does not reflect the sign of the time interval that *d* represents; to display the sign as well, you must affix it to the string by separate string manipulation. For example:

```
if d.seconds >= 0.0: return d.strftime(fmt)
else: return '-' + d.strftime(fmt)
```

Format is a synonym of `strftime`.

tuple   `d.tuple()`

Returns a tuple (*day*,*hour*,*minute*,*second*) where each item is a signed number in the respective range. *second* is a floating-point number, and the other items are integers.

Attributes of DateTimeDelta instances

A `DateTimeDelta` instance *d* supplies the following attributes (all read-only):

day, hour, minute, second
  Like the four items of the tuple returned by `d.tuple()`

days, hours, minutes, seconds
  Each is a floating-point value expressing *d*'s value in the given unit of measure, so that:

```
d.seconds == 60.0*d.minutes == 3600.0*d.hours == 86400.0*d.days
```

Arithmetic on DateTimeDelta instances

You can add or subtract two `DateTimeDelta` instances *d1* and *d2*, to add or subtract the signed time intervals they represent. You can use binary operators + and - between a `DateTimeDelta` instance *d* and a number *n*: *n* is taken as a number of seconds (and fraction of a second, if *n* is a floating-point value). You can also multiply or divide *d* by *n*, to scale the time interval *d* represents. Each of these operations yields another `DateTimeDelta` instance. You can also add or subtract a `DateTimeDelta` instance *dd* to or from a `DateTime` instance *d*, yielding another `DateTime` instance *d1* that differs from *d* by the signed time interval indicated by *dd*.

Other Attributes

Module mx.DateTime also supplies many constant attributes. The attributes used most often are:

oneWeek, oneDay, oneHour, oneMinute, oneSecond
: Instances of DateTimeDelta representing the indicated durations

Monday, Tuesday, Wednesday, Thursday, Friday, Saturday, Sunday
: Integers representing the weekdays: Monday is 0, Tuesday is 1, and so on

Weekday
: A dictionary that maps integer weekday numbers to their string names and vice versa: 0 maps to 'Monday', 'Monday' maps to 0, and so on

January, February, March, April, May, June, July, August, September, October, November, December
: Integers representing the months: January is 1, February is 2, and so on

Month
: A dictionary that maps integer month numbers to their string names and vice versa: 1 maps to 'January', 'January' maps to 1, and so on

Module mx.DateTime supplies one other useful function.

cmp	cmp(*obj1*,*obj2*,*accuracy*=0.0) Compares two DateTime or DateTimeDelta instances *obj1* and *obj2*, and returns -1, 0, or 1, like the built-in function cmp. It also returns 0 (meaning that *obj1* and *obj2* are "equal") if the two instants or durations differ by less than *accuracy* seconds.

Submodules

Module mx.DateTime also supplies several submodules for specialized purposes. Module mx.DateTime.ISO supplies functions to parse and generate date and time strings in ISO 8601 formats. Module mx.DateTime.ARPA supplies functions to parse and generate date and time strings in the ARPA format that is widely used on the Internet:

[*Day*,]*DD Mon YYYY HH:MM*[:*SS*] [*ZONE*]

Module mx.DateTime.Feasts supplies functions to compute the date of Easter Sunday, and other moveable feast days that depend on it, for any given year. If your machine is connected to the Internet, you can use module mx.DateTime.NIST to access the accurate world standard time provided by NIST atomic clocks. Thanks to NIST's atomic clocks, the module is able to compute the current date and time very accurately. The module calibrates your computer's approximate clock with reference to NIST's clocks and compensates for any network delays incurred while accessing NIST.

13

Controlling Execution

Python directly exposes many of the mechanisms it uses internally. This helps you understand Python at an advanced level, and means you can hook your own code into such documented Python mechanisms and control those mechanisms to some extent. For example, Chapter 7 covered the import statement and the way Python arranges for built-ins to be made implicitly visible. This chapter covers other advanced techniques that Python offers for controlling execution, while Chapter 17 covers execution-control possibilities that apply specifically to the three crucial phases of development: testing, debugging, and profiling.

Dynamic Execution and the exec Statement

With Python's exec statement, it is possible to execute code that you read, generate, or otherwise obtain during the running of a program. The exec statement dynamically executes a statement or a suite of statements. exec is a simple keyword statement with the following syntax:

    exec code[in globals[,locals]]

code can be a string, an open file-like object, or a code object. *globals* and *locals* are dictionaries. If both are present, they are the global and local namespaces, respectively, in which *code* executes. If only *globals* is present, exec uses *globals* in the role of both namespaces. If neither *globals* nor *locals* is present, *code* executes in the current scope. Running exec in current scope is not good programming practice, since it can bind, rebind, or unbind any name. To keep things under control, you should use exec only with specific, explicit dictionaries.

Avoiding exec

More generally, use exec only when it's really indispensable. Most often, it is better avoided in favor of more specific mechanisms. For example, a frequently asked question is, "How do I set a variable whose name I just read or constructed?" Strictly speaking, exec lets you do this. For example, if the name of the variable you want to set is in variable *varname*, you might use:

```
exec varname+'=23'
```

Don't do this. An exec statement like this in current scope causes you to lose control of your namespace, leading to bugs that are extremely hard to track and more generally making your program unfathomably difficult to understand. An improvement is to keep the "variables" you need to set, not as variables, but as entries in a dictionary, say *mydict*. You can then use the following variation:

```
exec varname+'=23' in mydict
```

While this is not as terrible as the previous example, it is still a bad idea. The best approach is to keep such "variables" as dictionary entries and not use exec at all to set them. You can just use:

```
mydict[varname] = 23
```

With this approach, your program is clearer, more direct, more elegant, and faster. While there are valid uses of exec, they are extremely rare and they should always use explicit dictionaries.

Restricting Execution

If the global namespace is a dictionary without key '__builtins__', exec implicitly adds that key, referring to module __builtin__ (or to the dictionary thereof), as covered in Chapter 8. If the global namespace dictionary has a key '__builtins__' and the value doesn't refer to the real module __builtin__, *code*'s execution is restricted, as covered in the upcoming section "Restricted Execution."

Expressions

exec can execute an expression because any expression is also a valid statement (called an expression statement). However, Python ignores the value returned by an expression statement in this case. To evaluate an expression and obtain the expression's value, see built-in function eval, covered in Chapter 8.

Compile and Code Objects

To obtain a code object to use with exec, you normally call built-in function compile with the last argument set to 'exec' (as covered in Chapter 8). I recommend using compile on statements held in a string and then using exec on the resulting code object, rather than giving exec the string to compile and execute. This separation lets you check for syntax errors separately from evaluation-time errors. You can often arrange things so the string is compiled once and the code object is executed repeatedly, speeding things up. eval can also benefit from such separation.

A code object has a read-only attribute co_names, the tuple of the names used in the code. Knowing what names the code is about to access may sometimes help you optimize the preparation of the dictionary you pass to exec or eval as the namespace. Since you need to provide values only for those names, you may save work by not preparing other entries.

For example, your application may dynamically accept code from the user with the convention that variable names starting with data_ refer to files residing in subdirectory *data* that user-written code doesn't need to read explicitly. User-written code may in turn compute and leave results in global variables with names starting with result_, which your application will write back as files in subdirectory *data*. Thanks to this convention, you may later move the data elsewhere (e.g., to BLOBs in a database), and user-written code won't be affected. Here's how you might implement these conventions efficiently:

```
def exec_with_data(user_code_string):
    user_code = compile(user_code_string, '<user code>', 'exec')
    datadict = { }
    for name in user_code.co_names:
        if name.startswith('data_'):
            datafile = open('data/%s' % name[5:], 'rb')
            datadict[name] = datafile.read( )
            datafile.close( )
    exec user_code in datadict
    for name in datadict:
        if name.startswith('result_'):
            datafile = open('data/%s' % name[7:], 'wb')
            datafile.write(datadict[name])
            datafile.close( )
```

Restricted Execution

Python code executed dynamically normally suffers no special restrictions. Python's general philosophy is to give the programmer tools and mechanisms that make it easy to write good, safe code, and trust the programmer to use them appropriately. Sometimes, however, trust might not be warranted. When code to execute dynamically comes from an untrusted source, the code itself is untrusted. In such cases it's important to selectively restrict the execution environment so that such code cannot accidentally or maliciously inflict damage. If you never need to execute untrusted code, you can skip this section. However, Python makes it easy to impose appropriate restrictions on untrusted code if you ever do need to execute it.

When the __builtins__ item in the global namespace isn't the standard __builtin__ module (or the latter's dictionary), Python knows the code being run is restricted. Restricted code executes in a sandbox environment, previously prepared by the trusted code, that requests the restricted code's execution. Standard modules rexec and Bastion help you prepare an appropriate sandbox. To ensure that restricted code cannot escape the sandbox, a few crucial internals (e.g., the __dict__ attributes of modules, classes, and instances) are not directly available to restricted code.

There is no special protection against restricted code raising exceptions. On the contrary, Python diagnoses any attempt by restricted code to violate the sandbox restrictions by raising an exception. Therefore, you should generally run restricted code in the try clause of a try/except statement, as covered in Chapter 6. Make sure you catch all exceptions and handle them appropriately if your program needs to keep running in such cases.

There is no built-in protection against untrusted code attempting to inflict damage by consuming large amounts of memory or time (so-called denial-of-service attacks). If you need to ward against such attacks, you can run untrusted code in a separate process. The separate process uses the mechanisms described in this section to restrict the untrusted code's execution, while the main process monitors the separate one and terminates it if and when resource consumption becomes excessive. Processes are covered in Chapter 14. Resource monitoring is currently supported by the standard Python library only on Unix-like platforms (by platform-specific module resource), and this book covers only cross-platform Python.

As a final note, you need to know that there are known, exploitable security weaknesses in the restricted-execution mechanisms, even in the most recent versions of Python. Although restricted execution is better than nothing, at the time of this writing there are no known ways to execute untrusted code that are suitable for security-critical situations.

The rexec Module

The rexec module supplies the RExec class, which you can instantiate to prepare a typical restricted-execution sandbox environment in which to run untrusted code.

Controlling
Execution

RExec   class RExec(*hooks*=None,*verbose*=False)

Returns an instance of the RExec class, which corresponds to a new restricted-execution environment, also known as a sandbox. *hooks*, if not None, lets you exert fine-grained control on import statements executed in the sandbox. This is an advanced and rarely used functionality, and I do not cover it further in this book. *verbose*, if true, causes additional debugging output to be sent to standard output for many kinds of operations in the sandbox.

Methods

An instance r of RExec provides the following methods. Versions of RExec's methods whose names start with s_ rather than r_ are also available. An r_ method and its s_ variant are equivalent, but the latter also ensures that untrusted code can call only safe methods on standard file objects sys.stdin, sys.stdout, and sys.stderr. This is needed only in the unusual case in which you have replaced the standard file objects with file-like objects that also expose additional, unsafe methods or attributes.

r_add_module   *r*.r_add_module(*modname*)

Adds and returns a new empty module if no module yet corresponds to name *modname* in the sandbox. If the sandbox already contains a module object that corresponds to name *modname*, r_add_module returns that module object.

r_eval,
s_eval
	`r.r_eval(expr)`
	`r.s_eval(expr)`
	
	r_eval executes *expr*, which must be an expression or a code object, in the restricted environment and returns the expression's result.

r_exec,
s_exec
	`r.r_exec(code)`
	`r.s_exec(code)`
	
	r_exec executes *code*, which must be a string of code or a code object, in the restricted environment.

r_execfile,
s_execfile
	`r.r_execfile(filename)`
	`r.s_execfile(filename)`
	
	r_execfile executes the file identified by *filename*, which must contain Python code, in the restricted environment.

r_import,
s_import
	`r.r_import(modname[,globals[,locals[,fromlist]]])`
	`r.s_import(modname[,globals[,locals[,fromlist]]])`
	
	Imports the module *modname* into the restricted environment. All parameters are just like for built-in function __import__, covered in Chapter 7. r_import raises ImportError if the module is considered unsafe. A subclass of RExec may override r_import, to change the set of modules available to import statements in untrusted code and/or to otherwise change import functionality for the sandbox.

r_open	`r.r_open(filename[,mode[,bufsize]])` Executes when restricted code calls the built-in open. All parameters are just like for the built-in open, covered in Chapter 10. The version of r_open in class RExec opens any file for reading, but none for writing or appending. A subclass may ease or tighten these restrictions.

r_reload,
s_reload
	`r.r_reload(module)`
	`r.s_reload(module)`
	
	Reloads the module object *module* in the restricted-execution environment, similarly to built-in function reload, covered in Chapter 7.

r_unload,
s_unload
	`r.r_unload(module)`
	`r.s_unload(module)`
	
	Unloads the module object *module* from the restricted-execution environment (i.e., removes it from the dictionary sys.modules as seen by untrusted code executing in the sandbox).

Attributes

When RExec's defaults don't fully correspond to your application's specific needs, you can easily customize the restricted-execution sandbox. Class RExec has several attributes that are tuples of strings. The items of these tuples are names of functions, modules, or directories to be specifically allowed or disallowed, as follows:

nok_builtin_names
    Built-in functions not to be supplied in the sandbox

ok_builtin_modules
    Built-in modules that the sandbox can import

ok_path
    Used as sys.path for the sandbox's import statements

ok_posix_names
    Attributes of os that the sandbox may import

ok_sys_names
    Attributes of sys that the sandbox may import

When you instantiate RExec, the new instance uses class attributes to prepare the sandbox. If you need to customize the sandbox, subclass RExec and instantiate the subclass. Your subclass can override RExec's attributes, typically by copying the value that each attribute has in RExec and selectively adding or removing specific items.

Using rexec

In the simplest case, you can instantiate RExec and call the instance's r_exec and r_eval methods instead of using statement exec and built-in function eval. For example, here's a somewhat safer variant of built-in function input:

```
import rexec
rex = rexec.RExec( )
def rexinput(prompt):
    expr = raw_input(prompt)
    return rex.r_eval(expr)
```

Function rexinput in this example is roughly equivalent to built-in function input, covered in Chapter 8. However, rexinput wards against some of the abuses that are possible if you don't trust the user who's supplying input. For example, with the normal, unrestricted eval, an expression such as __import__('os').system('xx') lets the interactive user run any external program xx. Built-in function input implicitly uses normal, unrestricted eval on the user's input. Function rexinput uses restricted execution instead, so that the same expression fails and raises AttributeError, claiming that module os has no attribute named system. This example does not use a try/except around the r_eval call, but of course your application code that calls rexinput should use try/except if you need your program to keep executing when the user makes mistakes or unsuccessful attempts to break security. Mistakes and attempts to break security both get diagnosed through exceptions.

This example's usefulness comes from the fact that a restricted-execution sandbox can hide some functionality from untrusted code, so that untrusted code cannot take advantage of that functionality to wreak havoc. Function os.system is a prime example of functionality that should always be prohibited to untrusted code, so class RExec forbids it by default.

After creating a new restricted-execution environment *r* with *r*=rexec.RExec( ), you can optionally complete *r*'s initialization by inserting modules into *r*'s sandbox with add_module, then inserting attributes in those modules with built-in function setattr. Simple assignment statements also work just fine if the attributes have names that you know at the time you're writing your sandbox-preparation code. Here's how to enrich the previous example to let the user-entered expressions use all functions from module math (covered in Chapter 15) as if they were built-ins, since you know that none of the functions presents any security risk:

```
import rexec, math
rex = rexec.RExec( )
burex = rex.add_module('__builtins__')
for function in dir(math):
    if function[0] != '_':
        setattr(burex, function, getattr(math, function))
def rich_input(prompt):
    expr = raw_input(prompt)
    return rex.r_eval(expr)
```

Function rich_input in this example is now both richer and safer than the built-in input. It's richer because the user can now also input expressions such as sin(1.0). It's safer, just like rexinput in the previous example, because it uses restricted execution to limit untrusted code.

Normally, you use add_module, and then add attributes, only for the modules named '__main__' and '__builtins__'. If the untrusted code needs other modules that it is allowed to import (based on the ok_builtin_modules and ok_path attributes of the RExec subclass you instantiated), the untrusted code can import those other modules normally, usually with an import statement or a call to built-in function __import__. However, you can also choose to use add_module for other module names in order to synthesize, restrict, or otherwise modify modules that later get imported by the untrusted code.

Once you have populated the sandbox, untrusted code can call the functions and other callables that you added to the sandbox. When called, such functions and other callables execute in the normal (non-sandbox) environment, without constraints. You should therefore ensure that untrusted code cannot cause damage by misusing such callables. Module Bastion, covered in the next section, deals with the specific task of selectively exposing object methods.

The Bastion Module

The Bastion module supplies a class, each of whose instances wraps an object and selectively exposes some of the wrapped object's methods, but no other attributes.

Bastion   class Bastion(*obj*,*filter*=lambda *n*: *n*[:1]!='_',*name*=None)

A Bastion instance *b* wrapping object *obj* exposes only those methods of *obj* for whose name *filter* returns true. An access *b.attr* works like:

```
if filter('attr'): return obj.attr
else: raise AttributeError, 'attr'
```

plus a check that *b.attr* is a method, not an attribute of any other type.

The default *filter* accepts all method names that do not start with an underscore (_) (i.e., all methods that are neither private nor special methods). When *name* is not None, repr(*b*) is the string '<Bastion for *name*>'. When *name* is None, repr(*b*) is '<Bastion for %s>' % repr(*obj*).

Suppose, for example, that your application supplies a class MyClass whose public methods are all safe, while private and special methods, as well as attributes that are not methods, should be hidden from untrusted code. In the sandbox, you can provide a factory function that supplies safely wrapped instances of MyClass to untrusted code as follows:

```
import rexec, Bastion
rex = rexec.RExec( )
burex = rex.add_module('__builtins__')
def SafeMyClassFactory(*args, **kwds):
    return Bastion.Bastion(MyClass(*args, **kwds))
burex.MyClass = SafeMyClassFactory
```

Now, untrusted code that you run with rex.r_exec can instantiate and use safely wrapped instances of MyClass:

```
m = MyClass(1,2,3)
m.somemethod(4,5)
```

However, any attempt by the untrusted code to access private or special methods, even indirectly (e.g., *m*[6]=7 indirectly tries to use special method __setitem__), raises AttributeError, whether the real MyClass supplies such methods or not. Suppose you want a slightly less tight wrapping, allowing untrusted code to use special method __getitem__, as well as normal public methods, but no other. You just need to provide a custom *filter* function when you instantiate Bastion:

```
import rexec, Bastion
rex = rexec.RExec( )
burex = rex.add_module('__builtins__')
def SafeMyClassFactory(*args, **kwds):
    def is_safe(n): n=='__getitem__' or n[0]!='_'
    return Bastion.Bastion(MyClass(*args, **kwds), is_safe)
burex.MyClass = SafeMyClassFactory
```

Now, untrusted code that is run in sandbox rex can get, but not set, items of the instances of MyClass it builds with the factory function (assuming, of course, that your class MyClass does supply method __getitem__).

Internal Types

Some of the internal Python objects that I mention in this section are hard to use. Using such objects correctly requires some study of Python's own C (or Java) sources. Such black magic is rarely needed, except to build general-purpose development frameworks and similar wizardly tasks. Once you do understand things in depth, Python empowers you to exert control, if and when you need to. Since Python exposes internal objects to your Python code, you can exert that control by coding in Python, even when a nodding acquaintance with C (or Java) is needed to understand what is going on.

Type Objects

The built-in type named type acts as a factory object, returning objects that are types themselves (type was a built-in function in Python 2.1 and earlier). Type objects don't need to support any special operations except equality comparison and representation as strings. Most type objects are callable, and return new instances of the type when called. In particular, built-in types such as int, float, list, str, tuple, and dict all work this way. The attributes of the types module are the built-in types, each with one or more names. For example, types.DictType and types.DictionaryType both refer to type({ }), also known since Python 2.2 as the built-in type dict. Besides being callable to generate instances, type objects are useful in Python 2.2 and later because you can subclass them, as covered in Chapter 5.

The Code Object Type

As well as by using built-in function compile, you can also get a code object via the func_code attribute of a function or method object. A code object's co_varnames attribute is the tuple of names of local variables, including the formal arguments; the co_argcount attribute is the number of arguments. Code objects are not callable, but you can rebind the func_code attribute of a compatible function object in order to wrap a code object into callable form. Module new supplies a function to create a code object, as well as other functions to create instances, classes, functions, methods, and modules. Such needs are both rare and advanced, and are not covered further in this book.

The frame Type

Function _getframe in module sys returns a frame object from Python's call stack. A frame object has attributes that supply information about the code executing in the frame and the execution state. Modules traceback and inspect help you access and display information, particularly when an exception is being handled. Chapter 17 provides more information about frames and tracebacks.

Garbage Collection

Python's garbage collection normally proceeds transparently and automatically, but you can choose to exert some direct control. The general principle is that Python collects each object *x* at some time after *x* becomes unreachable, that is, when no chain of references can reach *x* by starting from a local variable of a function that is executing, nor from a global variable of a loaded module. Normally, an object *x* becomes unreachable when there are no references at all to *x*. However, a group of objects can also be unreachable when they reference each other.

Classic Python keeps in each object *x* a count, known as a *reference count*, of how many references to *x* are outstanding. When *x*'s reference count drops to 0, CPython immediately collects *x*. Function getrefcount of module sys accepts any object and returns its reference count (at least 1, since getrefcount itself has a reference to the object it's examining). Other versions of Python, such as Jython, rely on different garbage collection mechanisms, supplied by the platform they run on (e.g., the JVM). Modules gc and weakref therefore apply only to CPython.

When Python garbage-collects *x* and there are no references at all to *x*, Python then finalizes *x* (i.e., calls *x*.__del__( )) and makes the memory that *x* occupied available for other uses. If *x* held any references to other objects, Python removes the references, which in turn may make other objects collectable by leaving them unreachable.

The gc Module

The gc module exposes the functionality of Python's garbage collector. gc deals only with objects that are unreachable in a subtle way, being part of mutual reference loops. In such a loop, each object in the loop refers to others, keeping the reference counts of all objects positive. However, an outside reference no longer exists to the whole set of mutually referencing objects. Therefore, the whole group, also known as cyclic garbage, is unreachable, and therefore garbage collectable. Looking for such cyclic garbage loops takes time, which is why module gc exists.

gc exposes functions you can use to help you keep garbage collection times under control. These functions can sometimes help you track down a memory leak—objects that are not getting collected even though there should be no more references to them—by letting you discover what other objects are in fact holding on to references to them.

collect	collect( ) Forces a full cyclic collection run to happen immediately.
disable	disable( ) Suspends automatic garbage collection.

enable   enable( )

Re-enables automatic garbage collection previously suspended with disable.

garbage   A read-only attribute that lists the uncollectable but unreachable objects. This happens if any object in a cyclic garbage loop has a __del__ special method, as there may be no safe order in which Python can finalize such objects.

get_debug   get_debug( )

Returns an integer, a bit string corresponding to the garbage collection debug flags set with set_debug.

get_objects   get_objects( )   New as of Python 2.2

Returns a list whose items are all the objects currently tracked by the cyclic garbage collector.

get_referrers   get_referrers(*objs)

Returns a list whose items are all the container objects, currently tracked by the cyclic garbage collector, that refer to any one or more of the arguments.

get_threshold   get_threshold( )

Returns a three-item tuple (thresh0, thresh1, thresh2) corresponding to the garbage collection thresholds set with set_threshold.

isenabled   isenabled( )

Returns True if cyclic garbage collection is currently enabled. When collection is currently disabled, isenabled returns False.

set_debug   set_debug(flags)

Sets the debugging flags for garbage collection. flags is an integer, a bit string composed by ORing (with Python's normal bitwise-OR operator |) zero or more of the following constants exposed by module gc:

DEBUG_COLLECTABLE
    Prints information on collectable objects found during collection

DEBUG_INSTANCES
    Meaningful only if DEBUG_COLLECTABLE and/or DEBUG_UNCOLLECTABLE are also set: prints information on objects found during collection that are instances of classic Python classes

DEBUG_LEAK
: The set of debugging flags that make the garbage collector print all information that can help you diagnose memory leaks, equivalent to the inclusive-OR of all other constants (except DEBUG_STATS, which serves a different purpose)

DEBUG_OBJECTS
: Meaningful only if DEBUG_COLLECTABLE and/or DEBUG_UNCOLLECTABLE are also set: prints information on objects found during collection that are not instances of classic Python classes

DEBUG_SAVEALL
: Saves all collectable objects to list garbage (uncollectable ones are always saved there) to help diagnose leaks

DEBUG_STATS
: Prints statistics during collection to help tune the thresholds

DEBUG_UNCOLLECTABLE
: Prints information on uncollectable objects found during collection

set_threshold   set_threshold(*thresh0*[,*thresh1*[,*thresh2*]])

Sets the thresholds that control how frequently cyclic garbage collection cycles run. If you set *thresh0* to 0, garbage collection is disabled. Garbage collection is an advanced topic, and the details of the generational garbage collection approach used in Python and its thresholds are beyond the scope of this book.

When you know you have no cyclic garbage loops in your program, or when you can't afford the delay of a cyclic garbage collection run at some crucial time, you can suspend automatic garbage collection by calling gc.disable(). You can enable collection again later by calling gc.enable(). You can test whether automatic collection is currently enabled by calling gc.isenabled(), which returns True or False. To control when the time needed for collection is spent, you can call gc.collect() to force a full cyclic collection run to happen immediately. An idiom for wrapping some time-critical code is therefore:

```
import gc
gc_was_enabled = gc.isenabled()
if gc_was_enabled:
    gc.collect()
    gc.disable()
# insert some time-critical code here
if gc_was_enabled:
    gc.enable()
```

The other functionality in module gc is more advanced and rarely used, and can be grouped into two areas. Functions get_threshold and set_threshold and the debug flag DEBUG_STATS can help you fine-tune garbage collection to optimize your program's performance. The rest of gc's functionality is there to help you diagnose memory leaks in your program. While gc itself can automatically fix many such leaks, your program will be faster if it can avoid creating them in the first place.

The weakref Module

Careful design can often avoid reference loops. However, at times you need certain objects to know about each other, and avoiding mutual references would distort and complicate design. For example, a container has references to its items, yet it can often be useful for an object to know about some main container that holds it. The result is a reference loop: due to the mutual references, the container and items keep each other alive, even when all other objects forget about them. Weak references solve this problem by letting you have objects that mutually reference each other as long as both are alive, but do not keep each other alive.

A *weak reference* is a special object w that refers to some other object x without incrementing x's reference count. When x's reference count goes down to 0, Python finalizes and collects x, then informs w of x's demise. The weak reference w can now either disappear or become invalid in a controlled way. At any time, a given weak reference w refers to either the same target object x as when w was created, or to nothing at all: a weak reference is never re-targeted. Not all types of objects support being the target x of a weak reference w, but class instances and functions do.

Module weakref exposes functions and types to let you create and manage weak references.

getweakref count	getweakrefcount(x) Returns len(getweakrefs(x)).
getweakrefs	getweakrefs(x) Returns a list of all weak references and proxies whose target is x.
proxy	proxy(x[,f]) Returns a weak proxy p of type ProxyType (CallableProxyType, if x is callable), with object x as the target. In most contexts, using p is just like using x, except that if you use p after x has been deleted, Python raises ReferenceError. p is never hashable (therefore you cannot use p as a dictionary key), even when x is. If f is present, it must be callable with one argument, and is the finalization callback for p (i.e., right before finalizing x, Python calls f(p)). Note that when f is called, x is no longer reachable from p.
ref	ref(x[,f]) Returns a weak reference w of type ReferenceType, with object x as the target. w is callable: calling w( ) returns x if x is still alive, otherwise w( ) returns None. w is hashable if x is hashable. You can

compare weak references for equality (==, !=), but not for order (<, >, <=, >=). Two weak references *x* and *y* are equal if their targets are alive and equal, or if *x* is *y*. If *f* is present, it must be callable with one argument, and is the finalization callback for *w* (i.e., right before finalizing *x*, Python calls *f(w)*). Note that when *f* is called, *x* is no longer reachable from *w*.

WeakKey Dictionary	class WeakKeyDictionary(*adict*={ })

A WeakKeyDictionary *d* is a mapping that references its keys weakly. When the reference count of a key *k* in *d* goes to 0, item *d[k]* disappears. *adict* is used to initialize the mapping.

WeakValue Dictionary	class WeakValueDictionary(*adict*={ })

A WeakValueDictionary *d* is a mapping that references its values weakly. When the reference count of a value *v* in *d* goes to 0, all items of *d* such that *d[k]* is *v* disappear. *adict* is used to initialize the mapping.

WeakKeyDictionary and WeakValueDictionary are useful when you need to non-invasively associate additional data with objects without changing the objects. Weak mappings are also useful to non-invasively record transient associations between objects and to build caches. In each case, the specific consideration that can make a weak mapping preferable to a normal dictionary is that an object that is otherwise garbage-collectable is not kept alive just by being used in a weak mapping.

A typical use could be a class that keeps track of its instances, but does not keep them alive just in order to keep track of them:

```
import weakref
class Tracking:
    _instances_dict = weakref.WeakValueDictionary( )
    _num_generated = 0
    def __init__(self):
        Tracking._num_generated += 1
        Tracking._instances_dict[Tracking._num_generated] = self
    def instances( ): return _instances_dict.values( )
    instances = staticmethod(instances)
```

Termination Functions

The atexit module lets you register termination functions (i.e., functions to be called at program termination, last in, first out). Termination functions are similar to clean-up handlers established by try/finally. However, termination functions are globally registered and called at the end of the whole program, while clean-up handlers are established lexically and called at the end of a specific try clause. Both termination functions and clean-up handlers are called whether the program terminates normally or abnormally, but not when the termination is caused by calling os._exit. Module atexit supplies a single function called register.

register	register(*func,*args,**kwds*)
	Ensures that func(*args,**kwds) is called at program termination time.

Site and User Customization

Python provides a specific hook to let each site customize some aspects of Python's behavior at the start of each run. Customization by each single user is not enabled by default, but Python specifies how programs that want to run user-provided code at startup can explicitly request such customization.

The site and sitecustomize Modules

Python loads standard module site just before the main script. If Python is run with option -S, Python does not load site. -S allows faster startup, but saddles the main script with initialization chores. site's tasks are:

1. Putting sys.path in standard form (absolute paths, no duplicates).

2. Interpreting each *.pth* file found in the Python home directory, adding entries to sys.path, and/or importing modules, as each *.pth* file indicates.

3. Adding built-ins used to display information in interactive sessions (quit, exit, copyright, credits, and license).

4. Setting the default Unicode encoding to 'ascii'. site's source code includes two blocks, each guarded by if 0:, one to set the default encoding to be locale dependent, and the other to disable default encoding and decoding between Unicode and plain strings. You may optionally edit *site.py* to select either block.

5. Trying to import sitecustomize (should import sitecustomize raise an ImportError exception, site catches and ignores it). sitecustomize is the module that each site's installation can optionally use for further site-specific customization beyond site's tasks. It is generally best not to edit *site.py*, as any Python upgrade or reinstallation might overwrite your customizations. sitecustomize's main task is often to set the correct default encoding for the site. Western European sites, for example, may choose to call sys.setdefaultencoding('iso-8859-1').

6. After sitecustomize is done, removing from module sys the attribute sys.setdefaultencoding.

Thus, Python's default Unicode encoding can be set only at the start of a run, not changed in midstream during the run. In an emergency, if a specific main script desperately needs to break this guideline and set a different default encoding from that used by all other scripts, you may place the following snippet at the start of the main script:

```
import sys                              # get the sys module object
reload(sys)                            # restore module sys from disk
sys.setdefaultencoding('iso-8859-15')  # or whatever codec you need
del sys.setdefaultencoding             # ensure against later accidents
```

However, this is not good style. You should refactor your script so that it can accept whatever default encoding the site has chosen, and pass the encoding name explicitly in those spots where a specific codec is necessary.

User Customization

Each interactive Python interpreter session runs the script indicated by environment variable PYTHONSTARTUP. Outside of interactive interpreter sessions, there is no automatic per-user customization. To request per-user customization, a Python main script can explicitly import user. Standard module user, when loaded, first determines the user's home directory, as indicated by environment variable HOME (or, failing that, HOMEPATH, possibly preceded by HOMEDRIVE on Windows systems only). If the environment does not indicate a home directory, user uses the current directory. If module user locates a file named *.pythonrc.py* in the indicated directory, user executes that file, with built-in function execfile, in module user's own global namespace.

Scripts that don't import user do not load *.pythonrc.py*. Of course, any given script is free to arrange other specific ways to load whatever startup or plug-in user-supplied files it requires. Such application-specific arrangements are more common than importing user. A generic *.pythonrc.py*, as loaded via import user, needs to be usable with any application that loads it. Specialized, application-specific startup and plug-in user-supplied files only need to follow whatever convention a specific application documents.

For example, your application *MyApp.py* could document that it looks for a file named *.myapprc.py* in the user's home directory, as indicated by environment variable HOME, and loads it in the application main script's global namespace. You could then have the following code in your main script:

```
import os
homedir = os.environ.get('HOME')
if homedir is not None:
    userscript = os.path.join(homedir, '.myapprc.py')
    if os.path.isfile(userscript):
        execfile(userscript)
```

In this case, the *.myapprc.py* user customization script, if present, has to deal only with MyApp-specific user customization tasks.

14

Threads and Processes

A *thread* is a flow of control that shares global state with other threads; all threads appear to execute simultaneously. Threads are not easy to master, but once you do, they may offer a simpler architecture or better performance (faster response, but typically not better throughput) for some problems. This chapter covers the facilities that Python provides for dealing with threads, including the thread, threading, and Queue modules.

A *process* is an instance of a running program. Sometimes you get better results with multiple processes than with threads. The operating system protects processes from one another. Processes that want to communicate must explicitly arrange to do so, via local inter-process communication (IPC). Processes may communicate via files (covered in Chapter 10) or via databases (covered in Chapter 11). In both cases, the general way in which processes communicate using such data storage mechanisms is that one process can write data, and another process can later read that data back. This chapter covers the process-related parts of module os, including simple IPC by means of pipes, and a cross-platform IPC mechanism known as memory-mapped files, supplied to Python programs by module mmap.

Network mechanisms are well suited for IPC, as they work between processes that run on different nodes of a network as well as those that run on the same node. Chapter 19 covers low-level network mechanisms that provide a flexible basis for IPC. Other, higher-level mechanisms, known as distributed computing, such as CORBA, DCOM/COM+, EJB, SOAP, XML-RPC, and .NET, make IPC easier, whether locally or remotely. However, distributed computing is not covered in this book.

Threads in Python

Python offers multithreading on platforms that support threads, such as Win32, Linux, and most variants of Unix. The Python interpreter does not freely switch threads. Python uses a global interpreter lock (GIL) to ensure that switching between threads happens only between bytecode instructions or when C code deliberately releases the GIL (Python's C code releases the GIL around blocking I/O and sleep operations). An action is said to be *atomic* if it's guaranteed that no thread switching within Python's process occurs between the start and the end of the action. In practice, an operation that looks atomic actually is atomic when executed on an object of a built-in type (augmented assignment on an immutable object, however, is not atomic). However, in general it is not a good idea to rely on atomicity. For example, you never know when you might be dealing with a derived class rather than an object of a built-in type, meaning there might be callbacks to Python code.

Python offers multithreading in two different flavors. An older and lower-level module, thread, offers a bare minimum of functionality, and is not recommended for direct use by your code. The higher-level module threading, built on top of thread, was loosely inspired by Java's threads, and is the recommended tool. The key design issue in multithreading systems is most often how best to coordinate multiple threads. threading therefore supplies several synchronization objects. Module Queue is very useful for thread synchronization as it supplies a synchronized FIFO queue type, which is extremely handy for communication and coordination between threads.

The thread Module

The only part of the thread module that your code should use directly is the lock objects that module thread supplies. Locks are simple thread-synchronization primitives. Technically, thread's locks are non-reentrant and unowned: they do not keep track of what thread last locked them, so there is no specific owner thread for a lock. A lock is in one of two states, locked or unlocked.

To get a new lock object (in the unlocked state), call the function named allocate_lock without arguments. This function is supplied by both modules thread and threading. A lock object L supplies three methods. .

acquire	L.acquire(*wait*=True)
	When *wait* is True, acquire locks L. If L is already locked, the calling thread suspends and waits until L is unlocked, then locks L. Even if the calling thread was the one that last locked L, it still suspends and waits until another thread releases L. When *wait* is False and L is unlocked, acquire locks L and returns True. When *wait* is False and L is locked, acquire does not affect L, and returns False.
locked	L.locked( )
	Returns True if L is locked, otherwise False.

release	`L.release( )`
	Unlocks L, which must be locked. When L is locked, any thread may call L.release, not just the thread that last locked L. When more than one thread is waiting on L (i.e., has called L.acquire, finding L locked, and is now waiting for L to be unlocked), release wakes up an arbitrary waiting thread. The thread that calls release is not suspended: it remains ready and continues to execute.

The Queue Module

The Queue module supplies first-in, first-out (FIFO) queues that support multi-thread access, with one main class and two exception classes.

Queue	`class Queue(maxsize=0)`
	Queue is the main class for module Queue and is covered in the next section. When *maxsize* is greater than 0, the new Queue instance *q* is deemed full when *q* has *maxsize* items. A thread inserting an item with the *block* option, when *q* is full, suspends until another thread extracts an item. When *maxsize* is less than or equal to 0, *q* is never considered full, and is limited in size only by available memory, like normal Python containers.

Empty	Empty is the class of the exception that *q*.get(False) raises when *q* is empty.

Full	Full is the class of the exception that *q*.put(*x*,False) raises when *q* is full.

An instance *q* of class Queue supplies the following methods.

empty	`q.empty( )`
	Returns True if *q* is empty, otherwise False.

full	`q.full( )`
	Returns True if *q* is full, otherwise False.

get, get_nowait	`q.get(block=True)`
	When *block* is False, get removes and returns an item from *q* if one is available, otherwise get raises Empty. When *block* is True, get removes and returns an item from *q*, suspending the calling

thread, if need be, until an item is available. _q_.get_nowait( ) is like _q_.get(False). get removes and returns items in the same order as put inserted them (first in, first out).

put, **put_nowait**	_q_.put(_item,block=_True) When _block_ is False, put adds _item_ to _q_ if _q_ is not full, otherwise put raises Full. When _block_ is True, put adds _item_ to _q_, suspending the calling thread, if need be, until _q_ is not full. _q_.put_nowait(_item_) is like _q_.put(_item_,False).
qsize	_q_.qsize( ) Returns the number of items that are currently in _q_.

Queue offers a good example of the idiom "it's easier to ask forgiveness than permission" (EAFP), covered in Chapter 6. Due to multithreading, each non-mutating method of _q_ can only be advisory. When some other thread executes and mutates _q_, things can change between the instant a thread gets the information and the very next moment, when the thread acts on the information. Relying on the "look before you leap" (LBYL) idiom is futile, and fiddling with locks to try and fix things is a substantial waste of effort. Just avoid LBYL code such as:

```
if q.empty( ): print "no work to perform"
else: x=q.get_nowait( )
```

and instead use the simpler and more robust EAFP approach:

```
try: x=q.get_nowait( )
except Queue.Empty: print "no work to perform"
```

The threading Module

The threading module is built on top of module thread and supplies multi-threading functionality in a more usable form. The general approach of threading is similar to that of Java, but locks and conditions are modeled as separate objects (in Java, such functionality is part of every object), and threads cannot be directly controlled from the outside (meaning there are no priorities, groups, destruction, or stopping). All methods of objects supplied by threading are atomic.

threading provides numerous classes for dealing with threads, including Thread, Condition, Event, RLock, and Semaphore. Besides factory functions for the classes detailed in the following sections of this chapter, threading supplies the currentThread factory function.

currentThread	currentThread( ) Returns a Thread object for the calling thread. If the calling thread was not created by module threading, currentThread creates and returns a semi-dummy Thread object with limited functionality.

Thread Objects

A Thread object *t* models a thread. You can pass *t*'s main function as an argument when you create *t*, or you can subclass Thread and override the run method (you may also override __init__, but should not override other methods). *t* is not ready to run when you create it: to make *t* ready (active), call *t*.start( ). Once *t* is active, it terminates when its main function ends, either normally or by propagating an exception. A Thread *t* can be a daemon, meaning that Python can terminate even if *t* is still active, while a normal (non-daemon) thread keeps Python alive until the thread terminates. Class Thread exposes the following constructor and methods.

Thread	class Thread(*name*=None,*target*=None,*args*=( ),*kwargs*={ }) Always call Thread with named arguments: the number and order of formal arguments may change in the future, but the names of existing arguments are guaranteed to stay. When you instantiate class Thread itself, you should specify *target*: *t*.run calls *target*(**args*,***kwargs*). When you subclass Thread and override run, you normally don't specify *target*. In either case, execution doesn't begin until you call *t*.start( ). *name* is *t*'s name. If *name* is None, Thread generates a unique name for *t*. If a subclass T of Thread overrides __init__, T.__init__ must call Thread.__init__ on self before any other Thread method.
getName, setName	*t*.getName( ) *t*.setName(*name*) getName returns *t*'s name, and setName rebinds *t*'s name. The *name* string is arbitrary, and a thread's name need not be unique among threads.
isAlive	*t*.isAlive( ) Returns True if *t* is active (i.e., if *t*.start has executed and *t*.run has not yet terminated). Otherwise, isAlive returns False.
isDaemon, setDaemon	*t*.isDaemon( ) *t*.setDaemon(*daemonic*) isDaemon returns True if *t* is a daemon (i.e., Python can terminate the whole process even if *t* is still active—such a termination also terminates *t*); otherwise isDaemon returns False. Initially, *t* is a daemon if and only if the thread creating *t* is a daemon. You can call *t*.setDaemon only before *t*.start: it sets *t* to be a daemon if *daemonic* is true.
join	*t*.join(*timeout*=None) The calling thread (which must not be *t*) suspends until *t* terminates. *timeout* is covered in the upcoming section "Timeout parameters." You can call *t*.join only after *t*.start.

run	`t.run( )`
	run is the method that executes *t*'s main function. Subclasses of Thread often override run. Unless overridden, run calls the target callable passed on t's creation. Do *not* call `t.run` directly—calling `t.run` appropriately is the job of `t.start`!

start	`t.start( )`
	start makes *t* active and arranges for `t.run` to execute in a separate thread. You must call `t.start` only once for any given thread object *t*.

Thread Synchronization Objects

The threading module supplies several synchronization primitives, which are objects that let threads communicate and coordinate. Each primitive has specialized uses. However, as long as you avoid global variables that several threads access, Queue can often provide all the coordination you need. "Threaded Program Architecture" later in this chapter shows how to use Queue objects to give your multithreaded programs simple and effective architectures, often without needing any synchronization primitives.

Timeout parameters

Synchronization primitives Condition and Event supply wait methods that accept a *timeout* argument. A Thread object's join method also accepts a *timeout* argument. A *timeout* argument can be None, the default, to obtain normal blocking behavior (the calling thread suspends and waits until the desired condition is met). If not None, a *timeout* argument is a floating-point value that indicates an interval of time in seconds (*timeout* can have a fractional part and so can indicate any time interval, even a very short one). If *timeout* seconds elapse, the calling thread becomes ready again, even if the desired condition has not been met. *timeout* lets you design systems that are able to overcome occasional anomalies in one or a few threads, and thus are more robust. However, using *timeout* may also make your program slower.

Lock and RLock objects

The Lock objects exposed by module threading are the same as those supplied by module thread and covered in "The thread Module" earlier in this chapter. RLock objects supply the same methods as Lock objects. The semantics of an RLock object *r* are, however, often more convenient. When *r* is locked, it keeps track of the owning thread (i.e., the thread that locked it). The owning thread can call *r*.acquire again without blocking: *r* just increments an internal count. In a similar situation involving a Lock object, the thread would block forever (until the lock is released by some other thread).

An RLock object *r* is unlocked only when release has been called as many times as acquire. Only the thread owning *r* should call *r*.release. An RLock is useful to ensure exclusive access to an object when the object's methods call each other; each method can acquire at the start, and release at the end, the same RLock instance. try/finally is a good way to ensure the lock is indeed released.

Condition objects

A Condition object *c* wraps a Lock or RLock object *L*. Class Condition exposes the following constructor and methods.

Condition	class Condition(*lock*=None) Condition creates and returns a new Condition object *c* with the lock *L* set to *lock*. If *lock* is None, *L* is set to a newly created RLock object.
acquire, release	*c*.acquire(*wait*=1) *c*.release( ) These methods call *L*'s corresponding methods. A thread must never call any other method on *c* unless the thread holds lock *L*.
notify, notifyAll	*c*.notify( ) *c*.notifyAll( ) notify wakes up one of the threads waiting on *c*. The calling thread must hold *L* before it calls *c*.notify( ), and notify does not release *L*. The woken-up thread does not become ready until it can acquire *L* again. Therefore, the calling thread normally calls release after calling notify. notifyAll is like notify, but wakes up all waiting threads, not just one.
wait	*c*.wait(*timeout*=None) wait releases *L*, then suspends the calling thread until some other thread calls notify or notifyAll on *c*. The calling thread must hold *L* before it calls *c*.wait( ). *timeout* is covered earlier in "Timeout parameters." After a thread wakes up, either by notification or timeout, the thread becomes ready when it acquires *L* again. When wait returns, the calling thread always holds *L* again.

In typical use, a Condition object *c* regulates access to some global state *s* that is shared between threads. When a thread needs to wait for *s* to change, the thread loops as follows:

```
c.acquire( )
while not is_ok_state(s):
    c.wait( )
do_some_work_using_state(s)
c.release( )
```

Meanwhile, each thread that modifies s calls notify (or notifyAll, if it needs to wake up all waiting threads, not just one) each time s changes:

```
c.acquire( )
do_something_that_modifies_state(s)
c.notify( )     # or, c.notifyAll( )
c.release( )
```

As you see, you always need to acquire and release c around each use of c's methods, which makes using Condition somewhat error-prone.

Event objects

Event objects let any number of threads suspend and wait. All threads waiting on Event object e become ready when some other thread calls e.set( ). e has a flag recording whether the event happened, initially False when e is created. Event is thus a bit like a simplified Condition. Event objects are useful to signal one-shot changes, but are brittle for more general uses, as resetting an event object (i.e., relying on calls to e.clear( )) is quite error-prone. Class Event exposes the following methods.

Event	class Event( )
	Event creates and returns a new Event object e.
clear	e.clear( )
	Sets e's flag to False.
isSet	e.isSet( )
	Returns the value of e's flag, True or False.
set	e.set( )
	Sets e's flag to True. All threads waiting on e, if any, become ready to run.
wait	e.wait(timeout=None)
	If e's flag is True, wait returns immediately. Otherwise, wait suspends the calling thread until some other thread calls set. timeout is covered earlier in "Timeout parameters."

Semaphore objects

Semaphores are a generalization of locks. The state of a Lock can be seen as True or False; the state of a Semaphore s is a number between 0 and some n set when s is created. Semaphores can be useful to manage a fixed pool of resources (e.g., four printers or twenty sockets), although it's often more robust to use a Queue. A semaphore object s exposes the following methods.

Semaphore	class Semaphore(*n*=1)
	Semaphore creates and returns a semaphore object *s* with the state set to *n*.

acquire	*s*.acquire(*wait*=True)
	When *s*'s state is greater than 0, acquire decrements the state by 1 and returns True. When *s*'s state is 0 and *wait* is True, acquire suspends the calling thread and waits until some other thread calls *s*.release. When *s*'s state is 0 and *wait* is False, acquire immediately returns False.

release	*s*.release( )
	When *s*'s state is greater than 0 or when the state is 0 but no thread is waiting on *s*, release increments the state by 1. When *s*'s state is 0 and some thread is waiting on *s*, release leaves *s*'s state at 0 and wakes up an arbitrary waiting thread. The thread that calls release is not suspended: it remains ready and continues to execute normally.

Threaded Program Architecture

A threaded program should always arrange for a *single* thread to deal with any given object or subsystem that is external to the program (such as a file, a database, a GUI, or a network connection). Having multiple threads that deal with the same external object can often cause unpredictable problems.

Whenever your threaded program must deal with some external object, devote a thread to such dealings, using a Queue object from which the external-interfacing thread gets work requests that other threads post. The external-interfacing thread can return results by putting them on one or more other Queue objects. The following example shows how to package this architecture into a general, reusable class, assuming that each unit of work on the external subsystem can be represented by a callable object:

```
import Threading, Queue
class ExternalInterfacing(Threading.Thread):
    def __init__(self, externalCallable, **kwds):
        Threading.Thread.__init__(self, **kwds)
        self.setDaemon(1)
        self.externalCallable = externalCallable
        self.workRequestQueue = Queue.Queue( )
        self.resultQueue = Queue.Queue( )
        self.start( )
    def request(self, *args, **kwds):
        "called by other threads as externalCallable would be"
        self.workRequestQueue.put((args,kwds))
```

```
        return self.resultQueue.get( )
    def run(self):
        while 1:
            args, kwds = self.workRequestQueue.get( )
            self.resultQueue.put(self.externalCallable(*args, **kwds))
```

Once some ExternalInterfacing object *ei* is instantiated, all other threads may now call *ei*.request just like they would call *someExternalCallable* without such a mechanism (with or without arguments as appropriate). The advantage of the ExternalInterfacing mechanism is that all calls upon *someExternalCallable* are now serialized. This means they are performed by just one thread (the thread object bound to *ei*) in some defined sequential order, without overlap, race conditions (hard-to-debug errors that depend on which thread happens to get there first), or other anomalies that might otherwise result.

If several callables need to be serialized together, you can pass the callable as part of the work request, rather than passing it at the initialization of class ExternalInterfacing, for greater generality. The following example shows this more general approach:

```
import Threading, Queue
class Serializer(Threading.Thread):
    def __init__(self, **kwds):
        Threading.Thread.__init__(self, **kwds)
        self.setDaemon(1)
        self.workRequestQueue = Queue.Queue( )
        self.resultQueue = Queue.Queue( )
        self.start( )
    def apply(self, callable, *args, **kwds):
        "called by other threads as callable would be"
        self.workRequestQueue.put((callable, args,kwds))
        return self.resultQueue.get( )
    def run(self):
        while 1:
            callable, args, kwds = self.workRequestQueue.get( )
            self.resultQueue.put(callable(*args, **kwds))
```

Once a Serializer object *ser* has been instantiated, other threads may call *ser*.apply(*someExternalCallable*) just like they would call *someExternalCallable* without such a mechanism (with or without further arguments as appropriate). The Serializer mechanism has the same advantages as ExternalInterfacing, except that all calls to the same or different callables wrapped by a single *ser* instance are now serialized.

The user interface of the whole program is an external subsystem and thus should be dealt with by a single thread, specifically the main thread of the program (this is mandatory for some user interface toolkits and advisable even when not mandatory). A Serializer thread is therefore inappropriate. Rather, the program's main thread should deal only with user interface issues, and farm out actual work to worker threads that accept work requests on a Queue object and return results on another. A set of worker threads is also known as a *thread pool*. As shown in the following example, all worker threads should share a single queue of requests and a single queue of results, since the main thread will be the only one posting work requests and harvesting results:

```
import Threading
class Worker(Threading.Thread):
    requestID = 0
    def __init__(self, requestsQueue, resultsQueue, **kwds):
        Threading.Thread.__init__(self, **kwds)
        self.setDaemon(1)
        self.workRequestQueue = requestsQueue
        self.resultQueue = resultsQueue
        self.start()
    def performWork(self, callable, *args, **kwds):
        "called by the main thread as callable would be, but w/o return"
        Worker.requestID += 1
        self.workRequestQueue.put((Worker.requestID, callable, args,kwds))
        return Worker.requestID
    def run(self):
        while 1:
            requestID, callable, args, kwds = self.workRequestQueue.get()
            self.resultQueue.put((requestID, callable(*args, **kwds)))
```

The main thread creates the two queues, then instantiates worker threads as follows:

```
import Queue
requestsQueue = Queue.Queue()
resultsQueue = Queue.Queue()
for i in range(numberOfWorkers):
    worker = Worker(requestsQueue, resultsQueue)
```

Now, whenever the main thread needs to farm out work (execute some callable object that may take substantial time to produce results), the main thread calls *worker*.performWork(*callable*) much like it would call *callable* without such a mechanism (with or without further arguments as appropriate). However, performWork does not return the result of the call. Instead of the results, the main thread gets an *id* that identifies the work request. If the main thread needs the results, it can keep track of that *id*, since the request's results will be tagged with that *id* when they appear. The advantage of the mechanism is that the main thread does not block waiting for the callable's lengthy execution to complete, but rather becomes ready again at once and can immediately return to its main business of dealing with the user interface.

The main thread must arrange to check the resultsQueue, since the result of each work request eventually appears there, tagged with the request's *id*, when the worker thread that took that request from the queue finishes computing the result. How the main thread arranges to check for both user interface events and the results coming back from worker threads onto the results queue depends on what user interface toolkit is used, or, if the user interface is text-based, on the platform on which the program runs.

A widely applicable general strategy is for the main thread to *poll* (i.e., check the state of the results queue periodically). On most Unix-like platforms, function alarm of module signal allows polling. The Tkinter GUI toolkit supplies method after, usable for polling. Some toolkits and platforms afford more effective strategies, letting a worker thread alert the main thread when it places some result on the results queue, but there is no generally available, cross-platform, and cross-toolkit way to arrange for this. Therefore, the following artificial example ignores user interface events, and just simulates work by evaluating random expressions, with random delays, on several worker threads, thus completing the previous example:

```
import random, time
def makeWork( ):
    return "%d %s %d"%(random.randrange(2,10),
        random.choice(('+', '-', '*', '/', '%', '**')),
        random.randrange(2,10))
def slowEvaluate(expressionString):
    time.sleep(random.randrange(1,5))
    return eval(expressionString)
workRequests = { }
def showResults( ):
    while 1:
        try: id, results = resultsQueue.get_nowait( )
        except Queue.Empty: return
        print 'Result %d: %s -> %s' % (id, workRequests[id], results)
        del workRequests[id]
for i in range(10):
    expressionString = makeWork( )
    id = worker.performWork(slowEvaluate, expressionString)
    workRequests[id] = expressionString
    print 'Submitted request %d: %s' % (id, expressionString)
    time.sleep(1)
    showResults( )
while workRequests:
    time.sleep(1)
    showResults( )
```

Process Environment

The operating system supplies each process *P* with an *environment*, which is a set of environment variables whose names are identifiers (most often, by convention, uppercase identifiers) and whose contents are strings. For example, in Chapter 3, we covered environment variables that affect Python's operations. Operating system shells offer various ways to examine and modify the environment, by such means as shell commands and others mentioned in Chapter 3.

The environment of any process *P* is determined when *P* starts. After startup, only *P* itself can change *P*'s environment. Nothing that *P* does affects the environment of *P*'s parent process (the process that started *P*), nor those of child processes previously started from *P* and now running, nor of processes unrelated to *P*. Changes to *P*'s environment affect only *P* itself: the environment is *not* a means of IPC. Child processes of *P* normally get a copy of *P*'s environment as their starting environment: in this sense, changes to *P*'s environment do affect child processes that *P* starts after such changes.

Module os supplies attribute environ, a mapping that represents the current process's environment. os.environ is initialized from the process environment when Python starts. Changes to os.environ update the current process's environment if the platform supports such updates. Keys and values in os.environ must be strings. On Windows, but not on Unix-like platforms, keys into os.environ are implicitly uppercased. For example, here's how to try to determine what shell or command processor you're running under:

```
import os
shell = os.environ.get('COMSPEC')
if shell is None: shell = os.environ.get('SHELL')
if shell is None: shell = 'an unknown command processor'
print 'Running under', shell
```

If a Python program changes its own environment (e.g., via os.environ['X']='Y'), this does not affect the environment of the shell or command processor that started the program. Like in other cases, changes to a process's environment affect only the process itself, not others.

Running Other Programs

The os module offers several ways for your program to run other programs. The simplest way to run another program is through function os.system, although this offers no way to control the external program. The os module also provides a number of functions whose names start with exec. These functions offer fine-grained control. A program run by one of the exec functions, however, replaces the current program (i.e., the Python interpreter) in the same process. In practice, therefore, you use the exec functions mostly on platforms that let a process duplicate itself by fork (i.e., Unix-like platforms). Finally, os functions whose names start with spawn and popen offer intermediate simplicity and power: they are cross-platform and not quite as simple as system, but simple and usable enough for most purposes.

The exec and spawn functions run a specified executable file given the executable file's path, arguments to pass to it, and optionally an environment mapping. The system and popen functions execute a command, a string passed to a new instance of the platform's default shell (typically /bin/sh on Unix, command.com or cmd.exe on Windows). A command is a more general concept than an executable file, as it can include shell functionality (pipes, redirection, built-in shell commands) using the normal shell syntax specific to the current platform.

execl, execle, execlp, execv, execve, execvp, execvpe	execl(path,*args) execle(path,*args) execlp(path,*args) execv(path,args) execve(path,args,env) execvp(path,args) execvpe(path,args,env)

These functions run the executable file (program) indicated by string *path*, replacing the current program (i.e., the Python interpreter) in the current process. The distinctions encoded in the function names (after the prefix exec) control three aspects of how the new program is found and run:

- Does *path* have to be a complete path to the program's executable file, or can the function also accept just a name as the *path* argument and search for the executable in several directories, like operating system shells do? execlp, execvp, and execvpe can accept a *path* argument that is just a filename rather than a complete path. In this case, the functions search for an executable file of that name along the directories listed in os.environ['PATH']. The other functions require *path* to be a complete path to the executable file for the new program.

- Are arguments for the new program accepted as a single sequence argument *args* to the function or as separate arguments to the function? Functions whose names start with execv take a single argument *args* that is the sequence of the arguments to use for the new program. Functions whose names start with execl take the new program's arguments as separate arguments (execle, in particular, uses its last argument as the environment for the new program).

- Is the new program's environment accepted as an explicit mapping argument *env* to the function, or is os.environ implicitly used? execle, execve, and execvpe take an argument *env* that is a mapping to be used as the new program's environment (keys and values must be strings), while the other functions use os.environ for this purpose.

Each exec function uses the first item in *args* as the name under which the new program is told it's running (for example, argv[0] in a C program's main); only *args*[1:] are passed as arguments proper to the new program.

---

popen

popen(*cmd,mode='r',bufsize=-1*)

Runs the string command *cmd* in a new process *P*, and returns a file-like object *f* that wraps a pipe to *P*'s standard input or from *P*'s standard output (depending on *mode*). *mode* and *bufsize* have the same meaning as for Python's built-in open function, covered in Chapter 10. When *mode* is 'r' (or 'rb', for binary-mode reading), *f* is read-only and wraps *P*'s standard output. When mode is 'w' (or 'wb', for binary-mode writing), *f* is write-only and wraps *P*'s standard input.

The key difference of *f* with respect to other file objects is the behavior of method *f*.close. *f*.close waits for *P* to terminate, and returns None, as close methods of file-like objects normally do, when *P*'s termination is successful. However, if the operating system associates an integer error code with *P*'s termination indicating that *P*'s termination was unsuccessful, *f*.close also returns *c*. Not all operating systems support this mechanism: on some platforms, *f*.close therefore always returns None. On Unix-like platforms, if *P* terminates with the system call exit(*n*) (e.g., if *P* is a Python program and terminates by calling sys.exit(*n*)), *f*.close receives from the operating system, and returns to f.close's caller, the code 256*n.

popen2,	popen2(*cmd*,*mode*='t',*bufsize*=-1)
popen3,	popen3(*cmd*,*mode*='t',*bufsize*=-1)
popen4	popen4(*cmd*,*mode*='t',*bufsize*=-1)

Each of these functions runs the string command *cmd* in a new process P, and returns a tuple of file-like objects that wrap pipes to P's standard input and from P's standard output and standard error. *mode* must be 't' to get file-like objects in text mode, or 'b' to get them in binary mode. On Windows, *bufsize* must be -1. On Unix, *bufsize* has the same meaning as for Python's built-in open function, covered in Chapter 10.

popen2 returns a pair (*fi*,*fo*), where *fi* wraps P's standard input (so the calling process can write to *fi*) and *fo* wraps P's standard output (so the calling process can read from *fo*). popen3 returns a tuple with three items (*fi*,*fo*,*fe*), where *fe* wraps P's standard error (so the calling process can read from *fe*). popen4 returns a pair (*fi*,*foe*), where *foe* wraps both P's standard output and error (so the calling process can read from *foe*). While popen3 is in a sense the most general of the three functions, it can be difficult to coordinate your reading from *fo* and *fe*. popen2 is simpler to use than popen3 when it's okay for *cmd*'s standard error to go to the same destination as your own process's standard error, and popen4 is simpler when it's okay for *cmd*'s standard error and output to be mixed with each other.

File objects *fi*, *fo*, *fe*, and *foe* are all normal ones, without the special semantics of the close method as covered for function popen. In other words, there is no way in which the caller of popen2, popen3, or popen4 can learn about P's termination code.

Depending on the buffering strategy of command *cmd* (which is normally out of your control, unless you're the author of *cmd*), there may be nothing to read on files *fo*, *fe*, and/or *foe* until your process has closed file *fi*. Therefore, the normal pattern of usage is something like:

```
import os
def pipethrough(cmd, list_of_lines):
    fi, fo = os.popen2(cmd, 't')
    fi.writelines(list_of_lines)
    fi.close()
    result_lines = fo.readlines()
    fo.close()
    return result_lines
```

Functions in the popen group are generally not suitable for driving another process interactively (i.e., writing something, then reading *cmd*'s response to that, then writing something else, and so on). The first time your program tries to read the response, if *cmd* is following a typical buffering strategy, everything blocks. In other words, your process is waiting for *cmd*'s output but *cmd* has already placed its pending output in a memory buffer, which your process can't get at, and is now waiting for more input. This is a typical case of deadlock.

If you have some control over *cmd*, you can try to work around this issue by ensuring that *cmd* runs without buffering. For example, if *cmd.py* is a Python program, you can run *cmd* without buffering as follows:

```
C:/> python -u cmd.py
```

Other possible approaches include module `telnetlib`, covered in Chapter 18, if your platform supports *telnet*; and third-party, Unix-like-only extensions such as *expectpy.sf.net* and packages such as *pexpect.sf.net*. There is no general solution applicable to all platforms and all *cmd*s of interest.

---

spawnv,
spawnve

spawnv(*mode,path,args*)
spawnve(*mode,path,args,env*)

These functions run the program indicated by *path* in a new process *P*, with the arguments passed as sequence *args*. spawnve uses mapping *env* as *P*'s environment (both keys and values must be strings), while spawnv uses os.environ for this purpose. On Unix-like platforms only, there are other variations of os.spawn, corresponding to variations of os.exec, but spawnv and spawnve are the only two that exist on Windows.

mode must be one of two attributes supplied by the os module: os.P_WAIT indicates that the calling process waits until the new process terminates, while os.P_NOWAIT indicates that the calling process continues executing simultaneously with the new process. When *mode* is os.P_WAIT, the function returns the termination code *c* of *P*: 0 indicates successful termination, *c* less than 0 indicates *P* was killed by a *signal*, and *c* greater than 0 indicates normal but unsuccessful termination. When *mode* is os.P_NOWAIT, the function returns *P*'s process ID (on Windows, *P*'s process handle). There is no cross-platform way to use *P*'s ID or handle; platform-specific ways (not covered further in this book) include function os.waitpid on Unix-like platforms and the win32all extensions (*starship. python.net/crew/mhammond*) on Windows.

For example, your interactive program can give the user a chance to edit a text file that your program is about to read and use. You must have previously determined the full path to the user's favorite text editor, such as *c:\\windows\\notepad.exe* on Windows or */bin/ vim* on a Unix-like platform. Say that this path string is bound to variable *editor*, and the path of the text file you want to let the user edit is bound to *textfile*:

```
import os
os.spawnv(os.P_WAIT, editor, [textfile])
```

When os.spawnv returns, the user has closed the editor (whether or not he has made any changes to the file), and your program can continue by reading and using the file as needed.

system	system(*cmd*)
	Runs the string command *cmd* in a new process, and returns 0 if the new process terminates successfully (or if Python is unable to ascertain the success status of the new process's termination, as happens on Windows 95 and 98). If the new process terminates unsuccessfully (and Python is able to ascertain this unsuccessful termination), system returns an integer error code not equal to 0.

The mmap Module

The mmap module supplies memory-mapped file objects. An mmap object behaves similarly to a plain (not Unicode) string, so you can often pass an mmap object where a plain string is expected. However, there are differences:

- An mmap object does not supply the methods of a string object
- An mmap object is mutable, while string objects are immutable
- An mmap object also corresponds to an open file and behaves polymorphically to a Python file object (as covered in Chapter 10)

An mmap object *m* can be indexed or sliced, yielding plain strings. Since *m* is mutable, you can also assign to an indexing or slicing of *m*. However, when you assign to a slice of *m*, the right-hand side of the assignment statement must be a string of exactly the same length as the slice you're assigning to. Therefore, many of the useful tricks available with list slice assignment (covered in Chapter 4) do not apply to mmap slice assignment.

Module mmap supplies a factory function that is different on Unix-like systems and Windows.

mmap	mmap(*filedesc,length,tagname=''*) # Windows mmap(*filedesc,length,flags*=MAP_SHARED, *prot*=PROT_READ|PROT_WRITE) # Unix
	Creates and returns an mmap object *m* that maps into memory the first *length* bytes of the file indicated by file descriptor *filedesc*. *filedesc* must normally be a file descriptor opened for both reading and writing (except, on Unix-like platforms, when argument *prot* requests only reading or only writing). File descriptors are covered in "File Descriptor Operations" in Chapter 10. To get an mmap object *m* that refers to a Python file object *f*, use *m*=mmap.mmap(*f*.fileno( ),*length*).
	On Windows only, you can pass a string *tagname* to give an explicit tag name for the memory mapping. This tag name lets you have several memory mappings on the same file, but this functionality is rarely necessary. Calling mmap with only two arguments has the advantage of keeping your code portable between Windows and Unix-like platforms. On Windows, all memory mappings are readable and writable and shared between processes, so that all

processes with a memory mapping on a file can see changes made by each such process.

On Unix-like platforms only, you can pass mmap.MAP_PRIVATE as the *flags* argument to get a mapping that is private to your process and copy-on-write. mmap.MAP_SHARED, the default, gets a mapping that is shared with other processes, so that all processes mapping the file can see changes made by one process (same as on Windows). You can pass mmap.PROT_READ as the *prot* argument to get a mapping that you can only read, not write. Passing mmap.PROT_WRITE gets a mapping that you can only write, not read. The bitwise-OR mmap.PROT_READ|mmap.PROT_WRITE, the default, gets a mapping that you can both read and write (same as on Windows).

Methods of mmap Objects

An mmap object *m* supplies the following methods.

close

    m.close( )

    Closes the file of *m*.

find

    m.find(*str*,*start*=0)

    Returns the lowest index *I* greater than or equal to *start* such that *str*==*m*[*i*:*i*+len(*str*)]. If no such *i* exists, *m*.find returns -1. This is the same functionality as for the find method of string objects, covered in Chapter 9.

flush

    m.flush([*offset*,*n*])

    Ensures that all changes made to *m* also exist on *m*'s file. Until you call *m*.flush, it's uncertain whether the file reflects the current state of *m*. You can pass a starting byte offset *offset* and a byte count *n* to limit the flushing effect's guarantee to a slice of *m*. You must pass both arguments, or neither: it is an error to call *m*.flush with exactly one argument.

move

    m.move(*dstoff*,*srcoff*,*n*)

    Like the slicing *m*[*dstoff*:*dstoff*+*n*]=*m*[*srcoff*:*srcoff*+*n*], but potentially faster. The source and destination slices can overlap. Apart from such potential overlap, move does not affect the source slice (i.e., the move method *copies* bytes but does not move them, despite the method's name).

read

    m.read(*n*)

    Reads and returns a string *s* containing up to *n* bytes starting from *m*'s file pointer, then advances *m*'s file pointer by len(*s*). If there are less than *n* bytes between *m*'s file pointer and *m*'s length, returns the bytes available. In particular, if *m*'s file pointer is at the end of *m*, returns the empty string ' '.

---

read_byte   `m.read_byte( )`

Returns a string of length 1 containing the character at *m*'s file pointer, then advances *m*'s file pointer by 1. `m.read_byte( )` is similar to `m.read(1)`. However, if *m*'s file pointer is at the end of *m*, `m.read(1)` returns the empty string ' ', while `m.read_byte( )` raises a `ValueError` exception.

---

readline   `m.readline( )`

Reads and returns one line from the file of *m*, from *m*'s current file pointer up to the next `'\n'`, included (or up to the end of *m*, if there is no `'\n'`), then advances *m*'s file pointer to point just past the bytes just read. If *m*'s file pointer is at the end of *m*, `readline` returns the empty string ' '.

---

resize   `m.resize(n)`

Changes the length of *m*, so that `len(m)` becomes *n*. Does not affect the size of *m*'s file. *m*'s length and the file's size are independent. To set *m*'s length to be equal to the file's size, call `m.resize(m.size( ))`. If *m*'s length is larger than the file's size, *m* is padded with null bytes (`\x00`).

---

seek   `m.seek(pos,how=0)`

Sets the file pointer of *m* to the integer byte offset *pos*. *how* indicates the reference point (point 0): when *how* is 0, the reference point is the start of the file; when 1, *m*'s current file pointer; when 2, the end of *m*. A seek that tries to set *m*'s file pointer to a negative byte offset, or to a positive offset beyond *m*'s length, raises a `ValueError` exception.

---

size   `m.size( )`

Returns the length (number of bytes) of the file of *m*, not the length of *m* itself. To get the length of *m*, use `len(m)`.

---

tell   `m.tell( )`

Returns the current position of the file pointer of *m*, as a byte offset from the start of *m*'s file.

---

write   `m.write(str)`

Writes the bytes in *str* into *m* and at the current position of *m*'s file pointer, overwriting the bytes that were there, and then advances *m*'s file pointer by `len(str)`. If there aren't at least `len(str)` bytes between *m*'s file pointer and the length of *m*, `write` raises a `ValueError` exception.

---

write_byte   *m*.write_byte(*byte*)

Writes *byte*, which must be a single-character string, into mapping *m* at the current position of *m*'s file pointer, overwriting the byte that was there, and then advances *m*'s file pointer by 1. When *x* is a single-character string, *m*.write_byte(*x*) is similar to *m*.write(*x*). However, if *m*'s file pointer is at the end of *m*, *m*.write_byte(*x*) silently does nothing, while *m*.write(*x*) raises a ValueError exception. Note that this is the reverse of the relationship between read and read_byte at end-of-file: write and read_byte raise ValueError, while read and write_byte don't.

Using mmap Objects for IPC

The way in which processes communicate using mmap is similar to IPC using files: one process can write data, and another process can later read the same data back. Since an mmap object rests on an underlying file, you can also have some processes doing I/O directly on the file, as covered in Chapter 10, while others use mmap to access the same file. You can choose between mmap and I/O on file objects on the basis of convenience: the functionality is the same. For example, here is a simple program that uses file I/O to make the contents of a file equal to the last line interactively typed by the user:

```
fileob = open('xxx','w')
while True:
    data = raw_input('Enter some text:')
    fileob.seek(0)
    fileob.write(data)
    fileob.truncate()
    fileob.flush()
```

And here is another simple program that, when run in the same directory as the former, uses mmap (and the time.sleep function, covered in Chapter 12) to check every second for changes to the file and print out the file's new contents:

```
import mmap, os, time
mx = mmap.mmap(os.open('xxx',os.O_RDWR), 1)
last = None
while True:
    mx.resize(mx.size())
    data = mx[:]
    if data != last:
        print data
        last = data
    time.sleep(1)
```

15

Numeric Processing

In Python, you can perform numeric computations with operators (as covered in Chapter 4) and built-in functions (as covered in Chapter 8). Python also provides the math, cmath, operator, and random modules, which support additional numeric computation functionality, as documented in this chapter.

You can represent arrays in Python with lists and tuples (covered in Chapter 4), as well as with the array standard library module, which is covered in this chapter. You can also build advanced array manipulation functions with loops, list comprehensions, iterators, generators, and built-ins such as map, reduce, and filter, but such functions can be complicated and slow. Therefore, when you process large arrays of numbers in these ways, your program's performance can be below your machine's full potential.

The Numeric package addresses these issues, providing high-performance support for multidimensional arrays (matrices) and advanced mathematical operations, such as linear algebra and Fourier transforms. Numeric does not come with standard Python distributions, but you can freely download it at *http://sourceforge.net/ projects/numpy*, either as source code (which is easy to build and install on many platforms) or as a prebuilt self-installing *.exe* file for Windows. Visit *http://www. pfdubois.com/numpy/* for an extensive tutorial and other resources, such as a mailing list about Numeric. Note that the Numeric package is not just for numeric processing. Much of Numeric is about multidimensional arrays and advanced array handling that you can use for any Python sequence.

Numeric is a large, rich package. For full understanding, study the tutorial, work through the examples, and experiment interactively. This chapter presents a reference to an essential subset of Numeric on the assumption that you already have some grasp of array manipulation and numeric computing issues. If you are unfamiliar with this subject, the Numeric tutorial can help.

The math and cmath Modules

The math module supplies mathematical functions on floating-point numbers, while the cmath module supplies equivalent functions on complex numbers. For example, math.sqrt(-1) raises an exception, but cmath.sqrt(-1) returns 1j.

Each module also exposes two attributes of type float bound to the values of fundamental mathematical constants, pi and e.

acos	acos(x)	math and cmath
	Returns the arccosine of x in radians.	
acosh	acosh(x)	cmath only
	Returns the arc hyperbolic cosine of x in radians.	
asin	asin(x)	math and cmath
	Returns the arcsine of x in radians.	
asinh	asinh(x)	cmath only
	Returns the arc hyperbolic sine of x in radians.	
atan	atan(x)	math and cmath
	Returns the arctangent of x in radians.	
atanh	atanh(x)	cmath only
	Returns the arc hyperbolic tangent of x in radians.	
atan2	atan2(y,x)	math only
	Like atan(y/x), except that when x equals 0, atan2 returns pi/2, while dividing by x would raise ZeroDivisionError.	
ceil	ceil(x)	math only
	Returns the lowest integer i such that i is greater than or equal to x as a floating-point value.	
cos	cos(x)	math and cmath
	Returns the cosine of x in radians.	
cosh	cosh(x)	math and cmath
	Returns the hyperbolic cosine of x in radians.	

e	The mathematical constant *e*.	math and cmath

exp	`exp(x)` Returns e**x.	math and cmath

fabs	`fabs(x)` Returns the absolute value of *x*.	math only

floor	`floor(x)` Returns the highest integer *i* such that *i* is less than or equal to *x* as a floating-point value.	math only

fmod	`fmod(x,y)` Returns *x*%*y* (on most platforms).	math only

frexp	`frexp(x)` Returns a pair (*m,e*) with the mantissa and exponent of *x*. *m* is a floating-point number and *e* is an integer such that $x==m*(2**e)$ and `0.5<=abs(m)<1`, except that `frexp(0)` returns `(0.0,0)`.	math only

hypot	`hypot(x,y)` Returns `sqrt(x*x+y*y)`.	math only

ldexp	`ldexp(x,i)` Returns $x*(2**i)$.	math only

log	`log(x)` Returns the natural logarithm of *x*.	math and cmath

log10	`log10(x)` Returns the base-10 logarithm of *x*.	math and cmath

modf	`modf(x)` Returns a pair (*f,i*) with fractional and integer parts of *x*, each a floating-point value with the same sign as *x*.	math only

pi	The mathematical constant π.	math and cmath

pow	`pow(x,y)` Returns $x**y$.	math only

sin	sin(x)	math and cmath
	Returns the sine of x in radians.	

sinh	sinh(x)	math and cmath
	Returns the hyperbolic sine of x in radians.	

sqrt	sqrt(x)	math and cmath
	Returns the square root of x.	

tan	tan(x)	math and cmath
	Returns the tangent of x in radians.	

tanh	tanh(x)	math and cmath
	Returns the hyperbolic tangent of x in radians.	

The operator Module

The operator module supplies functions that are equivalent to Python's operators. These functions are handy for use with map and reduce, and in other cases where callables must be stored, passed as arguments, or returned as function results. The functions in operator have the same names as the corresponding special methods (covered in Chapter 5). Each function is available with two names, with and without the leading and trailing double underscores (e.g., both operator.add(a,b) and operator.__add__(a,b) return a+b). Table 15-1 lists the functions supplied by operator.

Table 15-1. Functions supplied by operator

Method	Signature	Behaves like
abs	abs(a)	abs(a)
add	add(a,b)	a+b
and_	and_(a,b)	a&b
concat	concat(a,b)	a+b
contains	contains(a,b)	b in a
countOf	countOf(a,b)	a.count(b)
delitem	delitem(a,b)	del a[b]
delslice	delslice(a,b,c)	del a[b:c]
div	div(a,b)	a/b
getitem	getitem(a,b)	a[b]
getslice	getslice(a,b,c)	a[b:c]
indexOf	indexOf(a,b)	a.index(b)

Table 15-1. *Functions supplied by operator (continued)*

Method	Signature	Behaves like
invert, inv	invert(a), inv(a)	~a
lshift	lshift(a,b)	a<<b
mod	mod(a,b)	a%b
mul	mul(a,b)	a*b
neg	neg(a)	-a
not_	not_(a)	not a
or_	or_(a,b)	a|b
pos	pos(a)	+a
repeat	repeat(a,b)	a*b
rshift	rshift(a,b)	a>>b
setitem	setitem(a,b,c)	a[b]=c
setslice	setslice(a,b,c,d)	a[b:c]=d
sub	sub(a,b)	a-b
truth	truth(a)	not not a
xor_	xor(a,b)	a^b

The random Module

The random module generates pseudo-random numbers with various distributions. The underlying uniform pseudo-random generator uses the Whichmann-Hill algorithm, with a period of length 6,953,607,871,644. The resulting pseudo-random numbers, while quite good, are not of cryptographic quality. If you want physically generated random numbers rather than algorithmically generated pseudo-random numbers, you may use */dev/random* or */dev/urandom* on platforms that support such pseudo-devices (such as recent Linux releases). For an alternative, see *http://www.fourmilab.ch/hotbits*.

All functions of module random are methods of a hidden instance of class random. Random. You can instantiate Random explicitly to get multiple generators that do not share state. Explicit instantiation is advisable if you require random numbers in multiple threads (threads are covered in Chapter 14). This section documents the most frequently used functions exposed by module random.

choice
choice(*seq*)

Returns a random item from non-empty sequence *seq*.

getstate
getstate( )

Returns an object S that represents the current state of the generator. You can later pass S to function setstate in order to restore the generator's state.

jumpahead	jumpahead(n)
	Advances the generator state as if *n* random numbers had been generated. Computing the new state is faster than generating *n* random numbers would be.
random	random( )
	Returns a random floating-point number *r* from a uniform distribution, such that 0<=r<1.
randrange	randrange([*start*,]*stop*[,*step*])
	Like choice(range(*start*,*stop*,*step*)), but faster, since randrange does not need to build the list that range would create.
seed	seed(*x*=None)
	Initializes the generator state. *x* can be any hashable object. When *x* is None, and also automatically when module random is first loaded, seed uses the current system time to get a seed. *x* is normally a long integer up to 27814431486575L. Larger *x* values are accepted, but may produce the same generator states as smaller ones.
setstate	setstate(*S*)
	Restores the generator state. *S* must be the result of a previous call to getstate.
shuffle	shuffle(*alist*)
	Shuffles, in place, mutable sequence *alist*.
uniform	uniform(*a*,*b*)
	Returns a random floating-point number *r* from a uniform distribution, such that *a*<=r<*b*.

Module random also supplies functions that generate pseudo-random floating-point numbers from many other probability distributions (Beta, Gamma, exponential, Gauss, Pareto, etc.). All of these functions internally call random.random as their source of randomness.

The array Module

The array module supplies a type, also called array, whose instances are mutable sequences, like lists. An array *a* is a one-dimensional sequence whose items can be only characters, or only numbers of one specific numeric type that is fixed when *a* is created.

The extension module Numeric, covered later in this chapter, also supplies a type called array that is far more powerful than array.array. For advanced array operations and multidimensional arrays, I recommend Numeric even if your array elements are not numbers.

array.array is a simple type, whose main advantage is that, compared to a list, it can save memory to hold objects all of the same (numeric or character) type. An array object *a* has a one-character read-only attribute *a*.typecode, set when *a* is created, that gives the type of *a*'s items. Table 15-2 shows the possible type codes for array.

Table 15-2. Type codes for the array module

Type code	C type	Python type	Minimum size
'c'	char	str (length 1)	1 byte
'b'	char	int	1 byte
'B'	unsigned char	int	1 byte
'h'	short	int	2 bytes
'H'	unsigned short	int	2 bytes
'i'	int	int	2 bytes
'I'	unsigned	long	2 bytes
'l'	long	int	4 bytes
'L'	unsigned long	long	4 bytes
'f'	float	float	4 bytes
'd'	double	float	8 bytes

The size in bytes of each item may be larger than the minimum, depending on the machine's architecture, and is available as the read-only attribute *a*.itemsize. Module array supplies just one function, a factory function called array.

array	array(*typecode,init=''*)
	Creates and returns an array object *a* with the given *typecode*. *init* can be a plain string whose length is a multiple of itemsize; the string's bytes, interpreted as machine values, directly initialize *a*'s items. Alternatively, *init* can be a list (of characters when *typecode* is 'c', otherwise of numbers): each item of the list initializes one item of *a*.

Array objects expose all the methods and operations of mutable sequences, as covered in Chapter 4, except method sort. Concatenation (with both + and extend) and assignment to slices require both operands to be arrays with the same type code (i.e., there is no implicit coercion between sequences). In addition to the methods of mutable sequences, an array object *a* also exposes the following methods.

byteswap	*a*.byteswap( )
	Swaps the byte order of each item of *a*.

fromfile	*a*.fromfile(*f,n*)
	Reads *n* items, taken as machine values, from file object *f*, and appends the items to *a*. Note that *f* should be open for reading in binary mode, for example with mode 'rb'. When less than *n* items are available in *f*, fromfile raises EOFError after appending the items that are available.

fromlist	*a*.fromlist(*L*)
	Appends to *a* all items of list *L*.

fromstring	*a*.fromstring(*s*)
	Appends to *a* the bytes, interpreted as machine values, of string *s*. len(*s*) must be a multiple of *a*.itemsize.

tofile	*a*.tofile(*f*)
	Writes all items of *a*, taken as machine values, to file object *f*. Note that *f* should be open for reading in binary mode, for example with mode 'rb'.

tolist	*a*.tolist( )
	Creates and returns a list object with the same items as *a*.

tostring	*a*.tostring( )
	Returns the string with the bytes from all items of *a*, taken as machine values. For any *a*, len(*a*.tostring( )) always equals len(*a*)*a.itemsize. *f*.write(*a*.tostring( )) is the same as *a*.tofile(*f*).

The Numeric Package

The main module in the Numeric package is the Numeric module, which provides the array object type, a set of functions that manipulate these objects, and universal functions that operate on arrays and other sequences. The Numeric package also supports a variety of optional modules for things like linear algebra, random numbers, masked arrays, and Fast Fourier Transforms.

Numeric is one of the rare Python packages often used with the idiom from Numeric import *. You can also use import Numeric and qualify each name by preceding it with Numeric. However, if you need many of the package's names, importing all the names at once is handy. Another popular alternative is to import Numeric with a shorter name (e.g., import Numeric as N) and qualify each name by preceding it with N.

Although quite solid and stable, Numeric is under continuous development, with functionality being added and limitations removed. This chapter describes specifically Numeric Version 21.3, the latest released version at the time of this writing. A successor to Numeric, named numarray, is being developed by the Numeric community, and is not quite ready for production use yet. numarray is not totally compatible with Numeric, but shares most of Numeric's functionality and enriches it further. Information on numarray is available at *http://stsdas.stsci.edu/numarray/*.

Array Objects

Numeric provides an array type that represents a grid of items. An array object *a* has a specified number of dimensions, known as its *rank*, up to some arbitrarily high limit (normally 40, when Numeric is built with default options). A scalar (i.e., a single number) has rank 0, a vector has rank 1, a matrix has rank 2, and so forth.

Type Codes

The values that occupy cells in the grid of an array object, known as the *elements* of the array, are homogeneous, meaning they are all of the same type, and all element values are stored within one memory area. This contrasts with a list or tuple, where the items may be of different types and each is stored as a separate Python object. This means a Numeric array occupies far less memory than a Python list or tuple with the same number of items. The type of *a*'s elements is encoded as *a*'s type code, a one-character string, as shown in Table 15-3. Factory functions that build array instances, covered in "Factory Functions" later in this chapter, take a *typecode* argument that is one of the values in Table 15-3.

Table 15-3. Type codes for Numeric arrays

Type code	C type	Python type	Synonym
'c'	char	str (length 1)	Character
'b'	unsigned char	int	UnsignedInt8
'1'	signed char	int	Int8
's'	short	int	Int16
'i'	int	int	Int32
'l'	long	int	Int
'f'	float	float	Float32
'F'	two floats	complex	Complex32
'd'	double	float	Float
'D'	two doubles	complex	Complex
'O'	PyObject*	any	PyObject

Numeric supplies readable attribute names for each type code, as shown in the last column of Table 15-3. Numeric also supplies, on all platforms, the names Int0,

Float0, Float8, Float16, Float64, Complex0, Complex8, Complex16, and Complex64. In each case, the name refers to the smallest type of the requested kind with at least that many bits. For example, Float8 is the smallest floating-point type of at least 8 bits (generally the same as Float32, but some platforms may provide very small floating-point types), while Complex0 is the smallest complex type. On some platforms, but not all, Numeric also supplies the names Int64, Int128, Float128, and Complex128, with similar meanings. These names are not supplied on all platforms because not all platforms provide numbers with that many bits. The next release of Numeric will also support unsigned integer types.

A type code of '0' indicates that elements are references to Python objects. In this case, elements can be of different types. This lets you use Numeric array objects as Python containers, for advanced array-processing tasks that may have nothing to do with numeric processing. When you build an array a with one of Numeric's factory functions, you can either specify a's type code explicitly or accept a default data-dependent type code.

To get the type code of an array a, call a.typecode(). a's type code determines how many bytes each element of a takes up in memory. Call a.itemsize() to get this information. When the type code is '0', the item size is small (e.g., 4 bytes on a 32-bit platform), but this size accounts only for the reference held in each of a's cells. The objects indicated by the references are stored elsewhere as separate Python objects; each such object may occupy an arbitrary amount of extra memory, which is not accounted for in the item size of an array with type code '0'.

Shape and Indexing

Each array object a has an attribute a.shape, which is a tuple of integer values. len(a.shape) is a's rank, so for example, a one-dimensional array of numbers (also known as a *vector*) has rank 1, and a.shape has just one item. More generally, each item of a.shape is the length of the corresponding dimension of a. a's number of elements, known as its *size*, is the product of all items of a.shape. Each dimension of a is also known as an *axis*. Axis indices are from 0 up, as usual in Python. Negative axis indices are allowed and count from the right, so -1 is the last (rightmost) axis.

Each array a is a Python sequence. Each item $a[i]$ of a is a subarray of a, meaning it is an array with a rank one less than a's:

    $a[i]$.shape==a.shape[1:]

For example, if a is a two-dimensional matrix (a is of rank 2), $a[i]$, for any valid index i, is a one-dimensional subarray of a corresponding to a row of the matrix. When a's rank is 1 or 0, a's items are a's elements. Since a is a sequence, you can index a with normal indexing syntax to access or change a's items. Note that a's items are a's subarrays; only for an array of rank 1 or 0 are the array's items the same thing as the array's elements.

You can also use a in a for loop, as for any other sequence. For example:

```
for x in a:
    process(x)
```

means the same thing as:

```
for i in range(len(a)):
    x = a[i]
    process(x)
```

In these examples, each item *x* of *a* in the for loop is a subarray of *a*. For example, if *a* is a two-dimensional matrix, each *x* in either of these loops is a one-dimensional subarray of *a* corresponding to a row of the matrix.

You can also index *a* by a tuple. For example, if *a*'s rank is at least 2, you can write $a[i][j]$ as $a[i,j]$ for any valid *i* and *j*, for rebinding as well as for access. Tuple indexing is faster and more convenient. You do not need to use parentheses inside the brackets in order to indicate that you are indexing *a* by a tuple: it suffices to write the indices one after the other, separated by commas. In other words, $a[i,j]$ means the same thing as $a[(i,j)]$, but the syntax without the parentheses is more natural and readable.

If the result of indexing is a single number, Numeric implicitly converts the result from a rank-zero array to a scalar quantity of the appropriate Python type. In other words, as a result of such an indexing you get a number, not an array with one number in it. While this makes it convenient to pass array elements to other non-Numeric software, it also has unfortunate consequences, and this behavior will change in numarray. With the present behavior, special-casing is required. For example:

```
a[i].shape==a.shape[1:]
```

does not execute correctly as Python code when *a*'s rank is 1. In this case, $a[i]$ is just a number, and numbers don't have a shape attribute. Thus, an AttributeError exception results.

Storage

An array object *a* is usually stored in a continuous memory area, with the elements one after the other in what is traditionally called row-major order. This means that, for example, when *a*'s rank is 2, the elements of *a*'s first row ($a[0]$) come first, immediately followed by those of *a*'s second row ($a[1]$), and so on.

An array can be noncontiguous when it shares some of the storage of a larger array, as covered in the following section "Slicing." For example, if *a*'s rank is 2, the slice $b=a[:,0]$ is the first column of *a*, and is stored noncontiguously because it occupies some of the same storage as *a*. In other words, $b[0]$ occupies the same storage as $a[0,0]$, while $b[1]$ occupies the same storage as $a[1,0]$, which cannot be adjacent to the memory occupied by $a[0,0]$ when *a* has more than one column.

Numeric handles both contiguous and noncontiguous arrays transparently in most cases. In the rest of this chapter, I will point out the rare exceptions where a contiguous array is needed. When you want to copy a noncontiguous array *b* into a new contiguous array *c*, use method copy, covered in "Attributes and Methods" later in this chapter.

Slicing

Arrays may share some or all of their data with other arrays. Numeric shares data between arrays whenever feasible. If you want Numeric to copy data, explicitly ask for a copy. Data sharing particularly applies to slices. For built-in Python lists and standard library array objects, slices are copies, but for Numeric array objects, slices share data with the array they're sliced from:

```
from Numeric import *
alist=range(10)
list_slice=alist[3:7]
list_slice[2]=22
print list_slice, alist        # prints: [3,4,22,6] [0,1,2,3,4,5,6,7,8,9]
anarray=array(alist)
arr_slice=anarray[3:7]
arr_slice[2]=33
print arr_slice, anarray        # prints: [ 3 4 33 6] [ 0 1 2 3 4 33 6 7 8 9]
```

Rebinding an item of list_slice does not affect the list alist that list_slice is sliced from, since for built-in lists, slicing performs a copy. However, because for Numeric arrays, slicing shares data, assigning to an item of arr_slice does affect the array object anarray that arr_slice is sliced from. This behavior may be unexpected for a beginner, but was chosen to enable high performance.

Slicing examples

You can use a tuple to slice an array, just as you can to index it. For arrays, slicing and indexing blend into each other. Each item in a slicing tuple can be an integer, and the slice has one fewer axis than the array being sliced. Slicing removes the axis for which you give a number by selecting the indicated plane of the array.

A slicing tuple item can also be a slice expression; the general syntax is *start:stop:step*, and you can omit one or more of the three parts (see "Sequence Operations" in Chapter 4, and function slice in Chapter 8, for details on slice semantics and defaults). Here are some example slicings:

```
# a is [[ 0, 1, 2, 3, 4, 5],
#       [10,11,12,13,14,15],
#       [20,21,22,23,24,25],
#       [30,31,32,33,34,35],
#       [40,41,42,43,44,45],
#       [50,51,52,53,54,55]]
a[0,2:4)              # array([2,3])
a[3:,3:]              # array([[33,34,35],
                      #        [43,44,45],
                      #        [53,54,55]])
a[:,4]                # array([4,14,24,34,44,54])
a[2::2,::2]           # array([[20,22,24],
                      #        [40,42,44]])
```

A slicing-tuple item can also use an ellipsis (...) to indicate that the following items in the slicing tuple apply to the last (rightmost) axes of the array you're slicing. For example, consider slicing an array b of rank 3:

```
b.shape                      # (4,2,3)
b[1].shape                   # (2,3)
b[...,1].shape               # (4,2)
```

When we slice with b[1] (equivalent to indexing), we give an integer index for axis 0, and therefore we select a specific plane along b's axis 0. By selecting a specific plane, we remove that axis from the result's shape. Therefore, the result's shape is b.shape[1:]. When we slice with b[...,1], we select a specific plane along b's axis -1 (the rightmost axis of b). Again, by selecting a specific plane, we remove that axis from the result's shape. Therefore, the result's shape in this case is b.shape[:-1].

A slicing-tuple item can also be the pseudo-index NewAxis. The resulting slice has an additional axis at the point at which you use NewAxis, with a value of 1 in the corresponding item of the shape tuple. Continuing the previous example:

```
b[NewAxis,...,NewAxis].shape      # (1,4,2,3,1)
```

Here, rather than selecting and thus removing some of b's axes, we have added two new axes, one at the start of the shape and one at the end, thanks to the ellipsis.

Axis removal and addition can both occur in the same slicing. For example:

```
b[NewAxis,:,0,:,NewAxis].shape      # (1,4,3,1)
```

Here, we both add new axes at the start and end of the shape, and select a specific index from the middle axis (axis 1) of b by giving an index for that axis. Therefore, axis 1 of b is removed from the result's shape. The colons (:) used as the second and fourth items in the slicing tuple in this example are slice expressions with both *start* and *stop* omitted, meaning that all of the corresponding axis is included in the slice. In all these examples, all slices share some or all of b's data. Slicing affects only the shape of the resulting array. No data is copied, and no operations are performed on the data.

Assigning to array slices

Assignment to array slices is less flexible than assignment to list slices. Normally, you can assign to an array slice only another array of the same shape as the slice. However, if the right-hand side of the assignment is not an array, Numeric implicitly creates a temporary array from it. Each element of the right-hand side is coerced to the left-hand side's type. If the right-hand side array is not the same shape as the left-hand side slice, broadcasting applies, as covered in "Operations on Arrays" later in this chapter. So, for example, you can assign a scalar (a single number) to any slice of a numeric array. In this case, the right-hand side number is coerced, then broadcast (replicated) as needed to make the assignment succeed.

When you assign to an array slice (or indexing) a right-hand side of a type different from that of the left-hand side, Numeric coerces the values to the left-hand side's type, for example by truncating floating-point numbers to integers. This does not apply if the right-hand side values are complex. Full coercion does not apply to in-place operators, which can only cast the right-hand side values upwards (for example, an integer right-hand side may be used for in-place operations with a

---

floating-point left-hand side, but not vice versa), as covered in "In-place operations" later in this chapter.

Truth Values

Although an array object *a* is a Python sequence, in recent versions of Numeric *a* does not follow Python's normal rule for truth values of sequences, where bool(*a*) depends only on len(*a*) and not on *a*'s elements (i.e., the rule by which any sequence is false only when empty, otherwise it is true). Rather, *a* is false when *a* has no elements or all of *a*'s elements are numeric 0. This lets you test for element-wise equality of arrays in the natural way:

```
if a==b:
```

Without this proviso, such an if condition would be satisfied by any non-empty comparable arrays *a* and *b*.

Do remember, however, that you have to be explicit when you want to test whether *a* has any items or whether *a* has any elements, as these are two different conditions:

```
a = Numeric.array( [ [], [], [] ] )
if a: print 'a is true'
else: print 'a is false'                # prints: a is false
if len(a): print 'a has some items'
else: print 'a has no items'            # prints: a has some items
if Numeric.size(a): print 'a has some elements'
else: print 'a has no elements'         # prints: a has no elements
```

In most cases, the best way to compare arrays of numbers is for approximate equality with function allclose, covered later in this chapter.

Factory Functions

Numeric supplies numerous factory functions that create array objects.

array   array(*data*,*typecode*=None,*copy*=True,*savespace*=False)

Returns a new array object *a*. *a*'s shape depends on *data*. When *data* is a number, *a* has rank 0 and *a*.shape is the empty tuple ( ). When *data* is a sequence of numbers, *a* has rank 1 and *a*.shape is the singleton tuple (len(*data*),). When *data* is a sequence of sequences of numbers, all of *data*'s items must have the same length, *a* has rank 2, and *a*.shape is the pair (len(*data*),len(*data*[0])). This idea generalizes to any nesting level of *data* as a sequence of sequences, up to the arbitrarily high limit on rank mentioned earlier in this chapter. If data is nested over that limit, array raises TypeError. (This is unlikely to be a problem in practice, as an array of rank at least 40, with each axis of length at least 2, would have well over a million of millions of elements).

typecode can be any of the values shown in Table 15-2 or None. When *typecode* is None, array chooses a default type code depending on the types of the elements of *data*. When any one or more elements in *data* are long integer values or are neither numbers nor plain strings (e.g., None or Unicode strings), the type code is PyObject. When all elements are plain strings, the type code is Character. When any one or more elements (but not all) are plain strings, all others are numbers (not long integers), and *typecode* is None, array raises TypeError. You must explicitly pass '0' or PyObject as argument *typecode* if you want to have array build an array from some plain strings and some non-long integers. When all elements are numbers (not long integers), the default type code depends on the widest numeric type among the elements. When any of the elements is a complex, the type code is Complex. When no elements are complex but some are floating-point values, the type code is Float. When all elements are integers, the type code is Int.

Function array, by default, returns an array object *a* that doesn't share data with others. If *data* is an array object, and you explicitly pass a false value for argument *copy*, array returns an array object *a* that shares data with *data*, if feasible.

By default, an array object with a numeric type code is implicitly cast up when operated with numbers of wider numeric types. When you do not need this implicit casting, you can save some memory by explicitly passing a true value for argument *savespace* to the array factory function, to set the resulting array object *a* into space-saving mode. For example:

```
array(range(4),typecode='b')+2.0     # array([2.,3.,4.,5.])
array(range(4),typecode='b',savespace=True)+2.0
# array([2,3,4,5])
array(range(4),typecode='b',savespace=True)+258.7
# array([2,3,4,5])
```

The first statement creates an array of floating-point values, as *savespace* is not specified and thus each element is implicitly cast up to a float when added to 2.0. The second and third statements create arrays of 8-bit integers, since *savespace* is specified. Therefore, instead of implicit casting up of the array's element, we get implicit casting down of the float added to each element. 258.7 is cast down to 2: the fractional part .7 is lost because of the cast to an integer, and the resulting 258 becomes 2 because, since the cast is to 8-bit integers, only the lowest 8 bits are kept. The *savespace* mode can be very useful for large arrays, but be careful lest you suffer unexpected loss of precision when using it.

arrayrange,
arange

arrayrange([*start*,]*stop*[,*step*=1],*typecode*=None)

Like array(range(*start*,*stop*,*step*),*typecode*), but faster. See built-in function range, covered in Chapter 8, for details about *start*, *stop*, and *step*. arrayrange allows float values for these arguments, not just int values. Be careful when exploiting this feature, since the approximations inherent in floating-point arithmetic may lead to a result with one more or fewer items than you might expect. arange is a synonym of arrayrange.

fromstring   fromstring(*data*,*count*=None,*typecode*=Int)

Returns a one-dimensional array *a* of shape (*count*,) with data copied from the bytes of string *data*. When *count* is None, len(*data*) must be a multiple of *typecode*'s item size, and *a*'s shape is (len(*data*)/*a*.itemsize( ),). When *count* is not None, len(*data*) must be greater than or equal to *count**a.itemsize( ), and fromstring ignores *data*'s trailing bytes, if any.

Together with methods *a*.tostring and *a*.byteswapped (covered in the following section "Attributes and Methods"), function fromstring allows binary input/output of array objects. When you need to save arrays and later reload them, and don't need to use the saved form in non-Python programs, it's simpler and faster to use module cPickle, covered in Chapter 11. Many experienced users prefer to use a portable self-describing file format such as netCDF (see *http://met-www.cit.cornell.edu/noon/ncmodule.html*).

identity   identity(*n*,*typecode*=Int)

Returns a two-dimensional array *a* of shape (*n*,*n*). *a*'s elements are 0, except those on the main diagonal (*a*[*j*,*j*] for *j* in range(*n*)), which are 1.

ones   ones(*shapetuple*,*typecode*=Int,*savespace*=False)

Returns an array *a* such that *a*.shape==*shapetuple*. All of *a*'s elements are 1.

zeros   zeros(*shapetuple*,*typecode*=Int,*savespace*=False)

Returns an array *a* such that *a*.shape==*shapetuple*. All of *a*'s elements are 0.

Note that, by default, identity, ones, and zeros all return arrays whose type is Int. Be sure to specify explicitly a different type code, such as Float, if that is what you really want. For example, be sure to avoid the following common mistake:

```
a = zeros(3)
a[0] = 0.3                    # a is array([0,0,0])
```

Since a is Int in this snippet, the 0.3 we assign to one of its items gets truncated to the integer 0. Instead, you typically want something closer to the following:

```
a = zeros(3,Float)
a[0] = 0.3                    # a is array([0.3,0.,0.])
```

Here, we have explicitly specified Float as the type code for a, and therefore no truncation occurs when we assign 0.3 to one of a's items.

Attributes and Methods

For most array manipulations, `Numeric` supplies functions you can call with array arguments. You can also use Python lists as arguments; this polymorphism offers flexibility that is not available for functionality packaged up as array attributes and methods. Each `array` object *a* also supplies some methods and attributes, for direct access to functionality that would not benefit from polymorphic possibilities.

astype	*a*.astype(*typecode*)
	Returns a new array *b* with the same shape as *a*. *b*'s elements are *a*'s elements coerced to the type indicated by *typecode*. *b* does not share *a*'s data, even if *typecode* equals *a*.typecode( ).
byteswapped	*a*.byteswapped( )
	Returns a new `array` object *b* with the same type code and shape as *a*. Each element of *b* is copied from the corresponding element of *a*, inverting the order of the bytes in the value. This swapping transforms each value from little-endian to big-endian or vice versa. Together with function `fromstring` and method *a*.tostring, this helps when you have binary data from one kind of machine and need them for the other kind (for example, Intel platforms are little-endian, while Sun platforms are big-endian).
copy	*a*.copy( )
	Returns a new contiguous array object *b*, identical to *a*, but not sharing *a*'s data.
flat	*a*.flat is an attribute that contains an array with rank of one less than *a* and of the same size as *a*, sharing *a*'s data. Indexing or slicing *a*.flat lets you access or change *a*'s elements through this alternate view of *a*. Trying to access *a*.flat raises a `TypeError` exception if *a* is noncontiguous. When *a* is contiguous, *a*.flat is in row-major order. This means that, for example, when *a*'s shape is $(7,4)$ (i.e., *a* is a two-dimensional matrix with seven rows and four columns), *a*.flat[*i*] is the same as *a*[divmod(*i*,4)] for all *i* in range(28).
imag, **imaginary,** **real**	Trying to access the *a*.real and *a*.imag attributes raises a `TypeError` exception unless *a*'s type code is complex. When *a*'s type code is complex, each of *a*.real and *a*.imag is a noncontiguous array with the same shape as *a* and a `float` type code, sharing data with *a*. By accessing or modifying *a*.real or *a*.imag, you access or modify the real or imaginary parts of *a*'s complex-number elements. `imaginary` is a synonym of `imag`.

iscontiguous

`a.iscontiguous( )`

Returns True if *a*'s data occupies contiguous storage, otherwise False. This matters particularly when interfacing to C-coded extensions. *a*.copy( ) makes a contiguous copy of *a*. Noncontiguous arrays arise when slicing or transposing arrays, as well as for attributes *a*.real and *a*.imag of an array *a* with a complex type code.

itemsize

`a.itemsize( )`

Returns the number of bytes of memory used by each of *a*'s elements (not by each of *a*'s items, which are subarrays of *a*).

savespace

`a.savespace(flag=True)`

Sets or resets the space-saving mode of array *a*, depending on the truth value of *flag*. When *flag* is true, *a*.savespace(*flag*) sets *a*'s space-saving mode so that *a*'s elements are not implicitly cast up when operated with arrays of wider numeric types. For more details on this, see the discussion of *savespace* for function array earlier in this chapter. When *flag* is false, *a*.savespace(*flag*) resets *a*'s space-saving mode so that *a*'s elements *are* implicitly cast up when needed.

shape

The *a*.shape attribute is a tuple with one item per axis of *a*, giving the length of that axis. You can assign a sequence of integers to *a*.shape to change the shape of *a*, but *a*'s size (the total number of elements) must remain the same. When you assign to *a*.shape another sequence *s*, one of *s*'s items can be -1, meaning that the length along that axis is whatever is needed to keep *a*'s size unchanged. However, the product of the other items of *s* must evenly divide *a*'s size, or else the reshaping raises an exception. When you need to change the total number of elements in *a*, call function resize (covered in "Functions" later in this chapter).

spacesaver

`a.spacesaver( )`

Returns True if space-saving mode is on for array *a*, otherwise False. See the discussion of *savespace* for function array earlier in this chapter.

tolist

`a.tolist( )`

Returns a list *L* equivalent to *a*. For example, if *a*.shape is (2,3) and *a*'s type code is 'd', *L* is a list of two lists of three float values each. In other words, for each valid *i* and *j*, *L*[*i*][*j*]==*a*[*i,j*]. Note that list(*a*) converts only the top-level (axis 0) of array *a* into a list, and thus is not equivalent to *a*.tolist( ) if *a*'s rank is 2 or more. For example:

```
a=array([[1,2,3],[4,5,6]],typecode='d')
print a.shape          # prints: (2,3)
```

```
print a                       # prints: [[1. 2. 3.]
                              #          [4. 5. 6.]]
print list(a)
# prints: [array([1.,2.,3.]), array([4.,5.,6.])]
print a.tolist()
# prints: [[1.0,2.0,3.0],[4.0,5.0,6.0]]
```

---

tostring   *a*.tostring( )

Returns a binary string *s* whose bytes are a copy of the bytes of *a*'s elements.

---

typecode   *a*.typecode( )

Returns the type code of *a* as a one-character string.

Operations on Arrays

Arithmetic operators +, -, *, /, %, and **, comparison operators >, >=, <, <=, ==, and !=, and bitwise operators &, |, ^, and ~ (all covered in Chapter 4) also apply to arrays. If both operands *a* and *b* are arrays with equal shapes and type codes, the result is a new array *c* with the same shape and type code. Each element of *c* is the result of the operator on corresponding elements of *a* and *b* (element-wise operation).

Arrays do not follow sequence semantics for * (replication) and + (concatenation), but rather use * and + for element-wise arithmetic. Similarly, * does not mean matrix multiplication, but element-wise multiplication. Numeric supplies functions to perform replication, concatenation, and matrix multiplication; all operators on arrays perform element-wise operations.

When the type codes of *a* and *b* differ, the narrower numeric type is converted to the wider one, like for other Python numeric operations. As usual, operations between numeric and non-numeric values are disallowed. In the case of arrays, you can inhibit casting up by setting an array into space-saving mode with method savespace. Use space-saving mode with care, since it can result in silent loss of significant data. For more details on this, see the discussion of *savespace* for function array earlier in this chapter.

Broadcasting

Element-wise operations between arrays of different shapes are generally not possible: attempting such operations raises an exception. Numeric allows some such operations by broadcasting (replicating) a smaller array up to the shape of the larger one when feasible. To make broadcasting efficient, the replication is only conceptual: Numeric does not need to physically copy the data being broadcast (i.e., you need not worry that performance will be degraded because an operation involves broadcasting).

The simplest case of broadcasting is when one operand, *a*, is a scalar (an array of rank 0), while *b*, the other operand, is an array. In this case, Numeric conceptually builds a temporary array *t*, with shape *b*.shape, where each element of *t* equals *a*. Numeric then performs the requested operation between *t* and *b*. In practice, therefore, when you operate an array *b* with a scalar *a*, as in *a+b* or *b+a*, the resulting array has the same shape as *b*, and each element is the result of applying the operator to the corresponding element of *b* and the single number *a*.

More generally, broadcasting can also apply when both operands *a* and *b* are arrays. Conceptually, broadcasting works according to rather complicated general rules:

1. When *a* and *b* differ in rank, the one whose shape tuple is shorter is padded up to the other's rank by adding leading axes, each with a length of 1.
2. *a*.shape and *b*.shape, padded to the same length as per rule 1, are compared starting from the right (i.e., from the length of the last axis).
3. When the axis length along the axis being examined is the same for *a* and *b*, that axis is okay, and examination moves leftward to the previous axis.
4. When the lengths of the axes differ and both are greater than 1, Numeric raises an exception.
5. When one axis length is 1, Numeric broadcasts the corresponding array by replication along that plane to the axis length of the other array.

Broadcasting's rules are complicated because of their generality, but most typical applications of broadcasting are in simple cases. For example, say we compute *a+b*, and *a*.shape is (5,3) (a matrix of five rows, three columns). Further, say typical values for *b*.shape include ( ) (a scalar), (3,) (a one-dimensional vector with three elements), and (5,1) (a matrix with five rows, one column). In each of these cases, *b* is broadcast up to a temporary array *t* with shape (5,3) by replicating *b*'s elements along the needed axis (both axes, when *b* is a scalar), and Numeric computes *a+t*. The simplest and most frequent case, of course, is when *b*. shape is (5,3), the same shape as *a*'s. In this case, no broadcasting is needed.

In-place operations

Arrays support in-place operations through augmented assignment operators +=, -=, and so on. The left-hand side array or slice cannot be broadcast, but the right-hand side can be. Similarly, the left-hand side cannot be cast up, but the right-hand side can be. In other words, in-place operations treat the left-hand side as rigid in both shape and type, but the right-hand side is subject to the normal, more lenient rules.

Functions

Numeric defines several functions that operate on arrays, or polymorphically on Python sequences, conceptually forming temporary arrays from non-array operands.

allclose

allclose(*x*,*y*,*rtol*=1.e-5,*atol*=1.e-8)

Returns True when every element of *x* is close to the corresponding element of *y*, otherwise False. Two elements *ex* and *ey* are defined to be close if:

abs(*ex-ey*)<*atol*+*rtol**abs(*ey*)

In other words, *ex* and *ey* are close if both are tiny (less than *atol*) or if the relative difference is small (less than *rtol*). allclose is generally a better way to check array equality than ==, since floating-point arithmetic requires some comparison tolerance. However, allclose is not applicable to complex arrays, only to floating-point and integer arrays. To compare two complex arrays *x* and *y* for approximate equality, you can use:

allclose(x.real, y.real) and allclose(x.imag, y.imag)

argmax,
argmin

argmax(*a*,*axis*=-1)
argmin(*a*,*axis*=-1)

argmax returns a new integer array *m* whose shape tuple is *a*.shape minus the indicated *axis*. Each element of *m* is the index of a maximal element of *a* along *axis*. argmin is similar, but indicates minimal elements rather than maximal ones.

argsort

argsort(*a*,*axis*=-1)

Returns a new integer array *m* with the same shape as *a*. Each vector of *m* along *axis* is the index sequence needed to sort the corresponding axis of *a*. In particular, if *a* has rank 1, the most common case, take(*a*,argsort(*a*))==sort(*a*). For example:

```
x = [52, 115, 99, 111, 114, 101, 97, 110, 100, 55]
print Numeric.argsort(x)   # prints: [0 9 6 2 8 5 7 3 4 1]
print Numeric.sort(x)
# prints: [52 55 97 99 100 101 110 111 114 115]
print Numeric.take(x, Numeric.argsort(x))
# prints: [52 55 97 99 100 101 110 111 114 115]
```

Here, the result of Numeric.argsort(*x*) tells us that *x*'s smallest element is *x*[0], the second smallest is *x*[9], the third smallest is *x*[6], and so on. The call to Numeric.take in the last print statement takes *x*'s elements exactly in this order, and therefore produces the same sorted array as the call to Numeric.sort in the second print statement.

array2string

array2string(*a*,*max_line_width*=None,*precision*=None,
                suppress_small=None,*separator*=' ',
                array_output=False)

Returns a string representation *s* of array *a*, showing elements within brackets, separated by string *separator*. The last dimension is horizontal, the penultimate one vertical, and further dimensions are denoted by bracket nesting. If *array_output* is true, *s* starts with 'array(' and ends with ')'. *s* ends with ", 'X')" instead if X, which is *a*'s type code, is not Float, Complex, or Int, which lets you later use eval(*s*) if *separator* is ','.

Lines longer than *max_line_width* (by default, 77) are broken up. *precision* determines how many digits are used per element (by default, 8). If *suppress_small* is true, very small numbers are shown as 0. You can change these defaults by binding attributes of module sys named output_line_width, float_output_precision, and float_output_suppress_small.

str(*a*) is like array2string(*a*). repr(*a*) is like array2string(*a*,separator=', ',array_output=True).

---

average

average(*a*,axis=0,weights=None,returned=False)

Returns *a*'s average along *axis*. When *axis* is None, returns the average of all *a*'s elements. When *weights* is not None, *weights* must be an array with *a*'s shape, or a one-dimensional array with the length of *a*'s given *axis*, and average computes a weighted average. When *returned* is true, returns a pair: the first item is the average, the second item is the sum of weights (the count of values, when *weights* is None).

---

choose

choose(*a*,*values*)

Returns an array *c* with the same shape as *a*. *values* is a sequence. *a*'s elements are integers between 0, included, and len(*values*), excluded. Each element of *c* is the item of *values* whose index is the corresponding element of *a*. For example:

```
print Numeric.choose(Numeric.identity(3),'ox')
# prints: [[x o o]
#          [o x o]
#          [o o x]]
```

---

clip

clip(*m*,*min*,*max*)

Returns an array *c* with the same type code and shape as *a*. Each element *ec* of *c* is the corresponding element *ea* of *a*, where *min*<=*ea*<=*max*. Where *ea*<*min*, *ec* is *min*; where *ea*>*max*, *ec* is *max*. For example:

```
print Numeric.clip(Numeric.arange(10),2,7)
# prints: [2 2 2 3 4 5 6 7 7 7]
```

---

compress

compress(*condition*,*a*,axis=0)

Returns an array *c* with the same type code and rank as *a*. *c* includes only the elements of *a* for which the item of *condition*, corresponding along the given *axis*, is true. For example, compress((1,0,1),*a*) == take(*a*,(0,2),0) since (1,0,1) has true values only at indices 0 and 2. Here's how to get only the even numbers from an array:

```
a = Numeric.arange(10)
print Numeric.compress(a%2==0, a)   # prints: [0 2 4 6 8]
```

concatenate   concatenate(*arrays, axis=0*)

arrays is a sequence of arrays, all with the same shape except possibly along the given *axis*. concatenate returns an array that is the concatenation of the *arrays* along the given *axis*. In particular, concatenate((s,)*n) has the same sequence replication semantics that s*n would have if s were a generic Python sequence rather than an array. For example:

```
print Numeric.concatenate([Numeric.arange(5),
                           Numeric.arange(3)])
# prints: [0 1 2 3 4 0 1 2]
```

---

convolve   convolve(*a,b,mode=2*)

Returns an array c with rank 1, the linear convolution of rank 1 arrays a and b. Linear convolution is defined over unbounded sequences. convolve conceptually extends a and b to infinite length by padding with 0, then clips the infinite-length result to its central part, yielding c. When mode is 2, the default, convolve clips only the padding, so c's shape is (len(a)+len(b)-1,). Otherwise, convolve clips more. Say len(a) is greater than or equal to len(b): when mode is 0, len(c) is len(a)-len(b)+1; when mode is 1, len(c) is len(a). When len(a) is less than len(b), the effect is symmetrical. For example:

```
a = Numeric.arange(6)
b = Numeric.arange(4)
print Numeric.convolve(a, b)
# prints: [0 0 1 4 10 16 22 22 15]
print Numeric.convolve(a, b, 1)
# prints: [0 1 4 10 16 22]
print Numeric.convolve(a, b, 0)       # prints: [4 10 16]
```

---

cross_correlate   cross_correlate(*a,b,mode=0*)

Like convolve(*a,b[::-1],mode*).

---

diagonal   diagonal(*a,k=0,axis1=0,axis2=1*)

Returns the elements of a whose index along *axis1* and index along *axis2* differ by k. When a has rank 2, this means the main diagonal when k equals 0, subdiagonals above the main one when k is greater than 0, and subdiagonals below the main one when k is less than 0. For example:

```
# a is [[0 1 2 3]
#       [4 5 6 7]
#       [8 9 10 11]
#       [12 13 14 15]]
print Numeric.diagonal(a)        # prints: [0 5 10 15]
print Numeric.diagonal(a,1)      # prints: [1 6 11]
print Numeric.diagonal(a,-1)     # prints: [4 9 14]
```

As shown, diagonal(a) is the main diagonal, diagonal(a,1) the subdiagonal just above the main one, and diagonal(a,-1) the subdiagonal just below the main one.

indices

indices(*shapetuple*,*typecode*=None)

Returns an integer array x of shape (len(*shapetuple*),)+*shapetuple*. Each element of subarray $x[i]$ is equal to the element's i index in the subarray. For example:

```
print Numeric.indices((2,4))   # prints: [[[0 0 0 0]
                               #           [1 1 1 1]]
                               #          [[0 1 2 3]
                               #           [0 1 2 3]]]
```

innerproduct

innerproduct(a,b)

Returns an array m with the result of the inner product of a and b, like matrixmultiply(a,transpose(b)). a.shape[-1] must equal b.shape[-1], and m.shape is the tuple a.shape[:-1]+b.shape[0:-1:-1].

matrixmultiply

matrixmultiply(a,b)

Returns an array m with a times b in the matrix-multiplication sense, rather than element-wise multiplication. a.shape[-1] must equal b.shape[0], and m.shape is the tuple a.shape[:-1]+b.shape[1:].

nonzero

nonzero(a)

Returns the indices of those elements of a that are not equal to 0, like the expression:

```
array([i for i in range(len(a)) if a[i] != 0])
```

a must be a sequence or one-dimensional array.

put

put(a,*indices*,*values*)

a must be a contiguous array. *indices* is a sequence of integers, taken as indices into a.flat. *values* is a sequence of values that can be converted to a's type code (if shorter than *indices*, *values* is repeated as needed). Each element of a indicated by an item in *indices* is replaced by the corresponding item in *values*. put is therefore similar to (but faster than) the loop:

```
for i,v in zip(indices,values*len(indices)):
    a.flat[i]=v
```

putmask

putmask(a,*mask*,*values*)

a must be a contiguous array. *mask* is a sequence with the same length as a.flat. *values* is a sequence of values that can be converted to a's type code (if shorter than *mask*, *values* is repeated as needed). Each element of a corresponding to a true item in *mask* is replaced by the corresponding item in *values*. putmask is therefore similar to (but faster than) the loop:

```
for i,v in zip(xrange(len(mask)),values*len(mask)):
    if mask[i]: a.flat[i]=v
```

---

rank

rank(*a*)

Returns the rank of *a*, just like len(array(*a*,copy=False).shape).

---

ravel

ravel(*a*)

Returns the flat form of *a*, just like array(*a*,copy=False).flat.

---

repeat

repeat(*a*,*repeat*,*axis*=0)

Returns an array with the same type code and rank as *a*, where each of *a*'s elements is repeated along *axis* as many times as the value of the corresponding element of *repeat*. *repeat* is an integer, or an integer sequence of length *a*.shape[*axis*].

---

reshape

reshape(*a*,*shapetuple*)

Returns an array *r* with shape *shapetuple*, sharing *a*'s data. *r*=reshape(*a*,*shapetuple*) is just like *r*=*a*;*r*.shape=*shapetuple*. The product of *shapetuple*'s items must equal the product of *a*.shape's, but one of *shapetuple*'s items may be -1 to ask for adaptation of that axis's length. For example:

```
print Numeric.reshape(range(12),(3,-1))
# prints: [[0 1 2 3]
#          [4 5 6 7]
#          [8 9 10 11]]
```

---

resize

resize(*a*,*shapetuple*)

Returns an array *r* with shape *shapetuple* and data copied from *a*. If *r*'s size is smaller than *a*'s size, *r*.flat is copied from the start of ravel(*a*); if *r*'s size is larger, the data in ravel(*a*) is replicated as many times as needed. In particular, resize(*s*,(*n**len(*s*),)) has the sequence replication semantics that *s*n* would have if *s* were a generic Python sequence rather than an array. For example:

```
print Numeric.resize(range(5),(3,4))
# prints: [[0 1 2 3]
#          [4 0 1 2]
#          [3 4 0 1]]
```

---

searchsorted

searchsorted(*a*,*values*)

a must be a sorted rank 1 array. searchsorted returns an array of integers *s* with the same shape as *values*. Each element of *s* is the index in *a* where the corresponding element of *values* would fit in the sorted order of *a*. For example:

```
print Numeric.searchsorted([0,1],
    [0.2,-0.3,0.5,1.3,1.0,0.0,0.3])
# prints: [1 0 1 2 1 0 1]
```

This specific idiom returns an array with 0 in correspondence to each element *x* of *values* when *x* is less than or equal to 0; 1 when *x* is greater than 0 and less than or equal to 1; and 2 when *x* is greater than 1. With slight generalization, and with appropriate thresholds as the elements of sorted array *a*, this idiom allows very fast classification of what subrange each element *x* of *values* falls into.

shape shape(*a*)

Returns the shape of *a*, just like array(*a*,copy=False).shape.

size size(*a*,*axis*=None)

When *axis* is None, returns the total number of elements in *a*. Otherwise, returns the number of elements of *a* along *axis*, like array(*a*,copy=False).shape[*axis*].

sort sort(*a*,*axis*=-1)

Returns an array *s* with the same type code and shape as *a*, with elements along each plane of the given *axis* reordered so that the plane is sorted in increasing order. For example:

```
# x is [[0 1 2 3]
#       [4 0 1 2]
#       [3 4 0 1]]
print Numeric.sort(x)      # prints: [[0 1 2 3]
                           #          [0 1 2 4]
                           #          [0 1 3 4]]
print Numeric.sort(x,0)    # prints: [[0 0 0 1]
                           #          [3 1 1 2]
                           #          [4 4 2 3]]
```

sort(*x*) returns a result where each row is sorted. sort(*x*,0) returns a result where each column is sorted.

swapaxes swapaxes(*a*,*axis1*,*axis2*)

Returns an array *s* with the same type code, rank, and size as *a*, sharing *a*'s data. *s*'s shape is the same as *a*, but with the lengths of axes *axis1* and *axis2* swapped. In other words, *s*=swapaxes(*a*,*axis1*,*axis2*) is like:

```
swapped_shape=range(length(a.shape))
swapped_shape[axis1]=axis2
swapped_shape[axis2]=axis1
s=transpose(a,swapped_shape)
```

take take(*a*,*indices*,*axis*=0)

Returns an array *t* with the same type code and rank as *a*, containing the subset of *a*'s elements that would be in a slice along *axis* comprising the given *indices*. For example, after t=take(*a*,(1,3)), *t*.shape==(2,)+*a*.shape[1:], and *t*'s elements are those in the second and fourth rows of *a*.

trace	trace(*a*,*k*=0) Returns the sum of *a*'s elements along the *k* diagonal, like sum(diagonal(*a*,*k*)).
transpose	transpose(*a*,*axes*=None) Returns an array *t*, with the same type code, rank, and size as *a*, sharing *a*'s data. *t*'s axes are permuted with respect to *a*'s by the axis indices in sequence *axes*. When *axes* is None, *t*'s axes invert the order of *a*'s, as if *axes* were *a*.shape[::-1].
where	where(*condition*,*x*,*y*) Returns an array *w* with the same shape as *condition*. Where an element of *condition* is true, the corresponding element of *w* is the corresponding element of *x*; otherwise it is the corresponding element of *y*. For example, clip(*a*,*min*,*max*) is the same as where(greater(*a*,*max*),*max*,where(greater(*a*,*min*),*a*,*min*)).

Universal Functions (ufuncs)

Numeric supplies named functions with the same semantics as Python's arithmetic, comparison, and bitwise operators. Similar semantics (element-wise operation, broadcasting, coercion) are also available with other mathematical functions, both binary and unary, that Numeric supplies. For example, Numeric supplies typical mathematical functions similar to those supplied by built-in module math, such as sin, cos, log, and exp.

These functions are objects of type ufunc (which stands for universal function) and share several traits in addition to those they have in common with array operators. Every ufunc instance *u* is callable, is applicable to sequences as well as to arrays, and lets you specify an optional *output* argument. If *u* is binary (i.e., if *u* accepts two operand arguments), *u* also has four callable attributes, named *u*.accumulate, *u*.outer, *u*.reduce, and *u*.reduceat. The ufunc objects supplied by Numeric apply only to arrays with numeric type codes (i.e., not to arrays with type code '0' or 'c').

Any ufunc *u* applies to sequences, not just to arrays. When you start with a list *L*, it's faster to call *u* directly on *L* rather than to convert *L* to an array. *u*'s return value is an array *a*; you can perform further computation, if any, on *a*, and then, if you need a list result, you can convert the resulting array to a list by calling its method tolist. For example, say you must compute the logarithm of each item of a list and return another list. On my system, with N set to 2222 and using python -O, a list comprehension such as:

```
def logsupto(N):
    return [math.log(x) for x in range(2,N)]
```

takes about 5.6 milliseconds. Using Python's built-in map:

```
def logsupto(N):
    return map(math.log, range(2,N))
```

takes around half the time, 2.8 milliseconds. Using Numeric's ufunc named log:

```
def logsupto(N):
    return Numeric.log(range(2,N)).tolist()
```

reduces the time to about 2.0 milliseconds. Taking some care to exploit the *output* argument to the log ufunc:

```
def logsupto(N):
    temp = Numeric.arange(2, N, typecode=Numeric.Float)
    Numeric.log(temp, temp)
    return temp.tolist()
```

further reduces the time, down to just 0.9 milliseconds. The ability to accelerate such simple but massive computations (here by about 6 times) with so little effort is a good part of the attraction of Numeric, and particularly of Numeric's ufunc objects.

The Optional output Argument

Any ufunc *u* accepts an optional last argument *output* that specifies an output array. If supplied, *output* must be an array or array slice of the right shape and type for *u*'s results (i.e., no coercion, no broadcasting). *u* stores results in *output* and does not create a new array. *output* can be the same as an input array argument *a* of *u*. Indeed, *output* is normally specified in order to substitute common idioms such as *a=u(a,b)* with faster equivalents such as *u(a,b,a)*. However, *output* cannot share data with *a* without being *a* (i.e., *output* can't be a different view of some or all of *a*'s data). If you pass such a disallowed *output* argument, Numeric is normally unable to diagnose your error and raise an exception, so instead you get wrong results.

Whether you pass the optional *output* argument or not, a ufunc *u* returns its results as the function's return value. When you do not pass *output*, *u* stores the results it returns in a new array object, so you normally bind *u*'s return value to some reference in order to be able to access *u*'s results later. When you pass the *output* argument, *u* stores the results in *output*, so you need not bind *u*'s return value. You can later access *u*'s results as the new contents of the array object passed as *output*.

Callable Attributes

Every binary ufunc *u* supplies four attributes that are also callable objects.

accumulate   `u.accumulate(a,axis=0)`

Returns an array r with the same shape and type code as a. Each element of r is the accumulation of elements of a along the given *axis* with the function or operator underlying u. For example:

```
print add.accumulate(range(10))
# prints: [0 1 3 6 10 15 21 28 36 45]
```

Since add's underlying operator is +, and a is sequence $0,1,2,\ldots,9$, r is $0,0+1,0+1+2,\ldots,0+1+\ldots+8+9$. In other words, $r[0]$ is $a[0]$, $r[1]$ is $r[0] + a[1]$, $r[2]$ is $r[1] + a[2]$, and so on (i.e., each $r[i]$ is $r[i-1] + a[i]$).

outer   `u.outer(a,b)`

Returns an array r whose shape tuple is $a.shape+b.shape$. For each tuple *ta* indexing a and *tb* indexing b, $a[ta]$, operated (with the function or operator underlying u) with $b[tb]$, is put in $r[ta+tb]$ (the + here indicates tuple concatenation). The overall operation is known in mathematics as the outer product when u is multiply. For example:

```
a = Numeric.arange(3, 5)
b = Numeric.arange(1, 6)
c = Numeric.multiply.outer(a, b)
print a.shape, b.shape, c.shape # prints: (2,) (5,) (2,5)
print c                         # prints: [[3 6 9 12 15]
                                #          [4 8 12 16 20]]
```

$c.shape$ is $(2,5)$, the concatenation of the shape tuples of operands a and b. Each i row of c is the whole of b multiplied by the corresponding i element of a.

reduce   `u.reduce(a,axis=0)`

Returns an array r with the same type code as a and rank one less than a's rank. Each element of r is the reduction of the elements of a, along the given *axis*, with the function or operator underlying u. The functionality of $u.reduce$ is therefore close to that of Python's built-in reduce function, covered in Chapter 8. For example, since $0+1+2+\ldots+9$ is 45, add.reduce(range(10)) is 45. This is just like, when using built-in reduce and import operator, reduce(operator.add,range(10)) is also 45.

reduceat   `u.reduceat(a,indices)`

Returns an array r with the same type code as a and the same shape as *indices*. Each element of r is the reduction, with the function or operator underlying u, of elements of a starting from the corresponding item of *indices* up to the next one excluded (up to the end, for the last one). For example:

```
print add.reduceat(range(10),(2,6,8)) # prints: [14 13 17]
```

Here, r's elements are the partial sums 2+3+4+5, 6+7, and 8+9.

ufunc Objects Supplied by Numeric

Numeric supplies several ufunc objects, as listed in Table 15-4.

Table 15-4. ufunc objects supplied by Numeric

ufunc	Behavior
absolute	Behaves like the abs built-in function
add	Behaves like the + operator
arccos	Behaves like the acos function in math and cmath
arccosh	Behaves like the acosh function in cmath
arcsin	Behaves like the asin function in math and cmath
arcsinh	Behaves like the asinh function in cmath
arctan	Behaves like the atan function in math and cmath
arctanh	Behaves like the atanh function in cmath
bitwise_and	Behaves like the & operator
bitwise_not	Behaves like the ~ operator
bitwise_or	Behaves like the | operator
bitwise_xor	Behaves like the ^ operator
ceil	Behaves like the ceil function in math
conjugate	Computes the complex conjugate of each element (unary)
cos	Behaves like the cos function in math and cmath
cosh	Behaves like the cosh function in cmath
divide	Behaves like the / operator
equal	Behaves like the = = operator
exp	Behaves like the exp function in math and cmath
fabs	Behaves like the fabs function in math
floor	Behaves like the floor function in math
fmod	Behaves like the fmod function in math
greater	Behaves like the > operator
greater_equal	Behaves like the /= operator
less	Behaves like the < operator
less_equal	Behaves like the <= operator
log	Behaves like the log function in math and cmath
log10	Behaves like the log10 function in math and cmath
logical_and	Behaves like the & operator; always returns an array containing 0s and 1s, the truth values of the operands' elements
logical_not	Returns an array of 0s and 1s, logical negations of the operand's elements
logical_or	Behaves like the | operator; always returns an array containing 0s and 1s, the truth values of the operands' elements
logical_xor	Behaves like the ^ operator; always returns an array containing 0s and 1s, the truth values of the operands' elements
maximum	Returns element-wise the larger of the two elements being operated on
minimum	Returns element-wise the smaller of the two elements being operated on
multiply	Behaves like the * operator
not_equal	Behaves like the != operator

Table 15-4. ufunc objects supplied by Numeric (continued)

ufunc	Behavior
power	Behaves like the ** operator
remainder	Behaves like the % operator
sin	Behaves like the sin function in math and cmath
sinh	Behaves like the sinh function in cmath
sqrt	Behaves like the sqrt function in math and cmath
subtract	Behaves like the - operator
tan	Behaves like the tan function in math and cmath
tanh	Behaves like the tanh function in cmath

Here's how you might use the maximum ufunc to get a numeric ramp that goes down and then back up again:

```
print Numeric.maximum(range(1,20),range(20,1,-1))
# prints: [20 19 18 17 16 15 14 13 12 11 11 12 13 14 15 16 17 18 19]
```

Shorthand for Commonly Used ufunc Methods

Numeric defines function synonyms for some commonly used methods of ufunc objects, as listed in Table 15-5.

Table 15-5. Synonyms for ufunc methods

Synonym	Stands for
alltrue	logical_and.reduce
cumproduct	multiply.accumulate
cumsum	add.accumulate
product	multiply.reduce
sometrue	logical_or.reduce
sum	add.reduce

Optional Numeric Modules

Many other modules are built on top of Numeric or cooperate with it. You can download some of them from the same URL as Numeric (*http://sourceforge.net/projects/numpy*). Some of these extra modules may already be included in the package you have downloaded. Documentation for the modules is also part of the documentation for Numeric. A rich library of scientific tools that work well with Numeric is SciPy, available at *http://www.scipy.org*. I highly recommend it if you are using Python for scientific or engineering computing.

Here are some key optional Numeric modules:

MLab
    MLab supplies many Python functions written on top of Numeric. MLab's functions are similar in name and operation to functions supplied by the product Matlab.

FFT

FFT supplies Python-callable Fast Fourier Transforms (FFTs) of data held in Numeric arrays. FFT can wrap either the well-known *FFTPACK* Fortran-coded library or the compatible C-coded *fftpack* library.

LinearAlgebra

LinearAlgebra supplies Python-callable functions, operating on data held in Numeric arrays, that wrap either the well-known *LAPACK* Fortran-coded library or the compatible C-coded *lapack_lite* library. LinearAlgebra lets you invert matrices, solve linear systems, compute eigenvalues and eigenvectors, perform singular value decomposition, and least-squares-solve overdetermined linear systems.

RandomArray

RandomArray supplies fast, high-quality pseudo-random number generators, using various random distributions, that work with Numeric arrays.

MA

MA supports masked arrays (i.e., arrays that can have missing or invalid values). MA supplies a large subset of Numeric's functionality, albeit sometimes at reduced speed. The extra functionality of MA is the ability to associate to each array an optional mask, an auxiliary array of False and True, where True indicates array elements that are missing, unknown, or invalid. Computations propagate masks, and you can turn masked arrays into plain Numeric ones by using a fill-in value for invalid elements. MA is widely applicable because experimental data quite often has missing or inapplicable elements. Furthermore, when you need to extend or specialize some aspect of Numeric's behavior for your application's purposes, it often turns out to be simplest and most effective to start with MA's sources rather than with Numeric's. The latter are often quite hard to understand and modify, due to the extreme degree of optimization applied to them over the years.

16

Tkinter GUIs

Most professional applications interact with users through a graphical user interface (GUI). A GUI is normally programmed through a *toolkit*, which is a library that implements *controls* (also known as *widgets*) that are visible objects such as buttons, labels, text entry fields, and menus. A GUI toolkit lets you compose controls into a coherent whole, display them on-screen, and interact with the user, receiving input via such devices as the keyboard and mouse.

Python gives you a choice among many GUI toolkits. Some are platform-specific, but most are cross-platform to different degrees, supporting at least Windows and Unix-like platforms, and often the Macintosh as well. Check *http://starbase. neosoft.com/~claird/comp.lang.python/python_GUI.html* for a list of dozens of GUI toolkits available for Python. One package, anygui (*http://anygui.org*), lets you program simple GUIs to one common programming interface and deploy them with any of a variety of backends.

The most widespread Python GUI toolkit is Tkinter. Tkinter is an object-oriented Python wrapper around the cross-platform toolkit Tk, which is also used with other scripting languages such as Tcl (for which it was originally developed) and Perl. Tkinter, like the underlying Tcl/Tk, runs on Windows, Macintosh, and Unix-like platforms. Tkinter itself comes with standard Python distributions. On Windows, the standard Python distribution also includes the Tcl/Tk components needed to run Tkinter. On other platforms, you must obtain and install Tcl/Tk separately.

This chapter covers an essential subset of Tkinter, sufficient to build simple graphical frontends for Python applications. A richer introduction is available at *http://www.pythonware.com/library/tkinter/introduction/*.

Tkinter Fundamentals

The Tkinter module makes it easy to build simple GUI applications. You simply import Tkinter, create, configure, and position the widgets you want, and then enter the Tkinter main loop. Your application becomes *event-driven*, which means that the user interacts with the widgets, causing events, and your application responds via the functions you installed as handlers for these events.

The following example shows a simple application that exhibits this general structure:

```
import sys, Tkinter
Tkinter.Label(text="Welcome!").pack( )
Tkinter.Button(text="Exit", command=sys.exit).pack( )
Tkinter.mainloop( )
```

The calls to Label and Button create the respective widgets and return them as results. Since we specify no parent windows, Tkinter puts the widgets directly in the application's main window. The named arguments specify each widget's configuration. In this simple case, we don't need to bind variables to the widgets. We just call the pack method on each widget, handing control of the widget's geometry to a layout manager object known as the packer. A *layout manager* is an invisible component whose job is to position widgets within other widgets (known as *container* or *parent* widgets), handling geometrical layout issues. The previous example passes no arguments to control the packer's operation, so therefore the packer operates in a default way.

When the user clicks on the button, the command callable of the Button widget executes without arguments. The example passes function sys.exit as the argument named command when it creates the Button. Therefore, when the user clicks on the button, sys.exit( ) executes and terminates the application (as covered in Chapter 8).

After creating and packing the widgets, the example calls Tkinter's mainloop function, and thus enters the Tkinter main loop and becomes event-driven. Since the only event for which the example installs a handler is a click on the button, nothing happens from the application's viewpoint until the user clicks the button. Meanwhile, however, the Tkinter toolkit responds in the expected way to other user actions, such as moving the Tkinter window, covering and uncovering the window, and so on. When the user resizes the window, the packer layout manager works to update the widgets' geometry. In this example, the widgets remain centered, close to the upper edge of the window, with the label above the button.

All strings going to or coming from Tkinter are Unicode strings, so be sure to review "Unicode" in Chapter 9 if you need to show, or accept as input, characters outside of the ASCII encoding (you may then need to use some other appropriate codec).

Note that all the scripts in this chapter are meant to be run standalone (i.e., from a command line or in a platform-dependent way, such as by double clicking on a script's icon). Running a GUI script from inside another program that has its own

GUI, such as a Python integrated development environment (e.g., IDLE or PythonWin), can cause various anomalies. This can be a particular problem when the GUI script attempts to terminate (and thus close down the GUI), since the script's GUI and the other program's GUI may interfere with each other.

Note also that this chapter refers to several all-uppercase, multi-letter identifiers (e.g., LEFT, RAISED, ACTIVE). All these identifiers are constant attributes of module Tkinter, used for a wide variety of purposes. If your code uses from Tkinter import *, you can then use the identifiers directly. If your code uses import Tkinter instead, you need to qualify those identifiers, just like all others you import from Tkinter, by preceding them with 'Tkinter.'. Tkinter is one of the rare Python modules designed to support from Tkinter import *, but of course you may choose to use import Tkinter anyway, sacrificing some convenience and brevity in favor of greater clarity. A good compromise between convenience and clarity is often to import Tkinter with a shorter name (e.g., import Tkinter as Tk).

Widget Fundamentals

The Tkinter module supplies many kinds of widgets, and most of them have several things in common. All widgets are instances of classes that inherit from class Widget. Class Widget itself is *abstract*; that is, you never instantiate Widget itself. You only instantiate concrete subclasses corresponding to specific kinds of widgets. Class Widget's functionality is common to all the widgets you instantiate.

To instantiate any kind of widget, call the widget's class. The first argument is the parent window of the widget, also known as the widget's *master*. If you omit this positional argument, the widget's master is the application's main window. All other arguments are in named form, *option=value*. You can also set or change options on an existing widget w by calling w.config(*option=value*). You can get an option of w by calling w.cget('*option*'), which returns the option's value. Each widget w is a mapping, so you can also get an option as w['*option*'] and set or change it with w['*option*']=*value*.

Common Widget Options

Many widgets accept some common options. Some options affect a widget's colors, others affect lengths (normally in pixels), and there are various other kinds. This section details the most commonly used options.

Color options

Tkinter represents colors with strings. The string can be a color name, such as 'red' or 'orange', or it may be of the form '#RRGGBB', where each of R, G, and B is a hexadecimal digit, to represent a color by the values of red, green, and blue components on a scale of 0 to 255. Don't worry; if your screen can't display millions of different colors, as implied by this scheme; Tkinter maps any requested color to the closest color that your screen can display. The common color options are:

`activebackground`

Background color for the widget when the widget is *active*, meaning that the mouse is over the widget and clicking on it makes something happen

`activeforeground`

Foreground color for the widget when the widget is active

`background` *(also* bg*)*

Background color for the widget

`disabledforeground`

Foreground color for the widget when the widget is *disabled*, meaning that clicking on the widget is ignored

`foreground` *(also* fg*)*

Foreground color for the widget

`highlightbackground`

Background color of the highlight region when the widget has focus

`highlightcolor`

Foreground color of the highlight region when the widget has focus

`selectbackground`

Background color for the selected items of the widget, for widgets that have selectable items, such as `Listbox`

`selectforeground`

Foreground color for the selected items of the widget

Length options

Tkinter normally expresses a length as an integer number of pixels; other units of measure are possible, but rarely used. The common length options are:

`borderwidth`

Width of the border (if any), giving a 3D look to the widget

`highlightthickness`

Width of the highlight rectangle when the widget has focus (when 0, the widget does not draw a highlight rectangle)

`padx, pady`

Extra space the widget requests from its geometry manager beyond the minimum the widget needs to display its contents, in the x and y directions

`selectborderwidth`

Width of the 3D border (if any) around selected items of the widget

`wraplength`

Maximum line length for widgets that perform word wrapping (when less than or equal to 0, no wrapping: the widget breaks lines of text only at '\n')

Options expressing numbers of characters

Some options indicate a widget's requested geometry not in pixels, but rather as a number of characters, using average width or height of the widget's fonts:

height
Desired height of the widget; must be greater than or equal to 1

underline
Index of the character to underline in the widget's text (0 is the first character, 1 the second one, and so on). The underlined character also determines what shortcut key reaches or activates the widget.

width
Desired width of the widget (when less than or equal to 0, desired width is just enough to hold the widget's current contents)

Other common options

Other options accepted by many kinds of widgets are a mixed bag, dealing with both behavior and presentation issues.

anchor
Where the information in the widget is displayed; must be N, NE, E, SE, S, SW, W, NW, or CENTER (all except CENTER are compass directions)

command
Callable without arguments; executes when the user clicks on the widget (only for widgets Button, Checkbutton, and Radiobutton)

font
Font for the text in this widget (see "Fonts" later in this chapter)

image
An image to display in the widget instead of text; the value must be a Tkinter image object (see "Tkinter Images" later in this chapter)

justify
How lines are justified when a widget shows more than a line of text; must be LEFT, CENTER, or RIGHT

relief
The 3D effect that indicates how the interior of the widget appears relative to the exterior; must be RAISED, SUNKEN, FLAT, RIDGE, SOLID, or GROOVE

state
Widget look and behavior on mouse and keyboard clicks; must be NORMAL, ACTIVE, or DISABLED

takefocus
If true, the widget accepts focus when the user navigates among widgets by pressing the Tab or Shift-Tab keys

text
The text string displayed by the widget

textvariable
The Tkinter variable object associated with the widget (see "Tkinter Variable Objects" later in this chapter)

Common Widget Methods

A widget *w* supplies many methods. Besides event-related methods, mentioned in "Events" later in this chapter, commonly used widget methods are the following.

cget	`w.cget(`*`option`*`)` Returns the value configured in *w* for *option*.
config	`w.config(**`*`options`*`)` `w.config( )`, without arguments, returns a dictionary where each possible option of *w* is mapped to a tuple that describes it. Called with one or more named arguments, `config` sets those options in *w*'s configuration.
focus_set	`w.focus_set( )` Sets focus to *w*, so that all keyboard events for the application are sent to *w*.

grab_set,
grab_release
	`w.grab_set( )`
	`w.grab_release( )`
	
	`grab_set` ensures that all of the application's events are sent to *w* until a corresponding call to `grab_release`.

mainloop	`w.mainloop( )` Enters a Tkinter event loop. Event loops may be nested; each call to `mainloop` enters one further-nested level of the event loop.
quit	`w.quit( )` Quits a Tkinter event loop. When event loops are nested; each call to `quit` exits one nested level of the event loop.
update	`w.update( )` Handles all pending events. *Never* call this while handling an event!
update_ idletasks	`w.update_idletasks( )` Handles those pending events that would normally be handled only when the event loop is idle (such as layout-manager updates and widget redrawing) but does not perform any callbacks. You can safely call this method at any time.
wait_variable	`w.wait_variable(`*`v`*`)` *v* must be a Tkinter variable object (covered in the next section). `wait_variable` returns only when the value of *v* changes. Meanwhile, other parts of the application remain active.

wait_visibility	`w.wait_visibility(w1)`
	w1 must be a widget. `wait_visibility` returns only when *w1* becomes visible. Meanwhile, other parts of the application remain active.
wait_window	`w.wait_window(w1)`
	w1 must be a widget. `wait_window` returns only when *w1* is destroyed. Meanwhile, other parts of the application remain active.
winfo_height	`w.winfo_height( )`
	Returns *w*'s height in pixels.
winfo_width	`w.winfo_width( )`
	Returns *w*'s width in pixels.

w supplies many other methods whose names start with `winfo_`, but the two above are the most often called, typically after calling `w.update_idletasks`. They let you ascertain a widget's dimensions after the user has resized a window, causing the layout manager to rearrange the widgets' geometry.

Tkinter Variable Objects

The `Tkinter` module supplies classes whose instances represent variables. Each class deals with a specific data type: `DoubleVar` for `float`, `IntVar` for `int`, `StringVar` for `str`. You can instantiate any of these classes without arguments to obtain an instance *x*, also known in `Tkinter` as a *variable object*. Then, *x*.`set`(*datum*) sets *x*'s value to the given value, and *x*.`get( )` returns *x*'s current value.

You can pass *x* as the `textvariable` or `variable` configuration option for a widget. Once you do this, the widget's text changes to track any change to *x*'s value, and *x*'s value, in turn, tracks changes to the widget (for some kinds of widgets). Further, a single `Tkinter` variable can control more than one widget. `Tkinter` variables let you control widget contents more transparently, and sometimes more conveniently, than explicitly querying and setting widget properties. The following example shows how to use a `StringVar` to connect an `Entry` widget and a `Label` widget automatically:

```
import Tkinter

root = Tkinter.Tk( )
tv = Tkinter.StringVar( )
Tkinter.Label(textvariable=tv).pack( )
Tkinter.Entry(textvariable=tv).pack( )
tv.set('Welcome!')
Tkinter.Button(text="Exit", command=root.quit).pack( )

Tkinter.mainloop( )
print tv.get( )
```

As you edit the Entry, you'll see the Label change automatically. This example instantiates the Tkinter main window explicitly, binds it to name *root*, and then sets as the Button's command the bound method *root.quit*, which quits Tkinter's main loop but does not terminate the Python application. Thus, the example ends with a print statement, to show on standard output the final value of variable object *tv*.

Tkinter Images

The Tkinter class PhotoImage supports Graphical Interchange Format (GIF) and Portable PixMap (PPM) images. You instantiate class PhotoImage with a keyword argument file=*path* to load the image's data from the image file at the given *path* and get an instance *x*.

You can set *x* as the image configuration option for one or more widgets. When you do this, the widget displays the image rather than text. If you need image processing functionality and support for many image formats (including JPEG, PNG, and TIFF), use PIL, the Python Imaging Library (*http://www.pythonware. com/products/pil/*), designed to work with Tkinter. I do not cover PIL further in this book.

Tkinter also supplies class BitmapImage, whose instances are usable wherever instances of PhotoImage are. BitmapImage supports some file formats known as bitmaps. I do not cover BitmapImage further in this book.

Being set as the image configuration option of a widget does not suffice to keep instances of PhotoImage and BitmapImage alive. Be sure to hold such instances in a Python container object, typically a list or dictionary, to ensure that the instances are not garbage-collected. The following example shows how to display GIF images:

```
import os
import Tkinter

root = Tkinter.Tk( )
L = Tkinter.Listbox(selectmode=Tkinter.SINGLE)
gifsdict = { }

dirpath = 'imgs'
for gifname in os.listdir(dirpath):
    if not gifname[0].isdigit( ): continue
    gifpath = os.path.join(dirpath, gifname)
    gif = Tkinter.PhotoImage(file=gifpath)
    gifsdict[gifname] = gif
    L.insert(Tkinter.END, gifname)

L.pack( )
img = Tkinter.Label( )
img.pack( )
def list_entry_clicked(*ignore):
    imgname = L.get(L.curselection( )[0])
img.config(image=gifsdict[imgname])
L.bind('<ButtonRelease-1>', list_entry_clicked)
root.mainloop( )
```

Assuming you have in some directory ('imgs' in the example) several GIF files whose filenames start with digits, the example loads the images into memory, shows the filenames in a Listbox instance, and shows in a Label instance the GIF whose filename you click on. Note that for simplicity, the example does not give the Listbox widget a Scrollbar (we'll see how to equip a Listbox with a Scrollbar shortly).

Commonly Used Simple Widgets

The Tkinter module provides a number of simple widgets that cover most needs of basic GUI applications. This section documents the Button, Checkbutton, Entry, Label, Listbox, Radiobutton, Scale, and Scrollbar widgets.

Button

Class Button implements a *pushbutton*, which the user clicks to execute an action. Instantiate Button with option text=*somestring* to let the button show text, or image=*imageobject* to let the button show an image. You normally use option command=*callable* to have *callable* execute without arguments when the user clicks the button. *callable* can be a function, a bound method of an object, an instance of a class with a __call__ method, or a lambda.

Besides methods common to all widgets, an instance *b* of class Button supplies two button-specific methods.

flash   *b*.flash( )

           Draws the user's attention to button *b* by redrawing *b* a few times, alternatively in normal and active states.

invoke   *b*.invoke( )

           Calls without arguments the callable object that is *b*'s command option, just like *b*.cget('command')( ). This can be handy when, within some other action, you want the program to act just as if the button had been clicked.

Checkbutton

Class Checkbutton implements a *checkbox*, which is a little box, optionally displaying a checkmark, that the user clicks to toggle on or off. You normally instantiate Checkbutton with exactly one of the two options text=*somestring*, to label the box with text, or image=*imageobject*, to label the box with an image. Optionally, use option command=*callable* to have *callable* execute without arguments when the user clicks the box. *callable* can be a function, a bound method of an object, an instance of a class with a __call__ method, or a lambda.

An instance *c* of Checkbutton must be associated with a Tkinter variable object *v*, using configuration option variable=*v* of *c*. Normally, *v* is an instance of IntVar, and *v*'s value is 0 when the box is unchecked, and 1 when the box is checked. The value of *v* changes when the box is checked or unchecked (either by the user clicking on it, or by your code calling *c*'s methods deselect, select, toggle). Vice versa, when the value of *v* changes, *c* shows or hides the checkmark as appropriate.

Besides methods common to all widgets, an instance *c* of class Checkbutton supplies five checkbox-specific methods.

deselect   `c.deselect( )`

Removes *c*'s checkmark, like `c.cget('variable').set(0)`.

flash   `c.flash( )`

Draws the user's attention to checkbox *c* by redrawing *c* a few times, alternately in normal and active states.

invoke   `c.invoke( )`

Calls without arguments the callable object that is *c*'s command option, just like `c.cget('command')( )`.

select   `c.select( )`

Shows *c*'s checkmark, like `c.cget('variable').set(1)`.

toggle   `c.deselect( )`

Toggles the state of *c*'s checkmark, as if the user had clicked on *c*.

Entry

Class Entry implements a *text entry field* (i.e., a widget in which the user can input and edit a line of text). An instance *e* of Entry supplies several methods and configuration options allowing fine-grained control of widget operation and contents, but in most GUI programs you can get by with just three Entry-specific idioms:

```
e.delete(0, END)          # clear the widget's contents
e.insert(END, somestring) # append somestring to the widget's contents
somestring = e.get( )     # get the widget's contents
```

An Entry instance with state=DISABLED is a good way to display a line of text while letting the user copy it to the clipboard. To display more than one line of text, use an instance of class Text, covered later in this chapter. DISABLED stops your program, as well as the user, from altering *e*'s contents. To perform any alteration, temporarily set state=NORMAL:

```
e.config(state=NORMAL)    # allow alteration of e's contents
# call e.delete and/or e.insert as needed
e.config(state=DISABLED)  # make e's contents inalterable again
```

Tkinter

Label

Class Label implements a widget that just displays text or an image without inter-acting with user input. Instantiate Label either with option text=*somestring* to let the widget display text, or image=*imageobject* to let the widget display an image.

An instance L of class Label does not let the user copy text from L to the clip-board. L is therefore not the right widget to use when you show text that the user may want to copy, say in order to paste it into an email or some other document. Instead, use an instance e of class Entry, with option state=DISABLED to avoid alteration of e's contents, as discussed in the previous section.

Listbox

Class Listbox displays textual items and lets the user select one or more items. To set the text items for an instance L of class Listbox, in most GUI programs you can get by with just two Listbox-specific idioms:

```
L.delete(0, END)          # clear the listbox's items
L.insert(END, somestring) # add somestring to the listbox's items
```

To get the text item at index *idx*, call L.get(*idx*). To get a list of all text items between indices *idx1* and *idx2*, call L.get(*idx1,idx2*). To get the list of all text items, call L.get(0,END).

Option selectmode defines the selection mode of a Listbox instance L. The selec-tion mode indicates how many items the user can select at once: only one in modes SINGLE and BROWSE, more than one in modes MULTIPLE and EXTENDED. Secondarily, selectmode also defines the details of what user actions cause items to be selected or unselected. BROWSE mode is the default; it differs from SINGLE mode in that the user may change the one selected item by moving up and down while holding down the left mouse button. In MULTIPLE mode, each click on a list item selects or deselects the item without affecting the selection state of other items. In EXTENDED mode, a normal click on a list item selects that item and deselects all other items; however, clicking while holding down a Ctrl key selects an item without deselecting others, and clicking while holding down a Shift key selects a contiguous range of items.

An instance L of class Listbox supplies three selection-related methods.

---

curselection   L.curselection( )

Returns a sequence of zero or more indices, from 0 upwards, of selected items. Depending on the underlying release of Tk, curselection may return string representations of the integer indices, rather than the integers themselves. To remove this uncer-tainty, you can use:

indices = [int(*x*) for *x* in L.curselection( )]

However, [L.get(*x*) for *x* in L.curselection( )] is always the list of the zero or more text items that are selected, no matter what form of indices curselection returns. Therefore, if you're interested in selected text items rather than selected indices, the uncertainty may not be an issue.

select_clear   *L*.select_clear(*i*,*j*=None)

Deselects the *i* item (all items from the *i* to the *j*, if *j* is not None).

select_set   *L*.select_set(*i*,*j*=None)

Selects the *i* item (all items from the *i* to the *j*, if *j* is not None). select_set does not automatically deselect other items, even if *L*'s selection mode is SINGLE or BROWSE.

Radiobutton

Class Radiobutton implements a little box that is optionally checked. The user clicks the radiobutton to toggle it on or off. Radiobuttons come in groups: checking a radiobutton automatically unchecks all other radiobuttons of the same group. Instantiate Radiobutton with option text=*somestring* to label the button with text, or image=*imageobject* to label the button with an image. Optionally, use option command=*callable* to have *callable* execute without arguments when the user clicks the radiobutton. *callable* can be a function, a bound method of an object, an instance of a class with a __call__ method, or a lambda.

An instance *r* of Radiobutton must be associated with a Tkinter variable object *v*, using configuration option variable=*v* of *r*, and with a designated value *X*, using option value=*X* of *r*. Most often, *v* is an instance of IntVar. The value of *v* changes to *X* when *r* is checked, either by the user clicking on *r* or by your code calling *r*.select( ). Vice versa, when the value of *v* changes, *r* is checked if, and only if, *v*.get( )==*X*. Several instances of Radiobutton form a group if they have the same variable and different values; selecting an instance changes the variable's value, and therefore automatically unchecks whichever other instance was previously checked.

Note that Radiobutton instances form a group if, and only if, they share the same value for the variable option. There is no special container to use to make Radiobutton instances into a group, nor is it even necessary for the Radiobutton instances to be children of the same widget. However, it would be confusing to the user if you dispersed a group of Radiobutton instances among several disparate locations.

Besides methods common to all widgets, an instance *r* of class Radiobutton supplies four radiobutton-specific methods.

deselect   *r*.deselect( )

Unchecks *r* and sets the associated variable object to an empty string, like *r*.cget('variable').set('').

flash   *c*.flash( )

Draws the user's attention to *r* by redrawing *r* a few times, alternately in normal and active states.

Tkinter

invoke	`c.invoke( )`
	Calls without arguments the callable object that is *r*'s command option, just like `r.cget('command')( )`.

select	`r.select( )`
	Checks *r* and sets the associated variable object to *r*'s value, like `r.cget('variable').set(r.cget('value'))`.

Scale

Class Scale implements a widget in which the user can input a value by sliding a cursor along a line. Scale supports configuration options to control the widget's looks and the value's range, but in most GUI programs the only option you specify is `orient=HORIZONTAL` when you want the line to be horizontal (by default, the line is vertical).

Besides methods common to all widgets, an instance *s* of class Scale supplies two scale-specific methods.

get	`s.get( )`
	Returns the current position of *s*'s cursor, normally on a scale of 0 to 100.

set	`s.set(p)`
	Sets the current position of *s*'s cursor, normally on a scale of 0 to 100.

Scrollbar

Class Scrollbar implements a widget similar to class Scale, almost always used to scroll another widget (most often a Listbox, covered earlier, or a Text or Canvas, covered later) rather than to let the user input a value.

A Scrollbar instance *s* is connected to the widget that *s* controls (e.g., a Listbox instance *L*) through one configuration option on each of *s* and *L*. Exactly for this purpose, the widgets most often associated with a scrollbar supply a method named yview and a configuration option named yscrollcommand for vertical scrolling. (For horizontal scrolling, widgets such as Text, Canvas, and Entry supply a method named xview and a configuration option named xscrollcommand.) For vertical scrolling, use *s*'s option `command=L.yview` so that user actions on *s* call *L*'s bound method yview to control *L*'s scrolling, and also use *L*'s option `yscrollcommand=s.set` so that changes to *L*'s scrolling, in turn, adjust the way *s* displays by calling s's bound method set. The following example uses a Scrollbar to control vertical scrolling of a Listbox:

```
import Tkinter
s = Tkinter.Scrollbar( )
L = Tkinter.Listbox( )
s.pack(side=Tkinter.RIGHT, fill=Tkinter.Y)
L.pack(side=Tkinter.LEFT, fill=Tkinter.Y)
s.config(command=L.yview)
L.config(yscrollcommand=s.set)
for i in range(30): L.insert(Tkinter.END, str(i)*3)
Tkinter.mainloop( )
```

Since s and L need to refer to each other, we cannot set their respective options on construction in both cases, so for uniformity we call their config methods to set the options later for both. Clearly, in this example we do need to bind names to the widgets in order to be able to call pack and config methods of the widgets, use the widgets' bound methods, and populate the Listbox. Note that L=Tkinter. Listbox( ).pack( ) does not bind L to the Listbox, but rather to the result of method pack (i.e., None). Therefore, code this in two statements instead (as shown in the previous example):

```
L = Tkinter.Listbox( )
L.pack( )
```

Container Widgets

The Tkinter module supplies widgets whose purpose is to contain other widgets. A Frame instance does nothing more than act as a container. A Toplevel instance (including Tkinter's *root window*, also known as the application's main window) is a top-level window, so your window manager interacts with it (typically by supplying suitable decoration and handling certain requests). To ensure that a widget *parent*, which must be a Frame or Toplevel instance, is the parent (also known as master) of another widget *child*, pass *parent* as the first parameter when you instantiate *child*.

Frame

Class Frame represents a rectangular area of the screen contained in other frames or top-level windows. Frame's only purpose is to contain other widgets. Option borderwidth defaults to 0, so an instance of Frame normally displays no border. You can configure the option with borderwidth=1 if you want the frame border's outline to be visible.

Toplevel

Class Toplevel represents a rectangular area of the screen that is a top-level window and therefore receives decoration from whatever window manager handles your screen. Each instance of Toplevel can interact with the window manager and can contain other widgets. Every program using Tkinter has at least one top-level window, known as the root window. You can instantiate Tkinter's root window explicitly using *root*=Tkinter.Tk( ); otherwise Tkinter instantiates its root window implicitly as and when first needed. If you want to have more than one top-level window, first instantiate the main one with *root*=Tkinter.Tk( ). Later in your program, you can instantiate other top-level windows as needed, with calls such as *another_toplevel*=Tkinter.Toplevel( ).

An instance *T* of class Toplevel supplies many methods enabling interaction with the window manager. Many are platform-specific, relevant only with some window managers for the X Windowing System (used mostly on Unix and Unix-like systems). The cross-platform methods used most often are as follows.

deiconify   *T*.deiconify( )

Makes *T* display normally, even if previously *T* was iconic or invisible.

geometry   *T*.geometry([*geometry_string*])

T.geometry( ), without arguments, returns a string encoding *T*'s size and position: *widthxheight+x_offset+y_offset*, with *width*, *height*, *x_offset*, and *y_offset* being the decimal forms of the corresponding numbers of pixels. *T*.geometry(*S*), with one argument *S* (a string of the same form), sets *T*'s size and position according to *S*.

iconify   *T*.deiconify( )

Makes *T* display as an icon (in Windows, as a button in the taskbar).

maxsize   *T*.maxsize([*width*,*height*])

T.maxsize( ), without arguments, returns a pair of integers whose two items are *T*'s maximum width and height in pixels. *T*.maxsize(*W*,*H*), with two integer arguments *W* and *H*, sets *T*'s maximum width and height in pixels to *W* and *H*, respectively.

minsize   *T*.minsize([*width*,*height*])

T.minsize( ), without arguments, returns a pair of integers whose two items are *T*'s minimum width and height in pixels. *T*.minsize(*W*,*H*), with two integer arguments *W* and *H*, sets *T*'s minimum width and height in pixels to *W* and *H*, respectively.

overrideredirect   *T*.overrideredirect([*avoid_decoration*])

T.overrideredirect( ), without arguments, returns False for a normal window, True for a window that has asked the window manager to avoid decorating it. *T*.overrideredirect(*x*), with one argument *x*, asks the window manager to avoid decorating *T* if, and only if, *x* is true. A top-level window without decoration has no title. The user cannot act via the window manager to close, move, or resize such an undecorated top-level window.

| protocol | `T.protocol(protocol_name,callable)` |

By calling protocol with a first argument of `'WM_DELETE_WINDOW'` (the only meaningful protocol on most platforms), you install *callable* as the handler for attempts by the user to close *T* through the window manager (for example by clicking on the X in the upper right corner on Windows and KDE). Python then calls *callable* without arguments when the user makes such an attempt. *callable* itself must call `T.destroy( )` in order to close *T*, otherwise *T* stays open. By default, if `T.protocol` has not been called, such attempts implicitly call `T.destroy( )` and thus unconditionally close *T*.

| resizable | `T.resizable([width,height])` |

`T.resizable( )`, without arguments, returns a pair of integers (each 0 or 1) whose two items indicate if user action via the window manager can change *T*'s width and height, respectively. `T.resizable(W,H)`, with two integer arguments *W* and *H* (each 0 or 1), sets the user's ability to change *T*'s width and height according to the truth values of *W* and *H*. With some releases of Tk, resizable, when called without arguments, returns a string such as `'1 1'` rather than a pair of integers such as `(1,1)`. To remove this uncertainty, use:

```
resizable_wh = T.resizable( )
if len(resizable_wh) != 2: resizable_wh = map(int,
resizable_wh.split( ))
resizable_w, resizable_h = resizable_wh
```

| state | `T.state( )` |

Returns `'normal'` if *T* is displaying normally, `'withdrawn'` if *T* is invisible, `'icon'` or `'iconic'` (depending on the window manager) if *T* is displaying as an icon (e.g., in Windows, only as a button in the taskbar).

| title | `T.title([title_string])` |

`T.title( )`, without arguments, returns a string that is *T*'s window title. `T.title(title_string)`, with one argument *title_string*, sets *T*'s window title to string *title_string*.

| withdraw | `T.withdraw( )` |

Makes *T* invisible.

The following example shows a root window with an Entry widget that lets the user edit the window's title and buttons to perform various root window operations.

```
import Tkinter
root = Tkinter.Tk( )
var = Tkinter.StringVar( )
entry = Tkinter.Entry(root, textvariable=var)
entry.focus_set( )
entry.pack( )
var.set(root.title( ))
def changeTitle( ): root.title(var.get( ))
Tkinter.Button(root, text="Change Title", command=changeTitle).pack( )
Tkinter.Button(root, text="Iconify", command=root.iconify).pack( )
Tkinter.Button(root, text="Close", command=root.destroy).pack( )
Tkinter.mainloop( )
```

Menus

Class Menu implements all kinds of menus: menubars of top-level windows, submenus, and pop-up menus. To use a Menu instance *m* as the menubar for a top-level window *w*, set *w*'s configuration option menu=*m*. To use *m* as a submenu of a Menu instance *x*, call *x*.add_cascade with a named argument menu=*m*. To use *m* as a pop-up menu, call method *m*.post.

Besides configuration options covered in "Common Widget Options" earlier in this chapter, a Menu instance *m* supports option postcommand=*callable*. Tkinter calls *callable* without arguments each time it is about to display *m* (whether because of a call to *m*.post or because of user actions). You can use this option to update a dynamic menu just in time when necessary.

By default, a Tkinter menu shows a tear-off entry (a dashed line before other entries), which lets the user get a copy of the menu in a separate Toplevel window. Since such tear-offs are not part of user interface standards on popular platforms, you may want to disable tear-off functionality by using configuration option tearoff=0 for the menu.

Menu-Specific Methods

Besides methods common to all widgets, an instance *m* of class Menu supplies several menu-specific methods.

add, **add_cascade,** **add_** **checkbutton,** **add_command,** **add_** **radiobutton,** **add_separator**	*m*.add(*entry_kind*, **entry_options)
	Adds after *m*'s existing entries a new entry whose kind is the string *entry_kind*, which is one of the strings 'cascade', 'checkbutton', 'command', 'radiobutton', or 'separator'. "Menu Entries" later in this chapter covers entry kinds and options.
	Methods whose names start with add_ work just like method add, but they accept no positional argument; what kind of entry each method adds is implied by the method's name.

delete	*m*.delete(*i*[,*j*])
	m.delete(*i*) removes *m*'s *i* entry. *m*.delete(*i*,*j*) removes *m*'s entries from the *i* one to the *j* one, included. The first entry has index 0.

entryconfigure,	*m*.entryconfigure(*i*, **entry_options*)
entryconfig	Changes entry options for *m*'s *i* entry. entryconfig is an exact synonym.

insert,	*m*.insert(*i*,*entry_kind*, **entry_options*)
insert_cascade,	Adds before *m*'s entry *i* a new entry whose kind is the string *entry_*
insert_	*kind*, which is one of the strings 'cascade', 'checkbutton',
checkbutton,	'command', 'radiobutton', or 'separator'. "Menu Entries" later in
insert_	this chapter covers entry kinds and options.
command,	Methods whose names start with insert_ work just like method
insert_	insert, except that they don't accept a second positional argu-
radiobutton,	ment; what kind of entry each method inserts is implied by the
insert_separator	method's name.

invoke	*m*.invoke(*i*)
	Invokes *m*'s *i* entry, just as if the user clicked on it.

post	*m*.post(*x*,*y*)
	Displays *m* as a pop-up menu, with *m*'s upper left corner at coordinates *x*,*y* (offsets in pixels from upper left corner of Tkinter's root window).

unpost	*m*.unpost( )
	Closes *m* if *m* was displaying as a pop-up menu, otherwise does nothing.

Menu Entries

When a menu *m* displays, it shows a vertical (horizontal for a menubar) list of entries. Each entry can be one of the following kinds:

cascade
  A submenu; option menu=*x* must give as *x* another Menu instance

checkbutton
  Similar to a Checkbutton widget; typical options are variable (which must indicate a Tkinter variable object), onvalue, offvalue, and optionally command, quite similarly to a Checkbutton instance

command
Similar to a Button widget; typical option is command=*callable*

radiobutton
Similar to a Radiobutton widget; typical options are variable (which must indicate a Tkinter variable object), value, and optionally command, quite similarly to a Radiobutton instance

separator
A line segment that separates groups of other entries

Other entry options often used with menu entries are:

image
Option image=*x* uses *x*, a Tkinter image object, to label the entry with an image rather than text

label
Option label=*somestring* labels the entry with a text string

underline
Option underline=*x* gives *x* as the index of the character to underline within the entry's label (0 is the first character, 1 the second one, and so on)

Menu Example

The following example shows how to add a menubar with typical File and Edit menus:

```
import Tkinter

root = Tkinter.Tk( )
bar = Tkinter.Menu( )

def show(menu, entry): print menu, entry

fil = Tkinter.Menu( )
for x in 'New', 'Open', 'Close', 'Save':
    fil.add_command(label=x,command=lambda x=x:show('File',x))
bar.add_cascade(label='File',menu=fil)

edi = Tkinter.Menu( )
for x in 'Cut', 'Copy', 'Paste', 'Clear':
    edi.add_command(label=x,command=lambda x=x:show('Edit',x))
bar.add_cascade(label='Edit',menu=edi)
```

In this example, each menu command just outputs information to standard output for demonstration purposes. Note the *x=x* idiom to snapshot the value of *x* at the time we create each lambda. Otherwise, the current value of *x* at the time a lambda executes, 'Clear', would show up at each menu selection. A good alternative to the lambda expressions would be a closure. Instead of def show, use:

```
def mkshow(menu):
    def emit(entry, menu=menu): print menu, entry
    return emit
```

and use command=mkshow('File') and command=mkshow('Edit'), respectively, in the calls to the add_command methods of *fil* and *edi*.

The Text Widget

Class Text implements a powerful multiline text editor, able to display images and embedded widgets as well as text in one or more fonts and colors. An instance *t* of Text supports many ways to refer to specific points in *t*'s contents. *t* supplies methods and configuration options allowing fine-grained control of operations, content, and rendering. This section covers a large, frequently used subset of this vast functionality. In some very simple cases, you can get by with just three Text-specific idioms:

```
t.delete('1.0', END)           # clear the widget's contents
t.insert(END, astring)         # append astring to the widget's contents
somestring = t.get('1.0', END) # get the widget's contents as a string
```

END is an index on any Text instance *t*, indicating the end of *t*'s text. '1.0' is also an index, indicating the start of *t*'s text (first line, first column). For more about indices, see "Indices" later in this chapter.

Text Widget Methods

An instance *t* of class Text supplies many methods. Methods dealing with marks and tags are covered in later sections. Many methods accept one or two indices into *t*'s contents. The most frequently used methods are the following.

delete   *t*.delete(*i*[,*j*])

Deletes *t*.delete(*i*) removes *t*'s character at index *i*. *t*.delete(*i*,*j*) removes all characters from index *i* to index *j*, included.

get   *t*.get(*i*[,*j*])

t.get(*i*) returns *t*'s character at index *i*. *t*.get(*i*,*j*) returns a string made up of all characters from index *i* to index *j*, included.

image_create *t*.image_create(*i*,**window_options*)

Inserts an embedded image in *t*'s contents at index *i*. Call image_create with option image=*e*, where *e* is a Tkinter image object, as covered in "Tkinter Images" earlier in this chapter.

insert   *t*.insert(*i*,*s*[,*tags*])

Inserts string *s* in *t*'s contents at index *i*. *tags*, if supplied, is a sequence of strings to attach as tags to the new text, as covered in "Tags" later in this chapter.

search   *t*.search(*pattern*,*i*,**search_options)

Finds the first occurrence of string *pattern* in *t*'s contents not earlier than index *i* and returns a string that is the index of the occurrence, or an empty string ' ' if not found. Option nocase=True makes the search case-insensitive; by default, or with an explicit option nocase=False, the search is case-sensitive. Option stop=*j* makes the search stop at index *j*; by default, the search wraps around to the start of *t*'s contents. When you need to avoid wrapping, you can use stop=END.

see   *t*.see(*i*)

Scrolls *t*, if needed, to make sure the contents at index *i* are visible. If the contents at index *i* are already visible, see does nothing.

window_create   *t*.window_create(*i*,**window_options)

Inserts an embedded widget in *t*'s contents at index *i*. *t* must be the parent of the widget *w* that you are inserting. Call window_create either with option window=*w* to insert an already existing widget *w*, or with option create=*callable*. If you use option create, Tkinter calls *callable* without arguments the first time the embedded widget needs to be displayed, and *callable* must create a widget *w* (with *t* as *w*'s parent) and return *w* as *callable*'s result. Option create lets you arrange creation of embedded widgets just in time and only if needed, and is useful as an optimization when you have many embedded widgets in a very long text.

xview, yview   *t*.xview([...])
t.yview([...])

xview and yview handle scrolling in horizontal and vertical directions respectively, and accept several different patterns of arguments. *t*.xview( ), without arguments, returns a tuple of two floats between 0.0 and 1.0 indicating the fraction of *t*'s contents corresponding to the first (leftmost) and last (rightmost) currently visible columns. *t*.xview(MOVETO,*frac*) scrolls *t* left or right so that the first (leftmost) visible column becomes the one corresponding to fraction *frac* of *t*'s contents, between 0.0 and 1.0. yview supports the same patterns of arguments, but uses lines rather than columns, and scrolls up and down rather than left and right. yview supports one more pattern of arguments: *t*.yview(*i*), for any index *i*, scrolls *t* up or down so that the first (topmost) visible line becomes the one of index *i*.

Giving Text a Scrollbar

You'll often want to couple a Scrollbar instance to a Text instance in order to let the user scroll through the text. The following example shows how to use a Scrollbar *s* to control vertical scrolling of a Text instance *T*:

```
import Tkinter

root = Tkinter.Tk( )
s = Tkinter.Scrollbar(root)
T = Tkinter.Text(root)
T.focus_set( )
s.pack(side=Tkinter.RIGHT, fill=Tkinter.Y)
T.pack(side=Tkinter.LEFT, fill=Tkinter.Y)
s.config(command=T.yview)
T.config(yscrollcommand=s.set)
for i in range(40): T.insert(Tkinter.END, "This is line %d\n" % i)
Tkinter.mainloop( )
```

Marks

A *mark* on a Text instance *t* is a symbolic name indicating a point within the contents of *t*. INSERT and CURRENT are predefined marks on any Text instance *t*, with special predefined meanings. INSERT names the point where the *insertion cursor* (also known as the text caret) is located in *t*. By default, when the user enters text at the keyboard with the focus on *t*, *t* inserts the text at index INSERT. CURRENT names the point in *t* that was closest to the mouse cursor when the user last moved the mouse within *t*. By default, when the user clicks the mouse on *t*, *t* gets focus and sets INSERT to CURRENT.

To create other marks on *t*, call method *t*.mark_set. Each mark is an arbitrary string containing no whitespace. To avoid any confusion with other forms of index, use no punctuation in a mark. A mark is an index, as covered in "Indices" later in this chapter; you can pass a string that is a mark on *t* wherever a method of *t* accepts an index argument.

When you insert or delete text before a mark *m*, *m* moves accordingly. Deleting a portion of text that surrounds *m* does not remove *m*. To remove a mark on *t*, call method *t*.mark_unset. What happens when you insert text at a mark *m* depends on *m*'s gravity setting, which can be RIGHT (the default) or LEFT. When *m* has gravity RIGHT, *m* moves to remain at the end (i.e., to the right) of text inserted at *m*. When *m* has gravity LEFT, *m* does not move when you insert text at *m*: text inserted at *m* goes after *m*, and *m* itself remains at the start (i.e., to the left) of such inserted text.

A Text instance *t* supplies the following methods related to marks on *t*.

mark_gravity   *t*.mark_gravity(*mark*[,*gravity*])

> *mark* is a mark on *t*. *t*.mark_gravity(*mark*) returns *mark*'s gravity setting, RIGHT or LEFT. *t*.mark_gravity(*mark*,*gravity*) sets *mark*'s gravity to *gravity*, which must be RIGHT or LEFT.

mark_set	`t.mark_set(mark,i)`
	If *mark* was not yet a mark on *t*, mark_set creates *mark* at index *i*. If *mark* was already a mark on *t*, mark_set moves *mark* to index *i*.

mark_unset	`t.mark_unset(mark)`
	mark is a user-defined mark on *t* (not one of the predefined marks INSERT or CURRENT). mark_unset removes *mark* from among the marks on *t*.

Tags

A *tag* on a Text instance *t* is a symbolic name indicating zero or more regions (ranges) in the contents of a Text instance *t*. SEL is a predefined tag on any Text instance *t*, and names a single range of *t* that is selected, normally by the user dragging over it with the mouse. Tkinter typically displays the SEL range with distinctive background and foreground colors. To create other tags on *t*, call the `t.tag_add` or `t.tag_config` method, or use optional parameter *tags* of method `t.insert`. Ranges of various tags on *t* may overlap. *t* renders text having several tags by using options from the uppermost tag, according to calls to methods `t.tag_raise` or `t.tag_lower`. By default, a tag created more recently is above one created earlier.

Each tag is an arbitrary string containing no whitespace. Each tag has two indices, first (start of the tag's first range) and last (end of the tag's last range). You can pass a tag's index wherever a method of *t* accepts an index argument. SEL_FIRST and SEL_LAST indicate the first and last indices of predefined tag SEL.

A Text instance *t* supplies the following methods related to tags on *t*.

tag_add	`t.tag_add(tag,i[,j])`
	`t.tag_add(tag,i)` adds tag *tag* to the single character at index *i* in *t*. `t.tag_add(tag,i,j)` adds tag *tag* to characters from index *i* to index *j*.

tag_bind	`t.tag_bind(tag,event_name,callable[,'+'])`
	`t.tag_bind(tag,event_name,callable)` sets *callable* as the callback object for *event_name* on *tag*'s ranges. `t.tag_bind(tag,event_name,callable,'+')` adds *callable* to the previous bindings. Events, callbacks, and bindings are covered in "Tkinter Events" later in this chapter.

tag_cget	`t.tag_cget(tag,tag_option)`
	Returns the value currently associated with option *tag_option* for tag *tag*. For example, `t.tag_cget(SEL,'background')` returns the color that *t* is using as the background of *t*'s selected range.

tag_config   `t.tag_config(tag,**tag_options)`

Sets or changes tag options associated with tag *tag*, determining the way *t* renders text in *tag*'s region. The most frequently used tag options are:

`background, foreground`
Background and foreground colors

`bgstipple, fgstipple`
Background and foreground stipples, typically `'gray12'`, `'gray25'`, `'gray50'`, or `'gray75'`; by default, solid colors (no stippling)

`borderwidth`
Width in pixels of the text border; default is 0 (no border)

`font`
Font used for text in the tag's ranges (see "Fonts" later in this chapter)

`justify`
Text justification, `LEFT` (default), `CENTER`, or `RIGHT`

`lmargin1, lmargin2, rmargin`
Left margin (first line, other lines) and right margin (all lines), in pixels; default is 0 (no margin)

`offset`
Offset from baseline in pixels (greater than 0 for superscript, less than 0 for subscript); default is 0 (no offset, i.e., text aligned with the baseline)

`overstrike`
If true, draw a line right over the text

`relief`
Text relief: `FLAT` (default), `SUNKEN`, `RAISED`, `GROOVE`, or `RIDGE`

`spacing1, spacing2, spacing3`
Extra spacing in pixels (before first line, between lines, after last line); default is 0 (no extra spacing)

`underline`
If true, draw a line under the text

`wrap`
Wrapping mode: `WORD` (default), `CHAR`, or `NONE`

For example:

    t.tag_config(SEL,background='black',foreground='yellow')

tells *t* to display *t*'s selected range with yellow text on a black background.

tag_delete   `t.tag_delete(tag)`

Forgets all information associated with tag *tag* on *t*.

tag_lower	`t.tag_lower(tag)`
	Gives *tag*'s options minimum priority for ranges overlapping with other tags.
tag_names	`t.tag_names([i])`
	Returns a sequence of strings whose items are all the tags that include index *i*. Called without arguments, returns a sequence of strings whose items are all the tags that currently exist on *t*.
tag_raise	`t.tag_raise(tag)`
	Gives *tag*'s options maximum priority for ranges overlapping with other tags.
tag_ranges	`t.tag_ranges(tag)`
	Returns a sequence with an even number of strings (zero if *tag* is not a tag on *t* or has no ranges), alternating start and stop indices of *tag*'s ranges.
tag_remove	`t.tag_remove(tag,i[,j])`
	`t.tag_remove(tag,i)` removes tag *tag* from the single character at index *i* in *t*. `t.tag_remove(tag,i,j)` removes tag *tag* from characters from index *i* to index *j*. Removing a tag from characters that do not have that tag is not an error; it's an innocuous no-operation.
tag_unbind	`t.tag_unbind(tag,event)`
	`t.tag_unbind(tag,event)` removes any binding for *event* on *tag*'s ranges. Events and bindings are covered in "Tkinter Events" later in this chapter.

Indices

All ways to indicate a spot in the contents of a Text instance *t* are known as *indices* on *t*. The basic form of an index is a string of the form `'%d.%d'%(L,C)`, indicating the spot in the text that is at line *L* (the first line is 1), column *C* (the first column is 0). For example, `'1.0'` is a basic-form index indicating the start of text for any *t*. `t.index(i)` returns the basic-form equivalent to an index *i* of any form.

END is an index indicating the end of text for any *t*. `'%d.end'%L`, for any line number *L*, is an index indicating the end (the `'\n'` end-of-line marker) of line *L*. For example, `'1.end'` indicates the end of the first line. To get the number of characters in line number *L* of a Text instance *t*, you can use:

```
def line_length(t, L):
    return int(t.index('%d.end'%L).split('.')[-1])
```

'@%d,%d'%(x,y) is also an index on *t*, where *x* and *y* are coordinates in pixels within *t*'s window.

Any tag on *t* is associated with two indices, strings '%s.first'%*tag* (the start of *tag*'s first range) and '%s.last'%*tag* (the end of *tag*'s last range). For example, right after *t*.tag_add('mytag',*i,j*), 'mytag.first' indicates the same spot in *t* as index *i*, and 'mytag.last' indicates the same spot in *t* as index *j*. Trying to use an index such as 'x.first' or 'x.last' when no characters in *t* are tagged with 'x' raises an exception.

SEL_FIRST and SEL_LAST are indices (the start and end of the selection, the SEL tag). Trying to use SEL_FIRST or SEL_LAST when there is no selected range on *t*, however, raises an exception.

Marks (covered earlier), including predefined marks INSERT and CURRENT, are also indices. Moreover, any image or widget embedded in *t* is also an index on *t* (methods image_create and window_create are also covered earlier in this chapter).

Another form of index, *index expressions*, are obtained by concatenating to the string form of any index one or more of the following modifier string literals:

'+*n* chars', '-*n* chars'
    n characters toward the end or start of the text (including newlines)

'+*n* lines', '-*n* lines'
    n lines toward the end or start of the text

'linestart', 'lineend'
    Column 0 in the index's line or the '\n' in the index's line

'wordstart', 'wordend'
    Start or end of the word that comprises the index (in this context, a *word* is a sequence of letters, digits, and underscores)

You can optionally omit spaces and abbreviate keywords (even down to one character). For example, '%s-4c'%END means "four characters before the end of *t*'s text contents," and '%s+1line linestart'%SEL_LAST means "the start of the line immediately after the line where *t*'s selection ends."

A Text instance *t* supplies two methods related to indices on *t*.

---

compare   *t*.compare(*i*,*op*,*j*)

    Returns True or False reflecting the comparison of indices *i* and *j*, where a lower number means earlier, and *op* is one of '<', '>', '<=', '>=', '==', or '!='. For example, *t*.compare('1.0+90c','<',END) returns True if *t* contains more than 90 characters, counting each line end as a character.

---

index   *t*.index(*i*)

    Returns the basic form '*L.C*' of index *i* where *L* and *C* are decimal string forms of the line and column of *i* (lines start from 1, columns start from 0).

Fonts

You can change fonts on any Tkinter widget with option font=*font*. In most cases it makes no sense to change widgets' fonts. However, in Text instances, and for specific tags on them, changing fonts can be quite useful.

Module tkFont supplies class Font, attributes BOLD, ITALIC, and NORMAL to define font characteristics, and functions families (returns a sequence of strings naming all families of available fonts) and names (returns a sequence of strings naming all user-defined fonts). Frequently used font options are:

family
: Font family (e.g. 'courier' or 'helvetica')

size
: Font size (in points if positive, in pixels if negative)

slant
: NORMAL (default) or ITALIC

weight
: NORMAL (default) or BOLD

An instance F of Font supplies the following frequently used methods.

---

actual   F.actual([*font_option*])

F.actual( ), without arguments, returns a dictionary with all options actually used in F (best available approximations to those requested). F.actual(*font_option*) returns the value actually used in F for the option *font_option*.

---

cget   F.cget(*font_option*)

Returns the value configured (i.e., requested) in F for *font_option*.

---

config   F.config(**font_options*)

F.config( ), without arguments, returns a dictionary with all options configured (i.e., requested) in F. Called with one or more named arguments, config sets font options in F's configuration.

---

copy   F.copy( )

Returns a font G that is a copy of F. You can then modify either or both of F and G separately, and any modifications on one do not affect the other.

Text Example

To exemplify some of the many features of class Text, the following example shows one way to highlight all occurrences of a string in the text:

```
from Tkinter import *

root = Tk()

# at top of root, left to right, put a Label, an Entry, and a Button
fram = Frame(root)
Label(fram,text='Text to find:').pack(side=LEFT)
edit = Entry(fram)
edit.pack(side=LEFT, fill=BOTH, expand=1)
edit.focus_set()
butt = Button(fram, text='Find')
butt.pack(side=RIGHT)
fram.pack(side=TOP)

# fill rest of root with a Text and put some text there
text = Text(root)
text.insert('1.0',
'''Nel mezzo del cammin di nostra vita
mi ritrovai per una selva oscura
che la diritta via era smarrita
''')
text.pack(side=BOTTOM)

# action-function for the Button: highlight all occurrences of string
def find():
    # remove previous uses of tag `found', if any
    text.tag_remove('found', '1.0', END)
    # get string to look for (if empty, no searching)
    s = edit.get()
    if s:
        # start from the beginning (and when we come to the end, stop)
        idx = '1.0'
        while 1:
            # find next occurrence, exit loop if no more
            idx = text.search(s, idx, nocase=1, stopindex=END)
            if not idx: break
            # index right after the end of the occurrence
            lastidx = '%s+%dc' % (idx, len(s))
            # tag the whole occurrence (start included, stop excluded)
            text.tag_add('found', idx, lastidx)
            # prepare to search for next occurrence
            idx = lastidx
        # use a red foreground for all the tagged occurrences
        text.tag_config('found', foreground='red')
    # give focus back to the Entry field
    edit.focus_set()
```

```
# install action-function to execute when user clicks Button
butt.config(command=find)

# start the whole show (go event-driven)
root.mainloop()
```

This example also shows how to use a Frame to perform a simple widget layout task (put three widgets side by side, with the Text below them all). Figure 16-1 shows this example in action.

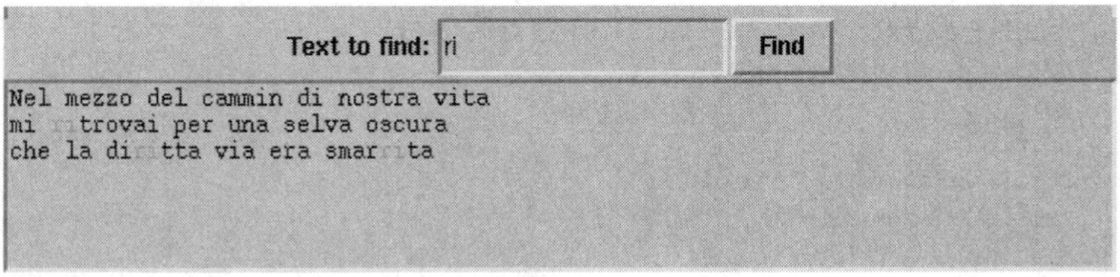

Figure 16-1. Highlighting in a Text instance

The Canvas Widget

Class Canvas is a powerful, flexible widget used for many purposes, including plotting and, in particular, building custom widgets. Building custom widgets is an advanced topic, and I do not cover it further in this book. This section covers only a subset of Canvas functionality used for the simplest kind of plotting.

Coordinates within a Canvas instance *c* are in pixels, with the origin at the upper left corner of *c* and positive coordinates growing rightward and downward. There are advanced methods that let you change *c*'s coordinate system, but I do not cover them in this book.

What you draw on a Canvas instance *c* are canvas items, which can be lines, polygons, Tkinter images, arcs, ovals, texts, and others. Each item has an *item handle* by which you can refer to the item. You can also assign symbolic names called *tags* to sets of canvas items (the sets of items with different tags can overlap). ALL is a predefined tag that applies to all items; CURRENT is a predefined tag that applies to the item under the mouse pointer.

Tags on a Canvas instance are different from tags on a Text instance. The canvas tags are nothing more than sets of items with no independent existence. When you perform any operation, passing a Canvas tag as the item identifier, the operation occurs on those items that are in the tag's current set. It makes no difference if items are later removed from or added to that tag's set.

You create a canvas item by calling on *c* a method with a name of the form create_*kindofitem*, which returns the new item's handle. Methods itemcget and itemconfig of *c* let you get and change items' options.

Canvas Methods on Items

A Canvas instance *c* supplies methods that you can call on items. The *item* argument can be an item's handle, as returned for example by *c*.create_line, or a tag, meaning all items in that tag's set (or no items at all, if the tag's set is currently empty), unless otherwise indicated in the method's description.

bbox   *c*.bbox(*item*)

Returns an approximate bounding box for *item*, a tuple of four integers: the pixel coordinates of minimum x, minimum y, maximum x, maximum y, in this order. For example, *c*.bbox(ALL) returns the minimum and maximum x and y coordinates of all items on *c*. When *c* has no items at all, *c*.bbox(ALL) returns None.

coords   *c*.coords(*item*,**coordinates*)

Changes the coordinates for *item*. Operates on just one item. If *item* is a tag, coords operates on an arbitrary one of the items currently in the tag's set. If *item* is a tag with an empty set, coords is an innocuous no-operation.

delete   *c*.delete(*item*)

Deletes *item*. For example, *c*.delete(ALL) deletes all items on *c*.

gettags   *c*.gettags(*item*)

Returns the sequence of all tags whose sets include *item* (but not tag ALL, which includes all items, nor CURRENT, whether or not it includes *item*).

itemcget   *c*.itemcget(*item*,*option*)

Returns the value of *option* for *item*. Operates on just one item. If *item* is a tag, itemcget returns the value of *option* for an arbitrary one of the items currently in the tag's set. If *item* is a tag with an empty set, itemcget returns the empty string ' '.

itemconfig   *c*.itemconfig(*item*,***options*)

Sets or changes the value of *options* for *item*. For example, *c*.itemconfig(ALL, fill='red') sets all items on *c* to color red.

tag_bind   *c*.tag_bind(*tag*,*event_name*,*callable*[,'+'])

c.tag_bind(*tag*,*event_name*,*callable*) sets *callable* as the callback object for *event_name* on the items currently in *tag*'s set. Calling *c*.tag_bind(*tag*,*event_name*,*callable*,'+') adds *callable* to the previous bindings. Events, callbacks, and bindings are covered in "Tkinter Events" later in this chapter.

tag_unbind   `c.tag_unbind(`*tag*`,`*event*`)`

                        `c.tag_unbind(`*tag*`,`*event*`)` removes any binding for *event* on the items currently in *tag*'s set. Events and bindings are covered in "Tkinter Events" later in this chapter.

The Line Canvas Item

A Canvas instance *c* supplies one method to create a `line` item.

create_line   `c.create_line(*`*coordinates*`, **`*line_options*`)`

                  Creates a line item with vertices at the given *coordinates* and returns the item's handle. *coordinates* must be an even number of positional parameters, alternately x and y values for each vertex of the line. Canvas coordinates, by default, are in pixels, with the origin (coordinates 0,0) in the upper left corner, the x coordinate growing rightward, and the y coordinate growing downward. You may set different coordinate systems on *c*, but I do not cover these possibilities in this book. *line_options* may include:

                  `arrow`
                        Sets which ends of the line have arrow heads; may be `NONE` (default), `FIRST`, `LAST`, or `BOTH`

                  `fill`
                        The line's color (default is black)

                  `smooth`
                        If true, the line is drawn as a smooth curve (a B-spline); otherwise (default), the line is drawn as a polygonal (a sequence of line segments)

                  `tags`
                        A string (to assign a single tag to this item) or a tuple of strings (to assign multiple tags to this item)

                  `width`
                        Width of the line in pixels (default 1)

                  For example:

```
x=c.create_line(0,150, 50,100, 0,50, 50,0 smooth=1)
```

                  draws a somewhat S-like curve on *c*, and binds the curve's handle to variable *x*. You can then change the curve's color to blue with:

```
c.itemconfig(x,fill='blue')
```

The Polygon Canvas Item

A Canvas instance *c* supplies one method to create a polygon item.

create_polygon   `c.create_polygon(*coordinates, **poly_options)`

Creates a polygon item with vertices at the given *coordinates* and returns the item's handle. *coordinates* must be an even number of positional parameters, alternately x and y values for each vertex of the polygon, and there must be at least six positional parameters (three vertices). *poly_options* may include:

fill
> The polygon's interior color (default is black)

outline
> The polygon's perimeter color (default is black)

smooth
> If true, the polygon is drawn as a smooth curve (a B-spline); otherwise (default), the line is drawn as a normal polygon (a sequence of sides)

tags
> A string (to assign a single tag to this item) or a tuple of strings (to assign multiple tags to this item)

width
> Width of the perimeter line in pixels (default 1)

For example:

```
x=c.create_polygon(0,150, 50,100, 0,50, 50,0 fill='',
                    outline='red')
```

draws two empty red triangles on *c* as a single polygon, and binds the polygon's handle to variable *x*. You can then fill the triangles with blue using:

```
c.itemconfig(x,fill='blue')
```

The Rectangle Canvas Item

A Canvas instance *c* supplies one method to create a rectangle item.

create_ rectangle   `c.create_rectangle(x0,y0,x1,y1,**rect_options)`

Creates a rectangle item with vertices at the given coordinates and returns the item's handle. *rect_options* may include:

fill
> The rectangle's interior color (default is empty)

outline
> The rectangle's perimeter color (default is black)

tags
> A string (to assign a single tag to this item) or a tuple of strings (to assign multiple tags to this item)

width
> Width of the perimeter line in pixels (default 1)

The Text Canvas Item

A Canvas instance *c* supplies one method to create a text item.

create_text   `c.create_text(x,y,**text_options)`

Creates a text item at the given *x* and *y* coordinates and returns the item's handle. *text_options* may include:

anchor
> The exact spot of the text's bounding box that *x* and *y* refer to: may be N, E, S, W, NE, NW, SE, or SW, compass directions indicating the corners and sides of the bounding box, or CENTER (the default)

fill
> The text's color (default is black)

font
> Font to use for this text

tags
> A string (to assign a single tag to this item) or a tuple of strings (to assign multiple tags to this item)

text
> The text to display

A Simple Plotting Example

The following example shows how to use a Canvas to perform an elementary plotting task, graphing a user-specified function:

```
from Tkinter import *
import math

root = Tk()

# first, a row for function entry and action button
fram = Frame(root)
Label(fram,text='f(x):').pack(side=LEFT)
func = Entry(fram)
func.pack(side=LEFT, fill=BOTH, expand=1)
```

```
butt = Button(fram, text='Plot')
butt.pack(side=RIGHT)
fram.pack(side=TOP)

# then a row to enter bounds in
fram = Frame(root)
bounds = [ ]
for label in 'minX', 'maxX', 'minY', 'maxY':
    Label(fram,text=label+':').pack(side=LEFT)
    edit = Entry(fram, width=6)
    edit.pack(side=LEFT)
    bounds.append(edit)
fram.pack(side=TOP)

# and finally the canvas
c = Canvas(root)
c.pack(side=TOP, fill=BOTH, expand=1)

def minimax(values=[0.0, 1.0, 0.0, 1.0]):
    "Adjust and display X and Y bounds"
    for i in range(4):
        edit = bounds[i]
        try: values[i] = float(edit.get())
        except: pass
        edit.delete(0, END)
        edit.insert(END, '%.2f'%values[i])
    return values

def plot():
    "Plot given function with given bounds"
    minx, maxx, miny, maxy = minimax()

    # get and compile the function
    f = func.get()
    f = compile(f, f, 'eval')

    # get Canvas X and Y dimensions
    CX = c.winfo_width()
    CY = c.winfo_height()

    # compute coordinates for line
    coords = [ ]
    for i in range(0,CX,5):
        coords.append(i)
        x = minx + ((maxx-minx)*i)/CX
        y = eval(f, vars(math), {'x':x})
        j = CY*(y-miny)/(maxy-miny)
        coords.append(j)

    # draw line
    c.delete(ALL)
    c.create_line(*coords)
```

```
butt.config(command=plot)

# give an initial sample in lieu of docs
f = 'sin(x) + cos(x)'
func.insert(END, f)
minimax([0.0, 10.0, -2.0, 2.0])

root.mainloop()
```

Figure 16-2 shows the output resulting from this example.

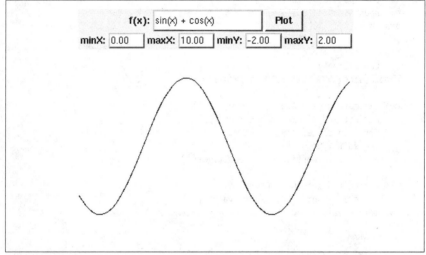

Figure 16-2. A sample Canvas

Geometry Management

In all the examples so far, we have made each widget visible by calling method pack on the widget. This is representative of real-life Tkinter usage. However, two other layout managers exist and are sometimes useful. This section covers all three layout managers provided by the Tkinter module.

Never mix geometry managers for the same container widget: all children of each given container widget must be handled by the same geometry manager, or very strange effects (including Tkinter going into infinite loops) may result.

The Packer

Calling method pack on a widget delegates widget geometry management to a simple and flexible layout manager component called the Packer. The Packer sizes and positions each widget within a container (parent) widget, according to each widget's space needs (including options padx and pady). Each widget w supplies the following Packer-related methods.

pack   w.pack(**pack_options)

Delegates geometry management to the packer. *pack_options* may include:

expand
>   When true, *w* expands to fill any space not otherwise used in *w*'s parent.

fill
>   Determines whether *w* fills any extra space allocated to it by the packer, or keeps its own minimal dimensions: NONE (default), X (fill only horizontally), Y (fill only vertically), or BOTH (fill both horizontally and vertically).

side
>   Determines which side of the parent *w* packs against: TOP (default), BOTTOM, LEFT, or RIGHT. To avoid confusion, don't mix different values for option side= in widgets that are children of the same container. When more than one child requests the same side (for example TOP), the rule is first come, first served: the first child packs at the top, the second child packs second from the top, and so on.

---

pack_forget   w.pack_forget( )

The packer forgets about *w*. *w* remains alive but invisible, and you may show *w* again later (by calling *w*.pack again, or perhaps *w*.grid or *w*.place).

---

pack_info   w.pack_info( )

Returns a dictionary with the current *pack_options* of *w*.

The Gridder

Calling method grid on a widget delegates widget geometry management to a specialized layout manager component called the Gridder. The Gridder sizes and positions each widget into cells of a table (grid) within a container (parent) widget. Each widget *w* supplies the following Gridder-related methods.

---

grid   w.grid(**grid_options)

Delegates geometry management to the gridder. *grid_options* may include:

column
>   The column to put *w* in; default 0 (leftmost column).

columnspan
>   How many columns *w* occupies; default 1.

ipadx, ipady
> How many pixels to pad *w*, horizontally and vertically, inside *w*'s borders.

padx, pady
> How many pixels to pad *w*, horizontally and vertically, outside *w*'s borders.

row
> The row to put *w* in; default the first row that is still empty.

rowspan
> How many rows *w* occupies; default 1.

sticky
> What to do if the cell is larger than *w*. By default, with sticky='', *w* is centered in its cell. sticky may be the string concatenation of zero or more of N, E, S, W, NE, NW, SE, and SW, compass directions indicating the sides and corners of the cell to which *w* sticks. For example, sticky=N means that *w* sticks to the cell's top and is centered horizontally, while sticky=N+S means that *w* expands vertically to fill the cell and is centered horizontally.

For example:

```
import Tkinter
root = Tkinter.Tk( )
for r in range(3):
    for c in range(4):
        Tkinter.Label(root, text='R%s/C%s'%(r,c),
            borderwidth=1 ).grid(row=r,column=c)
root.mainloop( )
```

displays 12 labels arrayed in a 3 × 4 grid.

---

grid_forget   w.grid_forget( )

The gridder forgets about *w*. *w* remains alive but invisible, and you may show *w* again later (by calling w.grid again, or perhaps w.pack or w.place).

---

grid_info   w.grid_info( )

Returns a dictionary with the current *grid_options* of *w*.

The Placer

Calling method place on a widget explicitly handles widget geometry management, thanks to a simple layout manager component called the Placer. The Placer sizes and positions each widget *w* within a container (parent) widget exactly as *w* explicitly requires. Other layout managers are usually preferable, but

---

the `Placer` can help you implement custom layout managers. Each widget *w* supplies the following `Placer`-related methods.

---

place   `w.place(**place_options)`

Delegates geometry management to the placer. *place_options* may include:

anchor
> The exact spot of *w* other options refer to: may be N, E, S, W, NE, NW, SE, or SW, compass directions indicating the corners and sides of *w*; default is NW (the upper left corner of *w*)

bordermode
> INSIDE (the default) to indicate that other options refer to the parent's inside (ignoring the parent's border); OUTSIDE otherwise

height, width
> Height and width in pixels

relheight, relwidth
> Height and width as a float between 0.0 and 1.0, as a fraction of the height and width of the parent widget

relx, rely
> Horizontal and vertical offset as a float between 0.0 and 1.0, as a fraction of the height and width of the parent widget

x, y
> Horizontal and vertical offset in pixels

---

place_forget   `w.place_forget( )`

The placer forgets about *w*. *w* remains alive but invisible, and you may show *w* again later (by calling `w.place` again, or perhaps `w.pack` or `w.grid`).

---

place_info   `w.place_info( )`

Returns a dictionary with the current *place_options* of *w*.

Tkinter Events

So far, we've seen only the most elementary kind of event handling: the callbacks performed on callables installed with the `command=` option of buttons and menu entries of various kinds. `Tkinter` also lets you install callables to call back when needed to handle a variety of events. However, `Tkinter` does not let you create your own custom events; you are limited to working with events predefined by `Tkinter` itself.

The Event Object

General event callbacks must accept one argument *event* that is a Tkinter event object. Such an event object has several attributes describing the event:

char
> A single-character string that is the key's code (only for keyboard events)

keysym
> A string that is the key's symbolic name (only for keyboard events)

num
> Button number (only for mouse-button events); 1 and up

x, y
> Mouse position, in pixels, relative to the upper left corner of the widget

x_root, y_root
> Mouse position, in pixels, relative to the upper left corner of the screen

widget
> The widget in which the event has occurred

Binding Callbacks to Events

To bind a callback to an event in a widget w, call w.bind, describing the event with a string, usually enclosed in angle brackets ('<...>'). The following example prints 'Hello World' each time the user presses the Enter key:

```
from Tkinter import *

root = Tk( )
def greet(*ignore): print 'Hello World'
root.bind('<Return>', greet)
root.mainloop( )
```

Method tag_bind of classes Canvas and Text, covered earlier in this chapter, lets you bind event callbacks to specific sets of items of a Canvas instance, or to ranges within a Text instance.

Event Names

Frequently used event names, which are almost all enclosed in angle brackets, fall into a few categories.

Keyboard events

Key
> The user clicked any key. The event object's attribute char tells you which key, but for normal keys only, not for special keys. The event object's attribute keysym is equal to attribute char for letters and digits, is the character's name for punctuation characters, and is the key name for special keys, as covered in the next paragraph.

Special keys

Special keys are associated with event names: F1, F2, ..., up to F12 for function keys; Left, Right, Up, Down for arrow keys; Prior, Next for page-up, page-down; BackSpace, Delete, End, Home, Insert, Print, Tab, for keys so labeled; Escape for the key often labeled Esc; Return for the key often labeled Enter; Caps_Lock, Num_Lock, Scroll_Lock for locking-request keys; Alt_L, Control_L, Shift_L for the modifier keys Alt, Ctrl, Shift (without distinction among the multiple instances of such modifier keys in a typical keyboard). All of these event names are placed within angle brackets, like almost all event names.

Normal keys

Normal keys are associated with event names without surrounding angle brackets—the only event names to lack such brackets. The event name of each normal key is just the associated character, such as 'w', '1', or '+'. Two exceptions are the Space key, whose event name is '<space>', and the key associated with the less-than character, whose event name is '<less>'.

All key event names can be modified by prefixing 'Alt-', 'Shift-', or 'Control-'. In this case, the whole event name does always have to be surrounded with '<...>'. For example, '<Control-Q>' and '<Alt-Up>' name events corresponding to normal or special keys with modifiers.

Mouse events

Button-1, Button-2, Button-3

The user pressed the left, middle, or right mouse-button. A two-button mouse produces only events Button-1 and Button-3, since it has no middle button.

B1-Motion, B2-Motion, B3-Motion

The user moved the mouse while pressing the left, middle, or right mouse button (there is no mouse event for mouse motion without pressing a button, except for Enter and Leave).

ButtonRelease-1, ButtonRelease-2, ButtonRelease-3

The user released the left, middle, or right mouse button.

Double-Button-1, Double-Button-2, Double-Button-3

The user double-clicked the left, middle, or right mouse button (such an action also generates Button-1, Button-2, or Button-3 before the double-click event).

Enter

The user moved the mouse so that the mouse entered the widget.

Leave

The user moved the mouse so that the mouse exited the widget.

Event-Related Methods

Each widget *w* supplies the following event-related methods.

bind	w.bind(*event_name,callable*[,'+'])
	w.bind(*event_name,callable*) sets *callable* as the callback for *event_name* on w. w.bind(*event_name,callable*,'+') adds *callable* to the previous bindings for *event_name* on w.
bind_all	w.bind_all(*event_name,callable*[,'+'])
	w.bind_all(*event_name,callable*) sets *callable* as the callback for *event_name* on any widget of the application, whatever widget w you call the method on. w.bind_all(*event_name,callable*,'+') adds *callable* to the previous bindings for *event_name* on any widget.
unbind	w.unbind(*event_name*)
	Removes all callbacks for *event_name* on w.
unbind_all	w.unbind_all(*event_name*)
	Removes all callbacks for *event_name* on any widget, previously set by calling method bind_all on any widget.

An Events Example

The following example shows how to detect key presses and mouse-button presses and releases using the bind_all method:

```
import Tkinter
from Tkinter import *

root = Tk( )
prompt='Click any button, or press a key'
L = Label(root, text=prompt, width=len(prompt))
L.pack( )

def key(event):
    if event.char==event.keysym:
        msg ='Normal Key %r' % event.char
    elif len(event.char)==1:
        msg ='Punctuation Key %r (%r)' % (event.keysym, event.char)
    else:
        msg ='Special Key %r' % event.keysym
    L.config(text=msg)
L.bind_all('<Key>', key)

def do_mouse(eventname):
    def mouse_binding(event):
        msg = 'Mouse event %s' % eventname
        L.config(text=msg)
    L.bind_all('<%s>'%eventname, mouse_binding)
```

```
for i in range(1,4):
    do_mouse('Button-%s'%i)
    do_mouse('ButtonRelease-%s'%i)
    do_mouse('Double-Button-%s'%i)

root.mainloop()
```

Other Callback-Related Methods

Each widget *w* supplies the following other callback-related methods.

---

after   `w.after(ms,callable,*args)`

Starts a timer that calls *callable(*args)* about *ms* milliseconds from now. Returns an ID that you can pass to after_cancel to cancel the timer. The timer is one-shot: for a function to be called periodically, the function itself must call after to install itself as a callback again.

---

after_cancel `w.after_cancel(id)`

Cancels the timer identified by *id*.

---

after_idle   `w.after_idle(callable,*args)`

Registers a callback to *callable(*args)* to be performed when the event loop is idle (i.e., when all pending events have been processed).

The following example shows how to use after to implement a simple digital clock:

```
import Tkinter
import time

curtime = ''
clock = Tkinter.Label()
clock.pack()

def tick():
    global curtime
    newtime = time.strftime('%H:%M:%S')
    if newtime != curtime:
        curtime = newtime
        clock.config(text=curtime)
    clock.after(200, tick)

tick()
clock.mainloop()
```

Tkinter

The kind of polling that method after lets you establish is an important Tkinter technique. Several Tkinter widgets have no callbacks to let you know about user actions on them, so if you want to track such actions in real-time, polling may be your only option. For example, here's how to use polling established with after to track a Listbox selection in real time:

```
import Tkinter

F1 = Tkinter.Frame()
s = Tkinter.Scrollbar(F1)
L = Tkinter.Listbox(F1)
s.pack(side=Tkinter.RIGHT, fill=Tkinter.Y)
L.pack(side=Tkinter.LEFT, fill=Tkinter.Y)
s['command'] = L.yview
L['yscrollcommand'] = s.set
for i in range(30): L.insert(Tkinter.END, str(i))
F1.pack(side=Tkinter.TOP)

F2 = Tkinter.Frame()
lab = Tkinter.Label(F2)
def poll():
    lab.after(200, poll)
    sel = L.curselection()
    lab.config(text=str(sel))
lab.pack()
F2.pack(side=Tkinter.TOP)

poll()
Tkinter.mainloop()
```

17

Testing, Debugging, and Optimizing

You're not finished with a programming task when you're done writing the code: you're finished when your code is running correctly and with acceptable performance. *Testing* means verifying that your code is running correctly by exercising the code under known conditions and checking that the results are as expected. *Debugging* means discovering the causes of incorrect behavior and removing them (the removal is often easy once you have figured out the causes).

Optimizing is often used as an umbrella term for activities meant to ensure acceptable performance. Optimizing breaks down into *benchmarking* (measuring performance for given tasks and checking that it's within acceptable bounds), *profiling* (instrumenting the program to find out what parts are performance bottlenecks), and optimizing proper (removing bottlenecks to make overall program performance acceptable). Clearly, you can't remove performance bottlenecks until you've found out where they are (using profiling), which in turn requires knowing that there *are* performance problems (using benchmarking).

All of these tasks are large and important, and each could fill a book by itself. This chapter does not explore every related technique and implication; it focuses on Python-specific techniques, approaches, and tools.

Testing

In this chapter, I distinguish between two rather different kinds of testing: unit testing and system testing. Testing is a rich and important field, and even more distinctions could be drawn, but my goal is to focus on the issues of most immediate importance to software developers.

Unit Testing and System Testing

Unit testing means writing and running tests to exercise a single module or an even smaller unit, such as a class or function. *System testing* (also known as functional testing) involves running an entire program with known inputs. Some classic books on testing draw the distinction between *white-box testing*, done with knowledge of a program's internals, and *black-box testing*, done from the outside. This classic viewpoint parallels the modern one of unit versus system testing.

Unit and system testing serve different goals. Unit testing proceeds apace with development; you can and should test each unit as you're developing it. Indeed, one modern approach is known as *test-first coding*: for each feature that your program must have, you first write unit tests, and only then do you proceed to write code that implements the feature. Test-first coding seems a strange approach, but it has several advantages. For example, it ensures that you won't omit unit tests for some feature. Further, test-first coding is helpful because it urges you to focus first on what tasks a certain function, class, or method should accomplish, and to deal only afterwards with implementing that function, class, or method. In order to test a unit, which may depend on other units not yet fully developed, you often have to write *stubs*, which are fake implementations of various units' interfaces that give known and correct responses in cases needed to test other units.

System testing comes afterwards, since it requires the system to exist with some subset of system functionality believed to be in working condition. System testing provides a sanity check: given that each module in the program works properly (passes unit tests), does the whole program work? If each unit is okay but the system as a whole is not, there is a problem with integration between units. For this reason, system testing is also known as integration testing.

System testing is similar to running the system in production use except that you fix the inputs in advance, so any problems you find are easy to reproduce. The cost of failure in system testing is lower than in production use, since outputs from system testing are not used to make decisions, control external systems, and so on. Rather, outputs from system testing are systematically compared with the outputs that the system should produce given the known inputs. The purpose of the whole procedure is to find discrepancies between what the program should do and what the program actually does in a cheap and reproducible way.

Failures discovered by system testing, just like system failures in production use, reveal defects in unit tests as well as defects in the code. Unit testing may have been insufficient; a module's unit tests may have failed to exercise all needed functionality of that module. In this case, the unit tests clearly need to be beefed up.

More often, failures in system testing reveal communication problems within the development team: a module may correctly implement a certain interface functionality, but another module expects different functionality. This kind of problem (an integration problem in the strict sense) is harder to pinpoint in unit testing. In good development practice, unit tests must run often, so it is crucial that they run fast. It's therefore essential that each unit can assume other units are working correctly and as expected.

Unit tests that are run in reasonably late stages of development can reveal integration problems if the system architecture is hierarchical, a common and reasonable organization. In such an architecture, lower-level modules depend on no others (except perhaps library modules, which you can assume to be correct), and thus their unit tests, if complete, suffice to assure correctness. Higher-level modules depend on lower-level ones, and therefore also depend on correct team communication about what interfaces each module expects and supplies. Running complete unit tests on higher-level modules, using the true lower-level modules rather than stubs, automatically exercises the interface between modules, as well as the higher-level modules' own code.

Unit tests for higher-level modules are thus run in two ways. You run the tests with stubs for the lower levels during the early stages of development when the lower-level modules are not yet ready, or, later, when you need to check correctness of the higher levels only. During later stages of development, you also regularly run the higher-level modules' unit tests using the true lower-level modules. In this way, you check the correctness of the whole subsystem, from the higher levels downwards.

System testing is similar to running the program in normal ways. You need special support only to ensure that known inputs are supplied and that outputs are captured for comparison with expected outputs. This is easy for programs whose I/O uses files, but terribly hard for programs whose I/O relies on a GUI, network, or other communication with independent external entities. To simulate such external entities and make them predictable and entirely observable, platform-dependent infrastructure is generally necessary.

Another useful piece of supporting infrastructure for system testing is a *testing framework* that automates the running of system tests, including logging of successes and failures. Such a framework can also help testers prepare sets of known inputs and corresponding expected outputs.

Both free and commercial programs for these purposes exist, but they are not dependent on what programming languages are used in the system under test. As mentioned, system testing is akin to what was classically known as black-box testing—testing independent of the implementation of the system under test, and therefore, in particular, of the programming languages used for implementation. Instead, testing frameworks usually depend on the operating system platform on which they run, since the tasks they perform are platform-dependent: running programs with given inputs, capturing their outputs, and particularly simulating and capturing GUI, network, and other interprocess communication I/O. Since frameworks for system testing depend on the platform and not on programming languages, I do not cover them further in this book.

The doctest Module

The doctest module has the primary purpose of letting you create good usage examples in your code's docstrings, by checking that the examples do in fact produce the results that your docstrings show for them.

As you're developing a module, keep the docstrings up to date, and gradually enrich them with examples. Each time part of the module (e.g., a function) is ready, or even partially ready, make it a habit to add examples to the docstrings. Import the module into an interactive session, and interactively use the parts you just developed in order to provide examples with a mix of typical cases, limit cases, and failing cases. For this specific purpose only, use from module import * so that your examples don't prefix *module.* to each name the module supplies. Copy and paste the text of the interactive session into the docstring in your favorite editor, adjust any mistakes, and you're almost done.

Your documentation is now enriched with examples, and readers will have an easier time following it, assuming you chose a good mix of examples and seasoned it wisely with non-example text. Make sure you have docstrings, with examples, for your module as a whole, and for each function, class, and method that the module exports. You may skip functions, classes, and methods whose names start with _, since, as their names indicate, they're meant to be private implementation details; doctest by default ignores them, and so should most readers of your module's sources.

Examples that don't match the way your code works are worse than useless. Documentation and comments are useful only if they match reality. Docstrings and comments often get out of date as code changes, and then they become misinformation, hampering rather than helping any reader of the source. Better to have no comments and docstrings at all than to have ones that lie. doctest can help, at least, with the examples in your docstrings. A failing doctest run will often prompt you to review the whole docstring that contains the failing examples, thus reminding you to keep the docstring's text updated, too.

At the end of your module's source, insert the following small snippet:

```
if __name__ == '__main__':
    import doctest, sys
    doctest.testmod(sys.modules[__name__])
```

This code calls function testmod of module doctest on your module when you run your module as the main program. testmod examines all relevant docstrings (the module docstring, and docstrings of all public functions, public classes, and public methods of public classes). In each docstring, testmod finds all examples (by looking for occurrences of the interpreter prompt '>>> ', possibly preceded by whitespace) and runs each example. testmod checks that each example's results are equal to the output given in the docstring right after the example. In the case of exceptions, testmod ignores the traceback, but checks that the expected and observed error messages are equal.

When everything goes right, testmod terminates silently. Otherwise, it outputs detailed messages about examples that failed, showing expected and actual output. Example 17-1 shows a typical example of doctest at work on a module *mod.py*.

Example 17-1. Using doctest

```
"""
This module supplies a single function reverseWords that reverses
a string by words.

>>> reverseWords('four score and seven years')
'years seven and score four'
>>> reverseWords('justoneword')
'justoneword'
>>> reverseWords('')
''
```

Example 17-1. Using doctest (continued)

You must call reverseWords with one argument, and it must be a string:

```
>>> reverseWords( )
Traceback (most recent call last):
    ...
TypeError: reverseWords( ) takes exactly 1 argument (0 given)
>>> reverseWords('one', 'another')
Traceback (most recent call last):
    ...
TypeError: reverseWords( ) takes exactly 1 argument (2 given)
>>> reverseWords(1)
Traceback (most recent call last):
    ...
AttributeError: 'int' object has no attribute 'split'
>>> reverseWords(u'however, unicode is all right too')
u'too right all is unicode however,'
```

As a side effect, reverseWords eliminates any redundant spacing:

```
>>> reverseWords('with    redundant    spacing')
'spacing redundant with'

"""
def reverseWords(astring):
    words = astring.split( )
    words.reverse( )
    return ' '.join(words)
if __name__=='__main__':
    import doctest, sys
    doctest.testmod(sys.modules[__name__])
```

I have snipped the tracebacks from the docstring, as is commonly done, since doctest ignores them and they add nothing to the explanatory value of each failing case. Apart from this, the docstring is the copy and paste of an interactive session, with the addition of some explanatory text and empty lines for readability. Save this source as *mod.py*, and then run it with python mod.py. It produces no output, meaning that all examples work just right. Also try python mod.py -v to get an account of all tests tried and a verbose summary at the end. Finally, try altering the example results in the module docstring, making them incorrect, to see the messages doctest provides for errant examples.

doctest is not meant for general-purpose unit testing, but can nevertheless be a convenient tool for the purpose. The recommended way to do unit testing in Python is with module unittest, covered in the next section. However, unit testing with doctest can be easier and faster to set up, since it requires little more than copy and paste from an interactive session. If you need to maintain a module that lacks unit tests, retrofitting such tests into the module with doctest may be a reasonable compromise. It's certainly better to have doctest-based unit tests than not to have any unit tests at all, as might otherwise happen should you decide that setting up tests properly with unittest would take you too long.

Debugging

If you do decide to use doctest for unit testing, don't cram extra tests into your module's docstrings. That would damage the docstrings by making them too long and hard to read. Keep in the docstrings the right amount and kind of examples, strictly for explanatory purposes, just as if unit testing was not in the picture. Instead, put the extra tests into a global variable of your module, a dictionary named __test__. The keys in __test__ are strings used as arbitrary test names, and the corresponding values are strings that doctest picks up and uses just as it uses docstrings. The values in __test__ may also be function and class objects, in which case doctest examines their docstrings for tests to run. This is also a convenient way to run doctest on objects with private names, which doctest skips by default.

The unittest Module

The unittest module is the Python version of a unit-testing framework originally developed by Kent Beck for Smalltalk. Similar and equally widespread versions of the same framework also exist for other programming languages (e.g., the JUnit package for Java).

To use unittest, you don't put your testing code in the same source file as the tested module, but instead write a separate test module per module being tested. A popular convention is to name the test module the same as the module being tested, with a prefix such as 'test_', and put it in a subdirectory named *test* of the directory where you keep your sources. For example, the test module for *mod.py* can be *test/test_mod.py*. You need a simple and consistent naming convention to make it easy for you to write and maintain auxiliary scripts that find and run all unit tests for a package.

Separation between a module's source code and its unit-testing code lets you refactor the module more easily, including possibly recoding its functionality in C, without perturbing the unit-testing code. Knowing that *test_mod.py* stays intact, whatever changes you make to *mod.py*, enhances your confidence that passing the tests in *test_mod.py* indicates that *mod.py* still works correctly after the changes.

A unit-testing module defines one or more subclasses of unittest's TestCase class. Each subclass may define a single *test case* by overriding method runTest. Better yet, the subclass may define one or more test cases, not by overriding runTest, but rather by defining *test-case methods*, which are methods that are callable without arguments and whose names start with test. The subclass may also override methods setUp, which the framework calls to prepare a new instance for each test case, and tearDown, which the framework calls to clean things up after each test case. Each test-case method calls methods of class TestCase whose names start with assert, in order to express the conditions that the test must meet. unittest runs the test-case methods within a TestCase subclass in arbitrary order, running setUp just before each test case and tearDown just after each test case.

unittest provides other facilities, such as grouping test cases into test suites, and other more advanced functionality. You do not need such extras unless you're defining a custom unit-testing framework or, at the very least, structuring complicated testing procedures for equally complicated packages. In almost all cases, the concepts and details covered in this section are sufficient to perform effective and systematic unit testing. Example 17-2 shows how to use unittest to provide unit tests for the module *mod.py* of Example 17-1. For illustration purposes, this example uses unittest to perform exactly the same tests that Example 17-1 encoded as examples in docstrings using doctest.

Example 17-2. Using unittest

```
""" This module tests function reverseWords provided by module mod.py. """
import unittest
import mod

class ModTest(unittest.TestCase):

    def testNormalCase(self):
        self.assertEqual(mod.reverseWords('four score and seven years'),
            'years seven and score four')

    def testSingleWord(self):
        self.assertEqual(mod.reverseWords('justoneword'), 'justoneword')

    def testEmpty(self):
        self.assertEqual(mod.reverseWords(''), '')

    def testRedundantSpacing(self):
        self.assertEqual(mod.reverseWords('with    redundant    spacing'),
            'spacing redundant with')

    def testUnicode(self):
        self.assertEqual(mod.reverseWords(u'unicode is all right too'),
            u'too right all is unicode')

    def testExactlyOneArgument(self):
        self.assertRaises(TypeError, mod.reverseWords)
        self.assertRaises(TypeError, mod.reverseWords, 'one', 'another')

    def testMustBeString(self):
        self.assertRaises((AttributeError,TypeError), mod.reverseWords, 1)

if __name__=='__main__':
    unittest.main( )
```

Running this module with python test_mod.py is by default a bit more verbose, than using python mod.py to run doctest, as in Example 17-1. *test_mod.py* outputs a single . for each test-case method it runs, then a separator line of dashes, and finally a summary line, such as "Ran 7 tests in 0.110s", and a final line of "OK" if every test was indeed okay.

Each test-case method makes one or more calls to methods whose names start with assert (or their synonyms whose names start with fail). Here, we have only one test-case method in which we make two such calls, method testExactly1Argument. In more complicated cases, such multiple calls to assert methods from a single test-case method can be quite common.

Even in a case as simple as this, one minor aspect shows that, for unit testing, unittest is more powerful and flexible than doctest. In method testMustBeString, we pass as the first argument to assertRaises a pair of exception classes, meaning we accept either kind of exception. *test_mod.py* therefore accepts as valid different implementations of *mod.py*. It accepts the implementation in Example 17-1, which tries calling method split on its argument, and therefore raises AttributeError when called with an argument that is not a string. However, it also accepts a different hypothetical implementation, one that raises TypeError instead when called with an argument of the wrong type. It would be possible to code this testing functionality with doctest, but it would be awkward and non-obvious, while unittest makes it simple and natural.

This kind of flexibility is crucial for real-life unit tests, which essentially act as executable specifications for their modules. You could, pessimistically, view the need for flexibility as indicating that the interface of the code we're testing is not well defined. However, it's best to view the interface as being defined with a useful amount of flexibility for the implementer: under circumstance *X* (argument of invalid type passed to function reverseWords, in this example), either of two things (raising AttributeError or TypeError) is allowed to happen.

Thus, implementations with either of the different behaviors can be correct, and the implementer can choose between them on the basis of such considerations as performance and clarity. By viewing unit tests as executable specifications for their modules (the modern view, and the basis of test-first coding) rather than as white-box tests strictly constrained to a specific implementation (as in some traditional taxonomies of testing), the tests become a more vital component of the software development process.

The TestCase class

With unittest, you write test cases by subclassing class TestCase and adding methods, callable without arguments, whose names start with test. Such test-case methods, in turn, call methods that your subclass inherits from TestCase, whose names start with assert (or their synonyms, whose names start with fail), to indicate conditions that must hold for the test to succeed.

Class TestCase also defines two methods that your subclass can optionally override in order to group actions to perform right before and right after each test-case method runs. This doesn't exhaust TestCase's functionality, but you won't need the rest unless you're developing testing frameworks or performing some similarly advanced task. The frequently called methods in a TestCase instance *t* are the following.

assert_,
failUnless

t.assert_(*condition*,*msg*=None)

Fails and outputs *msg* if *condition* is false, otherwise does nothing. The underscore in the name is needed because assert is a Python keyword. failUnless is a synonym.

assertEqual, **failUnlessEqual**	`t.assertEqual(first,second,msg=None)` Fails and outputs *msg* if *first*!=*second*, otherwise does nothing. failUnlessEqual is a synonym.
assertNotEqual, **failIfEqual**	`t.assertNotEqual(first,second,msg=None)` Fails and outputs *msg* if *first*==*second*, otherwise does nothing. failIfEqual is a synonym.
assertRaises, **failUnlessRaises**	`t.assertRaises(exceptionSpec,callable,*args)` Calls *callable(*args)*. Fails if the call doesn't raise any exception. If the call raises an exception not meeting *exceptionSpec*, assertRaises propagates the exception. If the call raises an exception meeting *exceptionSpec*, assertRaises does nothing. *exceptionSpec* can be an exception class or a tuple of classes, just like the first argument to the except clause of a try/except statement. failUnlessRaises is a synonym.
fail	`t.fail(msg=None)` Fails unconditionally and outputs *msg*.
failIf	`t.failIf(condition, msg=None)` Fails and outputs *msg* if *condition* is true, otherwise does nothing.
setUp	`t.setUp()` The framework calls `t.setUp()` just before calling a test-case method. The implementation in TestCase does nothing. This method is provided in order to let your subclass override it if it needs to perform some preparation for each test.
tearDown	`t.tearDown()` The framework calls `t.tearDown()` just after calling a test-case method. The implementation in TestCase does nothing. This method is provided in order to let your subclass override it if it needs to perform some cleanup after each test.

Unit tests dealing with large amounts of data

Unit tests must be fast, since they are run frequently during development. Therefore, it's best to unit-test each aspect of your modules' functionality on small amounts of data when possible. This makes each unit test faster, and also lets you conveniently embed all needed data in the test's source code. When you test a function that reads from or writes to a file object, in particular, you normally use an instance of class cStringIO (covered in Chapter 10) to simulate a file object while holding the data in memory.

However, in some rare cases, it may be impossible to fully exercise a module's functionality without supplying and/or comparing data in quantities larger than can be reasonably embedded in a test's source code. In such cases, your unit test will have to rely on auxiliary external data files to hold the data it needs to supply to the module it tests, and/or the data it needs to compare to the tested module's output. Even then, you're generally better off reading the data into instances of cStringIO rather than directing the tested module to perform actual disk I/O. Similarly, I suggest you generally use stubs to test modules meant to interact with other external entities, such as a database, a GUI, or some other program over a network. It's easier for you to control all aspects of the test when using stubs rather than real external entities. Also, to reiterate, the speed at which you can run tests is important, and it's invariably faster to perform simulated operations in stubs, rather than real operations.

Debugging

Since Python's development cycle is so fast, the most effective way to debug is often to edit your code to make it output relevant information at key points. Python has many ways to let your code explore its own state in order to extract information that may be relevant for debugging. The inspect and traceback modules specifically support such exploration, which is also known as reflection or introspection.

Once you have obtained debugging-relevant information, statement print is often the simplest way to display it. You can also log debugging information to files. Logging is particularly useful for programs that run unattended for a long time, as is typically the case for server programs. Displaying debugging information is like displaying other kinds of information, as covered in Chapters 10 and 16, and similarly for logging it, as covered in Chapters 10 and 11. Python 2.3 will also include a module specifically dedicated to logging. As covered in Chapter 8, rebinding attribute excepthook of module sys lets your program log detailed error information just before your program is terminated by a propagating exception.

Python also offers hooks enabling interactive debugging. Module pdb supplies a simple text-mode interactive debugger. Other interactive debuggers for Python are part of integrated development environments (IDEs), such as IDLE and various commercial offerings. However, I do not cover IDEs in this book.

The inspect Module

The inspect module supplies functions to extract information from all kinds of objects, including the Python call stack (which records all function calls currently executing) and source files. At the time of this writing, module inspect is not yet available for Jython. The most frequently used functions of module inspect are as follows.

getargspec,
formatargspec

getargspec(*f*)

f is a function object. getargspec returns a tuple with four items (*arg_names, extra_args, extra_kwds, arg_defaults*). *arg_names* is the sequence of names of *f*'s formal arguments. *extra_args* is the name of the special formal argument of the form **args*, or None if *f* has no such special argument. *extra_kwds* is the name of the special formal argument of the form ***kwds*, or None if *f* has no such special argument. *arg_defaults* is the tuple of default values for *f*'s arguments. You can deduce other details about *f*'s signature from getargspec's results. For example, *f* has len(*arg_names*)-len(*arg_defaults*) mandatory arguments, and the names of *f*'s optional arguments are the strings that are the items of the list slice *arg_names*[-len(*arg_defaults*):].

formatargspec accepts one to four arguments that are the same as the items of the tuple that getargspec returns, and returns a formatted string that displays this information. Thus, formatargspec(*getargspec(*f*)) returns a formatted string with *f*'s formal arguments (i.e., *f*'s *signature*) in parentheses, as used in the def statement that created *f*.

getargvalues,
formatargvalues

getargvalues(*f*)

f is a frame object, for example the result of a call to the function _getframe in module sys (covered in Chapter 8) or to function currentframe in module inspect. getargvalues returns a tuple with four items (*arg_names, extra_args, extra_kwds, locals*). *arg_names* is the sequence of names of *f*'s function's formal arguments. *extra_args* is the name of the special formal argument of form **args*, or None if *f*'s function has no such special argument. *extra_kwds* is the name of the special formal argument of form ***kwds*, or None if *f*'s function has no such special argument. *locals* is the dictionary of local variables for *f*. Since arguments, in particular, are local variables, the value of each actual argument can be obtained from *locals* by indexing the *locals* dictionary with the argument's name.

formatargvalues accepts one to four arguments that are the same as the items of the tuple that getargvalues returns, and returns a formatted string that displays this information. formatargvalues(*getargvalues(*f*)) returns a formatted string with *f*'s actual arguments in parentheses, in named (keyword) form, as used in the call statement that created *f*. For example:

```
def f(x=23): return inspect.currentframe( )
print inspect.formatargvalues(inspect.getargvalues(f( )))
# prints: (x=23)
```

currentframe

currentframe( )

Returns the frame object for the current function (caller of currentframe). formatargvalues(getargvalues(currentframe( )), for example, returns a formatted string with the actual arguments of the calling function.

getdoc	getdoc(*obj*)
	Returns the docstring for *obj*, with tabs expanded to spaces and redundant whitespace stripped from each line.

getfile, **getsourcefile**	getfile(*obj*)
	Returns the name of the file that defined *obj*, and raises TypeError when unable to determine the file. For example, getfile raises TypeError if *obj* is built-in. getfile returns the name of a binary or source file. getsourcefile returns the name of a source file, and raises TypeError when it can determine only a binary file, not the corresponding source file.

getmembers	getmembers(*obj*, *filter*=None)
	Returns all attributes (members) of *obj*, a sorted list of (*name*,*value*) pairs. When *filter* is not None, returns only attributes for which callable *filter* returns a true result when called on the attribute's *value*, like:

```
[ (n, v) for n, v in getmembers(obj) if filter(v) ]
```

getmodule	getmodule(*obj*)
	Returns the module object that defined *obj*, or None if unable to determine it.

getmro	getmro(*c*)
	Returns a tuple of bases and ancestors of class *c* in method resolution order. *c* is the first item in the tuple. Each class appears only once in the tuple.

getsource, **getsourcelines**	getsource(*obj*)
	Returns a single multiline string that is the source code for *obj*, and raises IOError if unable to determine or fetch it. getsourcelines returns a pair: the first item is the source code for *obj* (a list of lines), and the second item is the line number of the list's first line in the source file it comes from.

isbuiltin, **isclass,** **iscode,** **isframe,** **isfunction,** **ismethod,** **ismodule,** **isroutine**	isbuiltin(*obj*)
	Each of these functions accepts a single argument *obj* and returns True if *obj* belongs to the type indicated in the function name. Accepted objects are, respectively: built-in (C-coded) functions, class objects, code objects, frame objects, Python-coded functions (including lambda expressions), methods, modules, and, for isroutine, all methods or functions, either C-coded or Python-coded. These functions are often used as the *filter* argument to getmembers.

stack   stack(*context*=1)

Returns a list of six-item tuples. The first tuple is about stack's caller, the second tuple is about the caller's caller, and so on. Each tuple's items, in order, are: frame object, filename, line number, function name, list of *context* source code lines around the current line, and index of current line within the list.

For example, suppose that at some point in your program you execute a statement such as:

```
x.f( )
```

and unexpectedly receive an AttributeError informing you that object *x* has no attribute named *f*. This means that object *x* is not as you expected, so you want to determine more about *x* as a preliminary to ascertaining why *x* is that way and what you should do about it. Change the statement to:

```
try: x.f( )
except AttributeError:
    import sys, inspect
    sys.stderr.write('x is type %s(%r)\n'%(x,type(x)))
    sys.stderr.write("x's methods are: ")
    for n, v in inspect.getmembers(x, callable):
        sys.stderr.write('%s '%n)
    sys.stderr.write('\n')
    raise
```

This example uses sys.stderr (covered in Chapter 8), since it's displaying diagnostic information related to an error, not program results. Function getmembers of module inspect obtains the name of all methods available on *x* in order to display them. Of course, if you need this kind of diagnostic functionality often, you should package it up into a separate function, such as:

```
import sys, inspect
def show_obj_methods(obj, name, show=sys.stderr.write):
    show('%s is type %s(%r)\n'%(name,obj,type(obj)))
    show("%s's methods are: "%name)
    for n, v in inspect.getmembers(obj, callable):
        show('%s '%n)
    show('\n')
```

And then the example becomes just:

```
try: x.f( )
except AttributeError:
    show_obj_methods(x, 'x')
    raise
```

Good program structure and organization are just as necessary in code intended for diagnostic and debugging purposes as they are in code that implements your program's functionality. See also "The __debug__ Built-in Variable" in Chapter 6 for a good technique to use when defining diagnostic and debugging functions.

The traceback Module

The traceback module lets you extract, format, and output information about tracebacks as normally produced by uncaught exceptions. By default, module traceback reproduces the formatting Python uses for tracebacks. However, module traceback also lets you exert fine-grained control. The module supplies many functions, but in typical use you will use only one of them.

print_exc	`print_exc(limit=None, file=sys.stderr)`
	Call `print_exc` from an exception handler or a function directly or indirectly called by an exception handler. `print_exc` outputs to file-like object *file* the traceback information that Python outputs to stderr for uncaught exceptions. When *limit* is not None, `print_exc` outputs only *limit* traceback nesting levels. For example, when, in an exception handler, you want to cause a diagnostic message just as if the exception propagated, but actually stop the exception from propagating any further (so that your program keeps running, and no further handlers are involved), call `traceback.print_exc()`.

The pdb Module

The pdb module exploits the Python interpreter's debugging and tracing hooks to implement a simple, command-line-oriented interactive debugger. pdb lets you set breakpoints, single-step on sources, examine stack frames, and so on.

To run some code under pdb's control, you import pdb and then call pdb.run, passing as the single argument a string of code to execute. To use pdb for post-mortem debugging (meaning debugging of code that terminated by propagating an exception at an interactive prompt), call pdb.pm( ) without arguments. When pdb starts, it first reads text files named *.pdbrc* in your home directory and in the current directory. Such files can contain any pdb commands, but most often they use the alias command in order to define useful synonyms and abbreviations for other commands.

When pdb is in control, it prompts you with the string '(Pdb) ', and you can enter pdb commands. Command help (which you can also enter in the abbreviated form h) lists all available commands. Call help with an argument (separated by a space) to get help about any specific command. You can abbreviate most commands to the first one or two letters, but you must always enter commands in lowercase: pdb, like Python itself, is case-sensitive. Entering an empty line repeats the previous command. The most frequently used pdb commands are the following.

!	`! statement`
	Executes Python statement *statement* in the currently debugged context.

alias, unalias	alias [*name* [*command*]]
	alias without arguments lists currently defined aliases. alias *name* outputs the current definition of the alias *name*. In the full form, *command* is any pdb command, with arguments, and may contain %1, %2, and so on to refer to arguments passed to the new alias *name* being defined, or %* to refer to all such arguments together. Command unalias *name* removes an alias.
args, a	args
	Lists all actual arguments passed to the function you are currently debugging.
break, b	break [*location* [,*condition*]]
	break without arguments lists currently defined breakpoints and the number of times each breakpoint has triggered. With an argument, break sets a breakpoint at the given *location*. *location* can be a line number or a function name, optionally preceded by *filename*: to set a breakpoint in a file that is not the current one or at the start of a function whose name is ambiguous (i.e., a function that exists in more than one file). When *condition* is present, *condition* is an expression to evaluate (in the debugged context) each time the given line or function is about to execute; execution breaks only when the expression returns a true value. When setting a new breakpoint, break returns a breakpoint number, which you can then use to refer to the new breakpoint in any other breakpoint-related pdb command.
clear, cl	clear [*breakpoint-numbers*]
	Clears (removes) one or more breakpoints. clear without arguments removes all breakpoints after asking for confirmation. To deactivate a breakpoint without removing it, see disable.
condition	condition *breakpoint-number* [*expression*]
	condition *n* *expression* sets or changes the condition on breakpoint *n*. condition *n*, without *expression*, makes breakpoint *n* unconditional.
continue, c, cont	continue
	Continues execution of the code being debugged, up to a breakpoint if any.
disable	disable [*breakpoint-numbers*]
	Disables one or more breakpoints. disable without arguments disables all breakpoints (after asking for confirmation). This differs

Debugging

from clear in that the debugger remembers the breakpoint, and you can reactivate it via enable.

down, d   down

Moves one frame down in the stack (i.e., toward the most recent function call). Normally, the current position in the stack is at the bottom (i.e., at the function that was called most recently and is now being debugged). Therefore, command down can't go further down. However, command down is useful if you have previously executed command up, which moves the current position upward.

enable   enable [*breakpoint-numbers*]

Enables one or more breakpoints. enable without arguments enables all breakpoints after asking for confirmation.

ignore   ignore *breakpoint-number* [*count*]

Sets the breakpoint's ignore count (to 0, if *count* is omitted). Triggering a breakpoint whose ignore count is greater than 0 just decrements the count. Execution stops, presenting you with an interactive pdb prompt, only when you trigger a breakpoint whose ignore count is 0. For example, say that module *fob.py* contains the following code:

```
def f( ):
    for i in range(1000):
        g(i)

def g(i):
    pass
```

Now, consider the following interactive pdb session:

```
>>> import pdb
>>> import fob
>>> pdb.run('fob.f( )')
> <string>(0)?( )
(Pdb) break fob.g
Breakpoint 1 at C:\mydir\fob.py:6
(Pdb) ignore 1 500
Will ignore next 500 crossings of breakpoint 1.
(Pdb) continue
> <string>(1)?( )
(Pdb) continue
> C:\mydir\fob.py(6)g( )
-> pass
(Pdb) print i
500
```

The ignore command, as pdb shows in response to it, asks pdb to ignore the next 500 hits on breakpoint 1, which we just set at *fob.g* in the previous break statement. Therefore, when execution finally stops, function g has already been called 500 times, as we show by printing its argument i, which indeed is now 500. Note that the ignore count of breakpoint 1 is now 0; if we give another continue and print i, i will then show as 501. In other words, once the ignore count is decremented back to 0, execution stops every time the breakpoint is hit. If we want to skip some more hits, we need to give pdb another ignore command, in order to set the ignore count of breakpoint 1 at some value greater than 0 yet again.

list, l	list [*first* [, *last*]] list without arguments lists 11 lines centered on the current one, or the next 11 lines if the previous command was also a list. By giving arguments to the list command, you may explicitly specify the first and last lines to list within the current file. The list command deals with physical lines, including comments and empty lines, not with logical lines.
next, n	next Executes the current line, without stepping into any function called from the current line. However, hitting breakpoints in functions called directly or indirectly from the current line does stop execution.
p	p *expression* Evaluates *expression* in the current context and displays the result.
quit, q	quit Immediately terminates both pdb and the program being debugged.
return, r	return Executes the rest of the current function, stopping only at breakpoints if any.
step, s	step Executes the current line, stepping into any function called from the current line.
tbreak	tbreak [*location* [,*condition*]] Like break, but the breakpoint is temporary (i.e., pdb automatically removes the breakpoint as soon as the breakpoint is triggered).
up, u	up Moves one frame up in the stack (i.e., away from the most recent function call and toward the calling function).

Debugging

where, w	where
	Shows the stack of frames and indicates the current one (i.e., in what frame's context command ! executes statements, command args shows arguments, command *p* evaluates expressions, etc.).

Debugging in IDLE

IDLE, the Interactive DeveLopment Environment that comes with Python, offers debugging functionality similar to that of pdb, although not quite as powerful. Thanks to IDLE's GUI, however, you may find the functionality easier to access. For example, instead of having to ask for source lists and stack lists explicitly with such pdb commands as list and where, you just activate one or more of four checkboxes in the Debug Control window to see source, stack, locals, and globals always displayed in the same window at each step.

To start IDLE's interactive debugger, use menu Debug → Debugger in IDLE's *Python Shell* window. IDLE opens the Debug Control window, outputs [DEBUG ON] in the shell window, and gives you another >>> prompt in the shell window. Keep using the shell window as you normally would—any command you give at the shell window's prompt now runs under the debugger. To deactivate the debugger, use Debug → Debugger again; IDLE then toggles the debug state, closes the Debug Control window, and outputs [DEBUG OFF] in the shell window. To control the debugger when the debugger is active, use the GUI controls in the Debug Control window. You can toggle the debugger away only when it is not busy actively tracking code: otherwise, IDLE disables the Quit button in the Debug Control window.

The warnings Module

Warnings are messages about errors or anomalies that may not be serious enough to be worth disrupting the program's control flow (as would happen by raising a normal exception). The warnings module offers you fine-grained control over which warnings are output and what happens to them. Your code can conditionally output a warning by calling function warn in module warnings. Other functions in the module let you control how warnings are formatted, set their destinations, and conditionally suppress some warnings (or transform some warnings into exceptions).

Classes

Module warnings supplies several exception classes representing warnings. Class Warning subclasses Exception and is the base class for all warnings. You may define your own warning classes; they must subclass Warning, either directly or via one of its other existing subclasses, which are:

DeprecationWarning
    Using deprecated features only supplied for backward compatibility

RuntimeWarning
    Using features whose semantics are error-prone

SyntaxWarning
    Using features whose syntax is error-prone

UserWarning
    Other user-defined warnings that don't fit any of the above cases

Objects

In the current version of Python, there are no concrete warning objects. A warning is composed of a *message* (a text string), a *category* (a subclass of Warning), and two pieces of information that identify where the warning was raised from: *module* (name of the module raising the warning) and *lineno* (line number of the source code line raising the warning). Conceptually, you may think of these as attributes of a warning object *w*, and I use attribute notation later for clarity, but no specific warning object *w* actually exists.

Filters

At any time, module warnings keeps a list of active filters for warnings. When you import warnings for the first time in a run, the module examines sys.warnoptions to determine the initial set of filters. You can run Python with option -W to set sys.warnoptions for a given run. Do not rely on the initial set of filters being held specifically in sys.warnoptions, as this is an implementation aspect that may change in future releases of Python.

As each warning *w* occurs, warnings tests *w* against each filter until a filter matches. The matching filter determines what happens to *w*. Each filter is a tuple of five items. The first item, *action*, is a string that defines what happens on a match. The other four items, *message*, *category*, *module*, and *lineno*, control what it means for *w* to match the filter, and all conditions must be satisfied for a match. Here are the meanings of these items (using attribute notation to indicate conceptual attributes of *w*):

message
    A regular expression object; the match condition is *message*.match(*w*.message) (the match is case-insensitive)

category
    Warning or a subclass of Warning; the match condition is issubclass(*w*.category,*category*)

module
    A regular expression object; the match condition is *module*.match(*w*.module) (the match is case-sensitive)

lineno
    An integer; the match condition is *lineno* in (0, *w*.lineno), i.e., either *lineno* is 0, meaning *w*.lineno does not matter, or *w*.lineno must exactly equal *lineno*

Upon a match, the first field of the filter, the *action*, determines what happens:

`'always'`
> w.message is output whether or not w has already occurred

`'default'`
> w.message is output if, and only if, this is the first time w occurs from this specific location (i.e., this specific w.module, w.location pair)

`'error'`
> w.category(w.message) is raised as an exception

`'ignore'`
> w is ignored

`'module'`
> w.message is output if, and only if, this is the first time w occurs from w.module

`'once'`
> w.message is output if, and only if, this is the first time w occurs from any location

Functions

Module warnings supplies the following functions.

filterwarnings `filterwarnings(action,message='.*',category=Warning, module='.*',lineno=0, append=False)`

Adds a filter to the list of active filters. When *append* is true, filterwarnings adds the filter after all other existing filters (i.e., appends the filter to the list of existing filters); otherwise filterwarnings inserts the filter before any other existing filter. All components, save *action*, have default values meaning match everything. As detailed above, *message* and *module* are pattern strings for regular expressions, *category* is some subclass of Warning, *lineno* is an integer, and *action* is a string that determines what happens when a message matches this filter.

formatwarning `formatwarning(message,category,filename,lineno)`

Returns a string that represents the given warning with standard formatting.

resetwarnings `resetwarnings()`

Removes all filters from the list of filters. resetwarnings also discards any filters originally added with the -W command-line option.

showwarning `showwarning(message,category,filename,lineno,file=sys.stderr)`

Outputs the given warning to the given file object. Filter actions that output warnings call showwarning, letting argument *file* default to sys.stderr. To change what happens when filter actions output warnings, code your own function with this signature and bind it to warnings.showwarning.

warn   warn(*message,category*=UserWarning,*stacklevel*=1)

Sends a warning, so that the filters examine and possibly output it. The location of the warning is the current function (caller of warn) if *stacklevel* is 1, or its caller if *stacklevel* is 2. Thus, passing 2 as the value of *stacklevel* lets you write functions that send warnings on their caller's behalf, such as:

```
def toUnicode(astr):
    try:
        return unicode(astr)
    except UnicodeError:
        warnings.warn("Invalid characters in (%s)"%astr,
                      stacklevel=2)
        return unicode(astr, errors='ignore')
```

Thanks to parameter *stacklevel*=2, the warning appears as coming from the caller of toUnicode, rather than from function toUnicode itself. This is particularly important when the *action* of the filter matching this warning is *default* or *module*, since these actions output a warning only the first time the warning occurs from a given location or module.

Optimization

"First make it work. Then make it right. Then make it fast." This quotation, often with slight variations, is widely known as the golden rule of programming. As far as I've been able to ascertain, the quotation is attributed to Kent Beck, who credits his father with it. Being widely known makes the principle no less important, particularly because it's more honored in the breach than in the observance. A negative form, slightly exaggerated for emphasis, is in a quotation by Don Knuth: "Premature optimization is the root of all evil in programming."

Optimization is premature if your code is not working yet. First make it work. Optimization is also premature if your code is working but you are not satisfied with the overall architecture and design. Remedy structural flaws before worrying about optimization: first make it work, then make it right. These first two steps are not optional—working, well-architected code is always a must.

In contrast, you don't always need to make it fast. Benchmarks may show that your code's performance is already acceptable after the first two steps. When performance is not acceptable, profiling often shows that all performance issues are in a small subset, perhaps 10% to 20% of the code where your program spends 80% or 90% of the time. Such performance-crucial regions of your code are also known as its *bottlenecks*, or *hot spots*. It's a waste of effort to optimize large portions of code that account for, say, 10% of your program's running time. Even if you made that part run 10 times as fast (a rare feat), your program's overall runtime would only decrease by 9%, a speedup no user will even notice. If optimization is needed, focus your efforts where they'll matter, on bottlenecks. You can optimize bottlenecks while keeping your code 100% pure Python. In some cases, you can resort to recoding some computational bottlenecks as Python extensions, potentially gaining even better performance.

Developing a Fast-Enough Python Application

Start by designing, coding, and testing your application in Python, often using some already available extension modules. This takes much less time than it would take with a classic compiled language. Then benchmark the application to find out if the resulting code is fast enough. Often it is, and you're done—congratulations!

Since much of Python itself is coded in highly optimized C, as are many of its standard and extension modules, your application may even turn out to be already faster than typical C code. However, if the application is too slow, you need to re-examine your algorithms and data structures. Check for bottlenecks due to application architecture, network traffic, database access, and operating system interactions. For typical applications, each of these factors is more likely than language choice to cause slowdowns. Tinkering with large-scale architectural aspects can often speed up an application dramatically, and Python is an excellent medium for such experimentation.

If your program is still too slow, you should profile it to find out where the time is going. Applications often exhibit computational bottlenecks—small areas of the source code, generally between 10% and 20%, which account for 80% or more of the running time. You can now optimize the bottlenecks, applying the techniques suggested in the rest of this chapter.

If normal Python-level optimizations still leave some outstanding computational bottlenecks, you can recode them as Python extension modules, as covered in Chapter 24. In the end, your application will run at roughly the same speed as if you had coded it all in C, C++, or Fortran—or faster, when large-scale experimentation has let you find a better architecture. Your overall programming productivity with this process is not much less than if you coded everything in Python. Future changes and maintenance are easy, since you use Python to express the overall structure of the program, and lower-level, harder-to-maintain languages only for a few specific computational bottlenecks.

As you produce applications in a given area according to this process, you will accumulate a library of reusable Python extension modules for that area. You therefore become more and more productive at developing other fast-running Python applications in the same field.

Even if external constraints should eventually force you to recode the whole application in a lower-level language, you're still better off for having started in Python. Rapid prototyping has long been acknowledged as the best way to get a software architecture just right. A working prototype lets you check that you have identified the right problems and taken the best path to their solution. A prototype affords the kind of large-scale architectural experimentation that can make a real difference to performance. Starting your prototype with Python allows a gradual migration to other languages by way of extension modules. The application remains in a fully functional and testable state at each stage. This ensures against the risk of compromising a design's architectural integrity in the coding stage. The resulting software is likely to be faster and more robust than if all of the coding had been lower-level from the start, and your productivity, while not quite as good as with a pure Python or mostly Python application, is still better than if you had been coding at a lower level throughout.

Benchmarking

Benchmarking is similar to system testing: both activities are like running the program as it's meant to be run for production purposes. In both cases, you need to have at least some subset of the program's intended functionality working, and you need to use known, reproducible inputs. In the case of benchmarking, you don't need to capture and check your program's output: since you make it work and make it right before you make it fast, you are already confident about your program's correctness by the time you benchmark it. You do need inputs that are representative of typical system operations, particularly those that may be most challenging for your program's performance. If your program performs several kinds of operations, make sure you run one or two benchmarks for each different kind of operation.

Elapsed time as measured by your wristwatch is probably precise enough to benchmark most programs. Programs with hard real-time constraints are obviously another matter, but they have needs very different from those of normal programs in most respects. A 5% or 10% difference in performance, except for programs with very peculiar constraints, makes no practical difference to a program's real-life usability.

When you benchmark "toy" programs in order to help you choose an algorithm or data structure, you may need more precision. In that case, you may want to set up an artificial environment, with a machine as quiescent as possible, no network activity, and accurate timekeeping. Python time operations are covered in Chapter 12. The benchmarking discussed in this section is a different kind of issue: an approximation of real-life program operation, for the sole purpose of checking whether the program's performance at each task is acceptable, before embarking on profiling and other optimization activities. For such system benchmarking, a situation that approximates the program's normal operating conditions is best, and accuracy in timing is not particularly important.

Large-Scale Optimization

The aspects of your program that are most important for performance are large-scale ones: choice of algorithms, overall architecture, and choice of data structures.

The performance issues that you must almost always take into account are those connected with the traditional big-O notation of computer science. Informally, if you call N the input size of an algorithm, big-O notation expresses algorithm performance, for large values of N, as proportional to a function of N (in precise computer science lingo, this should actually be called big-Theta, but in practical use programmers in the field call this big-O). An O(N) algorithm is one where, for large enough N, handling twice as much data takes about twice as much time, three times as much data three times as much time, and so on, growing linearly with N. An O(N^2) algorithm is one where, for large enough N, handling twice as much data takes about four times as much time, three times as much data nine times as much time, and so on, growing with N squared.

You will find more information on big-O notation, as well as other issues about algorithms and their complexity, in any good book about algorithms and data structures. Unfortunately, at the time of this writing, there aren't yet any such books using Python. However, if you are at least moderately familiar with C, I can recommend *Mastering Algorithms with C*, by Kyle Loudon (O'Reilly).

To understand the practical importance of big-O considerations in your programs, consider two different ways to accept all items from an input iterator and accumulate them into a list in reverse order:

```
def slow(it):
    result = [ ]
    for item in it: result.insert(0, item)
    return result

def fast(it):
    result = [ ]
    for item in it: result.append(item)
    result.reverse( )
    return result
```

We could express each of these functions more concisely, but the key difference is best appreciated by presenting them in these elementary terms. Function slow builds the result list by inserting each input item before all previously received ones. Function fast appends each input item after all previously received ones, then reverses the result list just before returning it. Intuitively, one might think that the final reversing represents extra work, and therefore slow should be faster than fast. But that's not the way things work out.

Each call to result.append takes roughly the same amount of time, independent of how many items are already in list result, since there is always a free slot for an extra item at the end of the list. The for loop in function fast executes N times to receive N items. Since each iteration of the loop takes a constant time, overall loop time is O(N). result.reverse also takes time O(N), as it is directly proportional to the total number of items. Thus, the total running time of fast is also O(N). (If you don't understand why a sum of two quantities, each O(N), is also O(N), consider that the sum of two linear functions of N is also a linear function of N).

In contrast, each call to result.insert must make space at slot 0 for the new item to insert, by moving all items that are already in list result forward one slot. That takes a time proportional to the number of items that are already in the list. The overall amount of time to receive N items is therefore proportional to 1+2+3+...N-1, a sum whose value is O(N^2). Therefore, the total running time of slow is also O(N^2).

It's almost always worth replacing an $O(N^2)$ solution with an $O(N)$ one, unless you can somehow assign rigorous limits to the input size N. If N can grow without bounds, the $O(N^2)$ solution will inevitably turn out to be disastrously slower than the $O(N)$ one for large enough values of N, no matter what the proportionality constants in each case may be (and no matter what profiling tells you). Unless you have other $O(N^2)$ or even worse bottlenecks elsewhere that you cannot eliminate, a part of the program that is $O(N^2)$ will inevitably turn into the program's bottle-neck and dominate runtime for large enough values of N. Do yourself a favor and watch out for the big O: all other performance issues, in comparison, are insignificant.

Incidentally, function fast can be made substantially faster by expressing it in more idiomatic Python. Just replace the first two lines with the single statement:

```
result = list(it)
```

This change does not affect fast's big-O character (fast is still $O(N)$ after the change), but does speed things up by a constant factor. Often, in Python, the simplest, clearest, most idiomatic way to express something is also the fastest.

Choosing algorithms with good big-O characteristics is roughly the same task in Python as in any other language. You just need a few indications about the big-O performance of Python's elementary building blocks.

List operations

Python lists are internally implemented with vectors (also known as arrays), not with linked lists. This fundamental implementation choice determines just about all performance characteristics of Python lists, in big-O terms.

Chaining two lists of length N1 and N2 is $O(N1+N2)$. Multiplying a list of length N by the number M is $O(N*M)$. Accessing or rebinding any list item is $O(1)$ (also known as constant time, meaning that the time taken does not depend on how many items are in the list). len( ) on a list is also $O(1)$. Accessing any slice of length M is $O(M)$. Rebinding a slice of length M with one of identical length is also $O(M)$. Rebinding a slice of length M1 with one of different length M2 is $O(M1+M2+N1)$, where N1 is the number of items after the slice in the target list.

Most list methods, as shown way back in Table 4-3, are equivalent to slice rebind-ings and have the same big-O performance. Methods count, index, remove, and reverse, and operator in, are $O(N)$. Method sort is generally $O(N*\log(N))$, but has optimizations that let it be $O(N)$ in some important special cases, like when the list is already sorted, reverse sorted, or sorted except for a few items at the end (in Python 2.3, sort will also be $O(N)$ in a few more important special cases). range(a,b,c) is $O((b-a)/c)$. xrange(a,b,c) is $O(1)$, but looping on xrange's result is $O((b-a)/c)$.

String operations

Most methods on a string of length N (be it plain or Unicode) are $O(N)$. len(astring) is $O(1)$. The fastest way to produce a copy of a string with transliter-ations and/or removal of specified characters is the string's method translate.

The most practically important big-O consideration involving strings is covered in "Small-Scale Optimization" later in this chapter.

Dictionary operations

Python dictionaries are internally implemented with hash tables. This fundamental implementation choice determines just about all performance characteristics of Python dictionaries, in big-O terms.

Accessing, rebinding, adding, or removing a dictionary item is generally O(1), as are methods has_key, get, setdefault, and popitem, and operator in. *d1*.update(*d2*) is O(len(*d2*)). len(*adict*) is O(1). Methods keys, items, and values are O(N). Methods iterkeys, iteritems, and itervalues are O(1), but looping on the iterators that those methods return is O(N). When the keys in a dictionary are instances of classes that define __hash__ and equality comparison methods, dictionary performance is of course affected by those methods. The indications presented in this paragraph are valid only if both hashing and equality comparison are O(1).

Profiling

Most programs have hot spots (i.e., regions of source code that account for most of the time elapsed during a program run). Don't try to guess where your program's hot spots are; programmers' intuition is notoriously unreliable in this field. Use module profile to collect profile data over one or more runs of your program, with known inputs. Then, use module pstats to collate, interpret, and display that profile data. To gain accuracy, you can calibrate the Python profiler for your machine (i.e., determine what overhead profiling incurs on your machine). Module profile can then subtract this overhead from the times it measures so that the profile data you collect is closer to reality.

The profile module

The profile module supplies one function you will often use.

run	run(*code*,*filename*=None)
	code is a string such as you could use with statement exec, normally a call to the main function of the program you're profiling. *filename* is the path of a file that run creates or rewrites with profile data. Usually you call run a few times, specifying different filenames, and possibly different arguments to your program's main function, in order to exercise various program parts proportionately. Then, you use module pstats to display collated results.
	You may call run without a *filename* to obtain a summary report, similar to the one module pstats could give you, directly on standard output. However, this approach gives no control at all over output format, nor does it offer any way to consolidate several runs into one report. In practice, you rarely use this feature: collecting profile data into files is generally preferable.

Module profile also supplies class Profile, mentioned in the next section. By instantiating Profile directly, you can access advanced functionality, such as the ability to run a command in specified local and global dictionaries. I do not cover such advanced functionality of class profile.Profile further in this book.

Calibration

To calibrate profile for your machine, you need to use class Profile, which module profile supplies and internally uses in function run. An instance *p* of Profile supplies one method you use for calibration.

calibrate   *p*.calibrate(*N*)

Loops *N* times, then returns a number that is the profiling overhead per call on your machine. *N* must be large if your machine is fast. Call *p*.calibrate(10000) a few times and check that the various numbers it returns are very close to each other, then pick the smallest one of them. If the numbers exhibit substantial variation, try again with larger values of *N*.

The calibration procedure can be time consuming. However, you need to perform it only once, repeating it only when you make changes that could alter your machine's characteristics, such as applying patches to your operating system, adding memory, or changing Python version. Once you know your machine's overhead, you can tell profile about it each time you import it, right before using profile.run. The simplest way to do this is as follows:

```
import profile
profile.Profile.bias = ...the overhead you measured...
profile.run('main( )', 'somefile')
```

The pstats module

The pstats module supplies a single class, Stats, that you use to analyze, consolidate, and report on the profile data contained in one or more files written by function profile.run.

Stats   class Stats(*filename,*filenames*)

Instantiates Stats with one or more filenames of files of profile data written by function profile.run.

An instance *s* of class Stats provides methods to add profile data and sort and output results. Each method returns *s*, so you can chain several calls in the same expression. *s*'s main methods are as follows.

add	`s.add(filename)`
	Adds another file of profile data to the set that *s* is holding for analysis.
print_callees, print_callers	`s.print_callees(*restrictions)`
	Outputs the list of functions in *s*'s profile data, sorted according to the latest call to `s.sort_stats`, and subject to the given restrictions, if any. You can call each printing method with zero or more *restrictions*, which are applied one after the other, in order, to reduce the number of output lines. A restriction that is an integer *n* limits the output to the first *n* lines. A restriction that is a floating-point value *f* between 0.0 and 1.0 limits the output to a fraction *f* of the lines. A restriction that is a string is compiled as a regular expression (as covered in Chapter 9); only lines satisfying a search method call on the regular expressions are output. Restrictions are cumulative. For example, `s.print_calls(10,0.5)` outputs the first 5 lines (half of 10). Output restrictions apply only after the summary and header lines: summary and header are output unconditionally.
	Each function *f* that is output is accompanied by the list of *f*'s callers (the functions that called *f*) or *f*'s callees (the functions that *f* called) according to the name of the method.
print_stats	`s.print_stats(*restrictions)`
	Outputs statistics about *s*'s profile data, sorted according to the latest call to `s.sort_stats`, and subject to the given restrictions, if any, as covered in `print_callees`. After a few summary lines (date and time on which profile data was collected, number of function calls, and sort criteria used), the output, absent restrictions, is one line per function, with six fields per line, labeled in a header line. For each function *f*, `print_stats` outputs six fields:

1. Total number of calls to function *f*
2. Total time spent in function *f*, exclusive of other functions that *f* called
3. Total time per call (i.e., field 2 divided by field 1)
4. Cumulative time spent in function *f*, and in all functions directly or indirectly called from *f*
5. Cumulative time per call (i.e., field 4 divided by field 1)
6. The name of function *f*

sort_stats	`s.sort_stats(key, *keys)`
	Gives one or more keys (primary first, if more than one) on which to sort future output. Each key is a string. The sort is descending for keys indicating times or numbers, alphabetical (ascending) for key `'nfl'`. The most frequently used keys when calling `sort_stats` are:

'calls'
> Number of calls to the function (like field 1 covered in print_
> stats)

'cumulative'
> Cumulative time spent in the function and all functions it
> called (like field 4 i covered in print_stats)

'nfl'
> Name of the function, its module, line number of the function
> in its file (like field 6 covered in print_stats)

'time'
> Total time spent in the function itself, exclusive of functions it
> called (like field 2 covered in print_stats)

strip_dirs	s.strip_dirs()

> Alters s by stripping directory names from all the module names
> that s holds, to make future output more compact. s is unsorted
> after s.strip_dirs(), and therefore you normally call s.sort_stats
> with the arguments you desire right after calling s.strip_dirs.

Small-Scale Optimization

Fine tuning of program operations is rarely important. Such tuning may make a small but meaningful difference in some particularly hot spot, but hardly ever is it a decisive factor. And yet, such fine tuning, in the pursuit of mostly irrelevant microefficiencies, is where a programmer's instincts are likely to lead. It is in good part because of this that most optimization is premature and best avoided. The most that can be said in favor of fine tuning is that, if one idiom is always speedier than another when the difference is measurable, it's worth getting into the habit of always using the former and not the latter.

Most often, in Python, if you do what comes naturally and choose simplicity and elegance, you end up with code that has good performance as well as clarity and maintainability. In a few cases, an approach that may not be intuitive offers performance advantages, as discussed in the rest of this section.

The simplest possible optimization is to run your Python programs using python -O or -OO. -OO makes little direct difference to performance compared to -O, but -OO may save memory, since it removes docstrings from the bytecode, and memory availability is sometimes (indirectly) a performance bottleneck. The optimizer is not very powerful in current releases of Python, but it may still gain you performance advantages on the order of 10%, sometimes as large as 20% (potentially even larger, if you make heavy use of assert statements and if __debug__: guards as suggested in Chapter 6). The best aspect of -O is that it costs nothing—as long as your optimization isn't premature, of course. -O does impede use of debuggers, such as pdb, and may thus make debugging somewhat harder if your program isn't fully tested and working correctly. So, don't use -O on a program you're still developing.

Debugging

Building up a string from pieces

The single Python anti-idiom that's likeliest to kill your program's performance, to the point that you should never use it, is to build up a large string from pieces by looping on string concatenation statements such as *big_string+=piece*. Since Python strings are immutable, such a concatenation makes Python free the M bytes previously allocated for *big_string*, and allocate and fill M+K bytes for the new version. Doing this repeatedly in a loop, you end up with roughly $O(N^2)$ performance, where N is the total number of characters. More often than not, $O(N^2)$ performance where $O(N)$ is available is a performance disaster. On some platforms, things may be even bleaker due to memory fragmentation effects caused by freeing many memory areas, all of different sizes, and allocating progressively larger ones.

To achieve $O(N)$ performance, accumulate intermediate pieces in a list rather than building up the string piece by piece. Lists, unlike strings, are mutable, so appending to a list has $O(1)$ performance (amortized). Change each occurrence of *big_string+=piece* into *temp_list*.append(*piece*). Then, when you're done accumulating, use the following to build your desired string result in $O(N)$ time:

    big_string = ''.join(temp_list)

Other $O(N)$ ways to build up big strings are to concatenate the pieces to an instance of array.array('c'), or to write the pieces to an instance of cStringIO. StringIO.

In the special case where you want to output the resulting string, you may gain a further small slice of performance by using writelines on *temp_list* (never building *big_string* in memory). When feasible (i.e., when you have the output file object open and available in the loop), it's at least as effective to perform a write call for each *piece*, without any accumulation.

Although not nearly as crucial as += on a big string in a loop, another case where removing string concatenation may give a slight performance improvement is when you're concatenating several values in an expression:

    oneway = str(x)+' eggs and '+str(y)+' slices of '+k+' ham'
    another = '%s eggs and %s slices of %s ham' % (x, y, k)

Using operator % for string formatting is often a good performance choice.

Searching and sorting

Operator in, the most natural tool for searching, is $O(1)$ when the right-hand side operand is a dictionary, but $O(N)$ when the right-hand side operand is a list. If you need to perform many searches on a container, you're generally much better off using a dictionary, rather than a list, as the container. Python dictionaries are highly optimized for searching and fetching items by key.

Method sort of Python lists is also a highly optimized and sophisticated tool. You can rely on sort's performance. Performance dramatically degrades, however, if you pass sort a custom callable to perform comparisons in order to sort a list based on anything but built-in comparisons. To satisfy such needs, consider using

---

the decorate-sort-undecorate (DSU) idiom instead. This idiom has the following steps:

decorate
Build an auxiliary list A where each item is a tuple made up of the sort keys, ending with the item of the original list L or with the item's index

sort
Call A.sort( ) without arguments

undecorate
Extract the items in order from the now-sorted A

The decorate and undecorate steps are most often handily performed with list comprehensions. If you need the sort to be in-place, assign the final sorted list to L[:]. Otherwise, DSU provides a sorted copy, without disturbing the original list L.

For example, say we have in L a large list of strings, each of at least two words, and we want to sort L in-place by the second word of each string:

```
A = [ (s.split( )[1], s) for s in L ]
A.sort( )
L[:] = [ t[1] for t in A ]
```

This is much faster than passing to L.sort a function that compares two strings by their second words, as in:

```
def cmp2ndword(a, b): return cmp(a.split( )[1], b.split( )[1])
L.sort(cmp2ndword)
```

On a series of benchmarks with Python 2.2 on lists of 10,000 strings, I measured the DSU version as 7 to 10 times faster than the non-DSU one.

Avoiding exec and from ... import *

If a function contains an exec statement without explicit dictionaries, the whole function slows down substantially. The presence of such an exec statement forces the Python compiler to avoid the modest but precious optimizations it normally performs because such an exec might cause any alteration at all to the function's namespace. A from statement of the form:

```
from MyModule import *
```

causes similar performance loss, since it, too, can alter a function's namespace unpredictably.

exec itself is also quite slow, particularly if you apply it to a string of source code rather than to a code object. By far the best approach, for performance, for correctness, and for clarity, is to avoid exec altogether. It's most often possible to find better (faster, more solid, and clearer) solutions. If you must use exec, always use it with explicit dictionaries. If you need to exec a dynamically obtained string more than once, compile the string one time and repeatedly exec the resulting code object.

eval works on expressions, not on statements; therefore, although it's still slow, at least it avoids some of the worst performance impacts of exec. With eval, too, you're best advised to use explicit dictionaries, and, if you need repeated evaluation of the same dynamically obtained string, compile the string just once, then repeatedly eval the resulting code object.

Optimizing loops

Most of your program's bottlenecks will be in loops, particularly nested loops, because loop bodies often execute repeatedly. Python does not implicitly perform any code hoisting: if you have any code inside a loop that might be executed just once by hoisting it out of the loop, and the loop is a performance bottleneck, hoist the code out yourself. Sometimes the presence of code to hoist may not be immediately obvious:

```
def slower(anobject, ahugenumber):
    for i in xrange(ahugenumber): anobject.amethod(i)
def faster(anobject, ahugenumber):
    themethod = anobject.amethod
    for i in xrange(ahugenumber): themethod(i)
```

In this case, the code that faster hoists out of the for loop is the attribute lookup anobject.amethod. slower repeats the lookup each and every time, while faster performs it just once. The two functions are not 100% equivalent: it is (just barely) conceivable that executing amethod might cause such changes on anobject that the next lookup for the same named attribute fetches a different method object. This is part of why Python doesn't perform such optimizations itself. In practice, such subtle, obscure, and tricky cases happen far less than one time in ten thousand. So you're quite safe performing such optimizations yourself, when you're trying to squeeze the last drop of performance out of some crucial bottleneck.

It's faster for Python to use local variables than global ones. So, if one of your loops is repeatedly accessing a global variable whose value does not change between iterations of the loop, put the value in a local variable and have the loop access the local variable instead. This also applies to built-in functions:

```
def slightly_slower(asequence, adict):
    for x in asequence: adict[x] = hex(x)
def slightly_faster(asequence, adict):
    myhex = hex
    for x in asequence: adict[x] = myhex(x)
```

Here, the speedup is very modest, on the order of 5% or so.

Do not cache None. None is currently an ordinary built-in identifier, but it is scheduled to become a keyword in Python 2.3 or 2.4, so no further optimization will be needed.

List comprehensions can be faster than loops, and so can map and filter. For optimization purposes, try changing loops into list comprehensions or map and filter calls where feasible. However, the performance advantage of map and filter is nullified if you have to use a lambda or an extra level of function call. Only when you pass to map or filter a built-in function, or a function you'd have to call anyway even from an explicit loop, do you stand to gain.

The loops that you can replace most naturally with list comprehensions, or map and filter calls, are loops that build up a list by repeatedly calling append on the list. In such cases, if you know in advance the length of the resulting list, a further optimization is available. Predefine the result list to the right length (e.g., with result=[None]*N), introduce an explicit index i that starts at 0 and grows by one at each iteration of the loop, and change each call to result.append(x) into result[i]=x. The following example shows this optimization in the context of a typical microperformance benchmark script:

```
import time

def slow(asequence):
    result = [ ]
    for x in asequence: result.append(-x)
    return result

def middling(asequence):
    return [ -x for x in asequence ]

def fast(asequence):
    result = [None]*len(asequence)
    for i in xrange(len(asequence)): result[i] = -asequence[i]
    return result

biggie = xrange(500*1000)
tentimes = [None]*10
def timit(afunc):
    lobi = biggie
    start = time.clock( )
    for x in tentimes: afunc(lobi)
    stend = time.clock( )
    return "%-10s: %.2f" % (afunc.__name__, stend-start)

for afunc in slow, middling, fast, fast, middling, slow:
    print timit(afunc)
```

Running this example with python -O (on a PC with a 1.2 GHz Athlon CPU, Python 2.2.1) shows fast taking 4.30 seconds, middling 4.81 to 4.84 seconds, and slow 6.50 to 7.02 seconds, on Windows 98. The time ranges on Linux are 4.19–4.20, 5.15–5.20, and 6.91–7.00, respectively. With the current alpha version of Python 2.3 on Linux, the time ranges are 3.35–3.37 for fast, 4.61–4.64 for middling, and 6.43–6.44 for slow. In summary, on this machine, slow is 35%–40% slower than middling, and middling is about 15%–25% slower than fast (and Python 2.2 is 10%–25% slower than the current alpha of Python 2.3).

Optimizing I/O

If your program does substantial amounts of I/O, it's likely that performance bottlenecks are due to I/O, not to computation. Such programs are said to be I/O bound, rather than CPU bound. Your operating system tries to optimize I/O performance, but you can help it in a couple of ways. One such way is to perform your I/O in chunks of a size that is optimal for performance, rather than simply being convenient for your program's operations. Another way is to use threading.

From the point of view of a program's convenience and simplicity, the ideal amount of data to read or write at a time is generally small (one character or one line) or very large (an entire file at a time). That's often okay, because Python and your operating system work behind the scenes to let your program use convenient logical chunks for I/O, while arranging physical I/O operations with chunk sizes that are more attuned to performance. Reading and writing a whole file at a time is quite likely to be okay for performance as long as the file is not inordinately large. Specifically, file-at-a-time I/O is fine as long as the file's data fits in your machine's physical memory, leaving enough physical memory available for your program and operating system to perform whatever other tasks they need to perform at the same time. The hard problems of I/O-bound program performance tend to come with huge files.

If performance is an issue, don't use a file object's readline method, which is limited in the amount of chunking and buffering it can perform. Using writeline, on the other hand, gives no performance problem when that method is the one most convenient for your program. Loop directly on the file object (in Python 2.2) to get one line at a time with the best performance. If the file isn't too huge, time two versions of your program, one that loops directly on the file object and one that calls method readlines, which reads the whole file into memory. Either solution may prove faster. In Python 2.1, you can't loop directly on the file object. Instead, use method xreadlines in a for loop. xreadlines will be deprecated in Python 2.3, but if you need top performance in this specific case and need to support Python 2.1, there is no alternative.

For binary files, specifically large binary files of whose contents you need just a part on each run of your program, module mmap, covered in Chapter 14, can often give you both good performance and program simplicity.

Making an I/O-bound program multithreaded may sometimes afford substantial performance gains if you can arrange your program's architecture accordingly. Start a few worker threads devoted exclusively to I/O, have the computational threads request I/O operations from the I/O threads via Queue instances, and try to post the request for each input operation as soon as you know you'll eventually need that data. Performance will increase only if there are other tasks your computational threads can perform while an I/O thread is blocked waiting for data. Basically, you get better performance this way if you can manage to overlap computation and waiting for data, by having different threads do the computing and the waiting. See Chapter 14 for detailed coverage of Python threading and a suggested architecture.

IV

Network and Web Programming

18

Client-Side Network Protocol Modules

A program can work on the Internet as a *client* (a program that accesses resources) or as a *server* (a program that makes services available). Both kinds of program deal with protocol issues, such as how to access and communicate data, and with data formatting issues. For order and clarity, the Python library deals with these issues in several different modules. This book will cover the topics in separate chapters. This chapter deals with the modules in the Python library that support protocol issues of client programs.

Nowadays, data access can often be achieved most simply through Uniform Resource Locators (URLs). Python supports URLs with modules urlparse, urllib, and urllib2. For rarer cases, when you need fine-grained control of data access protocols normally accessed via URLs, Python supplies modules httplib and ftplib. Protocols for which URLs are often insufficient include mail (modules poplib and smtplib), Network News (module nntplib), and Telnet (module telnetlib). Python also supports the XML-RPC protocol for distributed computing with module xmlrpclib.

URL Access

A URL identifies a resource on the Internet. A URL is a string composed of several optional parts, called components, known as scheme, location, path, query, and fragment. A URL with all its parts looks something like:

```
scheme://lo.ca.ti.on/pa/th?query#fragment
```

For example, in *http://www.python.org:80/faq.cgi?src=fie*, the scheme is *http*, the location is *www.python.org:80*, the path is */faq.cgi*, the query is *src=fie*, and there is no fragment. Some of the punctuation characters form a part of one of the components they separate, while others are just separators and are part of no component. Omitting punctuation implies missing components. For example, in *mailto:me@you.com*, the scheme is *mailto*, the path is *me@you.com*, and there is no location, query, or fragment. The missing // means the URL has no location part, the missing *?* means it has no query part, and the missing # means it has no fragment part.

The urlparse Module

The urlparse module supplies functions to analyze and synthesize URL strings. In Python 2.2, the most frequently used functions of module urlparse are urljoin, urlsplit, and urlunsplit.

---

urljoin

urljoin(*base_url_string*,*relative_url_string*)

Returns a URL string *u*, obtained by joining *relative_url_string*, which may be relative, with *base_url_string*. The joining procedure that urljoin performs to obtain its result *u* may be summarized as follows:

- When either of the argument strings is empty, *u* is the other argument.

- When *relative_url_string* explicitly specifies a scheme different from that of *base_url_string*, *u* is *relative_url_string*. Otherwise, *u*'s scheme is that of *base_url_string*.

- When the scheme does not allow relative URLs (e.g., *mailto*), or *relative_url_string* explicitly specifies a location (even when it is the same as the location of *base_url_string*), all other components of *u* are those of *relative_url_string*. Otherwise, *u*'s location is that of *base_url_string*.

- *u*'s path is obtained by joining the paths of *base_url_string* and *relative_url_string* according to standard syntax for absolute and relative URL paths. For example:

```
import urlparse
urlparse.urljoin(
    'http://somehost.com/some/path/here',
    '../other/path')
# Result is: 'http://somehost.com/some/other/path'
```

---

urlsplit

urlsplit(*url_string*,*default_scheme*='',*allow_fragments*=True)

Analyzes *url_string* and returns a tuple with five string items: scheme, location, path, query, and fragment. *default_scheme* is the first item when the *url_string* lacks a scheme. When *allow_fragments* is False, the tuple's last item is always '', whether or not *url_string* has a fragment. Items corresponding to missing parts are always ''. For example:

```
urlparse.urlsplit(
    'http://www.python.org:80/faq.cgi?src=fie')
# Result is:
# ('http','www.python.org:80','/faq.cgi','src=fie','')
```

urlunsplit   urlunsplit(*url_tuple*)

url_tuple is a tuple with exactly five items, all strings. For example, any return value from a urlsplit call is an acceptable argument for urlunsplit. urlunsplit returns a URL string with the given components and the needed separators, but with no redundant separators (e.g., there is no # in the result when the fragment, *url_tuple*'s last item, is ' '). For example:

```
urlparse.urlunsplit(('http','www.python.org:80',
    '/faq.cgi','src=fie',''))
# Result is: 'http://www.python.org:80/faq.cgi?src=fie'
```

urlunsplit(urlsplit(*x*)) returns a normalized form of URL string *x*, not necessarily equal to *x* because *x* need not be normalized. For example:

```
urlparse.urlunsplit(
    urlparse.urlsplit('http://a.com/path/a?'))
# Result is: 'http://a.com/path/a'
```

In this case, the normalization ensures that redundant separators, such as the trailing *?* in the argument to urlsplit, are not present in the result.

Module urlparse also supplies functions urlparse and urlunparse. In Python 2.1, urlparse did not supply urlsplit and urlunsplit, so you had to use urlparse and urlunparse instead. urlparse and urlunparse are akin to urlsplit and urlunsplit, but are based on six components rather than five. The parse functions insert a *parameters* component between *path* and *query* using an older standard for URLs, where parameters applied to the entire path. According to the current standard, parameters apply to each part of the path separately. Therefore, the path URL component may now include parameters to subdivide in further phases of the analysis. For example:

```
u.urlsplit('http://a.com/path;with;some;params?anda=query')
# Result is: ('http','a.com','/path;with;some;params','anda=query','')
u.urlparse('http://a.com/path;with;some;params?anda=query')
# Result is: ('http','a.com','/path;with;some','params','anda=query','')
```

In this code, urlparse is able to split off the ';params' part of the parameters, but considers the '/path;with;some' substring to be the path. urlsplit considers the entire '/path;with;some;params' to be the path, returned as the third item in the result tuple. Should you then need to separate the 'with' and 'params' parameters parts of the path component, you can perform further string processing on the third item of urlsplit's return tuple, such as splitting on / and then on ;. In practice, very few URLs on the Net make use of parameters, so you may not care about this subtle distinction.

The urllib Module

The urllib module supplies simple functions to read data from URLs. urllib supports the following protocols (schemes): *http*, *https*, *ftp*, *gopher*, and *file*. *file* indicates a local file. urllib uses *file* as the default scheme for URLs that lack an explicit scheme. You can find simple, typical examples of urllib use in Chapters 22 and 23, where urllib.urlopen is used to fetch HTML and XML pages that various examples parse and analyze.

Functions

Module urllib supplies a number of functions, with urlopen being the most frequently used.

quote	quote(*str*,*safe*='/')
	Returns a copy of *str* where special characters are changed into Internet-standard quoted form %*xx*. Does not quote alphanumeric characters, spaces, any of the characters '_,.-', nor any of the characters in string *safe*.
quote_plus	quote_plus(*str*, *safe*='/')
	Like quote, but also changes spaces into plus signs.
unquote	unquote(*str*)
	Returns a copy of *str* where each quoted form %*xx* is changed into the corresponding character.
unquote_plus	unquote_plus(*str*)
	Like unquote, but also changes plus signs into spaces.
urlcleanup	urlcleanup( )
	Clears the cache of function urlretrieve, covered later in this section.
urlencode	urlencode(*query*,*doseq*=False)
	Returns a string with the URL-encoded form of *query*. *query* can be either a sequence of (*name, value*) pairs, or a mapping, in which case the resulting string encodes the mapping's (*key, value*) pairs. For example:

```
urllib.urlencode([('ans',42),('key','val')])
# 'ans=42&key=val'
urllib.urlencode({'ans':42, 'key':'val'})
# 'key=val&ans=42'
```

Remember that the order of items in a dictionary is not defined: if you need the URL-encoded form to have the key/value pairs in a specific order, use a sequence as the *query* argument, as in the first call in this example.

When *doseq* is true, any *value* in *query* that is a sequence is encoded as separate parameters, one per item in *value*. For example:

```
u.urlencode([('K',('x','y','z'))],1)
# 'K=x&K=y&K=z'
u.urlencode([('K',('x','y','z'))],0)
# 'K=%28%27x%27%2C+%27y%27%2C+%27z%27%29'
```

When *doseq* is false (the default), each value is encoded as the quote_plus of its string form given by built-in str, whether the value is a sequence or not.

---

urlopen

urlopen(*urlstring,data*=None)

Accesses the given URL and returns a read-only file-like object *f*. *f* supplies file-like methods read, readline, readlines, and close, as well as two others:

f.geturl( )

> Returns the URL of *f*. This may differ from *urlstring* both because of normalization (as mentioned for function urlunsplit earlier) and because the server may issue HTTP redirects (i.e., indications that the requested data is located elsewhere). urllib supports redirects transparently, and method geturl lets you check for them if you want.

f.info( )

> Returns an instance *m* of class Message of module mimetools, covered in Chapter 21. The main use of *m* is as a container of headers holding metadata about *f*. For example, *m*['Content-Type'] is the MIME type and subtype of the data in *f*. You can also access this information by calling *m*'s methods *m*.gettype( ), *m*.getmaintype( ), and *m*.getsubtype( ).

When *data* is None and *urlstring*'s scheme is *http*, urlopen sends a GET request. When *data* is not None, *urlstring*'s scheme must be *http*, and urlopen sends a POST request. *data* must then be in URL-encoded form, and you normally prepare it with function urlencode, covered earlier in this section.

urlopen can transparently use proxies that do not require authentication. Set environment variables http_proxy, ftp_proxy, and gopher_proxy to the proxies' URLs to exploit this. You normally perform such settings in your system's environment, in platform-dependent ways, before you start Python. On the Macintosh only, urlopen transparently and implicitly retrieves proxy URLs from your Internet configuration settings. urlopen does not support proxies that require authentication—for such advanced needs, use the richer and more complicated library module urllib2, covered in a moment.

urlretrieve urlretrieve(*urlstring*,*filename*=None,*reporthook*=None,*data*=None)

Similar to urlopen(*urlstring*,*data*), but instead returns a pair (*f*,*m*). *f* is a string that specifies the path to a file on the local file-system. *m* is an instance of class Message of module mimetools, like the result of method info called on the result value of urlopen, covered earlier in this section.

When *filename* is None, urlretrieve copies retrieved data to a temporary local file, and *f* is the path to the temporary local file. When *filename* is not None, urlretrieve copies retrieved data to the file named *filename*, and *f* is *filename*. When *reporthook* is not None, it must be a callable with three arguments, as in the function:

```
def reporthook(block_count, block_size, file_size):
    print block_count
```

urlretrieve calls *reporthook* zero or more times while retrieving data. At each call, it passes *block_count*, the number of blocks of data retrieved so far; *block_size*, the size in bytes of each block; and *file_size*, the total size of the file in bytes. urlretrieve passes *file_size* as -1 when unable to determine file size, which depends on the protocol involved and on how completely the server implements that protocol. The purpose of *reporthook* is to let your program give graphical or textual feedback to the user about the progress of the file retrieval operation that urlretrieve performs.

The FancyURLopener class

You normally use module urllib through the functions it supplies (most often urlopen). To customize urllib's functionality, however, you can subclass urllib's FancyURLopener class and bind an instance of your subclass to attribute _urlopener of module urllib. The customizable aspects of an instance *f* of a subclass of FancyURLopener are the following.

---

prompt_user_ *f*.prompt_user_passwd(*host*,*realm*)
passwd
Returns a pair (*user*,*password*) to use to authenticate access to *host* in the security *realm*. The default implementation in class FancyURLopener prompts the user for this data in interactive text mode. Your subclass can override this method for such purposes as interacting with the user via a GUI or fetching authentication data from persistent storage.

---

version *f*.version

The string that *f* uses to identify itself to the server, for example via the User-Agent header in the HTTP protocol. You can override this attribute by subclassing, or rebind it directly on an instance of FancyURLopener.

The urllib2 Module

The urllib2 module is a rich, highly customizable superset of module urllib. urllib2 lets you work directly with rather advanced aspects of protocols such as HTTP. For example, you can send requests with customized headers as well as URL-encoded POST bodies, and handle authentication in various realms, in both Basic and Digest forms, directly or via HTTP proxies.

In the rest of this section, I cover only the ways in which urllib2 lets your program customize these advanced aspects of URL retrieval. I do not try to impart the advanced knowledge of HTTP and other network protocols, independent of Python, that you need to make full use of urllib2's rich functionality. As an HTTP tutorial, I recommend *Python Web Programming*, by Steve Holden (New Riders): it offers good coverage of HTTP basics with examples coded in Python, and a good bibliography if you need further details about network protocols.

Functions

urllib2 supplies a function urlopen basically identical to urllib's urlopen. To customize urllib2's behavior, you can install, before calling urlopen, any number of handlers grouped into an opener using the build_opener and install_opener functions.

You can also optionally pass to urlopen an instance of class Request instead of a URL string. Such an instance may include both a URL string and supplementary information on how to access it, as covered shortly in "The Request class."

---

build_opener   build_opener(*handlers*)

Creates and returns an instance of class OpenerDirector, covered later in this chapter, with the given *handlers*. Each handler can be a subclass of class BaseHandler, instantiable without arguments, or an instance of such a subclass, however instantiated. build_opener adds instances of various handler classes provided by module urllib2 in front of the handlers you specify, to handle proxies, unknown schemes, the *http*, *file*, and *https* schemes, HTTP errors, and HTTP redirects. However, if you have instances or subclasses of said classes in *handlers*, this indicates that you want to override these defaults.

---

install_opener   install_opener(*opener*)

Installs *opener* as the opener for further calls to urlopen. *opener* can be an instance of class OpenerDirector, such as the result of a call to function build_opener, or any signature-compatible object.

---

urlopen   urlopen(*url*,*data*=None)

Almost identical to the urlopen function in module urllib. However, you customize behavior via the opener and handler classes of urllib2, covered later in this chapter, rather than via class FancyURLopener as in module urllib. Argument *url* can be a

URL string, like for the urlopen function in module urllib. Alternatively, *url* can be an instance of class Request, covered in the next section.

The Request class

You can optionally pass to function urlopen an instance of class Request instead of a URL string. Such an instance can embody both a URL and, optionally, other information on how to access the target URL.

Request

class Request(*urlstring,data*=None,*headers*={})

urlstring is the URL that this instance of class Request embodies. For example, if there are no *data* and *headers*, calling:

urllib2.urlopen(urllib2.Request(*urlstring*))

is just like calling:

urllib2.urlopen(*urlstring*)

When *data* is not None, the Request constructor implicitly calls on the new instance *r* its method *r*.add_data(*data*). *headers* must be a mapping of header names to header values. The Request constructor executes the equivalent of the loop:

for *k,v* in *headers*.items( ): *r*.add_header(*k,v*)

An instance *r* of class Request supplies the following methods.

add_data

r.add_data(*data*)

Sets *data* as *r*'s data. Calling urlopen(*r*) then becomes like calling urlopen(*r,data*), i.e., it requires *r*'s scheme to be *http*, and uses a POST request with a body of *data*, which must be a URL-encoded string.

Despite its name, method add_data does not necessarily add the *data*. If *r* already had data, set in *r*'s constructor or by previous calls to *r*.add_data, the latest call to *r*.add_data replaces the previous value of *r*'s data with the new given one. In particular, *r*.add_data(None) removes *r*'s previous data, if any.

add_header

r.add_header(*key,value*)

Adds a header with the given *key* and *value* to *r*'s headers. If *r*'s scheme is *http*, *r*'s headers are sent as part of the request. When you add more than one header with the same *key*, later additions overwrite previous ones, so out of all headers with one given *key*, only the one given last matters.

get_data	`r.get_data( )`
	Returns the data of `r`, either `None` or a URL-encoded string.
get_full_url	`r.get_full_url( )`
	Returns the URL of `r`, as given in the constructor for `r`.
get_host	`r.get_host( )`
	Returns the host component of `r`'s URL.
get_selector	`r.get_selector( )`
	Returns the selector components of `r`'s URL (i.e., the path and all following components).
get_type	`r.get_type( )`
	Returns the scheme component of `r`'s URL (i.e., the protocol).
has_data	`r.has_data( )`
	Like `r.get_data( )` is not `None`.
set_proxy	`r.set_proxy(host,scheme)`
	Sets `r` to use a proxy at the given *host* and *scheme* for accessing `r`'s URL.

The OpenerDirector class

An instance *d* of class `OpenerDirector` collects instances of handler classes and orchestrates their use to open URLs of various schemes and to handle errors. Normally, you create *d* by calling function `build_opener`, and then install it by calling function `install_opener`. For advanced uses, you may also access various attributes and methods of *d*, but this is a rare need and I do not cover it further in this book.

Handler classes

Module `urllib2` supplies a class `BaseHandler` to use as the superclass of any custom handler classes you write. `urllib2` also supplies many concrete subclasses of `BaseHandler` that handle schemes *gopher*, *ftp*, *http*, *https*, and *file*, as well as authentication, proxies, redirects, and errors. Writing custom handlers is an advanced topic and I do not cover it further in this book.

Handling authentication

`urllib2`'s default opener does not include authentication handlers. To get authentication, call `build_opener` to build an opener that includes instances of classes

HTTPBasicAuthHandler, ProxyBasicAuthHandler, HTTPDigestAuthHandler, and/or ProxyDigestAuthHandler, depending on whether you need the authentication to be directly in HTTP or to a proxy, and on whether you need Basic or Digest authentication.

To instantiate each of these authentication handlers, use an instance *x* of class HTTPPasswordMgrWithDefaultRealm as the only argument to the authentication handler's constructor. You normally use the same *x* to instantiate all the authentication handlers you need. To record users and passwords for given authentication realms and URLs, call *x*.add_password one or more times.

add_password	*x*.add_password(*realm,URLs,user,password*)

Records in *x* the pair (*user,password*) as the authentication in the given *realm* of applicable URLs, as determined by argument *URLs*. *realm* is either a string, the name of an authentication realm, or None, to apply this authentication as the default for any realm not specifically recorded. *URLs* is a URL string or a sequence of URL strings. A URL *u* is deemed applicable for this authentication if there is an item *u1* of *URLs* such that the location components of *u* and *u1* are equal, and the path component of *u1* is a prefix of that of *u*. Note that other components (scheme, query, and fragment) don't matter to applicability for authentication purposes.

The following example shows how to use urllib2 with basic HTTP authentication:

```
import urllib2

x = urllib2.HTTPPasswordMgrWithDefaultRealm( )
x.add_password(None, 'http://myhost.com/', 'auser',
               'apassword')
auth = urrlib2.HTTPBasicAuthHandler(x)
opener = urllib2.build_opener(auth)
urllib2.install_opener(opener)

flob = urllib2.urlopen('http://myhost.com/index.html')
for line in flob.readlines( ): print line,
```

Email Protocols

Most email today is sent via servers that implement the Simple Mail Transport Protocol (SMTP) and received via servers that implement the Post Office Protocol Version 3 (POP3). These protocols are supported by the Python standard library modules smtplib and poplib, respectively. Some servers, instead of or in addition to POP3, implement the richer and more advanced Internet Message Access Protocol Version 4 (IMAP4), supported by the Python standard library module imaplib, which I do not cover in this book.

The poplib Module

The poplib module supplies a class POP3 to access a POP mailbox.

POP3   class POP3(*host,port*=110)

Returns an instance *p* of class POP3 connected to the given *host* and *port*.

Instance *p* supplies many methods, of which the most frequently used are the following.

---

dele   *p*.dele(*msgnum*)

Marks message *msgnum* for deletion. The server performs deletions when this connection terminates by a call to method *quit*. Returns the response string.

---

list   *p*.list(*msgnum*=None)

Returns a pair (*response,messages*) where *response* is the response string and *messages* is a list of strings, each of two words '*msgnum bytes*', giving the message number and the length in bytes of each message in the mailbox. When *msgnum* is not None, list *messages* has only one item, a string with two words: *msgnum* as requested, and the length *bytes*.

---

pass_   *p*.pass_(*password*)

Sends the password. Must be called after method user. The trailing underscore in the function's name is necessary because pass is a Python keyword. Returns the response string.

---

quit   *p*.quit( )

Ends the session and performs the deletions that were requested by calls to method dele. Returns the response string.

---

retr   *p*.retr(*msgnum*)

Returns a three-item tuple (*response,lines,bytes*), where *response* is the response string, *lines* is a list of all lines in message *msgnum*, and *bytes* is the total number of bytes in the message.

---

set_debuglevel   *p*.set_debuglevel(*debug_level*)

Sets the debug level to integer *debug_level*: 0, the default, for no debugging; 1 to get a modest amount of debugging output; 2 or more to get a complete output trace of all control information exchanged with the server.

---

stat	`p.stat( )`
	Returns a pair (*num_messages,bytes*), where *num_messages* is the number of messages in the mailbox, and *bytes* is the total number of bytes.

top	`p.top(msgnum,maxlines)`
	Like retr, but returns no more than *maxlines* lines of text from the message after the headers. Can be useful to view the start of long messages.

user	`p.user(username)`
	Sends the username. Must be followed by a call to method pass_.

The smtplib Module

The smtplib module supplies a class SMTP to send mail to any SMTP server.

SMTP	class `SMTP([host,port=25])`
	Returns an instance *s* of class SMTP. When *host* (and optionally *port*) is given, implicitly calls *s*.connect(*host,port*).

Instance *s* supplies many methods, of which the most frequently used are the following.

connect	`s.connect(host=127.0.0.1,port=25)`
	Connects to an SMTP server on the given *host* (by default, the local host) and *port* (port 25 is the default port for the SMTP service).

login	`s.login(user,password)`
	Logs in to the server with the given *user* and *password*. Needed only if the SMTP server requires authentication.

quit	`s.quit( )`
	Terminates the SMTP session.

sendmail	`s.sendmail(from_addr,to_addrs,msg_string)`
	Sends mail message *msg_string* from the sender whose email address is in string *from_addr* to each of the recipients whose email addresses are the items of list *to_addrs*. *msg_string* must be a

complete RFC-822 message in a single multiline string: the headers, an empty line for separation, followed by the body. *from_addr* and *to_addrs* are used only to direct the mail transport, not to add or change headers within *msg_string*. To prepare RFC-822-compliant messages, use package email, covered in Chapter 21.

The HTTP and FTP Protocols

Modules urllib and urllib2 are most often the handiest ways to access servers for *http*, *https*, and *ftp* protocols. The Python standard library also supplies specific modules to use for these data access protocols.

The httplib Module

Module httplib supplies a class HTTPConnection to connect to an HTTP server.

HTTPConnection	class HTTPConnection(*host,port*=80)

Returns an instance *h* of class HTTPConnection, ready for connection (but not yet connected) to the given *host* and *port*.

Instance *h* supplies several methods, of which the most frequently used are the following.

close	*h*.close( )

Closes the connection to the HTTP server.

getresponse	*h*.getresponse( )

Returns an instance *r* of class HTTPResponse, which represents the response received from the HTTP server. Call after method request has returned. Instance *r* supplies the following attributes and methods:

r.getheader(*name,default*=None)
   Returns the contents of header *name*, or *default* if no such header exists.

r.msg
   An instance of class Message of module mimetools, covered in Chapter 21. You can use *r*.msg to access the response's headers and body.

r.read( )
   Returns a string that is the body of the server's response.

r.reason

The string that the server gave as the reason for errors or anomalies. If the request was successful, r.reason could, for example, be 'OK'.

r.status

An integer, the status code that the server returned. If the request was successful, r.status should be between 200 and 299 according to the HTTP standards. Values between 400 and 599 are typical error codes, again according to HTTP standards. For example, 404 is the error code that a server sends when the page you request cannot be found.

r.version

10 if the server supports only HTTP 1.0, 11 if the server supports HTTP 1.1.

---

request h.request(*command,URL,data*=None,*headers*={})

Sends a request to the HTTP server. *command* is an HTTP command string, such as 'GET' or 'POST'. *URL* is an HTTP selector (i.e., a URL string without the scheme and location components—just the path component, possibly followed by query and/or fragment components). *data*, if not None, is a string sent as the body of the request, normally meaningful only for such commands as 'POST' and 'PUT'. request computes and sends the Content-Length header to describe the length of *data*. To send other headers, pass them as part of dictionary argument *headers*, with the header name as the key and the header contents as the corresponding value.

Module httplib also supplies class HTTPSConnection, used in exactly the same way as class HTTPConnection but supporting connections that use protocol *https* rather than protocol *http*.

The ftplib Module

The ftplib module supplies a class FTP to connect to an FTP server.

FTP class FTP([*host*[,*user,passwd*='']])

Returns an instance *f* of class FTP. When *host* is given, implicitly calls *f*.connect(*host*). When *user* (and optionally *passwd*) is also given, implicitly calls *f*.login(*user,passwd*) afterward.

Instance *f* supplies many methods, of which the most frequently used are the following.

connect

f.connect(*host,port*=21)

Connects to an FTP server on the given *host* and *port*. Call once per instance f, as f's first method call. Don't call if *host* was given on creation.

cwd

f.cwd(*pathname*)

Sets the current directory on the FTP server to *pathname*.

delete

f.delete(*filename*)

Tells the FTP server to delete a file, and returns a string, the server's response.

login

f.login(*user*='anonymous',*passwd*='')

Logs in to the FTP server. When *user* is 'anonymous' and *passwd* is '', login determines the real user and host and sends *user@host* as the password, as normal anonymous FTP conventions require. Call once per instance of f, as the first method call on f after connecting.

mkd

f.mkd(*pathname*)

Makes a new directory, named *pathname*, on the FTP server.

pwd

f.pwd( )

Returns the current directory on the FTP server.

quit

f.quit( )

Closes the connection to the FTP server. Call as the last method call on f.

rename

f.rename(*oldname,newname*)

Tells the FTP server to rename a file from *oldname* to *newname*.

retrbinary

f.retrbinary(*command,callback,blocksize*=8192,*rest*=None)

Retrieves data in binary mode. *command* is a string with an appropriate FTP command, typically 'RETR *filename*'. *callback* is a callable that retrbinary calls for each block of data returned, passing the block of data, a string, as the only argument. *blocksize* is the maximum size of each block of data. When *rest* is not None, it's the offset in bytes from the start of the file at which you want to start the retrieval, if the FTP server supports the 'REST' command. When *rest* is not None and the FTP server does not support the 'REST' command, retrbinary raises an exception.

retrlines f.retrlines(*command*,*callback*=None)

Retrieves data in text mode. *command* is a string with an appropriate FTP command, typically 'RETR *filename*' or 'LIST'. *callback* is a callable that retrlines calls for each line of text returned, passing the line of text, a string, as the only argument (without the end-of-line marker). When *callback* is None, retrlines writes the lines of text to sys.stdout.

rmd f.rmd(*pathname*)

Removes directory *pathname* on the FTP server.

sendcmd f.sendcmd(*command*)

Sends string *command* as a command to the server and returns the server's response string. Suitable only for commands that don't open data connections.

set_pasv f.set_pasv(*pasv*)

Sets passive mode on if *pasv* is true, off if false. Passive mode defaults to on.

size f.size(*filename*)

Returns the size in bytes of the named file on the FTP server, or None if unable to determine the file's size.

storbinary f.storbinary(*command*,*file*,*blocksize*=8192)

Stores data in binary mode. *command* is a string with an appropriate FTP command, typically 'STOR *filename*'. *file* is a file open in binary mode, which storbinary reads, repeatedly calling *file*.read(*blocksize*), to obtain the data to transfer to the FTP server.

storlines f.storlines(*command*,*file*)

Stores data in text mode. *command* is a string with an appropriate FTP command, typically 'STOR *filename*'. *file* is a file open in text mode, which storlines reads, repeatedly calling *file*.readline( ), to obtain the data to transfer to the FTP server.

Here is a typical, simple example of ftplib use in an interactive interpreter session:

```
>>> import ftplib
>>> f = ftplib.FTP('ftp.python.org')
>>> f.login( )
'230 Anonymous access granted, restrictions apply.'
```

```
>>> f.retrlines('LIST')
drwxrwxr-x   4 webmaster webmaster        512 Oct 12  2001 pub
'226 Transfer complete.'
>>> f.cwd('pub')
'250 CWD command successful.'
>>> f.retrlines('LIST')
drwxrwsr-x   2 barry      webmaster       512 Oct 12  2001 jython
lrwx------   1 root       ftp             25 Aug  3  2001 python -> www.python.
org/ftp/python
drwxrwxr-x  43 webmaster webmaster       2560 Sep  3 17:22 www.python.org
'226 Transfer complete.'
>>> f.cwd('python')
'250 CWD command successful.'
>>> f.retrlines('LIST')
drwxrwxr-x   2 webmaster webmaster        512 Aug 23  2001 2.0
  [ many result lines snipped ]
drwxrwxr-x   2 webmaster webmaster        512 Aug  2  2001 wpy
'226 Transfer complete.'
>>> f.retrlines('RETR README')
Python Distribution
====================

Most subdirectories have a README or INDEX files explaining the
contents.
  [ many result lines snipped ]
gzipped version of this file, and 'get misc.tar.gz' will fetch a
gzipped tar archive of the misc subdir.
'226 Transfer complete.'
```

In this case, the following far simpler code is equivalent:

```
print urllib.urlopen('ftp://ftp.python.org/pub/python/README').read( )
```

However, ftplib affords much more detailed control of FTP operations than urllib does. Thus, in some cases, ftplib may be useful for your programs.

Network News

Network News, also known as Usenet News, is mostly transmitted with the Network News Transport Protocol (NNTP). The Python standard library supports this protocol in its module nntplib. The nntplib module supplies a class NNTP to connect to an NNTP server.

NNTP   class NNTP(
                  host,port=119,user=None,passwd=None,readermode=False)

                Returns an instance *n* of class NNTP connected to the given *host* and
                port, and optionally authenticated with the given *user* and *passwd* if
                user is not None. When *readermode* is True, also sends a 'mode
                reader' command; you may need this, depending on what NNTP
                server you connect to and on what NNTP commands you send to
                that server.

Response Strings

An instance *n* of NNTP supplies many methods. Each of *n*'s methods returns a tuple whose first item is a string (referred to as *response* in the following section) that is the response from the NNTP server to the NNTP command corresponding to the method (method post just returns the *response* string, not a tuple). Each method returns the *response* string just as the NNTP server supplies it. The string starts with an integer in decimal form (the integer is known as the return code), followed by a space, followed by more text.

For some commands, the extra text after the return code is just a comment or explanation supplied by the NNTP server. For other commands, the NNTP standard specifies the format of the text that follows the return code on the response line. In those cases, the relevant method also parses the text in question, yielding other items in the method's resulting tuple, so your code need not perform such parsing itself; rather, you can just access further items in the method's result tuple, as specified in the following sections.

Return codes of the form 2*xx*, for any two digits *xx*, are success codes (i.e., they indicate that the corresponding NNTP command succeeded). Return codes of other forms, such as 4*xx* and 5*xx*, indicate failures in the corresponding NNTP command. In these cases, the method does not return a result. Rather, the method raises an instance of exception class nntplib.NNTPError or some appropriate subclass of it, such as NNTPTemporaryError for errors that may (or may not) be automatically resolved if you try the operation again, or NNTPPermanentError for errors that are sure to occur again if you retry. When a method of an NNTP instance raises an NNTPError instance *e*, the server's response string, starting with a return code such as 4*xx*, is accessible as str(*e*).

Methods

The most frequently used methods of an NNTP instance *n* are as follows.

---

article   *n*.article(*id*)

id is a string, either an article ID enclosed in angle brackets (<>) or an article number in the current group. Returns a tuple of three strings and a list (*response,number,id,list*), where *number* is the article number in the current group, *id* is the article ID enclosed in angle brackets, and *list* is a list of strings that are the lines in the entire article (headers then body, with an empty-line separator, and without end-of-line characters).

---

body   *n*.body(*id,file*)

id is a string, either an article ID enclosed in angle brackets (<>) or an article number in the current group. Returns a tuple of three strings and a list (*response,number,id,list*), where *number* is the article number in the current group, *id* is the article ID enclosed in angle brackets, and *list* is a list of strings that are the lines in the article's body, without end-of-line characters. When *file* is not None, it can be either a string naming a file that head then opens for

---

writing, or a file object already open for writing. In either case, body writes the article's body to the file, and *list* in the tuple it returns is an empty list.

group   *n*.group(*group_name*)

Makes *group_name* the current group, and returns a tuple of five strings (*response,count,first,last,group_name*), where *count* is the total number of articles in the group, *last* is the number of the most recent article, *first* is the number of the oldest article, and *group_name* is the group's name. Normally, the *group_name* that is the last item in the returned tuple will be the same as the one you requested (i.e., the argument to *n*.group). However, an NNTP server could conceivably set up aliases, or synonyms; therefore, you should always check the last item of the returned tuple to ascertain what newsgroup has been in fact set as the current one.

head   *n*.head(*id*)

Returns an article's headers. *id* is a string, either an article ID enclosed in angle brackets (<>) or an article number in the current group. head returns a tuple of three strings and a list (*response,number,id,list*), where *number* is the article number in the current group, *id* is the article ID enclosed in angle brackets, and *list* is a list of strings that are the lines in the article's headers, without end-of-line characters.

last   *n*.last( )

Returns a tuple of three strings (*response,number,id*), where *number* is the article number in the current group and *id* is the article ID, enclosed in angle brackets, for the last article in the current group.

list   *n*.list( )

Returns a pair (*response,group_stats*), where *group_stats* is a list of tuples with information about each group on the server. Each item of *group_stats* is a tuple of four strings (*group_name,last,first,group_flag*), where *group_name* is the group's name, *last* is the number of the most recent article, *first* is the number of the oldest article, and *group_flag* is 'y' when you're allowed to post, 'n' when you're not allowed to post, and 'm' when the group is moderated.

newgroups   *n*.newgroups(*date,time*)

date is a string indicating a date, of the form 'yymmdd'. *time* is a string indicating a time, of the form 'hhmmss'. newgroups returns a pair (*response,group_names*), where *group_names* is the list of the names of groups created since the given date and time.

newnews   *n*.newnews(*group,date,time*)

group is a string that is either a group name, meaning you only want data about articles in that group, or '*', meaning you want data about articles in any newsgroup on the server. *date* is a string indicating a date, of the form 'yymmdd'. *time* is a string indicating a time, of the form 'hhmmss'. newnews returns a pair (*response,article_ids*), where *article_ids* is the list of the identifiers of articles received since the given date and time.

next   *n*.next( )

Returns a tuple of three strings (*response,number,id*), where *number* is the article number in the current group and *id* is the article ID, enclosed in angle brackets, for the next article in the current group. The current group is set by calling *n*.group. Each time you call *n*.next, you receive information about another article (i.e., *n* implicitly maintains a pointer to a current article within the group and advances the pointer on each call to *n*.next). When there is no next article (i.e., the current article is the last one in the current group), *n*.next raises NNTPTemporaryError.

post   *n*.post(*file*)

Posts an article to the current group, reading it from *file*. *file* is a file-like object open for reading; post reads the article's headers and body from the file by repeatedly calling *file*.readline. Note that *file* must contain all needed headers, then an empty-line separator, then the body. post returns a string, the *response* from the server to the posting request.

quit   *n*.quit( )

Closes the connection to the NNTP server. Call as the last method call on *n*.

stat   *n*.stat(*id*)

id is a string, either an article ID enclosed in angle brackets, or an article number in the current group. Returns a tuple of three strings (*response,number,id*), where *number* is the article number in the current group and *id* is the article ID enclosed in angle brackets.

Example

Here is a typical, simple example of nntplib use in an interactive interpreter session, using the free public NNTP server at sunsite.dk:

```
>>> import nntplib
>>> n = nntplib.NNTP('sunsite.dk')
```

```
>>> response, groups = n.list( )
>>> print response
215 Newsgroups in form "group high low flags".
>>> print 'sunsite.dk carries', len(groups), 'newsgroups'
sunsite.dk carries 679 newsgroups
>>> linux_groups = [g for g in groups if g[0].startswith('linux')]
>>> print 'sunsite.dk carries', len(linux_groups), 'newsgroups about linux'
sunsite.dk carries 311 newsgroups about linux
>>> n.group('linux.postgres')
('211 13 974 986 linux.postgres', '13', '974', '986', 'linux.postgres')
>>> response, artnum, artid, headers = n.head('974')
>>> len(headers)
17
>>> [h for h in headers if h.startswith('Subject:')]
['Subject: newbie question on networking in postgresql']
>>> n.quit( )
'205 .'
```

Telnet

Telnet is an old protocol, specified by RFC 854 (see *http://www.faqs.org/rfcs/ rfc854.html*), and normally used for interactive user sessions. The Python standard library supports this protocol in its module telnetlib. Module telnetlib supplies a class Telnet to connect to a Telnet server.

Telnet	class Telnet(*host*=None,*port*=23)
	Returns an instance *t* of class Telnet. When *host* (and optionally *port*) is given, implicitly calls *t*.open(*host*,*port*).

Instance *t* supplies many methods, of which the most frequently used are as follows.

close	*t*.close( )
	Closes the connection.

expect	*t*.expect(*res*,*timeout*=None)
	Reads data from the connection until it matches any of the regular expressions that are the items of list *res*, or until *timeout* seconds elapse when *timeout* is not None. Regular expressions and match objects are covered in Chapter 9. Returns a tuple of three items (*i*,*mo*,*txt*), where *i* is the index in *res* of the regular expression that matched, *mo* is the match object, and *txt* is all the text read until the match, included. Raises EOFError when the connection is closed and no data is available; otherwise, when it gets no match, returns (-1,None,*txt*), where *txt* is all the text read, or possibly '' if nothing was read before a timeout. Results are non-deterministic

if more than one item in *res* can match, or if any of the items in *res* include greedy parts (such as '.*').

interact   `t.interact( )`

Enters interactive mode, connecting standard input and output to the two channels of the connection, like a dumb Telnet client.

open   `t.open(host,port=23)`

Connects to a Telnet server on the given *host* and *port*. Call once per instance *t*, as *t*'s first method call. Don't call if *host* was given on creation.

read_all   `t.read_all( )`

Reads data from the connection until the connection is closed, then returns all available data. Blocks until the time the connection is closed.

read_eager   `t.read_eager( )`

Reads and returns everything that can be read from the connection without blocking; may be the empty string ''. Raises EOFError if the connection is closed and no data is available.

read_some   `t.read_some( )`

Reads and returns at least one byte of data from the connection, unless the connection is closed, in which case it returns ''. Blocks until at least one byte of data is available.

read_until   `t.read_until(expected,timeout=None)`

Reads data from the connection until it encounters string *expected*, or until *timeout* seconds elapse when *timeout* is not None. Returns whatever data is available at that time, or possibly the empty string ''. Raises EOFError if the connection is closed and no data is available.

write   `t.write(astring)`

Writes string *astring* to the connection.

Distributed Computing

There are many standards for distributed computing, from simple Remote Procedure Call (RPC) ones to rich object-oriented ones such as CORBA. You can find several third-party Python modules supporting these standards on the Internet.

The Python standard library comes with support for both server and client use of a simple yet powerful standard known as XML-RPC. For in-depth coverage of XML-RPC, I recommend the book *Programming Web Services with XML-RPC*, by Simon St. Laurent and Joe Johnson (O'Reilly). XML-RPC uses HTTP as the underlying transport and encodes requests and replies in XML. For server-side support, see "The SimpleXMLRPCServer module" in Chapter 19. Client-side support is supplied by module xmlrpclib.

The xmlrcplib module supports a class ServerProxy, which you instantiate to connect to an XML-RPC server. An instance *s* of ServerProxy is a proxy for the server it connects to. In other words, you call arbitrary methods on *s*, and *s* packages up the method name and argument values as an XML-RPC request, sends the request to the XML-RPC server, receives the server's response, and unpackages the response as the method's result. The arguments to such method calls can be of any type supported by XML-RPC:

Boolean
> Constant attributes True and False of module xmlrpclib (since module xlmrpclib predates the introduction of bool into Python, it does not use Python's built-in True and False values for this purpose)

Integers, floating-point numbers, strings, arrays
> Passed and returned as Python int, float, Unicode, and list values

Structures
> Passed and returned as Python dict values whose keys must be strings

Dates
> Passed as instances of class xmlrpclib.DateTime; value is represented in seconds since the epoch, as in module time (see Chapter 12)

Binary data
> Passed as instances of class xmlrpclib.Binary; value is an arbitrary string of bytes

Module xmlrpclib supplies two factory functions.

---

binary   binary(*bytestring*)

> Creates and returns an instance of Binary wrapping the given *bytestring*.

---

boolean   boolean(*x*)

> Creates and returns an instance of Boolean with the truth value of *x*.

===

Module xmlrpclib supplies several classes.

Binary   class Binary(*x*)

> *x* is a Python string of arbitrary bytes. *b* represents the same bytes as an XML-RPC binary object.

Boolean	class Boolean(*x*)
	x is any Python value, and *b* has the same truth value as *x*.

DateTime	class DateTime(*x*)
	x is a number of seconds since the epoch, as used in module time, covered in Chapter 12.

ServerProxy	class ServerProxy(*url*)

If the server at the given *url* supports introspection, *s* supplies an attribute *s*.server that in turn supplies three methods:

s.server.listMethods( )
> Returns a list of strings, one per each method supported by the server.

s.server.methodSignature(*name*)
> Returns a list of strings, each a signature of method *name* on the server. A signature string is composed of type names separated by commas: first the type of the return value, then the type of each argument. When method *name* has no defined signature, *s*.server.methodSignature(*name*) returns some object that is not a list.

s.server.methodHelp(*name*)
> Returns a string with help about method *name*. The string can be either plain text or HTML. When the method *name* has no defined help, *s*.server.methodHelp(*name*) returns an empty string ' '.

The following example uses xmlrpclib to access O'Reilly's Meerkat open wire service (see *http://www.oreillynet.com/meerkat/* for more information about Meerkat) and displays the last few news items about Python.

```
import xmlrpclib

proxy = xmlrpclib.ServerProxy(
    'http://www.oreillynet.com/meerkat/xml-rpc/server.php')
results = proxy.meerkat.getItems({'search':'Python', 'num_items':7})

want_keys = 'title link description'.split( )
n = 0
for result in results:
    n = n + 1
    for key in want_keys:
        print '%d. %s: %s' % (n, key.title( ), result.get(key))
    print
```

19

Sockets and Server-Side Network Protocol Modules

To communicate with the Internet, programs use devices known as *sockets*. The Python library supports sockets through module socket, as well as wrapping them into higher-level modules covered in Chapter 18. To help you write server programs, the Python library also supplies higher-level modules to use as frameworks for socket servers. Standard and third-party Python modules and extensions also support timed and asynchronous socket operations. This chapter covers socket, the server-side framework modules, and the essentials of other, more advanced modules.

The modules covered in this chapter offer many conveniences compared to C-level socket programming. However, in the end, the modules rely on native socket functionality supplied by the underlying operating system. While it is often possible to write effective network clients by using just the modules covered in Chapter 18, without needing to understand sockets, writing effective network servers most often does require some understanding of sockets. Thus, the lower-level module socket is covered in this chapter and not in Chapter 18, even though both clients and servers use sockets.

However, I only cover the ways in which module socket lets your program access sockets; I do not try to impart the detailed understanding of sockets, and of other aspects of network behavior independent of Python, that you may need to make use of socket's functionality. To understand socket behavior in detail on any kind of platform, I recommend W. Richard Stevens' *Unix Network Programming, Volume 1* (Prentice-Hall). Higher-level modules are simpler and more powerful, but a detailed understanding of the underlying technology is always useful, and sometimes it can prove indispensable.

The socket Module

The socket module supplies a factory function, also named socket, that you call to generate a socket object s. You perform network operations by calling methods on s. In a client program, you connect to a server by calling s.connect. In a server program, you wait for clients to connect by calling s.bind and s.listen. When a client requests a connection, you accept the request by calling s.accept, which returns another socket object $s1$ connected to the client. Once you have a connected socket object, you transmit data by calling its method send, and receive data by calling its method recv.

Python supports both current Internet Protocol (IP) standards. IPv4 is more wide-spread, while IPv6 is newer. In IPv4, a network address is a pair (*host,port*), where *host* is a Domain Name System (DNS) hostname such as 'www.python.org' or a dotted-quad IP address string such as '194.109.137.226'. *port* is an integer indicating a socket's port number. In IPv6, a network address is a tuple (*host, port, flowinfo, scopeid*). Since IPv6 infrastructure is not yet widely deployed, I do not cover IPv6 further in this book. When *host* is a DNS hostname, Python implicitly looks up the name, using your platform's DNS infrastructure, and uses the dotted-quad IP address corresponding to that name.

Module socket supplies an exception class error. Functions and methods of the module raise error instances to diagnose socket-specific errors. Module socket also supplies many functions. Several of these functions translate data, such as integers, between your host's native format and network standard format. The higher-level protocol that your program and its counterpart are using on a socket determines what kind of conversions you must perform.

socket Functions

The most frequently used functions of module socket are as follows.

getfqdn

getfqdn(*host*='')

Returns the fully qualified domain name string for the given *host*. When *host* is '', returns the fully qualified domain name string for the local host.

gethostbyaddr

gethostbyaddr(*ipaddr*)

Returns a tuple with three items (*hostname, alias_list, ipaddr_list*). *hostname* is a string, the primary name of the host whose IP dotted-quad address you pass as string *ipaddr*. *alias_list* is a list of 0 or more alias names for the host. *ipaddr_list* is a list of one or more dotted-quad addresses for the host.

gethostbyname _ex

gethostbyname_ex(*hostname*)

Returns the same results as gethostbyaddr, but takes as an argument a *hostname* string that can be either an IP dotted-quad address or a DNS name.

htonl

htonl(*i32*)

Converts the 32-bit integer *i32* from this host's format into network format.

htons	htons(*i16*)
	Converts the 16-bit integer *i16* from this host's format into network format.
inet_aton	inet_aton(*ipaddr_string*)
	Converts IP dotted-quad address string *ipaddr_string* to 32-bit network packed format and returns a string of 4 bytes.
inet_ntoa	inet_ntoa(*packed_string*)
	Converts the 4-byte network packed format string *packed_string* and returns an IP dotted-quad address string.
ntohl	htonl(*i32*)
	Converts the 32-bit integer *i32* from network format into this host's format, and returns a normal native integer.
ntohs	htons(*i16*)
	Converts the 16-bit integer *i16* from network format into this host's format, and returns a normal native integer.
socket	socket(*family,type*)
	Creates and returns a socket object with the given family and type. *family* is usually the constant attribute AF_INET of module socket, indicating you want a normal, Internet (i.e., TCP/IP) kind of socket. Depending on your platform, *family* may also be another constant attribute of module socket. For example, AF_UNIX, on Unix-like platforms only, indicates that you want a Unix-kind socket. This book does not cover sockets that are not of the Internet kind, since it focuses on cross-platform Python. *type* is one of a few constant attributes of module socket; generally, *type* is SOCK_STREAM to create a TCP (connection-based) socket, or SOCK_DGRAM to create a UDP (datagram-based) socket.

The socket Class

A socket object *s* supplies many methods. The most frequently used ones are as follows.

accept	*s*.accept( )
	Accepts a connection request and returns a pair (*s1*,(*ipaddr*,*port*)), where *s1* is a new connected socket and *ipaddr* and *port* are the IP address and port number of the counterpart. *s* must be of type SOCK_STREAM, and you must have previously called

s.bind and s.listen. If no client is trying to connect, accept blocks until some client tries to connect.

bind s.bind((*host,port*))

Binds socket s to accept connections from host *host* serving on port number *port*. *host* can be the empty string ' ' to accept connections from any host. It's an error to call s.bind twice on any given socket object s.

close s.close()

Closes the socket, terminating any listening or connection on it. It's an error to call any other method on s after s.close.

connect s.connect((*host,port*))

Connects socket s to the server on the given *host* and *port*. Blocks until the server accepts or rejects the connection attempt.

getpeername s.getpeername()

Returns a pair (*ipaddr,port*), giving the IP address and port number of the counterpart. s must be connected, either because you called s.connect or because s was generated by another socket's accept method.

listen s.listen(*maxpending*)

Listens for connection attempts to the socket, allowing up to *maxpending* queued attempts at any time. *maxpending* must be greater than 0 and less than or equal to a system-dependent value, which on all contemporary systems is at least 5.

makefile s.makefile(*mode*='r')

Creates and returns a file object *f*, as covered in Chapter 10, that reads from and/or writes to the socket. You can close *f* and s independently; Python closes the underlying socket only when both *f* and s are closed.

recv s.recv(*bufsize*)

Receives up to *bufsize* bytes from the socket and returns a string with the data received. Returns an empty string when the socket is disconnected. If there is currently no data, blocks until the socket is disconnected or some data arrives.

recvfrom s.recvfrom(*bufsize*)

Receives up to *bufsize* bytes from the socket and returns a tuple (*data,(ipaddr,port)*), where *data* is a string with the data received, and *ipaddr* and *port* are the IP address and port number of the sender. Useful with datagram-oriented sockets, which can receive data from different senders. If there is currently no data in the socket, blocks until some data arrives.

send   s.send(*string*)

Sends the bytes of *string* on the socket. Returns the number *n* of bytes sent. *n* may be lower than len(*string*); your program must check, and resend the unsent substring *string*[*n*:] if non-empty. If there is no space in the socket's buffer, blocks until some space appears.

sendall   s.sendall(*string*)

Sends the bytes of *string* on the socket, blocking until all the bytes are sent.

sendto   s.sendto(*string*,(*host*,*port*))

Sends the bytes of *string* on the socket to the destination *host* and *port*, and returns the number *n* of bytes sent. Useful with data-gram-oriented sockets, which can send data to various destinations. You must not have previously called method s.bind. *n* may be lower than len(*string*); your program must check, and resend the unsent substring *string*[*n*:] if non-empty.

Echo Server and Client Using TCP Sockets

Example 19-1 shows a TCP server that listens for connections on port 8881. When connected, the server loops, echoing all data back to the client, and goes back to accept another connection when the client is finished. To terminate the server, hit the interrupt key with the focus on the server's terminal window (console). The interrupt key combination, depending on your platform and settings, may be Ctrl-Break (typical on Windows) or Ctrl-C.

Example 19-1. TCP echo server

```
import socket
sock = socket.socket(socket.AF_INET, socket.SOCK_STREAM)
sock.bind(('', 8881))
sock.listen(5)

# loop waiting for connections
# terminate with Ctrl-Break on Win32, Ctrl-C on Unix
try:
    while True:
        newSocket, address = sock.accept( )
        print "Connected from", address
        while True:
            receivedData = newSocket.recv(8192)
```

Example 19-1. TCP echo server (continued)

```
            if not receivedData: break
            newSocket.sendall(receivedData)
        newSocket.close( )
        print "Disconnected from", address
finally:
    sock.close( )
```

The argument passed to the newSocket.recv call, here 8192, is the maximum number of bytes to receive at a time. Receiving up to a few thousand bytes at a time is a good compromise between performance and memory consumption, and it's usual to specify a power of 2 (e.g., 8192==2**13) since memory allocation tends to round up to such powers anyway. It's important to close sock (to ensure we free its well-known port number 8881 as soon as possible), so we use a try/finally statement to ensure sock.close is called. Closing newSocket, which is system-allocated on any suitable free port, is not of the same importance; therefore we do not use a try/finally for it, although it would be fine to do so.

Example 19-2 shows a simple TCP client that connects to port 8881 on the local host, sends lines of data, and prints what it receives back from the server.

Example 19-2. TCP echo client

```
import socket
sock = socket.socket(socket.AF_INET, socket.SOCK_STREAM)
sock.connect(('localhost', 8881))
print "Connected to server"
data = """A few lines of data
to test the operation
of both server and client."""
for line in data.splitlines( ):
    sock.sendall(line)
    print "Sent:", line
    response = sock.recv(8192)
    print "Received:", response
sock.close( )
```

Run the server of Example 19-1 on a terminal window, and try a few runs of Example 19-2 while the server is running.

Echo Server and Client Using UDP Sockets

Examples 19-3 and 19-4 implement an echo server and client with UDP (i.e., using datagram rather than stream sockets).

Example 19-3. UDP echo server

```
import socket
sock = socket.socket(socket.AF_INET, socket.SOCK_DGRAM)
sock.bind(('', 8881))

# loop waiting for datagrams
(terminate with Ctrl-Break on Win32, Ctrl-C on Unix)
```

Example 19-3. UDP echo server (continued)

```
try:
    while True:
        data, address = sock.recvfrom(8192)
        print "Datagram from", address
        sock.sendto(data, address)
finally:
    sock.close( )
```

Example 19-4. UDP echo client

```
import socket
sock = socket.socket(socket.AF_INET, socket.SOCK_DGRAM)
data = """A few lines of data
to test the operation
of both server and client."""
for line in data.splitlines( ):
    sock.sendto(line, ('localhost', 8881))
    print "Sent:", line
    response = sock.recv(8192)
    print "Received:", response
sock.close( )
```

Run the server of Example 19-3 on a terminal window, and try a few runs of Example 19-4 while the server is running. Examples 19-3 and 19-4, as well as 19-1 and 19-2, can run independently at the same time. There is no interference nor interaction, even though all are using port number 8881 on the local host, because TCP and UDP ports are separate. Note that if you run Example 19-4 when the server of Example 19-3 is not running, you don't receive an error message: the client of Example 19-4 hangs forever, waiting for a response that will never arrive. Datagrams are not as robust and reliable as connections.

The timeoutsocket Module

Standard sockets, as supplied by module socket, have no concept of timing out. By default, each socket operation blocks until it either succeeds or fails. There are advanced ways to ask for non-blocking sockets and to ensure that you perform socket operations only when they can't block (relying on module select, covered later in this chapter). However, explicitly arranging for such behavior, particularly in a cross-platform way, can be complicated and difficult.

It's generally simpler to deal with socket objects enriched by a timeout concept. Each operation on such an object fails, with an exception indicating a timeout condition, if the operation still has neither succeeded nor failed after a timeout period has elapsed. Such objects are internally implemented by using non-blocking sockets and selects, but your program is shielded from the complexities and deals only with objects that present a simple and intuitive interface.

In Python 2.3, sockets with timeout behavior will be part of the standard Python library. However, you can use such objects with earlier releases of Python by downloading Timothy O'Malley's timeoutsocket module from *http://www.timo-tasi.org/*

python/timeoutsocket.py. Copy the file to your library directory (e.g., *C:\Python22\ Lib*). Then, have your program execute a statement:

    import timeoutsocket

before the program imports socket or any other module using sockets, such as urllib and others covered in Chapter 18. Afterwards, any creation of a connection-oriented (TCP) socket creates instead an instance *t* of class timeoutsocket. TimeoutSocket. In addition to socket methods, *t* supplies two additional methods.

get_timeout	*t*.get_timeout( )
	Returns the timeout value of *t*, in seconds.

set_timeout	*t*.set_timeout(*s*)
	Sets the timeout value of *t* to *s* seconds. *s* is a float or None.

The default timeout value of each new instance *t* of TimeoutSocket is None, meaning that there is no timeout—*t* behaves like an ordinary socket instance. To change this, module timeoutsocket supplies two functions.

getDefault SocketTimeout	getDefaultSocketTimeout( )
	Returns the default timeout value, in seconds, used for newly created instances of class TimeoutSocket. Initially returns None.

setDefault SocketTimeout	setDefaultSocketTimeout(*s*)
	Sets the default timeout value, used for newly created instances of class TimeoutSocket, to *s* seconds. *s* is a float or None.

Socket methods that may block and wait forever when you call them on normal sockets, such as connect, accept, recv, and send, may time out when you call them on an instance *t* of TimeoutSocket with a timeout value *s* that is not None. If *s* seconds elapse after the call, and the wait is still going on, then *t* stops waiting and raises timeoutsocket.Timeout.

The SocketServer Module

The Python library supplies a framework module, SocketServer, to help you implement Internet servers. SocketServer supplies server classes TCPServer, for connection-oriented servers using TCP, and UDPServer, for datagram-oriented servers using UDP, with the same interface.

An instance *s* of either TCPServer or UDPServer supplies many attributes and methods, and you can subclass either class and override some methods to architect your own specialized server framework. However, I do not cover such advanced and rarely used possibilities in this book.

Classes TCPServer and UDPServer implement synchronous servers, able to serve one request at a time. Classes ThreadingTCPServer and ThreadingUDPServer implement threaded servers, spawning a new thread per request. You are responsible for synchronizing the resulting threads as needed. Threading is covered in Chapter 14.

The BaseRequestHandler Class

For normal use of SocketServer, subclass the BaseRequestHandler class provided by SocketServer and override the handle method. Then, instantiate a server class, passing the address pair on which to serve and your subclass of BaseRequestHandler. Finally, call method serve_forever on the server class instance.

An instance *h* of BaseRequestHandler supplies the following methods and attributes.

client_address	The *h*.client_address attribute is the pair (*host*,*port*) of the client, set by the base class at connection.
handle	*h*.handle( ) Your subclass overrides this method, called by the server, on a new instance of your subclass for each new incoming request. Typically, for a TCP server, your implementation of handle conducts a conversation with the client on socket *h*.request to service the request. For a UDP server, your implementation of handle examines the datagram in *h*.request[0] and sends a reply string with *h*.request[1].sendto.
request	For a TCP server, the *h*.request attribute is the socket connected to the client. For a UDP server, the *h*.request attribute is a pair (*data*,*sock*), where *data* is the string of data the client sent as a request (up to 8192 bytes) and *sock* is the server socket. Your handle method typically calls method sendto on *sock* to send a reply to the client.
server	The *h*.server attribute is the instance of the server class that instantiated this handler object.

Example 19-5 uses module SocketServer to reimplement the server of Example 19-1 with the added ability to serve multiple clients simultaneously by threading.

Example 19-5. Threaded TCP echo server using SocketServer

```
import SocketServer
class EchoHandler(SocketServer.BaseRequestHandler):
    def handle(self):
        print "Connected from", self.client_address
        while True:
            receivedData = self.request.recv(8192)
            if not receivedData: break
            self.request.sendall(receivedData)
        self.request.close()
        print "Disconnected from", self.client_address
srv = SocketServer.ThreadingTCPServer(('',8881),EchoHandler)
srv.serve_forever()
```

Run the server of Example 19-5 on a terminal window, and try a few runs of Example 19-2 while the server is running. Try also *telnet localhost 8881* on other terminal windows (or other platform-dependent Telnet-like programs) to verify the behavior of longer-term connections.

HTTP Servers

The `BaseHTTPServer`, `SimpleHTTPServer`, `CGIHTTPServer`, and `SimpleXMLRPCServer` modules implement HTTP servers of different completeness and sophistication on top of module `SocketServer`.

The BaseHTTPServer module

The `BaseHTTPServer` module supplies a server class `HTTPServer` that subclasses `SocketServer.TCPServer` and is used in the same way. It also provides a request handler class `BaseHTTPRequestHandler`, which subclasses `SocketServer.BaseRequestHandler` and adds attributes and methods useful for HTTP servers, of which the most commonly used are as follows.

command	The *h*.command attribute is the HTTP verb of the client's request, such as 'get', 'head', or 'post'.
handle	*h*.handle( )
	Overrides the superclass's method handle and delegates request handling to methods whose names start with 'do_', such as do_get, do_head, and do_post. Class BaseHTTPRequestHandler supplies no do_ methods; you must subclass it to supply the methods you want to implement.
end_headers	*h*.end_headers( )
	Terminates the response's MIME headers by sending a blank line.
path	The *h*.path attribute is the HTTP path of the client's request, such as '/index.html'.

rfile
The *h*.rfile attribute is a file-like object open for reading, from which you can read optional data sent as the body of the client's request (e.g., URL-encoded form data for a POST).

send_header
h.send_header(*keyword*,*value*)

Adds to the response a MIME header with the given *keyword* and *value*. Each time send_header is called, another header is added to the response. Even when send_header is called repeatedly with the same *keyword*, multiple headers with that *keyword* are added, one per call to send_header, in the same order as the calls to send_header.

send_error
h.send_error(*code*,*message*=None)

Sends a complete error reply with HTTP code *code* and, optionally, more specific text from string *message*, when *message* is not None.

send_response
h.send_response(*code*,*message*=None)

Sends a response header with HTTP code *code* and, optionally, more specific text from string *message*, when message is not None. The headers sent automatically are Server and Date.

wfile
The *h*.wfile attribute is a file-like object open for writing, to which you can write the response body after calling send_response, optionally send_header, and end_headers.

As an example, here's a trivial HTTP server that just answers every request with the 404 error code and the corresponding message 'File not found'.

```
import BaseHTTPServer

class TrivialHTTPRequestHandler(BaseHTTPServer.BaseHTTPRequestHandler):
    """Trivial HTTP request handler, answers not found to every request"""

    server_version = "TrivialHTTP/1.0"

    def do_GET(self):
        """Serve a GET request."""
        self.send_error(404, "File not found")

    do_HEAD = do_POST = do_GET
```

The SimpleHTTPServer module

The SimpleHTTPServer module builds on top of BaseHTTPServer, supplying what's needed to serve GET HTTP requests for files in a given directory. It is most useful as an example of how to use `BaseHTTPServer` for a real, although simple, HTTP serving task.

The CGIHTTPServer module

The `CGIHTTPServer` module builds on top of `SimpleHTTPServer`, supplying the ability to serve GET and POST HTTP requests via CGI scripts, covered in Chapter 20. You can use it to debug CGI scripts on your local machine.

The SimpleXMLRPCServer module

XML-RPC is a higher-level protocol that runs on top of HTTP. Python supports XML-RPC clients with module `xmlrpclib`, covered in Chapter 18. The `SimpleXMLRPCServer` module, introduced in Python 2.2, supplies class `SimpleXMLRPCServer` to instantiate with the address pair on which to serve.

In Python 2.2 and 2.2.1, `SimpleXMLRPCServer` as supplied in the standard Python library has a defect: when a method called via XML-RPC raises an exception, the server does not correctly communicate exception details to the XML-RPC client. The defect is fixed in Python 2.3 and later. To get a fixed version for Python 2.2, download *SimpleXMLRPCServer.py* from URL *http://www.sweetapp.com/xmlrpc* to replace the file of the same name in the Python library directory (e.g., *c:\python22\Lib* for a standard Python 2.2 installation on Windows).

An instance *x* of class `SimpleXMLRPCServer` supplies two methods to call before `x.serve_forever( )`.

register_ function	`x.register_function(callable,name=None)` Registers *callable*, callable with a single argument, to respond to XML-RPC requests for *name*. *name* can be an identifier or a sequence of identifiers joined by dots. When *name* is None, uses name `callable.__name__`. The argument to *callable* is the result of `xmlrpclib.loads(payload)` where *payload* is the request's payload.
register_ instance	`x.register_instance(inst)` Registers *inst* to respond to XML-RPC requests with names not registered via `register_function`. When *inst* supplies a method `_dispatch`, `inst._dispatch` is called with the request's name and parameters as arguments. When *inst* does not supply `_dispatch`, the request's name is used as an attribute name to search on *inst*. When the request's name contains dots, the search repeats recursively for each component. The attribute found by this search is then called with the request's parameters as arguments. Only one instance at a time can be registered with `register_instance`: if you call `x.register_instance` again, the instance passed in the previous call to `x.register_instance` is replaced by the one passed in the later call.

Simple examples of all typical usage patterns for impleXMLRPCServer are given in the docstring of module *SimpleXMLRPCServer.py*, which you can find in the *Lib* directory of your Python installation (Python 2.2 and later only). Here is a toy example of using the _dispatch method. In one terminal window, run the following tiny script:

```
import SimpleXMLRPCServer
class with_dispatch:
    def _dispatch(self, *args):
        print '_dispatch', args
        return args
server = SimpleXMLRPCServer.SimpleXMLRPCServer(('localhost',8888))
server.register_instance(with_dispatch())
server.serve_forever()
```

From a Python interactive session on another terminal window of the same machine (or an IDLE interactive session on the same machine), you can now run:

```
>>> import xmlrpclib
>>> proxy = xmlrpclib.ServerProxy('http://localhost:8888')
>>> print proxy.whatever.method('any', 'args')
['whatever.method', ['any', 'args']]
```

Event-Driven Socket Programs

Socket programs, particularly servers, must often be ready to perform many tasks at once. Example 19-1 accepts a connection request, then serves a single client until that client has finished—other connection requests must wait. This is not acceptable for servers in production use. Clients cannot wait too long: the server must be able to service multiple clients at once.

One approach that lets your program perform several tasks at once is threading, covered in Chapter 14. Module SocketServer optionally supports threading, as covered earlier in this chapter. An alternative to threading that can offer better performance and scalability is *event-driven* (also known as *asynchronous*) programming.

An event-driven program sits in an event loop, where it waits for events. In networking, typical events are "a client requests connection," "data arrived on a socket," and "a socket is available for writing." The program responds to each event by executing a small slice of work to service that event, then goes back to the event loop to wait for the next event. The Python library supports event-driven network programming with low-level select module and higher-level asyncore and asynchat modules. Even more complete support for event-driven programming is in the Twisted package (available at *http://www.twistedmatrix.com*), particularly in subpackage twisted.internet.

The select Module

The select module exposes a cross-platform low-level function that lets you implement high-performance asynchronous network servers and clients. Module select offers additional platform-dependent functionality on Unix-like platforms, but I cover only cross-platform functionality in this book.

select   select(*inputs,outputs,excepts,timeout*=None)

inputs, *outputs*, and *excepts* are lists of socket objects waiting for input events, output events, and exceptional conditions, respectively. *timeout* is a float, the maximum time to wait in seconds. When *timeout* is None, there is no maximum wait: select waits until one or more objects receive events. When *timeout* is 0, select returns at once, without waiting.

select returns a tuple with three items (*i,o,e*). *i* is a list of zero or more of the items of *inputs*, those that received input events. *o* is a list of zero or more of the items of *outputs*, those that received output events. *e* is a list of zero or more of the items of *excepts*, those that received exceptional conditions (i.e., out-of-band data). Any or all of *i*, *o*, and *e* can be empty, but at least one of them is non-empty if *timeout* is None.

In addition to sockets, you can have in lists *inputs*, *outputs*, and *excepts* other objects that supply a method fileno, callable without arguments, returning a socket's file descriptor. For example, the server classes of module SocketServer, covered earlier in this chapter, follow this protocol. Therefore, you can have instances of those classes in the lists. On Unix-like platforms, select.select has wider applicability, since it can also accept file descriptors that do not refer to sockets. On Windows, however, select.select can accept only file descriptors that do refer to sockets.

Example 19-6 uses module select to reimplement the server of Example 19-1 with the added ability to serve any number of clients simultaneously.

Example 19-6. Asynchronous TCP echo server using select

```
import socket
import select
sock = socket.socket(socket.AF_INET, socket.SOCK_STREAM)
sock.bind(('', 8881))
sock.listen(5)

# lists of sockets to watch for input and output events
ins = [sock]
ous = []
# mapping socket -> data to send on that socket when feasible
data = {}
# mapping socket -> (host, port) on which the client is running
adrs = {}

try:
    while True:
```

Example 19-6. Asynchronous TCP echo server using select (continued)

```
        i, o, e = select.select(ins, ous, [])  # no excepts nor timeout
        for x in i:
            if x is sock:
                # input event on sock means client trying to connect
                newSocket, address = sock.accept()
                print "Connected from", address
                ins.append(newSocket)
                adrs[newSocket] = address
            else:
                # other input events mean data arrived, or disconnections
                newdata = x.recv(8192)
                if newdata:
                    # data arrived, prepare and queue the response to it
                    print "%d bytes from %s" % (len(newdata), adrs[x])
                    data[x] = data.get(x, '') + newdata
                    if x not in ous: ous.append(x)
                else:
                    # a disconnect, give a message and clean up
                    print "disconnected from", adrs[x]
                    del adrs[x]
                    try: ous.remove(x)
                    except ValueError: pass
                    x.close()
        for x in o:
            # output events always mean we can send some data
            tosend = data.get(x)
            if tosend:
                nsent = x.send(tosend)
                print "%d bytes to %s" % (nsent, adrs[x])
                # remember data still to be sent, if any
                tosend = tosend[nsent:]
            if tosend:
                print "%d bytes remain for %s" % (len(tosend), adrs[x])
                data[x] = tosend
            else:
                try: del data[x]
                except KeyError: pass
                ous.remove(x)
                print "No data currently remain for", adrs[x]
finally:
    sock.close()
```

Programming at such a low level incurs substantial complications, as shown by the complexity of Example 19-6 and its data structures. Run the server of Example 19-6 on a terminal window and try a few runs of Example 19-2 while the server is running. You should also try *telnet localhost 8881* on other terminal windows (or other platform-dependent Telnet-like programs) to verify the behavior of longer-term connections.

The asyncore and asynchat Modules

The asyncore and asynchat modules help you implement high-performance asynchronous network servers and clients at a higher, more productive level than module select affords.

The asyncore module

Module asyncore supplies one function.

loop
          loop( )

Implements the asynchronous event loop, dispatching all network events to previously instantiated dispatcher objects. loop terminates when all dispatcher objects (i.e., all communication channels) are closed.

Module asyncore also supplies class dispatcher, which supplies all methods of socket objects, plus specific methods for event-driven programming, with names starting with 'handle_'. Your class X subclasses dispatcher and overrides the handle_ methods for all events you need to handle. To initialize an instance *d* of dispatcher, you can pass an argument *s*, an already connected socket object. Otherwise, you must call:

    d.create_socket(socket.AF_INET,socket.SOCK_STREAM)

and then call on *d* either connect, to connect to a server, or bind and listen, to have *d* itself be a server. The most frequently used methods of an instance *d* of a subclass X of dispatcher are the following.

create_socket
          d.create_socket(*family,type*)

Creates *d*'s socket with the given family and type. *family* is generally socket.AF_INET. *type* is generally socket.SOCK_STREAM, since class dispatcher normally uses a TCP (i.e., connection-based) socket.

handle_accept
          d.handle_accept( )

Called when a new client has connected. Your class X normally responds by calling self.accept, then instantiating another subclass Y of dispatcher with the resulting new socket, in order to handle the new client connection.

Your implementation of handle_accept need not return the resulting instance of Y: all instances of subclasses of dispatcher register themselves with the asyncore framework in method dispatcher.__init__, so that asyncore calls back to their methods as appropriate.

handle_close	*d*.handle_close( )
	Called when the connection is closing.

handle_connect	*d*.handle_connect( )
	Called when the connection is starting.

handle_read	*d*.handle_read( )
	Called when the socket has new data that you can read without blocking.

handle_write	*d*.handle_write( )
	Called when the socket has buffer space, so you can write without blocking.

Module asyncore also supplies class dispatcher_with_send, a subclass of dispatcher that overrides one method.

send	*d*.send(*data*)
	In class dispatcher_with_send, method *d*.send is equivalent to a socket object's method send_all in that it sends all the data. However, *d*.send does not send all the data at once and does not block; rather, *d* sends the data in small packets of 512 bytes each in response to handle_write events (callbacks). This strategy ensures good performance in simple cases.

Example 19-7 uses module asyncore to reimplement the server of Example 19-1, with the added ability to serve any number of clients simultaneously.

Example 19-7. Asynchronous TCP echo server using asyncore

```
import asyncore
import socket

class MainServerSocket(asyncore.dispatcher):
    def __init__(self, port):
        asyncore.dispatcher.__init__(self)
        self.create_socket(socket.AF_INET, socket.SOCK_STREAM)
        self.bind(('',port))
        self.listen(5)
    def handle_accept(self):
        newSocket, address = self.accept( )
        print "Connected from", address
        SecondaryServerSocket(newSocket)
```

Example 19-7. Asynchronous TCP echo server using asyncore (continued)

```python
class SecondaryServerSocket(asyncore.dispatcher_with_send):
    def handle_read(self):
        receivedData = self.recv(8192)
        if receivedData: self.send(receivedData)
        else: self.close()
    def handle_close(self):
        print "Disconnected from", self.getpeername()

MainServerSocket(8881)
asyncore.loop()
```

The complexity of Example 19-7 is modest, comparable with that of Example 19-1. The additional functionality of serving multiple clients simultaneously, with the high performance and scalability of asynchronous event-driven programming, comes quite cheaply thanks to asyncore's power.

Note that method handle_read of SecondaryServerSocket can freely use self.send without precautions because SecondaryServerSocket subclasses dispatcher_with_send, which overrides method send to ensure that it sends all data passed to it. We could not do that if we had instead chosen to subclass asyncore.dispatcher directly.

The asynchat module

The asynchat module supplies class async_chat, which subclasses asyncore.dispatcher and adds methods to support data buffering and line-oriented protocols. You subclass async_chat with your class *X* and override some methods. The most frequently used additional methods of an instance *x* of a subclass of async_chat are the following.

collect_ incoming_data	*x*.collect_incoming_data(*data*) Called whenever a byte string *data* of data arrives. Normally, *x* adds *data* to some buffer that *x* keeps, most often a list using the list's append method.
found_ terminator	*x*.found_terminator() Called whenever the terminator, set by method set_terminator, is found. Normally, *x* processes the buffer it keeps, then clears the buffer.
push	*x*.push(*data*) Your class *X* normally doesn't override this method. The implementation in base class async_chat adds string *data* to an output buffer that it sends as appropriate. Method push is therefore quite similar to method send of class asyncore.dispatcher_with_send, but method push has a more sophisticated implementation to ensure good performance in more cases.

set_terminator   *x*.set_terminator(*terminator*)

Your class *X* normally doesn't override this method. *terminator* is normally '\r\n', the line terminator specified by most Internet protocols. *terminator* can also be None, to disable calls to found_ terminator.

Example 19-8 uses module asynchat to reimplement the server of Example 19-7, with small differences due to using class asynchat.async_chat instead of class asyncore.dispatcher_with_send. To highlight async_chat's typical use, Example 19-8 responds (by echoing the received data back to the client, like all other server examples in this chapter) only when it has received a complete line (i.e., one ending with \n).

Example 19-8. Asynchronous TCP echo server using asynchat

```
import asyncore, asynchat, socket

class MainServerSocket(asyncore.dispatcher):
    def __init__(self, port):
        print 'initing MSS'
        asyncore.dispatcher.__init__(self)
        self.create_socket(socket.AF_INET, socket.SOCK_STREAM)
        self.bind(('',port))
        self.listen(5)
    def handle_accept(self):
        newSocket, address = self.accept()
        print "Connected from", address
        SecondaryServerSocket(newSocket)

class SecondaryServerSocket(asynchat.async_chat):
    def __init__(self, *args):
        print 'initing SSS'
        asynchat.async_chat.__init__(self, *args)
        self.set_terminator('\n')
        self.data = []
    def collect_incoming_data(self, data):
        self.data.append(data)
    def found_terminator(self):
        self.push(''.join(self.data))
        self.data = []
    def handle_close(self):
        print "Disconnected from", self.getpeername()
        self.close()

MainServerSocket(8881)
asyncore.loop()
```

To try out Example 19-8, we cannot use Example 19-2 as it stands because it does not ensure that it sends only entire lines terminated with \n. It doesn't take much to fix that, however. The following client program, for example, is quite suitable for testing Example 19-8, as well as any of the other server examples in this chapter:

```
import socket
sock = socket.socket(socket.AF_INET, socket.SOCK_STREAM)
sock.connect(('localhost', 8881))
print "Connected to server"
data = """A few lines of data
to test the operation
of both server and client."""
for line in data.splitlines():
    sock.sendall(line+'\n')
    print "Sent:", line
    response = sock.recv(8192)
    print "Received:", response
sock.close()
```

The only difference in this code with respect to Example 19-2 is the change to the argument in the call to sock.sendall, in the first line of the loop body. This code simply adds a line terminator '\n', to ensure it interoperates with Example 19-8.

The Twisted Framework

The Twisted package (available at *http://www.twistedmatrix.com*) is a freely available framework for network clients and servers. Twisted includes powerful, high-level components such as a web server, a user authentication system, a mail server, instant messaging, and so on. Each is highly scalable and easily customizable, and all are integrated to interoperate smoothly. It's a tribute to the power of Python and to the ingenuity of Twisted's developers that so much can be accomplished within the small compass of half a megabyte's worth of download.

The twisted.internet and twisted.protocols packages

The twisted.internet package is the low-level, highly stable part of Twisted that supports event-driven clients and servers. twisted.internet supplies module protocol, supporting protocol handlers and factories, and object reactor, embodying the concept of an event loop. Note that to make fully productive use of twisted.internet, you need a good understanding of the design patterns used in distributed computing. Douglas Schmidt, of the Center for Distributed Object Computing of Washington University, documents such design patterns at *http://www.cs.wustl.edu/~schmidt/patterns-ace.html*.

twisted.protocols implements many protocols that use twisted.internet's infrastructure, including SSH, DNS, FTP, HTTP, IRC, NNTP, POP3, SMTP, SocksV4, and Telnet.

Reactors

A reactor object allows you to establish protocol factories as listeners (servers) on given TCP/IP ports (or other transports, such as SSL), and to connect protocol handlers as clients. You can choose different reactor implementations. The default reactor uses the select module covered earlier in this chapter. Other specialized reactors integrate with GUI toolkits' event loops, or use platform-specific techniques such as the Windows event loop or the poll system call support available in the select module on some Unix-like systems. The default reactor is often sufficient, but the extra flexibility of being able to use other implementations can help you to integrate GUIs or other platform-specific capabilities, or to achieve even higher performance and scalability.

A reactor object r supplies many methods. Client TCP APIs should be finalized by the time you read this book, but they're not definitive yet, so I do not cover them. The reactor methods most frequently used for programs that implement TCP/IP servers with twisted.internet are the following.

callLater r.callLater(*delay,callable,*args,**kwds*)

Schedules a call to callable(**args,**kwds*) to happen *delay* seconds from now. *delay* is a float, so it can also express fractions of a second. Returns an ID that you may pass to method cancelCallLater.

cancelCallLater r.cancelCallLater(*ID*)

Cancels a call scheduled by method callLater. *ID* must be the result of a previous call to r.callLater.

listenTCP r.listenTCP(*port,factory,backlog*=5)

Establishes *factory*, which must be an instance of class Factory (or any subclass of Factory), as the protocol handler for a TCP server on the given *port*. No more than *backlog* clients can be kept waiting for connection at any given time.

run r.run( )

Runs the event loop until r.stop( ) is called.

stop r.stop( )

Stops the event loop started by calling r.run( ).

Transports

A transport object embodies a network connection. Each protocol object calls methods on self.transport to write data to its counterpart and to disconnect. A transport object *t* supplies the following methods.

getHost t.getHost( )

Returns a tuple identifying this side of the connection. The first item indicates the kind of connection, while other items depend on the kind of connection. For a TCP connection, returns ('INET', *host, port*).

getPeer	*t*.getPeer( ) Returns a tuple identifying the other side of the connection (easily confused by proxies, masquerading, firewalls, and so on), just like getHost's result.
loseConnection	*t*.loseConnection( ) Tells *t* to disconnect as soon as *t* has finished writing all pending data.
write	*t*.write(*data*) Transmits string *data* to the counterpart, or queues it up for transmission. *t* tries its best to ensure that all data you pass to write is eventually sent.

Protocol handlers and factories

The reactor instantiates protocol handlers using a factory, and calls methods on protocol handler instances when events occur. A protocol handler subclasses class Protocol and overrides some methods. A protocol handler may use its factory, available as self.factory, as a repository for state that needs to be shared among handlers or persist across multiple instantiations. A protocol factory may subclass class Factory, but this subclassing is not always necessary since in many cases the stock Factory supplies all you need. Just set the protocol attribute of a Factory instance *f* to a class object that is an appropriate subclass of Protocol, then pass *f* to the reactor.

An instance *p* of a subclass of Protocol supplies the following methods.

connectionLost	*p*.connectionLost(*reason*) Called when the connection to the counterpart has been closed. Argument *reason* is an object explaining why the connection has been closed. *reason* is not an instance of a Python exception, but has an attribute *reason*.value that normally is such an instance. You can use str(*reason*) to get an explanation string, including a brief traceback, or str(*reason*.value) to get just the explanation string without any traceback.
connectionMade	*p*.connectionMade( ) Called when the connection to the counterpart has just succeeded.
dataReceived	*p*.dataReceived(*data*) Called when string *data* has just been received from the counterpart.

Echo server using twisted

Example 19-9 uses twisted.internet to implement an echo server with the ability to serve any number of clients simultaneously.

Example 19-9. Asynchronous TCP echo server using twisted

```
import twisted.internet.protocol
import twisted.internet.reactor

class EchoProtocol(twisted.internet.protocol.Protocol):
    def connectionMade(self):
        self.peer = self.transport.getPeer( )[1:]
        print "Connected from", self.peer
    def dataReceived(self, data):
        self.transport.write(data)
    def connectionLost(self, reason):
        print "Disconnected from", self.peer, reason.value

factory = twisted.internet.protocol.Factory( )
factory.protocol = EchoProtocol

twisted.internet.reactor.listenTCP(8881, factory)
twisted.internet.reactor.run( )
```

Example 19-9 exhibits scalability at least as good as Example 19-7, yet it's easily the simplest of the echo server examples in this chapter—a good indication of Twisted's power and simplicity. Note the statement:

```
factory.protocol = EchoProtocol
```

This binds the class object EchoProtocol as the attribute protocol of object factory. The right-hand side of the assignment must not be EchoProtocol( ), with parentheses after the class name. Such a right-hand side would call, and therefore instantiate, class EchoProtocol, and therefore the statement would bind to factory.protocol a protocol instance object rather than a protocol class object. Such a mistake would make the server fail pretty quickly.

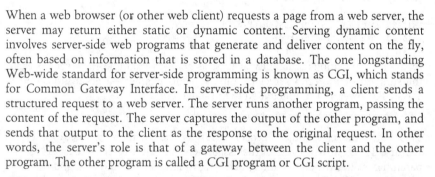

20

CGI Scripting and Alternatives

When a web browser (or other web client) requests a page from a web server, the server may return either static or dynamic content. Serving dynamic content involves server-side web programs that generate and deliver content on the fly, often based on information that is stored in a database. The one longstanding Web-wide standard for server-side programming is known as CGI, which stands for Common Gateway Interface. In server-side programming, a client sends a structured request to a web server. The server runs another program, passing the content of the request. The server captures the output of the other program, and sends that output to the client as the response to the original request. In other words, the server's role is that of a gateway between the client and the other program. The other program is called a CGI program or CGI script.

CGI enjoys the typical advantages of standards. When you program to the CGI standard, your program can be deployed on different web servers, and work despite the differences. This chapter focuses on CGI scripting in Python. It also mentions the downsides of CGI (basically, issues of scalability under high load) and some of the alternative, nonstandard server-side architectures that you can use instead of CGI.

This chapter assumes that you are familiar with both HTML and HTTP. For reference material on both of these standards, see *Webmaster in a Nutshell*, by Stephen Spainhour and Robert Eckstein (O'Reilly). For detailed coverage of HTML, I recommend *HTML & XHTML: The Definitive Guide*, by Chuck Musciano and Bill Kennedy (O'Reilly). And for additional coverage of HTTP, see the *HTTP Pocket Reference*, by Clinton Wong (O'Reilly).

CGI in Python

CGI's standardization lets you use any language to code CGI scripts. Python is a very-high-level, high-productivity language, and thus quite suitable for CGI coding. The Python standard library supplies modules to handle typical CGI-related tasks.

Form Submission Methods

CGI scripts are often used to handle HTML form submissions. In this case, the action attribute of the form tag specifies a URL for a CGI script to handle the form, and the method attribute is either GET or POST, indicating how the form data is sent to the script. According to the CGI standard, the GET method should be used for forms without side effects, such as asking the server to query a database and display the results, while the POST method is meant for forms with side effects, such as asking the server to update a database. In practice, however, GET is also often used to create side effects. The distinction between GET and POST in practical use is that GET encodes the form's contents as a query string joined to the action URL to form a longer URL, while POST transmits the form's contents as an encoded stream of data, which a CGI script sees as the script's standard input.

The GET method is slightly faster. You can use a fixed GET-form URL wherever you can use a hyperlink. However, GET cannot send large amounts of data to the server, since many clients and servers limit URL lengths (you're safe up to about 200 bytes). The POST method has no size limits. You must use POST when the form contains input tags with type=file—the form tag must then have enctype=multipart/form-data.

The CGI standard does not specify whether a single script can access both the query string (used for GET) and the script's standard input (used for POST). Many clients and servers let you get away with it, but relying on this nonstandard practice may negate the portability advantages that you would otherwise get from the fact that CGI is a standard. Python's standard module cgi, covered in the next section, recovers form data from the query string only, when any query string is present; otherwise, when no query string is present, cgi recovers form data from standard input.

The cgi Module

The cgi module supplies several functions and classes, mostly for backward compatibility or unusual needs. CGI scripts use one function and one class from module cgi.

escape	escape(*str*,*quote*=0)
	Returns a copy of string *str*, replacing each occurrence of characters &, <, and > with the appropriate HTML entity (&, <, >). When *quote* is true, escape also replaces double quote characters (") with ". Function escape lets a script prepare arbitrary text strings for output within an HTML document, whether or not the strings contain characters that HTML interprets in special ways.

FieldStorage   class FieldStorage(*keep_blank_values*=0)

When your script instantiates a FieldStorage instance *f*, module cgi parses the query string, and/or standard input, as appropriate. You need not determine whether the client used the POST or GET method, as cgi hides the distinction. Your script must instantiate FieldStorage only once, since the instantiation may consume standard input.

An instance *f* of class FieldStorage is a mapping. *f*'s keys are the name attributes of the form's controls. When *keep_blank_values* is true, *f* also includes controls whose values are blank strings. By default, *f* ignores such controls. *f* supplies methods *f*.has_key and *f*.keys, with normal mapping semantics. The value for each key *n*, *f*[*n*], can be either:

- A list of *k* FieldStorage instances, if name *n* occurs more than once in the form (*k* is the number of occurrences of *n*)

- A single FieldStorage instance, if name *n* occurs exactly once in the form

How often a name occurs in a form depends on HTML form rules. Groups of radio or checkbox controls share a name, but an entire group amounts to just one occurrence of the name.

Values in a FieldStorage instance are in turn FieldStorage instances, to let you handle nested forms. In practice, you don't need such complications. For each nested instance, just access the value (and occasionally other attributes), ignoring potential nested-mapping aspects. Avoid type tests: module cgi can optimize, using instances of MiniFieldStorage, a lightweight signature-compatible class instead of FieldStorage instances. You usually know what name values are repeated in the form, and thus you know which items of *f* can be lists. When you don't know, find out with try/except, not with type tests (see "Error-Checking Strategies" in Chapter 6 for details on this idiom).

An instance *f* of class FieldStorage supplies the following three methods.

---

getfirst   *f*.getfirst(*key*,*default*=None)

When *f*.has_key(*key*), and *f*[*key*].value is a single value, not a list of values, getfirst returns *f*[*key*].value. When *f*.has_key(*key*), and *f*[*key*].value is a list of values, getfirst returns *f*[*key*].value[0]. When *key* is not a key in *f*, getfirst returns *default*.

Use getfirst when you know that there should be just one input field (or at most one input field) named *key* in the form from which your script's input comes. getfirst was introduced in Python 2.2, so don't use it if your script must remain compatible with older versions of Python.

---

getlist

f.getlist(*key*)

When *f*.has_key(*key*), and *f*[*key*].value is a single value, not a list of values, getlist returns [*f*[*key*].value], i.e., a list whose only item is *f*[*key*].value. When *f*.has_key(*key*), and *f*[*key*].value is a list of values, getlist returns *f*[*key*].value. When *key* is not a key in *f*, getlist returns the empty list [].

Use getlist when you know that there can be more than one input field named *key* in the form from which your script's input comes. getlist was introduced in Python 2.2, so don't use it if your script must remain compatible with older versions of Python.

getvalue

f.getvalue(*key*,*default*=None)

Like *f*[*key*].value when *f*.has_key(*key*), otherwise returns *default*. getvalue is slightly less convenient than methods getfirst or getlist; the only reason to use getvalue is if your script must remain compatible with old versions of Python, since methods getfirst and getlist were introduced in Python 2.2.

An instance *f* of class FieldStorage supplies the following attributes:

disposition
    The Content-Disposition header, or None if no such header is present

disposition_options
    A mapping of all the options in the Content-Disposition header, if any

headers
    A mapping of all headers, normally an instance of the rfc822. Message class covered in Chapter 21

file
    A file-like object from which you can read the control's value, if applicable; None if the value is held in memory as a string, as happens for most controls

filename
    The filename as specified by the client, for file controls; otherwise None

name
    The name attribute of the control, or None if no such attribute is present

type
    The Content-Type header, or None if no such header is present

type_options
    A mapping of all the options in the Content-Type header, if any

value
> The control's value as a string; if *f* is keeping the control's value in a file, then *f* implicitly reads the file into memory each time you access *f*.value

In most cases, attribute value is all you need. Other attributes are useful for file controls, which may have very large values and metadata such as content type and content disposition headers. checkbox controls that share a name, and multiple-choice select controls, have values that are strings representing comma-separated lists of options. The idiom:

```
values=f.getfirst(n,'').split(',')
```

breaks apart such composite value strings into a list of their individual component strings.

CGI Output and Errors

When the server runs a CGI script to meet a request, the response to the request is the standard output of the script. The script must output the HTTP headers it needs, then an empty line, then the response's body. In particular, the script must always output the Content-Type header. Most often, the script outputs the Content-Type header as:

```
Content-Type: text/html
```

In this case, the response body must be HTML. However, the script may also choose to output a content type of text/plain (i.e., the response body must be plain text) or any other MIME type followed by a response body conforming to that MIME type. The MIME type must be compatible with the Accept header that the client sent, if any.

Here is the simplest possible Python CGI script in the tradition of "Hello World," ignoring its input and outputting just one line of plain text output:

```
print "Content-Type: text/plain"
print
print "Hello, CGI World!"
```

Most often, you want to output HTML, and this is similarly easy:

```
print "Content-Type: text/html"
print
print "<html><head><title>Hello, HTML</title></head>"
print "<body><p>Hello, CGI and HTML together!</p></body></html>"
```

Browsers are quite forgiving in parsing HTML: you could get by without the HTML structure tags that this code outputs. However, being fully correct costs little. For other ways to generate HTML output, see Chapter 22.

The web server collects all output from a CGI script, then sends it to the client browser in one gulp. Therefore, you cannot send to the client any progress information, just final results. If you need to output binary data (on a platform where binary and text files differ, such as Windows), you must ensure *python* is called with the -u switch, covered in Chapter 3. A more robust approach is to text-encode your output, using the encoding modules covered in Chapter 21 (typically with Base-64 encoding) and a suitable Content-Transfer-Encoding header. A standards-compliant browser will then decode your output according to the Content-Transfer-Encoding header and recover the binary data thus encoded.

Such encoding makes your output about 30% larger, which in some cases can give performance problems. In such cases, ensuring that your script's standard output stream is a binary file can be preferable. On Windows, specifically, an alternative to using the -u switch for this purpose is:

```
import msvcrt, os
msvcrt.setmode(1, os.OS_BINARY)
```

However, if you can ensure it's used, the -u switch is preferable, since it's cross-platform.

Error messages

If exceptions propagate from your script, Python outputs traceback diagnostics to standard error. With most web servers, error information ends up in error logs. The client browser receives a concise generic error message. This may be okay, if you can access the error logs. Seeing detailed error information in the client browser makes your life easier when you debug a CGI script. When you know that a script has bugs and you need an error trace for debugging, you can use a content type of text/plain and redirect standard error to standard output as shown here:

```
print "Content-Type: text/plain"
print
import sys
sys.stderr = sys.stdout
def witherror():
    return 1/0
print "Hello, CGI with an error!"
print "Trying to divide by 0 produces:",witherror()
print "The script does not reach this part..."
```

If your script fails only occasionally and you want to see HTML-formatted output up to the point of failure, you can use a more sophisticated approach based on the traceback module covered in Chapter 17, as shown here:

```
import sys
sys.stderr = sys.stdout
import traceback
print "Content-Type: text/html"
print
try:
    def witherror():
        return 1/0
    print "<html><head><title>Hello, traceback</title></head><body>"
    print "<p>Hello, CGI with an error traceback!"
    print "<p>Trying to divide by 0 produces:",witherror()
    print "<p>The script does not reach this part..."
```

```
except:
    print "<br><strong>ERROR detected:</strong><br><pre>"
    traceback.print_exc( )
    sys.stderr = sys.__stderr__
    traceback.print_exc( )
```

After imports, redirection, and content-type output, this example runs the script's substantial part in the try clause of a try/except statement. In the except clause, the script outputs a <br> tag, terminating any current line, and then a <pre> tag to ensure that further line breaks are honored. Function print_exc of module traceback outputs all error information. Lastly, the script restores standard error and outputs error information again. Thus, the information is also in the error logs for later study, not just transiently displayed in the client browser. These refinements are not very useful in this specific example, of course, since the error is repeatable, but they help track down real-life errors.

The cgitb module

The simplest way to provide good error reporting in CGI scripts is to use module cgitb. Module cgitb supplies two functions.

handle	handle(*exception*=None)
	Reports an exception's traceback to the browser. *exception* is a tuple with three items (*type,value,tb*), just like the result of calling sys.exc_info( ), covered in Chapter 8. When *exception* is None, handle calls exc_info to get the information about the exception to display.

enable	enable(*display*=True,*logdir*=None,*context*=5)
	Installs an exception hook, via sys.excepthook, to diagnose propagated exceptions. The hook displays the exception traceback on the browser if *display* is true. The hook logs the exception traceback to a file in directory *logdir* if *logdir* is not None. In the traceback, the hook shows *context* lines of source code per frame.

In practice, you can start all of your CGI scripts with:

```
import cgitb
cgitb.enable( )
```

and be assured of good error reporting to the browser with minimal effort on your part. Of course, when you don't want users of your page to see Python tracebacks from your scripts on their browsers, you can call cgitb(False,'/my/log/dir') and get the error reports, with exception tracebacks, as files in directory */my/log/dir* instead.

Installing Python CGI Scripts

Installation of CGI scripts depends on the web browser and host platform. A script coded in Python is no different in this respect from scripts coded in other languages. Of course, you must ensure that the Python interpreter and standard library are installed and accessible. On Unix-like platforms, you must set the x permission bits for the script and use a so-called shebang line as the script's first line. For example:

```
#!/usr/local/bin/python
```

depending on the details of your platform and Python installation. If you copy or share files between Unix and Windows platforms, make sure the shebang line does not end with a carriage return (\r), which might confuse the shell or web server that parses the shebang line to find out which interpreter to use for your script.

Python CGI scripts on Microsoft web servers

If your web server is Microsoft IIS 3 or 4 or Microsoft PWS (Personal Web Server), assign file extensions to CGI scripts via entries in registry path *HKLM\System\CurrentControlSet\Services\W3Svc\Parameters\Script_Map*. Each value in this path is named by a file extension, such as *.pyg* (each value's name starts with a period). The value is the interpreter command (e.g., C:\Python22\Python.Exe -u %s %s). You may also use file extensions such as *.cgi* or *.py* for this purpose, but I recommend a unique one such as *.pyg* instead. Assigning Python as the interpreter for all scripts named *.cgi* might interfere with your ability to use other interpreters for CGI purposes. Having all modules with a *.py* extension interpreted as CGI scripts is more accident-prone than dedicating a unique extension such as *.pyg* to this purpose, and may interfere with your ability to have your Python-coded CGI scripts import utility modules from the same directories.

With IIS 5, you can use the Administrative Tools → Computer Management applet to associate a file extension with an interpreter command line. This is performed via Services and Applications → Internet Information Services. Right-click either on [IISAdmin], for all sites, or on a specific web site, and choose Properties → Configuration → Add Mappings → Add. Enter the extension, such as *.pyg*, in the Extension field, and the interpreter command line, such as C:\Python22\Python.Exe -u %s %s, in the Executable field.

Python CGI scripts on Apache

The popular free web server Apache is configured via directives in a text file (by default, *httpd.conf*). When the configuration has ScriptAlias entries, such as:

```
ScriptAlias /cgi-bin/ /usr/local/apache/cgi-bin/
```

any executable script in the aliased directory can run as a CGI script. You may also enable CGI execution in a specific directory by using for that directory the Apache directive:

```
Options +ExecCGI
```

In this case, to let scripts with a certain extension run as CGI scripts, you may also add a global AddHandler directive, such as:

```
AddHandler cgi-script pyg
```

to enable scripts with extension *.pyg* to run as CGI scripts. Apache determines what interpreter to use for a script by the shebang line at the script's start. Another way to enable CGI scripts in a directory (if global directive AllowOverride Options is set) is to use Options +ExecCGI in a file named *.htaccess* in that directory.

Python CGI scripts on Xitami

The free, lightweight, simple web server Xitami (*http://www.xitami.org*) makes it easy to install CGI scripts. When any component of a URL is named *cgi-bin*, Xitami takes the URL as a request for CGI execution. Xitami determines what interpreter to use for a script by the shebang line at the script's start, even on Windows platforms.

Cookies

HTTP is a stateless protocol, meaning that it retains no session state between transactions. Cookies, as specified by the HTTP 1.1 standard, let web clients and servers cooperate to build a stateful session from a sequence of HTTP transactions.

Each time a server sends a response to a client's request, the server may initiate or continue a session by sending one or more Set-Cookie headers, whose contents are small data items called *cookies*. When a client sends another request to the server, the client may continue a session by sending Cookie headers with cookies previously received from that server or other servers in the same domain. Each cookie is a pair of strings, the name and value of the cookie, plus optional attributes. Attribute max-age is the maximum number of seconds the cookie should be kept. The client should discard saved cookies after their maximum age. If max-age is missing, then the client should discard the cookie when the user's interactive session ends.

Cookies have no intrinsic privacy nor authentication. Cookies travel in the clear on the Internet, and therefore are vulnerable to sniffing. A malicious client might return cookies different from cookies previously received. To use cookies for authentication or identification or to hold sensitive information, the server must encrypt and encode cookies sent to clients, and decode, decrypt, and verify cookies received back from clients.

Encryption, encoding, decoding, decryption, and verification may all be slow when applied to large amounts of data. Decryption and verification require the server to keep some amount of server-side state. Sending substantial amounts of data back and forth on the network is also slow. The server should therefore persist most state data locally, in files or databases. In most cases, a server should use cookies only as small, encrypted, verifiable keys confirming the identity of a user or session, using DBM files or a relational database (covered in Chapter 11) for session state. HTTP sets a limit of 2 KB on cookie size, but I suggest you normally use substantially smaller cookies.

The Cookie Module

The Cookie module supplies several classes, mostly for backward compatibility. CGI scripts normally use the following classes from module Cookie.

CGI

Morsel	A script does not directly instantiate class Morsel. However, instances of cookie classes hold instances of Morsel. An instance *m* of class Morsel represents a single cookie element: a key string, a value string, and optional attributes. *m* is a mapping. The only valid keys in *m* are cookie attribute names: `'comment'`, `'domain'`, `'expires'`, `'max-age'`, `'path'`, `'secure'`, and `'version'`. Keys into *m* are case-insensitive. Values in *m* are strings, each holding the value of the corresponding cookie attribute.

SimpleCookie	class SimpleCookie(*input*=None)
	A SimpleCookie instance *c* is a mapping. *c*'s keys are strings. *c*'s values are Morsel instances that wrap strings. `c[k]=v` implicitly expands to:
	`c[k]=Morsel(); c[k].set(k,str(v),str(v))`
	If *input* is not None, instantiating *c* implicitly calls `c.load(input)`.

SmartCookie	class SmartCookie(*input*=None)
	A SmartCookie instance *c* is a mapping. *c*'s keys are strings. *c*'s values are Morsel instances that wrap arbitrary values serialized with pickle. `c[k]=v` has the semantics:
	`c[k]=Morsel(); c[k].set(k,str(v),pickle.dumps(v))`
	Module pickle was covered in Chapter 11. Since you have little control on what code executes during implicit deserialization via pickle.loads, class SmartCookie offers correspondingly little security. Unless your script is exposed only on a trusted intranet, avoid SmartCookie—use SimpleCookie instead. You can use any cryptographic approach to build, and take apart again, the strings wrapped by Morsel instance values in SimpleCookie instances. Modules covered in Chapter 21 make it easy to encode arbitrary byte strings as text strings, quite apart from any cryptographic measures.
	SmartCookie is more convenient than SimpleCookie plus cryptography, encoding, and decoding. Convenience and security are often in conflict. The choice is yours. Do not labor under the misapprehension that your system is secure because "after all, nobody knows what I'm doing": security through obscurity isn't. Good cryptography is a necessary (but not sufficient) condition for strong security.

Cookie methods

An instance *c* of SimpleCookie or SmartCookie supplies the following methods.

js_output	*c*.js_output(*attrs*=None)

Returns a string *s*, a JavaScript snippet that sets document.cookie to the cookies held in *c*. You can embed *s* in an HTML response to simulate cookies without sending an HTTP Set-Cookie header if the client browser supports JavaScript. If *attrs* is not None, *s*'s Java-Script sets cookie attributes whose names are in *attrs*.

load	*c*.load(*data*)

When *data* is a string, load parses it and adds to *c* each parsed cookie. When *data* is a mapping, load adds to *c* a new Morsel instance for each item in *data*. Normally, *data* is string os.environ.get('HTTP_COOKIE',''), to recover the cookies the client sent.

output	*c*.output(*attrs*=None,*header*='Set–Cookie',*sep*='\n')

Returns a string *s* formatted as HTTP headers. You can print *c*.output( ) among your response's HTTP headers to send to the client the cookies held in *c*. Each header's name is string *header*, and headers are separated by string *sep*. If *attrs* is not None, *s*'s headers contain only cookie attributes whose names are in *attrs*.

Morsel attributes and methods

An instance *m* of class Morsel supplies three read-write attributes:

coded_value
The cookie's value, encoded as a string; *m*'s output methods use *m*.coded_ value

key
The cookie's name

value
The cookie's value, an arbitrary Python object

Instance *m* also supplies the following methods.

js_output	*m*.js_output(*attrs*=None)

Returns a string *s*, a JavaScript snippet that sets document.cookie to the cookie held in *m*. See also the js_output method of cookie instances.

output	*m*.output(*attrs*=None,*header*='Set–Cookie')
	Returns a string *s* formatted as an HTTP header that sets the cookie held in *m*. See also the output method of cookie instances.
OutputString	*m*.OutputString(*attrs*=['path','comment','domain','max-age', 'secure','version','expires'])
	Return a string *s* that represents the cookie held in *m*, without decorations. *attrs* can be any container suitable as the right-hand operand of in, such as a list or a dictionary.
set	*m*.set(*key*,*value*,*coded_value*)
	Sets *m*'s attributes. *key* and *coded_value* must be strings.

Using module Cookie

Module Cookie supports cookie handling in both client-side and server-side scripts. Typical usage is server-side, often in a CGI script. The following example shows a simple CGI script using cookies:

```
import Cookie, time, os, sys, traceback

sys.stderr = sys.stdout

try:
    # first, the script emits HTTP headers
    c = Cookie.SimpleCookie( )
    c["lastvisit"]=str(time.time( ))
    print c.output( )
    print "Content-Type: text/html"
    print
    # then, the script emits the response's body
    print "<html><head><title>Hello, visitor!</title></head><body>"
    # for the rest of the response, the scripts gets and decodes the cookie
    c = Cookie.SimpleCookie(os.environ.get("HTTP_COOKIE"))
    when = c.get("lastvisit")
    if when is None:
        print "<p>Welcome to this site on your first visit!</p>"
        print "<p>Please click the 'Refresh' button to proceed</p>"
    else:
        try: lastvisit = float(when.value)
        except:
            print "<p>Sorry, cannot decode cookie (%s)</p>"%when.value
            print "</br><pre>"
            traceback.print_exc( )
        else:
            formwhen = time.asctime(time.localtime(lastvisit))
            print "<p>Welcome back to this site!</p>"
            print "<p>You last visited on %s</p>"%formwhen
```

```
        print "</body></html>"
    except:
        print "Content-Type: text/html"
        print
        print "</br><pre>"
        traceback.print_exc( )
```

Each time a client visits the script, the script sets a cookie encoding the current time. On successive visits, if the client browser supports cookies, the script greets the visitor appropriately. Module time is covered in Chapter 12. Note that this example uses no cryptography or server-side persistence of state, since session state is small and not confidential.

Other Server-Side Approaches

A CGI script runs as a new process each time a client requests it. Process startup time, interpreter initialization, connection to databases, and script initialization all add up to measurable overhead. On fast, modern server platforms, the overhead is bearable for light to moderate loads. On a busy server, CGI may not scale up well. Web servers support server-specific ways to reduce overhead, running scripts in processes that can serve for several hits rather than starting up a new CGI process per hit.

Microsoft's ASP (Active Server Pages) is a server extension leveraging a lower-level library, ISAPI, and Microsoft's COM technology. Most ASP pages are coded in the VBScript language, but ASP is language-independent. As the reptilian connection suggests, Python and ASP go very well together, as long as Python is installed with the platform-specific win32all extensions, specifically ActiveScripting. Many other server extensions are cross-platform, not tied to specific operating systems.

The popular content server framework Zope (*http://www.zope.org*) is a Python application. If you need advanced content management features, Zope should definitely be among the solutions you consider. However, Zope is a large, rich, powerful system, needing a full book of its own to do it justice. Therefore, I do not cover Zope further in this book.

FastCGI

FastCGI lets you write scripts similar to CGI scripts, yet use each process to handle multiple hits, either sequentially or simultaneously in separate threads. FastCGI is available for Apache and other free web servers, but at the time of this writing not for Microsoft IIS. See *http://www.fastcgi.com* for FastCGI overviews and details. Go to *http://alldunn.com/python/fcgi.py* for a pure Python interface to FastCGI, letting scripts exploit FastCGI if available and fall back to normal CGI otherwise.

LRWP

Long-Running Web Processes (LRWP) are currently available only for Xitami (see *http://www.xitami.org*). Go to *http://alldunn.com/python/lrwp.py* for a pure Python module (by Robin Dunn, the architect of LRWP) that lets scripts exploit LRWP if available and fall back to normal CGI otherwise. LRWP peer processes connect to the web server via sockets. The server can use any number of peers that offer the same service. The server uses simple round-robin scheduling among equivalent available peers. If a request arrives when all peers are busy, the web server queues the request until a peer is free. This simple, clean protocol makes it easy to load-balance service requests among any number of hosts connected to the server's host by a fast, trusted local area network. Robin Dunn's article about LRWP, at *http://www.imatix.com/html/xitami/index12.htm*, gives architectural details and C and Python examples of LRWP peers.

PyApache and mod_python

Apache's architecture is modular. Besides CGI and FastCGI, other modules support Python server-side scripting with Apache. Simple, lightweight PyApache (*http://bel-epa.com/pyapache/*) focuses on letting you use CGI-like scripts with low overhead. mod_python (*http://www.modpython.org*) affords fuller access to Apache internals, including the ability to write authentication scripts. Both modules support the classic, widespread Apache 1.3 and the newer Apache 2.0.

Webware

Webware for Python (*http://webware.sf.net*) is a highly modular collection of software components for Python server-side web scripting. You can code Python scripts according to different programming models, such as CGI scripts with added-value wrappers, servlets, or Python Server Pages (PSP), and run them under Webware. Webware, in turn, can interface to your web server in many ways, including CGI, FastCGI, mod_python, the specialized Apache module mod_webkit, and special interfaces for Microsoft IIS and AOLServer. Webware offers you a lot of flexibility in architecting, coding, and deploying your server-side Python web scripts.

Among the many ways that Webware offers for you to generate web pages, one that will often be of interest is templating (i.e., automatic insertion of Python-computed values and some control logic in nearly formed HTML scripts). Webware supports templating via PSP, but also, with more power and sharper separation between logic and presentation parts, via the Cheetah package, covered in Chapter 22.

Quixote

Quixote (*http://www.mems-exchange.org/software/quixote/*) is another framework for Python web applications that can interface to your web server via CGI, FastCGI, or mod_python. Quixote defines a new language, the Python Template Language (PTL), and an import hook that lets your Python application directly import PTL-coded modules.

Quixote's PTL is nearly the same as Python, but has a few extras that may be handy in web applications. For example, PTL keyword template defines functions returning string results, automatically called to respond to web requests, with expression statements taken as appending strings to the function's return value. For example, the PTL code:

```
template hw( ):
    'hello'
    'world'
```

is roughly the same as the following Python code:

```
def hw( ):
    _result = []
    _result.append('hello')
    _result.append('world')
    return ''.join(_result)
```

Custom Pure Python Servers

In Chapter 19, we saw that the standard Python library includes modules that implement web servers. You can subclass BaseHTTPServer and implement special-purpose web servers with little effort. Such special-purpose servers are useful in low-volume applications, but they may not scale up well to handle moderate to high server loads.

Modules asyncore and asynchat, also covered in Chapter 19, exhibit very different performance characteristics. The event-driven architecture of asynchat-based applications affords high scalability and performance, beating applications that use lower-level languages and traditional architectures (multiprocess or multithreading).

The Twisted package, also covered in Chapter 19, has the same performance advantages as asyncore, and supplies much richer functionality. With Twisted, you can program a web site at high levels of abstraction and still obtain superb scalability and performance.

21

MIME and Network Encodings

What travels on a network are streams of bytes or text. However, what you want to send over the network often has more structure. The Multipurpose Internet Mail Extensions (MIME) and other encoding standards bridge the gap by specifying how to represent structured data as bytes or text. Python supports such encodings through many library modules, such as base64, quopri, uu, and the modules of the email package. This chapter covers these modules.

Encoding Binary Data as Text

Several kinds of media (e.g., email messages) contain only text. When you want to transmit binary data via such media, you need to encode the data as text strings. The Python standard library supplies modules that support the standard encodings known as Base 64, Quoted Printable, and UU.

The base64 Module

The base64 module supports the encoding specified in RFC 1521 as Base 64. The Base 64 encoding is a compact way to represent arbitrary binary data as text, without any attempt to produce human-readable results. Module base64 supplies four functions.

decode	decode(*infile*,*outfile*)
	Reads text-file-like object *infile*, by calling *infile*.readline until end of file (i.e, until a call to *infile*.readline returns an empty string), decodes the Base 64–encoded text thus read, and writes the decoded data to binary-file-like object *outfile*.

decodestring	decodestring(s)
	Decodes text string s, which contains one or more complete lines of Base 64–encoded text, and returns the byte string with the corresponding decoded data.

encode	encode(infile,outfile)
	Reads binary-file-like object infile, by calling infile.read (for a few bytes at a time—the amount of data that Base 64 encodes into a single output line) until end of file (i.e, until a call to infile.read returns an empty string). Then it encodes the data thus read in Base 64, and writes the encoded text as lines to text-file-like object outfile. encode appends \n to each line of text it emits, including the last one.

encodestring	encodestring(s)
	Encodes binary string s, which contains arbitrary bytes, and returns a text string with one or more complete lines of Base 64–encoded data. encodestring always returns a text string ending with \n.

The quopri Module

The quopri module supports the encoding specified in RFC 1521 as Quoted Printable (QP). QP can represent any binary data as text, but it's mainly intended for data that is textual, with a relatively modest amount of characters with the high bit set (i.e., characters outside of the ASCII range). For such data, QP produces results that are both compact and rather human-readable. Module quopri supplies four functions.

decode	decode(infile,outfile,header=False)
	Reads file-like object infile, by calling infile.readline until end of file (i.e., until a call to infile.readline returns an empty string), decodes the QP-encoded ASCII text thus read, and writes the decoded data to file-like object outfile. When header is true, decode also decodes _ (underscores) into spaces.

decodestring	decodestring(s,header=False)
	Decodes string s, which contains QP-encoded ASCII text, and returns the byte string with the decoded data. When header is true, decodestring also decodes _ (underscores) into spaces.

encode	encode(infile,outfile,spaces,header=False)
	Reads file-like object infile, by calling infile.readline until end of file (i.e, until a call to infile.readline returns an empty string),

encodes the data thus read in QP, and writes the encoded ASCII text to file-like object *outfile*. When *spaces* is true, encode also encodes spaces and tabs. When *header* is true, encode encodes spaces as _ (underscores).

encodestring	encodestring(*s*,*spaces*=False,*header*=False)
	Encodes string *s*, which contains arbitrary bytes, and returns a string with QP-encoded ASCII text. When *spaces* is true, encodestring also encodes spaces and tabs. When *header* is true, encodestring encodes spaces as _ (underscores).

The uu Module

The uu module supports the traditional Unix-to-Unix (UU) encoding, as implemented by Unix programs *uuencode* and *uudecode*. UU begins encoded data with a begin line, which also gives the filename and permissions of the file being encoded, and ends it with an end line. Therefore, UU encoding lets you embed encoded data in otherwise unstructured text, while Base 64 encoding relies on the existence of other indications of where the encoded data starts and finishes. Module uu supplies two functions.

decode	decode(*infile*,*outfile*=None,*mode*=None)
	Reads file-like object *infile*, by calling *infile*.readline until end of file (i.e, until a call to *infile*.readline returns an empty string) or until a terminator line (the string 'end' surrounded by any amount of whitespace). decode decodes the UU-encoded text thus read, and writes the decoded data to file-like object *outfile*. When *outfile* is None, decode creates the file specified in the UU-format begin line, with the permission bits given by *mode* (the permission bits specified in the begin line, when *mode* is None). In this case, decode raises an exception if the file already exists.

encode	encode(*infile*,*outfile*,*name*='-',*mode*=0666)
	Reads file-like object *infile*, by calling *infile*.read (for a few bytes at a time—the amount of data that UU encodes into a single output line) until end of file (i.e, until a call to *infile*.read returns an empty string). Then it encodes the data thus read in UU, and writes the encoded text to file-like object *outfile*. encode also writes a UU begin line before the encoded text, and a UU end line after the encoded text. In the begin line, encode specifies the filename as *name* and the mode as *mode*.

MIME and Email Format Handling

Python supplies the email package to handle parsing, generation, and manipulation of MIME files such as email messages, network news posts, and so on. The Python standard library also contains other modules that handle some parts of these jobs. However, the new email package offers a more complete and systematic approach to these important tasks. I therefore suggest you use package email, not the older modules that partially overlap with parts of email's functionality. Package email has nothing to do with receiving or sending email; for such tasks, see modules poplib and smtplib, covered in Chapter 18. Instead, package email deals with how you handle messages after you receive them or before you send them.

Functions in Package email

Package email supplies two factory functions returning an instance *m* of class email.Message.Message. These functions rely on class email.Parser.Parser, but the factory functions are handier and simpler. Therefore, I do not cover module Parser further in this book.

message_ **from_string**	message_from_string(*s*) Builds *m* by parsing string *s*.

message_ **from_file**	message_from_file(*f*) Builds *m* by parsing the contents of file-like object *f*, which must be open for reading.

The email.Message Module

The email.Message module supplies class Message. All parts of package email produce, modify, or use instances of class Message. An instance *m* of Message models a MIME message, including headers and a payload (data content). You can create *m*, initially empty, by calling class Message, which accepts no arguments. More often, you create *m* by parsing via functions message_from_string and message_from_file of module email, or by other indirect means such as the classes covered in "Creating Messages" later in this chapter. *m*'s payload can be a string, a single other instance of Message, or a list of other Message instances for a multipart message.

You can set arbitrary headers on email messages you're building. Several Internet RFCs specify headers that you can use for a wide variety of purposes. The main applicable RFC is RFC 2822 (see *http://www.faqs.org/rfcs/rfc2822.html*). An instance *m* of class Message holds headers as well as a payload. *m* is a mapping, with header names as keys and header value strings as values. The semantics of *m* as a mapping are rather different from those of a dictionary, to make *m* more convenient. *m*'s keys are case-insensitive. *m* keeps headers in the order in which you add them, and methods keys, values, and items return headers in that order. *m* can have more than one header named *key*—*m*[*key*] returns an arbitrary one of them, del *m*[*key*] deletes all of them. len(*m*) returns the total number of headers, counting duplicates, not just the number of distinct header names. If there is no header named *key*, *m*[*key*] returns None and does not raise KeyError (i.e., behaves like *m*.get(*key*)), and del *m*[*key*] is a no-operation.

An instance *m* of Message supplies the following attributes and methods dealing with *m*'s headers and payload.

---

add_header   *m*.add_header(*_name,_value,**_params*)

Like *m*[*_name*]=*_value*, but you can also supply header parameters as keyword arguments. For each keyword argument *pname=pvalue*, add_header changes underscores to dashes, then appends to the header's value a parameter of the form:

> ; *pname*="*pvalue*"

If *pvalue* is None, add_header appends only a parameter '; *pname*'.

---

add_payload   *m*.add_payload(*payload*)

Adds the *payload* to *m*'s payload. If *m*'s payload was None, *m*'s payload is now *payload*. If *m*'s payload was a list, appends *payload* to the list. If *m*'s payload was a single item *x*, *m*'s payload becomes the list [*x,payload*], but only if *m*'s Content-Type header is missing or has a main type of multipart. Otherwise, when *m* has a single payload and a Content-Type whose main type is not multipart, *m*.add_payload(*payload*) raises a MultipartConversionError exception.

---

as_string   *m*.as_string(*unixfrom=False*)

Returns the entire message as a string. When *unixfrom* is true, also includes a first line, normally starting with 'From ', known as the envelope header of the message.

---

epilogue   Attribute *m*.epilogue can be None, or a string that becomes part of the message's string form after the last boundary line. Mail programs normally don't display this text. epilogue is a normal attribute of *m*: your program can access it when you're examining an *m* that is fully built by whatever means, and your program can bind it when you're building or modifying *m* in your program.

---

get_all   *m*.get_all(*name,default=None*)

Returns a list with all values of headers named *name*, in the order in which the headers were added to *m*. When *m* has no header named *name*, get_all returns *default*.

---

get_boundary   *m*.get_boundary(*default=None*)

Returns the string value of the boundary parameter of *m*'s Content-Type header. When *m* has no Content-Type header, or the header has no boundary parameter, get_boundary returns *default*.

get_charsets	`m.get_charsets(`*default*`=None)`
	Returns the list *L* of string values of parameter charset of *m*'s Content-Type headers. When *m* is multipart, *L* has one item per part, otherwise *L* has length 1. For parts that have no Content-Type, no charset parameter, or a main type different from 'text', the corresponding item in *L* is *default*.
get_filename	`m.get_filename(`*default*`=None)`
	Returns the string value of the filename parameter of *m*'s Content-Disposition header. When *m* has no Content-Disposition, or the header has no filename parameter, get_filename returns *default*.
get_maintype	`m.get_maintype(`*default*`=None)`
	Returns *m*'s main content type, a string '*maintype*' taken from header Content-Type converted to lowercase. When *m* has no header Content-Type, get_maintype returns *default*.
get_param	`m.get_param(`*param*`,`*default*`=None,`*header*`='Content-Type')`
	Returns the string value of the parameter named *param* of *m*'s header named *header*. Returns the empty string for a parameter specified just by name. When *m* has no header *header*, or the header has no parameter named *param*, get_param returns *default*.
get_params	`m.get_params(`*default*`=None,`*header*`='Content-Type')`
	Returns the parameters of *m*'s header named *header*, a list of pairs of strings giving each parameter's name and value. Uses the empty string as the value for parameters specified just by name. When *m* has no header *header*, get_params returns *default*.
get_payload	`m.get_payload(`*i*`=None,`*decode*`=False)`
	Returns *m*'s payload. When `m.is_multipart()` is False, *i* must be None, and `m.get_payload()` returns *m*'s entire payload, a string or a Message instance. If *decode* is true, and the value of header Content-Transfer-Encoding is either 'quoted-printable' or 'base64', m.get_payload also decodes the payload. If *decode* is false, or header Content-Transfer-Encoding is missing or has other values, m.get_payload returns the payload unchanged.
	When `m.is_multipart()` is True, *decode* must be false. When *i* is None, `m.get_payload()` returns *m*'s payload as a list. Otherwise, m.get_payload() returns the *i*th item of the payload, and raises TypeError if *i* is less than 0 or is too large.
get_subtype	`m.get_subtype(`*default*`=None)`
	Returns *m*'s content subtype, a string '*subtype*' taken from header Content-Type converted to lowercase. When *m* has no header Content-Type, get_subtype returns *default*.

get_type	`m.get_type(default=None)`
	Returns *m*'s content type, a string `'maintype/subtype'` taken from header Content-Type converted to lowercase. When *m* has no header Content-Type, get_type returns *default*.
get_unixfrom	`m.get_unixfrom( )`
	Returns the envelope header string for *m*, or None if the envelope header was never set.
is_multipart	`m.is_multipart( )`
	Returns True when *m*'s payload is a list, otherwise False.
preamble	Attribute `m.preamble` can be None or a string that becomes part of the message's string form before the first boundary line. Only mail programs that don't support multipart messages display this text to the user, so you can use this attribute to alert the user that your message is multipart and that a different mail program is needed to view it. preamble is a normal attribute of *m*: your program can access it when you're examining an *m* that is fully built by whatever means, and your program can bind it when you're building or modifying *m* in your program.
set_boundary	`m.set_boundary(boundary)`
	Sets the boundary parameter of *m*'s Content-Type header to *boundary*. When *m* has no Content-Type header, raises HeaderParseError.
set_payload	`m.set_payload(payload)`
	Sets *m*'s payload to *payload*, which must be a string or list, as appropriate.
set_unixfrom	`m.set_unixfrom(unixfrom)`
	Sets the envelope header string for *m*. *unixfrom* is the entire envelope header line, including the leading `'From '` but not including the trailing `'\n'`.
walk	`m.walk( )`
	Returns an iterator on all parts and subparts of *m*, to walk the tree of parts depth-first.

The email.Generator Module

The email.Generator module supplies class Generator, which you can use to generate the textual form of a message *m*. *m*.as_string and str(*m*) may be sufficient, but class Generator gives you slightly more flexibility. You instantiate Generator with a mandatory argument and two optional ones.

Generator   class Generator(*outfp*,*mangle_from_*=False,*maxheaderlen*=78)

outfp is a file or file-like object supplying method write. When *mangle_from_* is true, *g* prepends a '>' to any line in a message's payload that starts with 'From ' This helps make the message's textual form more safely parseable. *g* wraps each header line at semicolons, into physical lines of no more than *maxheaderlen* characters, for readability. To use *g*, just call it:

> g(*m*, *unixfrom*=False)

This emits *m* in text form to *outfp*, like *outfp*.write(*m*.as_string(*unixfrom*)).

Creating Messages

Package email supplies modules with names starting with 'MIME', each module supplying a subclass of Message named like the module. These classes make it easier to create Message instances of various MIME types. The MIME classes are as follows.

MIMEAudio   class MIMEAudio(*_audiodata*,*_subtype*=None,*_encoder*=None, ***_params*)

_audiodata is a byte string of audio data to pack in a message of MIME type 'audio/*_subtype*'. When *_subtype* is None, *_audiodata* must be parseable by standard Python module sndhdr to determine the subtype; otherwise MIMEAudio raises a TypeError. When *_encoder* is None, MIMEAudio encodes data as Base 64, which is generally optimal. Otherwise, *_encoder* must be callable with one parameter *m*, the message being constructed; *_encoder* must then call *m*.get_payload( ) to get the payload, encode the payload, put the encoded form back by calling *m*.set_payload, and set *m*['Content-Transfer-Encoding'] appropriately. MIMEAudio passes the *_params* dictionary of keyword argument names and values to *m*.add_header to construct *m*'s Content-Type.

MIMEBase   class MIMEBase(*_maintype*,*_subtype*,***_params*)

The base class of all MIME classes; directly subclasses Message. Instantiating:

> *m* = MIMEBase(*main*,*sub*,**parms)

is equivalent to the longer and less convenient idiom:

```
m = Message( )
m.add_header('Content-Type','%s/%s'%(main,sub),**parms)
m.add_header('Mime-Version','1.0')
```

MIMEImage class MIMEAudio(_imagedata,_subtype=None,_encoder=None, **_params)

Like MIMEAudio, but with maintype 'image' and using standard Python module imghdr to determine the subtype if needed.

MIMEMessage class MIMEMessage(msg,_subtype='rfc822')

Packs msg, which must be an instance of Message (or a subclass), as the payload of a message of MIME type 'message/_subtype'.

MIMEText class MIMEText(_text,_subtype='plain',_charset='us-ascii', _encoder=None)

Packs text string _text as the payload of a message of MIME type 'text/_subtype' with the given charset. When _encoder is None, MIMEText does not encode the text, which is generally optimal. Otherwise, _encoder must be callable with one parameter m, the message being constructed; _encoder must then call m.get_payload( ) to get the payload, encode the payload, put the encoded form back by calling m.set_payload, and set m['Content-Transfer-Encoding'] appropriately.

The email.Encoders Module

The email.Encoders module supplies functions that take a message m as their only argument, encode m's payload, and set m's headers appropriately.

encode_base64 encode_base64(m)

Uses Base 64 encoding, optimal for arbitrary binary data.

encode_noop encode_noop(m)

Does nothing to m's payload and headers.

encode_quopri encode_quopri(m)

Uses Quoted Printable encoding, optimal for textual data that is not fully ASCII.

encode_7or8bit encode_7or8bit(*m*)

Does nothing to *m*'s payload, sets header Content-Transfer-Encoding to '8bit' if any byte of *m*'s payload has the high bit set, or otherwise to '7bit'.

The email.Utils Module

The email.Utils module supplies miscellaneous functions useful for email processing.

decode decode(*s*)

Decodes string *s* as per the rules in RFC 2047 and returns the resulting Unicode string.

dump_
address_pair dump_address_pair(*pair*)

pair is a pair of strings (*name*,*email_address*). dump_address_pair returns a string *s* with the address to insert in header fields such as To and Cc. When *name* is false (e.g., ''), dump_address_pair returns *email_address*.

encode encode(*s*,*charset*='iso-8859-1',*encoding*='q')

Encodes string *s* (which must use the given *charset*) as per the rules in RFC 2047. *encoding* must be 'q' to specify Quoted Printable, or 'b' to specify Base 64.

formatdate formatdate(*timeval*=None,*localtime*=False)

timeval is a number of seconds since the epoch. When *timeval* is None, formatdate uses the current time. When *localtime* is true, formatdate uses the local timezone; otherwise it uses UTC. formatdate returns a string with the given time instant formatted in the way specified by RFC 2822.

getaddresses getaddresses(*L*)

Parses each item of *L*, a list of address strings as used in header fields such as To and Cc, and returns a list of pairs of strings (*name*,*email_address*). When getaddresses cannot parse an item of *L* as an address, getaddresses uses (None,None) as the corresponding item in the list it returns.

mktime_tz mktime_tz(*t*)

t is a tuple with 10 items, the first 9 in the same format used in module time covered in Chapter 12, *t*[-1] is a time zone as an offset in seconds from UTC (with the opposite sign from time. timezone, as specified by RFC 2822). When $t[-1]$ is None, mktime_tz uses the local time zone. mktime_tz returns a float with the number of seconds since the epoch, in UTC, corresponding to the time instant that t denotes.

parseaddr	parseaddr(s)
	Parses string s, which contains an address as typically specified in header fields such as To and Cc, and returns a pair of strings (*name,email_address*). When parseaddr cannot parse s as an address, parseaddr returns (None,None).

parsedate	parsedate(s)
	Parses string s as per the rules in RFC 2822 and returns a tuple t with 9 items, as used in module time covered in Chapter 12 (the items $t[-3:]$ are not meaningful). parsedate also attempts to parse erroneous variations on RFC 2822 that widespread mailers use. When parsedate cannot parse s, parsedate returns None.

parsedate_tz	parsedate_tz(s)
	Like parsedate, but returns a tuple t with 10 items, where $t[-1]$ is s's time zone as an offset in seconds from UTC (with the opposite sign from time.timezone, as specified by RFC 2822), like in the argument that mktime_tz accepts. Items $t[-4:-1]$ are not meaningful. When s has no time zone, $t[-1]$ is None.

quote	quote(s)
	Returns a copy of string s where each double quote (") becomes '\"' and each existing backslash is repeated.

unquote	unquote(s)
	Returns a copy of string s where leading and trailing double quote characters (") and angle brackets (<>) are removed if they surround the rest of s.

The Message Classes of the rfc822 and mimetools Modules

The best way to handle email-like messages is with package email. However, other modules covered in Chapters 18 and 20 use instances of class rfc822.Message or its subclass mimetools.Message. This section covers the subset of these classes' functionality that you need to make effective use of the modules covered in Chapters 18 and 20.

An instance *m* of class Message is a mapping, with the headers' names as keys and the corresponding header value strings as values. Keys and values are strings, and keys are case-insensitive. *m* supports all mapping methods except clear, copy, popitem, and update. get and setdefault default to ' ', instead of None. Instance *m* also supplies convenience methods (e.g., to combine getting a header's value and parsing it as a date or an address). I suggest you use for such purposes the functions of module email.Utils, covered earlier in this chapter, and use *m* just as a mapping.

When *m* is an instance of mimetools.Message, *m* supplies additional methods.

---

getmaintype   *m*.getmaintype( )

Returns *m*'s main content type, taken from header Content-Type converted to lowercase. When *m* has no header Content-Type, getmaintype returns 'text'.

---

getparam   *m*.getparam(*param*)

Returns the string value of the parameter named *param* of *m*'s header Content-Type.

---

getsubtype   *m*.getsubtype( )

Returns *m*'s content subtype, taken from header Content-Type converted to lowercase. When *m* has no header Content-Type, getsubtype returns 'plain'.

---

gettype   *m*.gettype( )

Returns *m*'s content type, taken from header Content-Type converted to lowercase. When *m* has no header Content-Type, gettype returns 'text/plain'.

22

Structured Text: HTML

Most documents on the Web use HTML, the HyperText Markup Language. Markup is the insertion of special tokens, known as *tags*, in a text document to give structure to the text. HTML is an application of the large, general standard known as SGML, the Standard General Markup Language. In practice, many of the Web's documents use HTML in sloppy or incorrect ways. Browsers have evolved many practical heuristics over the years to try and compensate for this, but even so, it still often happens that a browser displays an incorrect web page in some weird way.

Moreover, HTML was never suitable for much more than presenting documents on a screen. Complete and precise extraction of the information in the document, working backward from the document's presentation, is often unfeasible. To tighten things up again, HTML has evolved into a more rigorous standard called XHTML. XHTML is very similar to traditional HTML, but it is defined in terms of XML and more precisely than HTML. You can handle XHTML with the tools covered in Chapter 23.

Despite the difficulties, it's often possible to extract at least some useful information from HTML documents. Python supplies the sgmllib, htmllib, and HTMLParser modules for the task of parsing HTML documents, whether this parsing is for the purpose of presenting the documents, or, more typically, as part of an attempt to extract information from them. Generating HTML and embedding Python in HTML are also frequent tasks. No standard Python library module supports HTML generation or embedding directly, but you can use normal Python string manipulation, and third-party modules can also help.

The sgmllib Module

The name of the sgmllib module is misleading: sgmllib parses only a tiny subset of SGML, but it is still a good way to get information from HTML files. sgmllib supplies one class, SGMLParser, which you subclass to override and add methods.

The most frequently used methods of an instance *s* of your subclass *X* of SGMLParser are as follows.

close	`s.close( )`
	Tells the parser that there is no more input data. When *X* overrides close, *x*.close must call SGMLParser.close to ensure that buffered data get processed.

do_tag	`s.do_tag(attributes)`
	X supplies a method with such a name for each *tag*, with no corresponding end tag, that *X* wants to process. *tag* must be in lowercase in the method name, but can be in any mix of cases in the parsed text. SGMLParser's handle_tag method calls do_*tag* as appropriate. *attributes* is a list of pairs (*name,value*), where *name* is each attribute's name, lowercased, and *value* is the value, processed to resolve entity references and character references and to remove surrounding quotes.

end_tag	`s.end_tag( )`
	X supplies a method with such a name for each *tag* whose end tag *X* wants to process. *tag* must be in lowercase in the method name, but can be in any mix of cases in the parsed text. *X* must also supply a method named start_*tag*, otherwise end_*tag* is ignored. SGMLParser's handle_endtag method calls end_*tag* as appropriate.

feed	`s.feed(data)`
	Passes to the parser some of the text being parsed. The parser may process some prefix of the text, holding the rest in a buffer until the next call to `s.feed` or `s.close`.

handle_charref	`s.handle_charref(ref)`
	Called to process a character reference `'&#ref;'`. SGMLParser's implementation of handle_charref handles decimal numbers in range(0,256), like:

```
def handle_charref(self, ref):
    try:
        c = chr(int(ref))
    except (TypeError, ValueError):
        self.unknown_charref(ref)
    else: self.handle_data(c)
```

Your subclass *X* may override handle_charref or unknown_charref in order to support other forms of character references `'&#...;'`.

handle_ comment	`s.handle_comment(`*`comment`*`)` Called to handle comments. *comment* is the string within '`<!--...-->`', without the delimiters. `SGMLParser`'s implementation of handle_comment does nothing.
handle_data	`s.handle_data(`*`data`*`)` Called to process each arbitrary string *data*. Your subclass *X* normally overrides handle_data. `SGMLParser`'s implementation of handle_data does nothing.
handle_endtag	`s.handle_endtag(`*`tag`*`,`*`method`*`)` Called to handle termination tags for which *X* supplies methods named start_*tag* and end_*tag*. *tag* is the tag string, lowercased. *method* is the bound method for end_*tag*. `SGMLParser`'s implementation of handle_endtag calls *method*( ).

**handle_
entityref**
	`s.handle_entityref(`*`ref`*`)`
	
	Called to process an entity reference '`&`*`ref`*`;`'. `SGMLParser`'s implementation of handle_entityref looks *ref* up in *s*.entitydefs, like:
	
	``
	def handle_entityref(self, ref):
	    try: t = self.entitydefs[ref]
	    except KeyError: self.unknown_entityref(ref)
	    else: self.handle_data(t)
	``
	
	Your subclass *X* may override handle_entityref or unknown_entityref in order to support entity references '`&...;`' in different ways. `SGMLParser`'s attribute entitydefs includes keys '`amp`', '`apos`', '`gt`', '`lt`', and '`quot`'.

handle_starttag	`s.handle_starttag(`*`tag, method, attributes`*`)` Called to handle tags for which *X* supplies a method start_*tag* or do_*tag*. *tag* is the tag string, lowercased. *method* is the bound method for start_*tag* or do_*tag*. *attributes* is a list of pairs (*name,value*), where *name* is each attribute's name, lowercased, and *value* is the value, processed to resolve entity references and character references and to remove surrounding quotes. When *X* supplies both start_*tag* and do_*tag* methods, start_*tag* has precedence and do_*tag* is ignored. `SGMLParser`'s implementation of handle_starttag calls *method*(*attributes*).
report_ unbalanced	`s.report_unbalanced(`*`tag`*`)` Called when tags terminate without being open. *tag* is the tag string, lowercased. `SGMLParser`'s implementation of report_unbalanced does nothing.

start_tag	*s*.start_tag(*attributes*)
	X supplies a method thus named for each *tag*, with an end tag, that *X* wants to process. *tag* must be in lowercase in the method name, but can be in any mix of cases in the parsed text. SGMLParser's handle_tag method calls start_tag as appropriate. *attributes* is a list of pairs (*name,value*), where *name* is each attribute's name, lowercased, and *value* is the value, processed to resolve entity references and character references and to remove surrounding quotes.
unknown_ charref	*s*.unknown_charref(*ref*)
	Called to process invalid or unrecognized character references. SGMLParser's implementation of unknown_charref does nothing.
unknown_ endtag	*s*.unknown_endtag(*tag*)
	Called to process termination tags for which *X* supplies no specific method. SGMLParser's implementation of unknown_endtag does nothing.
unknown_ entityref	*s*.unknown_entityref(*ref*)
	Called to process unknown entity references. SGMLParser's implementation of unknown_entityref does nothing.
unknown_ starttag	*s*.unknown_starttag(*tag, attributes*)
	Called to process tags for which *X* supplies no specific method. *tag* is the tag string, lowercased. *attributes* is a list of pairs (*name,value*), where *name* is each attribute's name, lowercased, and *value* is the value, processed to resolve entity references and character references and to remove surrounding quotes. SGMLParser's implementation of unknown_starttag does nothing.

The following example uses sgmllib for a typical HTML-related task: fetching a page from the Web with urllib, parsing it, and outputting the hyperlinks. The example uses urlparse to check the page's links, and outputs only links whose URLs have an explicit scheme of 'http'.

```
import sgmllib, urllib, urlparse

class LinksParser(sgmllib.SGMLParser):
    def __init__(self):
        sgmllib.SGMLParser.__init__(self)
        self.seen = {}
    def do_a(self, attributes):
        for name, value in attributes:
            if name == 'href' and value not in self.seen:
                self.seen[value] = True
```

```
        pieces = urlparse.urlparse(value)
        if pieces[0] != 'http': return
        print urlparse.urlunparse(pieces)
        return

p = LinksParser()
f = urllib.urlopen('http://www.python.org/index.html')
BUFSIZE = 8192
while True:
    data = f.read(BUFSIZE)
    if not data: break
    p.feed(data)
p.close()
```

Class `LinksParser` only needs to define method `do_a`. The superclass calls back to this method for all `<a>` tags, and the method loops on the attributes, looking for one named `'href'`, then works with the corresponding value (i.e., the relevant URL).

The htmllib Module

The `htmllib` module supplies a class named `HTMLParser` that subclasses `SGMLParser` and defines `start_tag`, `do_tag`, and `end_tag` methods for tags defined in HTML 2.0. `HTMLParser` implements and overrides methods in terms of calls to methods of a formatter object, covered later in this chapter. You can subclass `HTMLParser` to add or override methods. In addition to the `start_tag`, `do_tag`, and `end_tag` methods, an instance *h* of `HTMLParser` supplies the following attributes and methods.

---

anchor_bgn   *h*.`anchor_bgn(href,name,type)`

Called for each `<a>` tag. *href*, *name*, and *type* are the string values of the tag's attributes with the same names. `HTMLParser`'s implementation of `anchor_bgn` maintains a list of outgoing hyperlinks (i.e., *href* arguments of method *s*.`anchor_bgn`) in an instance attribute named *s*.`anchorlist`.

---

anchor_end   *h*.`anchor_end()`

Called for each `</a>` end tag. `HTMLParser`'s implementation of `anchor_end` emits to the formatter a footnote reference that is an index within *s*.`anchorlist`. In other words, by default, `HTMLParser` asks the formatter to format an `<a>`/`</a>` tag pair as the text inside the tag, followed by a footnote reference number that points to the URL in the `<a>` tag. Of course, it's up to the formatter to deal with this formatting request.

---

anchorlist   The *h*.`anchor_list` attribute contains the list of outgoing hyperlink URLs built by *h*.`anchor_bgn`.

---

formatter	The *h*.formatter attribute is the formatter object *f* associated with *h*, which you pass as the only argument when you instantiate HTMLParser(*f*).

handle_image	*h*.handle_image(*source,alt,ismap='',align='',width='',height=''*)
	Called for each <img> tag. Each argument is the string value of the tag's attribute of the same name. HTMLParser's implementation of handle_image calls *h*.handle_data(*alt*).

nofill	*h*.nofill
	The *h*.nofill attribute is false when the parser is collapsing whitespace, the normal case. It is true when the parser must preserve whitespace, typically within a <pre> tag.

save_bgn	*h*.save_bgn( )
	Diverts data to an internal buffer instead of passing it to the formatter, until the next call to *h*.save_end( ). *h* has only one buffer, so you cannot nest save_bgn calls.

save_end	*h*.save_end( )
	Returns a string with all data in the internal buffer, and directs data back to the formatter from now on. If save_bgn state was not on, raises TypeError.

The formatter Module

The formatter module defines formatter and writer classes. You instantiate a formatter by passing to the class a writer instance, and then you pass the formatter instance to class HTMLParser of module htmllib. You can define your own formatters and writers by subclassing formatter's classes and overriding methods appropriately, but I do not cover this advanced and rarely used possibility in this book. An application with special output requirements would typically define an appropriate writer, subclassing AbstractWriter and overriding all methods, and use class AbstractFormatter without needing to subclass it. Module formatter supplies the following classes.

Abstract Formatter	class AbstractFormatter(*writer*)
	The standard formatter implementation, suitable for most tasks.

AbstractWriter	class AbstractWriter( )
	A writer implementation that prints each of its method names when called, suitable for debugging purposes only.

DumbWriter	class DumbWriter(*file*=sys.stdout,*maxcol*=72)
	A writer implementation that emits text to file object *file*, with word wrapping to ensure that no text line is longer than *maxcol* characters.

NullFormatter	class NullFormatter(*writer*=None)
	A formatter implementation whose methods are do-nothing stubs. When *writer* is None, instantiates NullWriter. Suitable when you subclass HMTLParser to analyze an HTML document but don't want any output to happen.

NullWriter	class NullWriter( )
	A writer implementation whose methods are do-nothing stubs.

The htmlentitydefs Module

The htmlentitydefs module supplies just one attribute, a dictionary named entitydefs that maps each entity defined in HTML 2.0 to the corresponding string in the ISO-8859-1 (also known as Latin-1) encoding. Module htmllib uses module htmlentitydefs internally.

Parsing HTML with htmllib

The following example uses htmllib to perform the same task as in the previous example for sgmllib, fetching a page from the Web with urllib, parsing it, and outputting the hyperlinks:

```
import htmllib, formatter, urllib, urlparse

p = htmllib.HTMLParser(formatter.NullFormatter( ))
f = urllib.urlopen('http://www.python.org/index.html')
BUFSIZE = 8192
while True:
    data = f.read(BUFSIZE)
    if not data: break
    p.feed(data)
p.close( )

seen = {}
for url in p.anchorlist:
    if url in seen: continue
    seen[url] = True
    pieces = urlparse.urlparse(url)
    if pieces[0] == 'http':
        print urlparse.urlunparse(pieces)
```

The example exploits the anchorlist attribute of class htmllib.HTMLParser, and therefore does not need to perform any subclassing. htmllib.HTMLParser builds the anchorlist attribute as it parses the HTML page, so the code need only loop on the list and work with the list's items, each a relevant URL.

The HTMLParser Module

Module HTMLParser supplies one class, HTMLParser, that you subclass to override and add methods. HTMLParser.HTMLParser is similar to sgmllib.SGMLParser, but is simpler and able to parse XHTML as well. The main differences between HTMLParser and SGMLParser are the following:

- HMTLParser does not call back to methods named do_*tag*, start_*tag*, and end_ *tag*. To process tags and end tags, your subclass *X* of HTMLParser must override methods handle_starttag and/or handle_endtag and check explicitly for the tags it wants to process.

- HMTLParser does not keep track of, nor check, tag nesting in any way.

- HMTLParser does nothing, by default, to resolve character and entity references. Your subclass *X* of HTMLParser must override methods handle_charref and/or handle_entityref if it needs to perform processing of such references.

The most frequently used methods of an instance *h* of a subclass *X* of HTMLParser are as follows.

close	*h*.close( )
	Tells the parser that there is no more input data. When *X* overrides close, *h*.close must also call HTMLParser.close to ensure that buffered data gets processed.
feed	*h*.feed(*data*)
	Passes to the parser a part of the text being parsed. The parser processes some prefix of the text and holds the rest in a buffer until the next call to *h*.feed or *h*.close.
handle_charref	*h*.handle_charref(*ref*)
	Called to process a character reference '&#*ref*;'. HTMLParser's implementation of handle_charref does nothing.
handle_ comment	*h*.handle_comment(*comment*)
	Called to handle comments. *comment* is the string within '<!--...-->', without the delimiters. HTMLParser's implementation of handle_ comment does nothing.

handle_data	*h*.handle_data(*data*)
	Called to process each arbitrary string *data*. Your subclass *X* almost always overrides handle_data. HTMLParser's implementation of handle_data does nothing.
handle_endtag	*h*.handle_endtag(*tag*)
	Called to handle termination tags. *tag* is the tag string, lowercased. HTMLParser's implementation of handle_endtag does nothing.
handle_ entityref	*h*.handle_entityref(*ref*)
	Called to process an entity reference '&*ref*;'. HTMLParser's implementation of handle_entityref does nothing.
handle_starttag	*h*.handle_starttag(*tag*, *attributes*)
	Called to handle tags. *tag* is the tag string, lowercased. *attributes* is a list of pairs (*name,value*), where *name* is each attribute's name, lowercased, and *value* is the value, processed to resolve entity references and character references and to remove surrounding quotes. HTMLParser's implementation of handle_starttag does nothing.

The following example uses HTMLParser to perform the same task as our previous examples: fetching a page from the Web with urllib, parsing it, and outputting the hyperlinks.

```
import HTMLParser, urllib, urlparse

class LinksParser(HTMLParser.HTMLParser):
    def __init__(self):
        HTMLParser.HTMLParser.__init__(self)
        self.seen = {}
    def handle_starttag(self, tag, attributes):
        if tag != 'a': return
        for name, value in attributes:
            if name == 'href' and value not in self.seen:
                self.seen[value] = True
                pieces = urlparse.urlparse(value)
                if pieces[0] != 'http': return
                print urlparse.urlunparse(pieces)
                return

p = LinksParser( )
f = urllib.urlopen('http://www.python.org/index.html')
BUFSIZE = 8192
while True:
    data = f.read(BUFSIZE)
```

```
    if not data: break
    p.feed(data)

p.close( )
```

This example is similar to the one for sgmllib. However, since the HTMLParser. HTMLParser superclass performs no per-tag dispatching to methods, class LinksParser needs to override method handle_starttag and check that the *tag* is indeed 'a'.

Generating HTML

Python does not come with tools to generate HTML. If you want an advanced framework for structured HTML generation, I recommend Robin Friedrich's HTMLGen 2.2 (available at *http://starship.python.net/crew/friedrich/HTMLgen/ html/main.html*), but I do not cover the package in this book. To generate XHTML, you can also use the approaches covered in "Changing and Generating XML" in Chapter 23.

Embedding

If your favorite approach is to embed Python code within HTML in the manner made popular by JSP, ASP, and PHP, one possibility is to use Python Server Pages (PSP) as supported by Webware, mentioned in Chapter 20. Another package, focused more specifically on the embedding approach, is Spyce (available at *http:// spyce.sf.net/*). For all but the simplest problems, development and maintenance are eased by separating logic and presentation issues through templating, covered in the next section. Both Webware and Spyce optionally support templating in lieu of embedding.

Templating

To generate HTML, the best approach is often templating. With templating, you start with a *template*, which is a text string (often read from a file, database, etc.) that is valid HTML, but includes markers, also known as placeholders, where dynamically generated text must be inserted. Your program generates the needed text and substitutes it into the template. In the simplest case, you can use markers of the form '%(*name*)s'. Bind the dynamically generated text as the value for key '*name*' in some dictionary *d*. The Python string formatting operator %, covered in Chapter 9, now does all you need. If *t* is your template, *t%d* is a copy of the template with all values properly substituted.

The Cheetah Package

For advanced templating tasks, I recommend Cheetah (available at *http://www. cheetahtemplate.org*). Cheetah interoperates particularly well with Webware. When you have Webware installed, Cheetah's template objects are Webware servlets, so you can immediately deploy them under Webware. You can also use

Cheetah in other contexts, and Spyce can also optionally use Cheetah for templating. Cheetah can process HTML templates for any purpose whatsoever. In fact, I recommend Cheetah to process templates for any kind of structured text, HTML or not.

The Cheetah templating language

In a Cheetah template, use $*name* or ${*name*} to request the insertion of the value of a variable named *name*. *name* can contain dots to request lookups of object attributes or dictionary keys. For example, $a.b.c requests insertion of the value of attribute c of attribute b of the variable named a. When b is a dictionary, this translates to the Python expression *a.b*['*c*']. If an object encountered during $ substitution is callable, Cheetah calls the object, without arguments, as a part of the lookup. This high degree of polymorphism makes authoring and maintaining Cheetah templates easier for non-developers, as it saves them the need to learn and understand these distinctions.

A Cheetah template can contain *directives*, which are verbs starting with # that allow comments, file inclusion, flow control (conditionals, loops, exception handling), and more. Cheetah basically provides a rich templating language on top of Python. The most frequently used verbs in simple Cheetah templates are the following (mostly similar to Python, but with $ in front of names, no trailing :, and no mandatory indents, but #end clauses instead):

#break, #continue, #pass
> Like the Python statements with the same names

#echo *expression*
> Computes a Python expression (with $ in front of names) and outputs the result

#for $*variable* in $*container* ... #end for
> Like the Python for statement

#if ... #else if ... #else ... #end if
> Like the Python if statement

#repeat $*times* ... #end repeat
> Repeats some text $*times* times

#set $*variable* = *expression*
> Assigns a value to a variable (the variable is local to this template)

#silent *expression*
> Computes a Python expression (with $ in front of names) and hides the result

#slurp
> Consumes the following newline (i.e., joins the following line onto this one)

#while $*condition* ... #end while
> Like the Python while statement

Note the differences between #echo, #silent, and $ substitution. #echo $a(2) inserts in the template's output the result of calling function a with an argument of 2. Without the #echo, $a(2) inserts the string form of a (calling a( ) without arguments, if a is callable) followed by the three characters '(2)'. #silent $a(2) calls a with an argument of 2 and inserts nothing in the template's output.

Cheetah has many other verbs. A Cheetah template object is a class instance and may use inheritance, override methods, and so on. However, for simple templates you will most often not need such powerful mechanisms.

The Template class

The Cheetah.Template module supplies one class.

Template   class Template(*source*=None,*searchList*=[],*file*=None)

Always call Template with named arguments (except, optionally, the first one); number and order of formal arguments may change in the future, but the names are guaranteed to stay. You must pass either *source* or *file*, but not both. *source* is a template string. *file* is a file-like object open for reading, or the path to a file to open for reading.

searchList is a sequence of objects to use as top-level sources for $*name* insertion. An instance *t* of class Template is implicitly appended at the end of *t*'s search list (e.g., $a in the template inserts the value of *t*.a if no other object in the search list has an attribute a or an item with a key of 'a'). *searchList* defaults to the empty list, so, by default, *t*'s template expansion uses only *t*'s attributes as variables for $ substitution.

Class Template also allows other keyword arguments, but these are the most frequently used. The instance *t* supplies many methods, but normally you only call str(*t*), which returns the string form of the expanded template.

A Cheetah example

The following example uses Cheetah.Template to output HTML with dynamic content:

```
import Cheetah.Template
import os, time, socket

tt = Cheetah.Template.Template('''
<html><head><title>Report by $USER</title></head><body>
<h1>Report on host data</h1>
<p>Report written at $asctime:<br/>
#for $hostline in $uname
  $hostline<br/>
#end for
</p></body></html>
''', searchList=[time, os.environ])
```

```
try: tt.uname = os.uname
except AttributeError:
    tt.uname = [socket.gethostname( )]

print tt
```

This example instantiates and binds to name *tt* a Template instance, whose *source* is an HTML document string with some Cheetah placeholders (*$USER*, *$asctime*, *$uname*) and a Cheetah #for...#end for directive. The placeholder *$hostline* is the loop variable in the #for statement, so therefore the template does not search the search-list objects for name 'hostline' when it expands. The example instantiates *tt* with a *searchList* argument, which sets module time and dictionary os.environ as part of the search. For names that cannot be found in objects on the search list, *tt*'s expansion looks in instance *tt* itself. Therefore, the example binds attribute *tt.uname*, either to function os.uname (which returns a tuple of host description data, but exists only on certain platforms), if available, or else to a list whose only item is the hostname returned by function gethostname of module socket.

The last statement of the example is print *tt*. The print statement transforms its arguments into strings, as if str were called on each argument. Therefore, print *tt* expands *tt*. Some of the placeholders' expansions use dictionary lookup (*$USER* looks up os.environ['USER']); some need a function call (*$asctime* calls time.asctime( )); and some may behave in different ways (*$uname*, depending on what it finds as *tt.uname*, calls that attribute—if callable, as when it's os.uname—or just takes it as is, when it's already a list).

One important note applies to all templating tasks, not just to Cheetah. Templates are almost invariably not the right place for program logic to reside. Don't put more logic than strictly needed in your templates. Templating engines let you separate the task of computing results (best done in Python, outside of any template) from that of presenting the results as HTML or other kinds of structured text. Templates should deal just with presentation issues, and contain as little program logic as feasible.

23

Structured Text: XML

XML, the eXtensible Markup Language, has taken the programming world by storm over the last few years. Like SGML, XML is a metalanguage, a language to describe markup languages. On top of the XML 1.0 specification, the XML community (in good part inside the World Wide Web Consortium, W3C) has standardized other technologies, such as various schema languages, Namespaces, XPath, XLink, XPointer, and XSLT.

Industry consortia in many fields have defined industry-specific markup languages on top of XML, to facilitate data exchange among applications in the various fields. Such industry standards let applications exchange data even if the applications are coded in different languages and deployed on different platforms by different firms. XML, related technologies, and XML-based markup languages are the basis of interapplication, cross-language, cross-platform data interchange in modern applications.

Python has excellent support for XML. The standard Python library supplies the xml package, which lets you use fundamental XML technology quite simply. The third-party package PyXML (available at *http://pyxml.sf.net*) extends the standard library's xml with validating parsers, richer DOM implementations, and advanced technologies such as XPath and XSLT. Downloading and installing PyXML upgrades Python's own xml packages, so it can be a good idea to do so even if you don't use PyXML-specific features.

On top of PyXML, you can choose to install yet another freely available third-party package, 4Suite (available at *http://4suite.org*). 4Suite provides yet more XML parsers for special niches, advanced technologies such as XLink and XPointer, and code supporting standards built on top of XML, such as the Resource Description Framework (RDF).

As an alternative to Python's built-in XML support, PyXML, and 4Suite, you can try ReportLab's new pyRXP, a fast validating XML parser based on Tobin's RXP.

pyRXP is DOM-like in that it constructs an in-memory representation of the whole XML document you're parsing. However, pyRXP does not construct a DOM-compliant tree, but rather a lightweight tree of Python tuples to save memory and enhance speed. For more information on pyRXP, see *http://www. reportlab.com/xml/pyrxp.html.*

For coverage of all aspects of XML and of how you can process XML with Python, I recommend *Python & XML*, by Christopher Jones and Fred Drake (O'Reilly). In this chapter, I cover only the essentials of the standard library's xml package, taking some elementary knowledge of XML itself for granted.

An Overview of XML Parsing

When your application must parse XML documents, your first, fundamental choice is what kind of parsing to use. You can use *event-driven* parsing, where the parser reads the document sequentially and calls back to your application each time it parses a significant aspect of the document (such as an element). Or you can use *object-based* parsing, where the parser reads the whole document and builds in-memory data structures, representing the document, that you can then navigate. SAX is the main, normal way to perform event-driven parsing, and DOM is the main, normal way to perform object-based parsing. In each case there are alternatives, such as direct use of expat for event-driven parsing and pyRXP for object-based parsing, but I do not cover these alternatives in this book. Another interesting possibility is offered by pulldom, which is covered later in this chapter.

Event-driven parsing requires fewer resources, which makes it particularly suitable when you need to parse very large documents. However, event-driven parsing requires you to structure your application accordingly, performing your processing (and typically building auxiliary data structures) in your methods that are called by the parser. Object-based parsing gives you more flexibility about the ways in which you can structure your application. It may be more suitable when you need to perform very complicated processing, as long as you can afford the extra resources needed for object-based parsing (typically, this means that you are not dealing with very large documents). Object-based approaches also support programs that need to modify or create XML documents, as covered later in this chapter.

As a general guideline, when you are still undecided after studying the various trade-offs, I suggest you try event-driven parsing when you can see a reasonably direct way to perform your program's tasks through this approach. Event-driven parsing is more scalable; therefore, if your program can perform its task via event-driven parsing, it will be applicable to larger documents than it would be able to handle otherwise. If event-driven parsing is too confining, try pulldom instead. I suggest you consider (non-pull) DOM only when you think DOM is the only way to perform your program's tasks without excessive contortions. In that case DOM may be best, as long as you can accept the resulting limitations, in terms of the maximum size of documents that your program is able to support and the costs in time and memory for processing.

Parsing XML with SAX

In most cases, the best way to extract information from an XML document is to parse the document with a parser compliant with SAX, the Simple API for XML. SAX defines a standard API that can be implemented on top of many different underlying parsers. The SAX approach to parsing has similarities to the HTML parsers covered in Chapter 22. As the parser encounters XML elements, text contents, and other significant events in the input stream, the parser calls back to methods of your classes. Such event-driven parsing, based on callbacks to your methods as relevant events occur, also has similarities to the event-driven approach that is almost universal in GUIs and in some networking frameworks. Event-driven approaches in various programming fields may not appear natural to beginners, but enable high performance and particularly high scalability, making them very suitable for high-workload cases.

To use SAX, you define a content handler class, subclassing a library class and overriding some methods. Then, you build a parser object *p*, install an instance of your class as *p*'s handler, and feed *p* the input stream to parse. *p* calls methods on your handler to reflect the document's structure and contents. Your handler's methods perform application-specific processing. The xml.sax package supplies a factory function to build *p*, as well as convenience functions for simpler operation in typical cases. xml.sax also supplies exception classes, used to diagnose invalid input and other errors.

Optionally, you can also register with parser *p* other kinds of handlers besides the content handler. You can supply a custom error handler to use an error diagnosis strategy different from normal exception raising, and try to diagnose several errors during a parse. You can supply a custom DTD handler to receive information about notation and unparsed entities from the XML document's Document Type Definition (DTD). You can supply a custom entity resolver to handle external entity references in advanced, customized ways. These additional possibilities are advanced and rarely used, so I do not cover them in this book.

The xml.sax Package

The xml.sax package supplies exception class SAXException, and subclasses of it to support fine-grained exception handling. xml.sax also supplies three functions.

---

make_parser   make_parser(*parsers_list*=[])

parsers_list is a list of strings, names of modules from which you would like to build your parser. make_parser tries each module in sequence until it finds one that defines a suitable function create_ parser. After the modules in parsers_list, if any, make_parser continues by trying a list of default modules. make_parser terminates as soon as it can generate a parser *p*, and returns *p*.

---

parse   parse(*file,handler,error_handler*=None)

file is a filename or a file-like object open for reading, containing an XML document. handler is generally an instance of your own

---

subclass of class ContentHandler, covered later in this chapter. *error_handler*, if given, is generally an instance of your own subclass of class ErrorHandler. You don't necessarily have to subclass ContentHandler and/or ErrorHandler: you just need to provide the same interfaces as the classes do. Subclassing is often a convenient means to this end.

Function parse is equivalent to the code:

```
p = make_parser( )
p.setContentHandler(handler)
if error_handler is not None:
    p.setErrorHandler(error_handler)
p.parse(file)
```

This idiom is quite frequent in SAX parsing, so having it in a single function is convenient. When *error_handler* is None, the parser diagnoses errors by propagating an exception that is an instance of some subclass of SAXException.

parseString   parseString(*string,handler,error_handler*=None)

Like parse, except that *string* is the XML document in string form.

xml.sax also supplies a class, which you subclass to define your content handler.

ContentHandler   class ContentHandler( )

An instance *h* of a subclass of ContentHandler may override several methods, of which the most frequently useful are the following:

h.characters(*data*)
　　Called when textual content *data* is parsed. The parser may split each range of text in the document into any number of separate callbacks to *h*.characters. Therefore, your implementation of method characters usually buffers *data*, generally by appending it to a list attribute. When your class knows from some other event that all relevant data has arrived, your class calls ''.join on the list and processes the resulting string.

h.endDocument( )
　　Called once when the document finishes.

h.endElement(*tag*)
　　Called when the element named *tag* finishes.

h.endElementNS(*name,qname*)
　　Called when an element finishes and the parser is handling namespaces. *name* and *qname* are like for startElementNS, covered later in this chapter.

h.startDocument( )
　　Called once when the document begins.

h.startElement(*tag*,*attrs*)

Called when the element named *tag* begins. *attrs* is a mapping of attribute names to values, as covered in the next section.

h.startElementNS(*name*,*qname*,*attrs*)

Called when an element begins and the parser is handling namespaces. *name* is a pair (*uri*,*localname*), where *uri* is the namespace's URI or None, and *localname* is the name of the tag. *qname* (which stands for qualified name) is either None, if the parser does not supply the namespace prefixes feature, or the string *prefix*:*name* used in the document's text for this tag. *attrs* is a mapping of attribute names to values, as covered in the next section.

Attributes

The last argument of methods startElement and startElementNS is an attributes object *attr*, a read-only mapping of attribute names to attribute values. For method startElement, names are identifier strings. For method startElementNS, names are pairs (*uri*,*localname*), where *uri* is the namespace's URI or None, and *localname* is the name of the tag. The object *attr* also supports methods that let you work with the *qname* (qualified name) of each attribute.

getValueBy QName	attr.getValueByQName(*name*) Returns the attribute value for a qualified name *name*.
getNameBy QName	attr.getNameByQName(*name*) Returns the (*namespace, localname*) pair for a qualified name *name*.
getQNameBy Name	attr.getQNameByName(*name*) Returns the qualified name for *name*, which is a (*namespace, localname*) pair.
getQNames	attr.getQNames() Returns the list of qualified names of all attributes.

For startElement, each *qname* is the same string as the corresponding name. For startElementNS, a *qname* is the corresponding local name for attributes not associated with a namespace (i.e., attributes whose *uri* is None); otherwise, the *qname* is the string *prefix*:*name* used in the document's text for this attribute.

The parser may reuse in later processing the *attr* object that it passes to methods startElement and startElementNS. If you need to keep a copy of the attributes of an element, call *attr*.copy( ) to get the copy.

Incremental parsing

All parsers support a method parse, which you call with the XML document as either a string or a file-like object open for reading. parse does not return until the end of the XML document. Most SAX parsers, though not all, also support incremental parsing, letting you feed the XML document to the parser a little at a time, as the document arrives from a network connection or other source. A parser *p* that is capable of incremental parsing supplies three more methods.

close
    p.close( )
    Call when the XML document is finished.

feed
    p.feed(*data*)
    Passes to the parser a part of the document. The parser processes some prefix of the text and holds the rest in a buffer until the next call to *p*.feed or *p*.close.

reset
    p.reset( )
    Call after an XML document is finished or abandoned, before you start feeding another XML document to the parser.

The xml.sax.saxutils module

The saxutils module of package xml.sax supplies two functions and a class that are quite handy to generate XML output based on an input XML document.

escape
    escape(*data*,*entities*={})
    Returns a copy of string *data* with characters <, >, and & changed into entity references <, >, and &. *entities* is a dictionary with strings as keys and values; each substring *s* of *data* that is a key in *entities* is changed in escape's result string into string *entities*[*s*]. For example, to escape single and double quote characters, in addition to angle brackets and ampersands, you can call:

```
xml.sax.saxutils.escape(data,{'"':'&quot;', "'":"&apos;"})
```

quoteattr
    escape(*data*,*entities*={})
    Same as escape, but also quotes the result string to make it immediately usable as an attribute value, and escapes any quote characters that have to be escaped.

XMLGenerator class XMLGenerator(*out*=sys.stdout, *encoding*='iso-8859-1')

Subclasses xml.sax.ContentHandler and implements all that is needed to reproduce the input XML document on the given file-like object *out* with the specified *encoding*. When you must generate an XML document that is a small modification of the input one, you can subclass XMLGenerator, overriding methods and delegating most of the work to XMLGenerator's implementations of the methods. For example, if all you need to do is rename some tags according to a dictionary, XMLGenerator makes it quite simple, as shown in the following example:

```
import xml.sax, xml.sax.saxutils

def tagrenamer(infile, outfile, renaming_dict):
    base = xml.sax.saxutils.XMLGenerator

    class Renamer(base):
        def rename(self, name):
            return renaming_dict.get(name, name)
        def startElement(self, name, attrs):
            base.startElement(self, self.rename(name),
                              attrs)
        def endElement(self, name):
            base.endElement(self, self.rename(name))

    xml.sax.parse(infile, Renamer(outfile))
```

Parsing XHTML with xml.sax

The following example uses xml.sax to perform a typical XHTML-related task, very similar to the tasks performed in the examples of Chapter 22. The example fetches an XHTML page from the Web with urllib, parses it, and outputs all unique links from the page to other sites. The example uses urlparse to examine the links for the given site, and outputs only the links whose URLs have an explicit scheme of 'http':

```
import xml.sax, urllib, urlparse

class LinksHandler(xml.sax.ContentHandler):
    def startDocument(self):
        self.seen = {}
    def startElement(self, tag, attributes):
        if tag != 'a': return
        value = attributes.get('href')
        if value is not None and value not in self.seen:
            self.seen[value] = True
            pieces = urlparse.urlparse(value)
            if pieces[0] != 'http': return
            print urlparse.urlunparse(pieces)
```

```
p = xml.sax.make_parser( )
p.setContentHandler(LinksHandler( ))
f = urllib.urlopen('http://www.w3.org/MarkUp/')
BUFSIZE = 8192

while True:
    data = f.read(BUFSIZE)
    if not data: break
    p.feed(data)

p.close( )
```

This example is quite similar to the HTMLParser example in Chapter 22. With the xml.sax module, the parser and the handler are separate objects (while in the examples of Chapter 22 they coincided). Method names differ (startElement in this example versus handle_starttag in the HTMLParser example). The *attributes* argument is a mapping here, so its method get immediately gives us the attribute value we're interested in, while in the examples of Chapter 22 it was a sequence of (*name,value*) pairs, so we had to loop on the sequence until we found the right name. Despite these differences in detail, the overall structure is very close, and typical of simple event-driven parsing tasks.

Parsing XML with DOM

SAX parsing does not build any structure in memory to represent the XML document. This makes SAX fast and highly scalable, as your application builds exactly as little or as much in-memory structure as needed for its specific tasks. However, for particularly complicated processing tasks involving reasonably small XML documents, you may prefer to let the library build in-memory structures that represent the whole XML document, and then traverse those structures. The XML standards describe the DOM (Document Object Model) for XML. A DOM object represents an XML document as a tree whose root is the *document object,* while other nodes correspond to elements, text contents, element attributes, and so on.

The Python standard library supplies a minimal implementation of the XML DOM standard, xml.dom.minidom. minidom builds everything up in memory, with the typical pros and cons of the DOM approach to parsing. The Python standard library also supplies a different DOM-like approach in module xml.dom.pulldom. pulldom occupies an interesting middle ground between SAX and DOM, presenting the stream of parsing events as a Python iterator object so that you do not code callbacks, but rather loop over the events and examine each event to see if it's of interest. When you do find an event of interest to your application, you can ask pulldom to build the DOM subtree rooted in that event's node by calling method expandNode, and then work with that subtree as you would in minidom. Paul Prescod, pulldom's author and XML and Python expert, describes the net result as "80% of the performance of SAX, 80% of the convenience of DOM." Other DOM parsers are part of the PyXML and 4Suite extension packages, mentioned at the start of this chapter.

The xml.dom Package

The xml.dom package supplies exception class DOMException and subclasses of it to support fine-grained exception handling. xml.dom also supplies a class Node, typically used as a base class for all nodes by DOM implementations. Class Node only supplies constant attributes giving the codes for node types, such as ELEMENT_NODE for elements, ATTRIBUTE_NODE for attributes, and so on. xml.dom also supplies constant module attributes with the URIs of important namespaces: XML_NAMESPACE, XMLNS_NAMESPACE, XHTML_NAMESPACE, and EMPTY_NAMESPACE.

The xml.dom.minidom Module

The xml.dom.minidom module supplies two functions.

parse	parse(*file*,*parser*=None)
	file is a filename or a file-like object open for reading, containing an XML document. *parser*, if given, is an instance of a SAX parser class; otherwise, parse generates a default SAX parser by calling xml.sax.make_parser(). parse returns a minidom document object instance representing the given XML document.
parseString	parseString(*string*,*parser*=None)
	Like parse, except that *string* is the XML document in string form.

xml.dom.minidom also supplies many classes as specified by the XML DOM standard. Almost all of these classes subclass Node. Class Node supplies the methods and attributes that all kinds of nodes have in common. A notable class of module xml.dom.minidom that is not a subclass of Node is AttributeList, identified in the DOM standard as NamedNodeMap, which is a mapping that collects the attributes of a node of class Element.

For methods and attributes related to changing and creating XML documents, see "Changing and Generating XML" later in this chapter. Here, I present the classes, methods, and attributes that you use most often when traversing a DOM tree without changes, normally after the tree has been built by parsing an XML document. For concreteness and simplicity, I mention Python classes. However, the DOM specifications deal strictly with abstract interfaces, never with concrete classes. Your code must never deal with the class objects directly, only with instances of those classes. Do not type-test nodes (for example, don't use isinstance on them) and do not instantiate node classes directly (rather, use the factory methods covered later in "Changing and Generating XML"). This is good Python practice in general, but it's particularly important here.

Node objects

Each node *n* in the DOM tree is an instance of some subclass of Node; therefore *n* supplies all attributes and methods that Node supplies, with appropriate overriding implementations if needed. The most frequently used methods and attributes are as follows.

attributes
The *n*.attributes attribute is either None or an AttributeList instance with all attributes of *n*.

childNodes
The *n*.childNodes attribute is a list of all nodes that are children of *n*, possibly an empty list.

firstChild
The *n*.firstChild attribute is None when *n*.childNodes is empty, otherwise like *n*.childNodes[0].

hasChildNodes
n.hasChildNodes( )

Like len(*n*.childNodes)!=0, but possibly faster.

isSameNode
n.isSameNode(*other*)

True when *n* and *other* refer to the same DOM node, otherwise False. Do not use the normal Python idiom *n* is *other*: a Python DOM implementation is free to generate multiple Node instances that refer to the same DOM node. Therefore, to check the identity of DOM node references, always and exclusively use method isSameNode.

lastChild
The *n*.lastChild attribute is None when *n*.childNodes is empty, otherwise like *n*.childNodes[-1].

localName
The *n*.localName attribute is the local part of *n*'s qualified name (relevant when namespaces are involved).

namespaceURI
The *n*.namespaceURI attribute is None when *n*'s qualified name has no namespace part, otherwise the namespace's URI.

nextSibling
The *n*.nextSibling attribute is None when *n* is the last child of *n*'s parent, otherwise the next child of *n*'s parent.

nodeName
The *n*.nodeName attribute is *n*'s name string. The string is a node-specific name when that makes sense for *n*'s node type (e.g., the tag name when *n* is an Element), otherwise a string starting with '#'.

nodeType	The *n*.nodeType attribute is *n*'s type code, an integer that is one of the constant attributes of class Node.
nodeValue	The *n*.nodeValue attribute is None when *n* has no value (e.g., when *n* is an Element), otherwise *n*'s value (e.g., the text content when *n* is an instance of class Text).
normalize	*n*.normalize( ) Normalizes the entire subtree rooted at *n*, merging adjacent Text nodes. Parsing may separate ranges of text in the XML document into arbitrary chunks; normalize ensures that text ranges remain separate only when there is markup between them.
ownerDocument	The *n*.ownerDocument attribute is the Document instance that contains *n*.
parentNode	The *n*.parentNode attribute is *n*'s parent node in the DOM tree, or None for attribute nodes and nodes not in the tree.
prefix	The *n*.prefix attribute is None when *n*'s qualified name has no namespace prefix, otherwise the namespace prefix. Note that a name may have a namespace even if it has no namespace prefix.
previousSibling	The *n*.previousSibling attribute is None when *n* is the first child of *n*'s parent, otherwise the previous child of *n*'s parent.

Attr objects

The Attr class is a subclass of Node that represents an attribute of an Element. Besides attributes and methods of class Node, an instance *a* of Attr supplies the following attributes.

ownerElement	The *a*.ownerElement attribute is the Element instance of which *a* is an attribute.
specified	The *a*.specified attribute is true if *a* was explicitly specified in the document, false if obtained by default.

Document objects

The Document class is a subclass of Node whose instances are returned by the parse and parseString functions of module xml.dom.minidom. All nodes in the document refer to the same Document node as their ownerDocument attribute. To check this, you must use the isSameNode method, not Python identity checking (operator is). Besides the attributes and methods of class Node, d supplies the following attributes and methods.

doctype
The d.doctype attribute is the DocumentType instance corresponding to d's DTD. This attribute comes directly from the !DOCTYPE declaration in d's XML source.

document Element
The d.documentElement attribute is the Element instance corresponding to d's root element.

getElementById
d.getElementById(*elementId*)

Returns the Element instance within the document that has the given ID (what element attributes are IDs is specified by the DTD), or None if there is no such instance (or the underlying parser does not supply ID information).

getElementsBy TagName
d.getElementsByTagName(*tagName*)

Returns the list of Element instances within the document whose tag equals string *tagName*, in the same order as in the parsed XML document. May be the empty list. When *name* is '*', returns the list of all Element instances within the document, with any tag.

getElementsBy TagNameNS
d.getElementsByTagNameNS(*namespaceURI,localName*)

Returns the list of Element instances within the document with the given *namespaceURI* and *localName*, in the order found in the XML document. May be the empty list. A value of '*' for *namespaceURI*, *localName*, or both matches all values of the corresponding field.

Element objects

The Element class is a subclass of Node that represents tagged elements. Besides attributes and methods of Node, an instance e of Element supplies the following methods.

getAttribute
e.getAttribute(*name*)

Returns the value of e's attribute with the given *name*. Returns the empty string ' ' if e has no attribute with the given *name*.

getAttributeNS	`e.getAttributeNS(`*namespaceURI,localName*`)` Returns the value of *e*'s attribute with the given *namespaceURI* and *localName*.
getAttribute Node	`e.getAttributeNode(`*name*`)` Returns the Attr instance that is *e*'s attribute with the given *name*, or None if no attribute with that name is among *e*'s attributes.
getAttribute NodeNS	`e.getAttributeNodeNS(`*namespaceURI,localName*`)` Returns the Attr instance that is *e*'s attribute with the given *namespaceURI* and *localName*, or None if no such attribute is among *e*'s attributes.
getElementsBy TagName	`e.getElementsByTagName(`*tagName*`)` Returns the list of Element instances within the subtree rooted at *e* whose tag equals string *tagName*, in the same order as in the XML document. *e* is included in the list that getElementsbyTagName returns if *e*'s tag equals *tagName*. getElementsbyTagName may return the empty list when no node in the subtree rooted at *e* has a tag equal to *tagName*. When *tagName* is `'*'`, getElementsbyTagName returns the list of all Element instances within the subtree, with any tag, including *e*.
getElementsBy TagNameNS	`e.getElementsByTagNameNS(`*namespaceURI,localName*`)` Returns the list of Element instances within the subtree rooted at *e*, with the given *namespaceURI* and *localname*, in the same order as in the XML document. A value of `'*'` for *namespaceURI*, *localname*, or both matches all values of the corresponding field. The list may include *e* or may be empty, just as for method getElementsByTagName.
hasAttribute	`e.hasAttribute(`*name*`)` True if and only if *e* has an attribute with the given *name*. If the underlying parser extracts the relevant information from the DTD, hasAttribute is also true for attributes of *e* that have a default value, even when they are not explicitly specified.
hasAttributeNS	`e.hasAttributeNS(`*namespaceURI,localName*`)` True if and only if *e* has an attribute with the given *namespaceURI* and *localName*. Same as method hasAttribute regarding attributes with default values from the DTD.

Parsing XHTML with xml.dom.minidom

The following example uses xml.dom.minidom to perform the same task as in the previous example for xml.sax, fetching a page from the Web with urllib, parsing it, and outputting the hyperlinks:

```
import xml.dom.minidom, urllib, urlparse

f = urllib.urlopen('http://www.w3.org/MarkUp/')
doc = xml.dom.minidom.parse(f)
as = doc.getElementsByTagName('a')
seen = {}
for a in as:
    value = a.getAttribute('href')
    if value and value not in seen:
        seen[value] = True
        pieces = urlparse.urlparse(value)
        if pieces[0] == 'http' and pieces[1]!='www.w3.org':
            print urlparse.urlunparse(pieces)
```

In this example, we get the list of all elements with tag 'a', and the relevant attribute, if any, for each of them. We then work in the usual way with the attribute's value.

The xml.dom.pulldom Module

The xml.dom.pulldom module supplies two functions.

parse   parse(*file*,*parser*=None)

file is a filename or a file-like object open for reading, containing an XML document. *parser*, if given, is an instance of a SAX parser class; otherwise parse generates a default SAX parser by calling xml.sax.make_parser( ). parse returns a pulldom event stream instance representing the given XML document.

parseString   parseString(*string*,*parser*=None)

Like parse, except that *string* is the XML document in string form.

---

xml.dom.pulldom also supplies class DOMEventStream, an iterator whose items are pairs (*event*,*node*), where *event* is a string giving the event type, and *node* is an instance of an appropriate subclass of class Node. The possible values for *event* are constant uppercase strings that are also available as constant attributes of module xml.dom.pulldom with the same names: CHARACTERS, COMMENT, END_DOCUMENT, END_ELEMENT, IGNORABLE_WHITESPACE, PROCESSING_INSTRUCTION, START_DOCUMENT, and START_ELEMENT.

An instance *d* of class DOMEventStream supplies one other important method.

---

expandNode   *d*.expandNode(*node*)

node must be the latest instance of Node so far returned by iterating on *d*, i.e., the instance of Node returned by the latest call to *d*.next( ). expandNode processes that part of the XML document stream that corresponds to the subtree rooted at *node*, ensuring that you can then access the subtree with the usual minidom approach. *d* iterates on itself for the purpose so that after calling expandNode, the next call to next continues right after the subtree thus expanded.

Parsing XHTML with xml.dom.pulldom

The following example uses xml.dom.pulldom to perform the same task as our previous examples, fetching a page from the Web with urllib, parsing it, and outputting the hyperlinks:

```
import xml.dom.pulldom, urllib, urlparse

f = urllib.urlopen('http://www.w3.org/MarkUp/')
doc = xml.dom.pulldom.parse(f)
seen = {}
for event, node in doc:
    if event=='START_ELEMENT' and node.nodeName=='a':
        doc.expandNode(node)
        value = node.getAttribute('href')
        if value and value not in seen:
            seen[value] = True
            pieces = urlparse.urlparse(value)
            if pieces[0] == 'http' and pieces[1]!='www.w3.org':
                print urlparse.urlunparse(pieces)
```

In this example, we select only elements with tag 'a'. For each of them we request full expansion, and then proceed just like in the minidom example (i.e., we get the relevant attribute, if any, then work in the usual way with the attribute's value). The expansion is in fact not necessary in this specific case, since we do not need to work with the subtree rooted in each element with tag 'a', just with the attributes, and attributes can be accessed without calling expandNode. Therefore, this example works just as well if you change the call to doc.expandNode into a comment. However, I put the expandNode call in the example to show how this crucial method of pulldom is normally used in context.

Changing and Generating XML

Just like for HTML and other kinds of structured text, the simplest way to output an XML document is often to prepare and write it using Python's normal string and file operations, covered in Chapters 9 and 10. Templating, covered in

---

Chapter 22, is also often the best approach. Subclassing class XMLGenerator, covered earlier in this chapter, is a good way to generate an XML document that is like an input XML document, except for a few changes.

The xml.dom.minidom module offers yet another possibility, because its classes support methods to generate, insert, remove, and alter nodes in a DOM tree representing the document. You can create a DOM tree by parsing and then alter it, or you can create an empty DOM tree and populate it, and then output the resulting XML document with methods toxml, toprettyxml, or writexml of the Document instance. You can also output a subtree of the DOM tree by calling these methods on the Node that is the subtree's root.

Factory Methods of a Document Object

The Document class supplies factory methods to create new instances of subclasses of Node. The most frequently used factory methods of a Document instance *d* are as follows.

createComment   *d*.createComment(*data*)

Builds and returns an instance *c* of class Comment for a comment with text *data*.

createElement   *d*.createElement(*tagname*)

Builds and returns an instance *e* of class Element for an element with the given tag.

createTextNode   *d*.createTextNode(*data*)

Builds and returns an instance *t* of class TextNode for a text node with text *data*.

Mutating Methods of an Element Object

An instance *e* of class Element supplies the following methods to remove and add attributes.

removeAttribute   *e*.removeAttribute(*name*)

Removes *e*'s attribute with the given *name*.

setAttribute   *e*.setAttribute(*name*,*value*)

Changes *e*'s attribute with the given *name* to have the given *value*, or adds to *e* a new attribute with the given *name* and *value* if *e* had no attribute named *name*.

Mutating Methods of a Node Object

An instance *n* of class Node supplies the following methods to remove, add, and replace children.

appendChild   *n*.appendChild(*child*)

Makes *child* the last child of *n*, whatever *child*'s parent was (including *n* or None).

insertBefore   *n*.insertBefore(*child*,*nextChild*)

Makes *child* the child of *n* immediately before *nextChild*, whatever *child*'s parent was (including *n* or None). *nextChild* must be a child of *n*.

removeChild   *n*.removeChild(*child*)

Makes *child* parentless and returns *child*. *child* must be a child of *n*.

replaceChild   *n*.replaceChild(*child*,*oldChild*)

Makes *child* the child of *n* in *oldChild*'s place, whatever *child*'s parent was (including *n* or None). *oldChild* must be a child of *n*. Returns *oldChild*.

Output Methods of a Node Object

An instance *n* of class Node supplies the following methods to output the subtree rooted at *n*.

toprettyxml   *n*.toprettyxml(*indent*='\t',*newl*='\n')

Returns a string, plain or Unicode, with the XML source for the subtree rooted at *n*, using *indent* to indent nested tags and *newl* to end lines.

toxml   *n*.toxml( )

Like *n*.toprettyxml('',''), i.e., inserts no extraneous whitespace.

writexml   *n*.writexml(*file*)

Writes the XML source for the subtree rooted at *n* to file-like object *file*, open for writing. Note that *file*.write must accept Unicode strings (as covered in "The codecs Module" in Chapter 9), unless all text in the XML source produced can be converted implicitly to plain strings using the current default encoding (normally 'ascii').

Changing and Outputting XHTML with xml.dom.minidom

The following example uses xml.dom.minidom to analyze an XHTML page and output it to standard output with each hyperlink's destination URL shown, in three sets of parentheses, just before the hyperlink:

```
import xml.dom.minidom, urllib, sys

f = urllib.urlopen('http://www.w3.org/MarkUp/')
doc = xml.dom.minidom.parse(f)
as = doc.getElementsByTagName('a')
for a in as:
    value = a.getAttribute('href')
    if value:
        newtext = doc.createTextNode(' (((%s)))'%value)
        a.parentNode.insertBefore(newtext,a)

class UnicodeStdoutWriter:
    def write(self, data):
        sys.stdout.write(data.encode('utf-8'))

doc.writexml(UnicodeStdoutWriter())
```

This example wraps sys.stdout in a little UnicodeStdoutWriter class in order to encode Unicode output. Further, it uses encoding 'utf-8' because that is the encoding that the XML standard specifies as the default, and up to Python 2.2.2 we have no way of asking object *doc* to explicitly request a different encoding. In Python 2.3, method writexml accepts an optional keyword argument named encoding that lets us control the encoding attribute in the XML declaration.

XML

Extending and Embedding

Extending and Embedding Classic Python

Classic Python runs on a portable C-coded virtual machine. Python's built-in objects, such as numbers, sequences, dictionaries, and files, are coded in C, as are several modules in Python's standard library. Modern platforms support dynamic-load libraries, with file extensions such as *.dll* on Windows and *.so* on Linux, and building Python produces such binary files. You can code your own extension modules for Python in C, using the Python C API covered in this chapter, to produce and deploy dynamic libraries that Python scripts and interactive sessions can later use with the import statement, covered in Chapter 7.

Extending Python means building modules that Python code can import to access the features the modules supply. Embedding Python means executing Python code from your application. For such execution to be useful, Python code must in turn be able to access some of your application's functionality. In practice, therefore, embedding implies some extending, as well as a few embedding-specific operations.

Embedding and extending are covered extensively in Python's online documentation; you can find an in-depth tutorial at *http://www.python.org/doc/ext/ext.html* and a reference manual at *http://www.python.org/doc/api/api.html*. Many details are best studied in Python's extensively documented sources. Download Python's source distribution and study the sources of Python's core, C-coded extension modules and the example extensions supplied for study purposes.

This chapter covers the basics of extending and embedding Python with C. It also mentions, but does not cover, other possibilities for extending Python.

Extending Python with Python's C API

A Python extension module named *x* resides in a dynamic library with the same filename (*x.pyd* on Windows, *x.so* on most Unix-like platforms) in an appropriate directory (normally the *site-packages* subdirectory of the Python library directory). You generally build the *x* extension module from a C source file *x.c* with the overall structure:

```
#include <Python.h>

/* omitted: the body of the x module */

void
initx(void)
{
    /* omitted: the code that initializes the module named x */
}
```

When you have built and installed the extension module, a Python statement import *x* loads the dynamic library, then locates and calls the function named initx, which must do all that is needed to initialize the module object named *x*.

Building and Installing C-Coded Python Extensions

To build and install a C-coded Python extension module, it's simplest and most productive to use the distribution utilities, distutils, covered in Chapter 26. In the same directory as *x.c*, place a file named *setup.py* that contains at least the following statements:

```
from distutils.core import setup, Extension
setup(name='x', ext_modules=[ Extension('x',sources=['x.c']) ])
```

From a shell prompt in this directory, you can now run:

```
C:\> python setup.py install
```

to build the module and install it so that it becomes usable in your Python installation. The distutils perform all needed compilation and linking steps, with the right compiler and linker commands and flags, and copy the resulting dynamic library in an appropriate directory, dependent on your Python installation. Your Python code can then access the resulting module with the statement import *x*.

Overview of C-Coded Python Extension Modules

Your C function initx generally has the following overall structure:

```
void
initx(void)
{
    PyObject* thismod = Py_InitModule3("x", x_methods, "docstring for x");
    /* optional: calls to PyModule_AddObject(thismod, "somename", someobj)
        and other Python C API calls to finish preparing module object
        thismod and its types (if any) and other objects.
    */
}
```

More details are covered in the "Module Initialization" section later in this chapter. *x_methods* is an array of PyMethodDef structs. Each PyMethodDef struct in the *x_methods* array describes a C function that your module *x* makes available to

Python code that imports *x*. Each such C function has the following overall structure:

```
static PyObject*
func_with_named_arguments(PyObject* self, PyObject* args, PyObject* kwds)
{
    /* omitted: body of function, which accesses arguments via the Python C
       API function PyArg_ParseTupleAndKeywords, and returns a PyObject*
       result, NULL for errors */
}
```

or some simpler variant, such as:

```
static PyObject*
func_with_positional_args_only(PyObject* self, PyObject* args)
{
    /* omitted: body of function, which accesses arguments via the Python C
       API function PyArg_ParseTuple, and returns a PyObject* result,
       NULL for errors */
}
```

How C-coded functions access arguments passed by Python code is covered in the "Accessing Arguments" section later in this chapter. How such functions build Python objects is covered in the "Creating Python Values" section, and how they raise or propagate exceptions back to the Python code that called them is covered in "Exceptions." When your module defines new Python types (as well as or instead of Python-callable functions), your C code defines one or more instances of struct PyTypeObject. This subject is covered in the "Defining New Types" section later in this chapter.

A simple example that makes use of all these concepts is shown in "A Simple Extension Example" later in this chapter. A toy-level "Hello World" example could be as simple as:

```
#include <Python.h>

static PyObject*
helloworld(PyObject* self)
{
    return Py_BuildValue("s", "Hello, C-coded Python extensions world!");
}

static char helloworld_docs[] =
    "helloworld( ): return a popular greeting phrase\n";

static PyMethodDef helloworld_funcs[] = {
    {"helloworld", (PyCFunction)helloworld, METH_NOARGS, helloworld_docs},
    {NULL}
};

void
inithelloworld(void)
{
    Py_InitModule3("helloworld", helloworld_funcs,
                   "Toy-level extension module");
}
```

Save this as *helloworld.c*, and build it through a *setup.py* script with distutils. After you have run *python setup.py install*, you can use the newly installed module, for example from a Python interactive session, such as:

```
>>> import helloworld
>>> print helloworld.helloworld( )
Hello, C-coded Python extensions world!
>>>
```

Return Values of Python's C API Functions

All functions in the Python C API return either an int or a PyObject*. Most functions returning int return 0 in case of success, and -1 to indicate errors. Some functions return results that are true or false: those functions return 0 to indicate false and an integer not equal to 0 to indicate true, and never indicate errors. Functions returning PyObject* return NULL in case of errors. See "Exceptions" later in this chapter for more details on how C-coded functions handle and raise errors.

Module Initialization

Function initx must contain, at a minimum, a call to one of the module initialization functions supplied by the C API. You can always use the Py_InitModule3 function.

Py_InitModule3   PyObject* Py_InitModule3(char* *name*,PyMethodDef* *methods*, char* *doc*)

name is the C string name of the module you are initializing (e.g., "name"). *methods* is an array of PyMethodDef structures, covered next in this chapter. *doc* is the C string that becomes the docstring of the module. Py_InitModule3 returns a PyObject* that is a borrowed reference to the new module object, as covered in "Reference Counting" later in this chapter. In practice, this means that you can ignore the return value if you need to perform no more initialization operations on this module. Otherwise, assign the return value to a C variable of type PyObject* and continue initialization.

Py_InitModule3 initializes the module object to contain the functions described in table *methods*. Further initialization, if any, may add other module attributes, and is generally best performed with calls to the following convenience functions.

PyModule_   int PyModule_AddIntConstant(PyObject* *module*,char* *name*,
AddIntConstant   int *value*)

Adds to module *module* an attribute named *name* with integer value *value*.

PyModule_ **AddObject**	`int PyModule_AddObject(PyObject* module,char* name,` `PyObject* value)`
	Adds to module *module* an attribute named *name* with value *value* and steals a reference to value, as covered in "Reference Counting."

PyModule_ **AddString** **Constant**	`int PyModule_AddStringConstant(PyObject* module,char* name,` `char* value)`
	Adds to module *module* an attribute named *name* with string value *value*.

Some module initialization operations may be conveniently performed by executing Python code with `PyRun_String`, covered later in "Running Python Code," with the module's dictionary as both the *globals* and *locals* argument. If you find yourself using `PyRun_String` extensively, rather than just as an occasional convenience, consider the possibility of splitting your extension module in two: a C-coded extension module offering raw, fast functionality, and a Python module wrapping the C-coded extension to provide further convenience and handy utilities.

When you do need to get a module's dictionary, use the `PyModule_GetDict` function.

PyModule_ **GetDict**	`PyObject* PyModule_GetDict(PyObject* module)`
	Returns a borrowed reference to the dictionary of module *module*. You should not use `PyModule_GetDict` for the specific tasks supported by the `PyModule_Add` functions covered earlier in this section; I suggest using `PyModule_GetDict` only for such purposes as supporting the use of `PyRun_String`.

If you need to access another module, you can import it by calling the `PyImport_` `Import` function.

PyImport_ **Import**	`PyObject* PyImport_Import(PyObject* name)`
	Imports the module named in Python string object *name* and returns a new reference to the module object, like Python's `__import__` (*name*). `PyImport_Import` is the highest-level, simplest, and most often used way to import a module.
	Beware, in particular, of using function `PyImport_ImportModule`, which may often look more convenient because it accepts a `char*` argument. `PyImport_ImportModule` operates on a lower level, bypassing any import hooks that may be in force, so extensions that use it will be far harder to incorporate in packages such as those

built by tools py2exe and Installer, covered in Chapter 26. Therefore, always do your importing by calling PyImport_Import, unless
you have very specific needs and know exactly what you're doing.

To add functions to a module (or non-special methods to new types, as covered
later in "Defining New Types"), you must describe the functions or methods in an
array of PyMethodDef structures, and terminate the array with a *sentinel* (i.e., a
structure whose fields are all 0 or NULL). PyMethodDef is defined as follows:

```
typedef struct {
    char* ml_name;          /* Python name of function or method */
    PyCFunction ml_meth;    /* pointer to C function impl */
    int ml_flags;           /* flag describing how to pass arguments */
    char* ml_doc;           /* docstring for the function or method */
} PyMethodDef
```

You must cast the second field to (PyCFunction) unless the C function's signature
is exactly PyObject* *function*(PyObject* *self*, PyObject* *args*), which is the
typedef for PyCFunction. This signature is correct when ml_flags is METH_O,
meaning a function that accepts a single argument, or METH_VARARGS, meaning a
function that accepts positional arguments. For METH_O, *args* is the only argument. For METH_VARARGS, *args* is a tuple of all arguments, to be parsed with the C
API function PyArg_ParseTuple. However, ml_flags can also be METH_NOARGS,
meaning a function that accepts no arguments, or METH_KEYWORDS, meaning a function that accepts both positional and named arguments. For METH_NOARGS, the
signature is PyObject* *function*(PyObject* *self*), without arguments. For METH_
KEYWORDS, the signature is:

PyObject* *function*(PyObject* *self*, PyObject* *args*, PyObject* *kwds*)

args is the tuple of positional arguments, and *kwds* the dictionary of named arguments. *args* and *kwds* are parsed together with the C API function PyArg_
ParseTupleAndKeywords.

When a C-coded function implements a module's function, the self parameter of
the C function is always NULL for any value of the ml_flags field. When a C-coded
function implements a non-special method of an extension type, the self parameter points to the instance on which the method is being called.

Reference Counting

Python objects live on the heap, and C code sees them via PyObject*. Each
PyObject counts how many references to itself are outstanding, and destroys itself
when the number of references goes down to 0. To make this possible, your code
must use Python-supplied macros: Py_INCREF to add a reference to a Python
object, and Py_DECREF to abandon a reference to a Python object. The Py_XINCREF
and Py_XDECREF macros are like Py_INCREF and Py_DECREF, but you may also use
them innocuously on a null pointer. The test for a non-null pointer is implicitly
performed inside the Py_XINCREF and Py_XDECREF macros, which saves you from
needing to write out that test explicitly.

A `PyObject* p`, which your code receives by calling or being called by other functions, is known as a *new reference* if the code that supplies *p* has already called `Py_INCREF` on your behalf. Otherwise, it is called a *borrowed reference*. Your code is said to *own* new references it holds, but not borrowed ones. You can call `Py_INCREF` on a borrowed reference to make it into a reference that you own; you must do this if you need to use the reference across calls to code that might cause the count of the reference you borrowed to be decremented. You must always call `Py_DECREF` before abandoning or overwriting references that you own, but never on references you don't own. Therefore, understanding which interactions transfer reference ownership and which ones rely on reference borrowing is absolutely crucial. For most functions in the C API, and for all functions that you write and Python calls, the following general rules apply:

1. `PyObject*` arguments are borrowed references

2. A `PyObject*` returned as the function's result transfers ownership

For each of the two rules, there are occasional exceptions. `PyList_SetItem` and `PyTuple_SetItem` *steal* a reference to the item they are setting (but not to the list or tuple object into which they're setting it). So do the faster versions of these two functions that exist as C preprocessor macros, `PyList_SET_ITEM` and `PyTuple_SET_ITEM`. So does `PyModule_AddObject`, covered earlier in this chapter. There are no other exceptions to the first rule. The rationale for these exceptions, which may help you remember them, is that the object you're setting is most often one you created for the purpose, so the reference-stealing semantics save you from having to call `Py_DECREF` immediately afterward.

The second rule has more exceptions than the first one: there are several cases in which the returned `PyObject*` is a borrowed reference rather than a new reference. The abstract functions, whose names begin with `PyObject_`, `PySequence_`, `PyMapping_`, and `PyNumber_`, return new references. This is because you can call them on objects of many types, and there might not be any other reference to the resulting object that they return (i.e., the returned object might be created on the fly). The concrete functions, whose names begin with `PyList_`, `PyTuple_`, `PyDict_`, and so on, return a borrowed reference when the semantics of the object they return ensure that there must be some other reference to the returned object somewhere.

In this chapter, I indicate all cases of exceptions to these rules (i.e., the return of borrowed references and the rare cases of reference stealing from arguments) regarding all functions that I cover. When I don't explicitly mention a function as being an exception, it means that the function follows the rules: its `PyObject*` arguments, if any, are borrowed references, and its `PyObject*` result, if any, is a new reference.

Accessing Arguments

A function that has `ml_flags` in its `PyMethodDef` set to `METH_NOARGS` is called from Python with no arguments. The corresponding C function has a signature with only one argument, *self*. When `ml_flags` is `METH_O`, Python code must call the function with one argument. The C function's second argument is a borrowed reference to the object that the Python caller passes as the argument's value.

When `ml_flags` is `METH_VARARGS`, Python code can call the function with any number of positional arguments, which are collected as a tuple. The C function's second argument is a borrowed reference to the tuple. Your C code can then call the `PyArg_ParseTuple` function.

PyArg_
ParseTuple

`int PyArg_ParseTuple(PyObject* tuple, char* format,...)`

Returns 0 for errors, a value not equal to 0 for success. *tuple* is the PyObject* that was the C function's second argument. *format* is a C string that describes mandatory and optional arguments. The following arguments of `PyArg_ParseTuple` are the addresses of the C variables in which to put the values extracted from the tuple. Any PyObject* variables among the C variables are borrowed references. Table 24-1 lists the commonly used code strings, of which zero or more are joined to form string *format*.

Table 24-1. Format codes for PyArg_ParseTuple

Code	C type	Meaning
c	char	A Python string of length 1 becomes a C char
d	double	A Python float becomes a C double
D	Py_Complex	A Python complex becomes a C Py_Complex
f	float	A Python float becomes a C float
i	int	A Python int becomes a C int
l	long	A Python int becomes a C long
L	long long	A Python int becomes a C long long (or _int64 on Windows)
O	PyObject*	Gets non-NULL borrowed reference to a Python argument
O!	type + PyObject*	Like code O, plus type checking or TypeError (see below)
O&	convert + void*	Arbitrary conversion (see below)
s	char*	Python string without embedded nulls to C char*
s#	char* + int	Any Python string to C address and length
t#	char* + int	Read-only single-segment buffer to C address and length
u	Py_UNICODE*	Python Unicode without embedded nulls to C (UTF-16)
u#	Py_UNICODE* + int	Any Python Unicode C (UTF-16) address and length
w#	char* + int	Read-write single-segment buffer to C address and length
z	char*	Like code s, also accepts None (sets C's char* to NULL)
z#	char* + int	Like code s#, also accepts None (sets C's char* to NULL)
(...)	as per ...	A Python sequence is treated as one argument per item
|		The following arguments are optional
:		Format finished, followed by function name for error messages
;		Format finished, followed by entire error message text

Code formats d to L accept numeric arguments from Python. Python coerces the corresponding values. For example, a code of i can correspond to a Python float—the fractional part gets truncated, as if built-in function int had been called. Py_Complex is a C struct with two fields named real and imag, both of type double.

0 is the most general format code and accepts any argument, which you can later check and/or convert as needed. Variant O! corresponds to two arguments in the variable arguments: first the address of a Python type object, then the address of a PyObject*. O! checks that the corresponding value belongs to the given type (or any subtype of that type) before setting the PyObject* to point to the value. Variant O& also corresponds to two arguments in the variable arguments: first the address of a converter function you coded, then a void* (i.e., any address at all). The converter function must have signature int *convert*(PyObject*, void*). Python calls your conversion function with the value passed from Python as the first argument and the void* from the variable arguments as the second argument. The conversion function must either return 0 and raise an exception (as covered in "Exceptions" later in this chapter) to indicate an error, or return 1 and store whatever is appropriate via the void* it gets.

Code format s accepts a string from Python and the address of a char* (i.e., a char**) among the variable arguments. It changes the char* to point at the string's buffer, which your C code must then treat as a read-only, null-terminated array of chars (i.e., a typical C string; however, your code must not modify it). The Python string must contain no embedded null characters. s# is similar, but corresponds to two arguments among the variable arguments: first the address of a char*, then the address of an int to set to the string's length. The Python string can contain embedded nulls, and therefore so can the buffer to which the char* is set to point. u and u# are similar, but accept any Unicode string, and the C-side pointers must be Py_UNICODE* rather than char*. Py_UNICODE is a macro defined in *Python.h*, and corresponds to the type of a Python Unicode character in the implementation (this is often, but not always, the same as a wchar_t in C).

t# and w# are similar to s#, but the corresponding Python argument can be any object of a type that respects the buffer protocol, respectively read-only and read-write. Strings are a typical example of read-only buffers. mmap and array instances are typical examples of read-write buffers, and they are also acceptable where a read-only buffer is required (i.e., for a t#).

When one of the arguments is a Python sequence of known length, you can use format codes for each of its items, and corresponding C addresses among the variable arguments, by grouping the format codes in parentheses. For example, code (ii) corresponds to a Python sequence of two numbers, and, among the remaining arguments, corresponds to two addresses of ints.

The format string may include a vertical bar (|) to indicate that all following arguments are optional. You must initialize the C variables, whose addresses you pass among the variable arguments for later arguments, to suitable default values before you call PyArg_ParseTuple. PyArg_ParseTuple does not change the C variables corresponding to optional arguments that were not passed in a given call from Python to your C-coded function.

The format string may optionally end with :*name* to indicate that *name* must be used as the function name if any error messages are needed. Alternatively, the format string may end with ;*text* to indicate that *text* must be used as the entire error message if PyArg_ParseTuple detects errors (this is rarely used).

A function that has ml_flags in its PyMethodDef set to METH_KEYWORDS accepts positional and keyword arguments. Python code calls the function with any number of positional arguments, which get collected as a tuple, and keyword arguments, which get collected as a dictionary. The C function's second argument is a borrowed reference to the tuple, and the third one is a borrowed reference to the dictionary. Your C code then calls the PyArg_ParseTupleAndKeywords function.

PyArg_ **ParseTupleAnd** **Keywords**	int PyArg_ParseTupleAndKeywords(PyObject* *tuple*,PyObject* *dict*, char* *format*,char** *kwlist*,...) Returns 0 for errors, a value not equal to 0 for success. *tuple* is the PyObject* that was the C function's second argument. *dict* is the PyObject* that was the C function's third argument. *format* is like for PyArg_ParseTuple, except that it cannot include the (...) format code to parse nested sequences. *kwlist* is an array of char* terminated by a NULL sentinel, with the names of the parameters, one after the other. For example, the following C code:

```
static PyObject*
func_c(PyObject* self, PyObject* args, PyObject* kwds)
{
    static char* argnames[] = {"x", "y", "z", NULL};
    double x, y=0.0, z=0.0;
    if(!PyArg_ParseTupleAndKeywords(
        args,kwds,"d|dd",argnames,&x,&y,&z))
        return NULL;
    /* rest of function snipped */
```

is roughly equivalent to this Python code:

```
def func_py(x, y=0.0, z=0.0):
    x, y, z = map(float, (x,y,z))
    # rest of function snipped
```

Creating Python Values

C functions that communicate with Python must often build Python values, both to return as their PyObject* result and for other purposes, such as setting items and attributes. The simplest and handiest way to build a Python value is most often with the Py_BuildValue function.

Py_BuildValue	PyObject* Py_BuildValue(char* *format*,...) *format* is a C string that describes the Python object to build. The following arguments of Py_BuildValue are C values from which the result is built. The PyObject* result is a new reference. Table 24-2 lists the commonly used code strings, of which zero or more are joined into string *format*. Py_BuildValue builds and returns a tuple if *format* contains two or more format codes, or if *format* begins

with (and ends with). Otherwise, the result is not a tuple. When you pass buffers, as for example in the case of format code s#, Py_BuildValue copies the data. You can therefore modify, abandon, or free( ) your original copy of the data after Py_BuildValue returns. Py_BuildValue always returns a new reference (except for format code N). Called with an empty *format*, Py_BuildValue("") returns a new reference to None.

Table 24-2. Format codes for Py_BuildValue

Code	C type	Meaning
c	char	A C char becomes a Python string of length 1
d	double	A C double becomes a Python float
D	Py_Complex	A C Py_Complex becomes a Python complex
i	int	A C int becomes a Python int
l	long	A C long becomes a Python int
N	PyObject*	Passes a Python object and steals a reference
O	PyObject*	Passes a Python object and INCREFs it as per normal rules
O&	convert + void*	Arbitrary conversion (see below)
s	char*	C null-terminated char* to Python string, or NULL to None
s#	char* + int	C char* and length to Python string, or NULL to None
u	Py_UNICODE*	C wide (UCS-2) null-terminated string to Python Unicode, or NULL to None
u#	Py_UNICODE* + int	C wide (UCS-2) string and length to Python Unicode, or NULL to None
(...)	as per ...	Build Python tuple from C values
[...]	as per ...	Build Python list from C values
{...}	as per ...	Build Python dictionary from C values, alternating keys and values (must be an even number of C values)

Code O& corresponds to two arguments among the variable arguments: first the address of a converter function you code, then a void* (i.e., any address at all). The converter function must have signature PyObject* *convert*(void*). Python calls the conversion function with the void* from the variable arguments as the only argument. The conversion function must either return NULL and raise an exception (as covered in "Exceptions" later in this chapter) to indicate an error, or return a new reference PyObject* built from the data in the void*.

Code {...} builds dictionaries from an even number of C values, alternately keys and values. For example, Py_BuildValue("{issi}",23,"zig","zag",42) returns a dictionary like Python's {23:'zig','zag':42}.

Note the important difference between codes N and O. N steals a reference from the PyObject* corresponding value among the variable arguments, so it's convenient when you're building an object including a reference you own that you would otherwise have to Py_DECREF. O does no reference stealing, so it's appropriate when you're building an object including a reference you don't own, or a reference you must also keep elsewhere.

Exceptions

To propagate exceptions raised from other functions you call, return NULL as the PyObject* result from your C function. To raise your own exceptions, set the current-exception indicator and return NULL. Python's built-in exception classes (covered in Chapter 6) are globally available, with names starting with PyExc_, such as PyExc_AttributeError, PyExc_KeyError, and so on. Your extension module can also supply and use its own exception classes. The most commonly used C API functions related to raising exceptions are the following.

PyErr_Format	PyObject* PyErr_Format(PyObject* *type*,char* *format*,...)

Raises an exception of class *type*, a built-in such as PyExc_IndexError, or an exception class created with PyErr_NewException. Builds the associated value from format string *format*, which has syntax similar to printf's, and the following C values indicated as variable arguments above. Returns NULL, so your code can just call:

```
return PyErr_Format(PyExc_KeyError,
    "Unknown key name (%s)", thekeystring);
```

PyErr_ NewException	PyObject* PyErr_NewException(char* *name*,PyObject* *base*, PyObject* *dict*)

Subclasses exception class *base*, with extra class attributes and methods from dictionary *dict* (normally NULL, meaning no extra class attributes or methods), creating a new exception class named *name* (string *name* must be of the form "*modulename.classname*") and returning a new reference to the new class object. When *base* is NULL, uses PyExc_Exception as the base class. You normally call this function during initialization of a module object *module*. For example:

```
PyModule_AddObject(module, "error",
    PyErr_NewException("mymod.error", NULL, NULL));
```

PyErr_ NoMemory	PyObject* PyErr_NoMemory( )

Raises an out-of-memory error and returns NULL, so your code can just call:

```
return PyErr_NoMemory( );
```

PyErr_SetObject	void PyErr_SetObject(PyObject* *type*,PyObject* *value*)

Raises an exception of class *type*, a built-in such as PyExc_KeyError, or an exception class created with PyErr_NewException, with *value* as the associated value (a borrowed reference). PyErr_SetObject is a void function (i.e., returns no value).

PyErr_ SetFromErrno	PyObject* PyErr_SetFromErrno(PyObject* *type*)

Raises an exception of class *type*, a built-in such as PyExc_OSError, or an exception class created with PyErr_NewException. Takes all details from global variable errno, which C library functions and system calls set for many error cases, and the standard C library function strerror. Returns NULL, so your code can just call:

```
return PyErr_SetFromErrno(PyExc_IOError);
```

PyErr_SetFromErrno WithFilename	PyObject* PyErr_SetFromErrnoWithFilename(PyObject* *type*, char* *filename*) Like PyErr_SetFromErrno, but also provides string *filename* as part of the exception's value. When *filename* is NULL, works like PyErr_SetFromErrno.

Your C code may want to deal with an exception and continue, as a try/except statement would let you do in Python code. The most commonly used C API functions related to catching exceptions are the following.

PyErr_Clear	void PyErr_Clear( ) Clears the error indicator. Innocuous if no error is pending.

PyErr_Exception Matches	int PyErr_ExceptionMatches(PyObject* *type*) Call only when an error is pending, or the whole program might crash. Returns a value not equal to 0 when the pending exception is an instance of the given *type* or any subclass of *type*, or 0 when the pending exception is not such an instance.

PyErr_Occurred	PyObject* PyErr_Occurred( ) Returns NULL if no error is pending, otherwise a borrowed reference to the type of the pending exception. (Don't use the returned value; call PyErr_ExceptionMatches instead, in order to catch exceptions of subclasses as well, as is normal and expected.)

PyErr_Print	void PyErr_Print( ) Call only when an error is pending, or the whole program might crash. Outputs a standard traceback to sys.stderr, then clears the error indicator.

If you need to process errors in highly sophisticated ways, study other error-related functions of the C API, such as PyErr_Fetch, PyErr_Normalize, PyErr_GivenExceptionMatches, and PyErr_Restore. However, I do not cover such advanced and rarely needed possibilities in this book.

Abstract Layer Functions

The code for a C extension typically needs to use some Python functionality. For example, your code may need to examine or set attributes and items of Python objects, call Python-coded and built-in functions and methods, and so on. In most cases, the best approach is for your code to call functions from the abstract layer of Python's C API. These are functions that you can call on any Python object (functions whose names start with PyObject_), or any object within a wide category, such as mappings, numbers, or sequences (with names respectively starting with PyMapping_, PyNumber_, and PySequence_).

Some of the functions callable on objects within these categories duplicate functionality that is also available from PyObject_ functions; in these cases, you should use the PyObject_ function instead. I don't cover such redundant functions in this book.

Functions in the abstract layer raise Python exceptions if you call them on objects to which they are not applicable. All of these functions accept borrowed references for PyObject* arguments, and return a new reference (NULL for an exception) if they return a PyObject* result.

The most frequently used abstract layer functions are the following.

PyCallable_ Check	int PyCallable_Check(PyObject* x)
	True if x is callable, like Python's callable(x).
PyEval_ CallObject	PyObject* PyEval_CallObject(PyObject* x,PyObject* args)
	Calls callable Python object x with the positional arguments held in tuple args. Returns the call's result, like Python's return x(*args).
PyEval_ CallObjectWith Keywords	PyObject* PyEval_CallObjectWithKeywords(PyObject* x, PyObject* args,PyObject* kwds)
	Calls callable Python object x with the positional arguments held in tuple args and the named arguments held in dictionary kwds Returns the call's result, like Python's return x(*args,**kwds).
PyIter_Check	int PyIter_Check(PyObject* x)
	True if x supports the iterator protocol (i.e., if x is an iterator).
PyIter_Next	PyObject* PyIter_Next(PyObject* x)
	Returns the next item from iterator x. Returns NULL without raising any exception if x's iteration is finished (i.e., when Python's x.next( ) raises StopIteration).
PyNumber_ Check	int PyNumber_Check(PyObject* x)
	True if x supports the number protocol (i.e., if x is a number).

PyObject_ CallFunction	`PyObject* PyObject_CallFunction(PyObject* x,char* format,...)` Calls the callable Python object *x* with positional arguments described by format string *format*, using the same format codes as `Py_BuildValue`, covered earlier. When *format* is `NULL`, calls *x* with no arguments. Returns the call's result.

**PyObject_
CallMethod**
	`PyObject* PyObject_CallMethod(PyObject* x,char* method,`
	`char* format,...)`
	Calls the method named *method* of Python object *x* with positional arguments described by format string *format*, using the same format codes as `Py_BuildValue`. When *format* is `NULL`, calls the method with no arguments. Returns the call's result.

PyObject_Cmp	`int PyObject_Cmp(PyObject* x1,PyObject* x2,int* result)` Compares objects *x1* and *x2* and places the result (-1, 0, or 1) in **result*, like Python's *result=cmp(x1,x2)*.
PyObject_ DelAttrString	`int PyObject_DelAttrString(PyObject* x,char* name)` Deletes *x*'s attribute named *name*, like Python's del *x.name*.
PyObject_ DelItem	`int PyObject_DelItem(PyObject* x,PyObject* key)` Deletes *x*'s item with key (or index) *key*, like Python's del *x[key]*.
PyObject_ DelItemString	`int PyObject_DelItemString(PyObject* x,char* key)` Deletes *x*'s item with key *key*, like Python's del *x[key]*.
PyObject_ GetAttrString	`PyObject* PyObject_GetAttrString(PyObject* x,char* name)` Returns *x*'s attribute named *name*, like Python's *x.name*.
PyObject_ GetItem	`PyObject* PyObject_GetItem(PyObject* x,PyObject* key)` Returns *x*'s item with key (or index) *key*, like Python's *x[key]*.
PyObject_ GetItemString	`int PyObject_GetItemString(PyObject* x,char* key)` Returns *x*'s item with key *key*, like Python's *x[key]*.
PyObject_ GetIter	`PyObject* PyObject_GetIter(PyObject* x)` Returns an iterator on *x*, like Python's iter(*x*).
PyObject_ HasAttrString	`int PyObject_HasAttrString(PyObject* x,char* name)` True if *x* has an attribute named *name*, like Python's hasattr(*x,name*).

PyObject_IsTrue	`int PyObject_IsTrue(PyObject* x)` True if x is true for Python, like Python's `bool(x)`.
PyObject_Length	`int PyObject_Length(PyObject* x)` Returns x's length, like Python's `len(x)`.
PyObject_Repr	`PyObject* PyObject_Repr(PyObject* x)` Returns x's detailed string representation, like Python's `repr(x)`.
PyObject_RichCompare	`PyObject* PyObject_RichCompare(PyObject* x,PyObject* y,int op)` Performs the comparison indicated by *op* between x and y, and returns the result as a Python object. *op* can be `Py_EQ`, `Py_NE`, `Py_LT`, `Py_LE`, `Py_GT`, or `Py_GE`, corresponding to Python comparisons x==y, x!=y, x<y, x<=y, x>y, or x>=y, respectively.
PyObject_RichCompareBool	`int PyObject_RichCompareBool(PyObject* x,PyObject* y,int op)` Like `PyObject_RichCompare`, but returns 0 for false, 1 for true.
PyObject_SetAttrString	`int PyObject_SetAttrString(PyObject* x,char* name,PyObject* v)` Sets x's attribute named *name* to v, like Python's x.*name*=v.
PyObject_SetItem	`int PyObject_SetItem(PyObject* x,PyObject* k,PyObject *v)` Sets x's item with key (or index) *key* to v, like Python's x[*key*]=v.
PyObject_SetItemString	`int PyObject_SetItemString(PyObject* x,char* key,PyObject *v)` Sets x's item with key *key* to v, like Python's x[*key*]=v.
PyObject_Str	`PyObject* PyObject_Str(PyObject* x)` Returns x's readable string form, like Python's `str(x)`.
PyObject_Type	`PyObject* PyObject_Type(PyObject* x)` Returns x's type object, like Python's `type(x)`.
PyObject_Unicode	`PyObject* PyObject_Unicode(PyObject* x)` Returns x's Unicode string form, like Python's `unicode(x)`.
PySequence_Contains	`int PySequence_Contains(PyObject* x,PyObject* v)` True if v is an item in x, like Python's v in x.

PySequence_ **DelSlice**	`int PySequence_DelSlice(PyObject* x,int start,int stop)` Delete x's slice from start to stop, like Python's del x[start:stop].
PySequence_ **Fast**	`PyObject* PySequence_Fast(PyObject* x)` Returns a new reference to a tuple with the same items as x, unless x is a list, in which case returns a new reference to x. When you need to get many items of an arbitrary sequence x, it's fastest to call t=PySequence_Fast(x) once, then call PySequence_Fast_GET_ITEM(t,i) as many times as needed, and finally call Py_DECREF(t).
PySequence_ **Fast_GET_ITEM**	`PyObject* PySequence_Fast_GET_ITEM(PyObject* x,int i)` Returns the i item of x, where x must be the result of PySequence_Fast, x!=NULL, and 0<=i<PySequence_Fast_GET_SIZE(t). Violating these conditions can cause program crashes: this approach is optimized for speed, not for safety.
PySequence_ **Fast_GET_SIZE**	`int PySequence_Fast_GET_SIZE(PyObject* x)` Returns the length of x. x must be the result of PySequence_Fast, x!=NULL.
PySequence_ **GetSlice**	`PyObject* PySequence_GetSlice(PyObject* x,int start,int stop)` Returns x's slice from start to stop, like Python's x[start:stop].
PySequence_ **List**	`PyObject* PySequence_List(PyObject* x)` Returns a new list object with the same items as x, like Python's list(x).

PySequence_
SetSlice
	`int PySequence_SetSlice(PyObject* x,int start,int stop,`
	`PyObject* v)`
	Sets x's slice from start to stop to v, like Python's x[start:stop]=v. Just as in the equivalent Python statement, v must be a sequence of the same type as x.

PySequence_ **Tuple**	`PyObject* PySequence_Tuple(PyObject* x)` Returns a new reference to a tuple with the same items as x, like Python's tuple(x).

The functions whose names start with PyNumber_ allow you to perform numeric operations. Unary PyNumber functions, which take one argument PyObject* x and return a PyObject*, are listed in Table 24-3 with their Python equivalents.

Table 24-3. Unary PyNumber functions

Function	Python equivalent
PyNumber_Absolute	abs(x)
PyNumber_Float	float(x)
PyNumber_Int	int(x)
PyNumber_Invert	~x
PyNumber_Long	long(x)
PyNumber_Negative	-x
PyNumber_Positive	+x

Binary `PyNumber` functions, which take two `PyObject*` arguments *x* and *y* and return a `PyObject*`, are similarly listed in Table 24-4.

Table 24-4. Binary PyNumber functions

Function	Python equivalent
PyNumber_Add	x + y
PyNumber_And	x & y
PyNumber_Divide	x / y
PyNumber_Divmod	divmod(x, y)
PyNumber_FloorDivide	x // y
PyNumber_Lshift	x << y
PyNumber_Multiply	x * y
PyNumber_Or	x | y
PyNumber_Remainder	x % y
PyNumber_Rshift	x >> y
PyNumber_Subtract	x - y
PyNumber_TrueDivide	x / y (non-truncating)
PyNumber_Xor	x ^ y

All the binary `PyNumber` functions have in-place equivalents whose names start with `PyNumber_InPlace`, such as `PyNumber_InPlaceAdd` and so on. The in-place versions try to modify the first argument in-place, if possible, and in any case return a new reference to the result, be it the first argument (modified) or a new object. Python's built-in numbers are immutable; therefore, when the first argument is a number of a built-in type, the in-place versions work just the same as the ordinary versions. Function `PyNumber_Divmod` returns a tuple with two items (the quotient and the remainder) and has no in-place equivalent.

There is one ternary `PyNumber` function, `PyNumber_Power`.

PyNumber_Power

`PyObject* PyNumber_Power(PyObject* x,PyObject* y,PyObject* z)`

When *z* is Py_None, returns *x* raised to the *y* power, like Python's *x***y or equivalently pow(*x,y*). Otherwise, returns *x***y%*z*, like Python's pow(*x,y,z*). The in-place version is named `PyNumber_InPlacePower`.

Concrete Layer Functions

Each specific type of Python built-in object supplies concrete functions to operate on instances of that type, with names starting with Py*type*_ (e.g., PyInt_ for functions related to Python ints). Most such functions duplicate the functionality of abstract-layer functions or auxiliary functions covered earlier in this chapter, such as Py_BuildValue, which can generate objects of many types. In this section, I cover some frequently used functions from the concrete layer that provide unique functionality or substantial convenience or speed. For most types, you can check if an object belongs to the type by calling Py*type*_Check, which also accepts instances of subtypes, or Py*type*_CheckExact, which accepts only instances of *type*, not of subtypes. Signatures are as for functions PyIter_Check, covered earlier in this chapter.

PyDict_GetItem PyObject* PyDict_GetItem(PyObject* *x*,PyObject* *key*)

Returns a borrowed reference to the item with key *key* of dictionary *x*.

PyDict_
GetItemString

int PyDict_GetItemString(PyObject* *x*,char* *key*)

Returns a borrowed reference to the item with key *key* of dictionary *x*.

PyDict_Next int PyDict_Next(PyObject* *x*,int* *pos*,PyObject** *k*,PyObject** *v*)

Iterates over items in dictionary *x*. You must initialize **pos* to 0 at the start of the iteration: PyDict_Next uses and updates **pos* to keep track of its place. For each successful iteration step, returns 1; when there are no more items, returns 0. Updates **k* and **v* to point to the next key and value respectively (borrowed references) at each step that returns 1. You can pass either *k* or *v* as NULL if you are not interested in the key or value. During an iteration, you must not change in any way the set of *x*'s keys, but you can change *x*'s values as long as the set of keys remains identical.

PyDict_Merge int PyDict_Merge(PyObject* *x*,PyObject* *y*,int *override*)

Updates dictionary *x* by merging the items of dictionary *y* into *x*. *override* determines what happens when a key *k* is present in both *x* and *y*: if *override* is 0, then *x*[*k*] remains the same; otherwise *x*[*k*] is replaced by the value *y*[*k*].

PyDict_
MergeFromSeq2

int PyDict_MergeFromSeq2(PyObject* *x*,PyObject* *y*,int *override*)

Like PyDict_Merge, except that *y* is not a dictionary but a sequence of sequences, where each subsequence has length 2 and is used as a (*key*,*value*) pair.

PyFloat_AS_ DOUBLE	double `PyFloat_AS_DOUBLE(PyObject* x)`
	Returns the C double value of Python float *x*, very fast, without error checking.
PyList_New	PyObject* `PyList_New(int length)`
	Returns a new, uninitialized list of the given *length*. You must then initialize the list, typically by calling `PyList_SET_ITEM length` times.
PyList_GET_ ITEM	PyObject* `PyList_GET_ITEM(PyObject* x,int pos)`
	Returns the *pos* item of list *x*, without error checking.
PyList_SET_ ITEM	int `PyList_SET_ITEM(PyObject* x,int pos,PyObject* v)`
	Sets the *pos* item of list *x* to *v*, without error checking. Steals a reference to *v*. Use only immediately after creating a new list *x* with `PyList_New`.
PyString_AS_ STRING	char* `PyString_AS_STRING(PyObject* x)`
	Returns a pointer to the internal buffer of string *x*, very fast, without error checking. You must not modify the buffer in any way, unless you just allocated it by calling `PyString_ FromStringAndSize(NULL,size)`.
PyString_ AsStringAndSize	int `PyString_AsStringAndSize(PyObject* x,char** buffer, int* length)`
	Puts a pointer to the internal buffer of string *x* in **buffer*, and *x*'s length in **length*. You must not modify the buffer in any way, unless you just allocated it by calling `PyString_ FromStringAndSize(NULL,size)`.
PyString_ FromFormat	PyObject* `PyString_FromFormat(char* format,...)`
	Returns a Python string built from format string *format*, which has syntax similar to `printf`'s, and the following C values indicated as variable arguments above.
PyString_ FromStringAnd Size	PyObject* `PyString_FromFormat(char* data,int size)`
	Returns a Python string of length *size*, copying *size* bytes from *data*. When *data* is NULL, the Python string is uninitialized, and you must initialize it. You can get the pointer to the string's internal buffer by calling `PyString_AS_STRING`.
PyTuple_New	PyObject* `PyTuple_New(int length)`
	Returns a new, uninitialized tuple of the given *length*. You must then initialize the tuple, typically by calling `PyTuple_SET_ITEM length` times.

| PyTuple_GET_ ITEM | `PyObject* PyTuple_GET_ITEM(PyObject* x,int pos)` |
| | Returns the *pos* item of tuple *x*, without error checking. |

| PyTuple_SET_ ITEM | `int PyTuple_SET_ITEM(PyObject* x,int pos,PyObject* v)` |
| | Sets the *pos* item of tuple *x* to *v*, without error checking. Steals a reference to *v*. Use only immediately after creating a new tuple *x* with `PyTuple_New`. |

A Simple Extension Example

Example 24-1 exposes the functionality of Python C API functions `PyDict_Merge` and `PyDict_MergeFromSeq2` for Python use. The update method of dictionaries works like `PyDict_Merge` with *override*=1, but Example 24-1 is more general.

Example 24-1. A simple Python extension module merge.c

```c
#include <Python.h>

static PyObject*
merge(PyObject* self, PyObject* args, PyObject* kwds)
{
    static char* argnames[] = {"x","y","override",NULL};
    PyObject *x, *y;
    int override = 0;
    if(!PyArg_ParseTupleAndKeywords(args, kwds, "O!O|i", argnames,
        &PyDict_Type, &x, &y, &override))
            return NULL;
    if(-1 == PyDict_Merge(x, y, override)) {
        if(!PyErr_ExceptionMatches(PyExc_TypeError)):
            return NULL;
        PyErr_Clear();
        if(-1 == PyDict_MergeFromSeq2(x, y, override))
            return NULL;
    }
    return Py_BuildValue("");
}

static char merge_docs[] = "\
merge(x,y,override=False): merge into dict x the items of dict y (or the pairs\n\
    that are the items of y, if y is a sequence), with optional override.\n\
    Alters dict x directly, returns None.\n\
";

static PyObject*
mergenew(PyObject* self, PyObject* args, PyObject* kwds)
{
    static char* argnames[] = {"x","y","override",NULL};
    PyObject *x, *y, *result;
```

Example 24-1. A simple Python extension module merge.c (continued)

```
    int override = 0;
    if(!PyArg_ParseTupleAndKeywords(args, kwds, "O!O|i", argnames,
        &PyDict_Type, &x, &y, &override))
            return NULL;
    result = PyObject_CallMethod(x, "copy", "");
    if(!result)
        return NULL;
    if(-1 == PyDict_Merge(result, y, override)) {
        if(!PyErr_ExceptionMatches(PyExc_TypeError)):
            return NULL;
        PyErr_Clear();
        if(-1 == PyDict_MergeFromSeq2(result, y, override))
            return NULL;
    }
    return result;
}

static char merge_docs[] = "\
mergenew(x,y,override=False): merge into dict x the items of dict y (or\n\
    the pairs that are the items of y, if y is a sequence), with optional\n\
    override.  Does NOT alter x, but rather returns the modified copy as\n\
    the function's result.\n\
";

static PyMethodDef funcs[] = {
    {"merge", (PyCFunction)merge, METH_KEYWORDS, merge_docs},
    {"mergenew", (PyCFunction)mergenew, METH_KEYWORDS, mergenew_docs},
    {NULL}
};

void
initmerge(void)
{
    Py_InitModule3("merge", funcs, "Example extension module");
}
```

This example declares as static every function and global variable in the C source file, except initmerge, which must be visible from the outside to let Python call it. Since the functions and variables are exposed to Python via the PyMethodDef structures, Python does not need to see their names directly. Therefore, declaring them static is best: this ensures that names don't accidentally end up in the whole program's global namespace, as might otherwise happen on some platforms, possibly causing conflicts and errors.

The format string "O!O|i" passed to PyArg_ParseTupleAndKeywords indicates that function merge accepts three arguments from Python: an object with a type constraint, a generic object, and an optional integer. At the same time, the format string indicates that the variable part of PyArg_ParseTupleAndKeywords's arguments must contain four addresses: in order, the address of a Python type object, then two addresses of PyObject* variables, and finally the address of an int variable.

The int variable must have been previously initialized to its intended default value, since the corresponding Python argument is optional.

And indeed, after the *argnames* argument, the code passes &PyDict_Type (i.e., the address of the dictionary type object). Then it passes the addresses of the two PyObject* variables. Finally, it passes the address of variable *override*, an int that was previously initialized to 0, since the default, when the *override* argument isn't explicitly passed from Python, should be no overriding. If the return value of PyArg_ParseTupleAndKeywords is 0, the code immediately returns NULL to propagate the exception; this automatically diagnoses most cases where Python code passes wrong arguments to our new function merge.

When the arguments appear to be okay, it tries PyDict_Merge, which succeeds if *y* is a dictionary. When PyDict_Merge raises a TypeError, indicating that *y* is not a dictionary, the code clears the error and tries again, this time with PyDict_MergeFromSeq2, which succeeds when *y* is a sequence of pairs. If that also fails, it returns NULL to propagate the exception. Otherwise, it returns None in the simplest way (i.e., with return Py_BuildValue("")) to indicate success.

Function mergenew basically duplicates merge's functionality; however, mergenew does not alter its arguments, but rather builds and returns a new dictionary as the function's result. The C API function PyObject_CallMethod lets mergenew call the copy method of its first Python-passed argument, a dictionary object, and obtain a new dictionary object that it then alters (with exactly the same logic as function merge). It then returns the altered dictionary as the function result (thus, no need to call Py_BuildValue in this case).

The code of Example 24-1 must reside in a source file named *merge.c*. In the same directory, create the following script named *setup.py*:

```
from distutils.core import setup, Extension
setup(name='merge', ext_modules=[ Extension('merge',sources=['merge.c']) ])
```

Now, run *python setup.py install* at a shell prompt in this directory. This command builds the dynamically loaded library for the merge extension module, and copies it to the appropriate directory, depending on your Python installation. Now your Python code can use the module. For example:

```
import merge
x = { 'a':1,'b':2 }
merge.merge(x,[['b',3],['c',4]])
print x                           # prints: {'a':1, 'b':2, 'c':4 }
print merge.mergenew(x,{'a':5,'d':6},override=1)
# prints: {'a':5, 'b':2, 'c':4, 'd':6 }
print x                           # prints: {'a':1, 'b':2, 'c':4 }
```

This example shows the difference between merge (which alters its first argument) and mergenew (which returns a new object and does not alter its argument). It also shows that the second argument can be either a dictionary or a sequence of two-item subsequences. Further, it demonstrates default operation (where keys that are already in the first argument are left alone) as well as the override option (where keys coming from the second argument take precedence, as in Python dictionaries' update method).

Defining New Types

In your extension modules, you often want to define new types and make them available to Python. A type's definition is held in a large struct named PyTypeObject. Most of the fields of PyTypeObject are pointers to functions. Some fields point to other structs, which in turn are blocks of pointers to functions. PyTypeObject also includes a few fields giving the type's name, size, and behavior details (option flags). You can leave almost all fields of PyTypeObject set to NULL if you do not supply the related functionality. You can point some fields to functions in the Python C API in order to supply certain aspects of fundamental object functionality in standard ways.

The best way to implement a type is to copy from the Python sources the file *Modules/xxsubtype.c*, which Python supplies exactly for such didactical purposes, and edit it. It's a complete module with two types, subclassing from list and dict respectively. Another example in the Python sources, *Objects/xxobject.c*, is not a complete module, and the type in this file is minimal and old-fashioned, not using modern recommended approaches. See *http://www.python.org/dev/doc/devel/api/type-structs.html* for detailed documentation on PyTypeObject and other related structs. File *Include/object.h* in the Python sources contains the declarations of these types, as well as several important comments that you would do well to study.

Per-instance data

To represent each instance of your type, declare a C struct that starts, right after the opening brace, with macro PyObject_HEAD. The macro expands into the data fields that your struct must begin with in order to be a Python object. Those fields include the reference count and a pointer to the instance's type. Any pointer to your structure can be correctly cast to a PyObject*.

The PyTypeObject struct that defines your type's characteristics and behavior must contain the size of your per-instance struct, as well as pointers to the C functions you write to operate on your structure. Therefore, you normally place the PyTypeObject toward the end of your code, after the per-instance struct and all the functions that operate on instances of the per-instance struct. Each *x* that points to a structure starting with PyObject_HEAD, and in particular each PyObject* *x*, has a field *x*->ob_type that is the address of the PyTypeObject structure that is *x*'s Python type object.

The PyTypeObject definition

Given a per-instance struct such as:

```
typedef struct {
    PyObject_HEAD
    /* other data needed by instances of this type, omitted */
} mytype;
```

the corresponding PyTypeObject struct almost invariably begins in a way similar to:

```
static PyTypeObject t_mytype = {
/* tp_head */          PyObject_HEAD_INIT(NULL)   /* use NULL, for MSVC++ */
/* tp_internal */      0,                      /* must be 0 */
/* tp_name /           "mymodule.mytype",      /* type name with module */
/* tp_basicsize */     sizeof(mytype),
/* tp_itemsize */      0,                      /* 0 except variable-size type */
/* tp_dealloc */       (destructor)mytype_dealloc,
/* tp_print */         0,                      /* usually 0, use str instead */
/* tp_getattr */       0,                      /* usually 0 (see getattro) */
/* tp_setattr */       0,                      /* usually 0 (see setattro) */
/* tp_compare*/        0,                      /* see also richcompare */
/* tp_repr */          (reprfunc)mytype_str,   /* like Python's __repr__ */
    /* rest of struct omitted */
```

For portability to Microsoft Visual C++, the PyObject_HEAD_INIT macro at the start of the PyTypeObject must have an argument of NULL. During module initialization, you must call PyType_Ready(&t_mytype), which, among other tasks, inserts in t_mytype the address of its type (the type of a type is also known as a metatype), normally &PyType_Type. Another slot in PyTypeObject that points to another type object is tp_base, later in the structure. In the structure definition itself, you must have a tp_base of NULL, again for compatibility with Microsoft Visual C++. However, before you invoke PyType_Ready(&t_mytype), you can optionally set t_mytype.tp_base to the address of another type object. When you do so, your type inherits from the other type, just like a class coded in Python 2.2 can optionally inherit from a built-in type. For a Python type coded in C, inheriting means that for most fields in the PyTypeObject, if you set the field to NULL, PyType_Ready copies the corresponding field from the base type. A type must specifically assert in its field tp_flags that it is usable as a base type, otherwise no other type can inherit from it.

The tp_itemsize field is of interest only for types that, like tuples, have instances of different sizes, and can determine instance size once and forever at creation time. Most types just set tp_itemsize to 0. Fields such as tp_getattr and tp_setattr are generally set to NULL because they exist only for backward compatibility: modern types use fields tp_getattro and tp_setattro instead. Field tp_repr is typical of most of the following fields, which are omitted here: the field holds the address of a function, which corresponds directly to a Python special method (here, __repr__). You can set the field to NULL, indicating that your type does not supply the special method, or else set the field to point to a function with the needed functionality. If you set the field to NULL, but also point to a base type from the tp_base slot, you inherit the special method, if any, from your base type. You often need to cast your functions to the specific typedef type that a field needs (here, type reprfunc for field tp_repr) because the typedef has a first argument PyObject* self, while your functions, being specific to your type, normally use more specific pointers. For example:

```
static PyObject* mytype_str(mytype* self) { ... /* rest omitted */
```

Alternatively, you can declare mytype_str with a PyObject* self, then use a cast (mytype*)self in the function's body. Either alternative is acceptable, but it's more common to locate the casts in the PyTypeObject declaration.

Instance initialization and finalization

The task of finalizing your instances is split among two functions. The tp_dealloc slot must never be NULL, except for immortal types (i.e., types whose instances are never deallocated). Python calls *x*->ob_type->tp_dealloc(*x*) on each instance *x* whose reference count decreases to 0, and the function thus called must release any resource held by object *x*, including *x*'s memory. When an instance of mytype holds no other resources that must be released (in particular, no owned references to other Python objects that you would have to DECREF), mytype's destructor can be extremely simple:

```
static void mytype_dealloc(PyObject *x)
{
    x->ob_type->tp_free((PyObject*)x);
}
```

The function in the tp_free slot has the specific task of freeing *x*'s memory. In Python 2.2, the function has signature void *name*(PyObject*). In Python 2.3, the signature has changed to void *name*(void*). One way to ensure your sources compile under both versions of Python is to put in slot tp_free the C API function _PyObject_Del, which has the right signature in each version.

The task of initializing your instances is split among three functions. To allocate memory for new instances of your type, put in slot tp_alloc the C API function PyType_GenericAlloc, which does absolutely minimal initialization, clearing the newly allocated memory bytes to 0 except for the type pointer and reference count. Similarly, you can often set field tp_new to the C API function PyType_GenericNew. In this case, you can perform all per-instance initialization in the function you put in slot tp_init, which has the signature:

int *init_name*(PyObject *self*,PyObject *args*,PyObject *kwds*)

The positional and named arguments to the function in slot tp_init are those passed when calling the type to create the new instance, just like, in Python, the positional and named arguments to __init__ are those passed when calling the class object. Again like for types (classes) defined in Python, the general rule is to do as little initialization as possible in tp_new and as much as possible in tp_init. Using PyType_GenericNew for tp_new accomplishes this. However, you can choose to define your own tp_new for special types, such as ones that have immutable instances, where initialization must happen earlier. The signature is:

PyObject* *new_name*(PyObject *subtype*,PyObject *args*,PyObject *kwds*)

The function in tp_new must return the newly created instance, normally an instance of *subtype* (which may be a type that inherits from yours). The function in tp_init, on the other hand, must return 0 for success, or -1 to indicate an exception.

If your type is subclassable, it's important that any instance invariants be established before the function in tp_new returns. For example, if it must be guaranteed that a certain field of the instance is never NULL, that field must be set to a non-NULL value by the function in tp_new. Subtypes of your type might fail to call your tp_init function; therefore such indispensable initializations should be in tp_new for subclassable types.

Attribute access

Access to attributes of your instances, including methods (as covered in Chapter 5) is mediated by the functions you put in slots tp_getattro and tp_setattro of your PyTypeObject struct. Normally, you put there the standard C API functions PyObject_GenericGetAttr and PyObject_GenericSetAttr, which implement standard semantics. Specifically, these API functions access your type's methods via the slot tp_methods, pointing to a sentinel-terminated array of PyMethodDef structs, and your instances' members via the slot tp_members, a similar sentinel-terminated array of PyMemberDef structs:

```
typedef struct {
    char* name;          /* Python-visible name of the member */
    int type;            /* code defining the data-type of the member */
    int offset;          /* offset of the member in the per-instance struct */
    int flags;           /* READONLY for a read-only member */
    char* doc;           /* docstring for the member */
} PyMemberDef
```

As an exception to the general rule that including *Python.h* gets you all the declarations you need, you have to include *structmember.h* explicitly in order to have your C source see the declaration of PyMemberDef.

type is generally T_OBJECT for members that are PyObject*, but many other type codes are defined in *Include/structmember.h* for members that your instances hold as C-native data (e.g., T_DOUBLE for double or T_STRING for char*). For example, if your per-instance struct is something like:

```
typedef struct {
    PyObject_HEAD
    double datum;
    char* name;
} mytype;
```

to expose to Python per-instance attributes *datum* (read/write) and *name* (read-only), you can define the following array and point your PyTypeObject's tp_members to it:

```
static PyMemberDef[] mytype_members = {
    {"datum", T_DOUBLE, offsetof(mytype, datum), 0, "The current datum"},
    {"name", T_STRING, offsetof(mytype, name), READONLY,
     "Name of the datum"},
    {NULL}
};
```

Using PyObject_GenericGetAttr and PyObject_GenericSetAttr for tp_getattro and tp_setattro also provides further possibilities, which I will not cover in detail in this book. Field tp_getset points to a sentinel-terminated array of PyGetSetDef structs, the equivalent of having property instances in a Python-coded class. If your PyTypeObject's field tp_dictoffset is not equal to 0, the field's value must be the offset, within the per-instance struct, of a PyObject* that points to a Python dictionary. In this case, the generic attribute access API functions use that dictionary to allow Python code to set arbitrary attributes on your type's instances, just like for instances of Python-coded classes.

Another dictionary is per-type, not per-instance: the PyObject* for the per-type dictionary is slot tp_dict of your PyTypeObject struct. You can set slot tp_dict to NULL, and then PyType_Ready initializes the dictionary appropriately. Alternatively, you can set tp_dict to a dictionary of type attributes, and then PyType_Ready adds other entries to that same dictionary, in addition to the type attributes you set. It's generally easier to start with tp_dict set to NULL, call PyType_Ready to create and initialize the per-type dictionary, and then, if need be, add any further entries to the dictionary.

Field tp_flags is a long whose bits determine your type struct's exact layout, mostly for backward compatibility. Normally, set this field to Py_TPFLAGS_DEFAULT to indicate that you are defining a normal, modern type. You should set tp_flags to Py_TPFLAGS_DEFAULT|Py_TPFLAGS_HAVE_GC if your type supports cyclic garbage collection. Your type should support cyclic garbage collection if instances of the type contain PyObject* fields that might point to arbitrary objects and form part of a reference loop. However, to support cyclic garbage collection, it's not enough to add Py_TPFLAGS_HAVE_GC to field tp_flags; you also have to supply appropriate functions, indicated by slots tp_traverse and tp_clear, and register and unregister your instances appropriately with the cyclic garbage collector. Supporting cyclic garbage collection is an advanced subject, and I do not cover it further in this book. Similarly, I do not cover the advanced subject of supporting weak references.

Field tp_doc, a char*, is a null-terminated character string that is your type's docstring. Other fields point to structs (whose fields point to functions); you can set each such field to NULL to indicate that you support none of the functions of that kind. The fields pointing to such blocks of functions are tp_as_number, for special methods typically supplied by numbers; tp_as_sequence, for special methods typically supplied by sequences; tp_as_mapping, for special methods typically supplied by mappings; and tp_as_buffer, for the special methods of the buffer protocol.

For example, objects that are not sequences can still support one or a few of the methods listed in the block to which tp_as_sequence points, and in that case the PyTypeObject must have a non-NULL field tp_as_sequence, even if the block of function pointers it points to is in turn mostly full of NULLs. For example, dictionaries supply a __contains__ special method so that you can check if x in d when d is a dictionary. At the C code level, the method is a function pointed to by field sq_contains, which is part of the PySequenceMethods struct to which field tp_as_sequence points. Therefore, the PyTypeObject struct for the dict type, named PyDict_Type, has a non-NULL value for tp_as_sequence, even though a dictionary supplies no other field in PySequenceMethods except sq_contains, and therefore all other fields in *(PyDict_Type.tp_as_sequence) are NULL.

Type definition example

Example 24-2 is a complete Python extension module that defines the very simple type intpair, each instance of which holds two integers named first and second.

Example 24-2. Defining a new intpair type

```c
#include "Python.h"
#include "structmember.h"

/* per-instance data structure */
typedef struct {
    PyObject_HEAD
    int first, second;
} intpair;

static int
intpair_init(PyObject *self, PyObject *args, PyObject *kwds)
{
    static char* nams[] = {"first","second",NULL};
    int first, second;
    if(!PyArg_ParseTupleAndKeywords(args, kwds, "ii", nams, &first, &second))
        return -1;
    ((intpair*)self)->first = first;
    ((intpair*)self)->second = second;
    return 0;
}

static void
intpair_dealloc(PyObject *self)
{
    self->ob_type->tp_free(self);
}

static PyObject*
intpair_str(PyObject* self)
{
    return PyString_FromFormat("intpair(%d,%d)",
        ((intpair*)self)->first, ((intpair*)self)->second);
}

static PyMemberDef intpair_members[] = {
    {"first", T_INT, offsetof(intpair, first), 0, "first item" },
    {"second", T_INT, offsetof(intpair, second), 0, "second item" },
    {NULL}
};

static PyTypeObject t_intpair = {
    PyObject_HEAD_INIT(0)       /* tp_head */
    0,                          /* tp_internal */
    "intpair.intpair",          /* tp_name */
    sizeof(intpair),            /* tp_basicsize */
    0,                          /* tp_itemsize */
    intpair_dealloc,            /* tp_dealloc */
    0,                          /* tp_print */
    0,                          /* tp_getattr */
    0,                          /* tp_setattr */
    0,                          /* tp_compare */
    intpair_str,                /* tp_repr */
```

Example 24-2. Defining a new intpair type (continued)

```
        0,                              /* tp_as_number */
        0,                              /* tp_as_sequence */
        0,                              /* tp_as_mapping */
        0,                              /* tp_hash */
        0,                              /* tp_call */
        0,                              /* tp_str */
        PyObject_GenericGetAttr,        /* tp_getattro */
        PyObject_GenericSetAttr,        /* tp_setattro */
        0,                              /* tp_as_buffer */
        Py_TPFLAGS_DEFAULT,
        "two ints (first,second)",
        0,                              /* tp_traverse */
        0,                              /* tp_clear */
        0,                              /* tp_richcompare */
        0,                              /* tp_weaklistoffset */
        0,                              /* tp_iter */
        0,                              /* tp_iternext */
        0,                              /* tp_methods */
        intpair_members,                /* tp_members */
        0,                              /* tp_getset */
        0,                              /* tp_base */
        0,                              /* tp_dict */
        0,                              /* tp_descr_get */
        0,                              /* tp_descr_set */
        0,                              /* tp_dictoffset */
        intpair_init,                   /* tp_init */
        PyType_GenericAlloc,            /* tp_alloc */
        PyType_GenericNew,              /* tp_new */
        _PyObject_Del,                  /* tp_free */
};

void
initintpair(void)
{
    static PyMethodDef no_methods[] = { {NULL} };
    PyObject* this_module = Py_InitModule("intpair", no_methods);
    PyType_Ready(&t_intpair);
    PyObject_SetAttrString(this_module, "intpair", (PyObject*)&t_intpair);
}
```

The intpair type defined in Example 24-2 gives just about no substantial benefits when compared to an equivalent definition in Python, such as:

```
class intpair(object):
    __slots__ = 'first', 'second'
    def __init__(self, first, second):
        self.first = first
        self.second = second
    def __repr__(self):
        return 'intpair(%s,%s)' % (self.first, self.second)
```

The C-coded version does ensure the two attributes are integers, truncating float or complex number arguments as needed. For example:

```
import intpair
x=intpair.intpair(1.2,3.4)          # x is: intpair(1,3)
```

Each instance of the C-coded version of intpair occupies somewhat less memory than an instance of the Python version in the above example. However, the purpose of Example 24-2 is purely didactic: to present a C-coded Python extension that defines a new type.

Extending Python Without Python's C API

You can code Python extensions in other classic compiled languages besides C. For Fortran, the choice is between Paul Dubois's Pyfort (available at *http://pyfortran.sf.net*) and Pearu Peterson's F2PY (available at *http://cens.ioc.ee/projects/f2py2e/*). Both packages support and require the Numeric package covered in Chapter 15, since numeric processing is Fortran's typical application area.

For C++, the choice is between Gordon McMillan's simple, lightweight SCXX (available at *http://www.mcmillan-inc.com/scxx.html*), which uses no templates and is thus suitable for older C++ compilers, Paul Dubois's CXX (available at *http://cxx.sf.net*), and David Abrahams's Boost Python Library (available at *http://www.boost.org/libs/python/doc*). Boost is a package of C++ libraries of uniformly high quality for compilers that support templates well, and includes the Boost Python component. Paul Dubois, CXX's author, recommends considering Boost. You may also choose to use Python's C API from your C++ code, using C++ in this respect as if it was C, and foregoing the extra convenience that C++ affords. However, if you're already using C++ rather than C anyway, then using SCXX, CXX, or Boost can substantially improve your programming productivity when compared to using Python's C API.

If your Python extension is basically a wrapper over an existing C or C++ library (as many are), consider SWIG, the Simplified Wrapper and Interface Generator (available at *http://www.swig.org*). SWIG generates the C source code for your extension based on the library's header files, generally with some help in terms of further annotations in an interface description file.

Greg Ewing is developing a language, Pyrex, specifically for coding Python extensions. Pyrex (found at *http://www.cosc.canterbury.ac.nz/~greg/python/Pyrex/*) is an interesting mix of Python and C concepts, and is already quite usable despite being a new development.

The weave package (available at *http://www.scipi.org/site_content/weave*), lets you run inline C/C++ code within Python. The blitz function, in particular, generates and runs C++ code from expressions using the Numeric package, and thus requires Numeric.

If your application runs only on Windows, the most practical way to extend and embed Python is generally through COM. In particular, COM is by far the best way to use Visual Basic modules (packaged as ActiveX classes) from Python. COM is also the best way to make Python-coded functionality (packaged as COM servers) available to Visual Basic programs. The standard Python distribution for Windows does not directly support COM: you also need to download and install the platform-specific win32all extension package (available at *http://starship. python.net/crew/mhammond/*). I do not cover Windows-specific functionality, including COM, any further in this book. For excellent coverage of platform-specific Python use on Windows, I recommend *Python Programming on Win32*, by Mark Hammond and Andy Robinson (O'Reilly).

Embedding Python

If you have an application already written in C or C++ (or any other classic compiled language), you may want to embed Python as your application's scripting language. To embed Python in languages other than C, the other language must be able to call C functions. In the following, I cover only the C view of things, since other languages vary widely regarding what you have to do in order to call C functions from them.

Installing Resident Extension Modules

In order for Python scripts to communicate with your application, your application must supply extension modules with Python-accessible functions and classes that expose your application's functionality. If these modules are linked with your application rather than residing in dynamic libraries that Python can load when necessary, register your modules with Python as additional built-in modules by calling the PyImport_AppendInittab C API function.

PyImport_ AppendInittab	int PyImport_AppendInittab(char* *name*,void (**initfunc*)(void)) *name* is the module name, which Python scripts use in import statements to access the module. *initfunc* is the module initialization function, taking no argument and returning no result, as covered earlier in this chapter (i.e., *initfunc* is the module's function that would be named *initname* for a normal extension module residing in a dynamic library). PyImport_AppendInittab must be called before calling Py_Initialize.

Setting Arguments

You may want to set the program name and arguments, which Python scripts can access as sys.argv, by calling either or both of the following C API functions.

Py_SetProgram Name	void Py_SetProgramName(char* *name*) Sets the program name, which Python scripts can access as sys. argv[0]. Must be called before calling Py_Initialize.

PySys_SetArgv   void PySys_SetArgv(int *argc*,char** *argv*)

Sets the program arguments, which Python scripts can access as sys.argv[1:]. Must be called after calling Py_Initialize.

Python Initialization and Finalization

After installing extra built-in modules and optionally setting the program name, your application initializes Python. At the end, when Python is no longer needed, your application finalizes Python. The relevant functions in the C API are as follows.

Py_Finalize   void Py_Finalize(void)

Frees all memory and other resources that Python is able to free. You should not make other Python C API calls after calling this function.

Py_Initialize   void Py_Initialize(void)

Initializes the Python environment. Make no other Python C API call before this one, except PyImport_AppendInittab and Py_SetProgramName, as covered earlier in this chapter.

Running Python Code

Your application can run Python source code from a character string or from a file. To run or compile Python source code, choose the mode of execution as one of the following three constants defined in *Python.h*:

Py_eval_input
    The code is an expression to evaluate (like passing 'eval' to Python built-in function compile)

Py_file_input
    The code is a block of one or more statements to execute (like 'exec' for compile—just like in that case, a trailing '\n' must close compound statements)

Py_single_input
    The code is a single statement for interactive execution (like 'single' for compile—implicitly outputs the results of expression statements)

Running Python source code directly is similar to passing a source code string to Python statement exec or built-in function eval, or a source code file to built-in function execfile. Two general functions you can use for this task are the following.

PyRun_File   PyObject* PyRun_File(FILE* *fp*,char* *filename*,int *start*,
                  PyObject* *globals*,PyObject* *locals*)

fp is a file of source code open for reading. *filename* is the name of
the file, to use in error messages. *start* is one of the constants that
define execution mode. *globals* and *locals* are dictionaries (may be
the same dictionary twice) to use as global and local namespace for
the execution. Returns the result of the expression when *start* is
Py_eval_input, a new reference to Py_None otherwise, or NULL to
indicate that an exception has been raised (often, but not always,
due to a syntax error).

PyRun_String   PyObject* PyRun_String(char* *astring*,int *start*,
                    PyObject* *globals*,PyObject* *locals*)

Like PyRun_File, but the source code is in null-terminated string
astring.

Dictionaries *locals* and *globals* are often new, empty dictionaries (most conveniently built by Py_BuildValue("{}")) or the dictionary of a module. PyImport_
Import is a convenient way to obtain an existing module object; PyModule_GetDict
obtains a module's dictionary. Sometimes you want to create a new module object
on the fly and populate it with PyRun_ calls. To create a new, empty module, you
can use the PyModule_New C API function.

PyModule_New   PyObject* PyModule_New(char* *name*)

Returns a new, empty module object for a module named *name*.
Before the new object is usable, you must add to the object a string
attribute named __file__. For example:

```
PyObject* newmod = PyModule_New("mymodule");
PyModule_AddStringConstant(newmod, "__file__",
    "<synthetic>");
```

After this code is run, module object *newmod* is ready; you can
obtain the module's dictionary with PyModule_GetDict(*newmod*) and
pass it directly to such functions as PyRun_String as the *globals* and
possibly also the *locals* argument.

To run Python code repeatedly, and to discern the diagnosis of syntax errors from
that of runtime exceptions raised by the code when it runs, you can compile the
Python source to a code object, then keep the code object and run it repeatedly.
This is just as true when using the C API as when dynamically executing from
Python, as covered in Chapter 13. Two C API functions you can use for this task
are the following.

Py_ CompileString	`PyObject* Py_CompileString(char* code,char* filename,int start)` *code* is a null-terminated string of source code. *filename* is the name of the file, to use in error messages. *start* is one of the constants that define execution mode. Returns the Python code object containing the bytecode, or `NULL` for syntax errors.

**PyEval_
EvalCode**
	`PyObject* PyEval_EvalCode(PyObject* co,PyObject* globals,`
	`PyObject* locals)`
	
	co is a Python code object, as returned by `Py_CompileString`, for example. *globals* and *locals* are dictionaries (may be the same dictionary twice) to use as global and local namespace for the execution. Returns the result of the expression when *co* was compiled with `Py_eval_input`, a new reference to `Py_None` otherwise, or `NULL` to indicate the execution has raised an exception.

25

Extending and Embedding Jython

Jython implements Python on a Java Virtual Machine (JVM). Jython's built-in objects, such as numbers, sequences, dictionaries, and files, are coded in Java. To extend Classic Python with C, you code C modules using the Python C API (as covered in Chapter 24). To extend Jython with Java, you do not have to code Java modules in special ways: every Java package on the Java CLASSPATH (or on Jython's sys.path) is automatically available to your Jython scripts and Jython interactive sessions for use with the import statement covered in Chapter 7. This applies to Java's standard libraries, third-party Java libraries you have installed, and Java classes you have coded yourself. You can also extend Java with C using the Java Native Interface (JNI), and such extensions will also be available to Jython code, just as if they had been coded in pure Java rather than in JNI-compliant C.

For details on advanced issues related to interoperation between Java and Jython, I recommend *Jython Essentials*, by Samuele Pedroni and Noel Rappin (O'Reilly). In this chapter, I offer a brief overview of the simplest interoperation scenarios, which suffices for a large number of practical needs. Importing, using, extending, and implementing Java classes and interfaces in Jython just works in most practical cases of interest. In some cases, however, you need to be aware of issues related to accessibility, type conversions, and overloading, as covered in this chapter. Embedding the Jython interpreter in Java-coded applications is similar to embedding the Python interpreter in C-coded applications (as covered in Chapter 24), but the Jython task is easier. Jython offers yet another possibility for interoperation with Java, using the *jythonc* compiler to turn your Python sources into classic, static JVM bytecode *.class* and *.jar* files. You can then use these byte-code files in Java applications and frameworks, exactly as if their source code had been in Java rather than in Python.

Importing Java Packages in Jython

Unlike Java, Jython does not implicitly and automatically import java.lang. Your Jython code can explicitly import java.lang, or even just import java, and then use classes such as java.lang.System and java.lang.String as if they were Python classes. Specifically, your Jython code can use imported Java classes as if they were Python classes with a __slots__ class attribute (i.e., you cannot create arbitrary new instance attributes). You can subclass a Java class with your own Python class, and instances of your class let you create new attributes just by binding them, as usual.

You may choose to import a top-level Java package (such as java) rather than specific subpackages (such as java.lang). Your Python code acquires the ability to access all subpackages when you import the top-level package. For example, after import java, your code can use classes java.lang.String, java.util.Vector, and so on.

The Jython runtime wraps every Java class you import in a transparent proxy, which manages communication between Python and Java code behind the scenes. This gives an extra reason to avoid the dubious idiom from *somewhere* import *, in addition to the reasons mentioned in Chapter 7. When you perform such a bulk import, the Jython runtime must build proxy wrappers for all the Java classes in package *somewhere*, spending substantial amounts of memory and time wrapping classes your code will probably not use. Avoid from ... import * except for occasional convenience in interactive exploratory sessions, and stick with the import statement. Alternatively, it's okay to use specific, explicit from statements for classes you know your Python code wants to use (e.g., from java.lang import System).

The Jython Registry

Jython relies on a *registry* of Java properties as a cross-platform equivalent of the kind of settings that would normally use the Windows registry, or environment variables on Unix-like systems. Jython's registry file is a standard Java properties file named *registry*, located in a directory known as the Jython root directory. The Jython root directory is normally the directory where *jython.jar* is located, but you can override this by setting Java properties python.home or install.root. For special needs, you may tweak the Jython registry settings via an auxiliary Java properties file named *.jython* in your home directory, and/or via command-line options to the *jython* interpreter command. The registry option python.path is equivalent to classic Python's PYTHONPATH environment variable. This is the option you may most often be interested in, as it can help you install extra Python packages outside of the Jython installation directories (e.g., sharing Python packages installed for CPython use).

Accessibility

Normally, your Jython code can access only public features (methods, fields, inner classes) of Java classes. You may choose to make private and protected features available by setting an option in the Jython registry before you run Jython:

```
python.security.respectJavaAccessibility=false
```

Such bending of normal Java rules should never be necessary for normal operation. However, the ability to access private and protected features may be useful to Jython scripts meant to thoroughly test a Java package, which is why Jython gives you this option.

Type Conversions

The Jython runtime converts data between Python and Java transparently. However, when a Java method expects a boolean argument, you have to pass an int or an instance of java.lang.Boolean in order to call that method from Python. In Python, any object can be taken as true or false, but Jython does not perform the conversion to boolean implicitly on method calls, to avoid confusion and the risk of errors.

Calling overloaded Java methods

A Java class can supply *overloaded* methods (i.e., several methods with the same name, distinguished by the number and types of their arguments). Jython resolves calls to overloaded methods at runtime, based on the number and types of arguments that Python code is passing in each given call. If Jython's automatic overload resolution is not giving the results you expect, you can help it along by explicitly passing instances of Java's java.lang wrapper classes, such as java.lang.Integer where the Java method expects an int argument, java.lang.Float where the Java method expects a float argument, and so on. For example, if a Java class C supplies a method named M in two overloaded versions, M(long x) and M(int x), consider the following Python code:

```
import C, java.lang

c = C()
c.M(23)                     # calls M(long)
c.M(java.lang.Integer(23))  # calls M(int)
```

c.M(23) calls the long overloaded method, due to the rules of Jython overload resolution. c.M(java.lang.Integer(23)), however, explicitly calls the int overloaded method.

The jarray module

When you pass Python sequences to Java methods that expect array arguments, Jython performs automatic conversion, copying each item of the Python sequence into an element of the Java array. When you call a Java method that accepts and modifies an array argument, the Python sequence that you pass cannot reflect any changes the Java method performs on its array argument. To let you effectively call methods that change their array arguments, Jython offers module jarray, which supplies two factory functions that let you build Java arrays directly.

array   array(*seq*,*typecode*)

seq is any Python sequence. *typecode* is either a Java class or a single character (specifying a primitive Java type according to Table 25-1). array creates a Java array *a* with the same length as *seq* and elements of the class or type given by *typecode*. array initializes *a*'s elements from *seq*'s corresponding items.

Table 25-1. Typecodes for the jarray module

Typecode	Java type
'b'	byte
'c'	char
'd'	double
'f'	float
'h'	short
'i'	int
'l'	long
'z'	boolean

zeros   zeros(*length*,*typecode*)

Creates a Java array *z* with length *length* and elements of the class or type given by *typecode*, which has the same meaning as in function array. zeros initializes each element of *z* to 0, null, or false, as appropriate for the type or class. Of course, when you access such elements from Jython code, you see them as the equivalent Python 0 values (or None as the Jython equivalent of Java null), but when Java code accesses the elements, it sees them with the appropriate Java types and values.

You can use instances created by functions array and zeros as Python sequences of fixed length. When you pass such an instance to a Java method that accepts an array argument and modifies the argument, the changes are visible in the instance, so your Python code can effectively call such methods.

The java.util collection classes

Jython performs no automatic conversion either way between Python containers and the collection classes of package java.util, such as java.util.Vector, java.util.Dictionary, and so on. However, Jython adds to the wrappers it builds for the Java collection classes a minimal amount of support to let you treat instances of collection classes as Python sequences, iterables, or mappings, as appropriate.

Subclassing a Java Class

A Python class may inherit from a Java class (equivalent to Java construct extends) and/or from Java interfaces (equivalent to Java construct implements), as well as from other Python classes. A Jython class cannot inherit, directly or indirectly, from more than one Java class. There is no limit on inheriting from interfaces. Your Jython code can access protected methods of the Java superclass, but not protected fields. You can override non-final superclass methods. In particular, you should always override the methods of interfaces you inherit from. If a method is overloaded in the superclass, your overriding method must support all of the signatures of the overloads. To accomplish this, you can define your method to accept a variable number of arguments (by having its last formal argument use special form *args) and check at runtime as needed for the number and types of arguments you receive on each call.

JavaBeans

Jython offers special support for the typical JavaBeans idiom of naming accessor methods get*SomeThing*, is*SomeThing*, set*SomeThing*. When such methods exist in a Java class, Python code can access and set a property named *someThing* on instances of that Java class, using the Python syntax of attribute access and binding. The Jython runtime transparently translates such accesses into calls to appropriate accessor methods.

Embedding Jython in Java

Your Java-coded application can embed the Jython interpreter in order to use Jython for scripting. *jython.jar* must be in your Java CLASSPATH. Your Java code must import org.python.core.* and org.python.util.* in order to access Jython's classes. To initialize Jython's state and instantiate an interpreter, use the Java statements:

```
PySystemState.initialize( );
PythonInterpreter interp = new PythonInterpreter( );
```

Jython also supplies several advanced overloads of this method and constructor in order to let you determine in detail how PySystemState is set up, and to control the system state and global scope for each interpreter instance. However, in typical, simple cases, the previous Java code is all your application needs.

The PythonInterpreter Class

Once you have an instance *interp* of class PythonInterpreter, you can call method *interp*.eval to have the interpreter evaluate a Python expression held in a Java string. You can also call any of several overloads of *interp*.exec and *interp*. execfile to have the interpreter execute Python statements held in a Java string, a precompiled Jython code object, a file, or a Java InputStream.

The Python code you execute can import your Java classes in order to access your application's functionality. Your Java code can set attributes in the interpreter namespace by calling overloads of *interp*.set, and get attributes from the interpreter namespace by calling overloads of *interp*.get. The methods' overloads give you a choice. You can work with native Java data and let Jython perform type conversions, or you can work directly with PyObject, the base class of all Python objects, covered later in this chapter. The most frequently used methods and overloads of a PythonInterpreter instance *interp* are the following.

eval

PyObject *interp*.eval(String *s*)

Evaluates, in *interp*'s namespace, the Python expression held in Java string *s*, and returns the PyObject that is the expression's result.

exec

void *interp*.exec(String *s*)
void *interp*.exec(PyObject *code*)

Executes, in *interp*'s namespace, the Python statements held in Java string *s* or in compiled PyObject *code* (produced by function _ _builtin_ _.compile of package org.python.core, covered later in this chapter).

execfile

void *interp*.execfile(String *name*)
void *interp*.execfile(java.io.InputStream *s*)
void *interp*.execfile(java.io.InputStream *s*,String *name*)

Executes, in *interp*'s namespace, the Python statements read from the stream *s* or from the file named *name*. When you pass both *s* and *name*, execfile reads the statements from *s*, and uses *name* as the filename in error messages.

get

PyObject *interp*.get(String *name*)
Object *interp*.get(String *name*,Class *javaclass*)

Fetches the value of the attribute named *name* from *interp*'s namespace. The overload with two arguments also converts the value to the specified *javaclass*, throwing a Java PyException exception that wraps a Python TypeError if the conversion is unfeasible. Either overload raises a NullPointerException if *name* is unbound. Typical use of the two-argument form might be a Java statement such as:

```
String s = (String)interp.get("attname", String.class);
```

set

void *interp*.set(String *name*,PyObject *value*)
void *interp*.set(String *name*,Object *value*)

Binds the attribute named *name* in *interp*'s namespace to *value*. The second overload also converts the value to a PyObject.

The org.python.core package supplies a class __builtin__ whose static methods let your Java code access the functionality of Python built-in functions. The compile method, in particular, is quite similar to Python built-in function compile, covered in Chapters 8 and 13. Your Java code can call compile with three String arguments (a string of source code, a filename to use in error messages, and a *kind* that is normally "exec"), and compile returns a PyObject instance *p* that is a precompiled Python bytecode object. You can repeatedly call *interp*.exec(*p*) to execute the Python statements in *p* without the overhead of compiling the Python source for each execution. The advantages are the same as covered in Chapter 13.

The PyObject Class

Seen from Java, all Jython objects are instances of classes that extend PyObject. Class PyObject supplies methods named like Python objects' special methods, such as __len__, __str__, and so on. Concrete subclasses of PyObject override some special methods to supply meaningful implementations. For example, __len__ makes sense for Python sequences and mappings, but not for numbers; __add__ makes sense for numbers and sequences, but not for mappings. When your Java code calls a special method on a PyObject instance that does not in fact supply the method, the call raises a Java PyException exception wrapping a Python AttributeError.

PyObject methods that set, get, and delete attributes exist in two overloads, as the attribute name can be a PyString or a Java String. PyObject methods that set, get, and delete items exist in three overloads, as the key or index can be a PyObject, a Java String, or an int. The Java String instances that you use as attribute names or item keys must be Java interned strings (i.e., either string literals or the result of calling *s*.intern( ) on any Java String instance *s*). In addition to the usual Python special methods __getattr__ and __getitem__, class PyObject also provides similar methods __findattr__ and __finditem__, the difference being that, when the attribute or item is not found, the __find methods return a Java null, while the __get methods raise exceptions.

Every PyObject instance *p* has a method __tojava__ that takes a single argument, a Java Class *c*, and returns an Object that is the value of *p* converted to *c* (or raises an exception if the conversion is unfeasible). Typical use might be a Java statement such as:

```
String s = (String)mypyobj.__tojava__(String.class);
```

Method __call__ of PyObject has several convenience overloads, but the semantics of all the overloads come down to __call__'s fundamental form:

```
PyObject p.__call__(PyObject args[], String keywords[]);
```

When array *keywords* has length *L*, array *args* must have length *N* greater than or equal to *L*, and the last *L* items of *args* are taken as named actual arguments, the names being the corresponding items in *keywords*. When *args* has length *N* greater than *L*, *args*'s first *N-L* items are taken as positional actual arguments. The equivalent Python code is therefore similar to:

```
def docall(p, args, keywords):
    assert len(args) >= len(keywords)
```

```
deltalen = len(args) - len(keywords)
return p(*args[:deltalen], ** dict(zip(keywords, args[deltalen:])))
```

Jython supplies concrete subclasses of PyObject that represent all built-in Python types. You can sometimes usefully instantiate a concrete subclass in order to create a PyObject for further use. For example, class PyList extends PyObject, implements a Python list, and has constructors that take an array or a java.util. Vector of PyObject instances, as well as an empty constructor that builds the empty list [ ].

The Py Class

The Py class supplies several utility class attributes and static methods. Py.None is Python's None. Method Py.java2py takes a single Java Object argument and returns the corresponding PyObject. Methods Py.py2*type*, for all values of *type* that name a Java primitive type (boolean, byte, long, short, etc.), take a single PyObject argument and return the corresponding value of the given primitive Java type.

Compiling Python into Java

Jython comes with the *jythonc* compiler. You can feed *jythonc* your *.py* source files, and *jythonc* compiles them into normal JVM bytecode and packages them into *.class* and *.jar* files. Since *jythonc* generates static, classic bytecode, it cannot quite cope with the whole range of dynamic possibilities that Python allows. For example, *jythonc* cannot successfully compile Python classes that determine their base classes dynamically at runtime, as the normal Python interpreters allow. However, except for such extreme examples of dynamically changeable class structures, *jythonc* does support compilation of essentially the whole Python language into Java bytecode.

The jythonc command

jythonc resides in the *Tools/jythonc* directory of your Jython installation. You invoke it from a shell (console) command line with the syntax:

```
jythonc options modules
```

options are zero or more option flags starting with --. *modules* are zero or more names of Python source files to compile, either as Python-style names of modules residing on Python's sys.path, or as relative or absolute paths to Python source files. Include the *.py* extension in each path to a source file, but not in a module name.

More often than not, you will specify the *jythonc* option --jar *jarfile*, to build a *.jar* file of compiled bytecode rather than separate *.class* files. Most other options deal with what to put in the *.jar* file. You can choose to make the file self-sufficient (for browsers and other Java runtime environments that do not support using multiple *.jar* files) at the expense of making the file larger. Option --all ensures all Jython core classes are copied into the *.jar* file, while --core tries to be more conservative, copying as few core classes as feasible. Option --addpackages

packages lets you list (in *packages*, a comma-separated list) those external Java packages whose classes are copied into the *.jar* file if any of the Python classes *jythonc* is compiling depends on them. An important alternative to --jar is --bean *jarfile*, which also includes a bean manifest in the *.jar* file as needed for Python-coded JavaBeans components.

Another useful *jythonc* option is --package *package*, which instructs Jython to place all the new Java classes it's creating in the given *package* (and any subpackages of *package* needed to reflect the Python-side package structure).

Adding Java-Visible Methods

The Java classes that *jythonc* creates normally extend existing classes from Java libraries and/or implement existing interfaces. Other Java-coded applications and frameworks instantiate the *jythonc*-created classes via constructor overloads, which have the same signatures as the constructors of their Java superclasses. The Python-side __init__ executes after the superclass is initialized, and with the same arguments (therefore, don't __init__ a Java superclass in the __init__ of a Python class meant to be compiled by *jythonc*). Afterward, Java code can access the functionality of instances of Python-coded classes by calling instance methods defined in known interfaces or superclasses and overridden by Python code.

Python code can never supply Java-visible static methods or attributes, only instance methods. By default, each Python class supplies only the instance methods it inherits from the Java class it extends or the Java interfaces it implements. However, Python code can also supply other Java-visible instance methods via the @sig directive.

To expose a method of your Python class to Java when *jythonc* compiles the class, code the method's docstring as @sig followed by a Java method signature. For example:

```
class APythonClass:
    def __init__(self, greeting="Hello, %s!"):
        "@sig public APythonClass(String greeting)"
        self.greeting = greeting
    def hello(self, name):
        "@sig public String hello(String name)"
        return self.greeting % name
```

To expose a constructor, use the @sig signature for the class, as shown in the previous example. All names of classes in @sig signatures must be fully qualified, except for names coming from java.lang and names supplied by the Python-coded module being compiled. When a Python method with a @sig has optional arguments, *jythonc* generates Java-visible overloads of the method with each legal signature, and deals with supplying the default argument values where needed. An __init__ constructor with a @sig, for a Python class that extends a Java class, initializes the superclass using the superclass's empty constructor.

Since a Python class cannot expose data attributes directly to Java, you may need to code accessors with the usual JavaBeans convention and expose them via the @sig mechanism. For example, instances of APythonClass in the above example do not allow Java code to directly access or change the `greeting` attribute. When such functionality is needed, you can supply it in a subclass as follows:

```
class APythonBean(APythonClass):
    def getGreeting(self):
        "@sig public String getGreeting( )"
        return self.greeting
    def setGreeting(self, greeting):
        "@sig public void setGreeting(String greeting)"
        self.greeting = greeting
```

Python Applets and Servlets

Two typical examples of using Jython within existing Java frameworks are applets and servlets. Applets are typical examples of *jythonc* use (with specific caveats), while servlets are specifically supported by a Jython-supplied utility.

Python applets

A Jython applet class must import `java.applet.Applet` and extend it, typically overriding method `paint` and others. You compile the applet into a *.jar* file by calling *jythonc* with options `--jar somejar.jar` and either `--core` or `--all`. Normally, Jython is installed in a modern Java 2 environment, which is okay for most uses. It is fine for applets, as long as the applets run only in browsers that support Java 2, typically with a Sun-supplied browser plug-in. However, if you need to support browsers that are limited to Java 1.1, you must ensure that the JDK you use is Release 1.1, and that you compile your applet with Jython under a JDK 1.1 environment. It's possible to share a single Jython installation between different JDKs, such as 1.1 and 1.4. However, I suggest you perform separate installations of Jython, one under each JDK you need to support, in separate directories, in order to minimize the risk of confusion and accidents.

Python servlets

You can use *jythonc* to build and deploy servlets. However, Jython also supports an alternative that lets you deploy Python-coded servlets as source *.py* files. Use the servlet class `org.python.util.PyServlet`, supplied with Jython, and a servlet mapping of all **.py* URLs to `PyServlet`. Each servlet *.py* file must reside in the *web-app* top-level directory, and must expose an object callable without arguments (normally a class) with the same name as the file. PyServlet uses that callable as a factory for instances of the servlet, and calls methods on the instance according to the Java Servlet API. Your servlet instance, in turn, accesses Servlet API objects such as the *request* and *response* objects, passed as method arguments, and those objects' attributes and methods such as *response*.`outputStream` and *request*.`getSession`. PyServlet provides an excellent, fast-turnaround way to experiment with servlets and rapidly deploy them.

26

Distributing Extensions and Programs

Python's distutils allow you to package Python programs and extensions in several ways, and to install programs and extensions to work with your Python installation. As I mentioned in Chapter 24, the distutils also afford the most effective way to build C-coded extensions you write yourself, even when you are not interested in distributing such extensions. This chapter covers the distutils, as well as third-party tools that complement the distutils and let you package Python programs for distribution as standalone applications, installable on machines with specific hardware and operating systems without a separate installation of Python.

Python's distutils

The distutils are a rich and flexible set of tools to package Python programs and extensions for distribution to third parties. I cover typical, simple use of the distutils for the most common packaging needs. For in-depth, highly detailed discussion of distutils, I recommend two manuals that are part of Python's online documentation: *Distributing Python Modules* (available at *http://www. python.org/doc/current/dist/*), and *Installing Python Modules* (available at *http:// www.python.org/doc/current/inst/*), both by Greg Ward, the principal author of the distutils.

The Distribution and Its Root

A *distribution* is the set of files to package into a single file for distribution purposes. A distribution may include zero, one, or more Python packages and other Python modules (as covered in Chapter 7), as well as, optionally, Python scripts, C-coded (and other) extensions, supporting data files, and auxiliary files containing metadata about the distribution itself. A distribution is said to be *pure* if all code it includes is Python, and *non-pure* if it also includes non-Python code (most often, C-coded extensions).

You should normally place all the files of a distribution in a directory, known as the *distribution root directory*, and in subdirectories of the distribution root. Mostly, you can arrange the subtree of files and directories rooted at the distribution root to suit your own organizational needs. However, remember from Chapter 7 that a Python package must reside in its own directory, and a package's directory must contain a file named *__init__.py* (or subdirectories with *__init__.py* files, for subpackages) as well as other modules belonging to that package.

The setup.py Script

The distribution root directory must contain a Python script that by convention is named *setup.py*. The *setup.py* script can, in theory, contain arbitrary Python code. However, in practice, *setup.py* always boils down to some variation of:

```
from distutils.core import setup, Extension

setup( many keyword arguments go here )
```

All the action is in the parameters you supply in the call to setup. You should not import Extension if your *setup.py* deals with a pure distribution. Extension is needed only for non-pure distributions, and you should import it only when you need it. It is fine to have a few statements before the call to setup, in order to arrange setup's arguments in clearer and more readable ways than could be managed by having everything inline as part of the setup call.

The distutils.core.setup function accepts only keyword arguments, and there are a large number of such arguments that you could potentially supply. A few deal with the internal operations of the distutils themselves, and you never supply such arguments unless you are extending or debugging the distutils, an advanced subject that I do not cover in this book. Other keyword arguments to setup fall into two groups: metadata about the distribution, and information about what files are in the distribution.

Metadata About the Distribution

You should provide metadata about the distribution by supplying some of the following keyword arguments when you call the distutils.core.setup function. The value you associate with each argument name you supply is a string that is intended mostly to be human-readable; therefore, any specifications about the string's format are just advisory. The explanations and recommendations about the metadata fields in the following are also non-normative, and correspond only to common, not universal, conventions. Whenever the following explanations refer to "this distribution," it can be taken to refer to the material included in the distribution, rather than to the packaging of the distribution.

author
> The name(s) of the author(s) of material included in the distribution. You should always provide this information, as the authors deserve credit for their work.

`author_email`

Email address(es) of the author(s) named in argument `author`. You should provide this information only if the author is willing to receive email about this work.

`contact`

The name of the principal contact person or mailing list for this distribution. You should provide this information if there is somebody who should be contacted in preference to people named in arguments `author` and `maintainer`.

`contact_email`

Email address of the contact named in argument `contact`. You should provide this information if and only if you supply the `contact` argument.

`description`

A concise description of this distribution, preferably fitting within one line of 80 characters or less. You should always provide this information.

`fullname`

The full name of this distribution. You should provide this information if the name supplied as argument `name` is in abbreviated or incomplete form (e.g., an acronym).

`keywords`

A list of keywords that would likely be searched for by somebody looking for the functionality provided by this distribution. You should provide this information if it might be useful to index this distribution in some kind of search engine.

`license`

The licensing terms of this distribution, in a concise form that may refer for details to a file in the distribution or to a URL. You should always provide this information.

`maintainer`

The name(s) of the current maintainer(s) of this distribution. You should normally provide this information if the maintainer is different from the author.

`maintainer_email`

Email address(es) of the maintainer(s) named in argument `maintainer`. You should provide this information only if you supply the `maintainer` argument and if the maintainer is willing to receive email about this work.

`name`

The name of this distribution as a valid Python identifier (this often requires abbreviations, e.g., by an acronym). You should always provide this information.

`platforms`

A list of platforms on which this distribution is known to work. You should provide this information if you have reasons to believe this distribution may not work everywhere. This information should be reasonably concise, so this field may refer for details to a file in the distribution or to a URL.

url

A URL at which more information can be found about this distribution. You should always provide this information if any such URL exists.

version

The version of this distribution and/or its contents, normally structured as *major.minor* or even more finely. You should always provide this information.

Distribution Contents

A distribution can contain a mix of Python source files, C-coded extensions, and other files. setup accepts optional keyword arguments detailing files to put in the distribution. Whenever you specify file paths, the paths must be relative to the distribution root directory and use / as the path separator. distutils adapts location and separator appropriately when it installs the distribution. Note, however, that the keyword arguments packages and py_modules do not list file paths, but rather Python packages and modules respectively. Therefore, in the values of these keyword arguments, use no path separators or file extensions. When you list subpackage names in argument packages, use Python syntax (e.g., *top_package.sub_package*).

Python source files

By default, setup looks for Python modules (which you list in the value of the keyword argument py_modules) in the distribution root directory, and for Python packages (which you list in the value of the keyword argument packages) as subdirectories of the distribution root directory. You may specify keyword argument package_dir to change these defaults. However, things are simpler when you locate files according to setup's defaults, so I do not cover package_dir further in this book.

The setup keyword arguments you will most frequently use to detail what Python source files to put in the distribution are the following.

packages	packages=[*list of package name strings*]
	For each package name string *p* in the list, setup expects to find a subdirectory *p* in the distribution root directory, and includes in the distribution the file *p/__init__.py*, which must be present, as well as any other file *p/*.py* (i.e., all the modules of package *p*). setup does not search for subpackages of *p*: you must explicitly list all subpackages, as well as top-level packages, in the value of keyword argument packages.

py_modules	py_modules=[*list of module name strings*]
	For each module name string *m* in the list, setup expects to find a file *m.py* in the distribution root directory, and includes *m.py* in the distribution.

scripts   scripts=[*list of script file path strings*]

Scripts are Python source files meant to be run as main programs (generally from the command line). The value of the scripts keyword lists the path strings of these files, complete with *.py* extension, relative to the distribution root directory.

Each script file should have as its first line a shebang line, that is, a line starting with #! and containing the substring python. When distutils install the scripts included in the distribution, distutils adjust each script's first line to point to the Python interpreter. This is quite useful on many platforms, since the shebang line is used by the platform's shells or by other programs that may run your scripts, such as web servers.

Other files

To put data files of any kind in the distribution, supply the following keyword argument.

data_files   data_files=[*list of pairs* (*target_directory*,[*list of files*])]

The value of keyword argument data_files is a list of pairs. Each pair's first item is a string and names a *target directory* (i.e., a directory where distutils places data files when installing the distribution); the second item is the list of file path strings for files to put in the target directory. At installation time, distutils places each target directory as a subdirectory of Python's sys.prefix for a pure distribution, or of Python's sys.exec_prefix for a non-pure distribution. distutils places the given files directly in the respective target directory, never in subdirectories of the target. For example, given the following data_files usage:

```
data_files = [ ('miscdata', ['conf/config.txt',
    'misc/sample.txt']) ]
```

distutils includes in the distribution the file *config.txt* from subdirectory *conf* of the distribution root, and the file *sample.txt* from subdirectory *misc* of the distribution root. At installation time, distutils creates a subdirectory named *miscdata* in Python's sys.prefix directory (or in the sys.exec_prefix directory, if the distribution is non-pure), and copies the two files into *miscdata/config. txt* and *miscdata/sample.txt*.

C-coded extensions

To put C-coded extensions in the distribution, supply the following keyword argument.

ext_modules	ext_modules=[*list of instances of class* Extension]
	All the details about each extension are supplied as arguments when instantiating the distutils.core.Extension class.

Extension's constructor accepts two mandatory arguments and many optional keyword arguments, as follows.

Extension	class Extension(*name, sources,* **kwds)
	name is the module name string for the C-coded extension. *name* may include dots to indicate that the extension module resides within a package. *sources* is the list of source files that the distutils must compile and link in order to build the extension. Each item of *sources* is a string giving a source file's path relative to the distribution root directory, complete with file extension *.c*. *kwds* lets you pass other, optional arguments to Extension, as covered later in this section.

The Extension class also supports other file extensions besides *.c*, indicating other languages you may use to code Python extensions. On platforms having a C++ compiler, file extension *.cpp* indicates C++ source files. Other file extensions that may be supported, depending on the platform and on add-ons to the distutils that are still in experimental stages at the time of this writing, include *.f* for Fortran, *.i* for SWIG, and *.pyx* for Pyrex files. See Chapter 24 for information about using different languages to extend Python.

In some cases, your extension needs no further information besides mandatory arguments *name* and *sources*. The distutils implicitly perform all that is necessary to make the Python headers directory and the Python library available for your extension's compilation and linking, and also provide whatever compiler or linker flags or options are needed to build extensions on a given platform.

When it takes additional information to compile and link your extension correctly, you can supply such information via the keyword arguments of class Extension. Such arguments may potentially interfere with the cross-platform portability of your distribution. In particular, whenever you specify file or directory paths as the values of such arguments, the paths should be relative to the distribution root directory—using absolute paths seriously impairs your distribution's cross-platform portability.

Program Distribution

Portability is not a problem when you just use the distutils as a handy way to build your extension, as suggested in Chapter 24. However, when you plan to distribute your extensions to other platforms, you should examine whether you really need to provide build information via keyword arguments to Extension. It is sometimes possible to bypass such needs by careful coding at the C level, and the already mentioned *Distributing Python Modules* manual provides important examples.

The keyword arguments that you may pass when calling Extension are the following:

define_macros = [(*macro_name*,*macro_value*) ...]
> Each of the items *macro_name* and *macro_value*, in the pairs listed as the value of define_macros, is a string, respectively the name and value for a C preprocessor macro definition, equivalent in effect to the C preprocessor directive:
>
> > #define *macro_name macro_value*
>
> *macro_value* can also be None, to get the same effect as the C preprocessor directive:
>
> > #define *macro_name*

extra_compile_args = [*list of compile_arg strings*]
> Each of the strings *compile_arg* listed as the value of extra_compile_args is placed among the command-line arguments for each invocation of the C compiler.

extra_link_args = [*list of link_arg strings*]
> Each of the strings *link_arg* listed as the value of extra_link_args is placed among the command-line arguments for the invocation of the linker.

extra_objects = [*list of object_name strings*]
> Each of the strings *object_name* listed as the value of extra_objects names an object file to add to the invocation of the linker. Do not specify the file extension as part of the object name: distutils adds the platform-appropriate file extension (such as *.o* on Unix-like platforms and *.obj* on Windows) to help you keep cross-platform portability.

include_dirs = [*list of directory_path strings*]
> Each of the strings *directory_path* listed as the value of include_dirs identifies a directory to supply to the compiler as one where header files are found.

libraries = [*list of library_name strings*]
> Each of the strings *library_name* listed as the value of libraries names a library to add to the invocation of the linker. Do not specify the file extension or any prefix as part of the library name: distutils, in cooperation with the linker, adds the platform-appropriate file extension and prefix (such as *.a* (and a prefix *lib*) on Unix-like platforms, and *.lib* on Windows) to help you keep cross-platform portability.

library_dirs = [*list of directory_path strings*]
> Each of the strings *directory_path* listed as the value of library_dirs identifies a directory to supply to the linker as one where library files are found.

runtime_library_dirs = [*list of directory_path strings*]
: Each of the strings *directory_path* listed as the value of runtime_library_dirs identifies a directory where dynamically loaded libraries are found at runtime.

undef_macros = [*list of macro_name strings*]
: Each of the strings *macro_name* listed as the value of undef_macros is the name for a C preprocessor macro definition, equivalent in effect to the C preprocessor directive:

```
#undef macro_name
```

The setup.cfg File

The distutils let the user who is installing your distribution specify many options at installation time. Most often the user will simply enter the following command at a command line:

```
C:\> python setup.py install
```

but the already mentioned manual *Installing Python Modules* explains many alternatives in detail. If you wish to provide suggested values for some installation options, you can put a *setup.cfg* file in your distribution root directory. *setup.cfg* can also provide appropriate defaults for options you can supply to build-time commands. For copious details on the format and contents of file *setup.cfg*, see the already mentioned manual *Distributing Python Modules*.

The MANIFEST.in and MANIFEST Files

When you run:

```
python setup.py sdist
```

to produce a packaged-up source distribution (typically a *.zip* file on Windows, or a *.tgz* file, also known as a tarball, on Unix), the distutils by default insert the following in the distribution:

- All Python and C source files, as well as data files, explicitly mentioned or directly implied by your *setup.py* file's options, as covered earlier in this chapter
- Test files, located at *test/test*.py* under the distribution root directory
- Files *README.txt* (if any), *setup.cfg* (if any), and *setup.py*

You can add yet more files in the source distribution *.zip* file or tarball by placing in the distribution root directory a *manifest template* file named *MANIFEST.in*, whose lines are rules, applied sequentially, about files to add (include) or subtract (prune) from the overall list of files to place in the distribution. The sdist command of the distutils also produces an exact list of the files placed in the source distribution as a text file named *MANIFEST* in the distribution root directory.

Creating Prebuilt Distributions with distutils

The packaged source distributions you create with python setup.py sdist are the most widely useful files you can produce with distutils. However, you can make life even easier for users with specific platforms by also creating prebuilt forms of your distribution with the command python setup.py bdist.

For a pure distribution, supplying prebuilt forms is merely a matter of convenience for the users. You can create prebuilt pure distributions for any platform, including ones different from those on which you work, as long as you have available on your path the needed commands (such as *zip*, *gzip*, *bzip2*, and *tar*). Such commands are freely available on the Net for all sorts of platforms, so you can easily stock up on them in order to provide maximum convenience to users who want to install your distribution.

For a non-pure distribution, making prebuilt forms available may be more than just an issue of convenience. A non-pure distribution, by definition, includes code that is not pure Python, generally C code. Unless you supply a prebuilt form, users need to have the appropriate C compiler installed in order to build and install your distribution. This is not a terrible problem on platforms where the appropriate C compiler is the free and ubiquitous *gcc*. However, on other platforms, the C compiler needed for normal building of Python extensions is commercial and costly. For example, on Windows, the normal C compiler used by Python and its C-coded extensions is Microsoft Visual C++ (Release 6, at the time of this writing). It is possible to substitute other compilers, including free ones such as the *mingw32* and *cygwin* versions of *gcc*, and Borland C++ 5.5, whose command-line version you can download from the Net at no cost. However, the process of using such alternative compilers, as documented in the Python online manuals, is rather complex and intricate, particularly for end users who may not be experienced programmers.

Therefore, if you want your non-pure distribution to be widely adopted on such platforms as Windows, it's highly advisable to make your distribution also available in prebuilt form. However, unless you have developed or purchased advanced cross-compilation environments, building a non-pure distribution and packaging it up in prebuilt form is only feasible on the target platform. You also need to have the necessary C compiler installed. When those conditions are satisfied, however, the distutils make the procedure quite simple. In particular, the command:

```
python setup.py bdist_wininst
```

creates an *.exe* file that is a Windows installer for your distribution. If your distribution is non-pure, the prebuilt distribution is dependent on the specific Python version. The distutils reflect this fact in the name of the *.exe* installer they create for you. Say, for example, that your distribution's name metadata is mydist, your distribution's version metadata is 0.1, and the Python version you use is 2.2. In this case, the distutils build a Windows installer named *mydist-0.1.win32-py2.2.exe*.

The py2exe Tool

The distutils help you package up your Python extensions and applications. However, an end user can install the resulting packaged form only after installing Python. This is particularly a problem on Windows, where end users want to run a single installer to get an application working on their machine. Installing Python first and then running your application's installer may prove too much of a hassle for such end users.

Thomas Heller has developed a simple solution, a distutils add-on named py2exe, freely available for download from *http://starship.python.net/crew/theller/ py2exe/*. This URL also contains detailed documentation of py2exe, and I recommend that you study that documentation if you intend to use py2exe in advanced ways. However, the simplest kinds of use, which I cover in the rest of this section, cover most practical needs.

After downloading and installing py2exe (on a Windows machine where Microsoft Visual C++ 6 is also installed), you just need to add the line:

```
import py2exe
```

at the start of your otherwise normal distutils script *setup.py*. Now, in addition to other distutils commands, you have one more option. Running:

```
python setup.py py2exe
```

builds and collects in a subdirectory of your distribution root directory an *.exe* file and one or more *.dll* files. If your distribution's name metadata is, for example, myapp, then the directory into which the *.exe* and *.dll* files are collected is named *dist\myapp*. Any files specified by option data_files in your *setup.py* script are placed in subdirectories of *dist\myapp*. The *.exe* file corresponds to your application's first or single entry in the scripts keyword argument value, and also contains the bytecode-compiled form of all Python modules and packages that your *setup.py* specifies or implies. Among the *.dll* files is, at minimum, the Python dynamic load library, for example *python22.dll* if you use Python 2.2, plus any other *.pyd* or *.dll* files that your application needs, excluding *.dll* files that py2exe knows are system files (i.e., guaranteed to be available on any Windows installation).

py2exe provides no direct means to collect the contents of the *dist\myapp* directory for easy distribution and installation. You have several options, ranging from a *.zip* file (which may be given an *.exe* extension and made self-extracting, in ways that vary depending on the *.zip* file handling tools you choose), all the way to a professional Windows installer construction system, such as those sold by companies such as Wise and InstallShield. One option that is particularly worth considering is Inno Setup, a free, professional-quality installer construction system (see *http://www.jrsoftware.org/isinfo.php*). Since the files to be packaged up for end user installation are an *.exe* file, one or more *.dll* files, and perhaps some data files in subdirectories, the issue becomes totally independent from Python. You may package up and redistribute such files just as if they had originally been built from sources written in any other programming language.

The Installer Tool

Gordon McMillan has developed a richer and more general solution to the same problem that py2exe solves—preparing compact ways to package up Python applications for installation on end user machines that may not have Python installed. The Installer tool, freely downloadable from *http://www.mcmillan-enterprises.com/installer*, is more general than py2exe, which supports only Windows platforms. Installer natively supports Linux as well as Windows. Also,

Installer's portable, cross-platform architecture may allow you to extend it to support other Unix-like platforms with a reasonable amount of effort.

Installer does not rely on distutils. To use Installer, you must learn its own specification files' syntax and semantics. Installer can do much more than py2exe, so it's not surprising that there is more for you to learn before making full use of it. However, I recommend studying and trying out Installer if you have the specific need of building standalone Python applications for Linux or other Unix-like architectures, or if you have tried py2exe and found it did not quite meet your needs.

Index

We'd like to hear your suggestions for improving our indexes. Send email to *index@oreilly.com*.

at sign (@), struct format strings, 195
atan/atan2 functions
    cmath module, 297
    math module, 297
atanh function
    cmath module, 297
    math module, 297
atexit module, 273
    register function, 274
atof function (locale module), 217
atoi function (locale module), 217
Attr class (minidom module), 504
    ownerElement attribute, 504
    specified attribute, 504
AttributeError exception, 76, 110
    array object, 306
AttributeList class (minidom
        module), 502
attributes, 40, 61
    binding, 136
        class attributes, 71
        instance attributes, 74
    of class objects, 71
    DBAPI-compliant modules, 239
    deleting, 131
        "deleting" class attributes, 81
    documentation strings, 61
    of file object, 189–191
    of module object, 117
    overriding, 80
    path-string (os module), 173
    references, 75
    Tkinter module, 366
    ufunc object, 323
    unbinding
        class attributes, 71
        instance attributes, 74
attributes attribute (Node object), 503
Attributes object (xml.sax package)
    getNameByQName method, 498
    getQNameByName method, 498
    getQNames method, 498
    getValueByQName method, 498
augmented assignment statements, 42
August attribute (mx.DateTime
        module), 259
authentication
    SMTP servers, 418
    URL access to network protocols, 415
author argument (distutils setup
        function), 561

author_email argument (distutils setup
        function), 562
average function (Numeric module), 317

B

backslash (\)
    directory paths, 21
        Windows, 173
    line continuation, 30
    regular expressions, 157
    string literals, 35
backtick (`), string conversion, 43
backward compatibility, 7
    exception objects, strings as, 109
base64 module, 469
    decode function, 469
    decodestring function, 470
    encode function, 470
    encodestring function, 470
BaseHandler class, 415
BaseHTTPRequestHandler class, 440
BaseHTTPServer module, 440
    web server implementation, 468
basename function (os.path
        module), 177
BaseRequestHandler class (SocketServer
        module), 439
    client_address method, 439
    handle method, 439
    request method, 439
    server method, 439
Bastion class (Bastion module), 266
Bastion module, 262
    Bastion class, 266
bbox method (Canvas object), 357
benchmarking, 371, 393
Berkeley Database library (see BSD DB)
binaries
    downloading, 17
    installing from, 16
    third-party installers for various
        platforms, 17
Binary class (xmlrpclib module), 429
binary data, encoding as text, 469–471
    base64 module, 469
    quopri module, 470
    uu module, 471
binary file mode, 188
binary function (xmlrpclib
        module), 429

environ attribute (os module), 288
environment variables
 name of, retrieving, 177
 process environment, 287
 Python interpreter and, 19
EnvironmentError exception, 109
epilogue attribute (Message object), 473
epoch, 245
__eq__ special method, 92
equal sign (=)
 comparisons, 44
 struct format strings, 195
erase method (Window object), 209
errno attribute (os module), 172
errno module, 172
error handling, 112–115
 assert statement, 115
 __debug__ variable, 115
 error-checking strategies, 112
 errors vs. special cases, 114
 in large programs, 113
 logging errors, 114
error messages
 CGI scripting, 459
 code numbers, 172
 file printed to, 107
 internationalization and, 216
 stderr attribute (sys module), 204
 traceback messages, 104
 (see also warnings module)
escape function
 cgi module, 455
 re module, 168
 saxutils module, 499
eval function (built-in), 131, 205
eval method (PythonInterpreter
  object), 555
Event class
 threading module, 279, 283
 Tkinter module, 366
Event object (threading module), 283
 clear method, 283
 isSet method, 283
 set method, 283
 wait method, 283
Event object (Tkinter module)
 attributes, 366
 char attribute, 366
 keysym attribute, 366
 num attribute, 366
 widget attribute, 366

x_root attribute, 366
y_root attribute, 366
event scheduler, 249
event-driven applications
 GUI applications, 329
 network programs, 443–453
events
 binding callbacks to, 366
 keyboard, 366
 mouse, 367
 (see also sockets, event-driven
  programs)
excepthook function (sys module), 114,
  138
Exception class (built-in), 109
exception classes
 custom, 111
 DBAPI, 237
 standard, 110–111
exception handling, 104
 exception propagation, 107
 sys.excepthook, 138
 try statement, 104–107
  try/except, 105–106
  try/finally, 106
exceptions, 104–115
 C-coded Python extensions, 526
 exception objects, 109–111
  custom exception classes, 111
  standard exception
   classes, 110–111
 IOError exceptions, 187
 pending, gathering information
  about, 112
 raise statement, 108
 standard, hierarchy of, 109
exc_info function, sys module, 112, 138
exclamation point (!)
 comparisons, 44
 pdb command, 384
 struct format strings, 195
exec method (PythonInterpreter
  object), 555
exec statement, 260–262
 limiting use of, 260, 401
execfile function (built-in), 132
execfile method (PythonInterpreter
  object), 555
execl function (os module), 288
execle function (os module), 288
execlp function (os module), 288

file attribute (FieldStorage object), 457
file descriptors
  duplicating, 185
  operations on, 184–186
  OS-level, 189
file extensions, order of, when searching
    filesystem for modules, 121
file object (file type), 140, 187–192, 198
  attributes, 189–191
  close method, 189
  closed attribute, 189
  creating, 187–189
    designating buffering, 188
    sequential/nonsequential
      access, 189
    specifying file mode, 187
  fileno method, 189
  flush method, 189
  isatty method, 189
  iteration on, 191
  memory-mapped (see mmap object)
  methods, 189–191
  mode attribute, 189
  mode of, 187
  name attribute, 190
  open, alternate way to create, 127
  polymorphism and, 191
  read method, 190
  readline method, 190
  readlines method, 190
  seek method, 190
  softspace attribute, 190
  tell method, 191
  truncate method, 191
  write method, 191
  writelines method, 191
  xreadlines method, 191
filecmp module, 182–183
  cmp function, 182
  cmpfiles function, 182
  dircmp function, 182
FileInput function (fileinput
    module), 193
fileinput module, 193
  close method, 193
  FileInput function, 193
  filelineno function, 193
  filename function, 193
  input function, 193
  isfirstline function, 194

isstdin function, 194
lineno function, 194
nextfile function, 194
filelineno function (fileinput
    module), 193
filename attribute
  FieldStorage object, 457
  os module, 172
  zipfile module, 200
filename function (fileinput module), 193
fileno method (file object), 189
files, 171, 187
  buffering, 188
  comparing, 182
  compressed, 198–203
    gzip module, 198
    tar archive, 13
    zipfile module, 200–203
    zlib module, 203
  copying, 183
  .cpp, 565
  creating/opening, 127
  .dll, 515
  HTML, getting information
    from, 481–485
  information about, retrieving, 176
  __init__.py, 561
  .jar, Jython and, 5
  jython.jar, 551
  MANIFEST, 567
  msvcrt.dll, 211
  .pythonrc.py, 275
  removing, 175
  renaming, 175
  setting time on, 177
  site.py, 274
  .so, 515
  as symbolic links, 181
  text, 171
  truncating, 191
  (see also file object)
file_size attribute (zipfile module), 200
filesystems, 171
  case-sensitive, 179
  operations of, 173–186
    permissions, 174
  searching for modules, 121
filter function (built-in), 132
filterwarnings function (warnings
    module), 390

About the Author

Alex Martelli spent eight years with IBM Research, winning three Outstanding Technical Achievement Awards. He then spent 13 years as a senior software consultant at think3 inc, developing libraries, network protocols, GUI engines, event frameworks, and web access frontends. He has also taught programming languages, development methods, and numerical computing at Ferrara University and other venues. He's a C++ MVP for Brainbench, a board member of the Python Business Forum, and a member of the Python Software Foundation. He currently works for AB Strakt (a Swedish Python-centered firm that develops new technologies for real-time workflow and groupware applications), mostly by telecommuting from his home in Bologna, Italy.

Alex's proudest achievement is the publication of two articles in *The Bridge World* (January/February 2000) that were hailed as giant steps toward solving issues that had haunted contract bridge theoreticians for decades.

Colophon

Our look is the result of reader comments, our own experimentation, and feedback from distribution channels. Distinctive covers complement our distinctive approach to technical topics, breathing personality and life into potentially dry subjects.

The animal on the cover of *Python in a Nutshell* is an African rock python, one of approximately 18 species of python. Pythons are nonvenomous constrictor snakes that live in tropical regions of Africa, Asia, Australia, and some Pacific Islands. Pythons live mainly on the ground, but they are also excellent swimmers and climbers. Both male and female pythons retain vestiges of their ancestral hind legs. The male python uses these vestiges, or spurs, when courting a female.

The python kills its prey by suffocation. While the snake's sharp teeth grip and hold the prey in place, the python's long body coils around its victim's chest, constricting tighter each time it breathes out. They feed primarily on mammals and birds. Python attacks on humans are extremely rare.

Emily Quill was the production editor and copyeditor for *Python in a Nutshell*. Linley Dolby and Tatiana Apandi Diaz provided quality control. Philip Dangler, Judy Hoer, and Genevieve d'Entremont provided production assistance. Nancy Crumpton wrote the index.

Emma Colby designed the cover of this book, based on a series design by Edie Freedman. The cover image is a 19th-century engraving from the Dover Pictorial Archive. Emma Colby produced the cover layout with QuarkXPress 4.1 using Adobe's ITC Garamond font.

Bret Kerr designed the interior layout, based on a series design by David Futato. This book was converted by Mike Sierra to FrameMaker 5.5.6 with a format conversion tool created by Erik Ray, Jason McIntosh, Neil Walls, and Mike Sierra that uses Perl and XML technologies. The text font is Linotype Birka; the heading font is Adobe Myriad Condensed; and the code font is LucasFont's TheSans Mono Condensed. The illustrations that appear in the book were produced by Robert Romano and Jessamyn Read using Macromedia FreeHand 9 and Adobe Photoshop 6. This colophon was written by Nicole Arigo.

Other Titles Available from O'Reilly

Scripting Languages

Programming Python, 2nd Edition

By Mark Lutz
2nd Edition March 2001
1256 pages, Includes CD-ROM
ISBN 0-596-00085-5

Programming Python, 2nd Edition, focuses on advanced applications of Python, an increasingly popular object-oriented scripting language. Endorsed by Python creator Guido van Rossum, it demonstrates advanced Python programming techniques, and addresses software design issues such as reusability and object-oriented programming. The enclosed platform-neutral CD-ROM has book examples and various Python-related packages, including the full Python Version 2.0 source code distribution.

Learning Python

By Mark Lutz & David Ascher
1st Edition April 1999
384 pages, ISBN 1-56592-464-9

Learning Python is an introduction to the increasingly popular Python programming language—an interpreted, interactive, object-oriented, and portable scripting language. This book thoroughly introduces the elements of Python: types, operators, statements, classes, functions, modules, and exceptions. It also demonstrates how to perform common programming tasks and write real applications.

Ruby in a Nutshell

By Yukihiro Matsumoto
With translated text by
David L. Reynolds Jr.
1st Edition November 2001
218 pages, ISBN 0-59600-214-9

Written by Yukihiro Matsumoto ("Matz"), creator of the language, Ruby in a Nutshell is a practical reference guide covering everything from Ruby syntax to the specifications of its standard class libraries. The book is based on Ruby 1.6, and is applicable to development versions 1.7 and the next planned stable version 1.8. As part of the successful "in a Nutshell" series Ruby in a Nutshell is for readers who want a single desktop reference for all their needs.

Python Cookbook

David Ascher & Alex Martelli,
Editors
1st Edition July 2002
608 pages, ISBN 0-596-00167-3

The Python Cookbook is a collection of problems, solutions, and practical examples written by Python programmers in the style of the popular Perl Cookbook. Its potential audience includes both Python programmers and experienced programmers who are new to Python and want to evaluate whether or not the language is suitable for their intended applications. Anyone interested in Python programming will want this wealth of practical advice, snippets of code, and patterns of program design that can be directly lifted out of the book and applied to everyday programming problems.

Exploring Expect

By Don Libes
1st Edition December 1994
602 pages, ISBN 1-56592-090-2

Written by the author of Expect, this is the first book to explain how this part of the Unix toolbox can be used to automate Telnet, FTP, passwd, rlogin, and hundreds of other interactive applications. Based on Tcl (Tool Command Language), Expect lets you automate interactive applications that have previously been extremely difficult to handle with any scripting language.

Jython Essentials

By Noel Rappin & Samuele
Pedroni
1st Edition March 2002
300 pages, ISBN 0-596-00247-5

Jython is an implementation of the Python programming language written in Java, allowing Python programs to integrate seamlessly with any Java code. The secret to Jython's popularity lies in the combination of Java's libraries and tools with Python's rapid development capabilities. Jython Essentials provides a solid introduction to the language, numerous examples of Jython/Java interaction, and valuable reference material on modules and libraries of use to Jython programmers.

O'REILLY®

To order: 800-998-9938 • order@oreilly.com • www.oreilly.com
Online editions of most O'Reilly titles are available by subscription at safari.oreilly.com
Also available at most retail and online bookstores.

How to stay in touch with O'Reilly

1. Visit our award-winning web site

http://www.oreilly.com/

★ "Top 100 Sites on the Web"—PC Magazine
★ CIO Magazine's Web Business 50 Awards

Our web site contains a library of comprehensive product information (including book excerpts and tables of contents), downloadable software, background articles, interviews with technology leaders, links to relevant sites, book cover art, and more. File us in your bookmarks or favorites!

2. Join our email mailing lists

Sign up to get email announcements of new books and conferences, special offers, and O'Reilly Network technology newsletters at:

http://elists.oreilly.com

It's easy to customize your free elists subscription so you'll get exactly the O'Reilly news you want.

3. Get examples from our books

To find example files for a book, go to:

http://www.oreilly.com/catalog

select the book, and follow the "Examples" link.

4. Work with us

Check out our web site for current employment opportunites:

http://jobs.oreilly.com/

5. Register your book

Register your book at:

http://register.oreilly.com

6. Contact us

O'Reilly & Associates, Inc.
1005 Gravenstein Hwy North
Sebastopol, CA 95472 USA
TEL: 707-827-7000 or 800-998-9938
(6am to 5pm PST)
FAX: 707-829-0104

order@oreilly.com
For answers to problems regarding your order or our products. To place a book order online visit:

http://www.oreilly.com/order_new/

catalog@oreilly.com
To request a copy of our latest catalog.

booktech@oreilly.com
For book content technical questions or corrections.

corporate@oreilly.com
For educational, library, government, and corporate sales.

proposals@oreilly.com
To submit new book proposals to our editors and product managers.

international@oreilly.com
For information about our international distributors or translation queries. For a list of our distributors outside of North America check out:

http://international.oreilly.com/distributors.html

adoption@oreilly.com
For information about academic use of O'Reilly books, visit:

http://academic.oreilly.com

O'REILLY®

To order: *800-998-9938* • *order@oreilly.com* • *www.oreilly.com*
Online editions of most O'Reilly titles are available by subscription at *safari.oreilly.com*
Also available at most retail and online bookstores.